P9-BIX-210

CRIME IN AMERICA

CRIME IN AMERICA

Perspectives on Criminal and Delinquent Behavior

Edited by
Bruce J. Cohen

MICHIGAN STATE UNIVERSITY

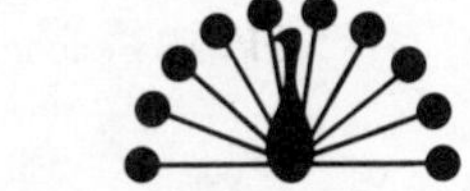

F. E. PEACOCK PUBLISHERS, INC. • ITASCA • ILLINOIS

Library of Congress
Catalog Card No. 78-94836
Second Printing 1971

FOR AUNT "B" AND UNCLE HARRY

Preface

Crime and delinquency is perhaps the most serious domestic problem facing the American people today. From August through November, 1968, the three major candidates for the presidency of the United States were asked repeatedly during their campaigns how they would handle the crime problem and what constructive steps they might take. Although their individual proposals varied widely, one series of responses was almost always in evidence—"our crime problem must be substantially reduced, streets must once again be made safe for all our citizens, solutions of social problems leading to unrest and disruption must be found, and all-out war against elements of organized crime must be lodged."

These reactions are easier said than done. For the past several decades technology has vastly improved police investigative techniques, formal education at the college level has been established as a standard requirement for appointment to many law enforcement agencies, citizen responsibilities have been emphasized time and time again, additional police personnel and equipment have been requisitioned and often granted, social scientists contributed the results of their extensive research, congressional committees held hearings, Presidential Commissions were established, and what has been the net result? Between 1960 and 1967 our crime rate rose seventy-one percent.

In the present volume I have selected three major areas of criminology to explore; the crime problem in the United States (its nature and extent), the range of criminal offenses, and the role of the victim. The bulk of the readings consist of a rather extensive study of ten major offense categories—aggressive crimes, abnormal sex offenses, drug addiction, alcoholism, white-collar crime, professional crime, organized crime, property offenders, juvenile and youthful offenders, and civil disorders. Because criminality exhibits such a heterogeneous range of antisocial behavior patterns, it is necessary to examine each specific category of criminal activity as a separate entity. Those who work in the field know all too well that it is rather difficult to compare the murderer with the drug addict or the kingpin of organized crime with the petty thief.

Selection of readings for a book such as this is a most difficult task for an editor. Many very excellent articles that were under consideration had to be deleted due to the practical matter of available space. The readings selected thus represent the subjective judgment of the editor and will hopefully serve the intended purpose well. Our authors comprise a list of distinguished scholars from the social sciences, law, and medicine, who have often been cited for their contributions in their appropriate fields. The selective nature of the articles will be of special interest to those studying criminology, deviant behavior, social problems, police science, and criminal law.

I would like to offer my wholehearted thanks to our authors for their scholarly research and reporting, to the several professional journals, magazines, and government publications for their cooperation and permissions to reprint, to my department chairman Dr. Douglas Dunham, and Dr. Jay Artis, Director of the Social Science Multidisciplinary Major Program at Michigan State University for their cooperation in scheduling of courses, thus granting me the opportunity to edit and prepare the manuscript, and finally to my parents for providing the inspiration and encouragement during my undergraduate and graduate years of study which made it possible to even contemplate such an undertaking.

September 17, 1969

BRUCE J. COHEN
East Lansing, Michigan

Contents

XIII. THE VICTIM 439

CHAPTER I

Our Crime Problem

TO ACCURATELY describe the magnitude of the crime problem in the United States is a most difficult task. We may use adjectives such as gigantic, huge, monstrous, immense, and enormous, but still fall far short of conveying the message. The problem is simply beyond belief. In its *Uniform Crime Report* for 1967 the Federal Bureau of Investigation has revealed some rather startling facts concerning criminality in our country:

1. Over 3.8 million serious crimes reported during 1967, a 16 percent rise over 1966.
2. Risk of becoming a victim of serious crime increased 15 percent in 1967 with almost 2 victims per each 100 inhabitants.
3. Firearms used to commit over 7,600 murders, 52,000 aggravated assaults and 73,000 robberies in 1967.
4. Since 1964 use of a firearm in murder up 47 percent; in aggravated assault up 76 percent. Armed robbery during same period up 58 percent.
5. Daytime burglaries of residences rose 187 percent from 1960 to 1967.
6. Property worth more than $1.4 billion stolen as a result of 202,050 robberies, 1,605,700 burglaries, 3,078,700 larcenies, and 654,900 auto thefts. Police recoveries, however, reduced this loss by 51 percent.
7. Careers in crime: Study disclosed 60 percent of offenders released to the street in 1963 rearrested within four years.

In addition to these isolated bits of data it is most interesting to examine the relationship between crime and population during the seven-year period 1960–67. As noted in Chart 1.1, while the population advanced only 10 percent in this rather short period, crime has increased 89 percent and the crime rate is up 71 percent. In Charts 1.2 and 1.3 we can easily trace the year by year surge of violent crimes and property offenses.

CHART 1.1

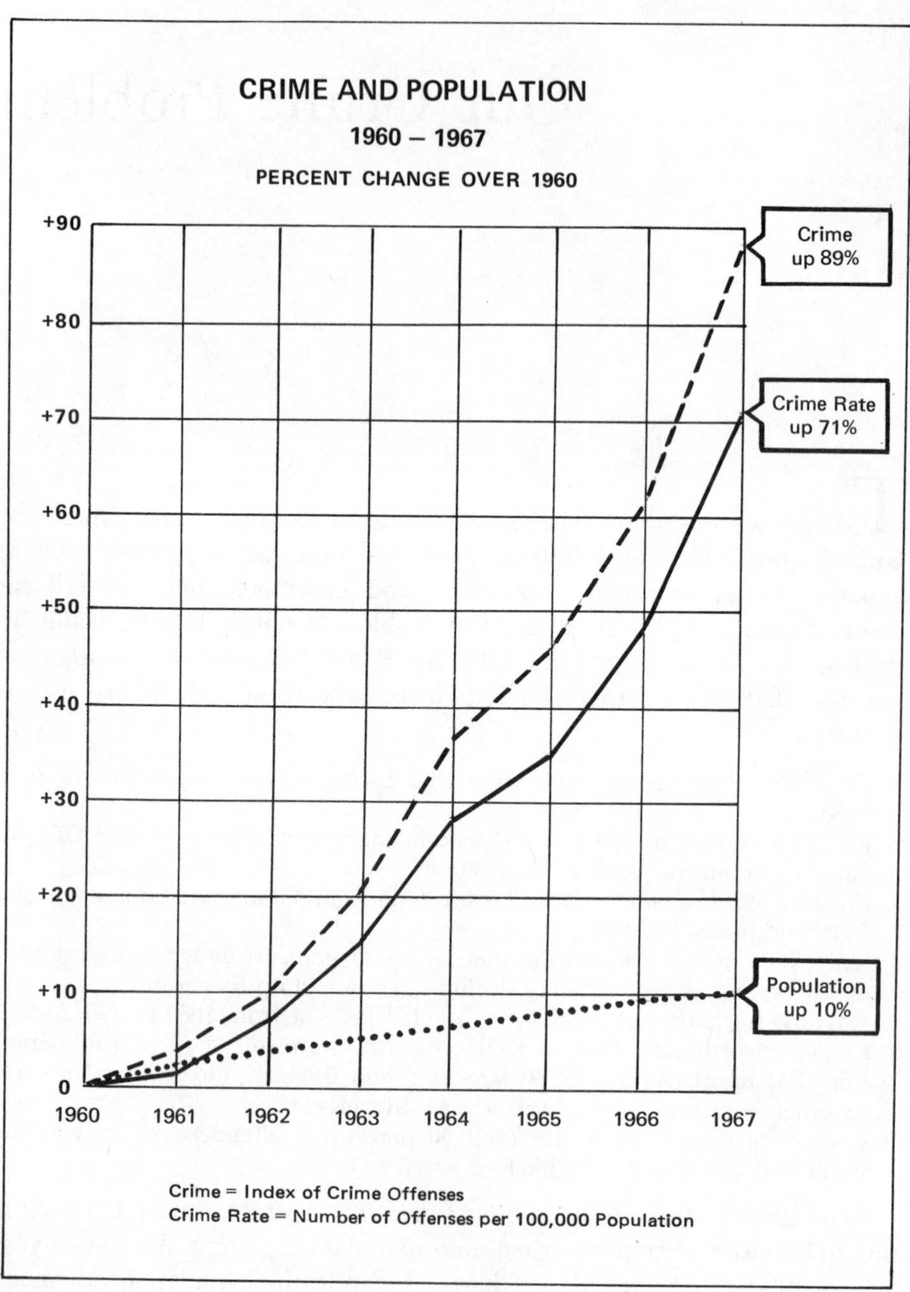

SOURCE: Federal Bureau of Investigation, U.S. Department of Justice, *1967 Uniform Crime Reports* (Washington, D.C.: U.S. Government Printing Office, 1968), p. 2.

CHART 1.2

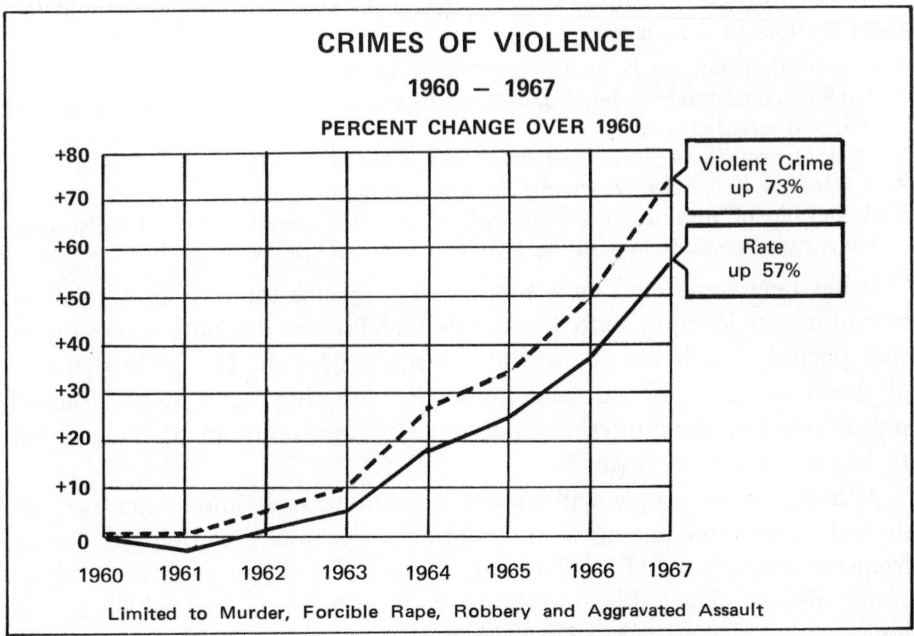

CHART 1.3

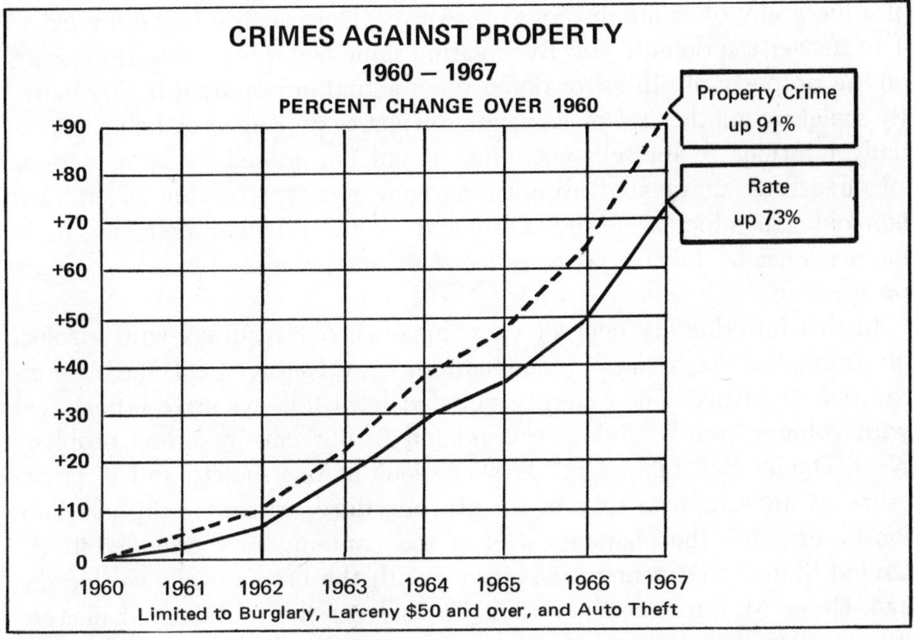

SOURCE: Federal Bureau of Investigation, U.S. Department of Justice, *1967 Uniform Crime Reports* (Washington, D.C.: U.S. Government Printing Office, 1968), p. 3.

When engaging in a scientific study of criminal behavior in the United States we are faced with several rather frustrating problems. Among the most serious problems are:

1. Inaccurate reporting by police agencies and victims.
2. Lack of consistency in legal definitions of criminal offenses among the several political jurisdictions.
3. Misinterpretations of the *Uniform Crime Reports*.
4. A selective bias directed against the lower classes.
5. A significant number of "white-collar" offenses handled by administrative boards and commissions rather than the criminal courts.

It has been suggested on a number of occasions that criminal behavior resembles an iceberg, with the number of known deviants representing that portion which shows itself above the waterline. The great majority of social deviants thus are unknown. Because they have had no official police contact, their interaction in society represents an obvious threat to life and property alike.

Although most people will commit a crime at one time or another, we do not look upon our entire population as criminal. Perhaps the most frequent infractions will fall within the area of traffic violations. Many young boys will act disorderly, or take a swim in a pool which is "off limits"; some are apprehended, others are not, and yet both groups were involved in identical behavior.

An inevitable question that must be posed concerns the existence of a hierarchy of crime in terms of severity. Does such a hierarchy exist? The answer is a definite yes. By violating some codes we are transgressing on the property of others, or doing them actual or potential bodily harm. By violating another set of laws, the deviant is perceived as being potentially injurious to himself. Gambling is not considered to be as serious an offense as aggravated assault; vagrancy is not as severe as criminal homicide. In caluculating the nature and extent of deviant behavior, these factors must be taken into consideration, and offenses placed in proper perspective.

In this introductory chapter we commence our readings with a selection from the President's Commission on Law Enforcement and Administration of Justice. The excerpts included from this extensive report deal with volume, trends, and factors related to our current crime problem. Next, Daniel Bell takes a rather sharp look at our society and discusses crime as an American way of life. In our third article, Irwin and Yablonsky examine the characteristics of the contemporary offender in the United States, contrasting his behavior with the criminal of two decades ago. Harry M. Shulman then critically analyzes the problems of measuring crime in this country. Among the many issues he discusses are: concealment and nonreporting, difficulties involved in bringing "white-collar" offenders into the criminal court, and the limitations of the police as a crime-reporting agency. Finally, Marvin E. Wolfgang dissects the *Uniform Crime Reports* and makes a most valuable critical appraisal.

1.

PRESIDENT'S COMMISSION ON LAW ENFORCEMENT AND ADMINISTRATION OF JUSTICE

CRIME IN AMERICA

* * *

THE AMOUNT OF CRIME

There are more than 2,800 Federal crimes and a much larger number of State and local ones. Some involve serious bodily harm, some stealing, some public morals or public order, some governmental revenues, some the creation of hazardous conditions, some the regulation of the economy. Some are perpetrated ruthlessly and systematically; others are spontaneous derelictions. Gambling and prostitution are willingly undertaken by both buyer and seller; murder and rape are violently imposed upon their victims. Vandalism is predominantly a crime of the young; driving while intoxicated, a crime of the adult. Many crime rates vary significantly from place to place.

The crimes that concern Americans the most are those that affect their personal safety—at home, at work, or in the streets. The most frequent and serious of these crimes of violence against the person are willful homicide, forcible rape, aggravated assault, and robbery. National statistics regarding the number of these offenses known to the police either from citizen complaints or through independent police discovery are collected from local police officials by the Federal Bureau of Investigation and published annually as a part of its report, *Crime in the United States, Uniform Crime Reports*. The FBI also collects "offenses known" statistics for three property crimes: Burglary, larceny of $50 and over and motor vehicle theft. These seven crimes are grouped together in the *UCR* to form an Index of serious crimes. . . .

SOURCE: *The Challenge of Crime in a Free Society*, A Report of the President's Commission on Law Enforcement and Administration of Justice (Washington, D.C.: U.S. Government Printing Office, February, 1967), pp. 18–31. Tables omitted.

THE RISK OF HARM

Including robbery, the crimes of violence make up approximately 13 percent of the Index. The Index reports the number of incidents known to the police, not the number of criminals who committed them or the number of injuries they caused.

The risk of sudden attack by a stranger is perhaps best measured by the frequency of robberies since, according to *UCR* and other studies, about 70 percent of all willful killings, nearly two-thirds of all aggravated assaults and a high percentage of forcible rapes are committed by family members, friends, or other persons previously known to their victims. Robbery usually does not involve this prior victim-offender relationship.

. . . Nationally, about one-half of all robberies are street robberies, and slightly more than one-half involve weapons. Attempted robberies are an unknown percentage of the robberies reported to the *UCR*. The likelihood of injury is also unknown, but a survey by the District of Columbia Crime Commission of 297 robberies in Washington showed that some injury was inflicted in 25 percent of them. The likelihood of injury was found higher for "yokings" or "muggings" (unarmed robberies from the rear) than for armed robberies. Injuries occurred in 10 of 91 armed robberies as compared with 30 of 67 yokings.

Aggravated assault . . . includes all cases of attempted homicide, but cases in which bodily injury is inflicted in the course of a robbery or a rape are included with those crimes rather than with aggravated assault. There are no national figures showing the percentage of aggravated assaults that involve injury, but a survey of 131 cases by the District of Columbia Crime Commission found injury in

84 percent of the cases; 35 percent of the victims required hospitalization. A 1960 *UCR* study showed that juvenile gangs committed less than 4 percent of all aggravated assaults.

Forcible rape includes only those rapes or attempted rapes in which force or threat of force is used. About one-third of the *UCR* total is attempted rape. In a District of Columbia Crime Commission survey of 151 cases, about 25 percent of all rape victims were attacked with dangerous weapons; the survey did not show what percentage received bodily harm in addition to the rape.

About 15 percent of all criminal homicides, both nationally and in the District of Columbia Crime Commission surveys, occurred in the course of committing other offenses. These offenses appear in the homicide total rather than in the total for the other offense. In the District of Columbia Crime Commission surveys, less than one-half of 1 percent of the robberies and about 1 percent of the forcible rapes ended in homicide.

Some personal danger is also involved in the property crimes. Burglary is the unlawful entering of a building to commit a felony or a theft, whether force is used or not. About half of all burglaries involve residences, but the statistics do not distinguish inhabited parts of houses from garages and similar outlying parts. About half of all residential burglaries are committed in daylight and about half at night. A *UCR* survey indicates that 32 percent of the entries into residences are made through unlocked doors or windows. When an unlawful entry results in a violent confrontation with the occupant, the offense is counted as a robbery rather than a burglary. Of course, even when no confrontation takes place there is often a risk of confrontation. Nationally such confrontations occur in only one-fortieth of all residential burglaries. They account for nearly one-tenth of all robberies.

In summary, these figures suggest that, on the average, the likelihood of a serious personal attack on any American in a given year is about 1 in 550; together with the studies available they also suggest that the risk of serious attack from spouses, family members, friends, or acquaintances is almost twice as great as it is from strangers on the street. Commission and other studies, moreover, indicate that the risks of personal harm are spread very unevenly. The actual risk for slum dwellers is considerably more; for most Americans it is considerably less.

Except in the case of willful homicide, where the figures describe the extent of injury as well as the number of incidents, there is no national data on the likelihood of injury from attack. More limited studies indicate that while some injury may occur in two-thirds of all attacks, the risk in a given year of injury serious enough to require any degree of hospitalization of any individual is about 1 in 3,000 on the average, and much less for most Americans. These studies also suggest that the injury inflicted by family members or acquaintances is likely to be more severe than that from strangers . . . the risk of death from willful homicide is about 1 in 20,000.

Criminal behavior accounts for a high percentage of motor vehicle deaths and injuries. In 1965 there were an estimated 49,000 motor vehicle deaths. Negligent manslaughter, which is largely a motor vehicle offense, accounted for more than 7,000 of these. Studies in several States indicate that an even higher percentage involve criminal behavior. They show that driving while intoxicated is probably involved in more than one-half of all motor vehicle deaths. These same studies show that driving while intoxicated is involved in more than 13 percent of the 1,800,000 nonfatal motor vehicle injuries each year.

For various statistical and other reasons, a number of serious crimes against or involving risk to the person, such as arson, kidnapping, child molestation, and simple assault, are not included in the *UCR* Index. In a study of 1,300 cases of delinquency in Philadelphia, offenses other than the seven Index crimes constituted 62 percent of all cases in which there was physical injury. Simple assault accounted for the largest percentage of these injuries. But its victims required medical attention in only one-fifth of the cases as opposed to three-fourths of the aggravated assaults, and hospitalization in 7 percent as opposed to 23 percent. Injury was more prevalent in conflicts between persons of the same age than in those in which the victim was older or younger than the attacker.

Property Crimes

The three property crimes of burglary, automobile theft, and larceny of $50 and over make up 87 percent of Index crimes. The Index is a reasonably reliable indicator of the total number of property crimes reported to the police, but not a particularly good indicator of the seriousness of monetary loss from all property crimes. Commission studies tend to indicate that such non-Index crimes as fraud and embezzlement are more significant in terms of dollar volume. Fraud can be a particularly pernicious offense. It is not only expensive in total but all too often preys on the weak.

Many larcenies included in the Index total are misdemeanors rather than felonies under the laws of their own States. Auto thefts that involve only unauthorized use also are misdemeanors in many States. Many stolen automobiles are abandoned after a few hours, and more than 85 percent are ultimately recovered according to *UCR* studies. Studies in California indicate that about 20 percent of recovered cars are significantly damaged.

* * *

Federal Crimes

More than 50 percent of all Federal criminal offenses relate to general law enforcement in territorial or maritime jurisdictions directly subject to Federal control, or are also State offenses (bank robberies, for example). Police statistics for these offenses are normally reported in the *UCR*, particularly when local law enforcement is involved. Such other Federal crimes as antitrust violations, food and drug violations and tax evasion are not included in the *UCR*. Although Federal crimes constitute only a small percentage of all offenses [these] . . . are an important part of the national crime picture.

The Extent of Unreported Crime

Although the police statistics indicate a lot of crime today, they do not begin to indicate the full amount. Crimes reported directly to prosecutors usually do not show up in the police statistics. Citizens often do not report crimes to the police. Some crimes reported to the police never get into the statistical system. Since better crime prevention and control programs depend upon a full and accurate knowledge about the amount and kinds of crime, the Commission initiated the first national survey ever made of crime victimization. The National Opinion Research Center of the University of Chicago surveyed 10,000 households, asking whether the person questioned, or any member of his or her household, had been a victim of crime during the past year, whether the crime had been reported and, if not, the reasons for not reporting.

More detailed surveys were undertaken in a number of high and medium crime rate precincts of Washington, Chicago, and Boston by the Bureau of Social Science Research of Washington, D.C., and the Survey Research Center of the University of Michigan. All of the surveys dealt primarily with households or individuals, although some data were obtained for certain kinds of businesses and other organizations.

These surveys show that the actual amount of crime in the United States today is several times that reported in the *UCR*. . . . The amount of personal injury crime reported to NORC is almost twice the *UCR* rate and the amount of property crime more than twice as much as the *UCR* rate for individuals. Forcible rapes were more than 3½ times the reported rate, burglaries three times, aggravated assaults and larcenies of $50 and over more than double, and robbery 50 percent greater than the reported rate. Only vehicle theft was lower and then by a small amount. (The single homicide reported is too small a number to be statistically useful.)

Even these rates probably understate the actual amounts of crime. The national survey was a survey of the victim experience of every member of a household based on interviews of one member. If the results are tabulated only for the family member who was interviewed, the amount of unreported victimization for some offenses is considerably higher. Apparently, the person interviewed remembered more of his own victimization than that of other members of his family. . . .

The survey in Boston and in one of the Chicago precincts indicated about three times as many Index crimes as the police statistics, in the other Chicago precinct about 1½ times as many. These survey rates are not fully comparable with the Washington results because adequate information did not exist for eliminating business and transient victims from the police statistics. If this computation could have been made, the Boston and Chicago figures would undoubtedly have shown a closer similarity to the Washington findings.

In the national survey of households those victims saying that they had not notified the police of their victimization were asked why. The reason most frequently given for all offenses was that the police could not do anything. . . . This reason was given by 68 percent of those not reporting malicious mischief, and by 60 or more percent of those not reporting burglaries, larcenies of $50 and over, and auto thefts. It is not clear whether these responses are accurate assessments of the victims' inability to help the police or merely rationalizations of their failure to report. The next most frequent reason was that the offense was a private matter or that the victim did not want to harm the offender. It was given by 50 percent or more of those who did not notify the police for aggravated and simple assaults, family crimes, and consumer frauds. Fear of reprisal, though least often cited, was strongest in the case of assaults and family crimes. The extent of failure to report to the police was highest for consumer fraud (90 percent) and lowest for auto theft (11 percent). . . .

TRENDS IN CRIME

There has always been too much crime. Virtually every generation since the founding of the Nation and before has felt itself threatened by the spectre of rising crime and violence.

A hundred years ago contemporary accounts of San Francisco told of extensive areas where "no decent man was in safety to walk the street after dark; while at all hours, both night and day, his property was jeopardized by incendiarism and burglary." Teenage gangs gave rise to the word "hoodlum"; while in one central New York City area, near Broadway, the police entered "only in pairs, and never unarmed." A noted chronicler of the period declared that "municipal law is a failure . . . we must soon fall back on the law of self preservation." "Alarming" increases in robbery and violent crimes were reported throughout the country prior to the Revolution. And in 1910 one author declared that "crime, especially its more violent forms, and among the young is increasing steadily and is threatening to bankrupt the Nation."

Crime and violence in the past took many forms. During the great railway strike of 1877 hundreds were killed across the country and almost 2 miles of railroad cars and buildings were burned in Pittsburgh in clashes between strikers and company police and the militia. It was nearly half a century later, after pitched battles in the steel industry in the late thirties, that the Nation's long history of labor violence subsided. The looting and take-over of New York for 3 days by mobs in the 1863 draft riots rivaled the violence of Watts, while racial disturbances in Atlanta in 1907, in Chicago, Washington, and East St. Louis in 1919, Detroit in 1943 and New York in 1900, 1935, and 1943 marred big city life in the first half of the 20th century. Lynchings took the lives of more than 4,500 persons throughout the country between 1882 and 1930. And the violence of Al Capone and Jesse James was so striking that they have left their marks permanently on our understanding of the eras in which they lived.

However, the fact that there has always been a lot of crime does not mean that the amount of crime never changes. It changes constantly, day and night, month to month, place to place. It is essential that society be able to tell when changes occur and what they are, that it be able to distinguish normal ups and downs from long-term trends. Whether the amount of crime is increasing or decreasing, and by how much, is an important question—for law enforcement, for the individual citizen who must run the risk of crime, and for the official who must plan and establish prevention and control programs. If it is true, as the Commission surveys tend to indicate, that society has not yet found fully reliable methods for measuring the volume of crime, it is even more true that it has failed to find such methods for measuring the trend of crime.

Unlike some European countries, which have maintained national statistics for more than a century and a quarter, the United States has maintained national crime statistics only since 1930. Because the rural areas were slow in coming into the system and reported poorly when they did, it was not until 1958, when other major changes were made in the *UCR,* that reporting of rural crimes was sufficient to allow a total national estimate without special adjustments. Changes in overall estimating procedures and two offense categories—rape and larceny—were also made in 1958. Because of these problems figures prior to 1958 and particularly those prior to 1940, must be viewed as neither fully comparable with nor nearly so reliable as later figures.

For crimes of violence the 1933–65 period, based on newly adjusted unpublished figures from the *UCR,* has been . . . one of sharply divergent trends for the different offenses. Total numbers for all reported offenses have increased markedly; the Nation's population has increased also—by more than 47 percent since 1940. The number of offenses per 100,000 population has tripled for forcible rape and has doubled for aggravated assault during the period, both increasing at a fairly constant pace. The willful homicide rate has decreased somewhat to about 70 percent of its high in 1933, while robbery has fluctuated from a high in 1933 and a low during World War II to a point where it is now about 20 percent above the beginning of the postwar era. The overall rate for violent crimes, primarily due to the increased rate for aggravated assault, now stands at its highest point, well above what it has been throughout most of the period.

Property crime rates . . . are up much more sharply than the crimes of violence. The rate for larceny of $50 and over has shown the greatest increase of all Index offenses. It is up more than 550 percent over 1933. The burglary rate has nearly doubled. The rate for auto theft has followed an uneven course to a point about the same as the rate of the early thirties. . . .

Arrest rates are in general much less complete and are available for many fewer years than are rates for offenses known to the police. However, they do provide another measure of the trend of crime. For crimes of violence, arrest rates rose 16 percent during 1960–65, considerably less than the 25 percent increase indicated by offenses known to the police. For property crimes, arrest rates have increased about 25 percent, as opposed to a 36 percent increase in offenses known to the police during 1960–65. . . .

Trends for crimes against trust, vice crimes, and crimes against public order, based on arrest rates for 1960–65, follow a much more checkered pattern than do trends for Index offenses. For some offenses this is in part due to the fact that arrest patterns change significantly from time to time, as when New York recently decided not to make further arrests for public drunkenness. Based on comparable places covering about half the total population, arrest rates during 1960–65 rose 13 percent for simple assault, 13 percent for embezzlement and fraud, and 36 percent for narcotics violations, while for the same period, the rates declined 24 percent for gambling and 11 percent for drunkenness.

The picture portrayed by the official statistics in recent years, both in the total number of crimes and in the number of crimes per 100,000 Americans, is one of increasing crime. Crime always seems to be increasing, never going down. Up 5 percent this year, 10 the next, and the Commission's surveys have shown there is a great deal more crime than the official statistics show. The public can fairly wonder whether there is ever to be an end.

This official picture is also alarming because it seems so pervasive. Crimes of violence are up in both the biggest and smallest cities, in the suburbs as well as in the rural areas. The same is true for property crimes. Young people are being arrested in ever increasing numbers. Offense rates for most crimes are rising every year and in every section of the country. That there are some bright spots does not change this dismal outlook. Rates for some offenses are still below those of the early thirties and perhaps of earlier periods. Willful homicide rates have been below the 1960 level through most of the last few years. Robbery rates continue to decline in the rural areas and small towns, and arrest rates for many non-Index offenses have remained relatively stable.

Because the general picture is so disturbing and the questions it raises go to the very heart of concern about crime in the United States today, the Commission has made a special effort to evaluate as fully as possible the information available. . . .

What is known about the trend of crime—in the total number of offenses; in the ratio of offenses to population, which measures roughly the risk of victimization; and in the relationship of crime trends to changes in the composition of the population, which measures roughly the crime proneness of various kinds of people—is almost wholly a product of statistics. Therefore the Commission has taken a particularly hard look at the current sources of statistical knowledge.

Factors Affecting the Reporting of Crime

From the time that police statistics first began to be maintained in France in the 1820's, it has been recognized that the validity of calculations of changes in crime rates was dependent upon a constant relationship between reported and unreported crime. Until the Commission surveys of unreported crime, however, no systematic effort of wide scale had ever been made to determine what the relationship between reported and unreported crime was. . . . These surveys have now indicated that the actual amount of crime is several times that reported to the police, even in some of the precincts with the highest reported crime rates. This margin of unreported crime raises the possibility that even small changes in the way that crime is reported by the public to the police, or classified and recorded by the police, could have significant effects on the trend of reported crime. There is strong reason to believe that a number of such changes have taken place within recent years.

Changing Expectations. One change of importance in the amount of crime that is reported in our society is the change in the expectations of the poor and members of minority groups about civil rights and social protection. Not long ago there was a tendency to dismiss reports of all but the most serious offenses in slum areas and segregated minority group districts. The poor and the segregated minority groups were left to take care of their own problems. Commission studies indicate that whatever the past pattern was, these areas now have a strong feeling of need for adequate police protection. Crimes that were once unknown to the police, or ignored when complaints were received, are now much more likely to be reported and recorded as part of the regular statistical procedure. . . .

Police Practice. Perhaps the most important change for reporting purposes that has taken place in the last 25 years is the change in the police. Notable progress has been made during this period in the professionalization of police forces. With this change, Commission studies indicate, there is a strong trend toward more formal actions, more formal records and less informal disposition of individual cases. This trend is particularly apparent in the way the police handle juveniles, where the greatest increases are reported, but seems to apply to other cases as well. It seems likely that professionalization also results in greater police efficiency in looking for crime. Increases in the number of clerks and statistical personnel, better methods for recording information, and the use of more intensive patrolling practices also tend to increase the amount of recorded crime. Because this process of professionalization has taken place over a period of time and because it is most often a gradual rather than an abrupt change, it is difficult to estimate what its cumulative effect has been.

Wholly different kinds of changes have occurred in a number of cities. In 1953 Philadelphia reported 28,560 Index crimes plus negligent manslaughter and larceny under $50, an increase of more than 70 percent over 1951. This sudden jump in crime, however, was not due to an invasion by criminals but to the discovery by a new administration that crime records had for years minimized the amount of crime in the city. One district had actually handled 5,000 complaints more than it had recorded.

The Commission could not attempt an exhaustive study of such changes in reporting procedures. It has noted . . . [that] the *UCR* indicated changes in reporting procedures for major cities during 1959–65. All of these changes have resulted in an increase in the level of reporting for all subsequent years. It has also noted that changes of this sort are still taking place, being indicated in 1966 for Detroit, Chattanooga, Worcester, Mass., and New York City among others. . . .

The existence of the *UCR* system has been one of the strongest forces pushing toward the adoption of better and more complete reporting. The FBI has been alert both to the need to encourage better reporting and to the problem that sizable changes in reporting present to the national statistical system. Through a careful system of checks the FBI is able to identify the units that are reporting on a different basis than the previous year. It then restricts its computations of trends from one year to the next to those police agencies that have had comparable records and reporting practices. In 1965, for example, computation of changes from 1964 were limited to agencies representing 82 percent of the U.S. population; 147 reporting agencies representing about 10 percent of the population were eliminated because of changes in reporting practices.

In order to make comparisons for periods greater than 1 year the *UCR* assumes that the city that underwent the change in reporting practices has had the same experience as other cities of its size and State throughout the period and reestimates the amount of crime for all prior years back to its base period of the 1937–40 average. In the 1960–65 period, use of this system reduces the 36 percent increase in Index crimes against the person based on published rates to a 25 percent increase, and the 39 percent increase in crimes against property to 36 percent. Cities are returned to the trend computation after they have had 2 years of comparable experience under the new system.

This system is perhaps as good as can be devised. It is obviously very hard, however, to estimate how much crime would have been reported in a major city in the year prior to that in which the system of reporting was changed, and even harder to say what the crime rate was 5 years earlier. It seems unlikely that the level of robbery in New York today is 13 times what it was in 1940 or triple what it was in 1960, but how does one decide for the purpose of long-term comparisons? The cities that have significantly changed their reporting systems since 1959 account for nearly 25 percent of all reported Index crimes against the person and about 16 percent of all reported Index property crimes. The real question is not the method of estimation, but whether the yardstick at the present time is too changeable to allow significant trend comparisons to be made at the national level.

A further problem is raised by the fact that a number of other large cities have not yet adopted the central complaint bureaus and strong staff controls necessary for an effective reporting program. In one of these cities Commission staff members were informed of a precinct file 13, where citizen complaints not forwarded to the central statistical office were filed for the purpose of answering insurance inquiries. The President's Commission on Crime in the District of Columbia recently criticized Washington's failure to record all offenses reported to the police. It is not clear how large this group of cities is, but disparities between cities of the same size for each of the Index offenses are so great that they seem most unlikely in the absence of some variation in reporting practice.

The reporting problem arises at least in part from the tendency of some cities, noted in 1931 by the Wickersham Commission, to "use these reports in order to advertise their freedom from crime as compared with other municipalities." This tendency has apparently not yet been fully overcome. It sometimes arises from political pressure outside the police department and sometimes from the desire of the police to appear to be doing a good job of keeping the crime rate down. Defective or inefficient recording practices may also prevent crimes reported by citizens from becoming a part of the record. . . .

Factors Indicating an Increase in Crime

Many factors affect crime trends but they are not always easy to isolate. Murder is a seasonal offense. Rates are generally higher in the summer, except for December, which is often the highest month and almost always 5 to 20 percent above the yearly average. In December 1963, follow the assassination of President Kennedy, murders were below the yearly average by 4 percent, one of the few years in the history of the *UCR* that this occurred. Since 1950 the pace of auto thefts has increased faster than but in the same direction as car registrations. During World War II, however, when there was rationing and a shortage of cars, rates for auto theft rose sharply. And in 1946 when cars came back in production and most other crimes were increasing, auto thefts fell off rapidly.

The introduction to the *UCR* provides a checklist of some of the many factors that must be taken into account in interpreting changes in crime rates and in the amount and type of crime that occurs from place to place:

Density and size of the community population and the metropolitan area of which it is a part.
Composition of the population with reference particularly to age, sex, and race.
Economic status and mores of the population.
Relative stability of population, including commuters, seasonal, and other transient types.
Climate, including seasonal weather conditions.
Educational, recreational, and religious characteristics.
Effective strength of the police force.
Standards governing appointments to the police force.
Policies of the prosecuting officials and the courts.
Attitude of the public toward law enforcement problems.
The administrative and investigative efficiency of the local law enforcement agency.

A number of these factors have been changing in ways that would lead one to expect increases in the amounts of certain kinds of crime.

Changing Age Composition. One of the most significant factors affecting crime rates is the age composition of the population. In 1965 more than 44 percent of all persons arrested for forcible rape, more than 39 percent for robbery, and more than 26 percent for willful homicide and aggravated assault were in the 18- to 24-year-old age group. For property crimes the highest percentages are found in the under 18 group—nearly 50 percent of all those arrested for burglary and larceny and more than 60 percent for auto theft.

For most of these offenses the rate of offense per individual in these age groups is many times that in older groups. Of course the differences are based on arrest figures, and the national figures on offenses cleared by arrest show that 75 to 80 percent of burglaries, larcenies, and auto thefts are unsolved. It is possible that older persons committing offenses against property are more successful at evading arrest, so that the age figures for arrests give a somewhat biased picture.

Because of the unusual birthrate in the postwar years, the youthful high-risk group—those in their teens and early twenties—has been increasing much faster than other groups in the population. Beginning in 1961 nearly 1 million more youths have reached the ages of maximum risk each year than did so in the prior year. Thus the volume of crime and the overall crime rate could be expected to grow whether the rate for any given age increased or not.

Commission studies based on 1960 arrest rates indicate that between 1960 and 1965 about 40 to 50 percent of the total increase in the arrests reported by *UCR* could have been expected as the result of increases in population and changes in the age composition of the population.

Urbanization. Rates for most crimes are highest in the big cities. Twenty-six core cities of more than 500,000 people, with less than 18 percent of the total population, account for more than half of all reported Index crimes against the person and more than 30 percent of all reported Index property crimes. One of every three robberies and nearly one of every five rapes occurs in cities of more than 1 million. The average rate for every Index crime except burglary . . . is at least twice as great —and often more—in these cities as in the suburbs or rural areas. With a few exceptions, average rates increase progressively as the size of the city becomes larger.

Suburban rates are closest to those of the smaller cities except for forcible rape where suburban rates are higher. Suburban rates appear to be going up as business and industry increase—shopping centers are most frequently blamed by local police officials for rises in suburban crime.

Although rural rates are lower generally than those for cities, the differences have always been much greater for property crimes than for crimes against the person. Until the last few years rural rates for murder were close to those of the big cities, and rural rates for murder and rape still exceed those for small towns.

The country has for many years seen a steady increase in its urban population and a decline in the proportion of the population living in rural areas and smaller towns. Since 1930 the rural population has increased by less than 2 percent while the city population has increased by more than 50 percent. The increase in the cities and their suburbs since 1960 alone has been about 10 percent. Because of the higher crime rates in and around the larger cities, this trend toward urbanization has a considerable effect on the national rate for most Index crimes. Commission studies show that if metropolitan, small city, and rural crime rates for 1960 had remained constant through 1965, the increase that could have been expected due to urbanization would have been about 7 to 8 percent of the increase reported by the *UCR*.

It would obviously tell us a great deal about the trend of crime if we could analyze all together the changes that have been taking place in urbanization, age composition of the population, number of slum dwellers, and other factors such as sex, race, and level of income. The Commission has spent a considerable amount of time trying to make this kind of analysis. However, it was unable to analyze satisfactorily more than one or two factors in conjunction with each other on the basis of present information. As more factors were brought into the analysis the results differed in some instances substantially from those obtained when only one factor was analyzed. It also seemed clear that as the number of factors was increased, a more accurate picture of the effect of changing conditions on the rate of crime emerged.

On the basis of its study, the Commission estimates that the total expected increase in crime from 1960 to 1965 from these kinds of changes would be at least half, and possibly a great deal more, of the total increase in crime rates actually observed. The Commission's study clearly indicates the need for fuller reporting of arrest information and for the development of more compatibility between police statistics and information collected by other statistical agencies. The FBI has already made substantial progress in this direction in recent years but further steps are still needed.

* * *

Increased Affluence. Another change that may result in more crime is increasing affluence. There are more goods around to be stolen. National wealth and all categories of merchandise have increased in terms of constant dollars more than fourfold since 1940—significantly more than the population or the rate of reported theft.

Increased affluence may also have meant that property is now protected less well than formerly. More than 40 percent of all auto thefts involve cars with the keys inside or the switch left open. A substantial percentage of residential burglaries occur in unlocked houses. Bicycles, whose theft constitutes 15 percent of all reported larcenies, are frequently left lying around. Larceny of goods and accessories from cars accounts for another 40 percent of all reported larceny.

Some increased business theft seems directly due to less protection. The recent rise in bank robbery seems due in large part to the development of small, poorly protected branch banks in the suburbs.

In retail establishments, managers choose to tolerate a high percentage of shoplifting rather than pay for additional clerks. Discount stores, for example, experience an inventory loss rate almost double that of the conventional department store. Studies indicate that there is in general more public tolerance for theft of property and goods from large organizations than from small ones, from big corporations or utilities than from small neighborhood establishments. Restraints on conduct that were effective in a more personal rural society do not seem as effective in an impersonal society of large organizations.

Inflation has also had an impact on some property crimes. Larceny, for example, is any stealing that does not involve force or fraud. The test of the seriousness of larceny is the value of the property stolen. The dividing line between "grand" and "petty" larceny for national reporting purposes is $50. Larceny of $50 and over is the Index offense that has increased the most over the history of the *UCR*, more than 550 percent since 1933. Because the purchasing power of the dollar today is only 40 percent of what it was in 1933, many thefts that would have been under $50 then are over $50 now. *UCR* figures on the value of property stolen, for example, indicate that the average value of a larceny has risen from $26 in 1940 to $84 in 1965.

* * *

Assessing the Amount and Trend of Crime

Because of the grave public concern about the crime problem in America today, the Commission has made a special effort to understand the amount and trend of crime and has reached the following conclusions:

1. The number of offenses—crimes of violence, crimes against property and most others as well—has been increasing. Naturally, population growth is one of the significant contributing factors in the total amount of crime.

2. Most forms of crime—especially crimes against property—are increasing faster than population growth. This means that the risk of victimization to the individual citizen for these crimes is increasing, although it is not possible to ascertain precisely the extent of the increase. All the economic and social factors discussed above support, and indeed lead to, this conclusion.

The Commission found it very difficult to make accurate measurements of crime trends by relying solely on official figures, since it is likely that each year police agencies are to some degree dipping deeper into the vast reservoir of unreported crime. People are probably reporting more to the police as a reflection of higher expectations and greater confidence, and the police in turn are reflecting this in their statistics. In this sense more efficient policing may be leading to higher rates of reported crime. The diligence of the FBI in promoting more complete and accurate reporting through the development of professional police reporting procedures has clearly had an important effect on the completeness of reporting, but while this task of upgrading local reporting is under way, the FBI is faced with the problem, in computing national trends, of omitting for a time the places undergoing changes in reporting methods and estimating the amount of crime that occurred in those places in prior years.

3. Although the Commission concluded that there has been an increase in the volume and rate of crime in America, it has been unable to decide whether individual Americans today are more criminal than their counterparts 5, 10, or 25 years ago. To answer this question it would be necessary to make comparisons between persons of the same age, sex, race, place of residence, economic status and other factors at the different times: in other words, to decide whether the 15-year-old slum dweller or the 50-year-old businessman is inherently more criminal now than the 15-year-old slum dweller or the 50-year-old businessman in the past. Because of the many rapid and turbulent changes over these years in society as a whole and in the myriad conditions of life which affect crime, it was not possible for the Commission to make such a comparison. Nor do the data exist to make even simple comparisons of the incidence of crime among persons of the same age, sex, race, and place of residence at these different years.

4. There is a great deal of crime in America, some of it very serious, that is not reported to the police, or in some instances by the police. The national survey revealed that people are generally more likely to report serious crimes to the police, but the percent who indicated they did report to the police ranged from 10 percent for consumer fraud to 89 percent for auto theft. Estimates of the rate of victimization for Index offenses ranged from 2 per 100 persons in the national survey to 10 to 20 per 100 persons in the individual districts surveyed in 3 cities. The surveys produced rates of victimization that were from 2 to 10 times greater than the official rates for certain crimes.

5. What is needed to answer questions about the volume and trend of crime satisfactorily are a number of different crime indicators showing trends over a period of time to supplement the improved reporting by police agencies. The

Commission experimented with the development of public surveys of victims of crime and feels this can become a useful supplementary yardstick. Further development of the procedure is needed to improve the reliability and accuracy of the findings. However, the Commission found these initial experiments produced useful results that justify more intensive efforts to gather such information on a regular basis. They should also be supplemented by new types of surveys and censuses which would provide better information about crime in areas where good information is lacking such as crimes by or against business and other organizations. The Commission also believes that an improved and greatly expanded procedure for the collection of arrest statistics would be of immense benefit in the assessment of the problem of juvenile delinquency.

6. Throughout its work the Commission has noted repeatedly the sharp differences in the amount and trends of reported crimes against property as compared with crimes against persons. It has noted that while property crimes are far more numerous than crimes against the person, and so dominate any reported trends, there is much public concern about crimes against persons. The more recent reports of the *UCR* have moved far toward separating the reporting of these two classes of crime altogether.

The Commission recommends:

The present Index of reported crime should be broken into two wholly separate parts, one for crimes of violence and the other for crimes against property.

The Commission also recommends, in principle, the development of additional indices to indicate the volume and trend of such other important crime problems as embezzlement, fraud, and other crimes against trust, crimes of vice that are associated with organized crime, and perhaps others. The Commission urges that consideration be given to practical methods for developing such indices.

The Commission also urges that the public media and others concerned with crime be careful to keep separate the various crime problems and not to deal with them as a unitary phenomenon. Whenever possible, crime should be reported relative to population as well as by the number of offenses, so as to provide a more accurate picture of risks of victimization in any particular locality.

7. The Commission believes that age, urbanization, and other shifts in the population already under way will likely operate over the next 5 to 10 years to increase the volume of offenses faster than population growth. Further dipping into the reservoirs of unreported crime will likely combine with this real increase in crime to produce even greater increases in reported crime rates. Many of the basic social forces that tend to increase the amount of real crime are already taking effect and are for the most part irreversible. If society is to be successful in its desire to reduce the amount of real crime, it must find new ways to create the kinds of conditions and inducements—social, environmental, and psychological—that will bring about a greater commitment to law-abiding conduct and respect for the law on the part of all Americans and a better understanding of the great stake that all men have in being able to trust in the honesty and integrity of their fellow citizens.

2.

Daniel Bell

CRIME AS AN AMERICAN WAY OF LIFE

In the 1890's the Reverend Dr. Charles Parkhurst, shocked at the open police protection afforded New York's bordellos, demanded a state inquiry. In the Lexow investigation that followed, the young and dashing William Travers Jerome staged a set of public hearings that created sensation after sensation. He badgered "Clubber" Williams, First Inspector of the Police Department, to account for wealth and property far greater than could have been saved on his salary; it was earned, the Clubber explained laconically, through land speculation "in Japan." Heavy-set Captain Schmittberger, the "collector" for the "Tenderloin precincts"—Broadway's fabulous concentration of hotels, theaters, restaurants, gaming houses, and saloons—related in detail how protection money was distributed among the police force. Crooks, policemen, public officials, businessmen, all paraded across the stage, each adding his chapter to a sordid story of corruption and crime. The upshot of these revelations was reform—the election of William L. Strong, a stalwart businessman, as mayor, and the naming of Theodore Roosevelt as police commissioner.

It did not last, of course, just as previous reform victories had not lasted. Yet the ritual drama was re-enacted. Thirty years ago the Seabury investigation in New York uncovered the tin-box brigade and the thirty-three little McQuades. Jimmy Walker was ousted as Mayor and in came Fiorello LaGuardia. Tom Dewey became district attorney, broke the industrial rackets, sent Lucky Luciano to jail, and went to the governor's chair in Albany. Then reform was again swallowed up in the insatiable maw of corruption until in 1950 Kefauver and his committee counsel Rudolph Halley threw a new beam of light into the seemingly bottomless pit.

How explain this repetitious cycle? Obviously the simple moralistic distinction between "good guys" and "bad guys," so deep at the root of the reform impulse, bears little relation to the role of organized crime in American society. What, then, does?

THE QUEER LADDER

Americans have had an extraordinary talent for compromise in politics and extremism in morality. The most shameless political deals (and "steals") have been rationalized as expedient and realistically necessary. Yet in no other country have there been such spectacular attempts to curb human appetites and brand them as illicit, and nowhere else such glaring failures. From the start America was at one and the same time a frontier community where "everything goes," and the fair country of the Blue Laws. At the turn of the century the cleavage developed between the Big City and the small-town conscience. Crime as a growing business was fed by the revenues from prostitution, liquor, and gambling that a wide-open urban society encouraged and that a middle-class Protestant ethos tried to suppress with a ferocity unmatched in any other civilized country. Catholic cultures have rarely imposed such restrictions and have rarely suffered such excesses. Even in prim and proper Anglican England, prostitution is a commonplace of Piccadilly night life, and gambling is one of the largest and most popular industries. In America the enforcement of public morals has been a continuing feature of our history.

Some truth may lie in Max Scheler's generalization that moral indignation is a peculiar fact of middle-class psychology and represents a disguised form of repressed envy. The larger truth lies perhaps in the brawling nature of

---

Reprinted with permission of The Macmillan Company from *The End of Ideology* by Daniel Bell. *The Antioch Review,* Vol. XIII (Summer, 1953).

American development and in the social character of crime. Crime, in many ways, is a Coney Island mirror, caricaturing the morals and manners of a society. The jungle quality of the American business community, particularly at the turn of the century, was reflected in the mode of "business" practiced by the coarse gangster elements, most of them from new immigrant families, who were "getting ahead," just as Horatio Alger had urged. In the older, Protestant tradition the intensive acquisitiveness, such as that of Daniel Drew, was rationalized by a compulsive moral fervor. But the formal obeisance of the ruthless businessman in the workaday world to the church-going pieties of the Sabbath was one that the gangster could not make. Moreover, for the young criminal, hunting in the asphalt jungle of the crowded city, it was not the businessman with his wily manipulation of numbers but the "man with the gun" who was the American hero. "No amount of commercial prosperity," once wrote Teddy Roosevelt, "can supply the lack of the heroic virtues." The American was "the hunter, cowboy, frontiersman, the soldier, the naval hero"—and in the crowded slums, the gangster. He was a man with a gun, acquiring by personal merit what was denied him by complex orderings of stratified society. And the duel with the law was the morality play par excellence: the gangster, with whom ride our own illicit desires, and the prosecutor, representing final judgment and the force of the law.

Yet all this was acted out in a wider context. The desires satisfied in extra-legal fashion were more than a hunger for the "forbidden fruits" of conventional morality. They also involved, in the complex and ever shifting structure of group, class, and ethnic stratification, which is the warp and woof of America's "open" society, such "normal" goals as independence through a business of one's own, and such "moral" aspirations as the desire for social advancement and social prestige. For crime, in the language of the sociologists, has a "functional" role in the society, and the urban rackets—the illicit activity organized for continuing profit, rather than individual illegal acts—is one of the queer ladders of social mobility in American life. Indeed, it is not too much to say that the whole question of organized crime in America cannot be understood unless one appreciates (1) the distinctive role of organized gambling as a function of a mass-consumption economy; (2) the specific role of various immigrant groups as they, one after another, became involved in marginal business and crime; and (3) the relation of crime to the changing character of the urban political machines.

GATSBY'S MODEL

As a society changes, so does, in lagging fashion, its type of crime. As American society became more "organized," as the American businessman became more "civilized" and less "buccaneering," so did the American racketeer. And just as there were important changes in the structure of business enterprise, so the "institutionalized" criminal enterprise was transformed too.

In the America of the last fifty years the main drift of society has been toward the rationalization of industry, the domestication of the crude self-made captain of industry into the respectable man of manners, and the emergence of a mass-consumption economy. The most significant transformation in the field of "institutionalized" crime in the 1940's was the increasing importance of gambling as against other kinds of illegal activity. And, as a multi-billion-dollar business, gambling underwent a transition parallel to the changes in American enterprise as a whole. This parallel was exemplified in many ways: in gambling's industrial organization (e.g., the growth of a complex technology such as the national racing-wire service and the minimization of risks by such techniques as lay-off betting); in its respectability, as was evidenced in the opening of smart and popular gambling casinos in resort towns and in "satellite" adjuncts to metropolitan areas; in its functional role in a mass-consumption economy (for sheer volume of money changing hands, nothing has ever surpassed this feverish activity of fifty million American adults); in the social acceptance of the gamblers in the important status world of sport and entertainment, i.e., "café society."

In seeking to "legitimize" itself, gambling had quite often actually become a force against older and more vicious forms of illegal activity. In 1946, for example, when a Chicago mobster, Pat Manno, went down to Dallas, Texas, to take over gambling in the area for the Accardo-Guzik combine, he reassured the sheriff as follows: "Something I'm against, that's dope peddlers, pickpockets, hired killers. That's one thing I can't stomach, and that's one thing the fellows up there—the group won't stand for, things like that. They discourage it, they even go to headquarters and ask them why they don't do something about it."

Jimmy Cannon once reported that when the gambling raids started in Chicago the "combine" protested that, in upsetting existing stable relations, the police were only opening the way for ambitious young punks and hoodlums to start trouble. Nor is there today, as there was twenty or even forty years ago, prostitution of major organized scope in the United States. Aside from the fact that manners and morals have changed, prostitution *as an industry* doesn't pay as well as gambling. Besides, its existence threatened the tacit moral acceptance and quasi-respectability that gamblers and gambling have secured in the American way of life. It was, as any operator in the field might tell you, "bad for business . . ."

But in the last decade and a half, industrial racketeering has not offered much in the way of opportunity. *Like American capitalism itself, crime shifted its emphasis from production to consumption.* The focus of crime became the direct exploitation of the citizen as consumer, largely through gambling. And while the protection of these huge revenues was inextricably linked to politics, the relation between gambling and "the mobs" became more complicated.

BIG-BUSINESS BOOKIES

Although it never showed up in the gross national product, gambling in the last decade was one of the largest industries in the United States. The Kefauver Committee estimated it as a $20 billion business. This figure has been picked up and widely quoted, but in truth no one knows what the gambling "turnover" and "take" actually is, nor how much is bet legally (parimutuel, etc.) and how much illegally. In fact, the figure cited by the committee was arbitrary and was arrived at quite sloppily. As one staff member said: "We had no real idea of the money spent. . . . The California Crime Commission said twelve billion. Virgil Peterson of Chicago estimated thirty billion. We picked twenty billion as a balance between the two."

If comprehensive data is not available, we do know, from specific instances, the magnitude of many of the operations. Some indication can be seen from these items culled as random:

James Carroll and the M & G syndicate did a $20 million annual business in St. Louis. This was one of the two large books in the city.

The S & G syndicate in Miami did a $26 million volume yearly; the total for all books in the Florida resort reached $40 million.

Slot machines were present in 69,786 establishments in 1951 (each paid $100 for a license to the Bureau of Internal Revenue); the usual average is three machines to a license, which would add up to 210,000 slot machines in operation in the United States. In legalized areas, where the betting is higher and more regular, the average gross "take" per machine is $50 a week.

The largest policy wheel (i.e., "numbers") in Chicago's "Black Belt" reported taxable net profits for the four-year period from 1946 through 1949, after sizable deductions for "overhead," of $3,656,968. One of the large "white" wheels reported in 1947 a gross income of $2,317,000 and a net profit of $205,000. One CIO official estimated that perhaps 15 per cent of his union's lower-echelon officials are involved in the numbers racket (a steward, free to roam a plant, is in a perfect situation for organizing bets).

If one considers the amount of dollars bet on sports alone—an estimated six billion on baseball, a billion on football pools, another billion on basketball, six billion on horse racing—then Elmo Roper's judgment that "only the food, steel, auto, chemical, and machine-tool industries have a greater volume of business" does not seem too farfetched.

While gambling has long flourished in the United States, the influx of the big mobsters into the industry—and its expansion—started in the thirties, when repeal of Prohibition forced them to look about for new avenues of enterprise. (The change, one might say crudely, was in the "democratization" of gambling. In New York of the 1860's, 1870's, and 1880's, one found elegant establishments where the wealthy men of the city, bankers, and sportsmen gambled. The saloon was the home of the worker. The middle class of the time did not gamble. In the changing mores of America, the rise of gambling in the 1930's and 1940's meant the introduction of the middle class to gambling and casinos as a way of life.) Gambling, which had begun to flower under the nourishment of rising incomes, was the most lucrative field in sight. To a large extent the shift from bootlegging to gambling was a mere transfer of business operations. In the East, Frank Costello went into slot machines and the operation of a number of ritzy gambling casinos. He also became the "banker" for the Erickson "book," which "laid off" bets for other bookies. Joe Adonis, similarly, opened up a number of casinos, principally in New Jersey. Across the country, many other mobsters went into bookmaking. As other rackets diminished and gambling, particularly horse-race betting, flourished in the forties, a struggle erupted over the control of racing information.

Horse-race betting requires a peculiar industrial organization. The essential component is time. A bookie can operate only if he can get information on odds up to the very last minute before the race, so that he can "hedge" or "lay off" bets. With racing going on simultaneously on many tracks throughout the country, this information has to be obtained speedily and accurately. Thus, the racing wire is the nerve ganglion of race betting.

The racing-wire news service got started in the twenties through the genius of the late Moe Annenberg, who had made a fearful reputation for himself as Hearst's circulation manager in the rough-and-tough Chicago newspaper wars. Annenberg conceived the idea of a telegraphic news service which would gather information from tracks and shoot it immediately to scratch sheets, horse parlors, and bookie joints. In some instances, track owners gave Annenberg the rights to send news from tracks; more often, the news was simply "stolen" by crews operating inside or near the tracks. So efficient did this news distribution system become, that in 1942, when a plane knocked out a vital telegraph circuit which served an Air Force field as well as the gamblers, the Continental Press managed to get its racing wire service for gamblers resumed in fifteen minutes, while it took the Fourth Army, which was responsible for the defense of the entire West Coast, something like three hours. . . .

GAMBLERS AND GUYS

While Americans made gambling illegal, they did not in their hearts think of it as wicked—even the churches benefited from the bingo and lottery crazes. So they gambled—and gamblers flourished. Against this open canvas, the indignant tones of Senator Wiley and the shocked righteousness of Senator Tobey during the Kefauver investigation rang oddly. Yet it was probably this very tone of surprise that gave the activity of the Kefauver Committee its piquant quality. Here were some senators who seemingly did not know the facts of life, as most Americans did. Here, in the person of Senator Tobey, was the old New England Puritan conscience poking around in industrial America, in a world it had made but never seen. Here was old-fashioned moral indignation, at a time when cynicism was rampant in public life.

Commendable as such moralistic fervor was, it did not make for intelligent discrimination of fact. Throughout the Kefauver hearings, for example, there ran the presumption that all gamblers were invariably gangsters. This was true of Chicago's Accardo-Guzik combine, which in the past had its fingers in many kinds of rackets. It was not nearly so true of many large gamblers in America, most of whom had the feeling that they were satisfying a basic American urge for sport and looked upon their calling with no greater sense of guilt than did many bootleggers. After all, Sherman Billingsley did start out as a speakeasy proprietor, as did the Kreindlers of the "21" Club; and today the Stork Club and the former Jack and Charlie's are the most fashionable night and dining spots in America (one prominent patron of the Stork Club: J. Edgar Hoover). . . .

Most intriguing of all were the opinions of

James J. Carroll, the St. Louis "betting commissioner," who for years had been widely quoted on the sports pages of the country as setting odds on the Kentucky Derby winter book and the baseball pennant races. Senator Wiley, speaking like the prosecutor in Camus's novel, *The Stranger*, became the voice of official morality:

SENATOR WILEY: Have you any children?
MR. CARROLL: Yes, I have a boy.
SENATOR WILEY: How old is he?
MR. CARROLL: Thirty-three.
SENATOR WILEY: Does he gamble?
MR. CARROLL: No.
SENATOR WILEY: Would you like to see him grow up and become a gambler, either professional or amateur?
MR. CARROLL: No. . . .
SENATOR WILEY: All right. Is your son interested in your business?
MR. CARROLL: No, he is a manufacturer.
SENATOR WILEY: Why do you not get him into the business?
MR. CARROLL: Well, psychologically a great many people are unsuited for gambling.

Retreating from this gambit, the Senator sought to pin Carroll down on his contributions to political campaigns:

SENATOR WILEY: Now this morning I asked you whether you contributed any money for political candidates or parties, and you said not more than $200 at one time. I presume that does not indicate the total of your contributions in any one campaign, does it?

MR. CARROLL: Well, it might, might not, Senator. I have been an "againster" in many instances. I am a reader of *The Nation* for fifty years and they have advertisements calling for contributions for different candidates, different causes. . . . They carried an advertisement for George Norris; I contributed, I think, to that, and to the elder LaFollette.

Carroll, who admitted to having been in the betting business since 1899, was the sophisticated—but not immoral!—counterpoint to moralist Wiley. Here was a man without the stigmata of the underworld or underground; he was worldly, cynical of official rhetoric, jaundiced about people's motives; he was an "againster" who believed that "all gambling legislation originates or stems from some group or some individual seeking special interests for himself or his cause."

Asked why people gamble, Carroll distilled his experiences of fifty years with a remark that deserves a place in American social history: "I really don't know how to answer the question," he said. "I think gambling is a biological necessity for certain types. I think it is the quality that gives substances to their day-dreams."

In a sense, the entire Kefauver materials, unintentionally, seem to document that remark. For what the committee revealed time and time again was a picture of gambling as a basic institution in American life, flourishing openly and accepted widely. In many of the small towns, the gambling joint is as open as a liquor establishment. The town of Havana, in Mason County, Illinois, felt miffed when Governor Adlai Stevenson intervened against local gambling. In 1950, the town had raised $15,000 of its $50,000 budget by making friendly raids on the gambling houses every month and having the owners pay fines. "With the gambling fines cut off," grumbled Mayor Clarence Chester, "the next year is going to be tough."

Apart from the gamblers, there were the mobsters. But what Senator Kefauver and company failed to understand was that the mobsters, like the gamblers, and like the entire gangdom generally, were seeking to become quasi-respectable and establish a place for themselves in American life. For the mobsters, by and large, had immigrant roots, and crime, as the pattern showed, was a route of social ascent and place in American life.

THE MYTH OF THE MAFIA

The mobsters were able, where they wished, to "muscle in" on the gambling business because the established gamblers were wholly vulnerable, not being able to call on the law for protection. The senators, however, refusing to make any distinction between a gambler and a gangster, found it convenient to talk loosely of a nationwide conspiracy of "illegal" elements. Senator Kefauver asserted that a "nationwide crime syndicate does exist in the United States, despite the protestations of a strangely assorted company of criminals, self-serving politicians, plain blind fools, and others who may be honestly misguided, that there is no such combine." The Senate committee report states the matter more dogmatically: "There is a nationwide crime syndicate known as the Mafia. . . . Its leaders are usually found in control of the most lucrative rackets in their cities. There are indications of a centralized direction and control of these rackets. . . . The Mafia is the cement that helps to bind the Costello-Adonis-Lansky syndicate of New York and the Accardo-Guzik-Fischetti syndicate of Chicago. . . . These groups have kept in touch with Luciano since his deportation from the country."

Unfortunately for a good story—and the existence of the Mafia would be a whale of a story—neither the Senate Crime Committee in its testimony, nor Kefauver in his book, presented any real evidence that the Mafia exists as a functioning organization. One finds police officials asserting before the Kefauver committee their *belief* in the Mafia; the Narcotics Bureau *thinks* that a world-wide dope ring allegedly run by Luciano is part of the Mafia; but the only other "evidence" presented—aside from the incredulous responses both of Senator Kefauver and Rudolph Halley when nearly all the Italian gangsters asserted that they didn't know about the Mafia—is that certain crimes bear "the earmarks of the Mafia. . . ."

Why did the Senate Crime Committee plump so hard for its theory of a Mafia and a national crime syndicate? In part, they may have been misled by their own hearsay. The Senate committee was not in the position to do original research, and its staff, both legal and investigative, was incredibly small. Senator Kefauver had begun the investigation with the attitude that with so much smoke there must be a raging fire. But smoke can also mean a smoke screen. Mob activities is a field in which busy gossip and exaggeration flourish even more readily than in a radical political sect.

There is, as well, in the American temper, a feeling that "somewhere," "somebody" is pulling all the complicated strings to which this jumbled world dances. In politics the labor image is "Wall Street" or "Big Business"; while the business stereotype was the "New Dealers." In the field of crime, the side-of-the-mouth low-down was "Costello."

The salient reason, perhaps, why the Kefauver Committee was taken in by its own myth of an omnipotent Mafia and a despotic Costello was its failure to assimilate and understand three of the more relevant sociological facts about institutionalized crime in its relation to the political life of large urban communities in America, namely: (1) the rise of the American Italian community, as part of the inevitable process of ethnic succession, to positions of importance in politics, a process that has been occurring independently but also simultaneously in most cities with large Italian constituences—New York, Chicago, Kansas City, Los Angeles; (2) the fact that there are individual Italians who play prominent, often leading roles today in gambling and in the mobs; and (3) the fact that Italian gamblers and mobsters often possessed "status" within the Italian community itself and a "pull" in city politics. These three items are indeed related—but not so as to form a "plot." . . .

THE "NEW" MONEY—AND THE OLD

There is little question that men of Italian origin appeared in most of the leading roles in the high drama of gambling and mobs, just as twenty years ago the children of East European Jews were the most prominent figures in organized crime, and before that individuals of Irish descent were similarly prominent. To some extent statistical accident and the tendency of newspapers to emphasize the few sensational figures give a greater illusion about the domination of illicit activities by a single ethnic group than all the facts warrant. In many cities, particularly in the South and on the West Coast, the mob and gambling fraternity consisted of many other groups, and often, predominantly, of native white Protestants. Yet it is clear that in the major northern urban centers there was a distinct ethnic sequence in the modes of obtaining illicit wealth and that, uniquely in the case of the recent Italian elements, the former bootleggers and gamblers provided considerable leverage for the growth of political influence as well. A substantial number of Italian judges sitting on the bench in New York today are indebted in one fashion or another to Costello; so too are many Italian district leaders—as well as some Jewish and

Irish politicians. And the motive in establishing Italian political prestige in New York was generous rather than scheming for personal advantage. For Costello it was largely a case of ethnic pride. As in earlier American eras, organized illegality became a stepladder of social ascent.

To the world at large, the news and pictures of Frank Sinatra, for example, mingling with former Italian mobsters could come somewhat as a shock. Yet to Sinatra, and to many Italians, these were men who had grown up in their neighborhoods and who were, in some instances, bywords in the community for their helpfulness and their charities. The early Italian gangsters were hoodlums—rough, unlettered, and young (Al Capone was only twenty-nine at the height of his power). Those who survived learned to adapt. By now they are men of middle age or older. They learned to dress conservatively. Their homes are in respectable suburbs. They sent their children to good schools and sought to avoid publicity. Costello even went to a psychiatrist in his efforts to overcome a painful feeling of inferiority in the world of manners.

As happens with all "new" money in American society, the rough and ready contractors, the construction people, trucking entrepreneurs, as well as racketeers, polished up their manners and sought recognition and respectability in their own ethnic as well as in the general community. The "shanty" Irish became the "lace curtain" Irish, and then moved out for wider recognition. Sometimes acceptance came first in established "American" society, and this was a certificate for later recognition by the ethnic community, a process well illustrated by the belated acceptance in established Negro society of such figures as Sugar Ray Robinson and Joe Louis, as well as leading popular entertainers.

Yet, after all, the foundation of many a distinguished older American fortune was laid by sharp practices and morally reprehensible methods. The pioneers of American capitalism were not graduated from Harvard's School of Business Administration. The early settlers and founding fathers, as well as those who "won the West" and built up cattle, mining, and other fortunes, often did so by shady speculations and a not inconsiderable amount of violence. They ignored, circumvented, or stretched the law when it stood in the way of America's destiny and their own—or were themselves the law when it served their purposes. This has not prevented them and their descendants from feeling proper moral outrage when, under the changed circumstances of the crowded urban environments, latecomers pursued equally ruthless tactics. . . .

3.

John Irwin and Lewis Yablonsky

THE NEW CRIMINAL: A VIEW OF THE CONTEMPORARY OFFENDER

This paper will attempt to delineate the "basic character" of the new criminal, in contrast with the basic criminal type of the past. These conclusions about the new criminal are not based on any special study but upon the authors' close association with various offenders and the structure of the crime problem over the past ten years. The development of the theme of the new addict is taken from perceptions and studies of New York violent gangs, ex-addicts,

Source: *The British Journal of Criminology,* Vol. 5, No. 2 (April, 1965), pp. 183–90, Institute for the Study and Treatment of Delinquency. Reprinted by permission of the authors and the journal.

and ex-criminals currently living in an anti-criminal society at Synanon House (Santa Monica, California). Incorporated is one author's experience in running group psychotherapy sessions with offenders in custody in various institutions over the past ten years. Much valuable material was collected by John Irwin directly in over fifty depth interviews with various "old" and "new" criminals in and out of prison.

On the basis of varied evidence we would contend that the basic personality of the majority of criminals has shifted from the well-trained, resourceful, "ethical" offender of the past to a new, unskilled and reckless deviant type. Here reference is made to an overall shift of the basic personality and behaviour of the modern criminal. Old criminal types are still around; however, they represent a dying breed.

The new criminal's crimes tend to be more violent and "senseless." He lacks the skill in his profession that older criminals had. He is more apt to be involved with "kicks" or "thrills" and emotional gratification, and less with the material profit of his crimes. His training as a "good criminal" is sketchy and ill-defined, unlike the "breaking-in" process of the criminal of the past. Not all criminals of today fit this new mould; however, the pendulum has swung in this direction. It is important to diagnose correctly the modal quality of the problem which we attempt to correct. In the treatment of social problems, there is often a cultural lag between correct diagnosis of the problem and the development of treatment approach. By the time correct treatment is constructed it is often no longer appropriate to the problem at hand—since it has shifted. We would contend this is true of the current crime problem. This fact accentuates the need to speculate on the gross qualities of our social problems; in this case, the criminal.

The old criminal codes of "honour among thieves," "thou shalt not squeal," and standing up for one's "crime partner" are fast becoming criminal slogans of the past. The new criminal is more apt to turn in his partners, cheat on them and make technical errors in his crimes. He is also younger and more apt to be some type of addict (e.g., in California over 40 percent of the prison population has had some type of narcotics experience). The dimensions of the problem to be described are more hypothetical than hard research results; yet they seem to be confirmed by considerable evidence.

THE "NEW" AND "OLD" CRIMINAL

Sutherland's conception of the criminal remains as our current sociological model of the offender. This paper contends that, although the criminal type described by Sutherland still exists in some measure, in terms of numbers and character the old criminal is decreasing and is being increasingly replaced by a new breed of sociopathic offenders.

Sutherland's classic theory of "differential association," grossly over-simplified, states that criminals learn to become criminal from association with other offenders. They are trained into criminal patterns at an early age in a school of criminal *modus operandi,* which specifies certain criminal values and behaviour patterns. Sutherland (1947) cites the "professional thief" as a primary case example.

> Professional thieves make a regular business of theft. They use techniques which have been developed over a period of centuries and transmitted to them through traditions and personal association. They have codes of behavior, *esprit de corps,* and consensus. They have a high status among other thieves and in the political and criminal underworld in general. They have differential association in the sense that they associate with each other and not, on the same basis, with outsiders, and also in the sense that they select their colleagues.
>
> Because of this differential association they develop a common language or argot which is relatively unknown to persons not in the profession, and they have organization. A thief is a professional when he has these six characteristics: regular work at theft, technical skill, consensus, status, differential association, and organization.
>
> Professional thieves have their group ways of behavior for the principal situations which confront them in their criminal activities. Consequently professional theft is a behavior system and a sociological entity.

This modal image of the criminal characterises him as a resourceful, well-trained and effective felon—a member of a profession (albeit illegal) with certain ethics and values which dictate his conduct. In criminal jargon, the "professional thief" had "class" or "character." He would not "give his buddies up" and even certain victims were proscribed. Assault and violence were used as means to an end, not as ends in themselves.

When I was 16 or 17 I used to hang around a pool hall in our neighborhood a lot. I got so I could shoot pool pretty good and once in a while I would make a couple of bucks. But there were older guys there who were really doing good. They had "good reputations" in the neighborhood and they always had money, cars and broads. Me and some kids my age were doing a lot of petty stealing at this time, cars and things from cars, but we didn't know how to make any real money. What we wanted to do is get in with the older guys so we could learn something and make some money. One day, I remember, I had just got out of jail for some petty beef and one of the older thieves, a guy that was supposed to be one of the slickest safe men then, come over to me and talked to me for a while. This made me feel pretty good. Later one of his friends asked me if I wanted to help him carry a safe out of some office. We worked half a night on that safe and never did get it out of the place. But from then on I was in with the older bunch. Every once in a while one of them would get me to do some little job for him, like standing point (look out) or driving a car or something like that, and once in a while when they had snatched a safe, I would get to help them open it. I was learning pretty fast.

By the time I was 19 or 20, me and a couple of my buddies had real solid names with the older thieves. We were beating a lot of places on our own and we handled ourselves pretty well. But we were still willing to learn more. We used to sit around some coffee shop half the night or ride around in a car listening to a couple of the old hoodlums cut up different scores. We would talk about different scores other guys had pulled or scores we had pulled, and we would also talk about how you were supposed to act in other situations; how to spend your money, how to act when you got arrested. We discussed different trials we knew about, we even talked about San Quentin and Folsom and prisons in other states, because usually the older thieves had done time before. We talked about how much time each beef carried, how much time the parole board would give you for each beef. I guess we talked about everything that had anything to do with stealing. Of course we didn't talk about it all the time. Lots of the time we just shot the bull like anyone else. But by the time I was 21 I had a pretty good education in crime.

This well-trained type of offender is in sharp contrast with a young modern violent gang offender who commented as follows after being involved in a brutal homicide:

Momentarily, I started thinking about it inside; I have my mind made up I'm not going to be in no gang. Then I go on inside. Something comes up, then here all my friends coming to me. Like I said before, I'm intelligent and so forth. They be coming to me—then they talk to me about what they gonna do. Like, "Man, we'll go out here and kill this cat." I say, "Yeah." They kept on talkin'. I said, "Man, I just gotta go with you." Myself, I don't want to go, but when they start talkin' about what they gonna do, I say, "So, he isn't gonna take over my rep. I ain't gonna let him be known more than me." And I go ahead, just for selfishness. . . .

This type of offender at the moment is indeterminable. He is at the time, and is apt to remain, a new criminal. However, since he is young and not formed, he might become a more skilled offender with proper criminal training. However, as will be pointed out, since this type of offender generally grows up in a disorganised slum which contains few well-developed old criminal role-models, he is more apt to continue as a here-and-now new criminal.

The described senseless "other-directed" violence of the larger proportion of modern offenders is perpetrated for ego-status—for "kicks" or "thrills." The "kicks" involve and produce a type of emotional euphoria which, the new criminal maintains, "makes me feel good." He does it for "selfishness." The goals of the crime are self-orientated in a primary fashion with material gain as a very secondary consideration. The old criminal could never be induced to place himself in jeopardy for this type of senseless offence. He used violence as an instrument for material gain, rather than for an emotional charge.

If the tight, cohesive criminal gang involved in burglary and robbery represented the "professional" model criminal behaviour patterns of the past, the modern violent gang in many respects represents the prototype structure for the incipient new criminal. This is not to say that criminal gangs do not exist today or that violent gangs were not active in the past; but it is to say that the dominant emphasis has shifted to the wilder criminal and hence to the wilder gang organisation.

These violent gang structures as a modern criminal group prototype are characterised more specifically by many or all of the following factors: (1) there are no evidences of prior contact or interaction between the assailant(s) and his (their) victim; (2) the act occurs in an unpremeditated, generally spontaneous and impulsive manner; (3) in some cases (particularly, for example, in violent gang assault) there is a degree of prior build-up to the act; however, the final consequence (often homicide) is not really anticipated; (4) the violent assailant or collectivity has indicated by prior behaviour or personality factors for some period of time a potentiality for the commission of violence; (5) the post-rationale expressed by the offender(s) for the violent behaviour is usually without regret or inappropriate to the act which has been committed. The "old criminals" rationales and motives in their gangs were at the opposite pole.

Refocusing on the individual offender, the pendulum of criminal prototype or "basic personality type" has swung towards the "new criminal." In an ideal-type fashion he may be classified as follows. He has a persistent pattern of deviant behaviour characterized by an almost total disregard for the rights and feelings of others. A listing of overt personality and behaviour traits of this brand of sociopath would include most, if not all, of the following factors: *(a)* limited social conscience; *(b)* egocentrism dominating most interaction, "instrumental manipulation" of others for self-advantage (rather than affective relating); *(c)* inability to forego immediate pleasure for future goals; *(d)* a habit of pathological lying to achieve personal advantage (according to Hervey Cleckley in *The Mask of Sanity,* the sociopath's feelings and emotions are "word deep"); and *(e)* persistent violent physical and emotional outbursts when blocked from achieving momentary goals.

THE "INNER-DIRECTED" (OLD CRIMINAL) AND THE "OTHER-DIRECTED" (NEW CRIMINAL)

Taking a leaf from Riesman's *Lonely Crowd* (1950), another observed characteristic of the new criminal basic personality involves a shift from "inner-direction" to "other-direction." With this reference in mind we would speculate that the change in the basic personality which has taken place in the middle-class person in the United States (as described by Riesman) may be equated with this shift in the basic personality of the criminal. The overall shift of societal forces which form the causal context of this change in the middle-class man also appears to correspond to changes in the participant in criminal culture. In particular, there is a striking similarity between the inner-directed middle-class man and the old type criminal.

The "inner-directed" person (old criminal) was more concerned with concrete material gain and less with psychic emotional gratification characteristic of "other-directed" individuals (new criminals). The business of the criminal of the past was making money, and to make money took skill. Highly skilled professionals thus emerged within the criminal subcultures. As in the legitimate society, the skills were those that allowed the person to manipulate the material world. Burglary, robbery, hi-jacking, forgery, counterfeiting methods and other professional skills became highly developed. The criminal was more secure in himself and developed his professional craft. The "inner-directed" old criminal not only knew how to "pull a caper," but how to do it in the "cleanest" way possible. This implied a knowledge of law, of court proceedings, of police methods, and many other aspects of the "caper." Unlike the current flimsy relationships characteristic of the new criminal, the old criminal had to make contacts with trusted people whom he needed in the pursuit of his criminal work. He had to trust others to co-operate with his criminal venture. This often meant using a steady "fence" when he was dealing in merchandise. He often made contracts with lawyers whom he could trust, who were "right." Such a lawyer would afford him legal advice before a crime, and would be ready to go to bat for him if he was caught. There was even a right way to "do time" when he was caught and couldn't "beat the rap." This training entailed doing "easy time" and getting out with a minimum sentence. It also prescribed the correct behaviour in relation to other criminals and officials while "in stir."

THE "COOL," VIOLENT AND ADDICTED

There are several traits or styles of criminal action on the part of the new criminal. Since he has no strong "inner-direction" the new criminal will seize on "the scene" or behaviour pattern which is popular at the time. These entail being "cool" or "hip," as well as violence and drugs. Sometimes all of these behaviour patterns fit the offender, or he has several of these traits which shift.

Among New York delinquents the following symptomatic pattern change has been observed. The violent gang youth, utilising violence for "kicks" decides that being "hip or cool is the scene" and that "gang fights are for kids." He shifts to dressing and being sharp. This involves some "blowing pot" (smoking marijuana) and "short con" (petty hustling). If heroin drug addiction is the style, he shifts to it. Of course, after he becomes a heroin addict, the dictatorship of king heroin pushes him into other reckless petty theft directions. This sequence has been observed to occur in the evolution of the new criminal.

The new criminal style of being cool or "hip" (the "manipulative" principal of relating) has perhaps filtered down from the middle-class competitive system. For the new criminal, "how to win friends and influence people" becomes interpreted and related to how to beat a "mark" (victim). This new definition of how to earn money has a different emphasis from the former definition. The old thief was out to make money in the cleanest, quickest, fastest way. The new hip-criminal is out to make money but equally important is the process of beating someone, by manipulating them and looking sharp to "others." Here the emphasis is often on the sharpness, not on making money. The important thing is the "cat's" ability, through his conversation or his keenness to manipulate others. The means for theft becomes a "kicks"-oriented end in itself.

The central theme in hipsterism is "having a ball" or getting "kicks." "The main purpose of life for the 'cat' is to experience the 'kick.' A 'kick' may be any act tabooed by 'squares' which heightens and intensifies the present movement of experience and differentiates it as much as possible from the humdrum routine of daily life." "Kicks" may grossly be viewed as a method of existential validation. The bored-dull person on a death-life continuum is closer to being non-existent or the "death side." He seeks some means of self-feeling validation. This need requires some intense emotional experience—"kicks." Senseless violence or drugs can produce this change of feeling state. The "kicks" experience of intense "dyonisian" gratification may thus validate the individual feeling of *being* or *existing*.

In addition violence as a form of "kicks" provides status in the delinquent subculture. As a young gang-killer commented:

> If I would of got the knife, I would have stabbed him. That would of gave me more of a build-up. People would have respected me for what I've done and things like that. They would say, "There goes a cold killer."

Addiction is another adaptable pattern for the new criminal. If one views hipsterism, "coolness" and "kicks" as overt symptom patterns of an underdeveloped self, it is logical to anticipate how the drug addiction symptom could also take over. In many ways, addiction is a new fad which the "other-directed" new criminal has gravitated toward.

The basic personality of the "other-directed" new criminal makes him very susceptible to drug addiction. All that he requires to start using drugs is to come into contact with a drug-using collectivity. He is seeking "kicks," trying to keep up with the trends of *his* culture, trying to be "hip"; so if drugs are "the scene," the "other-directed" new criminal will "make it." Also drug addiction is a neat, problem-solving complex. As one "hip" new criminal stated: "Man, getting on drugs is like putting all your little bills in one easy package. When you become hooked, you only got one problem getting stuff."

In summary, the new criminal is "kicks"-oriented, be it violence, drugs or being a hipster. As an "other-directed" personality, he is amenable and susceptible to criminal fads or new scenes. As a sociopath, he is not totally disoriented to the larger society. However, he characteristically has a limited social conscience or concern for "others." He is under-socialised to the legal society and his own criminal subculture has few clear and binding rules or demands. This is in marked contrast with the well-trained old criminal who assumed the responsibility of relating positively to his cohorts in their criminal activities. He had "character" or "ethics" in his criminal pursuits. The new criminal in contrast would literally give his crime partner up for a "fix" or a pill, and does.

THE NEW CRIMINAL IN SOCIETY

For speculative purposes we would divide the criminal hierarchy into upper middle and lower-class offenders. At the top we would place the skilled syndicated criminal form, greatly controlled by old mobsters. Their criminal tentacles enter into labour unions and some big businesses. These criminals are intelligent and highly skilled professionals. The middle class would be comprised essentially of the professional thief or the "old criminal" as described here. In the lower class, we would place the unskilled grifter, sometimes addict or, as described, the "new criminal." In this context it is our contention that the middle-class old criminal is the category on the demise and that there is some increase in the described upper and lower-class criminals, with a limited bridge between the upper and lower world of crime.

The causal context of this shift of criminal modal personality may very well be connected to some of the following factors:

1. The shift from a stable slum condition of the past to a disorganised slum. The high delinquency areas of the past had a stable population. A criminal hierarchy could develop. There was room at the top for an enterprising "hood" if he trained with an older criminal and had vision. The modern scene emphasises "kicks" and achievement in the "here and now," partly because there is no criminal ladder to climb in the shifting slum. With the demise of the middle-class criminal, the bridge to the top, the new deviant is restricted to his bottom position.

2. Because of the current limited neighbourhood criminal hierarchy, there is a concomitant limited training or recruitment system for the youth personally predisposed towards a life of professional crime. As a corollary of this fact, good professional criminal role-models and educators are disappearing from the crime scene.

3. The downfall of the old criminal culture of the past may also partially be related to improved police methods. In the big cities police methods seem to have won the technological race with the professional criminal. New safes, new detection methods, fingerprint systems, etc., make it difficult for the old type professional criminal to operate effectively.

These, of course, are only partial explanations of the backdrop to the ascendancy of the new offender. The world picture of potential total destruction and manipulation of instruments of violence, although difficult to prove as a causal force, no doubt filters down to affect the problem. The acceleration of great social change currently affecting our society also plays an important role in producing the changed socio-cultural context which spawns the new criminal. There may be a close association between the rate of social change and the type of criminal a society produces. It would be our contention that rapid social change correlates with the proportion of "new criminals."

4.

Harry M. Shulman

THE MEASUREMENT OF CRIME IN THE UNITED STATES

Crime is by its very nature not easily measureable, being subject to concealment and nonreporting—concealment by victims and nonreporting by authorities—and, as a result, the reported statistics of crime are ordinarily far short of the full volume and range of offenses. This situation holds true for the United States, in which there is as yet no comprehensive, co-ordinated body of national crime statistics, and whose reported crime statistics, compiled by a variety of agencies, fail to provide an accurate statistical base for the analysis of the volume, categories, and trends of crime in the nation.

The primary reporting of crimes in the United States lies in the hands of local police departments, who submit statistics of complaints and arrests to the Federal Bureau of Investigation of the United States Department of Justice. There are many inadequacies in this reporting process, some of which will be described later, but the underlying defect of police reporting as a measure of the volume of crime is that the police have only a very limited function in crime control, and the crimes reported by the police are only a fraction of those that occur. Important segments of crime are dealt with, not by criminal justice agencies under the auspices of criminal law but by regulatory agencies under the auspices of administrative and civil law, whose findings are hidden in the obscure and diverse reports of fifty sovereign States and the Federal government. Finally, many aspects of crime result in no official complaint to any form of sanctioning authority—criminal, administrative or civil—but only come to light through the operations of public departments and private agencies concerned with education, health, welfare and safety, and of private agencies and associations that serve the economic interests of many different occupations and industries.

As the result of the lack of a national policy for the comprehensive co-ordinated reporting of crime in the United States, governmental commissions and agencies assigned to the study of law enforcement and crime prevention labor under the handicap of a lack of the fundamental scientific data necessary for the study of the relationships between social policy and crime control as well as the study of the efficacy of agencies for the administration of justice. At the same time, social scientists lack the data necessary for sound national epidemiological and etiological studies of crime.

THE CONCEALMENT AND NONREPORTING OF CRIME

Wide areas of criminal behavior fail to be included in crime statistics because of ambivalences and social resistances toward their reporting to sanctioning agencies, and because of opportunities for their concealment.

In sex and family relationships there is a myriad of unreported cases in which the criminal law is often in conflict with social norms and private human emotions, viz.: in homosexual relations, seduction and statutory rape, fornication and adultery, illegal abortion, bastardy (illegitimacy), miscegenation, and desertion and non-support.

Among the independent professions there are large numbers of unreported violations of law both among clients and practitioners. In the medical profession alone there are unreported illegal abortions, illegal prescriptions of narcotic drugs and illegal child adoption practices, to say nothing regarding unethical if not downright illegal practices of fee-splitting and un-

Source: *The Journal of Criminal Law, Criminology and Police Science,* Vol. 57, No. 4 (December, 1966), pp. 483–92. Based on President's Commission on Law Enforcement and Administration of Justice—Task Force Report, 1964—Crime and Its Impact, An Assessment. Reprinted by permission of the author and the journal.

necessary medical care. In the practice of law there are falsifications of claims, perjury and subornation of perjury, mingling of client's funds with those of the practitioner, and conflicts of interest.

Among the independent professions, in retail trade, and in fact wherever there is the opportunity for cash transactions, there are concealments of income for the purposes of income and excise tax evasions. Despite their undoubted frequency, very few criminal tax evasions actually become known as crimes.

Among employees there are frequent embezzlements and thefts of goods and materials commonly dealt with not by arrest and prosecution but by dismissal and sometimes by restitution. Embezzlements go unreported because supervisors are themselves guilty of related or comparable offenses. Many times, employee thefts, resulting in inventory shrinkages, are written off as customer dishonesty.

Dishonesty among customers, such as the common offenses of shoplifting and petty check forgery, are ordinarily not dealt with by criminal complaint and prosecution. Shoplifting, a common and widespread customer offense, committed by housewives and teenagers who are not necessarily poverty-stricken, as well as by indigents and experienced thieves, is often dealt with by department and specialty stores in the form of confiscation of the stolen goods, warnings, and sometimes by the requirement of signed confessions that are filed for the purpose of prosecution in the case of repetition of the offense on the same premises. The issuance of forged and fraudulent checks for small amounts by customers against local merchants is usually charged to profit and loss for fear of harm to community good-will arising from the prosecution of local residents.

The laws on public policy in the field of gambling are violated with impunity by millions of the general public in urban society, who in this fashion often unwittingly support criminal syndicates who monopolistically control dangerous subsidiary rackets in prostitution, narcotics, bootlegging, and usury, offenses that have their own nonreporting clientele and victims.

Among public officials and employees there are many criminal acts of omission and commission, the most common being the acceptance of bribes to grant favors in violation of law and to overlook violations. In municipal government, licensing authorities, housing inspectors, and inspectors of health hazards and dishonest weights and measures, engage often in practices of corruption without too great a danger of being caught.

Together, the crimes and offenses committed in the areas of sex and family relationship, and by professionals, businessmen, landlords, taxpayers, employees, customers and the general public probably number in the tens of millions of cases and must far outweigh in volume and monetary loss the offenses that are the subject of police action. Whereas there is little evidence of these offenses in the known criminal statistics, there is a large number of subsidiary sources of information from which estimates of volume and trend could be derived. There is evidence from the medical profession, the clergy, departments of education, health and welfare, and from private social agencies regarding the extent of unreported offenses in the areas of sex and family relationship, even though the identity of specific offenders may be shielded by the confidential status of the information and of the records in which they are located.

Investigative reports by legislative and other governmental commissions, in the fields of industrial medicine and insurance fraud, not to mention a variety of other violations in the fields of food and drugs, employer-employee relationships, union management, etc., are data sources. Reports of insurance underwriters and fire marshals give evidence of arson. The files of the Internal Revenue Service hold evidences of tax dishonesty, but they are not open to outside study; and relatively few have been prosecuted as crimes. Reports from trade associations throw light upon dishonest practices by employees and customers and give evidence of the extent of certain rackets, such as the bootleg manufacture, distribution, and sale of untaxed liquor.

The records of agencies of municipal government, such as those of health, housing and fire, could throw a flood of light upon violations of municipal codes on licensing and occupancy reported by inspectors but neither made the subject of sanctions nor reported in public statistics. Consumer complaints of dishonesties in retail advertising and of frauds in installment selling, reported to Better Business Bureaus, are a data source. At the present time hardly any of these sources, with the exception of legislative inquiries into organized crime, are tapped for national estimates of the amount of unreported, unrecorded, and unpunished crimes and offenses.

REPORTED CRIMES AND OFFENSES DEALT WITH UNDER ADMINISTRATIVE AND CIVIL LAW

There are many specialized forms of reported crimes and offenses whose punitive sanctions lie not in the criminal law but in the realm of administrative and civil law. Among these are offenses in commerce and industry, management-labor relations, union management, income tax reporting, and social security and public assistance. Some of these offenses are dealt with by regulatory agencies of the states, but the majority are dealt with by the federal government under its interstate commerce powers. These include the Internal Revenue division of the Department of the Treasury, the National Labor Relations Board, the Federal Trade Commission, the Securities and Exchange Commission, etc. Some of these offenses are dealt with under anti-monopoly laws, such as the Sherman Act, which specifically defines violations as misdemeanors and permits criminal sanctions against corporation officers, but many others are dealt with under other administrative laws whose sanctions are directed only against the corporations themselves, through stipulations and cease and desist orders, fines, and confiscations of goods deemed unfit for public sale or consumption. Still others are dealt with under civil laws that permit punitive damages to injured parties.

Among reported offenses in commerce and industry—in the fields of finance, securities, manufacturing, communications, real estate, etc.—are restraints of free competition through illegal mergers, collusive price-fixing and bidding, market control through cartels, discriminatory rebates to favored customers, fraudulent advertising claims, and violations of a wide range of legislation regulatory of real estate—including rent controls, non-discrimination in rentals, and the maintenance of commercial and dwelling structures—so as to assure the health, welfare and safety of tenants.

In management-labor relations offenses include collusive practices between management and racket-controlled unions that result in contracts below current wage scales in industries and geographic areas; management violations of the National Labor Relations Act, such as labor spying, improper pressures upon workers in connection with union representation elections, and the discharge of workers for labor unionization activities; and in labor union management, the use of force and illegality in the election of officers of locals and national unions, and corrupt practices in the administration of vast union pension and welfare funds.

In industry-consumer relations there are such offenses as false labelling, misrepresentation of products, false weights and measures, adulteration of products, manufacture under unhygienic conditions, etc.

In the area of taxation, aside from such violations as the evasions of payment of excise taxes (on liquor, cigarettes, tobacco, etc.) which carry criminal law penalties, there are many other offenses, particularly in the area of taxes on income, in which, despite the generally high level of tax collection at source, or of withholding at source, there is extensive misrepresentation of income and dishonesty in declaration of deductions. The majority of the latter offenses are dealt with as civil offenses and punished by fines, with no statistical reporting of their number.

In the areas of social legislation—unemployment and industrial compensation insurance, social security and public assistance—under whose umbrella tens of millions of citizens and residents have coverage, there are many violations which are rarely discovered; and when discovered they are rarely dealt with by criminal prosecution. In the area of public assistance alone, for example, aid to the indigent, handicapped, children, and elderly indigent, which covers some five millions of persons, the files of public agencies would disclose many forms of illegality dealt with by other than criminal prosecution.

As indicated earlier, the statistics of law violation in most of these categories of criminal offense lie buried in agency files, and sometimes they are to be found in the annual reports of public agencies, but so scattered are these information sources that they are not easily available to scientific investigators, much less the press. Moreover, much of this information has remained in bureaucratic concealment under the pleas of confidentiality or national security and it will be released only when "right to know" legislation makes them available to the public. In the rare instances in which violations of court orders have resulted in punishments for contempt, or where prosecutions under federal criminal law has resulted in conviction, the statistics of conviction are to be found in the annual reports of the administrative office of the federal court system, but even here the statistics are so garbled that specific offenses, small in number but qualitatively significant, are concealed through inclusion in broader categories. What the total of this range of offenses may be, in commerce and industry, taxation and social legislation, is open to conjecture. Their gross volume must run into the millions of cases, of which only a relatively few are reported and dealt with under administrative and civil law, so that even a well-organized access to the statistics of reported cases would afford but a slight glimpse of their volume and characteristics.

CRIMES KNOWN TO THE POLICE

Only one body of crimes and offenses that occur in the United States is systematically reported on a national scale. These are the crimes known to the police and reported by them to the Federal Bureau of Investigation for publication in *Uniform Crime Reports.* Included among them are the major so-called *common crimes* of homicide, assault, robbery, burglary, and theft. These statistics have been given national prominence through regular distribution for the past 35 or more years in quarterly and annual reports and through regular conspicuous publication in the national press. As a result of this focus upon common crimes, as well as the constant cultural reference to and repetitious use of common crime themes in newspaper articles, radio, television, novels, detective stories, etc., the term *crime* has come to have an application almost entirely restricted to common crimes, and so respected has police crime reporting become that until recently mass communication agencies have given to their readers the impression that the statistics of common crimes are a scientific measure of the American crime volume.

From our previous discussion it should already be clear that this is not the case, and that crimes known to the police are a highly unrepresentative sample of American criminal offenses. The nature of this sample, evidences of its nonrepresentativeness even of common crime, and the legal, administrative and sociological circumstances that limit the function of the police in dealing with crime, and hence limit their role in crime reporting, call for some further discussion.

The police reporting of common crime consists of two markedly different sets of data, one of citizen *complaints,* i.e., "crimes known to the police," and the other of *arrests.* One refers to offenses and the other to persons, and there is no necessary statistical relationship between them since in some crimes a number of individuals may be involved and for others a single individual may have committed more than one offense.

There is markedly incomplete police reporting of offenses. Only seven *serious* forms of crime are regularly reported in *Uniform Crime Reports*: murder and non-negligent manslaughter, forcible rape, robbery, aggravated assault, burglary, larceny of $50 and over, and auto theft.[1] The remaining citizen complaints to the police are, with one exception (larceny of $50 and under), not reported in *Uniform Crime Reports,* and are not comparable for either volume or trend, although the basic data exist in the files of individual police departments.

---

[1]The word *serious* as used in *Uniform Crime Reports* is somewhat of a value judgment, since it includes such offenses as the theft of automobiles for pleasure use, and petty thefts.

The police rationalization of this selective reporting of citizen complaints is that minor offenses tend not to be reported to the police and that only complaints of serious crimes, which are said to be more commonly reported, can serve as an *Index of Crime*. However, since the crime index concept is itself a dubious one, in the light of evidence that police records as a whole are a highly selective measure of crime, its use to explain the non-reporting of the majority of complaints in the 29-category schedule of crimes used in *Uniform Crime Reports* is itself highly dubious. This point will be elaborated.

The selective reporting of crime complaints leaves only one category of police crime data free from criticism on this score, i.e., that of arrest. By arrest is meant persons taken into custody and charged with a criminal offense, as differentiated from those merely questioned and released. In 1964, in a registration area comprising some 132 million persons, some 4,582,000 persons were arrested, of which close to 2,000,000 arrests were either for drunkenness (1,458,000 cases) or disorderly conduct (475,000 cases). An additional 378,000 cases involved other aspects of drinking, viz.: driving under the influence (225,000 cases), and liquor law violations (153,000 cases).[2] Thus, of 4,582,000 arrests, some 2,311,000, or more than 50 percent, involved either drunkenness or disorderliness, or both. It would thus be fair to state that the job of the police, as judged by these statistics, is largely to cope with drunken and disorderly persons, a task of some importance in the maintenance of public order and safety, but not one bulking large in criminal threat to the security of the society.

The next largest category of arrests is for larceny-theft (some 358,000 cases) of which the bulk were probably for thefts under $50, and since arrests for larceny-theft bear a ratio of one arrest to every five complaints, or 20 percent, it can properly be stated that for this category arrests are a disproportionately low measure of predatory crime.

However, it is in the category of public policy arrests—for gambling, prostitution, and narcotics (offenses almost lacking in citizen complaint)—that police arrest statistics can be most highly criticized as a measure of societal misconduct. In 1964, in an urban registration area of some 3,000 cities, these offenses resulted in some 160,000 arrests (98,000 of gambling; 27,000 of prostitution; and 35,000 of narcotics), a somewhat impressive total until subjected to closer analysis. First of all, public policy arrests represented less than 4 percent (3.9 percent) of all arrests. The relative unimpressiveness of the statistics on public policy arrests becomes more apparent when their average distribution by cities is analyzed.[3]

Some 98,000 gambling arrests, distributed among some 3,000 cities, averaged out to 32 arrests per city per year, a figure that would include syndicate and independent operators, bookmakers, policy runners and collectors, customers, and repeated arrests of all these. Some 27,000 prostitution and commercialized vice arrests in the same number of cities averaged out to 9 arrests per city per year, a figure that would include overlords, madams, pimps, establishment prostitutes and streetwalkers, and repeated arrests of all these, as well as (in some jurisdictions) patrons. Some 36,000 narcotic drug arrests in the same number of cities averaged out to some 12 arrests per city per year, for syndicate and independent operators, distributors, addict-sellers and addicts, plus repeated arrests.

The small number of arrests for public policy offenses in a field of criminal operation reputed to derive huge revenues (estimated from 7 to 22 billions of dollars per year for gambling alone) for syndicated operators known as "families" would suggest that these low arrest figures are not to be taken as a serious measure of the volume of public policy offenses in the United States. When compared to the high volume of arrests in connection with drinking, the small proportion of arrests on public policy charges in a crime area that operates as a cancer in the American society, is suggestive

[2]Federal Bureau of Investigation, U.S. Department of Justice *1964 Uniform Crime Reports* (Washington, D.C., U.S. Government Printing Office, 1965) p. 106.

[3]Inasmuch as arrest figures for individual cities were not reported, only averages can be calculated.

of selective arrest patterns among the police of the United States.

Even these statistics, however, do not tell the entire story of selective public policy offense arrest patterns. Negroes, with some 11 percent of the national population, experience some 72 percent of all urban arrests for gambling, 53 percent of all urban arrests for prostitution and 40 percent of all urban arrests for possession of narcotics.

The evidence thus far is that many areas of crime are infrequently reported to the police, that in exercising their primary assignment of law enforcement the police make arrests primarily for drunkenness and disorderly conduct, and that they make relatively few arrests for larceny-theft and very few public policy arrests. Thus, neither citizen complaints nor arrests would appear to be sound measures of the volume of common crime in the United States. At best, perhaps, police statistics are a sound measure of only a handful of serious common crimes (homicide, rape, robbery, aggravated assault) in which there is both a high level of complaint as well as of arrest. Such conclusions raise questions as to the reasons for the selective nature of police crime statistics.

LIMITATIONS OF THE POLICE AS A CRIME-REPORTING AGENCY

The police, although they are in theory assigned wide powers of law enforcement, yet limited by the laws of arrest and other civil liberties and constitutional rights of the citizenry, exercise in practice a very restricted law enforcement role. They are primarily a peace preservation body whose major functions are the protection of life, limb, and property on the streets and highways, in places of public assemblage and in commercial and private properties entered illegally from public ways. As we have seen, they exercise little or no enforcement functions in crimes of sex and the family, in commerce and industry, in tax evasion, in crimes by employees and customers, and in public policy crimes by the general public and the syndicates they support. For all of these other areas there exist alternate agencies of complaint and law enforcement, some within criminal law enforcement power, such as prosecutors and attorneys-general of the states and of the federal government, or within administrative law such as state and federal regulative agencies. Indeed, even in those areas of crime in which the police function most competently, those of common crime, the crime prevention function of the police is restricted to general patrol, and their detective function occurs after the crime has occurred in their absence. The only offenses in which they exercise both a preventive and a criminal justice function are those offenses which occur in their presence and those to which they are summoned while the offenses are in process.

The circumstances in American culture and social organization that assign to the police such a circumscribed function in law enforcement, and that permits a vast range of offenses to go unreported or to be dealt with by other investigative bodies, are numerous and, in a paper concerned primarily with the measurement of crime, can be mentioned only summarily. A wide operational range of powers for police is inconsistent with American ideological beliefs and principles of limited sovereignty. Our ideological attachment to civil liberties prevents assignment to the police of roving powers of investigation such as through the unregulated tapping of the mails and other instruments of communication. The police are restricted to the exercise of the police powers of the municipality or some other governmental body of which they are agents, and they have no national police powers such as are exercised by some European police. As a result, offenders whose operations extend beyond municipal, county, and state boundaries are not subject to arrest outside of the limited jurisdiction in which their primary offense occurred, except for purposes of extradition.

At the same time, the local police are subject to the rivalry of other separate and equal branches of government. Their authority is kept in close check by the legislative branch, which has invented alternate regulatory mechanisms via the administrative law for the control of a vast network of economic forces; they are in rivalry with prosecutor's offices in the handling of criminal complaints; and they are checked by the courts in their exercise of practices that interfere with civil liberties.

Local police departments in the United States

function in communities sharply divided in social values on many issues of civil rights and personal morals. Not themselves ordinarily a cross-section of the racial and ethnic composition of the local population, they are called upon to adjudicate conflicts involving breaches of the peace that have overtones on the one hand of racial and ethnic antagonisms and, on the other, of violations of civil rights. In communities in which public policy crimes are not only the subject of culture conflict, but of political protection by corrupt political machines that have venal ties with fabulously wealthy criminal syndicates, the police are subject to many malignant controls and temptations.

Finally, the recruitment and training of the police as a highly technical career body of superior men and women is a policy that has had much lip service in American politics and little implementation. Ill-trained as most of them are, lacking in standards of high general education, and rarely selected for outstanding general intelligence, they have never had the undivided admiration and loyalty of the American public or even of the press. Because of these circumstances, together with the aforesaid legal restrictions upon their functions, they are rarely called upon to handle investigations that call for technical skill, rare judgment, tact, and administrative knowledge. Under these circumstances it is not surprising that the measure of their efficiency, as determined by the relationship of citizen complaints to arrests, and by their selective patterns of law enforcement through onsight arrest, is low.

GAPS, DISCONTINUITIES AND LIMITATIONS IN THE REPORTING OF CRIME

We may now pull together some of the gaps, discontinuities and limitations in the reporting of American crime. As has been indicated, vast numbers of offenses in many areas of misconduct are not included in any systematic totals of American crime volume. Nor are there adequate bodies of criminal statistics even among those arising among criminal justice agencies, i.e., the police, prosecutors and courts. The most extensive reporting system, that of *Uniform Crime Reports,* is deficient in many ways. Citizen complaints are reported for only 8 of 29 categories of offense.[4] That series of categories, while appearing offhand to be sufficient for crime reporting, is actually very insufficient and conceals important categories of crime, which, because they are lumped with others, are in effect not reported at all. Thus, shoplifting, commercial crimes generally, and offenses involving landlords and tenants, are in this manner not reported. The latter category, which includes landlord complaints of vandalism and tenant complaints of persistent failure to provide basic services in housing tenancy, have a close involvement with other aspects of social disorganization and intergroup conflict in our rapidly urbanizing society and their reporting would serve a useful purpose in the study of conflicted human relationships in slum areas.

Other important offenses are not reported at all; for example, the only traffic offense reported is that of drunken driving. It is understandable that minor offenses involving stationary vehicles —parking ordinance violations, etc.,—can be safely ignored in national crime totals, but offenses involving moving vehicles, such as speeding, passing on curves, driving by unauthorized persons or in unsafe vehicles, demand national reporting by reason of the large number of deaths from vehicular "accidents," some 50,000 annually, not to mention the hundreds of thousands of injuries and the monetary losses in property destruction and damage, hospital and medical bills and the loss of income and earning ability.

The use of complaints on only seven offenses in the *Uniform Crime Reports* as an *index of crime* is unwarranted in the light of our knowledge of the limited law enforcement functions of the police, and of the highly selective reporting by police of even those offenses over which they have primary jurisdiction. Under pressure, the *Uniform Crime Reports* has modified its claims to define these complaints as an index of common crime, and it is hypothesized that all other common crimes reported in police statistics vary in level as these seven do. Unfortunately, however, this hypothesis is not verifiable,

[4]Since the present paper was originally delivered some few changes have taken place in the composition of the 29 categories, but the number remains the same.

because in order to use a sample as an index we must know the size and composition of the universe from which the sample was drawn and we must have assurances that the sample was a representative one. From our preceding discussion we know that the universe of crime in our society is largely unknown, both as a whole and in its particulars, and that the police sample is likely to be unrepresentative, not only in its concentration upon certain categories of crime, but owing to the fact that those categories are unduly drawn from the offenses of certain racial and ethnic minorities and social classes.

Actually, the so-called "index to crime" projects predictively only a part of even that portion of crime with which the police come into contact and serves no other predictive function than to suggest what the future of those seven offenses may be. Its claimed use as a general crime predictive instrument has never been verified, is not verifiable and should not be used by the federal government in any manner, since its use tends to conceal the fact that in truth we do not now know either the whole volume or trends of crime in the United States, in part because it is not knowable, and in part because that portion which is known has never been properly organized for analysis.

As has been indicated, many complaints bypass the police and are reported directly to prosecutors and attorneys-general of the states and federal government, and these often comprise offenses of far greater importance to the public than those reported to the police. Thus, the range of victims may be greater. They include, for example, complaints against conspiracies such as syndicated operations in public policy crime, in labor union management, in labor-management relations, in manager-consumer relationships, within industries, and conspiracies in the operation of criminal justice itself. Complaints to prosecutors and attorneys-general, however, tend not to be systematically reported, being usually anecdotal and focussed upon dramatic cases, rather than statistical and analytical.

The judicial statistics of those cases that come to trial in the courts could throw a great deal of light upon the criminal justice process, but in most of the states these are not reported on a state-wide basis and are, as a result, not accessible for reporting and analysis.

The listing of three levels of criminal statistics, those of the police, prosecutors, and courts, defines the structure of criminal statistics necessary for the reporting of criminal complaints in any geographical and political jurisdiction and for an analysis of the criminal justice process in that jurisdiction. The flat statement can be made that in most jurisdictions this structure of criminal statistics is not available in a form convenient for criminological purposes, and is therefore not used for analytical studies. This situation is almost as true for the federal government as it is for the states.

At the federal justice level there exist administrative data at each stratum of operation, but these are neither systematically reported as criminal statistics nor made available to any central collecting agency for reporting and analysis. A handful of federal offenses are dealt with by federal marshals, who function as police and have jurisdiction over federal lands and properties. They issue no systematic reports of complaints or arrests. The major body of important federal criminal law offenses is dealt with by federal prosecutors, who issue no systematic reports of criminal complaints and their dispositions, either individually or as a whole. Another significant body of criminal complaints and dispositions arises among the armed forces, consisting of violations of civil and military law among a large group of young men of high actuarial crime risk. However, the statistics of their offenses, as handled within the military chain of command, are not available for public use, being issued only for intramural information by the Department of Defense. And, as has been indicated, a wide range of offenses against administrative and civil law carrying punitive sanctions, and handled by administrative and regulatory agencies of the Federal government, are not available as collected statistics. Only the Administrative Office of the United States Courts issues valuable annual statistics of those criminal complaints that are tried in the United States District Courts, but in the absence of complaint totals and their dispositions from all federal prosecutors, these tell little regarding the volume of federal criminal law complaints and their processing. As a result of this failure to collect under one roof all statistics of federal offenses, even the United States government has no systematic information on its own system of criminal and administrative law procedures.

STEPS TOWARD THE IMPROVED COLLECTION AND ANALYSIS OF AMERICAN CRIMINAL STATISTICS

If American criminal statistics are to become available for *(a)* epidemiological studies of volume, distribution, and trends within functional settings of the cultural, economic and political organizations of the society; *(b)* administrative studies of the investigative and judicial process in this volume of cases; and *(c)* studies of the relationship of law enforcement policies and practices to crime prevention and control, it is apparent that significant changes in their collection, reporting and analysis will have to be made, involving at the very least the following procedures:

(1) Synthesis of the presently available statistics of sanctionable violations of criminal, administrative and civil law, now scattered in the many reports of Federal, State and local policing and regulatory agencies;

(2) The collection and synthesis from the files of many agencies of unreported data indicative of the volume of sanctionable law violations, not now the subject of complaint; and

(3) Raising the technical standards of the procedures for the measurement of American crime by placing its collection, analysis and reporting in the hands of criminologically trained research personnel qualified in the methods of social science research and statistical analysis.

The first step (1) requires the designation of a federal department or agency as the center of analysis and reporting of all available American criminal statistics. The second step (2) calls for such policies by that agency that the data indicative of unreported violations would be made available for study by other public and private agencies. The third step (3) the assignment of criminal statistics collection analysis and reporting to highly qualified social science analysts, calls for some discussion.

The sociological study of criminal statistics has by now reached a relatively high level of sophistication, both theoretically and methodologically.[5] But so far there has been little utilization of this available skill in the field of criminal justice. Not since the 1930's, when federal and state commissions for the study of justice and law enforcement made systematic studies of criminal statistics has there been a proper emphasis upon the public utilization of sound social science methods and of a qualified professional personnel in their collection and analysis.[6] Currently, at every level in the criminal justice process—in the police, prosecutors' offices, courts, correctional agencies, and rehabilitative agencies such as probation and parole departments—the task of criminal statistics has been largely in the hands of persons lacking the training for that exacting specialization.

It is conceivable that the steps here proposed may be initiated in the near future, but it is necessary that there be an awareness of the resistances in our society against systematic scientific reporting of crime. Some of these resistances originate in the opposition of strong vested interests, and others have their roots in our historical traditions. There are resistances, for example, among some criminal justice agencies who object to scientific measures of their efficiency. Thus the honesty of police reporting of complaints has been from time to time called into question by the Federal Bureau of Investigation, which has had to reject the statistics of police departments which have sought to increase the measure of their own efficiency through under-reporting of citizen complaints as compared to arrests. Other resistances are latent in the industries subject to regulation by governmental bodies. Still other resistances exist in the administration of criminal justice, which is increasingly under criticism for its very high proportion of convictions without formal trial, on a plea of guilt to lesser offenses. Supportive of these resistances is a public opinion on the subject of law enforcement having its origin in the crime definitions of an earlier simpler society. . . .

---

[5]Thorsten Sellin and Marvin E. Wolfgang, *The Measurement of Delinquency* (New York: John Wiley & Sons, Inc., 1964).

[6]National Commission on Law Observance and Enforcement, *Report on Criminal Statistics* (Washington, D.C., 1931).

5.

Marvin E. Wolfgang

UNIFORM CRIME REPORTS: A CRITICAL APPRAISAL

A Committee on Uniform Crime Records was appointed at a convention of the International Association of Chiefs of Police (IACP) in 1927. In 1929, after extensive study of crime reporting, statutory designations, and police recording of various offenses throughout the country, the Committee published an elaborate guide entitled *Uniform Crime Reporting: A Complete Manual for Police*. The manual attempted to establish standard categories of offenses for reporting purposes. In that same year the Committee instituted a system of uniform crime reporting on an experimental basis. The following year, the Federal Bureau of Investigation took over the system and incorporated the IACP's offense categories in its first bulletin of *Uniform Crime Reports*. The *Uniform Crime Reports* (*UCR*) were published monthly, then quarterly, until 1941. Between 1942 and 1957 they were published semi-annually, and since 1958 have been published annually with a brief, three-page quarterly preliminary report "issued for current information purposes." These reports regularly record, among other things, the volume of crimes known to the police, offenses cleared by arrest, persons held for prosecution, and persons released or found guilty of offenses.

The IACP Committee on Uniform Crime Records established a crime classification based on legal categories of offenses. The original survey of the Committee clearly showed the wide range of variation in statutory definitions of crime in the states. Therefore, offenses such as robbery, burglary, and larceny were broadly defined so that crimes committed under each of the varying state statutes could, for statistical purposes, be embraced by the uniform classification system. Crimes were divided into two categories. The first, originally known as Part I, included criminal homicide, rape, robbery, aggravated assault, burglary, larceny, and automobile theft. All other crimes were subsumed in Part II which came to include 20 subcategories, ranging from minor assaults to parking violations. Only Part I offenses were recorded under the term "crimes known to the police"; Part II offenses were reported according to the number of "persons charged" by the police. Part I offenses were traditionally referred to as the "major" or "more serious" offenses. These were assumed most likely to be reported to the police in some consistent fashion and to maintain, more than the other offenses, a constant ratio to the total number of committed offenses, most of which do not come to the attention of the police. The Part I offenses came to be used as a crime index, much like a price or cost-of-living index. The wisdom of using police statistics for such a purpose has best been expressed in modern times by Thorsten Sellin who suggested that "the value of criminal statistics as a basis for the measurement of criminality in geographic areas decreases as the procedure takes us farther away from the offence itself."

All of the arguments concerning the establishment of a crime index cannot be reviewed here although some of the major problems involved in a statistical analysis of index offenses will be considered in a later section. The use of the term "crime index" in the *UCR* did not appear until 1958, although Part I offenses were traditionally used in that sense. The offenses listed in Part II are, therefore, those which are assumed less likely to become known to the police—because of victims' unwillingness to report them, variations in police activity, and other similar factors.

Maintenance of this system of uniform crime reporting was assigned to the FBI on September 1, 1930, by Act of Congress and has been the

---

Source: *University of Pennsylvania Law Review*, Vol. 111, No. 6 (April, 1963), pp. 708–38. Reprinted by permission of the author and the *Review*.

responsibility of that Bureau ever since. In fact, the FBI has expanded the system to include data relevant to law enforcement agencies, such as the number of police personnel and the efficiency of police activity. The FBI has no authority to compel the transmission to it of crime data from cities and separate states; instead, police agencies throughout the country are asked to cooperate by submitting their reports to the central clearing house in Washington. The number of cooperating police agencies has increased regularly through the years, from 400 in 1930 to 7,800 law enforcement agencies in 1961, representing 96 percent of the total United States population. The offenses reported are violations of the criminal law of the separate states; no violations of federal law per se are tabulated or included in the *UCR*. Since 1958, when important revisions were made in the presentation of data, crimes have been reported by geographical areas, following as closely as is practical definitions used by the Bureaus of the Budget and the Census. Standard metropolitan statistical areas (SMSA)—generally made up of an entire county or counties having certain metropolitan characteristics and at least one core city of 50,000 or more inhabitants—have the largest absolute population and coverage as reported in the last *UCR* (1961). The SMSA's represented 117,152,600 people with 98.3 percent of these areas actually reporting to the FBI. "Other cities" are urban places outside the standard metropolitan statistical areas, most of which are incorporated communities of 2,500 or more inhabitants. In the last *UCR*, "other cities" contained a population of 24,185,300 with 90.7 percent of these areas actually reporting to Washington. Finally, "rural areas," which are made up of the unincorporated portions of counties outside of urban places and standard metropolitan statistical areas, had a population of 41,615,100 with 82.5 percent actually reporting. Sheriffs, county police, and many other state police report crimes committed within the limits of a county, but outside of cities, while the police departments within urban places report crimes committed within the city limits.

The problems of attaining uniform reporting by the 7,800 agencies which prepare crime reports on a voluntary basis are obvious. But in the past 32 years an elaborate machinery has been constructed to insure increasing uniformity. A special *Uniform Crime Reporting Handbook* instructing law enforcement agencies how to fill out monthly forms is provided by the FBI to all police agencies cooperating in the program. In addition, "it is standard operating procedure [for the FBI] to examine each incoming report not only for arithmetical accuracy but also, and possibly of even more importance, for reasonableness as a possible indication of errors."

All law enforcement agencies in the United States receive from the FBI a series of blanks, requesting information for the *UCR*. From completed forms returned by cooperating agencies, the Bureau tabulates crime rates and trends for presentation in the current quarterly preliminary reports and in the annual *UCR*. The kinds of data requested may be found in the *Uniform Crime Reporting Handbook*. For index crimes —formerly Part I offenses—the FBI requests the number of offenses reported to the police, the number of complaints that were found to be false, the number of actual or founded offenses, and the number of offenses cleared by arrest. "Cleared by arrest" means that one or more suspects have been taken into custody by the police and made available for prosecution. Only the number of founded offenses and the number of offenses cleared by arrest are reported in the *UCR*. The index crimes are the ones most completely tabulated by rates according to population groups: for instance, the age, sex, and race of persons charged; monthly variations; the type and value of property stolen and recovered; murder victims according to weapons used; and murder victims by age, sex, and race. The rural-urban distribution of index crimes is determined from the police department's location. For crimes other than those that appear in the index, the cooperating agencies report on the number of persons charged (held for prosecution) but not the number known to the police, as occurs with index crime.

The most fundamental and recent changes in the *Uniform Crime Reports* occurred after the recommendations of a Consultant Committee on Uniform Crime Reporting. This Committee was appointed in 1957 under the auspices of the FBI and the IACP to carry out a detailed and independent analysis of the uniform crime reporting system and to make concrete recommendations for its alteration. The Committee's report was published in 1958 as a *Special Issue* of the *UCR*. Twenty-two recommendations were made, all of which have been accepted as ultimate goals by the FBI and the IACP. However, only a few of the recommendations have thus far been carried out. The most important of these dealt with changes in statistical presentation and analysis, and with revisions in the classification of what has become known as the crime index.

* * *

For over a century, writers have considered the possibility of establishing an index of criminality from available criminal statistics. Quetelet, Mayr, Messedaglia, De Castro, and Sellin represent important names from the 1830's to the present who have written extensively about the problems of measuring the quantity and quality of crime. Establishing an index of any phenomenon is based upon the assumption that a subuniverse of items will reflect the total universe from which they come and, therefore, constitute a valid measurement of the total phenomenon. Unlike a cost-of-living index or index of production, a crime index is based upon a selection of items from an unknown volume—all crimes committed. Yet the underlying assumption in the use of criminal statistics for an index is that a constant ratio exists between the unknown universe and a properly selected portion of the known universe. As Adolphe Quetelet wrote in 1833: "I do not fear to say that everything we possess on statistics of crimes and misdemeanors would be of no utility if we did not tacitly assume that *there exists a nearly invariable relationship between offenses known and adjudicated and the total unknown sum of offenses committed.*" The Committee of the IACP had in mind such an assumption in 1929. In that same year, Bennett Mead, in charge of the section of Prison Statistics of the Bureau of the Census, wrote: "Statistics of the number of offenses known to the police form the best available means of measuring the extent of crime at a given time, and the changes from time to time in the prevalence of the more serious offenses against persons and against property." Two years later, the National Commission on Law Observance and Enforcement, better known as the Wickersham Commission, in its extensive *Report on Criminal Statistics* prepared by Sam Bass Warner, stated that "the best index of the number and nature of offenses committed is police statistics showing offenses known to the police." However, it recommended great caution in the use of such data until police agencies had become fully aware of the duty of accurate reporting. Also in 1931, Thorsten Sellin analyzed in some detail the reasons for relying on police statistics for the construction of an index to crime. Since those first years of the *UCR*, police statistics have generally been accepted as the best source for measurement, as may be seen by an inspection of any one of the numerous textbooks on criminology published in the United States.

Even so, there were many objections to the attempt by the *UCR* to provide accurate measurements of the amount of crime in the country as a whole and in the separate states and cities. Perhaps one of the earliest and most bitter articles appeared in 1931 in the *Harvard Law Review* by Sam Bass Warner. Mr. Warner argued that the *UCR* were likely to do more harm than good because of the inaccuracies and incompleteness of the police reports.

As efforts to improve the accuracy of reporting increased and as the proportion of the urban and rural areas voluntarily submitting criminal statistics grew, these early criticisms of Warner and others gradually diminished in importance. However, many writers continue to emphasize that crime statistics represent an unknown type of sample of a universe whose volume cannot be specified. Our knowledge of "hidden" delinquency and crimes which never come to the attention of the public authorities has raised many questions about the problems of using official criminal statistics for measuring the extent of the crime problem. But, although it is obvious that some crimes are not reported to the police, adequate and proper selection, classification, and statistical analysis of offenses can overcome most of the problems and produce a reasonably valid index of crime. At least it is generally agreed that if we are to have a continuous collection of delinquency and criminal statistics, police records are the best source of official information.

Perhaps a more damaging and direct criticism of the *UCR* is the fact that the number of crimes recorded as "known to the police" may be only a proportion of the crimes actually known to them. According to Donald Cressey, "police have an obligation to protect the reputation of their cities, and when this cannot be done efficiently under existing legal and administrative machinery, it is sometimes accomplished statistically." For example, in New York City until 1950, crimes known to the police were collected on a precinct level and the volume of offenses was grossly under-reported. Between 1949 and 1952, the FBI did not tabulate figures by that city because of incomplete data. After 1950 the collection of statistics was put on a centralized basis; consequently, there was an apparent increase in crime between 1948 and 1952 which was really a statistical artifact caused by great improvement in the collection of police statistics. Between those years burglaries rose from 2,726 to 42,491 and larcenies from 7,713 to 70,949. Moreover, the new recording system showed for the first quarter of 1952 that New York had a clearance level that was 50 percent below the national average.

The number of known robberies in Chicago increased from 1,263 to 14,544 between 1928 and 1931, and burglaries increased from 879 to 18,689 in the same period. Again, these changes were for the most part traceable to revisions in the recording practices of the police following an investigation by the Chicago Crime Commission. Philadelphia provides another startling example; in 1953 the city reported 28,560 Part I crimes as against 16,773 in 1951, an increase of over 70 percent.

It is true that the FBI eventually detected the under-reporting of offenses due to faulty communication and recording systems and therefore excluded the crime data of Philadelphia and New York from the national figures of crime in the *UCR*. Nonetheless, questions may be raised regarding the publication of crime reports from these communities prior to the refusal of the FBI to accept their reports, as well as about other communities, particularly rural areas, that have not yet been detected. Moreover, variations in police handling of violations of the law in different communities compound the problem of accuracy and completeness of police reporting. Differential statutory definitions and police procedures relating to such offenses as drunkenness, disorderly conduct, prostitution, vagrancy, assault and battery, and aggravated assault present particular problems along these lines. It has also been noted that except for embezzlement, fraud, and perhaps some categories of larceny, most of the "white collar crimes" referred to by Sutherland in his classic review of such offenses are not routinely collected by the FBI. Most of these crimes are adjudicated by "quasi-judicial bodies in order to avoid stigmatizing businessmen as criminals, in much the way that children's cases are heard in surroundings different from those of adults for the same reason."

Because "the primary objective [of the *UCR*] is to produce a reliable program of nationwide criminal statistics for administrative and operational use of law enforcement agencies," there are some problems in using these statistics safely for scientific research. Although it is suggested that the reports also provide meaningful data for social scientists and other scholars, there are many difficulties involved in trying to interpret table titles, locate the data used in various kinds of tables, and discover what raw data were used in presenting certain kinds of statistical analyses of crime trends. As one author has pointed out, "One who develops a criminological theory accounting for variations in crime rates risks his professional reputation, for the extent of statistical error in any observed variation is unknown."

* * *

1. Physical Harm

The index offenses, as reported in the *UCR*, give a false impression of the meaning of seriousness. As the Consultant Committee indicated in its 1958 special report to the FBI, the separation of offenses into more important and less important ones by using the designation of "major crime" to refer to Part I offenses conveyed the idea that Part II offenses were not major, and consequently were minor or less important. The term "serious crimes," however, was still used in the 1961 issue. The exact meanings of these terms—major and serious—have never been clear. Nor did the removal of negligent manslaughter, larceny under $50, and statutory rape remove the implications that are still found in describing the index offenses as major crimes, though it did improve the crime index. Such offenses as arson, kidnapping, and assault and battery, which do not appear in the index, may in fact involve more personal injury than forcible rape, aggravated assault, and others listed in the index. Research on the problem of constructing an index of delinquency, conducted by Thorsten Sellin and the writer, has revealed that in a carefully selected sample from over 13,000 delinquencies in a single year in Philadelphia, one-fifth of the cases which involved bodily injury occurred in offenses not generally recognized in the traditional *UCR* classification as involving physical harm. Moreover, of all bodily injury offenses, 62 percent occurred in what the *UCR* refers to as Part II offenses, those which are not now included in the crime index. As might be expected from the legal labels, the modal type of harm in cases of aggravated assault was more serious than in simple assaults. Nearly three-fourths of aggravated assaults required medical treatment as compared to one-fifth of simple assaults. Only 3 percent of aggravated assaults as compared to 72 percent of simple assaults involved minor injuries; and 23 percent of the former as compared to 7 percent of the latter required hospitalization. However, it is significant that as many as 28 percent of the bodily injury cases, classified by the *UCR* as simple assaults, were as serious or more serious in terms of the resultant harm than 76 percent of those cases classified as aggravated assaults. It should be remembered that simple assaults are not listed in the *UCR* crime index. If physical harm to the person of the victim is considered an important item in measuring the seriousness of a criminal act, then obviously a classificatory scheme that takes account of this fact is necessary.

2. Property Stolen or Damaged

The amount of property stolen or damaged may be much greater in many offenses not found in the index than in those classified even under the category of larceny over $50 which appears in the list of index offenses. Embezzlement, for example, is not an index crime. It is segregated from other types of larceny presumably because it is less reported or because it is committed by stealth. But pocket-picking, which is included in the crime index if over $50 in value, is also committed by stealth and rarely involves as much property loss as does embezzlement. Moreover, malicious mischief and disorderly conduct, which do not appear in the index, can on many occasions result in considerably more property damage and consequently more injury to the community than do some of the property offenses listed in the crime index.

3. Attempted Acts

Attempted acts are commingled with completed acts in the crime index. For example, attempted burglaries, robberies, and rapes, including assaults with intent to ravish, are index crimes even though no property damage or loss occurs and even though no personal injury ensues. If there is any value in having a collection of criminal statistics based upon objective criteria indicating the amount of actual harm or loss to a community, then criminal attempts should definitely be omitted from the crime index. They could be separately tabulated, for they may serve a useful purpose in some other capacity than that of an index; psychological motivations may be similar for persons who attempt as well as complete an act. But there are enough difficulties in providing operational definitions simply for observable behavior and completed crimes without mixing the two. These problems should not be compounded by incomplete reporting and police interpretations of intent and attempt.

4. Auto Theft and Joy Riding

Despite the fact that specific information is reported to the FBI, the category of automobile theft continues to include joy riding by juveniles, and the two are not separated in tabulations of the crime index.

5. Lack of Weighting Within the Index

The wide range of criminal behavior covered by the seven offenses in the index lacks any weighting by seriousness of offense. For index purposes, a $50 larceny is equated with a premeditated murder. Taken as a whole, in which each offense represents a unit of one, the total number of offenses in the seven categories is not a figure that can tell us anything meaningful about the crime problem. Moreover, it is possible that crime trends in the seven offenses do not reflect trends in the other types of offenses. Burglary, larceny, and auto theft constitute a large group of offenses, whereas criminal homicide and forcible rape involve small numbers. Offenses against the person constitute only 8 percent of all the index crimes; offenses against property comprise 92 percent. It is obvious that because burglary makes up 44 percent of the crime index, a slight increase in burglary offenses will substantially affect that total, regardless of the trends for the other six offenses. A marked decline in criminal homicides and rapes may, therefore, be offset by proportionately minor increases in burglaries, larcenies, and auto thefts. Under these circumstances, the total number of index crimes, or the crime index, represents an invalid, inaccurate measure of the amount and quality of criminality in a community.

6. Multiple Offenses

Because only the highest order of an index offense is used when there are multiple offenses committed in a single criminal event, the amount of physical harm or property loss and the duality of personal injury and property loss are altogether hidden. For example, if an offender simultaneously commits an aggravated assault and a burglary, aggravated assault is used for tabulation purposes, while burglary is dropped from the criminal statistic. Similarly, with an aggravated assault and robbery, any reference to the personal assault, and certainly to the degree of the injury, is lost by counting only the robbery, which is considered "more serious"—higher in the rank order of offenses listed for uniform crime reporting. In the *Uniform Crime Reporting Handbook* (1960), several examples of classification ("finding the proper crime classification from the facts about a crime") and scoring offenses ("counting the number of offenses after you find the classification") are presented, clearly illustrating these kinds of omissions:

1. *Problem.* A holdup man forces a husband and his wife to get out of their automobile. He shoots the husband, gun whips and rapes the wife and leaves in the automobile after taking money from the husband. The husband dies as a result of the shooting.

Solution. In the problem, we can recognize robbery, aggravated assault, rape, murder, as well as auto theft and larceny. Our Part I offenses are in order as follows:

1. Criminal homicide:
   (a) Murder, non-negligent manslaughter.
   (b) Manslaughter by negligence.
2. Rape
3. Robbery
4. Aggravated Assault
5. Burglary—breaking or entering
6. Larceny-Theft
7. Auto Theft

From the several crimes in the problem, you recognize Class 1a, murder and non-negligent manslaughter, as the first crime on the list. Stop at that classification—it is the only one that will be used for scoring the problem. (For crime reporting you ignore the other crimes in the set of facts—this does not affect the number of charges for which the defendant may be prosecuted in your courts.) You have classified the case. As you will see under "Scoring," only one offense of murder is scored.

2. *Problem.* Two thieves break into a warehouse and have loaded considerable merchandise on a truck belonging to the warehouse when surprised by a night watchman. The night watchman is knocked unconscious with some blunt instrument. The thieves drive away in a stolen truck.

Solution. Here is unlawful entry, theft and auto theft. Following the rule we find unlawful entry first (burglary—breaking or entering). This is the only classification used.

3. *Problem.* Three men break into a public garage after closing hours. They steal cash from the garage office lockbox and two automobiles from the shop.

Solution. Here is unlawful entry, theft and auto theft. Following the rule we find unlawful entry first (burglary—breaking or entering). This is the only classification used.

4. *Problem.* An automobile containing clothing and luggage valued at $375 is stolen. The car is recovered but the clothing and luggage are missing.

Solution. This is an *exception to the general rule* for classifying. It may help to remember that auto theft is only a special type of *larceny-theft* and was made a separate classification only because it is a special problem. When you have to choose between auto theft and larceny-theft in problems such as this classify as auto theft only.

In the first solution it is obvious that no accounting is made of the very serious criminal acts of aggravated assault upon, and rape of the woman, robbery, auto theft, and larceny. In the second, aggravated assault and auto theft are omitted; in the third, the theft of two automobiles; in the fourth, the theft of $375 worth of property. Not only are the qualifying characteristics of degree of physical harm and property loss ignored, *but even the tabulations by traditional legal categories are incomplete because of these particular classifying and scoring techniques.*

Despite the fact that rates based on annual population estimates have appeared since 1958, another kind of statistical misrepresentation persists. Percent changes in the total volume of index offenses from one year to the next are reported by single years or occasionally over longer time spans. Unwary readers receive a false image of the changes that are taking place in the amount of crime relative to population changes. The percent of change of the instant year over the preceding year is now given both according to population-based rates and according to the absolute number of offenses. Although this dual presentation is somewhat of an improvement, the rate changes are treated subordinately in all reports, especially in the introductory section that summarizes the data in the tricky alliteration of "crime capsule," "crime clock," "crime calender," and "crime count." This section is the one most used by newspapers, local police, and civic groups interested in crime. It is here, as well as in the current quarterly reports, that the percent change by total volume or absolute numbers, irrespective of the population base, continues to be given a prominent position and description. Trend analyses, bar charts, and pie charts are used to show how much crime has changed—usually increased—during the past year or past decade. Almost invariably these graphic presentations of criminal statistics are misleading.

We are regularly informed that a certain number of serious crimes occurs each minute in the United States. For example, in 1961, four serious crimes occurred each minute, one murder every hour, one forcible rape every 33 minutes, one robbery every 6 minutes, one aggravated assault every 4 minutes, one burglary every 37 seconds, one serious larceny ($50 and over) every minute, and one auto theft every one and one-half minutes. If the purpose of this "crime clock" is to frighten consumers of the *UCR*, the statements probably succeed, for they are reproduced in scores of newspapers and read by millions, including congressmen, state legislators, and city councilmen who appropriate funds for police budgets. But some other document should be used for this purpose, not a responsible publication that disseminates official statistics for use by social scientists and other analysts in scholarly research. Once again, the objections are obvious. Even if the proportion of crimes to the population remained stable, the "crime clock" would move more rapidly if the population is increasing. Contrariwise, if the population were decreasing and the volume of crime remained the same, the crime rate would increase but the "crime clock" would show no change.

When rates are presented in the *UCR*, they are computed per 100,000 population. This crude rate is based on an unstated assumption that all humans are equally capable of committing crimes. As Sellin has suggested, this assumption is erroneous, for criminal conduct is not evenly distributed over all segments of the population. By definition, criminal conduct generally cannot occur among children under 7 years of age, and is rare among children up to at least 12 years. It predominantly appears in males between 12 and 50 years of age. The custom in some foreign countries of computing rates on the basis of the population of "punishable age" or "capable of committing a crime" represents a slight improvement. What are actually needed, but have never appeared in the *UCR*, are refined rates calculated on a population standardized for age and sex, and perhaps for other factors, depending on the availability of accurate and properly sub-classified statistics of the population concerned.

I have previously noted statistical deficiencies of the *UCR* classification system, especially due to the method used by police departments in reporting and scoring offenses by that system. Attributing the same "weight" of seriousness (namely, a unit of one) to each index offense also has inherent weaknesses. Equally disturbing is the fact that different levels of criminal statistics are presented in the *UCR* in a fashion which does not permit analysis of their relationships. "Offenses known to the police," "offenses cleared by arrests," "persons charged," and "persons found guilty" are recorded, but it is impossible for an analyst to move directly from one statistic to another while retaining a base of offenses known. The *UCR* cannot tell us, for example, what proportion of offenses known to the police result in a conviction of one or more perpetrators.

* * *

The *UCR* crime classification and scheme for scoring offenses are based upon an allocation procedure which is derived a priori. Moreover, the statistics to which I have previously referred appear to indicate biases designed to suggest that crime is rapidly increasing and that police efficiency is greatly improving. To emphasize, without appropriate reference to the population base, that the absolute number of crimes in 1950 is greater than in 1940 and greater in 1960 than in 1950 is about as meaningful as saying that there are more crimes in California than in Rhode Island.

There are other items which indicate similar biases. Interesting use of adjectives is made in recent *Quarterly Reports*. We are told, for example, that serious crimes "substantially" increased by 7 percent; pocket-picking decreased by 18 percent, but with no adjective; while forcible rape had an "alarming" rise of 8 percent. "Murder" in rural counties was "sharply down" by 16 percent, but offenses against the person showed a "sharp" increase of 6 percent. At one time, index offenses increased "alarmingly" by 12 percent, and aggravated assault had a "sharp" increase of 7 percent, but at another time when "serious crimes" went up 11 percent, no adjective was used. This may be a relatively minor objection, but it is certainly difficult to know what is a "sharp," "substantial," or "alarming" change according to these *Reports*. If these terms are to be used at all, they should at least be applied with discrimination and consistency.

Keeping in mind what was said earlier about errors in reporting, no one can give very serious attention to the following statement: "Increases were recorded in all crime categories except robbery which was down one percent. This crime had the most significant rise in 1960 and the reversal of the trend indicates to some extent the success of police efforts to reduce its occurrence." That this change in absolute numbers of one percent could be a measurement of police efforts is a patently biased comment. Of course no mention is ever made about police efforts to reduce any type of crime when there is a percent increase, however "sharp" or "alarming." Moreover, the paradoxical situation may occur that when the police are making greater efforts in their activity, certain types of crime increase.

Ordinarily, the term "cleared by arrest" is used quite properly; but to say that a certain percentage of offenses known to the police have been "solved" is very doubtful language. The word "solved" may infer more efficient performance than would a more appropriate phrase. Equally annoying is the misuse of the term "murder" in text and tables when the proper term is "murder and non-negligent homicide" or "criminal homicide." It is difficult enough to excuse newspaper reporters for using "murder" when they mean the various types of criminal homicide, thus conjuring up in the public imagination the most reprehensible sort of first degree murder. To encourage this incorrect usage by its appearance in an official document is indefensible.

CONCLUSION

Although the *Uniform Crime Reports* represent efforts to provide good police statistics and a valid crime index and although they have been improved since 1958, these *Reports* and the changes in them are partial and inadequate. Limitations of the classification system and the recording and scoring techniques, and statistical deficiencies in presenting crime data—particularly changes over time—are serious and should be carefully examined by the Department of Justice in an effort to rectify them. To claim that changing some of these procedures would render difficult any comparisons with the past is to suggest perpetuation of many elements of error, omission, inconsistency, contradiction, deficiency, and bias.

CHAPTER II

Aggressive Crimes—I

In this book of readings two chapters have been devoted to the subject of aggressive crimes. In the present chapter our attention will be directed to an analysis of criminal homicide. In Chapter III we will explore assaultive crimes and forcible rape. Some students may feel that the criminal category of robbery has been ignored by the editor. However, robbery is considered both a crime against the person and a crime against property. Although it may be perfectly legitimate to discuss robbery in the following chapter, the choice has been made to defer this discussion until we reach Chapter X (Property Offenses).

Homicide, although a low-volume crime in terms of number (less than 3 percent of all crimes of violence, and less than one-half of 1 percent of all Crime Index offenses), is one of the most serious offenses that may be committed in our society. A person convicted of homicide in the United States faces the most severe legal penalties that the state may impose. Although capital punishment has long been employed in an attempt to deter the potential murderer from committing his act, statistical evidence suggests that even the threat of putting the convicted to death has not proven very successful.

Criminal homicide is typically an individual crime involving one victim and one offender who are intimately acquainted. It is not at all common in the United States for the participants in this act to be strangers. Quite often they are members of the same family, business acquaintances, drinking partners who frequent a neighborhood bar, or social companions who may vacation, party, and/or travel together. When large groups are involved in acts of killing, this is usually not defined as homicide, but rather as war or revolution. If the group conflict takes the form of a revolution, at its conclusion the victors will be accorded high rank and status within the society and the losers rather harshly dealt with, either executed or given extremely long prison terms.

In its *Uniform Crime Report,* the Federal Bureau of Investigation makes the distinction between all willful acts of murder and deaths caused by negligence. Criminal homicide is thus defined as:

(a) Murder and nonnegligent manslaughter: all willful felonious homicides as distinguished from deaths caused by negligence. Excludes attempts to kill, suicides, accidental deaths, or justifiable homicides. Justifiable homicides are limited to: (1) the killing of a person by a peace officer in line of duty; (2) the killing of a person in the act of committing a felony by a private citizen. (b) Manslaughter by negligence: any death which the police investigation establishes was primarily attributable to gross negligence of some individual other than the victim.

In Chart 2.1 below it is most interesting to follow the year by year increase in homicides through the 1960s and note that this offense category falls far below the overall increase in our national crime rate. While the homicide rate, 1960–67 is up 22 percent, the national crime rate for this same period rose by 71 percent, more than a 3 to 1 ratio. (See Chart 2.1).

In our country, firearms continue to be the predominant weapon used in acts of criminal homicide. As illustrated in Chart 2.2, over 63 percent of criminal homicides in 1967 involved the use of a handgun, rifle, or shotgun. At the present time a good deal of legislation aimed at controlling the shipment, purchase, and ownership of firearms has been proposed at both the national and state levels of government. However, because of various pressure group interests and some public sentiment regarding the right to bear arms, it has been most difficult to make any meaningful progress.

Selected Facts on Criminal Homicide[1]

1. Firearms were used to commit over 7,600 homicides.
2. More homicides were committed in the summer months, but December was the peak month.
3. 48 percent of the homicides were committed in the southern states.
4. Homicide increased 11 percent in 1967 over 1966.
5. Homicide victims were predominantly males by a 3 to 1 ratio.
6. Arrests for homicide were 5 males to every 1 female.
7. 54 percent of homicide victims were Negro. (Although Negroes represent only 12 percent of our population.)
8. Killings within the family constitute 28 percent of all criminal homicides. The wife was the victim in 55 percent of the cases, the husband in 45 percent.

[1]Based on 1967 statistics.

CHART 2.1

MURDER, 1960–1967
(Percent Change over 1960)

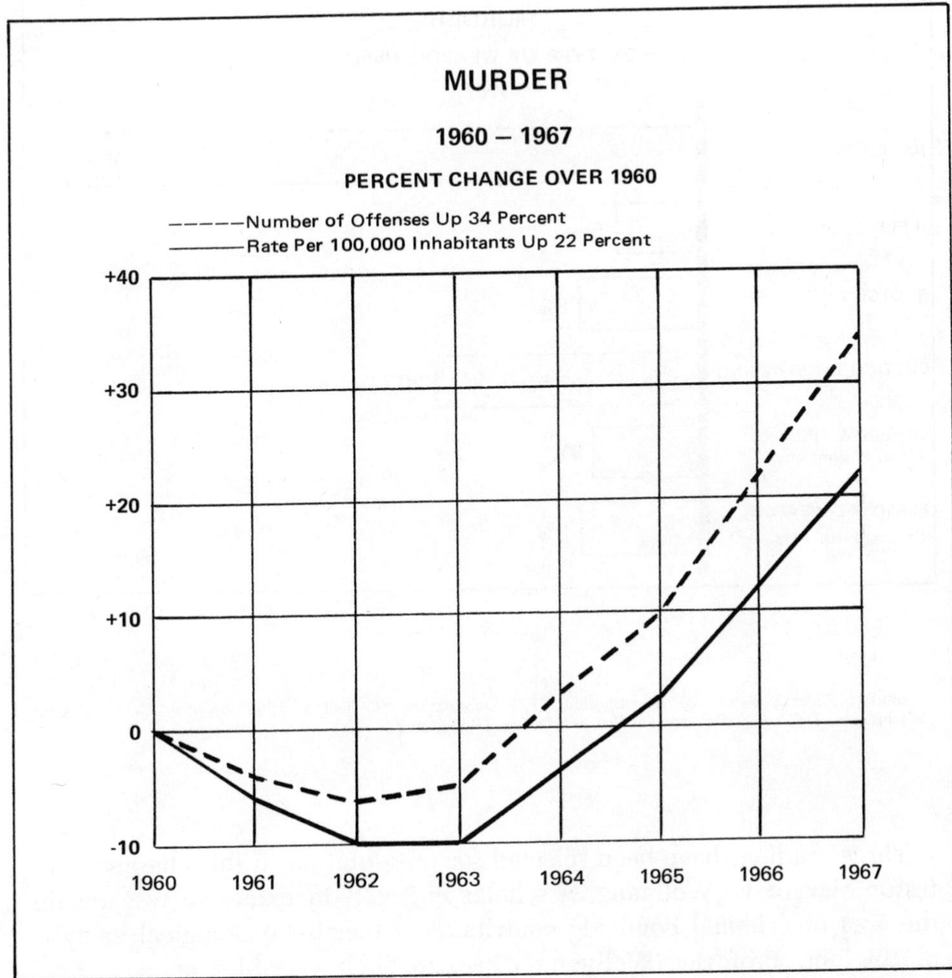

SOURCE: Federal Bureau of Investigation, U.S. Department of Justice, *1967 Uniform Crime Reports* (Washington, D.C.: U.S. Government Printing Office, 1968), p. 6.

9. One criminal homicide is committed every 43 minutes around the clock.
10. 88 percent of all homicide cases were cleared by arrest.[2] (The highest percentage of clearance of any criminal category.)

[2]"Cleared by arrest" means the arrest was made and the suspect made available for prosecution.

CHART 2.2

MURDER BY TYPE OF WEAPON USED—1967

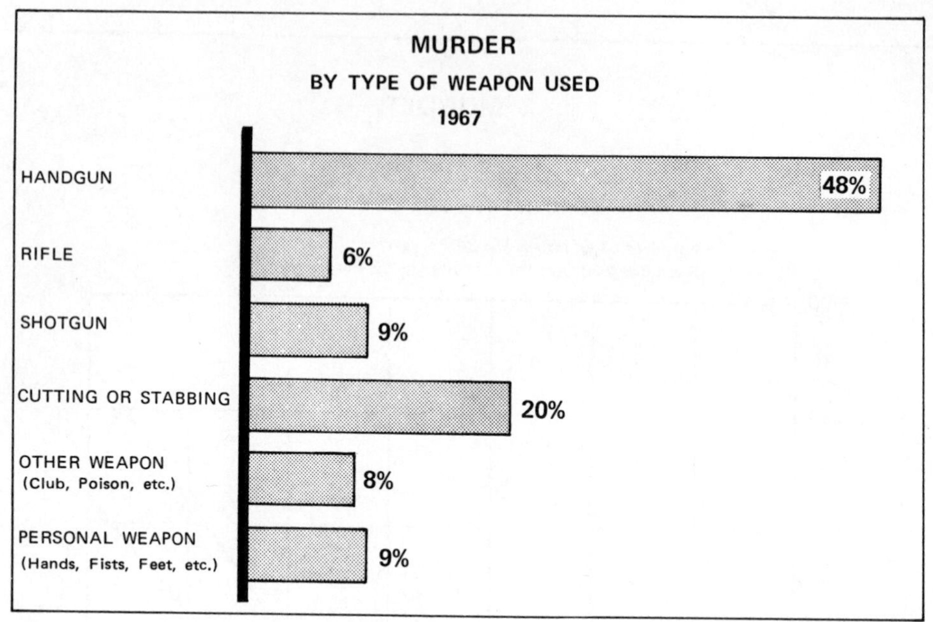

SOURCE: Federal Bureau of Investigation, U.S. Department of Justice, *1967 Uniform Crime Reports* (Washington, D.C.: U.S. Government Printing Office, 1968), p. 7.

Three readings have been selected for presentation in this chapter. Professor Marvin E. Wolfgang, a scholar engaged in extensive research in the area of criminal homicide contributes a concise sociological analysis of this act. Professor Wolfgang discusses such variables as race, age, sex, method used, time of day, place of occurrence, presence of alcohol, and the role of the victim in relation to the commission of an act of homicide. In the second article, Dr. Alex D. Pokorny, chief of Psychiatry and Neurology Services, Veterans Hospital, Houston, compares homicide data abstracted from the files of the Houston Police Department with Wolfgang's findings in his Philadelphia study. For the final reading, the editor turned to Professor Thomas F. Pettigrew and Rosalind B. Spier's study of "The Ecological Structure of Negro Homicide." Because the Negro is statistically overrepresented in arrests for murder and non-negligent manslaughter when compared with other racial groups (Negro —4,312 arrests, whites 2,188 in 1967), it was felt that this rather high involvement necessitated additional study of the black subculture and the Negroes' relations with other members of society.

6.

MARVIN E. WOLFGANG

A SOCIOLOGICAL ANALYSIS OF CRIMINAL HOMICIDE

Murder and other types of criminal homicide are deviations of the most serious and visible kind in our society. Public concern, the amount of time the police spend in detection and investigation, the ratio of the number of police to the number of these crimes, and the quantity of stories in literature and the drama that use murder as a central theme all attest to the interest we have in homicide. However, the television or literary mystery usually is concerned with the relatively rare premeditated type of killing. Most homicides have typical forms and are crimes of passion that arise from a world of violence.

The typical criminal slayer is a young man in his twenties who kills another man only slightly older. Both are of the same race; if Negro, the slaying is commonly with a knife, if white, it is a beating with fists and feet on a public street. Men kill and are killed between four and five times more frequently than women, but when a woman kills she most likely has a man as her victim and does it with a butcher knife in the kitchen. A woman killing a woman is extremely rare, for she is most commonly slain by her husband or other close friend by a beating in the bedroom.

These are some of the findings of a study more fully described in *Patterns in Criminal Homicide*.[1] Since publication of this book, a variety of requests for a summary discussion have come to my desk, partly, I imagine, because of the recent renewed interest in the sociopsychological aspects of criminal homicide reflected in Guttmacher's *The Mind of the Murderer*,[2] Palmer's *A Study of Murder*,[3] and in Bohannan's *African Homicide and Suicide*.[4] What follows, therefore, is an abbreviated analysis of my own sociological study with suggestive theoretical points of departure for additional research. For detailed information of the research methods and interpretive analysis of criminal homicide, the reader is referred to the present author's book.

WHAT IS CRIMINAL HOMICIDE?

The popular press and even some of our national, state, and municipal police officials sometimes confuse murder with other types of criminal homicide. As every capable policeman should know, homicide is the killing of another person and is divided into criminal and noncriminal homicide. The former category comprises murder (commonly in the first and second degree) as well as voluntary (nonnegligent) and involuntary (negligent) manslaughter. Noncriminal homicide is excusable, or a killing in self-defense, and justifiable homicide, or homicide performed as a legal duty by a peace officer or executioner. Confusion of these terms, mixing criminal with noncriminal cases, and mislabeling murder for other types of criminal homicides, has occurred in both professional and popular studies.

In order to produce some clarity among these terms and to provide a sociological and statistical analysis of criminal homicide, research was conducted in Philadelphia, using all criminal homicides recorded by the Philadelphia Homicide Squad from January 1, 1948 through December 31, 1952. Excusable and justifiable

SOURCE: *Federal Probation,* Vol. XXV, No. 1 (March, 1961), pp. 48–55. Reprinted by permission of the author and the journal.

[1] Marvin E. Wolfgang, *Patterns in Criminal Homicide* (Philadelphia, Pa.: University of Pennsylvania Press, 1958), p. 413.

[2] Manfred S. Guttmacher, *The Mind of the Murderer* (New York: Farrar, Strauss and Cudahy, 1960).

[3] Stuart Palmer, *A Study of Murder* (New York: Thomas Y. Crowell, 1960).

[4] Paul Bohannan (ed.), *African Homicide and Suicide* (Princeton, N.J.: Princeton University Press, 1960).

homicides were excluded from the study and concentration was only on criminal cases listed by the police. I spent many long hours over several years collecting the data and participating in arrest and interrogation of offenders, and I have the highest respect for the police officers with whom I came into contact during that period. The homicide detectives consistently showed due respect for the constitutional rights of persons they arrested as well as an attitude of understanding rather than that of vengeance and retribution. These are, of course, qualities desirable in all police officers, for their function is to protect as well as to apprehend, to make suspects available for prosecution, but not to judge guilty.

It is almost axiomatic in criminal statistics that for purposes of determining the amount and type of crime committed in a community, police statistics yield the most valid data.[5] Too many cases are lost through court trials to use court statistics, and to use prison data means a still further reduction of cases that are highly selected to result in incarceration instead of probation or some other form of disposition. For this reason, police statistics were used to obtain the most valid picture of criminal homicides over this 5-year period.

Another important aspect of the research design was to distinguish between victims and offenders in terms of their major social characteristics. Usually this distinction is not maintained in studies of homicide, especially in those that rely only on mortality statistics published by the Office of Vital Statistics from death certifications. The Philadelphia study and review of the literature on criminal homicide reveal that much confusion of terminology pervades the field; that data about victims often are confused with data about offenders; rates per population unit are sometimes confused with reports about proportionate distributions or percentages of criminal slayings. We have emphasized constantly the invalidity of inferring characteristics about victims from criminal statistics, some of which supply data only for offenders; or of inferring characteristics about offenders from mortality statistics, which supply data only for victims.

Most previous research has examined *either* the victim *or* the offender. In the present work, analysis has been made of *both* victims and offenders, separately, as distinct units, but also as mutual participants in the homicide. A broad social approach is interested both in the active, "to kill," and in the passive, "to be killed." It is one type of analysis to consider victims as a social group and offenders as another social group; it is quite a different and more refined type of analysis to consider specific victim-offender relationships, and to find race, sex, age, and other patterns among them.

During the period from 1948 through 1952 there were 588 cases of criminal homicide in Philadelphia; i.e., there were 588 victims. Because several people were sometimes involved in killing one person, there were 621 offenders arrested by the police and taken into custody. In terms of a mean annual rate per 100,000 population in the city, the victim rate was 5.7 and the offender rate 6.0. This is neither high nor low. Compared with 18 other cities across the country, each of which had a population of a quarter of a million or more in 1950, Philadelphia ranks ninth, with a range between Miami having a victim rate of 15.1 and Milwaukee having a low of 2.3. New York's rate was only 3.7, Los Angeles 4.0, and Chicago 7.8. The rate for Pennsylvania as a whole for 1950 was only 3.5, but the most fair comparison is between cities of comparable size.[6]

The years 1948–52 were advantageous years

[5]The advantages of police statistics and limitations of other sources of data for criminal homicide research have been discussed in: Thorsten Sellin, "The Basis of a Crime Index," *Journal of Criminal Law and Criminology*, Vol. 22 (September, 1931), pp. 335–56; T. Sellin, *Crime and the Depression* (New York: Social Science Research Council Memorandum, 1937), chap. 4; T. Sellin, "The Measurement of Criminality in Geographic Areas," *Proceedings of the American Philosophical Society*, Vol. 97 (April, 1953) pp. 163–67. For additional references, see Marvin E. Wolfgang, *Patterns in Criminal Homicide*, (University of Pennsylvania, 1958), p. 12, n. 1.

[6]It is obvious to any student in the field that there are many criminal offenses committed that are never reported or recorded by the public authorities. This generalization is applicable to criminal homicide as it is to other offenses. But a theoretical analysis of the social visibility of crime, or the varying degrees of high and low reportability of specific offenses, leads us to suggest that there is a relatively low ratio between offenses committed and those known to the police in cases of criminal homicide.

for research purposes because the census fell exactly in the middle of this period so that the population statistics for 1950 could be used for computing a rate for any of the single 5 years or for all of them together. Moreover, it should be noted that the data collected from police files and used to analyze suggested associations and questions are expressed in numerical and percentage frequency distributions, in rates per 100,000 population in some cases, and in ratios. In order to safeguard against loose generalizations, several tests of statistical significance were employed.[7]

SOME BASIC FINDINGS: RACE, SEX, AND AGE

Research has shown that although criminal homicide is largely an unplanned act, there are nonetheless in the act regular uniformities and patterns. We have found, as previous research has noted, that there is a statistically significant association between criminal homicide and the race and sex of both victim and offender. Negroes and males involved in homicide far exceed their proportions in the general population and rates for these two groups are many times greater than for whites and females. The rate per 100,000 by race and sex of offenders reveals the following rank order of magnitude: Negro males (41.7), Negro females (9.3), white males (3.4), and white females (0.4). Although Negroes of either sex, and males of either race, are positively related to criminal slayings, the association between race and homicide is statistically more significant than that between sex and homicide. This relationship of Negroes and males to criminal homicide confirms reports and studies made elsewhere in this country, although the proportion of female offenders is reportedly much higher in England. It should be noted, however, that the whole of the British Isles has no more criminal homicides in a year than the city of Philadelphia alone (or about 125 annually).

Among offenders, the age group 20–24 predominates with a rate of 12.6 per 100,000, while the highest rate for victims is in the age group 25–34. In short, victims are generally older than their offenders; the median age of the former being 35.1 years and of the latter 31.9 years. The importance of the race factor here is striking in view of the fact that the *lowest* 5-year age-specific rates for Negro males and females are similar to, or higher than the *highest* of such rates for white males and females, respectively. Although males of both races more frequently commit criminal homicide during their twenties than during any other period of life, Negro males in their early sixties kill as frequently as do white males in their early twenties.

The race factor in criminal homicide is alarming and should be the cause of both Negro and white community leaders to examine more closely the reasons for this differential. The child is not born with homicide tendencies in his genes, so that in no way can we infer a biological explanation for this difference. Negroes are a minority group that still suffer from residential and general cultural isolation from the rest of the community, despite recent advances in integration. So long as this ethnic group is socially isolated and required to live in restricted residential areas they will continue to constitute a "subcultural" area. This subculture is characterized by poor housing, high density of population, overcrowded home conditions, and by a system of values that often condones violence and physical aggression from childrearing processes to adult interpersonal relationships that sometimes end in criminal slayings. To a lesser degree, whites in the lower socioeconomic classes as well as Negroes become part of this *subculture of violence* and participate in criminal homicide. Only by breaking up this culturally isolated group and by integrating them into the general community of morality and values can society hope to reduce violence that results in homicide.

METHODS AND TIME OF ASSAULT

We have also noted significant associations between methods of inflicting death and the race and sex of both victims and offenders. In Phila-

[7] For the most part, the statistical tests involved use of the non-parametric technique of Chi-square (X^2) with corrections for continuity and a probability level of (P) less than 0.05.

delphia 39 percent of all homicides were due to stabbings, 33 percent to shooting, 22 percent to beatings, and 6 percent to other and miscellaneous methods. There appears to be a cultural preference for particular types of methods and weapons. Males, if Negro, usually stab and are stabbed to death; and if white, beat and are beaten to death. Females generally stab their victims with a butcher knife, but are very often beaten to death.

Although homicides tend to increase during the hot summer months, there is no significant association by seasons or months of the year. But homicide is significantly associated with days of the week and hours of the day. The weekend in general, and Saturday night in particular, are related to homicide, as are the hours between 8:00 p.m. and 2 a.m. Between 8:00 p.m. Friday and midnight Sunday there were, during the 5 years under review, 380 criminal homicides; but from the beginning of Monday morning to 8:00 p.m. Friday, there were only 208. Thus, on the average, 65 percent of all homicides occurred during the shorter time span of 52 hours, while only 35 percent occurred during the longer time span of 116 hours.

The time between assault and death of the victim varies according to the method employed by the offender. Relatively quick death (within 10 minutes after assault) occurred for half of the victims in a shooting, for less than three-tenths in a stabbing, and for only one-sixteenth in a beating. About a third of the victims were dead within 10 minutes after assault, slightly less than three-fifths after the first hour had passed, and four-fifths within a day. Only 5 percent lived more than 10 days after being assaulted. Probably fewer persons today die from aggravated assault wounds than was true a generation ago, for data suggest that (1) improved communication with the police, (2) more rapid transportation to a hospital (usually by the police), and (3) advanced medical technology have contributed to the decreasing homicide rates in this country during the last 25 years.

We do not know, of course, just how many aggravated assaults, assaults with intent to kill, and other violent assaults are today prevented from becoming classified as criminal homicides because of these three factors, but the steady increases of other crimes of personal violence, such as aggravated assaults and rapes, regularly reported in the *Uniform Crime Reports* lead us to suggest that something other than a greater repugnance to commit crimes of personal violence has entered our mores. Many factors are involved in changing rates of homicide, such as the age composition, business cycles, etc. But because crimes of violence against the person, excluding homicide, appear to have increased during the past two decades, it is logical to assume that if these gross social factors affect homicide, they should affect other crimes of violence in the same way.

Research testing the hypothesis suggested by the three factors mentioned above might be useful in explaining the general decrease in criminal homicide over the past 25 years.[8] It would be valuable, for example, to know the recovery rate for those who are today grievously assaulted but who would have probably died under medical and other conditions of a generation ago. Although this type of analysis fails to account for any psychological dimensions in the phenomenon of homicide, the approach nonetheless has the virtue of mensurability in testing the validity of the explanation.

PLACE WHERE CRIMES OCCUR

The place where the crime occurred is also important. The most dangerous single place is the highway (public street, alley, or field), although more slayings occur in the home than outside the home. Men kill and are killed most frequently in the street, while women kill most often in the kitchen but are killed in the bedroom. For victims and offenders of each race and sex group significant differences have been noted. Most cases of Negro males who kill Negro males involve a stabbing in a public street; most cases of white males who kill white males involve a beating in a public street. However, the high proportion of females who kill with a butcher knife in a kitchen, and of those who

[8]Some recent analysis of this hypothesis has been made for Ceylon. See Cleobis Jayewardene, "Criminal Homicide: A Study in Culture Conflict," Ph.D. thesis, University of Pennsylvania, 1960.

are killed in a bedroom by being beaten is associated with the fact that 84 percent of all female offenders slay males and 87 percent of all female victims are slain by males.

PRESENCE OF ALCOHOL

Either or both the victim and offender had been drinking immediately prior to the slaying in nearly two-thirds of the cases. The presence of alcohol in the homicide situation appears to be significantly associated with Negroes—either as victims or as offenders—and, separately, with Negro male and female victims. Particular caution[9] must be exercised in evaluating the presence of alcohol in these homicides, since drinking—particularly on Saturday night, the time of highest incidence of homicide—is an integral part of the mores of most groups involved in this crime. A significantly higher proportion of week-end homicides than of homicides occurring during the remainder of the week had alcohol present (in either the victim, the offender, or both). An association between alcohol, weekend slayings, and the payment of wages on Friday was indicated and crudely confirmed by the available data. We have, therefore, suggested that when the socioeconomic group most likely to commit homicide almost simultaneously receives its weekly wages, purchases alcohol, and meets together socially, it is not unlikely that the incidence of homicide should also rise.

PREVIOUS POLICE RECORD AND VICTIM-OFFENDER RELATIONSHIPS

Contrary to many past impressions, an analysis of offenders in criminal homicide reveals a relatively high proportion who have a previous police or arrest record. Of total offenders, nearly two-thirds have a previous arrest record, and of total victims, almost half have such a record. Having a previous record is also associated with males both among victims and offenders, and is obvious from the fact that more *male victims* have such a record than do *female offenders.* Moreover, when an offender has a previous record, he is more likely to have a record of offenses against the person than against property; and when he has a record of offenses against the person, he is more likely than not to have a record of having committed a serious assault offense, such as aggravated assault or assault with intent to kill. A greater proportion of Negro male and female victims have a previous arrest record than do white male and female offenders, respectively. In view of these facts, it is of interest to future attempts at prevention and control of potential offenders in criminal homicide that *a larger proportion of offenders with an arrest record have a record of aggravated assault than of all types of property offenses* combined. The courts should take special care not to release too hastily and without proper individualized treatment those persons arrested on charges of personal assault in order to prevent later homicides.

Criminal homicide usually results from a vaguely defined altercation, domestic quarrel, jealousy, argument over money, and robbery. These five police-recorded "motives" are involved in 8 out of 10 cases. Most of the identified victim-offender relationships may be classified as "primary group" relations, or those that include intimate, close, frequent contacts. Close friends and relatives accounted for over half of the contacts, and the combined categories which involve primary group contacts constitute 59 percent of all victim-offender relationships among males, but significantly as much as 84 percent among females. Because white males were killed more frequently than Negro males during the commission of a robbery, the former were also more frequently strangers to their slayers than the latter.

Mate slayings have been given special attention.[10] Of the 100 husband-wife homicides, 53 victims were wives and 47 were husbands. The number of wives killed by their husbands constitutes 41 percent of all women killed,

[9]Problems of analyzing the presence of alcohol in the victim and in the offender were particularly trying. In addition to Chapter 8 in the book, the reader is referred to Marvin E. Wolfgang's paper (with R. Strohm) for discussion of these problems in "The Relationship between Alcohol and Criminal Homicide," *Quarterly Journal of Studies in Alcohol,* Vol. 17 (September, 1956), pp. 411–25.

[10]See also Marvin E. Wolfgang's analysis of "Husband-Wife Homicides," *The Journal of Social Therapy,* Vol. 2 (1956), pp. 263–71.

whereas husbands slain by their wives make up only 11 percent of all men killed. Thus, when a woman commits homicide, she is more likely than a man to kill her mate; and when a man is killed by a woman, he is most likely to be killed by his wife. Husbands are often killed by their wives in the kitchen with a butcher knife, but nearly half of the wives are slain in the bedroom. More male than female offenders in these spouse slayings were found guilty, were convicted of more serious degrees of homicide, and committed suicide.

In 94 percent of the cases, the victim and offender were members of the same race, but in only 64 percent were they of the same sex. Thus, the ratio of intra- to interracial homicide is 15.2 to 1; but the ratio of intra- to intersex homicide is only 1.8 to 1. In general, it may be said that victims were homicidally assaulted most frequently by males of their own race, and least frequently by females of another race.

In 32 cases involving 57 offenders and 6 victims, a felony, in addition to the killing, was perpetrated at the time of the slaying. In most cases the other felony was robbery, and white males accounted for a larger proportion of these felony-murders than they did among all homicides in general.

VICTIM-PRECIPITATED HOMICIDE

The term *victim-precipitated homicide* has been introduced to refer to those cases in which the victim is a direct, positive precipitator in the crime—the first to use physical force in the homicide drama. After establishing a theoretical and legal basis for analysis, the Philadelphia data reveal several factors significantly associated with the 150 victim-precipitated homicides, which is 26 percent of all homicides. These factors are: Negro victims and offenders, male victims, female offenders, stabbings, victim-offender relationships involving male victims and female offenders, mate slayings, husbands who were victims in mate slayings, alcohol, victims with a previous arrest record, particularly an arrest record of assault. Thus, in most of these cases, the role and characteristics of the victim and offender are reversed, the victim assumes the role of determinant, and the victim makes a definite contribution to the genesis of his own victimization.[11]

Recently, I have extended the meaning of victim-precipitated homicide to include a sociological and psychoanalytic discussion of these 150 victims as being bent on suicide.[12] Although it is impossible to verify an assumption of subconscious suicide wishes among these victims, empirical data from broad social factors combine with psychological and sociological data suggesting that victims in many cases present themselves as willing targets for violent aggression leading to homicide. The material collected by John M. Macdonald at the Colorado Psychopathic Hospital on "The Murderer and His Victim"[13] sheds additional light on this area of analysis.

SUICIDE AFTER PERFORMING HOMICIDE

In 24 cases the offenders committed suicide after performing the homicide.[14] Of these, 22 were males, nearly half of whom were men who had killed their wives. Analysis and evaluation of these homicide-suicides indicate that half of the homicides would have been classified as first-degree murder had the offender experienced a court trial. As a result, even with the low amount of suicide after homicide in this country, more offenders inflict death upon themselves than are put to death by the social sanction of legal execution. Twelve persons who committed suicide appear to have committed first-degree murder. Thus the number of self-inflicted "executions" is greater than the 7 of-

---

[11]For more detailed treatment of this concept of victim-precipitation, which is increasingly becoming an important element in theoretical discussions of the poorly designated term, "victimology," see Chapter 14 in the book as well as "Victim-Precipitated Criminal Homicide," *Journal of Criminal Law, Criminology, and Police Science,* Vol. 48 (June, 1957), pp. 1–11.

[12]"Suicide by Means of Victim-Precipitated Homicide," *Journal of Clinical and Experimental Psychopathology,* Vol. 20 (October-December, 1959), pp. 335–49.

[13]*The Murderer and His Victim,* Charles C. Thomas, 1961.

[14]In addition to Chapter 15 in the book, see also Marvin E. Wolfgang's "An Analysis of Homicide-Suicide," *Journal of Clinical and Experimental Psychopathology,* Vol. 19 (July-September, 1958), pp. 208–18.

fenders who were sentenced to death by a court of record. However, suicide following homicide is 5 to 6 times more frequent in England than in the United States.

UNSOLVED HOMICIDES

Of particular importance to the police are unsolved homicides. The definition used in this study was not exactly like that of offenses not cleared by arrest, which is used for uniform crime reporting purposes, but there were similarities. Comparisons of the unsolved with solved cases reveal that the former have higher proportions of: white male and female victims, victims 65 years of age and over, robbery as a prelude to the slayings, victims who were strangers to their assailants, beatings, weekend slayings, and assaults that occurred in the public street.

COURT DISPOSITIONS

Finally, analysis has been made of the tempo of legal procedures, of court disposition, designation of the degree of homicide, insanity, and sentences imposed by the court. Two-thirds of the offenders were arrested on the same day that the crime was committed, and over half appeared in court for trial within 6 months after the crime. Two-thirds of those taken into police custody, and over three-quarters of those who experienced a court trial were declared guilty. Proportionately, Negroes and males were convicted more frequently than whites and females; but previous analysis of the nature of these cases reveals that Negroes and males had in fact committed more serious offenses, and that a charge of unjust race and sex discrimination in court would not necessarily be correct.[15] Of the 387 offenders convicted and sentenced, 30 percent were guilty of murder in the first degree, 29 percent of murder in the second degree, 36 percent of voluntary manslaughter, and 15 percent of involuntary manslaughter. Less than 3 percent of the offenders were declared insane by the courts, which is a proportion similar to that reported in other studies in this country, but considerably smaller than the 30 percent or more reported insane in England.

FURTHER RESEARCH

We have only touched on some of the highlights of this analysis of criminal homicide. There are many aspects of special importance to the police that can aid them in making investigations and particularly in working on cases in which it is difficult to determine suspects, or that are listed as unsolved cases. Each city and each police department has its own peculiar problems, of course, but studies of this sort can easily be made if proper records are kept. Other types of crime need the same kind of research attention, but ultimately all such research depends on the veracity and efficiency of the police in recording and reporting their information. The greatest service the police can make to scientific research is their cooperation with the social scientist and the maintenance of valid, efficient records of their cases.

The Baltimore Criminal Justice Commission, under the direction of Ralph Murdy, former agent of the Federal Bureau of Investigation, was engaged in a 5-year study (1960–1965) of criminal homicides in Baltimore—a study modeled on the kind of analysis made in Philadelphia. Dr. John Macdonald, Assistant Director of the Colorado Psychopathic Hospital, intends to collect similar data for Denver over a 5-year period. Professor Franco Ferracuti, from the Institute of Criminal Anthropology at the University of Rome, has proposed simultaneous analyses of criminal homicide in San Juan, Puerto Rico, and in Rome, Italy. On-going research like these that seek to duplicate and to expand on the Philadelphia study will confirm, reject, or modify the patterns in criminal homicide that have thus far been described and analyzed. Only in this way, as Albert Morris[16] has suggested, can science produce meaningful understanding of this delimited phenomenon,

[15]Cf. Edward Green, "An Analysis of the Sentencing Practices of Criminal Court Judges in Philadelphia," Ph.D. thesis, University of Pennsylvania, 1959.

[16]Albert Morris, *Homicide: An Approach to the Problem of Crime* (Boston: Boston University Press, 1955).

leading from empirical data to a meaningful sociopsychological theory of crimes of violence.[17]

CONCLUSION

On the basis of these findings thus far, it is obvious that homicides are principally crimes of passion, or violent slayings that are not premeditated or psychotic manifestations. Emerging out of the data is a theory that suggests a conflict between the prevailing middle class values of our society and the values of a subsocial or subcultural group. Previously we have referred to this group as constituting a "subculture of violence." If there exists a subculture of violence, then we must further propose that the greater the degree of integration of the individual into this subculture the higher the likelihood that his behavior will often be violent; or, we may assert that there is a direct relationship between rates of homicide and the degree of integration of the subculture of violence to which the individual belongs. The importance of human life in the scale of values, the kinds of expected reactions to certain types of stimuli, the perceptual differences in the evaluation of the stimuli, and the general personality structure are all factors of importance in this theory. As has been pointed out,

> . . . the significance of a jostle, a slightly derogatory remark, or the appearance of a weapon in the hands of an adversary are stimuli differentially perceived and interpreted by Negroes and whites, males and females. Social expectations of response in particular types of social interaction result in differential "definitions of the situation." A male is usually expected to defend the name and honor of his mother, the virtue of womanhood . . . and to accept no derogation about his race (even from a member of his own race), his age, or his masculinity. Quick resort to physical combat as a measure of daring, courage, or defense of status appears to be a cultural expression, especially for lower socioeconomic class males of both races. When such a culture norm response is elicited from an individual enga[ged in] social interplay with others who harbor the same response mechanism, physical assaults, altercations, and violent domestic quarrels that result in homicide are likely to be common. The upper-middle and upper social class value system defines and codifies behavioral norms into legal rules that often transcend subcultural mores, and considers many of the social and personal stimuli that evoke a combative reaction in the lower classes as "trivial." Thus, there exists a cultural antipathy between many folk rationalizations of the lower class, and of males of both races, on the one hand, and the middle-class legal norms under which they live, on the other.[18]

Highest rates of rape, aggravated assaults, persistency in arrests for assaults (recidivism) among these same groups with high rates of homicide are additional confirmations of the contention of a subculture of violence. Ready access to weapons may become essential for protection against others in this milieu who respond in similarly violent ways, and the carrying of knives or other protective devices becomes a common symbol of willingness to participate in and to expect violence, and to be ready for its retaliation. As in combat on the front lines during wartime where the "it-was-either-him-or-me" situation arises, there are similar attitudes and reactions among participants in homicide. The Philadelphia study shows that 65 percent of the offenders and 47 percent of the victims had a previous police record of arrests. Here, then, is a situation often not unlike that of combat in which two persons committed to the value of violence come together, and in which chance often dictates the identity of the slayer and of the slain.

We have not tried to explain the causes of this subculture of violence, but such an endeavor would involve analysis of social class and race relations that would include residential, occupational, and other forms of discrimination and social isolation as important factors. Some consideration of the groups from which the individual obtains a conception of himself and an analysis of child-rearing practices that employ punishment and promote early patterns of physical aggression would aid the search for causal factors and methods of treatment.

[17]The most recent theoretical statement about criminal homicide, based on data from the Philadelphia study, has been made by the author with the collaboration of Professor Ferracuti in "Subculture of Violence: An Interpretive Analysis of Homicide," paper presented before the Annual Meeting of the American Sociological Association, Section on The Sociology of Deviation, Marshall Clinard, chairman, New York, N. Y., August 29–31, 1960.

[18]Marvin E. Wolfgang, *Patterns in Criminal Homicide, op. cit.*, pp. 188–89.

As we have indicated, dispersing the group that shares the subculture of violence should weaken the value. Through wider economic opportunities, freedom of residential mobility, etc., integration of the group members into the larger society and its predominant value system should function to destroy or at least to reduce the subculture of violence. The work done in New York City in breaking up delinquent gangs has demonstrated the effectiveness of this approach. Similarly in correctional institutions, the treatment program, especially when using individual or group psychotherapy, should try to counterbalance or to eliminate the allegiance of the individual to the subculture of violence and his violent perception of the world.

7.

ALEX D. POKORNY

A COMPARISON OF HOMICIDES IN TWO CITIES

This study is a partial replication of the definitive analysis by Wolfgang[1] of criminal homicides in Philadelphia during 1948–1952. The cases analyzed in the present paper were collected for use in a comparative study of homicide, aggravated assault, suicide, and attempted suicide.[2] In view of the similarities of the data-securing approach to that of Wolfgang, it was decided to compare some of the findings in a Southern city with comparable ones in Philadelphia.

Wolfgang studied all of the criminal homicide cases occurring in Philadelphia during the years 1948 through 1952. There were 588 victims and 621 offenders. His book is crammed full of tables, maps, references, literature reviews, and scholarly discussions, and it is not possible to summarize it adequately here. Neither is it possible to replicate his entire study without creating another book. The present study seeks to confirm some of Wolfgang's more general findings.

In brief, Wolfgang studied all criminal homicides, using files of the Homicide Squad of the Philadelphia Police Department. He stated that police files were the most inclusive, in that they include the unsolved cases, those in which the offender committed suicide, etc. Homicide series collected from coroners' reports, court records, or prison commitments are progressively more selective (though they may be superior to police files in other respects). Wolfgang distinguishes clearly between homicide generally and criminal homicide, as well as between criminal homicide and the narrower category of murder. He points out that many studies fail to distinguish between these and between offender and victim; crime reports statistics generally refer to offenders, whereas mortality statistics refer to victims (the latter usually include non-criminal homicide too).

Wolfgang then presents a detailed analysis of offenders and victims by race, sex, age, previous criminal records, etc. He also analyzes methods, degree of violence, the contribution of alcohol, and motives. An important part of the study analyzes the victim-offender relationship, in terms of race, sex, the interpersonal relationship, and the possible role of the victim in precipitation of the homicide. In a final section he presents analyses of homicide-suicide, unsolved homicides, and the results of adjudication.

More specific findings from Wolfgang's study

[1]Marvin E. Wolfgang, *Patterns in Criminal Homicide* (Philadelphia: University of Pennsylvania Press, 1958).

[2]See research paper by Dr. Pokorny in Chapter 3.

will be presented later, in relation to findings from the present study.

PROCEDURE

All criminal homicides occurring in Houston, Texas, during the period March 15, 1958, through December 31, 1961, were abstracted from the files of the Houston Police Department.[3] "Murder by Auto" cases were excluded. The total number of the remaining cases was 438, with 430 offenders and 425 victims. The data on age, sex, race, home address, and method of homicide were available on virtually all of the known offenders and victims. The exact place where the offense occurred was usually identified fully in the case file. The personal or legal relationship between offender and victim was likewise identified in almost all of the cases where both parties were known.

Persons dealt with by the Houston Police Department are identified by race, except that a "Latin-American" category is separated from the other whites. In some of the subsequent analyses, the "White" category will be similarly subdivided into Latin-American and "Other White."

RESULTS

The main findings will be presented in the form of eight tables. These are arranged and patterned like eight comparable tables in the book by Wolfgang, and in most of the tables the corresponding Philadelphia data is included in parentheses, to facilitate comparisons. Most of the tabulated material is reported in percentages, and the actual number of cases is given at the top or bottom of each column. It should be noted that the "total white" category for the Houston data is comparable to Wolfgang's "white" group. Particular attention should be paid to whether the analysis is from the standpoint of the victim or the offender; this is stated in the title of the table.

1. Race, Ethnic Group, and Sex

Table 2.1 shows the numbers and rates of homicides broken down by race and sex. Although the percentage of Negroes in the population was larger in Houston (18% in Philadelphia in 1950, 23% in Houston in 1960), Negroes were the offenders in only 63% of Houston homicides as compared to 75% in Philadelphia.

An examination of Table 2.1, however, shows that the homicide rates in Houston are approximately double the Philadelphia rates. Although the Negro rates in Houston are somewhat higher than in Philadelphia, the most striking difference is in the White rates. When the Latin-American group is separated from the "Other Whites," their rate falls in an intermediate position. As usual, the female rates are far smaller than the male rates; in the Latin-American group, there were no female victims at all.

2. Method

Table 2.2 shows the principal method in homicides from the standpoint of the victim. One striking finding is that, in Houston, shooting accounts for almost two-thirds of the deaths; in Philadelphia, only one-third of the deaths are by shooting. Much of the difference is made up by the comparative infrequency of beating in Houston. In both series stabbing is more frequent among Negroes.

3. Hour of Day

Table 2.3 shows clearly that homicides are bunched in the hours from 8:00 p.m. to 2:00 a.m. with about half of the cases occurring during those six hours. By contrast, the half-day from 2:00 a.m. to 2:00 p.m. accounts for only about one-quarter of the homicides. There is a close similarity between the hourly distribution in Houston and in Philadelphia.

4. Place of Occurrence

The places where the homicides occurred are shown in Table 2.4. These are also summarized into sites at home and away from home. The classification of places is that of Wolfgang, and there were numerous instances in the Houston data in which the place did not fit one of these categories; these are listed under "other." It

[3]The author expresses his appreciation to the officials of the Houston Police Department for their cooperation, and particularly to Inspector Larry W. Fultz of the Records Division of the Department.

TABLE 2.1

NUMBERS AND RATES PER 100,000 POPULATION, VICTIMS AND OFFENDERS IN CRIMINAL HOMICIDE, HOUSTON, 1958–1961, BY RACE, ETHNIC GROUP, AND SEX

(Comparable Philadelphia rates in parentheses)

Race, Ethnic Group, Sex	*Victims*			*Offenders*		
	Number	*Rate per 100,000*	*(Philadelphia Rates)*	*Number*	*Rate per 100,000*	*(Philadelphia Rates)*
Negro						
Male	214	54.45	(36.9)	194	49.36	(41.7)
Female	49	11.60	(9.6)	70	16.58	(9.3)
Total	263	32.26	(22.5)	264	32.38	(24.6)
Latin-American						
Male	29	24.65		30	25.50	
Female	0	0.00		2	1.63	
Total	29	12.07		32	13.32	
Other White						
Male	96	7.87		93	7.62	
Female	35	2.75		27	2.12	
Total	131	5.26		120	4.39	
Total White						
Male	125	9.34	(2.9)	123	9.19	(3.4)
Female	35	2.51	(1.0)	29	2.08	(0.4)
Total	160	5.86	(1.9)	152	5.57	(1.8)
Other Races						
Male	2	43.96		0	0.0	
Female	0	0.00		0	0.0	
Total	2	20.02		0	0.0	
All Races						
Male	341	19.65	(9.0)	317	18.07	(10.2)
Female	84	4.61	(2.6)	99	5.24	(2.0)
Total	425	11.95	(5.7)	416	11.70	(6.0)

will be noted that in Houston, 58% of the homicides occurred away from home, whereas in Philadelphia the corresponding figure was 49%. This contrast is even more marked in the Negro group. The Philadelphia percentages show more homicides in the kitchen, living room, and in stairways. All of this may reflect different living arrangements in the two cities and perhaps differences in the amount of leisure time spent outdoors.

The Latin-American group, which had no female victims, also shows up quite different from all the others in regard to place. There were only 14% in the home, none in the bedroom, kitchen, etc.

5. TYPE OF INTERPERSONAL RELATIONSHIP

The type of interpersonal relationship existing between victim and offender is shown in Table 2.5. The classification used was again that of Wolfgang. Over 20% of the Houston cases fell into the "other categories" group, whereas only 3.7% of Wolfgang's cases did. Subject to this limitation, it appears that there were noticeably fewer "stranger" and "acquaintance" relationships in Houston. Otherwise the percentages tend to be about the same. It is noteworthy that a criminal homicide interaction occurs much more often between people who have had a personal relationship to each other than between strangers, in the course of a crime, etc.

TABLE 2.2

METHOD USED IN CRIMINAL HOMICIDE, BY RACE AND SEX OF VICTIM, 1958–1961
(In per cent)

Method	Victim								
	All Races			*Negro*			*White*		
	Total	*Male*	*Female*	*Total*	*Male*	*Female*	*Total*	*Male*	*Female*
Stabbing	25.4	25.5	25.0	29.9	27.8	38.8	17.9	21.2	5.7
Shooting	63.5	65.4	56.0	62.4	67.0	42.9	65.4	63.0	74.3
Beating	5.9	5.0	9.5	4.6	2.8	12.2	8.0	8.7	5.7
Other	5.2	4.1	9.5	3.1	2.4	6.1	8.7	7.1	14.3
Total	100.0 (425)	100.0 (341)	100.0 (84)	100.0 (261)	100.0 (212)	100.0 (49)	100.0 (162)	100.0 (127)	100.0 (35)
Comparable Philadelphia data from Table 5, page 84 (Ref. 1) [not reprinted in this article]									
Stabbing	38.8	40.3	33.8	46.8	48.3	41.7	17.4	17.8	16.3
Shooting	33.0	33.9	30.2	34.0	35.4	29.1	30.4	29.7	32.6
Beating	21.8	21.4	23.0	14.1	12.4	19.8	42.3	46.6	30.2
Other	6.4	4.4	13.0	5.1	3.9	9.4	9.9	5.9	20.9
Total	100.0 (588)	100.0 (449)	100.0 (139)	100.0 (427)	100.0 (331)	100.0 (96)	100.0 (161)	100.0 (118)	100.0 (43)

6. HUSBAND-WIFE CRIMINAL HOMICIDE

The 61 Houston homicides involving husband and wife (common-law marriages are omitted) are analyzed in Table 2.6. The comparable Philadelphia findings are also listed in the table. It is again seen that whites account for a greater proportion of the Houston husband-wife homicides, and that shooting is a much more common method in Houston. The differences in the place of the offense are about the same as have been noted in the entire group of homicides. The differences between the sexes appear to be minor.

TABLE 2.3

DISTRIBUTION OF CRIMINAL HOMICIDE BY FOUR SIX-HOUR PERIODS OF THE DAY AND BY RACE AND SEX OF VICTIM, HOUSTON, 1958–1961
(In per cent)

Hours	*Houston*			*(Philadelphia)*		
	All Races			*(All Races)*		
	Total	*Male*	*Female*	*Total*	*Male*	*Female*
8:00 p.m.–1:59 a.m.	49.9	52.1	40.0	49.7	50.6	46.7
2:00 a.m.–7:59 a.m.	10.5	9.9	13.3	16.5	16.2	17.3
8:00 a.m.–1:59 p.m.	11.7	11.7	12.0	9.2	7.6	8.0
2:00 p.m.–7:59 p.m.	27.9	26.3	34.7	24.7	25.6	21.6
	100.0 (409)	100.0 (334)	100.0 (75)	100.0 (588)	100.0 (449)	100.0 (139)

TABLE 2.4

PLACE OF OCCURRENCE OF CRIMINAL HOMICIDE, BY RACE AND SFX OF VICTIM, HOUSTON, 1958–1961

(In per cent)

Place	*Race and Ethnic Group*				*Sex*	
	Total	*Negro*	*Latin-American*	*Total White*	*Male*	*Female*
Bedroom	13.8	13.1	0.0	15.3	11.3	23.8
Kitchen	3.6	3.2	0.0	3.9	3.3	4.8
Living room	7.6	8.1	3.6	7.0	8.3	4.8
Stairway	3.3	4.2	0.0	1.9	3.9	1.1
Highway (public street, alley, or field)	26.1	30.0	46.4	19.7	29.0	14.3
Taproom	13.6	14.6	28.6	12.1	13.8	13.1
Other commercial place	3.6	3.8	0.0	3.2	3.9	2.4
Other—At home	13.6	11.5	10.7	17.2	13.1	15.5
—Away from home	14.8	11.5	10.7	19.7	13.4	20.2
Total	100.0	100.0	100.0	100.0	100.0	100.0
	(419)	(260)	(28)	(157)	(335)	(84)
In the home	41.9	40.0	14.3	45.2	40.0	50.0
Not in the home	58.1	60.0	85.7	54.8	60.0	50.0
(Comparable Philadelphia data, from Table 12, p. 123, Ref. 1) [not reprinted in this article]						
Bedroom	19.0	19.0		19.3	14.3	34.5
Kitchen	12.1	13.1		9.3	11.1	15.1
Living room	12.1	12.9		9.9	12.3	11.5
Stairway	6.8	8.7		1.9	6.9	6.5
Highway	30.1	31.4		26.7	33.2	20.1
Taproom	8.2	7.5		9.9	9.6	3.6
Other commercial place	8.0	4.9		16.2	8.5	6.5
Other	3.7	2.6		6.8	4.2	2.2
Total	100.0	100.0	100.0	100.0	100.0	100.0
	(588)	(427)		(161)	(399)	(139)
In the home	51.2	54.8		41.6	45.9	68.3
Not in the home	48.8	45.2		58.4	54.1	31.7

7. RELATIONSHIP BETWEEN VICTIM AND OFFENDER, IN TERMS OF RACE, ETHNIC GROUP, AND SEX

Perhaps the most interesting facet of Wolfgang's study is his detailed analysis of "who kills whom," the relationship between race and sex of victim and offender. In 94% of the 550 identified relationships, the victim and offender were members of the same race. To make the relationships completely clear, it is necessary to view the data from the standpoint of the victim, and then separately from the standpoint of the offender.

This has been repeated for the Houston data, as presented in Tables 2.7 and 2.8. It will be noted that there has been a further breakdown of the white category into Latin-American and "Other White" groupings, to see if this "segregated" characteristic of homicides would extend to these further subdivisions. Such has indeed proven to be the case. If one reads Table 2.7 or Table 2.8 on the diagonal from the upper left to lower right, it can be seen that most instances of homicide are intra-group: 97% of Negro victims are at the hands of Negro offenders; 86% of Latin-American victims are at the hands of Latin-American offenders; and 91% of "Other White" victims are at the hands of "Other White" offenders. Wolfgang's corresponding findings have not been reproduced

TABLE 2.5

TYPE OF INTERPERSONAL RELATIONSHIP BETWEEN VICTIM AND PRINCIPAL OFFENDER, BY RACE AND SEX OF VICTIM, CRIMINAL HOMICIDES, HOUSTON, 1958–1961

(In per cent)

(Philadelphia data from Table 24, p. 207, Ref. 1) [not reprinted in this article]

Interpersonal Relationship	*All Races*			*Negro*			*Total White*			*(Philadelphia) (Both Races)*		
	Total	*Male*	*Female*	*Total*	*Male*	*Female*	*Total*	*Male*	*Female*	*Total*	*Male*	*Female*
Close friend	27.9	28.4	26.2	28.9	29.9	24.5	26.3	25.6	28.6	28.2	34.0	9.3
Family relationship ...	22.9	19.1	38.2	20.2	16.8	34.7	27.5	23.2	42.8	24.7	16.4	51.9
Acquaintance	4.7	5.3	2.4	3.0	3.7	0.0	7.5	8.0	5.7	13.5	15.7	6.2
Stranger	1.4	1.4	1.2	1.9	1.9	2.0	0.6	0.8	0.0	12.2	14.2	5.4
Paramour, sex relationship	6.6	5.3	11.9	8.7	7.5	14.3	3.1	1.6	8.6	9.8	6.4	20.9
Sex rival	6.2	7.1	2.4	6.9	7.5	4.1	5.0	6.4	0.0	4.0	4.8	1.6
Enemy	5.7	6.5	2.4	6.1	6.5	4.1	5.0	6.4	0.0	2.9	3.6	0.8
Felon or police officer..	1.9	2.1	1.2	1.1	1.4	0.0	3.1	3.2	2.9	1.1	1.4	0.0
Other categories	22.7	24.8	14.1	23.2	24.8	16.3	21.9	24.8	11.4	3.7	3.5	2.3
Total	100.0 (423)	100.0 (339)	100.0 (84)	100.0 (263)	100.0 (214)	100.0 (49)	100.0 (160)	100.0 (125)	100.0 (35)	100.0 (550)	100.0 (421)	100.0 (129)

in the table because of crowding, but his comparable percentages are 97.6% for Negroes and 85.7% for whites. Thus the present study provides a striking confirmation of Wolfgang's finding, from which he concluded that only slight error results from using mortality (victim) statistics to make inferences about the racial distribution of offenders.

The Latin-American group again appears deviant in these tables, in that female victims are completely absent and there are only two female offenders.

8. COMPARISON WITH EARLIER HOUSTON STUDY

The findings in the present study are also of interest when compared with findings in an earlier study of Houston homicides by Bullock covering homicides in the years 1945–49, about 13 years earlier than the present study.[4] Bullock's cases were also drawn from records of the Houston Police Department. Though his was primarily an areal study, he also explored the relationship between assailant and victim and

[4]Henry A. Bullock, "Urban Homicide in Theory and Fact," *The Journal of Criminal Law, Criminology and Police Science*, Vol. 45 (1955), p. 565.

TABLE 2.6

HUSBAND-WIFE CRIMINAL HOMICIDE, BY RACE, METHOD, AND PLACE, HOUSTON, 1958–1961

(Per cent of Total)

(Philadelphia percentages calculated from Table 26, p. 213, Ref. 1 [not reprinted in this article], given in parentheses after each figure)

	Total		*Husband Killed by Wife*		*Wife Killed by Husband*	
Both races	100.0	(100.0)	52.4	(47)	47.6	(53)
Negro	57.4	(80)	31.1	(40)	26.3	(40)
White	42.6	(20)	21.3	(7)	21.3	(13)
Method						
Stabbing ...	16.4	(46)	8.2	(30)	8.2	(16)
Shooting ...	73.8	(34)	44.2	(15)	29.6	(19)
Beating	6.5	(15)	0.0	(0)	6.5	(15)
Other	3.3	(5)	0.0	(2)	3.3	(3)
Place						
Bedroom ...	34.4	(35)	14.7	(11)	19.7	(24)
Kitchen	8.2	(29)	4.9	(19)	3.3	(10)
Living room.	14.8	(11)	9.9	(4)	4.9	(7)
Stairway ...	3.3	(9)	3.3	(6)	0.0	(3)
Highway ...	4.9	(8)	1.6	(4)	3.3	(4)
Taproom ...	8.2	(3)	6.6	(2)	1.6	(1)
Commercial	1.6	(4)	1.6	(1)	0.0	(3)
Other	24.6	(1)	9.8	(0)	14.8	(1)
Total	100.0 (61)	(100)	52.4 (32)	(47)	47.6 (29)	(53)

TABLE 2.7

RACE, ETHNIC GROUP, AND SEX OF OFFENDER BY RACE, ETHNIC GROUP, AND SEX OF VICTIM, CRIMINAL HOMICIDE, HOUSTON, 1958–1961

(Per cent of Total)

Offender	*Victim*														
	All Races			*Negro*			*Latin-American*			*Other White*			*Total White*		
	Total	*Male*	*Female*	*Total*	*Male*	*Female*	*Total*	*Male*	*Female*	*Total*	*Male*	*Female*	*Total*	*Male*	*Female*
	(411)	(329)	(82)	(257)	(209)	(48)	(29)	(29)	(0)	(123)	(89)	(34)	(152)	(118)	(34)
All races	100.0	100.0	100.0	100.0	100.0	100.0	100.0	100.0	100.0	100.0	100.0	100.0	100.0	100.0	100.0
Male	76.0	74.8	80.5	72.8	73.2	70.8	89.7	89.7	0.0	78.9	73.0	94.1	80.9	77.1	94.1
Female	24.0	25.2	19.5	27.2	26.8	29.2	10.3	10.3	0.0	21.1	27.0	5.9	19.1	22.9	5.9
Negro	63.0	63.6	61.0	96.9	96.6	97.9	3.5	3.5	0.0	6.5	5.6	8.8	5.9	5.1	8.8
Male	46.0	46.6	43.9	69.6	69.8	68.7	3.5	3.5	0.0	6.5	5.6	8.8	5.9	5.1	8.8
Female	17.0	17.0	17.1	27.3	26.8	29.2	0.0	0.0	0.0	0.0	0.0	0.0	0.0	0.0	0.0
Latin-American	7.0	8.8	0.0	0.4	0.5	0.0	86.2	86.2	0.0	2.4	3.4	0.0	18.4	23.7	0.0
Male	6.6	8.2	0.0	0.4	0.5	0.0	79.4	79.4	0.0	2.4	3.4	0.0	17.1	22.0	0.0
Female	0.4	0.6	0.0	0.0	0.0	0.0	6.8	6.8	0.0	0.0	0.0	0.0	1.3	1.7	0.0
Other white	30.0	27.6	39.0	2.7	2.9	2.1	10.3	10.3	0.0	91.1	91.0	91.2	75.7	71.2	91.2
Male	23.3	20.1	36.6	2.7	2.9	2.1	6.8	6.8	0.0	69.9	64.0	85.3	57.9	50.0	85.3
Female	6.7	7.5	2.4	0.0	0.0	0.0	3.5	3.5	0.0	21.2	27.0	5.9	17.8	21.2	5.9
Total white	37.0	36.4	39.0	3.1	3.4	2.1	96.5	96.5	0.0	93.5	94.4	91.2	94.1	94.9	91.2
Male	29.9	28.3	36.6	3.1	3.4	2.1	86.2	86.2	0.0	72.4	67.4	85.3	75.0	72.0	85.3
Female	7.1	8.1	2.4	0.0	0.0	0.0	10.3	10.3	0.0	21.1	27.0	5.9	19.1	22.9	5.9

others factors included in the present paper.

There is a striking difference in the average homicide rate. Bullock's 1945–49 rate was 22.7, whereas the 1958–61 rate was 11.95, or approximately half (this is still more than double the Philadelphia rate).

Bullock also analyzed the relationship between race and ethnic group of the assailant and victim. He found that 108/119 (90.8%) of the victims of white (non-Spanish-American) offenders were white; 42/43 (97.7%) of the victims of Spanish Americans were Spanish American; 321/327 (98.2%) of the victims of Negroes were also Negroes. Considering this from the victim standpoint: when the victim was white, 108/114 (94.7%) of the assailants were white; when the victim was Spanish American, 42/46 (91.3%) of the assailants were Spanish American; when the victim was Negro, 321/329 (97.6%) of the assailants were Negro. Thus there was a very striking intra-class relationship here. A comparison of these percentages with Tables 2.7 and 2.8 shows that the findings for Other White and Negro are very similar. There is a drop in the intra-class percentage for the Latin-American group between 1945–49 and 1958–61; this suggests that this group may have become more assimilated into the general white group during this interval.

Bullock also studied the distance between home addresses of the two persons involved in homicide; he found that assailants and victims tended to live near each other. This same matter was examined in the 1958–61 homicides. Because the distance units used were different from Bullock's, it is not possible to give a full comparison; a summarized one, using approximately the same steps, is given in Table 2.9. In the more recent series, there is an even more marked tendency for the two persons to have lived near each other. Since a fourth of the homicides involve husband-wife and common-

TABLE 2.8

RACE, ETHNIC GROUP, AND SEX OF VICTIM BY RACE, ETHNIC GROUP, AND SEX OF OFFENDER, CRIMINAL HOMICIDE, HOUSTON, 1958–1961

(Per cent of Total)

Victim	*Offender*														
	All Races			*Negro*			*Latin-American*			*Other White*			*Total White*		
	Total	*Male*	*Female*	*Total*	*Male*	*Female*	*Total*	*Male*	*Female*	*Total*	*Male*	*Female*	*Total*	*Male*	*Female*
	(416)	(317)	(99)	(264)	(194)	(70)	(32)	(30)	(2)	(120)	(93)	(27)	(152)	(123)	(29)
All races	100.0	100.0	100.0	100.0	100.0	100.0	100.0	100.0	100.0	100.0	100.0	100.0	100.0	100.0	100.0
Male	80.8	79.8	83.8	81.1	81.4	80.0	100.0	100.0	100.0	75.0	69.9	92.6	80.2	77.3	93.1
Female	19.2	20.2	16.2	18.9	18.6	20.0	0.0	0.0	0.0	25.0	30.1	7.4	19.8	22.7	6.9
Negro	62.7	60.3	70.7	95.8	94.3	100.0	3.1	3.3	0.0	5.8	7.5	0.0	5.3	6.5	0.0
Male	51.2	49.6	56.7	78.0	77.3	80.0	3.1	3.3	0.0	5.0	6.5	0.0	4.6	5.7	0.0
Female	11.5	10.7	14.0	17.8	17.0	20.0	0.0	0.0	0.0	0.8	1.0	0.0	0.7	0.8	0.0
Latin-American	7.2	8.5	3.0	0.4	0.5	0.0	81.3	80.0	100.0	2.5	2.1	3.7	19.1	21.2	10.3
Male	7.2	8.5	3.0	0.4	0.5	0.0	81.3	80.0	100.0	2.5	2.1	3.7	19.1	21.2	10.3
Female	0.0	0.0	0.0	0.0	0.0	0.0	0.0	0.0	0.0	0.0	0.0	0.0	0.0	0.0	0.0
Other white	29.6	30.6	26.3	3.4	4.7	0.0	15.6	16.7	0.0	90.9	89.3	96.3	74.9	71.5	89.7
Male	21.9	21.1	24.2	2.3	3.2	0.0	15.6	16.7	0.0	66.7	60.2	88.9	55.8	49.6	82.8
Female	7.7	9.5	2.1	1.1	1.5	0.0	0.0	0.0	0.0	24.2	29.1	7.4	19.1	21.9	6.9
Total white	36.8	39.1	29.3	3.8	5.2	0.0	96.9	96.7	100.0	93.4	91.4	100.0	94.0	92.7	100.0
Male	29.1	29.6	27.3	2.7	3.7	0.0	96.9	96.7	100.0	69.2	62.4	92.6	74.9	70.8	93.1
Female	7.7	9.5	2.0	1.1	1.5	0.0	0.0	0.0	0.0	24.2	29.0	7.4	19.1	21.9	6.9
Other races	0.5	0.6	0.0	0.4	0.5	0.0	0.0	0.0	0.0	0.8	1.1	0.0	0.7	0.8	0.0
Male	0.5	0.6	0.0	0.4	0.5	0.0	0.0	0.0	0.0	0.8	1.1	0.0	0.7	0.8	0.0
Female	0.0	0.0	0.0	0.0	0.0	0.0	0.0	0.0	0.0	0.0	0.0	0.0	0.0	0.0	0.0

law partners, this accounts for much of this tendency (although not all the married couples or the common-law couples were shown as living at the same address). Table 2.10 shows a somewhat more detailed breakdown of distance for the 1958–61 data, and shows the effect of removing the married and common-law married couples. Even after the subtraction of the husband-wife and common-law cases, the residual group is made up of pairings who lived near each other (65% within one mile). To put this into proper context, it should be pointed out that the area of Houston is very large, the dimensions of the city being approximately 18 miles by 20 miles.

This same question was explored for the 1958–61 Houston cases using census tracts. The 360 criminal homicide cases in which the home address of both offender and victim were known, and in which both home addresses were within the city, were studied to determine the percentage of cases in which both parties had lived in the same tract (Houston had 120 census tracts at time of the 1960 census).[5]

With all 360 cases considered, there were 221 cases or 61.4% in which both parties lived in the same census tract. When the 90 husband-wife and common-law marriage cases were removed, the remainder showed 137 of 270, or 50.7%, instances in which both parties lived in the same census tract. Again it is evident that homicide tends to involve persons who live near to each other, and this holds true even after removal of the married group.

[5]U.S. Bureau of Census: *U.S. Census of Population and Housing*. Census Tracts. Final Report PHC (1)-63 (Washington, D.C.: U. S. Government Printing Office, 1962).

TABLE 2.9

COMPARISON OF 1945–1949 AND 1958–1961 HOUSTON HOMICIDES IN DISTANCE BETWEEN HOME ADDRESSES OF ACCUSED AND VICTIM

(Per cent of Cases)

Distance in Miles	*Bullock's (Ref. 4) Findings for 1945–1949 Houston Homicides*	*All Homicides, Houston, 1958–1961*
	(489)	(360)
Zero to one	57.5	72.8
One to two	12.7	7.8
Two and over	29.8	19.4
Total	100.0	100.0

TABLE 2.10

DISTANCE BETWEEN HOME ADDRESSES OF ACCUSED AND VICTIM IN CRIMINAL HOMICIDE, HOUSTON, 1958–1961

(Numbers of Cases)

Distance in Miles	*(1) All Homicides*	*(2) Husband-Wife and Common-Law Partners*	*(3) All Others Col. (1)–(2)*
Same address	126	77	49
0–.33	101	6	95
.34–.67	25	2	23
.68–1.00	10	1	9
1.01–2.00	28	0	28
Over 2.00	70	4	66
Total	360	90	270

SUMMARY

The 438 criminal homicides which occurred in Houston in 1958–61 were analyzed and examined in several ways to make it possible to do comparisons with the definitive study by Wolfgang of Philadelphia criminal homicides during 1948–52. In addition, the white race group was subdivided into Latin-American and "Other White."

It was found that homicide rates in Houston are about double those in Philadelphia. Negroes account for a smaller proportion of the Houston homicides than in Philadelphia. Negro homicide rates are about six times as high as those of "Other Whites," with Latin-Americans falling in between. In Houston, shootings accounted for almost two-thirds of the deaths, compared to one-third in Philadelphia; death by beating was less frequent in Houston. The distribution through the hours of the day was strikingly similar, with half of the homicides occurring between 8:00 p.m. and 2:00 a.m. and three-fourths of them occurring between 2:00 p.m. and 2:00 a.m.

Fifty-eight per cent of the Houston homicides occurred away from home, as compared to 49% in Philadelphia. There were also some differences in more specific sites, such as rooms of the house involved. The Latin-American group was deviant in that 86% of their homicides occurred away from home; this group also had no female victims at all.

The inter-personal relationships between offender and victim were broadly similar in the Houston and Philadelphia data, with somewhat fewer "stranger" and "acquaintance" relationships in Houston. The husband-wife homicides seem to be similar in the two studies, except that the Houston husband-wife cases reflect the differences found in the total homicide group (larger proportion of Whites, more shootings).

As in Wolfgang's study, it was found that criminal homicide is predominantly an intra-racial phenomenon. 97% of Negro victims were at the hands of Negro offenders, and 91% of the "Other White" victims were at the hands of "Other White" offenders. This relationship held true when it was extended to the Latin-American group. 86% of Latin-American victims were at the hands of Latin-American offenders.

The Houston data is then compared briefly with an earlier (1945–49) study of Houston homicides; except for a halving of the homicide rate in this interval, the other findings are rather similar.

Findings are presented concerning the distance between the home addresses of offender and victim. Almost three-quarters of the group lived within a mile of each other. Even after the married pairs were removed, two-thirds lived within two miles of each other. Over 60% of the pairs lived in the same census tract.

Thus it appears that in Houston as well as in Philadelphia, criminal homicide occurs most often between members of the same race; that the persons involved tend to be relatives or friends rather than strangers; that males are much more frequently involved, both as offenders and victims; and that the most likely hours are between 8:00 p.m. and 2:00 a.m. The persons involved typically live at the same address or within a mile or two of each other.

8.

Thomas F. Pettigrew and Rosalind B. Spier

THE ECOLOGICAL STRUCTURE OF NEGRO HOMICIDE

One of the most interesting characteristics of homicide among Negro Americans is the great range in rates across states. As Table 2.11 indicates, Negro homicide rates for 1949–51 were over four times as great in Missouri as in Massachusetts and two-and-a-half times as great in such states as Texas and Florida as in New Jersey and Connecticut. The present paper is an exploratory attempt to account for these wide state-rate discrepancies in terms of a variety of ecological variables.

Within the general hypothesis that Negro homicide rates are ecologically patterned in direct and meaningful ways, four specific hypotheses are tested: (1) Negro homicide rates are positively related to the states' general traditions of violence. (2) Negro homicide rates are positively related to the amounts of Negro in-migration to the states. (3) Negro homicide rates are negatively related to the states' socio-economic levels of Negroes. (4) Negro homicide rates are positively related to the states' degrees of family disorganization.

TABLE 2.11

Average Non-White Homicidal Death Rates, by States, 1949–51*

State	*Rank*	*Rate per 100,000*
Texas	1	39.5
Florida	2	39.2
Missouri	3	38.6
Delaware	4	36.9
West Virginia	5	36.1
Kentucky	6	35.4
Ohio	7	34.9
Indiana	8.5	34.3
Illinois	8.5	34.3
Tennessee	10	33.2
Georgia	11	33.0
Alabama	12	31.2
Michigan	13	27.8
Kansas	14	27.1
Virginia	15	26.3
Mississippi	16	26.1
Maryland	17	25.8
North Carolina	18	23.7
Arkansas	19	21.8
Louisiana	20.5	21.3
Pennsylvania	20.5	21.3
New York	22	20.4
South Carolina	23	19.9
New Jersey	24	16.9
Connecticut	25	16.4
Massachusetts	26	9.3

*At least 97 per cent of the non-white populations of the twenty-six states were Negro in 1950. The rates include both sexes and are not adjusted for age.

Source: National Office of Vital Statistics, *Death Rates for Selected Causes by Age, Color, and Sex: United States and Each State, 1949–51: Homicide* (Vol. LXIX, No. 62 [Washington, D.C.: Government Printing Office, 1959]), p. 937.

THE SAMPLE AND MEASURES

Sample. Twenty-six states comprise the units of analysis (see Table 2.11). The remaining

Source: *The American Journal of Sociology,* Vol. LXVII, No. 6 (May, 1962), pp. 621–29, University of Chicago Press.

states are excluded either because they had an insignificant Negro population in 1950 or, as in the cases of Arizona, California, New Mexico, Oklahoma, and Washington, because a significant proportion of their non-whites in 1950 were not Negro and consequently introduced considerable error into the non-white statistics provided by the Census Bureau and the National Office of Vital Statistics. The final sample's twenty-six states included 89.6 per cent of the nation's Negroes in 1950, with Negroes constituting at least 97 per cent of the non-whites in each of these states.

The Homicide Data. Following Henry and Short and other investigators, cause-of-death data for non-whites are employed as the measure of Negro homicide.[1] That is the number of non-whites listed by the National Office of Vital Statistics as *victims* of homicide during 1949–51 is used instead of crime statistics directly.[2] Though not without its own recording errors,[3] such an index has a number of advantages over crime data: more consistent definitions and recording across states, broader coverage over the nation, and less racial bias.

But cause-of-death data, when utilized to indicate a racial homicide rate, involve an important assumption: namely, that whites kill whites and Negroes kill Negroes. Actually, this assumption appears sound, since repeated studies have found that the overwhelming majority of homicides are in fact intraracial.[4] In Wolfgang's sample of 550 Philadelphia slayings, for instance, only thirty-four (6.2 per cent) were interracial; and even these thirty-four balanced off—fourteen Negro victims and twenty white victims—to make the error introduced by the intraracial assumption quite small.[5]

The Ecological Data. Two variables are employed as measures of the states' violent traditions: white homicide rates for 1949–51[6] and a "homicidal culture index." The latter index employs both white homicide rates and the 1950 Negro population's states of origin in an effort to achieve a rough measure of the degree to which "a homicidal culture" exists for Negroes living in any particular state. For example, homicidal culture for Michigan is computed by summing the products of the percentage of Negroes who were born in any particular state (e.g., Alabama, or Michigan itself) and who now reside in Michigan multiplied by the state of origin's 1949–51 white homicide rate (e.g., Alabama or Michigan). Note that this index includes *all* of a state's Negroes, both migrant and native. And note, too, that this index takes into account the violence patterns of the Negroes' formative environments. Thus, many Negroes now living in the North were born and reared in the South, a fact of some importance since homicide rates have been consistently higher in the South than the North over the years.[7]

Negro migration is measured by three census variables: the 1950 percentage of non-white males born outside of a state; the percentage increase in a state's non-white population, 1940 to 1950; and the percentage of *all* persons in a state who were in 1950 residing in the same county as they were in 1949.[8]

[1]Andrew F. Henry and James F. Short, Jr., *Suicide and Homicide* (Glencoe, Ill.: Free Press, 1954).

[2]National Office of Vital Statistics, *Death Rates for Selected Causes by Age, Color, and Sex: United States and Each State, 1949–51;* Homicide (Vol. LXIX, No. 62 [Washington, D.C.: Government Printing Office, 1959]). This measure and four of the ecological measures reported were subjected to minor normalizing transformations. The resulting correlations, however, were not significantly different from those obtained from the raw data.

[3]For an early discussion of these errors, see H. C. Brearley, *Homicide in the United States* (Chapel Hill, N.C.: University of North Carolina Press, 1932), pp. 12–14.

[4]Henry and Short, *op. cit.*, pp. 186–87.

[5]Marvin E. Wolfgang, *Patterns in Criminal Homicide* (Philadelphia: University of Pennsylvania Press, 1958). Similarly, Bensing and Schroeder noted only thirty-nine (8.4 per cent) interracial homicides in a sample of 462 Cleveland killings (Robert C. Bensing and Oliver Schroeder, Jr., *Homicide in an Urban Community* [Springfield, Ill.: Charles C. Thomas, Publisher, 1960], p. 51).

[6]This measure, too, is based on cause-of-death data from National Office of Vital Statistics, *op. cit.*

[7]See, e.g., Austin L. Porterfield and Robert H. Talbert, "A Decade of Differentials and Trends in Serious Crimes in 86 American Cities by Southern and Non-Southern Pairs," *Social Forces,* Vol. 31 (1952), pp. 60–68; and Lyle W. Shannon, "The Spatial Distribution of Criminal Offenses by States," *Journal of Criminal Law, Criminology and Police Science,* Vol. 45 (1954), pp. 264–71; and National Office of Vital Statistics, *op. cit.*

[8]These and other census data for the study come from United States Bureau of the Census, *United States Census of the Population: 1950,* Vols. II and

TABLE 2.12

CORRELATES OF 1949–51 STATE NEGRO HOMICIDE RATES

Variable	*Product Moment r's with Negro Homicide*	*Partial r's with Homicidal Culture Held Constant*
Violent tradition variables:		
Homicidal culture index, 1950	+.55†	.....
White homicide rate, 1949–51	+.50†	+.15
Migration variables:		
Per cent of non-white males born out of state, 1950	−.01	+.46*
Per cent increase of non-white population, 1940–50	−.36‡	−.20
Per cent residing in the same county, 1949–50	−.51†	−.18
Socioeconomic variables:		
Per cent of employed non-white males in the professions, 1950	.00	+.08
Median non-white education, 1950	−.16	+.24
Family-disorganization variable:		
Per cent of women over fourteen years of age who are divorced or separated, 1950	+.36‡	+.15

*$p < .05$.
†$p < .01$.
‡$p < .10$.

Two additional variables tap Negro socioeconomic levels. These are the 1950 state percentages of employed non-whites who are professionals and the 1950 state non-white education medians. The final specific hypothesis concerning family disorganization is tested with one further variable: the 1950 state percentages of *all* females over fourteen years of age who are either divorced or separated. . . .

FINDINGS

Table 2.12 presents the correlations between the Negro homicide rates and eight ecological variables.

The Violent-Tradition Hypothesis. Negro homicide rates are high when white homicide rates are high either in the state of residence or in the state of birth ("the homicidal culture index"). Indeed, the relatively large coefficient for homicidal culture suggests that this predictor should be held constant in inspecting the relationships between other variables and Negro homicide; Table 2.12 provides these partial correlations.

This support for the violent-tradition hypothesis led the authors to seek state measures of frontier culture, often credited as the historical origin of much of America's violent tradition.[9] One such measure is simply the absolute number of recorded lynchings performed from 1882 to the present in each of the twenty-six states.[10] Since this frontier technique was almost entirely a white crime, it is not surprising that it correlates significantly with the 1949–51 *white* homicide *rates* (Spearman rank order correlation, + .86, $p < .001$); but it is more interesting that this crude frontier measure is also modestly related to the 1949–51 Negro homicide rates (Spearman rank order correlation, + .35, $p < .05$). Similarly, the rank order in which the twenty-six states entered the Union offers another gross gauge of frontierism. This measure, too, correlates significantly with Negro

IV (Washington, D.C.: U.S. Government Printing Office).

[9]See H. C. Brearley, "The Pattern of Violence," in W. T. Couch (ed.), *Culture in the South* (Chapel Hill, N.C.: University of North Carolina Press, 1934), pp. 678–92; and Mabel Elliott, "Crime and the Frontier Mores," *American Sociological Review*, Vol. 9 (April, 1944), pp. 185–92.

[10]The lynching data were kindly provided by the Department of Records and Research, Tuskegee Institute, Tuskegee, Alabama.

TABLE 2.13

CORRELATIONAL MATRIX OF NEGRO HOMICIDE AND FIVE KEY VARIABLES

Variable	B	C	D	E	F
A. Negro homicide, 1949–51	+.55†	–.01	–.51†	–.16	+.36‡
B. Homicidal culture index, 1950		–.59†	–.73†	–.58†	+.46*
C. Non-white males born out of state, 1950			+.66†	+.90†	–.53†
D. Same county residents, 1949–50				+.72†	–.59†
E. Median non-white education, 1950					–.67†
F. Divorced or separated women, 1950					

*$p < .05$.
†$p < .01$.
‡$p < .10$.

homicide (Spearman rank order correlation, $-.52$, $p < .01$).[11]

The Migration Hypothesis. The results for the variables tapping migration are contingent upon whether the homicidal culture index is controlled (Table 2.12). While substantially related before the control is applied, neither the increase in non-white population nor the same county residence variables are significantly associated with Negro homicide once the effects of homicidal culture are partialled out.

By contrast, the most direct measure of Negro migration—the percentage of non-white males born out of state—does not covary with Negro homicide until the homicidal culture index is controlled. The out-of-state birth variable is particularly useful in separating low- and high-rate states with relatively small native Negro percentages; it relates significantly to Negro homicide (Spearman rank order correlation, $+.65$, $p < .05$) for nine northern states—Connecticut, Illinois, Indiana, Massachusetts, Michigan, New Jersey, New York, Ohio, and Pennsylvania. These data give at least qualified support to the hypothesis that Negro migration and homicide are positively related.

The Socioeconomic Hypothesis. Neither of the socioeconomic variables are significantly associated with Negro homicide rates (Table 2.12). What small relationships that do exist after homicidal culture is controlled are actually in the opposite direction from that hypothesized; for example, non-white education is positively correlated with homicide, rather than negatively as predicted.

The Family-Disorganization Hypothesis. A modest, positive coefficient exists between the percentage of divorced or separated women and Negro homicide rates, but once again the relationship becomes trivial after the homicidal culture index is partialled out (Table 2.12).

Factor-Analysis Results. Table 2.13 shows the correlational matrix of Negro homicide rates and five of the study's primary variables, and Table 2.14 presents the matrix's factorial solution. Using Thurstone's complete centroid method,[12] two tentative orthogonal factors emerge after rotation which clarify the pre-

TABLE 2.14

ROTATED ORTHOGONAL FACTORS

Variable	Factor Loadings I	II
A. Negro homicide, 1949–51	+.61	+.41
B. Homicidal culture index, 1950	+.85	.00
C. Non-white males born out of state, 1950	–.59	+.68
D. Same county residents, 1949–50	–.92	+.12
E. Median non-white education, 1950	–.68	+.70
F. Divorced or separated women, 1950	+.62	–.31

[11]This relationship would be lowered if the western states were included in the sample.

[12]L. L. Thurstone, *Multiple-Factor Analysis* (Chicago: University of Chicago Press, 1947).

vious findings considerably.[13] Factor I is a high southern rate–low northern rate factor; it has high Negro homicide rates strongly associated with high homicidal culture and high intercounty residential mobility together with high percentages of divorced or separated women, low percentages of non-white males born out of state, and low non-white education. Fringe southern states typify this pattern, particularly Texas (ranked first among the sample's twenty-six states in Negro homicide rates as indicated in Table 2.11) and Florida (second). The mirror opposite, low Negro homicide states are all in the East: Massachusetts (rank of 26), Connecticut (rank of 25), New Jersey (rank of 24), New York (rank of 22), and Pennsylvania (rank of 20.5).

Factor II is a high northern rate–low southern rate factor; it has high Negro homicide related to high percentages of non-white males born out of state and high non-white education. High-rate midwestern states evidence this pattern: Missouri (rank of 3), Ohio (rank of 7), Indiana (rank of 8.5), and Illinois (rank of 8.5). Such relatively low-rate southern states as South Carolina (rank of 23), Louisiana (rank of 20.5), Arkansas (rank of 19), North Carolina (rank of 18), and Mississippi (rank of 16) present the opposite configuration.

Multiple Correlations. As the results of Table 2.12 and the factorial solution suggest, the homicidal culture index combined with the out-of-state birth measure of non-white male migration offer the best two-variable prediction of the Negro state homicide rates; the multiple coefficient is .67. When a third variable–same county residence–is added, the correlation coefficient becomes .76, or roughly 58 per cent of the variance. Further additions of variables do not significantly raise this coefficient.

[13]No expansive claims can be made for these factorial results. Both the small number of cases and the small number of variables render these particular results quite tentative; i.e., the sampling fluctuation of the correlations combined with so few points mean that other possible rotations are probably as satisfactory as the one shown in Table 2.14. These results are shown, then, simply as a clarifying summary of the over-all findings, with the two factors providing a convenient point from which to view the two major trends in the data.

DISCUSSION

Research which employs ecological correlations and gross units to analyze an infrequent phenomenon is to some extent a deceptive art. It has two principal limitations. In the first place, all units, regardless of size, are given equal weight; at the extremes, Delaware with only 44,000 Negroes contributes as much to these data as Georgia with over a million Negroes.

Second, the procedure does not allow conclusions about *individual* Negroes who commit homicide. Ecological correlations, as Robinson, Selvin, and others have emphasized, are relevant only for the aggregate units used, not for individuals within the aggregates.[14] For example, just because Negro homicide rates in the North are highest in states with large percentages of non-white males born out of state, we cannot conclude that northern Negro males born out of state are more likely to be murderers than other Negro males born in state. Such an erroneous conclusion would be a classic example of the "ecological fallacy." The use of replicating in smaller units is a useful method of narrowing the bounds of such individual relationships;[15] but Selvin has pointed out that this alternative is not available to an analysis of a relatively rare phenomenon like homicide.[16]

In spite of these limitations, an exploratory ecological study offers a broad, comparative perspective not achieved in one-community case studies; apart from individuals, it is sociologically important to learn what the significant differences are between large aggregates of Negro Americans with sharply contrasting homicide rates.[17] Moreover, just as epidemiological studies

[14]W. S. Robinson, "Ecological Correlations and the Behavior of Individuals," *American Sociological Review,* Vol. 15 (June, 1950), pp. 351–57; and H. C. Selvin, "Durkheim's *Suicide* and Problems of Empirical Research," *American Journal of Sociology,* Vol. 63 (1958), pp. 607–19.

[15]Otis D. Duncan and Beverly Davis, "An Alternative to Ecological Correlation," *American Sociological Review,* Vol. 18 (1953), pp. 665–66.

[16]Selvin, *op. cit.*

[17]See, e.g., the arguments put forward by Otis D. Duncan and Leo F. Schnore, "Cultural, Behavioral, and Ecological Perspectives in the Study of Social Organization," *American Journal of Sociology,* Vol. 65 (1959), pp. 132–46; and Herbert Menzel, "Comment on Robinson's 'Ecological Correlations and the Behavior of Individuals,'" *American Sociological Review,* Vol. 15 (October, 1950), p. 674.

often provide clues of a disease's etiology, ecological studies are useful in generating hypotheses for future research on a social problem's individual factors.

From these data, it appears that the most prominent factor is simply the homicidal cultures, as measured by white homicidal rates, in which the various state populations of Negroes were reared. This finding coincides with a variety of other data. Shannon, for instance, has noted that the rank order of states over time is considerably more stable for homicide than for other crimes, a result which also suggests the importance of cultural traditions for homicide.[18] Similarly, the present authors constructed a "suicidal culture index" in the same manner as the homicidal culture index, but, unlike the index for homicide, the suicidal index only modestly correlates with the twenty-six states' Negro suicide rates (+ .30, not significant).

A considerable amount of historical evidence indicates that this traditional patterning of outwardly directed aggression stems from features of frontier life that have persisted in some areas, such as the South, longer than in others. Mabel Elliott and H. C. Brearley have both stressed in their discussions of twentieth-century homicide the importance of the frontier's use of firearms and its distrust of formal legal processes.[19] Other writers have documented how this frontier legacy of personal violence remained longest in the South, even longer than in the West. John Hope Franklin has offered a vast array of historical data to support his contention that the South had a uniquely developed violent tradition in the early nineteenth century, a tradition continued from frontier days by slavery and a restricted economy.[20] He cites the South's greater use of firearms, dueling, vigilante groups, local militia, military training, and military titles during this period. In addition, W. J. Cash has shown how the Civil War further impeded the erosion of frontier traits and maintained the romantic, individualistic, and violent "hell-of-a-fellow" as a valued personality type.[21] In short, first slavery and then the Civil War made certain that the South would be the nation's "last frontier."

Rapid industrialization and urbanization during the past generation in the "newest South" have erased most—but not all—of the traces of the violent tradition. For instance, Southerners still have somewhat different attitudes toward firearms than other Americans. A 1959 opinion poll asked: "Do you think it should be legal or illegal for private citizens to have loaded weapons in their homes?" Fifty-three per cent of the southern sample thought "it should be legal," compared with 42 per cent of the western sample, 35 per cent of the northeastern sample, and 33 per cent of the midwestern sample.[22] Though the standard errors for regional differences are large in such survey results, note that the percentage for the West falls roughly midway between the South and the other regions. This reminds us of the additional point that eastern states are further from their frontier beginnings than the rest of the nation.

Consistent with these considerations are the South's persistently higher homicide and aggravated assault rates over the years, though the region has not had unusually high rates for the non-frontier crimes against property.[23] Such considerations are consistent, too, with the findings of this study, including the significant associations between lynchings and both the 1949–51 white and Negro homicide rates and the significant relation between the states' entrances into the Union and their 1949–51 Negro homicide rates.

Factor I, with its high rates in the two youngest of the southern states and its low rates in the long-settled eastern states, also follows from a violent-tradition explanation of diverse state rates. There is one important qualification, however. Texas and Florida, the high-rate and high

[18]Shannon, *op. cit.*

[19]Elliott, *op. cit.;* Brearley, "The Pattern of Violence," *op. cit.*

[20]John H. Franklin, *The Militant South: 1800–1861* (Cambridge, Mass.: Harvard University Press, 1956).

[21]W. J. Cash, *The Mind of the South* (New York: Alfred A. Knopf, Inc., 1941).

[22]American Institute of Public Opinion, Poll No. 616K, July 21, 1959. The authors wish to thank Dr. Alfred Hero, World Peace Foundation, for bringing these data to our attention.

[23]Porterfield and Talbert, *op. cit.*; and Shannon, *op. cit.*

homicidal culture states, are also states that have been undergoing swift and sweeping changes in recent decades, particularly large influxes of out-of-state *whites*. The contrasting, low-rate eastern states have obviously not been changing at such a pace. Consequently, homicidal culture is not the only heavily weighted variable of Factor I; the factor has a very high and negative weighting on the percentage of residents who in 1950 were living in the same county as in 1949, a variable which included whites as well as Negroes. Put differently, this means that states like Texas (rank of 1) and Florida (rank of 2), with both rapid social change and high homicidal cultures, have considerably higher rates than states, like Tennessee, Georgia, and Alabama, (ranks 10, 11, and 12 respectively), with equally high homicidal cultures but not the same pace of sweeping change. This suggests an interesting causal hypothesis for future testing: *swift social change may be a triggering condition for making more manifest a developed homicidal culture.*

Factor II presents a sharply contrasting pattern. States with medium indexes of homicidal culture but vastly different Negro migration rates also tend to have diverse Negro homicide rates. Such states in the South, with little in-migration of Negroes, have a largely native Negro population; and they tend to have below average rates for Negro homicide, though not as low as those of Massachusetts and Connecticut. Such states in the North, with a constant influx of migrants from the South,, have large percentages of their Negroes born out of state; and they tend to have above-average rates for Negro homicide, though not as high as those of Texas and Florida. Moreover, the most common age range of these Negroes moving out of the South and into the North is precisely the same range with the greatest homicide rate: eighteen to thirty-five years old.

This migration aspect of Factor II explains the heavy positive weighting of non-white education; northern Negroes in general, though not southern-reared migrants in particular, are much better educated than southern Negroes as a whole. The "ecological fallacy" would be illustrated once again if Factor II were interpreted as indicating that highly educated Negroes are more likely than poorly educated Negroes to kill in northern states.

We can safely skirt the fallacy, however, by reviewing the results of the migration variable in previous northern Negro homicide research which employed individual rather than ecological measures. Adult Negro migrants, particularly southern-born Negro migrants, are more likely than native Negro adults to be incarcerated for violent crimes. Spirer, for example, studied the commitment rates of Negroes to Pennsylvania's Western State Penitentiary from 1906 through 1935; he noted that Negroes not born in the state had two and a half times the over-all incarceration rates of native Negroes, and four and a half times higher rates for violent crimes.[24] Likewise, Tulchin found in his 1920–27 Illinois prison research that among northern-born Negro inmates, only 19.1 per cent were convicted of murder as opposed to 28.7 per cent of the southern-born Negro inmates. A similar difference was uncovered by Tulchin among the Illinois reformatory delinquents of the same period.[25] More recent work with delinquents, however, has raised doubts concerning crime and migration at younger ages. Savitz has noted that delinquency, including crimes of violence in certain slum areas of Philadelphia, is actually more frequent among *native* than among migrant juveniles.[26]

But the association of migration with adult crime is not limited to the United States or Negro Americans. Amarista, for instance, in a study of five hundred inmates at a Venezuelan penitentiary reports that a high percentage of

---

[24]Jess Spirer, "Negro Crime," *Comparative Psychological Monographs*, Vol. 16, No. 81 (1940), pp. 1–81.

[25]Simon H. Tulchin, *Intelligence and Crime* (Chicago: University of Chicago Press, 1939), pp. 88–90.

[26]Leonard Savitz, *Delinquency and Migration* (Philadelphia: Commission of Human Relations, 1960). The definition of "migrant" becomes difficult when dealing with juveniles. If migrants who arrived in their teens are studied, there is the problem of migrants and natives not having had the same length of time to establish a police record. Or if only migrants who have arrived in the northern city by the age of seven are studied, as in Savitz's work, one wonders if such individuals meet the full definition of a migrant whose developing years were spent in a different environment. Only later research probing the full complexities of the problem can untangle this dilemma for juvenile research.

these prisoners were born in the rural provinces and committed their crimes in the cities.[27]

Nor is crime the only symptom of the drastic adjustment in life style required of migrants. The study by Malzberg and Lee revealed that age-standardized rates for all psychoses among whites were twice as high for migrants as for non-migrants; but the differential among non-whites was *three* times greater for migrants.[28]

All of these migration findings are confounded by socioeconomic variables. Negro migrants typically move in at the bottom rungs of urban society, below the native Negroes who have had the education and time to slowly make their way into better jobs, housing, etc. But racial discrimination in many areas places such a limit on the socioeconomic differences possible between Negro migrants and non-migrants that their discrepancies in adult rates for violent crime appear to be more than simply a function of socioeconomic status. At the very least, migration needs to be given careful attention in future studies of Negro homicide; at the present, neither of the most recent community studies of homicide have made a distinction between southern-born and northern-born Negro murderers.[29]

The present data, then, suggest two factors in answer to Wolfgang's crucial question concerning Negro homicide: "Why should a quantitatively unknown but presumed greater amount of frustration in the environment of the Negro . . . find aggressive outlet specifically in a high incidence of homicide?"[30] It might well be that the Negro turns to homicide because he is often a product of a region with a violent tradition, and because he is often a migrant in a new and threatening environment that makes it difficult for him to throw off this cultural predilection for homicide. Only future research using individual measures can properly evaluate the importance of these variables.

[27]F. J. Amarista, "Experiencia en la Prueba de Raven," Abstracted in *Psychological Abstracts*, Vol. 33 (October, 1959), p. 1034.

[28]These rates are for migrants who arrived in New York State five or less years before their hospital admission. See Benjamin Malzberg and Everett S. Lee, *Migration and Mental Disease* (New York: Social Science and Research Council, 1956).

[29]Wolfgang, *op. cit.*; and Bensing and Schroeder, *op. cit.*

[30]*Op. cit.*, p. 330.

CHAPTER III

Aggressive Crimes—II

IT HAS BEEN NOTED by criminologists that assaultive crimes and homicide share many common characteristics. Empirical investigation has revealed that the victim-offender relationship existent in assault cases is very similar to that found in murder, for assaults generally occur among neighbors or within the family unit where the participants are intimately acquainted.

If, as suggested in Chapter 1, we are to view homicide as one of the most serious offenses that may be committed in our society, we must view aggravated assault in the same light, for in most cases this criminal category realistically is attempted murder. The following definition published by the Federal Bureau of Investigation should clarify this position:

AGGRAVATED ASSAULT—Assault with intent to kill or for the purpose of inflicting severe bodily injury by shooting, cutting, stabbing, maiming, poisoning, scalding, or by the use of acids, explosives, or other means. Excludes simple assault, assault and battery, fighting, etc.[1]

Unlike criminal homicide, aggravated assault is not lacking in volume. In 1967, the 253,321 cases reported ranked fourth in number among the seven index offenses. As may be seen in Chart 3.1, aggravated assault cases are up 67 percent since 1960, representing a 51 percent increase in rate per 100,000 population.

Selected Facts on Aggravated Assault[2]

1. Comprised 51 percent of the crimes of violence.
2. Southern states recorded 40 percent of the total volume.

[1]Federal Bureau of Investigation, U.S. Department of Justice, *1967 Uniform Crime Reports* (Washington, D.C.: U. S. Government Printing Office, 1968), p. 57.

[2]Based on 1967 statistics.

CHART 3.1

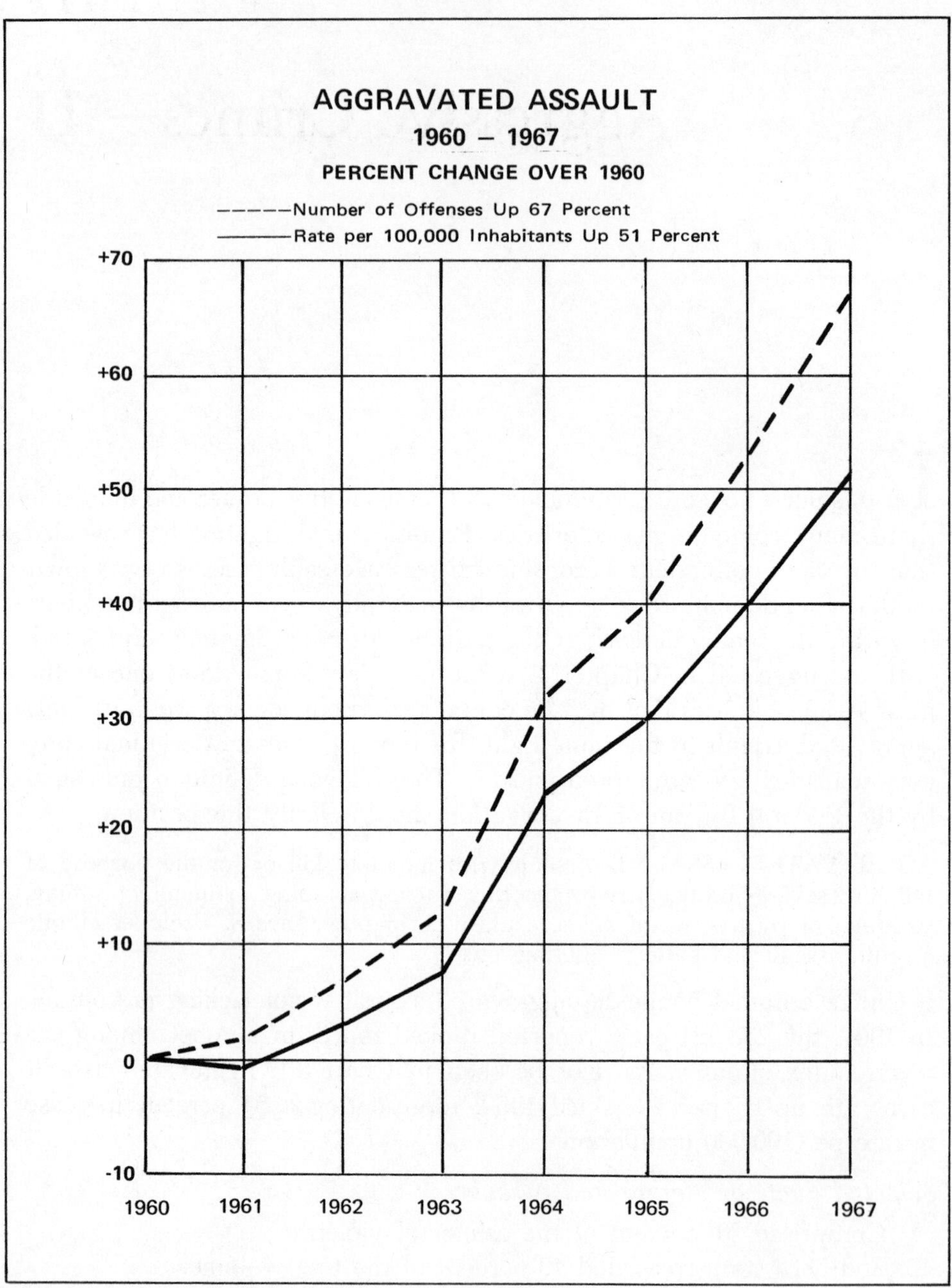

SOURCE: Federal Bureau of Investigation, U.S. Department of Justice, *1967 Uniform Crime Reports* (Washington, D.C.: U.S. Government Printing Office, 1968), p. 10.

3. One aggravated assault committed every two minutes.
4. 69 percent of cases cleared by arrest.
5. Since 1967 aggravated assaults increased 67 percent.
6. 21 percent of serious assaults committed with the use of a firearm, 33 percent with cutting instruments, 22 percent with blunt objects, 24 percent with personal weapons (fists, hands, etc.).
7. Since 1964 assaults with firearms increased 76 percent.
8. Since 1960 arrests of young persons under 18 years of age increased 121 percent.
9. Arrests for males outnumbered females by nearly 7 to 1.
10. 50 percent of persons arrested for aggravated assault were Negro. The Negro is also the primary victim.
11. The peak month for aggravated asaults was July.

Forcible rape is defined as unlawful sexual intercourse with a female without her consent. As an index crime, forcible rape is ranked directly below criminal homicide, with its seriousness reflected by the fact that 16 jurisdictions provide the death penalty for those convicted. Statutory rape (a far less serious offense) is applicable in cases involving a female below the legal age of consent who has voluntarily engaged in sexual intercourse.

Predictions concerning the volume of rape cases tend to be inconsistent. On the one hand there are many individuals who feel that this criminal category is probably the most underreported of all the serious offenses—the major reasons being fear on the part of the female involved and potential embarrassment for herself and her family. There are others who feel that rape is very much overreported. The Federal Bureau of Investigation confirms the fact that acquittals and dismissals run high, with almost 4 out of every 10 cases being dropped and only 48 percent of adults charged actually convicted for this offense. Quite often females offer little resistance when involved in the sexual act and sign a complaint only when discovered by a member of the family or overcome with feelings of guilt. At other times she may report a sexual assault after her boyfriend has abandoned her and she is left alone.

As can be seen in Chart 3.2, the incidence of forcible rape has increased significantly since 1960. In this seven-year period the number of offenses committed is up 61 percent with the rate per 100,000 inhabitants up 46 percent. For the violent crime category, this places forcible rape in between criminal homicide and aggravated assault in terms of percentage increase.

CHART 3.2

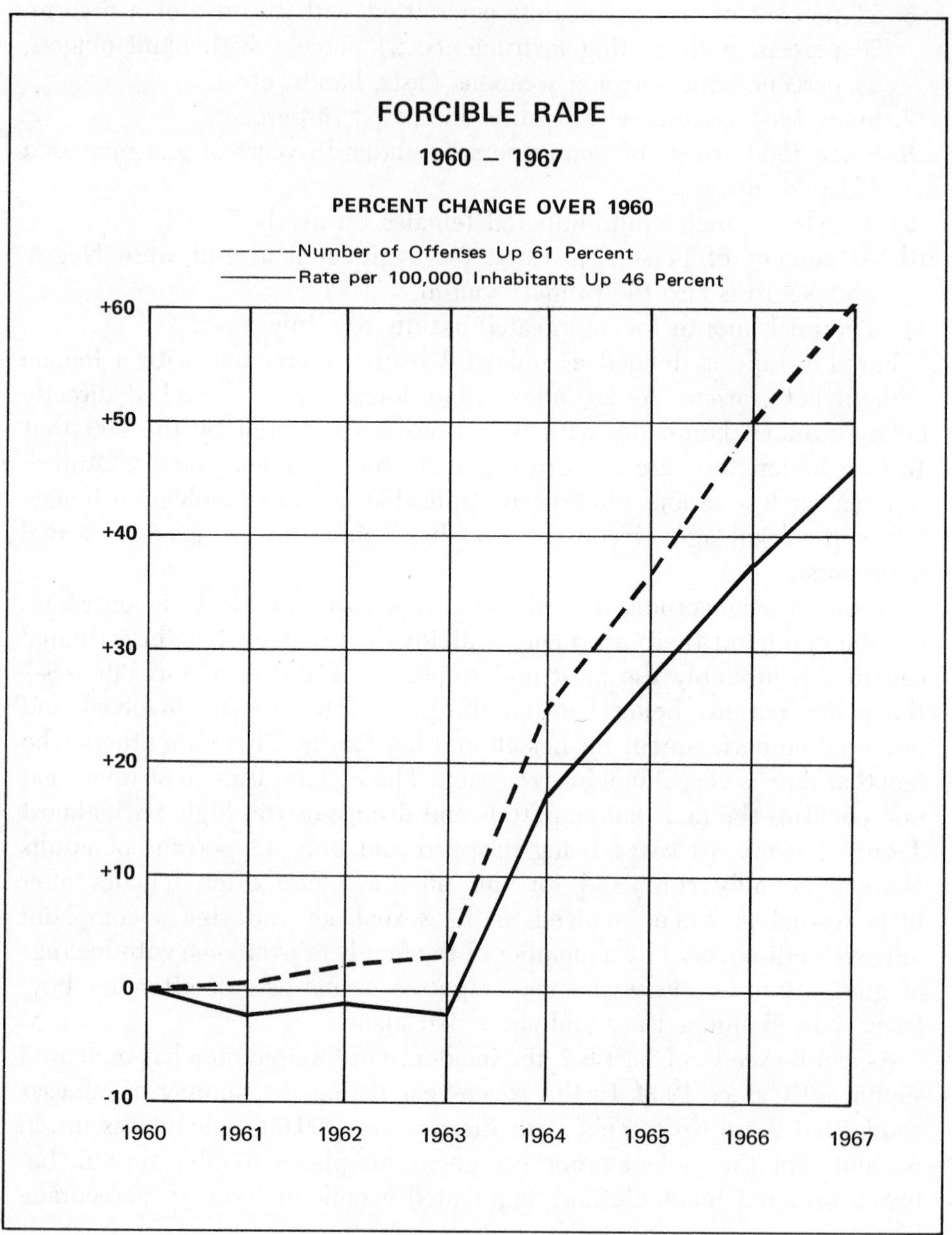

SOURCE: Federal Bureau of Investigation, U.S. Department of Justice, *1967 Uniform Crime Reports* (Washington, D.C.: U.S. Government Printing Office, 1968), p. 12.

Selected Facts on Forcible Rape[3]

1. Comprised 5 percent of the crimes of violence.
2. Southern states recorded the greatest volume—29 percent of the cases reported.
3. One forcible rape is committed every 19 minutes.
4. 61 percent of the cases are cleared by arrest.
5. Since 1960 forcible rape rates per 100,000 population have increased 46 percent.
6. 18 percent of all forcible rape cases reported to police were determined after investigation to be unfounded. (No offense took place.)
7. 64 percent of those arrested were under 25 years of age.
8. Whites comprised 51 percent of those arrested.
9. The peak month for forcible rape was July.

In the opening article Dr. Menachem Amir of the Institute of Criminology at the Hebrew University, Jerusalem, discusses the nature of forcible rape. Dr. Amir examines some common misconceptions about rape along with citing several characteristics associated with this offense. In the second selection David J. Pittman and William Handy examine several variables associated with aggravated assaults. Among these are time of day, location and season of the year, weapon used, alcohol involvement and the relationship between the victim and offender. In this study the authors attempted to test several of the homicide hypotheses proposed by Wolfgang in Chapter 2 against acts of aggravated assaults. In the final selection Alex D. Pokorny takes a broad look at the subject of human violence, comparing the characteristics of homicide, aggravated assault, suicide, and attempted suicide.

---

[3]Based on 1967 statistics.

9.

Menachem Amir

FORCIBLE RAPE

The term "rape" arouses hostile and aggressive feelings in many societies and in many countries. In a number of jurisdictions it is punishable by death. There is sympathy for the victim and hostility toward the offender. Since the crime of rape includes many elements other than sex, judicial decisions relating to punishment and treatment are difficult to render.

This article is based on an empirical study which was designed to explore and disclose the patterns of forcible rape among 646 cases occurring in Philadelphia, Pennsylvania, from January 1 to December 31, 1958, and from January 1 to December 31, 1960. The cases were those in the files of the Morals Squad of the Philadelphia Police Department where all complaints about rapes are recorded and centrally filed.

The emphasis in this study has not been on the psychological dynamics underlying the behavior of the individual offender and his victim but rather on their social characteristics, social relationships, and on the act itself, that is, the modus operandi of the crime and the situations in which rape is likely to occur.

The patterns which emerged were derived from a study of 646 victims and 1,292 offenders who were involved in single and multiple rape.[1] Patterns were sought regarding race, marital status, and employment differences, as well as seasonal and other temporal patterns, spatial patterns, the relationships between forcible rape and the presence of alcohol, and the previous arrest record of victims and offenders.

Further questions were raised relating to rape during the commission of another felony, the relationship between the victim and offender, victim-precipitated rape, and unsolved cases of rape. Finally, all of these aspects were related to group rape and to leadership functions in such situations.

METHOD OF STUDY

While we approached the study from a sociological viewpoint, i.e., crimes as learned behavior committed within socioculturally defined situations, we were not guided by a specific theoretical system for explaining the offense studied. Nor did we attempt to find specific causes and explanations for the offense. Rather, we undertook to learn what we could about the characteristics of the offense, the offenders, and the victims separately, but also as mutually interacting participants. The suggested associations were tested primarily by the chi-square test of significance.

At the outset of the study our hypothesis was that criminal behavior is a patterned and structured event. However, some unexpected empirical uniformities appeared, and the study was able to refute some of the misconceptions surrounding the crime of rape.

SOME MISCONCEPTIONS ABOUT RAPE

Following are some misconceptions about rape disclosed in this study:

1. *Negroes are more likely to attack white women than Negro women.* Rape, we found, is an intraracial act, especially between Negro men and women.

2. *Rape reflects a demographic strain due to sex-marital status imbalance in the community.* This theory was refuted, along with the derivative assumption about age-sex imbalance which might exist within the general populations.

3. *Rape is predominantly a hot-season crime.*

Source: *Federal Probation,* Vol. 31 (March, 1967), pp. 51–58. Reprinted by permission of the journal.

[1]The term "multiple rape" refers to cases where two or more offenders rape one victim. It includes the following two categories: "pair rape" where two offenders rape one victim, and "group rape" where three or more offenders rape one victim.

The "thermic law of delinquency" was not confirmed by the present study.

4. *Rape usually occurs between total strangers.* This assumption was challenged by the analysis of several variables.

5. *Rape is associated with drinking.* In two-thirds of our cases alcohol was absent from the rape situation.

6. *Rape victims are innocent persons.* One-fifth of the victims had a police record, especially for sexual misconduct. Another 20 percent had "bad" reputations.

7. *Rape is predominantly an explosive act.* In almost three-quarters of the cases rape was found to be a planned event.

8. *Rape is mainly a dead-end street or dark alley event.* Rape was found to occur in places where the victim and offender initially met each other (especially when the meeting was in the residence of one of the participants).

9. *Rape is a violent crime in which brutality is inflicted upon the victim.* In a large number of cases (87 percent) only temptation and verbal coercion were used initially to subdue the victim.

10. *Victims generally do not resist their attackers.* As it is commonly believed that almost no woman wants to be deprived of her sexual self-determination, it was surprising to find that over 50 percent of the victims failed to resist their attackers in any way.

11. *Victims are responsible for their victimization either consciously or by default.* The proportion of rape precipitated by the victim and the characteristics of such acts refute this claim.

FINDINGS OF THIS STUDY

In the following pages are discussed the major significant patterns emerging from the study:

Race. A significant association was found between forcible rape and the race of both victims and offenders. Negroes exceed whites both among victims and offenders in absolute numbers as well as in terms of their proportion in the general population. Negroes have four times their expected number of victims, and the proportion of Negro offenders was four times greater than their proportion in the general population of Philadelphia.

We have used Sellin's[2] concept of "potential population," that is, the members of each race whose age and sex are such that they could be an offender or a victim, respectively, and from which the involvement of the participants can be presumed.

When specific rates by age and sex were calculated on the basis of the "potential" population of each race, it was found that the rates for the Negro victims (on the basis of total Negro female population) is almost 12 times higher than that of the white women who were victims (on the basis of total white female population).

Similarly, for offenders, when the rates were computed on the basis of male population in each racial group, the proportion of Negro offenders was 12 times greater than that of white offenders. Furthermore, when the rates were figured on the basis of the "potential" race populations, the rate for Negro offenders turned out to be three times greater than that of Negro victims, a difference found to hold also for white offenders as compared to white victims.

The data on racial differences reveals that forcible rape is mainly an intraracial event. In this sample, forcible rape occurred significantly more often between Negroes than between whites.

Age. A statistical association existed between age and forcible rape, the age group 15-19 years having the highest rates among offenders and among victims. In examining the relative ages of the offenders and the victims, we found that the higher the age of the offender, the more likely it was that the victim would be in a lower age group. When the differences were broken down further by race it appeared that, regardless of the population basis, the top "risk" age group for Negro and white offenders is the same (15 to 19, and 20 to 25 years of age), but the rates for Negroes in these age levels are higher than for whites. For each age group, however, the rates show a greater proportion of Negro than of white males involved in forcible rape.

The age pattern for victims was found to be somewhat different from that of offenders. For victims there is a wider range of "critical" age

---

[2]Thorsten Sellin, "The Significance of Records of Crime," *Law Quarterly Review,* October, 1951, pp. 496–504.

groups, with the Negro victim rate exceeding that of the white victims in all age groups.

Examination of age differences according to race of victims and offender showed that mainly in Negro and white intraracial rape events, offenders and victims were at the same age level. However, white victims tend to be younger than their white assailants by at least 10 years, while Negro offenders tend to be at least 10 years younger than their victims. (The majority of cases of the latter description were felony-rape events.)

Marital Status. After examination of the marital status of both offenders and victims, it was found that both generally were unmarried. The highest rates for victims were in the "dependent" category (below marriageable age and still unmarried).

Offenders as a group, but Negroes more than whites, show the highest rate in the "single" group (above the age of marriage but not married and still living at parents' home) and the second highest rate in the "dependent" group. These results coincide with the age distribution of victims and offenders noted above.

Negro victims showed a greater concentration in the "single" and "dependent" groups than did white victims who were, however, also concentrated in these groups.

Demographic Imbalance. An attempt was made to check Von Hentig's[3] demographic explanation of forcible rape, i.e., a disturbed sex ratio for unmarried persons age 19 to 49 years resulting in a surplus of males, leads to rape as a solution to their problem of securing sexual partners. We found that the marital demographic structure of Philadelphia cannot explain the extent to which males, especially Negroes, resort to forcible rape. The same applies when marital status, age, and sex ratio were analyzed together.

Occupational Status. Examination of the occupational status of the offenders indicated that 90 percent of the offenders of both races belonged to the lower part of the occupational scale. The rate of Negro offenders in the unemployed category was twice as high as the rate of unemployed Negroes in Philadelphia at that time, and five times as high as that of white offenders.

Season. Although the number of forcible rapes tended to increase during the hot summer months, there was no significant association either with the season or with the month of the year. While Negro intraracial rapes were spread over the year, white intraracial events showed a more consistent increase during the summer. Summer was also found to be the season when multiple rapes were most likely to occur.

Days of the Week. Forcible rape was found to be significantly associated with days of the week. We found the highest concentration of rapes (53 percent) to be on weekends, with Saturday being the peak day.

Time of Day. A study of the distribution of forcible rapes by hours of the day found the top "risk" hours to be between 8:00 p.m. and 2:00 a.m. Almost half of all the rape events occurred during these hours. Finally, the highest number of weekend rapes occurred on Friday between 8:00 p.m. and midnight.

Ecological Patterns. The analysis of the ecology of forcible rape reveals that in various areas of Philadelphia there was a correspondence between high rates of crime against the person and the rates of forcible rape. Moreover, those police districts where Negroes are concentrated were also the areas where the rates of forcible rape were highest.

A check was made to determine whether the offenders lived in the vicinity of the victims or the offense. In the majority of cases (82 percent) offenders and victims lived in the same area, while in 68 percent a "neighborhood triangle" was observed, i.e., offenders lived in the vicinity of victim and offense. Also observed are the pattern of "residence mobility triangle," i.e., instances in which the site of the crime was in the area of the residence of the offender but not that of the victim. A new concept used in this study was a "crime mobility triangle." In 4 percent of the cases the offenders lived in the victim's vicinity, while the crime was committed outside the boundaries of their residential area. When correlating these ecological patterns with race and age factors we found that forcible rape was an interracial event between victims and offenders who were at the same age level

[3]Hans Von Hentig, "The Sex Ratio," *Social Forces*, March, 1951.

and who were ecologically bound, i.e., victims and offenders lived in the same area, which tended also to be the area of the offense. This was especially true for Negro intraracial rapes.

Drinking. Unlike previous studies the present one examined the consumption of alcohol by the offender and the victim separately and together. Alcohol was found only in one-third of all the rape events. In 63 percent of the 217 cases in which alcohol was present, it was present in both the victim and the offender.

The presence of alcohol in the rape situation appeared to be statistically associated with whites—both victims and offenders—and with Negro victims who had consumed alcohol alone before the offense. Alcohol was frequently found to be present in the victim, offender, or both in white intraracial rape events. Of the various combinations of drinking patterns, alcohol in the victim alone and in both victim and offender has stronger implications of causal relationships with the crime of rape than other drinking patterns.

Alcohol is a factor found to be strongly related to violence used in the rape situation, especially when present in the offender only. In terms of race, it was drinking Negro victims or the offenders who were involved most frequently in violent rapes. Also, alcohol was found to be significantly associated with sexual humiliation forced upon a drinking victim.

Finally, weekend rapes were found to be associated with the presence of alcohol in either the victim, the offender, or both. As an explanation, we offered (as did Wolfgang in his homicide study[4]) the fact that Friday is a payday with greater purchase of alcohol and the more intense social and leisure activities.

Previous Arrest Records of Offenders and Victims. A relatively high proportion of rapists in Philadelphia (50 percent) had previous arrest records. Contrary to past impressions, it was found that there are slight differences between the races, for offenders or victims, in terms of police or arrest record, although Negro offenders had a statistically significant higher proportion of two or more offenses in their past than white offenders.

When cases of persistence in violating the law were examined, it was found that over 50 percent of those who had an arrest record as adults also had a record as juveniles.

Analysis of the type of previous offenses committed by the offenders revealed that only 20 percent of those who had a past arrest record had previously committed a crime against the person, with Negro offenders outnumbering the whites in this respect. Among offenders with criminal records, 9 percent had committed rape in the past, and 4 percent had been arrested before for sexual offenses other than rape. When examining the continuity and persistence of offenses from juvenile to adult age, we found that the highest proportion in continuity was in offenses against the person. Thus, adults arrested for rape were found to be less likely first offenders than adults arrested for other types of offenses.

The analysis of the victim's criminal records revealed that 19 percent had an arrest record, the highest proportion of these arrests being for sexual misconduct (56 percent).

The victim's "bad" reputation was explored. It was found that 128, or 20 percent, of the 646 victims had such reputations, with significantly higher proportion of Negro victims having such a reputation. The assumption was made, and later confirmed, that a "bad" reputation, together with other factors such as ecological proximity, was a factor in what was termed "victim-precipitated" forcible rape.

Modus Operandi. The analysis of the modus operandi was made in terms of processes and characteristics of the rape situation, i.e., sequences and conjunctions of events which enter into the perpetration of the offense. Five phases were distinguished according to offender's behavior, victim's reaction, and situational factors which finally set the stage for the rape event.

In phase one we were concerned with the initial interaction between victim and offender, and the relevant problems such as the place meeting and the degree of planning of the offense. It was found that the most dangerous meeting places were the street, and the residence of the victims or offenders or place of sojourn. In

[4]Marvin E. Wolfgang, *Patterns in Criminal Homicide* (Philadelphia: University of Pennsylvania Press, 1958), pp. 142–43.

one-third of the cases, the offender met the victim at and committed the offense in the victim's home or place where she stayed. Such was especially the case in intraracial rape situations.

Planning of the Act. On the basis of the description of the event by the victim and offender, three degrees of planning were distinguished. Contrary to past impression, the analysis revealed that 71 percent of the rapes were planned. Most planned events were intraracial events when the meeting place was the residence of one of the participants or when the rape was a group affair. Explosive rapes were characterized as being single interracial rapes, with the street as the meeting place.

Location of the Event. Phase two concerned itself with the location of the offense and was found to be associated with the place of initial meeting. Thus, when the meeting place was outside the participant's residence or place of sojourn, the offense also took place there. Movement of the crime scene was mainly from outdoors to inside. The automobile, which was already found as a vehicle of crime commission, was revealed to be the location of the offense in only 15 percent of the cases, and more often when white offenders were involved. A significant association was also found between the location of the rape in the participant's place and use of violence in the commission of the offense, as well as the subjection of the victim to sexually humiliating practices.

Degrees of Violence. In phase three we examined various aspects in the actual commission of the offense: Nonphysical methods used to manipulate the victim into submission, the degrees of violence used against her, and sexual humiliating practices which she was forced to endure.

Besides temptation, three forms of nonphysical methods were distinguished: Verbal coercion, intimidation by physical gestures, and intimidation with a weapon or other physical object to force the victim into submission. Combined with verbal coercion, nonphysical aggression was used in the majority of cases (87 percent), with Negroes in significant proportion using both forms of intimidation against their Negro victims. No differences were found between intra- and interracial events in this respect.

Degrees of violence were classified into three main groups: roughness, beatings (brutal and nonbrutal), and choking. In 15 percent of the 646 rapes, no force was used. Of the cases in which force was used, 29 percent took the form of roughness, one-quarter were nonbrutal beatings, one-fifth were brutal beatings, and 12 percent involved choking the victim. Violence, especially in its extreme forms, was found to be significantly associated with Negro intraracial events and with cases in which the offender was Negro and the victim white. Also, a significant association was found between multiple rape and the use of force in the rape situation and between the latter and the outside as the place of rape.

Sexual Humiliation. It was not merely to forced intercourse that the female was subjected in rape, but also to various forms of sexual practices usually defined as sexual deviations. It was found that sexual humiliation existed in 27 percent of all rape cases, especially in the forms of fellatio, cunnilingus, or both, or in the form of repeated intercourse. Sexual humiliation was found to be significantly associated with white intraracial rapes, where the victims were subjected most frequently to fellatio and pederasty, and with Negro intraracial rapes where Negro victims were forced more often to repeated intercourse by their Negro assaulters. Sexual humiliation was found also to be significantly associated with multiplicity of offenders and with the presence of alcohol in the offender only or both by the offender and the victim. In these cases sexual humiliation appeared mainly in the form of fellatio.

Victim Behavior. The behavior of the victim —that is, whether she "consented" or resisted the offender—was, and still is, the basis in determining in the court whether the offender is guilty of forcible rape. This problematic dimension was, therefore, analyzed in the present work.

The varieties of victim behavior have been divided into three groups—submission, resistance, and fight. The analysis revealed that in over half of the rapes the victims displayed only submissive behavior; in 173, or 27 percent, victims resisted the offender; and in 116, or 18 percent, the victims put up a strong fight against their attackers.

In both intra- and interracial rapes Negro and white victims displayed the same proportion of either one of these forms of behavior. The highest proportion of the instances of submissive behavior were cases in which the victim was white and the offender Negro. These cases included almost all felony-rape situations. In most situations the victim was older than her attacker.

In terms of age the younger the age, the more submissive was the victim—mainly those 10 to 14 years. In the adult age (30 or over), victims showed significantly more resistance. Victims tended to fight more when they were more intimate in the initial encounter with the offender, or when force was used against them by the offenders. As expected, the presence of alcohol in the victim diminished her capacity to resist, and in such cases her behavior was found to be mainly submissive.

Multiple Rape. The phenomenon of multiple rape (see footnote 1), mentioned sometimes in the literature but nowhere analyzed, was given special attention in this study. We suggested a tentative theory, borrowing heavily from Redl's[5] theory, which emphasizes the role of the leader in group deviant behavior.

Multiple rape situations were divided into "pair rapes," in which two offenders rape one victim, and "group rapes," in which three or more males rape one victim. Of the 646 cases of forcible rape, 276 cases, or 43 percent, were multiple rapes. Of these cases, 105 were pair rapes and 171 were group rapes. Of 1,292 offenders, 210, or 16 percent, were involved in pair rapes and 712 or 55 percent, participated in group rapes.

The analysis of multiple rapes revealed the following characteristics: More white than Negro offenders participated in pair rapes and more Negro than white offenders were involved in group rapes. Multiple-rape situations were found to be mainly an intraracial affair, with no differences in proportions between Negro and white intraracial events.

The younger the offender, the less likely he is to participate in multiple rape. All of the offenders of ages 10 to 14 participated either in pair rapes or group rapes. The highest proportion of pair rapes or group rapes were perpetrated by offenders between the ages 14 to 19. Group rapes were also found to be characterized by victims being in the same age level as the offender.

Group rape shows a tendency to occur more on weekends and to occur in the evening as well as late at night.

In group rapes, alcohol was more likely to be present, especially in the victim only, while in pair rapes it was more often present only in the offender who was the leader.

A significant proportion of participants in multiple rapes, compared with single-rape offenders, had a previous arrest record either for offenses against the person, for sex offenses other than rape, or for forcible rape. This was true for pair-rape leaders, as compared to their partners, but not for group-rape leaders vis-à-vis their followers.

Turning to the modus operandi aspect in multiple-rape situations, it was observed that multiple-rape offenders are most likely to attack victims who live in their area (neighborhood or delinquency triangles). The initial interaction between victims and offenders usually occurred in the street, where the rape also took place. There was little "mobility of crime scene" in multiple-rape situations.

Multiple rapes, especially group rapes, were found to be planned events. Compared to group rapes, pair rapes showed a high proportion of cases of explosiveness or partial planning.

Turning to the problems of intimidation and coercion, it was found that multiple-rape situations, especially group rapes, are characterized by temptation and coercion, with intimidation more used in pair-rape events. The leader was found to be the initiator of the manipulating acts, i.e., he was the first to tempt or to intimidate the victim into submission.

A significant association existed between violence and multiple rapes, especially group rapes. Multiple rapes also are characterized by the greater use of nonbrutal beatings. Extreme violence and brutality characterize the single-rape events, since the lone offender must constantly subdue the victim alone. The leader in pair and group rapes was more violent than his

[5]Fritz Redl, "Group Emotion and Leadership," *Psychiatry,* July, 1942, pp. 573–96.

followers, and he was also the one to initiate the beatings.

Group rapes were also found to be characterized by tormenting the victim with perverted sexual practices. Testing the theory of "magical seduction"[6] we found that only the pair-rape leader inflicted sexual humiliation upon the victim.

When the association between leadership functions, such as "initiator" or magical seducer" was tested, it was found that both are significantly associated, i.e., those who first attacked the victim were also the first to rape her. However, "magical seduction" was found to be the more important role of the leader. Introducing another leadership function, that of "commanding" and organizing the situation, we found that in group rape the "true" leader was the one who performed all three functions. However, if the three functions were not performed by the same person, the one who first raped the victim was also likely to be the one who commanded the event.

The futility of resistance and fight by the group-rape victim is revealed by the fact that in group-rape situations the victim was more submissive or lightly resisted the offender but was less inclined to put up a strong fight. Pair-rape victims showed no definite pattern in this respect.

For many variables pair rapes and group rapes show some variations from the cluster of patterns which distinguished the multiple-rape situations. We found that in many instances pair rape resembled single rape more than group rape. Thus, it may be better to see pair rapes not as a form of group event but rather as a form of criminal "partnership."

Felony Rape. In 76 cases, or 4 percent, of the 646 rape situations, a felony in the form of burglary or robbery was committed in addition to the rape. These cases were mainly single rapes, and especially Negro intraracial rapes. A special trait of felony rape is the age disparity between victim and offender. In more than half of these cases the offender was at least 10 years younger than the victims, especially when the offender was Negro and the victim white.

Examination of the previous record of felony-rapists showed them to be more often recidivists than the offenders in rape generally. Felony rapes also were characterized by a greater proportion of cases in which sexual humiliation was inflicted upon the victim. Because of the age differences between victim and offenders, it was expected and, indeed, found that victims of felony rapes were more inclined to be submissive than victims of rape generally.

Victim-Offender Relationships. Almost half (48 percent) of the identified victim-offender relationships conformed to our definition of "primary" relationships. When the types of primary contacts were further divided into "acquaintanceship" and more "intimate" contacts, the former constituted 34 percent and the latter contributed 14 percent of all types of victim-offender relationships.

A detailed analysis of victim-offender relationships revealed that when primary relationships existed, a relatively large proportion of cases involved Negro victims whose assailants were their close neighbors, or victims who were drinking acquaintances of their white assaulters.

As expected, Negro intraracial events involved mainly close neighbors. White intraracial events occurred mainly between acquaintances who established their relations just before the offense. Again, as expected, acquaintanceships were formed mainly between victims and offenders who were at the same level.

Neighbors met initially in the residence of one of the participants and the rape also took place there. The automobile was the place of rape for those who were intimate.

Although nonphysical means of coercion in its light forms were used between acquaintances, the closer the relationship was between victim and offender the greater was the use of physical force against the victim, and neighbors and acquaintances were found to be the most dangerous people so far as brutal rape was concerned.

As hypothesized, a greater proportion of multiple than single rape was found to take place between strangers. In general, the analysis of the interpersonal relations between victim and offender lent support to those who reject the myth of the offender who attacks victims unknown to him. But, equally rejected is the notion that rape is generally an affair between, or

[6] *Ibid.*

a result of, intimate relations between victims and offenders.

Vulnerable Situations in Which Rape Occurred. After discussing the psychological approach to victim proneness and victim selection, we found it more fruitful to deal with vulnerable or "risk" situations rather than with psychological concepts like "victim proneness." We noted those factors which emerged in significant proportions as constituents of such situations. It is probable that women entering these risk situations will more likely become victims of rape regardless of their own psychological characteristics.

The following were the main features of vulnerable situations in which rape occurred:

1. Where victims and offenders of single and multiple-rape events were either of the same race or age or both;
2. Where victims of felony rape, who tended to be at least 10 years older than their assailants (Negro and white), lived as neighbors or acquaintances in the same area as their assailants, which tended to be also the area where the offense was committed;
3. Where offenders and victims of the same race and age level met during the summer months, mainly on weekends and/or during the evening and night hours, in places which allowed or encouraged the development of an acquaintanceship or relations between neighbors;
4. Where alcohol was present in both white offender and white victim, or in white offender and Negro victim, or in the victim only, especially when her assailant was white;
5. Where Negro victims with a "bad" reputation lived in the neighborhood of their Negro attackers, and where groups of offenders who planned the rape of victim of their own race live in the same vicinity;
6. Where victims and offenders were neighbors of the same race and age, between whom primary relations existed, and where victims and offenders established drinking relations just prior to the offense; and
7. Where a drinking victim was accosted in the street by a stranger, usually of her own race.

Victim-Precipitated Rape. The term "victim-precipitated," initiated by Wolfgang in his study of homicide,[7] was introduced to refer to those rape cases in which the victims actually—or so it was interpreted by the offender—agreed to sexual relations but retracted before the actual act or did not resist strongly enough when the suggestion was made by the offenders. The term applies also to cases in which the victim enters vulnerable situations charged with sexuality, especially when she uses what could be interpreted as indecent language and gestures or makes what could be taken as an invitation to sexual relations.

Philadelphia data revealed several significant factors associated with the 122 victim-precipitated rapes, which comprised 19 percent of all forcible rapes studied. These factors are:

1. White victims; white intraracial rapes; alcohol in the rape situation, particularly in the victim or both in offenders and victims;
2. Victims with a bad reputation; victims who live in residential proximity to the offenders and/or to the area of offense; victims who meet their offenders in a bar, picnic, or party;
3. Victims who were in "primary" relationships with the offenders but who were not their relatives;
4. Victims who were raped outside their or the offender's home or place of sojourn; and
5. Victims subjected to sexual humiliation.

Solved and Unsolved Rape. We distinguished two types of "unsolved" cases: the "undetected" —those cases in which the police could not attribute the recorded offense to any identifiable offender(s), and the "vanished"—those cases about which the police had some information on suspected, identified, or alleged offenders but which suspects were still at large. In 124, or 19 percent, of the rape events the offenders were classified as "undetected" and in 24, or 4 percent, as "vanished." Of 1,292 offenders, 405, or 33 percent, were classified as undetected.

In unsolved cases of rape in Philadelphia there was:

1. A higher proportion of Negro offenders involved in Negro intraracial rape than in solved cases;
2. A higher average age among the offenders than among offenders in general;

[7]Wolfgang, *op. cit.*, chap. 14, pp. 245–69.

3. A higher proportion of explosive types of rape;
4. A higher proportion of cases in which alcohol was present in the victim only or in the offender only;
5. A higher proportion of single-rape situations; and
6. A higher proportion where there was delay by the victim or others in reporting the offense to the police, especially because of fear of the offender or an inability to adequately describe him.

CONCLUSION

Discussing various theoretical explanations for the crime of forcible rape, a subculture theory of violence emerged as a possible interpretation of the patterns discerned in this study.

There can be little doubt that more studies are needed to give us more systematic and comparative knowledge of the characteristics of rapists and victims and of social conditions which may explain more accurately the crime of rape.

10.

David J. Pittman and William Handy

PATTERNS IN CRIMINAL AGGRAVATED ASSAULT

No crimes are considered more serious than homicide and aggravated assault, for homicide deprives an individual of his life, and aggravated assault is an attempt to deprive an individual of his life or to cause him serious injury.

The act of homicide has been analyzed in numerous studies, the most complete of these being Wolfgang's *Patterns in Criminal Homicide.*[1] In his study, Wolfgang formulated a series of hypotheses concerning the nature of acts of homicide, tested them through the use of police homicide data, and thereby established the "patterns" in criminal homicide.

As far as can be discerned no study of Wolfgang's type has been made of the crime of aggravated assault. The lack of such a study is remarkable, for often the line dividing aggravated assault from homicide is so thin that a factor such as the speed of an ambulance carrying the victim to the hospital will determine whether the crime will be aggravated assault or homicide. The purpose of this study is to analyze the crime of aggravated assault and to attempt to establish its "patterns," as Wolfgang did for homicide, by testing where possible Wolfgang's homicide hypotheses against acts of aggravated assaults.

The Federal Bureau of Investigation classifies the crime of aggravated assault as "assault with intent to kill or for the purpose of inflicting severe bodily injury by shooting, cutting, stabbing, maiming, poisoning, scalding, or by the use of acids, explosives, or others means."[2] In November, 1960, the FBI added a supplement to this definition by stating that aggravated assault was "an unlawful attack by one person upon another for the purpose of inflicting severe bodily injury accompanied by the use of a weapon or other means likely to produce death or great bodily harm. Attempts should be included since it is not necessary that any injury result from an aggravated assault."[3] The following guides were also given in this supplement:

Reprinted by special permission of the *Journal of Criminal Law, Criminology and Police Science* (Northwestern University School of Law), Copyright © 1964, Vol. 55, No. 4.

[1]Wolfgang, *Patterns in Criminal Homicide* (Philadelphia: University of Pennsylvania Press, 1958).

[2]Federal Bureau of Investigation, U.S. Department of Justice, *Uniform Crime Report 29* (Washington, D.C.: U.S. Government Printing Office, 1960).

[3]Federal Bureau of Investigation, U.S. Department of Justice, *Uniform Crime Reporting–Aggravated Assaults* (Washington, D.C.: U. S. Government Printing Office, Nov. 1960), Supp.

"Careful consideration of the following factors should clarify the classification of an aggravated assault. (1) The seriousness of the injury. (2) The type of weapon used or the use made of an object as a weapon. (3) The intent of the assailant to cause serious injury."[4] Furthermore all these factors should be weighed before the crime is classified as an aggravated assault.

Even with this clarification of the definition of aggravated assault, the crime remains one of the most difficult to classify. According to the Department of Justice of the State of California:

> Aggravated assault is an offense which is very difficult to classify. There has been a growth in the number of aggravated assaults reported over the years, but there does not seem to be a corresponding growth in the number of felonious assaults prosecuted. This would suggest that because of the relationship of the parties or the conditions under which the assaults occurred, many altercations, largely domestic quarrels, characterized in reports as aggravated assaults, do not seem to fall in the general area of felonious assault. There is a need to have a subclassifying of this type of offense in order to arrive at a true picture of assault.[5]

This statement was prepared before the supplement in the FBI definition and clearly states one of the many reasons for the refinement. However, other factors which are impossible to regulate by a clarification in definition will adversely affect the proper classification of aggravated assaults; the way in which the police officer fills out a report form and the difference of interpretation held by two clerks who classify these acts may cause variance. Such factors will have to be overlooked in this study, and the police classification of the crime will be accepted.

By popular definition, the crime of aggravated assault is known as "attempted murder," "assault with intent to kill," "assault with intent to do great bodily harm" or just "assault." All of these terms might be thought of as sub-classifications of the act, for they all more or less describe the purpose of the offender.

STUDY METHOD

The study group was composed of a random sample of 25 per cent of the 965 crimes classified by the St. Louis Metropolitan Police Department as aggravated assault for the period January 1, 1961, to December 31, 1961. Sampled cases totaled 241. Copies of the offense reports for each sampled case were obtained as well as the arrest records of the offender and the victim involved in the act. The information concerning the crime contained in offense reports was considered adequate, and the arrest records were also considered sufficient. Records such as those concerning the individual's prison, parole, and psychiatric status were unavailable, and the addresses of the individuals were not current and were difficult to determine. The collected data were analyzed in terms of a set of formulated hypotheses concerned with the variables of time, location and season of year, weapon, reporting, injury, police processing, alcohol involvement, victim-offender relationship, and arrest records.

In a few cases there were multiple offenders or victims. Generally, the additional offender or victim will not be considered, and the act will be analyzed as one crime, the emphasis being on the act and not on the individuals involved. In certain analyses, however, all offenders and all victims must be considered, and this accounts for the variable number of cases.

RESULTS

I. Time

During week days, interaction among people is limited by their work, and there is less leisure time than on the weekends. For this reason, it was hypothesized that the majority of the acts of aggravated assault would occur between 6:00 p.m. Friday and 6:00 a.m. Monday.

As shown in Table 3.1, 132 of the 241 acts occurred during the hypothesized time. The period between 10:00 p.m. and 11:00 p.m. contained more acts than any other hour. More aggravated assaults occurred on Saturday than on any other day of the week, with Friday and Sunday following in that order. The hours between 4:00 p.m. and 3:00 a.m. were those during which the largest number of acts occurred, confirming the view of the police that this period has the largest number of all types of crime, since they reach their climax under the cover of darkness.

[4] *Ibid.*

[5] California Department of Justice, Bureau of Criminal Statistics, *Crime in California* 18 (1958).

TABLE 3.1

DAY AND TIME OF OCCURRENCE OF AGGRAVATED ASSAULT CASES

	Mid-night-6:00 a.m.	*6:00 a.m.-Noon*	*Noon-6:00 p.m.*	*6:00 p.m.-Mid-night*	*Total*	*Per Cent*
Sunday	15	5	5	10	35	14.5
Monday	1	2	7	11	21	8.6
Tuesday	5	4	5	10	24	10.0
Wednesday ...	7	1	8	8	24	10.0
Thursday	5	0	6	10	21	8.6
Friday	10	5	5	24	44	18.4
Saturday	22	6	11	33	72	29.9
Total	65	23	47	106	241	
Per cent ...	27.0	9.6	19.5	43.9	100.0	100.0

Our second hypothesis concerning time factor was that the majority of the acts would occur between 8:00 p.m. on a given evening and 4:00 a.m. the following morning. This hypothesis was accepted. As shown in Table 3.2, the number of acts is the greatest between 8:00 p.m. and 4:00 a.m., the period of darkness and more interaction. Aggravated assaults decline sharply during the next eight hours, when most people are sleeping and then going to work. The number begins to rise again between noon and 8 p.m., as interaction after the working day slowly increases, and finally reaches its climax between 10:00 and 11:00 p.m. in the evening.

TABLE 3.2

TIME OF OCCURRENCE

8:00 p.m. 4:00 a.m.	*4:00 a.m.– Noon*	*Noon– 8:00 p.m.*	*Total*
140	31	70	241

Mean no. for 8-hour period = 80.3.

II. LOCATION AND SEASON OF THE YEAR

Criminal aggravated assaults may occur in a wide variety of places, but it was hypothesized that place of occurrence would be related to the season of the year, victim-offender relationship, and sex status. First, it was hypothesized that the largest number of acts would occur on public streets, rather than in taverns or bars, residences, or other places. This hypothesis was accepted (Table 3.3).

TABLE 3.3

PLACE OF OCCURRENCE BY MONTH

	Street	*Tavern or Bar*	*Residence*	*Other*	*Total*	*Per Cent*
Jan.	5	2	10	2	19	7.9
Feb.	12	2	6	1	21	8.7
March ..	10	3	3	0	16	6.6
April	11	1	6	1	19	7.9
May	8	1	7	2	18	7.5
June	9	2	6	0	17	7.1
July	7	5	12	0	24	10.0
Aug.	10	2	10	2	24	10.0
Sept. ...	10	1	8	3	22	9.1
Oct.	9	0	9	1	19	7.9
Nov.	13	4	6	0	23	9.5
Dec.	6	4	8	1	19	7.9
Total .	110	27	91	13	241	100.0
Per cent	45.6	11.2	37.8	5.4	100.0	

Also it was expected that more acts would occur during the winter than during other seasons. Summer months for St. Louis were defined as June, July, August, and September,[6] while winter months were defined as November, December, January, and February. Table 3.3 shows that 87 acts occurred during the four summer months, while 82 occurred during the winter months. Thus, this hypothesis was rejected.

In relation to location and season of year, it was hypothesized that during the winter months, a greater number of acts would occur indoors as against the summer, when the larger number would occur outdoors. For this testing, summer was defined as April through September, and winter as October through March, so that all of the acts might be included. This hypothesis was also rejected (see Table 3.4).

It was thought that since females spend the majority of their time indoors, the acts in which they were offenders would be likely to occur indoors, and this hypothesis was accepted (Table 3.5).

[6] In St. Louis, the month of September is regarded as a summer month.

Since related persons tend to have most of their interaction within their own home, it was hypothesized that if the offender and victim were related, the act of assault would take place within a residence. As shown in Table 3.6, the hypothesis was accepted.

TABLE 3.4

PLACE OF OCCURRENCE BY SEASON

	Summer	*Winter*	*Total*
Indoors	55	55	110
Outdoors	61	57	118
Total	116	112	228*

*For remaining 13 acts, location indoors or outdoors not assigned.

TABLE 3.5

PLACE OF OCCURRENCE BY SEX OF OFFENDER

	Female	*Male*	*Total*
Indoors	41	75	116
Outdoors	18	107	125
Total	59	182	241

Chi sq. = 14.27; P < .001. All cases assigned to outdoors-indoors categories.

TABLE 3.6

PLACE OF OCCURRENCE BY KIN RELATIONSHIP

	Kin	*Not Kin*	*Total*
In residence	42	49	91
Not in residence ..	5	145	150
Total	47	194	241

Chi sq. = 66.13; P < .001.

III. WEAPON

In choosing a weapon for assault, the offender's choice is almost unlimited, and any given weapon may be used in a variety of ways. A gun, for instance, may be employed as a firearm or as a club. The offender may choose one of the more common weapons, such as a gun or knife, or some unique concoction such as a curtain rod, bottle, meat cleaver, shovel, or can opener.

It was hypothesized that a knife, being readily accessible, would be used in more instances than any other weapon. In 126 of the 241 cases, the offender did choose a knife; guns were used in only 39 cases. Personal force (fists, feet, or any part of the body, but without the use of a weapon), although certainly more accessible than a knife, was used in only 14 cases, perhaps because the offender is more certain of inflicting injury upon his victim with a knife than with his own striking power. The remaining 62 cases involved weapons ranging from sharp instruments to fire, lye, and vases.

It was further hypothesized that, proportionately, white offenders would use personal force to a greater extent than would Negro offenders. The fact that in Negro neighborhoods, weapons for self-defense are commonly carried[7] gave rise to this proposition. The hypothesis was accepted (Table 3.7).

TABLE 3.7

TYPE OF FORCE BY RACE OF OFFENDER

	White Offender	*Negro Offender*	*Total*
Personal force	6	7	13
Weapon	36	189	225
Total	42	196	238*

Chi sq. = 7.72; P < .01.
*Three unknown.

It was hypothesized that white females would use guns more frequently than other weapons, since guns requires less strength to use and are "cleaner" than other weapons. This hypothesis was rejected, as no white female offender selected a gun, while four of them chose knives. Apparently the accessibility of knives and the lack of knowledge about guns took precedence over other factors.

IV. REPORTING

There are numerous ways in which a case of aggravated assault may become known to the police. The crime may be reported by the victim, the offender, a witness, a hospital, or a physician, or it may be observed by the police. The hypothesis that the victim would report the

[7]E.g., Leroy G. Schultz, *Why the Negro Carries Weapons*, Vol. 53, *Journal of Criminal Law, Criminology and Police Science* (1962), p. 476.

crime in the majority of cases proved acceptable, for such was the case in 146 of the 241 acts. In only 10 cases did the offender report his own crime, while in 41 cases a witness reported the act. In 16 cases the police observed the crime or its consequences, in 23 cases they were called by medical authorities, and in five cases by a relative of the victim. Acts in progress observed by the police were usually those occurring on a street where a crowd had gathered. In those cases in which a relative notified police, much time had elapsed since the act.

V. Injury

In the act of aggravated assault, the offender or the victim may be wounded, and the degree of injury varies. Although the extent of injury does determine, in some cases, whether or not the crime is classified as aggravated assault, it does not necessarily determine which party is the victim and which the offender. Sometimes the offender may be seriously wounded, and the victim only slightly injured, if at all.

In all of the sampled cases, the victim was wounded to some degree, and only when he refused medical attention was he not conveyed to a hospital. As was hypothesized, in more than half the cases, the victim was seriously wounded, while the offender was not (Table 3.8). Seriously wounded was defined as being incapacitated to the extent to require hospitalization.

TABLE 3.8

SERIOUSNESS OF WOUND BY VICTIM AND OFFENDER

	Seriously Wounded	*Not Seriously Wounded*	*Total*
Victim	134	117	251
Offender	35	222	257
Total	169	339	508*

Chi sq. $= 90.47$; $P < .001$.
*More than one offender or victim in 22 cases studied.

VI. Police Processing

Aggravated assault is generally a distinct crime; in other words, usually no other Index Crime is involved, since the assault follows some type of verbal argument. In only three of the 241 cases was another Index Crime involved—in all cases robbery. In these cases, the police reports contained information which led authorities to believe that robbery was an afterthought, with assault the primary motive of the offenders.

Sometimes, both the victim and the offender are charged by the police with aggravated assault. Both were charged in 10 of the sampled cases. In the remaining 231 cases, the victim was charged with either suspicion of affray or suspicion of peace disturbance. The charging of the victim with one of these counts was a police practice at the time of the study, and the charge was deleted only when it was ascertained that the victim was in no way responsible for the attack upon himself. Witnesses were often charged with affray or peace disturbance, depending on their role in the act. Clearance by arrest of aggravated assault cases is generally high, being surpassed only by homicide. In this sample, 77.2 per cent of the cases were cleared by arrest.

Elapsed time following a crime before the offender is apprehended is of importance to the police, for the longer the time lapse, the less the chance the police will arrest the offender. For aggravated assault, it was believed that the offender would usually be apprehended within an hour after the act, and such proved to be the case (Table 3.9). Of course a number of offenders were apprehended at the scene of the crime.

TABLE 3.9

LENGTH OF TIME BETWEEN THE ACT AND APPREHENSION OF THE OFFENDER

Time Elapsed	*Number Arrested*	*Percentage*
0.1 hour	116	62.3
1–5 hours	28	15.1
5–24 hours	19	10.2
Over 24 hours	23	12.4
Total	186	100.0

In 193 of the 241 cases, the identity of the offender was known to either the offender, the witness, or the police. This number corresponds closely with the number of clearances by arrest; in only seven cases was the offender not apprehended when his identity was known.

It was hypothesized that more female than male offenders would be apprehended, since a female would be less able to avoid arrest by escape, more likely to be known to the offender, a witness, or police, and less likely to take part in a street attack. The hypothesis was accepted (Table 3.10).

TABLE 3.10

CLEARANCE BY SEX

	Arrested	*Not Arrested*	*Total*
Female offender	60	2	62
Male offender	126	50	176
Total	186	52	238*

Chi sq. = 17.03; P < .001.
*Three unknown.

We hypothesized that a Negro offender would be more likely to be arrested than a white one, for the former would have less means at his disposal to avoid arrest and detection. The competing hypothesis would be that significantly fewer Negroes than whites would be arrested, in accordance with a popular belief in certain segments of the society that the police ignore Negro personal crimes of violence. Table 3.11 shows that both hypotheses were rejected. While Negroes were the offenders, 79 per cent of the cases were cleared by arrest; the comparable figure for whites was 74 per cent. This is not a statistically significant difference.

TABLE 3.11

CLEARANCE BY RACE

	Arrested	*Not Arrested*	*Total*
Negro offender	155	41	196
White offender	31	11	42
Total	186	52	238*

Chi sq. = .56; P < .50. Association not significant.
*Three unknown.

VII. Alcohol Involvement

It was hypothesized that prior alcohol ingestion by both the offender and the victim would be common in acts of aggravated assault. It was found, however, that alcohol ingestion was present in only slightly more than one-quarter (57 offenders and 58 victims) of all the cases. This, however, may be a consequence of either the inability to detect the presence of prior alcohol ingestion or the failure to report it. But in 41 cases the offender and victim had been drinking together prior to the crime. To discern the role of alcohol ingestion in aggravated assault, one would need more complete information than police records provide.

VIII. The Relationship of Offender and Victim

Prior to the act of aggravated assault, the offender and victim have generally been in interaction with each other. Verbal arguments (181 of 241 cases) usually precede the aggression. These quarrels may range from domestic incidents to tavern disputes over who was to sit on which bar stool. On the surface the quarrels appear to have little rationality. They must be understood in terms of the social and psychological mechanisms which the offenders and victims have developed to handle their aggressive impulses.

Furthermore, aggravated assault most often involves only one offender and one victim—in this sample, 219 cases of 241. In eight cases there was one offender and a multiplicity of victims, in 11 cases more than one offender but one victim, and in only three cases a multiplicity of both.

Since it was expected that there would be few interracial assaults (in this sample only 10 cases, of which only one was cross-sex and cross-race lines), it was hypothesized that if the offender and victim were of the same race, they would be of the same sex. Table 3.12 shows that the hypothesis was rejected.

Persons of the same age group are most likely to interact with each other, and for this reason it was hypothesized that the victim and offender would be within the same age category. The categories adopted were under 20, 20–34, 35–49, and 50+. The assumption was true in 146 of the 241 cases. Where offender and victim were in the same age category, there were more cases in the 20–34 age group than in any other

TABLE 3.12

RACE AND SEX RELATION OF OFFENDER AND VICTIM

	Same Race	*Different Race*	*Total*
Same sex	135	9	144
Different sex	93	1	94
Total	228	10	238*

Chi sq. = 3.65; P < .10. Association not significant.
*Three unknown.

single group. Also, more offenders and more victims, considered apart, were in the 20–34 group than in any other single age group. (Table 3.13.)

TABLE 3.13

AGES OF OFFENDERS AND VICTIMS

	Under 20	*20–34*	*35–49*	*50+*	*Not in Same Age Group*
Both offender and victim ..	22	75	33	16	77*
Offender only ..	35	105	71	30	—
Victim only	28	91	59	35	—

*Remainder unknown.

In 106 of the cases, the offender was older than the victim, while in 92 cases the victim was older. In 23 cases, they were of the same age, and in the remaining 20 cases the age of the offender was unknown.

It was expected that the majority of both offenders and victims would be in-migrants to St. Louis. This assumption was checked by ascertaining the place of birth of the arrestees. Of the offenders, 71 per cent were born outside St. Louis, and of the victims 62 per cent were born outside the city.

Of the known offenders (237), 139 were Negro males, while 118 of the victims were Negro males; the hypothesis was thus validated that in cases involving Negro male offenders, the majority of victims would be Negro males.

Of the 252 victims, 218 (86.5 per cent) were married, while only 143 (60.3 per cent) of the 237 offenders were married. This is a statistically significant difference between the two groups in reference to marital status. In cases involving spouses only, the wife was the victim in 21 cases, while the husband was the victim in the remaining 15.

It was expected that blue collar workers would be involved in more acts of aggravated assault than their white collar counterparts—a belief confirmed by the data. Two-hundred twelve of the 252 victims and 229 of the 237 offenders were blue collar workers. A housewife was considered to be a blue collar worker if her husband's socio-economic status was blue collar.

It was hypothesized that a female, being more likely to have interaction with a male to whom she was related than with an unrelated male, would commit aggravated assault against a male to whom she was related more frequently than would a male attack a female to whom he was related. Table 3.14 indicates that this hypothesis was rejected.

TABLE 3.14

KINSHIP RELATIONSHIP OF MALE AND FEMALE OFFENDER AND VICTIM

	Related	*Not Related*	*Total*
Male attacks female...	21	72	93
Female attacks male...	15	30	45
Total	36	102	138

Chi sq. = 1.82; P < .20. Association not significant.

In cases involving a male and a female not legally related, it was hypothesized that prior to the assault the two would have had a relationship of common-law marriage, sexual intimacy, or dating. Table 3.15 supports the hypothesis in cases involving a female attacking a male, but not in cases of a male attacking a female. This finding indicates that the female is more likely than a male to aggress against one with whom there is some intimate relationship.

Interracial assault was an uncommon occurrence in this sample. Only 10 of the 241 cases involved an offender and victim of different race. It was hypothesized that in an interracial assault, a white person would most likely be the victim. This hypothesis was accepted (Table 3.16).

TABLE 3.15

RELATION OF MALE AND FEMALE OFFENDER AND VICTIM

	Male Attacks Female	*Female Attacks Male*	*Total*
Former close relation . .	9	16	25
No former relation	16	9	25
Total	25	25	50

Chi sq. = 3.92; $P < .05$.

TABLE 3.16

INTERRACIAL ASSAULTS

	White Offender	*Negro Offender*	*Total*
White victim	40	8	48
Negro victim	2	188	190
Total	42	196	238

Chi sq. = 178.19; $P < .001$.

Only a small number (22 cases) of the victims had previous arrests for Index Crimes. Most offenders, however, had previous criminal records (Table 3.17), with the prior arrest most frequently being for peace disturbance. The record, however, does not indicate whether this prior act was a slight scuffle or affray or a reduced charge from a more serious offense. At least 37 of the offenders had at least one previous arrest on an assault charge.

TABLE 3.17

PRIOR ARREST RECORD OF OFFENDERS AND VICTIMS

	Offenders	*Victims*	*Total*
Prior arrest record	156	121	277
No prior arrest record . .	92	131	223
Total	248	252	500

Chi sq. = 11.21; $P < .001$.

It was hypothesized that Negro offenders would be no more likely to have prior arrest records than white offenders; this belief was confirmed (Table 3.18).

The last hypothesis was that there would be no correlation between the age of the offender and presence of a prior arrest record. Using the age categories previously cited, it was found that the age category 20–34, into which the largest number of offenders fell, had a higher percentage of prior records than did other groups, but the percentage did not sharply increase or decrease with a change in age. Forty-six per cent of the offenders under 20, 62 per cent of those 20–34, 48 per cent of those 35–49, and 57 per cent of those 50 or over had prior arrest records.

TABLE 3.18

PRIOR ARREST RECORD OF OFFENDERS BY RACE

	Negro Offender	*White Offender*	*Total*
Prior arrest record	128	28	156
No prior arrest record . .	68	24	92
Total	196	52	248*

Chi sq. = 2.32; $P < .20$. Association not significant.
*Remainder unknown.

AGGRAVATED ASSAULT, THE TYPICAL PATTERN

These patterns in aggravated assault are based on a random sample of 241 acts in 1961 drawn from the cases reported to the St. Louis Metropolitan Police Department. From the analysis presented here, it is possible to state the expected pattern of aggravated assault in the "typical" case.

An act of aggravated assault is more likely to occur on a weekend than during the week, specifically between 6:00 p.m. Friday and 6:00 a.m. Monday, with peak frequency on Saturday, between 10:00 p.m. and 11:00 p.m. While the event shows little likelihood of being more frequent in the four summer months considered together than in the winter, this type of assault peaks in the months of July and August.

The crime will occur on a public street, or, secondly, in a residence. If a female is the offender, the act will occur indoors, if a male offender, outdoors. When offender and victim are related, the act will more likely occur in a residence than elsewhere. The general neighborhood context is one populated by lower socioeconomic groups–especially Negroes of this class.

The weapon used by both men and women will in most cases be a knife, with a gun the second choice. In acts involving white offenders, personal force will be used more often than in those involving Negro offenders.

Generally, the act will be reported to the police by the victim. The victim will be wounded seriously enough to require hospitalization, but the offender will not. More than 75 per cent of the aggravated assault cases will be cleared by arrest within one hour after the crime occurs. A Negro is no more likely to be arrested for his crime than is a white.

These records indicate that neither the offender nor the victim will be under the influence of alcohol, nor will they have been drinking together, and neither will be a user of drugs.

The aggravated assault will be preceded by a verbal argument, most likely centering around a domestic quarrel.

The offender and victim will be of the same race and of the same sex; there will be only one offender and one victim, and both will have been born outside of the city in which the crime occurs. Both will be of the same age group, usually between the ages of 20 and 35, with the offender being older. The victim will more often be married than the offender, but both will be blue collar workers. A female offender is more likely to be related to her male victim than is the male offender to his female victim. Females assault males with whom they have had a previous close relationship (such as dating, sexual intimacy, or common-law marriage); but this is not the case with males assaulting females.

Negro offenders are no more likely than their white counterparts to have a prior arrest record. Offenders in the age bracket 20–34 will in the majority of cases have a prior arrest record.

AGGRAVATED ASSAULT COMPARED TO CRIMINAL HOMICIDE

Despite the lack of sociological studies of aggravated assault, it was believed that this offense had many similarities to homicide. A comparison of the findings in this study with those of Wolfgang[8] for criminal homicide reveals more similarities than differences, even though the two studies represent different time periods, cities, and police departments.

1. *Time.* For both aggravated assault and homicide, occurrences were higher on Saturdays, with the time of day being most frequently late evening and early morning hours; for homicide, between 8:00 p.m. and 2:00 a.m., and for aggravated assault, between 4:00 p.m. and 3:00 a.m. The next highest time for both acts were the hours immediately following the highest period.

2. *Location.* Both crimes occurred more often on a public street than in any other location, with residences second. Summer months accounted for a higher percentage of crimes in both cases, but to a greater extent for homicides. In winter these crimes occurred indoors. Females committed both acts more often indoors than outdoors. If the victim and offender were related, the crime most likely occurred in a residence. Both types of acts usually took place in a lower class, Negro neighborhood.

3. *Weapon.* The weapon most often used differed between homicide and aggravated assault; a pistol or revolver was most common in homicides, while a knife was most common in assaults. White females used a revolver or pistol most often in homicide, while they used a knife most often in assault.

4. *Police Processing.* No other Index Crime was involved in the majority of both crimes, and there was a high cleanup rate for both, although it was higher for homicides. The offender in both crimes was arrested within a short time of committing the act, and he was known to either witnesses or police. Clearance was higher for females and Negroes than for males and whites in both homicide and assault.

5. *Alcohol Involvement.* The ingestion of alcohol was more common in homicide than in assault, as was a drinking episode between offender and victim prior to the crime.

6. *Situational Context.* Verbal arguments preceded both crimes, but alcohol was involved in the arguments in homicide situations more often than in aggravated assault cases.

---

[8]Wolfgang, *op. cit.*

7. *Offender-Victim Relationship.* For both crimes, the victim and offender were typically of the same age, sex, and race. There were most often only one victim and one offender. Negro males were disproportionately involved in both types of crime. The participants in both acts were usually married, blue collar workers, and the victims of interracial assaults were white more often than Negroes. In acts of homicide, a wife attacked her husband more often than a husband attacked his wife, while the reverse was the case in aggravated assaults.

8. *Prior Arrest Records.* For both homicide and aggravated assault, the majority of the victims had no prior arrest record, while the majority of the offenders did. For homicide offenders, two-thirds had a prior record of a crime against the person, while for aggravated assault the number of offenders having this type of record, if one excepts peace disturbance, was negligible.

This comparison of findings concerning acts of homicide and aggravated assault indicates that the pattern for the two crimes is quite similar. Both acts, of course, are reflections of population sub-groupings which tend to externalize their aggression when confronted with conflict situations.

11.

Alex D. Pokorny

HUMAN VIOLENCE: A COMPARISON OF HOMICIDE, AGGRAVATED ASSAULT, SUICIDE, AND ATTEMPTED SUICIDE

Suicide-Homicide

One of the most familiar themes in discussions of suicide and homicide is that these behaviors are closely related. Not only do they both represent the taking of human life by a human, but it is held that they are related in their motivation, that they spring from the same soil.

Perhaps the best known of these views is that suicide is a kind of inverted or retroflexed homicide[1]: "Nobody kills himself who had not intended to kill somebody else."[2] The classical psychoanalytic view is that suicide represents a murder of an "incorporated object"—the internalized image of an ambivalently-regarded person.[3] Suicide and homicide are seen as having similar underlying and often unconscious motivations. Karl Menninger has emphasized that persons who commit suicide have a wish to kill as one of the necessary components; he speaks in terms of instinctual destructive tendencies, which may be directed inward or outward.[4]

A contrasting view is that suicide and homicide are just the opposite of each other.[5] Durkheim quotes Ferri and Morselli as insisting that the polar character of suicide and homicide is an absolutely general law, that they always change inversely with each other.[6] Durkheim expresses doubt about the universality of this inversion, but he lists a number of observations which are compatible with it: (1) With regard to rates in European countries, there is a good fit; Spain, Ireland, and Italy are the three coun-

Reprinted by special permission of the *Journal of Criminal Law, Criminology and Police Science* (Northwestern University School of Law), Copyright © 1965, Vol. 56, No. 4.

[1]Jackson, "Theories of Suicide," in Shneidman & Farberow, *Clues to Suicide* (1957).

[2]Fenichel, *The Psychoanalytic Theory of Neurosis* (1945).

[3]Cassity, "Personality Study of 200 Murderers," *Journal of Criminal Psychopathology,* Vol. 2 (1941), p. 296; Bromberg, *The Mold of Murder* (1961).

[4]Menninger, *Man Against Himself* (1938).

[5]Wolfgang, *Patterns in Criminal Homicide* (Philadelphia: University of Pennsylvania Press, 1958); Stengel & Cook, *Attempted Suicide* (1958).

[6]Durkheim, *Suicide* (1951).

tries with the least suicide, yet they have the most murders, whereas France and Prussia are are just the reverse; (2) Wars tend to decrease suicides but to increase homicides, and political crises have the same effect; (3) Suicide is more urban than rural, with homicide the opposite; (4) Catholic countries have high homicide and low suicide rates, whereas Protestant countries are just the opposite.[7]

Suicide and homicide clearly come from the same source in the dual act of homicide and suicide committed by the same person. As part of his study of Philadelphia homicides, Wolfgang has studied Homicide-Suicide, the instances in which a person committed a homicide and then committed suicide.[8] Of 621 Criminal Homicide offenders, 24 or 4% also killed themselves. It is pointed out that this is a low rate as compared to England, where a quarter to a third of homicide suspects commit suicide. The author quotes Cavan's belief that the homicide and suicide are really part of the same act, in which one eliminates one's self but simultaneously gets even with the cause of one's troubles. Another common hypothesis in such cases is that the person commits a homicide, then kills himself because of the resulting guilt. Suicide may also represent an attempt to escape punishment.

Series of homicide offenders usually contain some individuals who have previously made suicide attempts.[9] There are other instances where homicide offenders make unsuccessful suicide attempts at the time of the homicide.[10]

Suicide-Attempted Suicide

Suicide is also linked in contrasting ways with Attempted Suicide. For many decades the prevailing view was that Attempted Suicide was a kind of bungled or unsuccessful suicidal act, perhaps quantitatively different but essentially representing the same behavior. A great many of the published studies of Suicide are really based on Attempted Suicide cases, because they were the ones who survived to be studied, and the findings were generalized uncritically to Suicide.

More recently, the view has emerged that Attempted Suicide is mostly a different class of behavior than Suicide.[11] This view has been most clearly and convincingly stated by Stengel and Cook.[12] They find that those who attempt suicide and those who commit suicide are two different, though overlapping, populations. Suicide is intended to terminate life, whereas suicide attempts, in the majority of cases, are aimed at improving one's life. A suicide attempt is seen as a social behavior pattern which cannot be understood fully unless seen in relation to the human environment; it usually has widespread social effects. Frequently suicide attempt cases are "moving towards others" in the course of the act, in contrast to suicides who are withdrawing. Jackson has pointed out that suicide attempts are often intended to manipulate, force, or get revenge.[13]

Homicide-Aggravated Assault

Just as Suicide has a related and larger category of Attempted Suicide, Homicide has a related, larger category of Aggravated Assault. This has been defined as an attempt to deprive an individual of his life or to cause him serious injury.[14] Is Aggravated Assault properly viewed as a bungled or unsuccessful Homicide, with the same motivations and characteristics? Or is it possible that, as in Suicide-Attempted Suicide, it is a different, though perhaps overlapping, class of human violence?

It has been stated that homicide offenders have, as a long-term characteristic, greater impulsivity, less ability to control emotions.[15] It has been found that in many instances of homicide

[7]It should be noted that the United States has a far higher homicide rate than any of these European countries. Dublin & Bunzel, "Thou Shall Not Kill, A Study of Homicide in the United States," *Survey Graphic,* Vol. 24 (1935), p. 127.

[8]Wolfgang, "An Analysis of Homicide-Suicide," *Journal of Clinical and Experimental Psychopathology,* Vol. 19 (1958), p. 208; Wolfgang, *op. cit. supra* note 5.

[9]Lanzkron, "Murder and Insanity: A Survey," *American Journal of Psychiatry,* Vol. 119 (1963), p. 754.

[10]Adelson, "Slaughter of the Innocents," *North East Journal of Medicine,* Vol. 246 (1961), p. 1345.

[11]Schmid & Van Arsdol, "Completed and Attempted Suicides," *American Sociological Review,* Vol. 20 (1955), p. 273; Hendin, *Suicide in Scandinavia* (1964).

[12]Wolfgang, *Patterns in Criminal Homicide, op. cit.*

[13]Jackson, *op. cit.*

[14]Menninger, *op. cit.*

[15]Brearley, *Homicide in the United States* (1932).

fierce arguments precede the murder, with progressive escalation in emotion and violence.[16] It may therefore be largely a matter of chance that an offense becomes a homicide or an assault. Wolfgang points out that in the past generation there has been a lower rate of criminal homicide but an actual increase in offenses against the person—particularly Aggravated Assault;[17] he suggests that the decrease in homicides may be a function of more prompt attention and improved medical care. This can be likened to the lowered death rate from wounds in World War II as compared with World War I.

Pittman and Handy have recently published a thorough study of Aggravated Assault, using a random 25% sample of the 965 such cases seen by the St. Louis Police in 1961.[18] They investigated the time, place, relationship and kinship status, type of force, method of reporting, apprehension, disposition, etc. They then compared the typical patterns with those developed for Criminal Homicide by Wolfgang. In almost all respects, the patterns were similar, which would indicate that these were likely to be the same broad class of behavior.

GOAL OF PRESENT STUDY

Few of the various comparisons of types of violence which have been quoted are based on strictly comparable data. Even the excellent study by Pittman and Handy is limited to Aggravated Assault; they then compare their findings with the findings of the study on Homicide done by Wolfgang in another city.

The present study was undertaken to see whether these four categories of violent behavior would show similar or contrasting patterns when studied in the same city at approximately the same time, using case data from the same source. The general aim was to contrast the four types of violence, self-directed (complete and partial), and outward-directed (complete and partial), to see if they could be differentiated from each other by objective characteristics of the events and the persons involved. Among such promising objective factors appeared to be the place of the occurrence,[19] the time and various aspects of the persons such as age, sex, race and ethnic group.

PROCEDURE

Data for individual cases of Suicide, Attempted Suicide, and Criminal Homicide were abstracted from the files of the Houston Police Department.[20] Initially the complete year of 1960 was used, to make possible derivation of rates on the basis of the 1960 census.[21] There were 91 suicides in 1960, and this series is used in the analysis of the exact place of the offense. For most purposes, the study period for suicides was increased to July 1958 through 1961 (a 3½ year period centered on the census-taking date) in order to increase the number of cases. Similarly, all homicide cases were abstracted for the period March 15, 1958 through 1961. "Murder by Auto" cases were not included. This yielded a total of 400 Attempted Suicides (the round number is fortuitous), 320 Suicides, and 438 Homicides.

It should be pointed out that there is some loss in numbers as one shifts from one type of evaluation to another. In Homicide, there may be multiple victims or multiple offenders, making these totals unequal to each other and to the total number of homicide offenses. Fourteen of the homicide offenders were unknown, so that they do not appear in age, race, and sex tabulations. With regard to the hour of the day, this is sometimes vague or unknown, especially in suicide cases, so that these totals are smaller. For the census tract comparisons, the numbers are smaller because a number of the persons in-

[16]Berg & Fox, "Factors in Homicide Committed by 200 Males," *Journal of Social Psychology,* Vol. 26 (1947), p. 109.

[17]Wolfgang, *Patterns in Criminal Homicide, op. cit. supra* note 5.

[18]Pittman & Handy, "Patterns in Criminal Aggravated Assault," *Journal of Criminal Law, Criminology and Police Science,* Vol. 55 (1964), p. 462. (See pages 90–99 of this volume).

[19]Adelson, *op. cit.;* Wolfgang, *Patterns in Criminal Homicide, op. cit.;* Bullock, "Urban Homicide in Theory and Fact," *Journal of Criminal Law, Criminology and Police Science,* Vol. 45 (1955), p. 565.

[20]The author wishes to express his appreciation to the Houston Police Department, and particularly Inspector Larry W. Fultz of the Records Division for their cooperation, and to Dr. Fred B. Davis for his assistance in data collection and analysis.

[21]U. S. Bureau of Census: *U. S. Census of Population and Housing.* Final Report (1)–63 (Washington, D.C.: U. S. Government Printing Office, 1962).

TABLE 3.19

PLACE OF OCCURRENCE OF HOMICIDES, SUICIDES, AND ATTEMPTED SUICIDES
(In per cent)

	All Homicides	*Husband-Wife Plus Common Law Husband-Wife Homicides*	*Homicides Except Husband-Wife and Common Law*	*Suicides (1960 Only)*	*Attempted Suicide*
Total number of cases	438	89	349	91	400
Bedroom	13.8	33.7	8.6	30.7	12.0
Living or dining room	7.6	12.3	5.7	12.1	1.8
Kitchen	3.6	5.7	2.9	7.7	3.0
Bathroom	0.4	0.0	0.6	8.8	9.2
Porch or yard	8.0	10.1	7.4	2.2	0.7
Other area of home	3.4	1.1	4.0	9.9	1.8
Home, area unknown	5.0	9.0	4.3	4.4	50.7
Total at home	41.8	71.9	33.5	75.8	79.2
Club, bar, lounge	13.0	10.1	13.7	0.0	0.7
Sidewalk, parking lot, driveway	13.9	6.7	15.8	0.0	0.0
Street, alley	8.0	3.4	9.2	0.0	0.3
Car, away from home	4.8	3.4	5.2	6.6	1.5
Other areas away from home	16.9	4.5	20.6	15.4	18.3
Total away from home	56.6	28.1	64.5	22.0	20.8
Unknown	1.6	0.0	2.0	2.2	0.0
Overall total (Per cent)	100.0	100.0	100.0	100.0	100.0

volved lived outside the city. Aside from such losses, the tabulations represent all of the cases investigated by the Houston Police Department during the intervals specified.

The Aggravated Assault cases were not studied individually; rather the findings on Aggravated Assault are taken from the tables and summaries of the Police Department Annual Reports.[22] For this reason there are no data on place of residence of participants, or place (in the home, street, etc.) where the offense occurred.

In addition, certain data on Homicides, Suicides, and Attempted Suicides (day of week, month) were also taken from Police Department Reports; for these tabulations various combinations of years between 1955 and 1962 are used, as indicated in the individual tables.

The Homicide data has also been used in a partial replication of the definitive study of Criminal Homicide by Wolfgang, and the results of this are presented elsewhere.[23]

RESULTS

1. Place

a. *Place of Occurrence*. The various types of locations, such as rooms in the house, bars, etc., where Homicides, Suicides, and Attempted Suicides occurred are shown in Table 3.19. The Homicides are also subdivided into (1) a category of husband-wife (plus common-law husband-wife) killings, and (2) all the remaining Criminal Homicides. This was done because it was suspected that the large proportion (41.8%) of slayings in the home might be due mainly to these husband-wife cases. It will be noted in the table that husband-wife slayings do occur more frequently in the home (71.9%), while the residual group shows 33.5% of cases in the home.

[22]*Annual Report*, 1960 (1961, 1962), City of Houston, Tex. Police Dept. Bureau of Technical Services, Division of Records and Analytical Data.

[23]See author's research paper on pages 60–69 of this volume.

When one compares all three classes of behavior, it is readily apparent that Suicides and Attempted Suicides occur typically at home, whereas Homicides occur more typically away from home, in public places such as bars, streets, and sidewalks, places where suicides and suicide attempts are virtually unknown. This is consistent with the idea that Suicide is a "private affair," whereas Homicide requires a partner. In this respect Attempted Suicide seems more like suicide. Unfortunately, because the Police reporting of attempted suicide is less thorough, the room of the house was not known in a high proportion of these cases.

b. *Census Tract in Which Offense Occurred.* A tabulation was made for the 120 census tracts of Houston in terms of how many of the July 1958-1961 Homicides (N = 412) occurred in each. Similar data was available for the 1960 Aggravated Assault cases (N = 1559). The Pearson product-moment correlation coefficient between these two sets of figures is .946, indicating a very striking similarity in place of occurrence.

c. *Census Tract of Residence of Persons Involved.* A tabulation was made for the 120 census tracts, crediting each tract with its residents who were involved in Suicide, Attempted Suicide, and Homicide (offender and victim). In addition, the place of occurrence of Homicide was included. These values were then correlated, and the results are shown in Table 3.20.

TABLE 3.20

CORRELATIONS BETWEEN 120 CENSUS TRACTS, HOUSTON, IN TERMS OF NUMBERS OF HOMICIDES AND NUMBERS OF RESIDENTS INVOLVED IN SUICIDE, ATTEMPTED SUICIDE, AND HOMICIDE

	Suicide (294)	*Suicide Attempts (387)*	*Homicide Offenders (384)*	*Homicide Victims (378)*	*Homicide Place of Occurrence (412)*
Suicide		.425*	.114	.120	.129
Suicide attempts			.176	.195	.207
Homicide offenders				.940	.956
Homicide victims					.945
Homicide place of occurrence					

*Pearson product-moment coefficients of correlation (with an N of 120, a value of .181 is significant at the .05 level.)

It can be seen that the three Homicide figures show a very high positive correlation. Suicide and Suicide Attempts show a moderate positive correlation, but otherwise the relationships are unimpressive. It appears that Homicide occurs in certain areas of the city, and that the offenders and victims in homicide live in these same areas. The participants in Suicide and Attempted Suicide tend to come from the same areas, but these are different from the "Homicide Areas."

2. Time

a. *Hour of Occurrence.* The hours of the day at which the Suicides, Suicide Attempts, Homicides, and Assaults occurred have been plotted in Figure 3.1. It is evident that the curves for Homicides and Aggravated Assaults are quite similar, with the offenses bunched in the periods from 5:00 p.m. to 2:00 a.m. The hourly distribution for Suicide is strikingly different, with a peak in the morning and tapering off in the afternoon and evening. The hourly distribution of Attempted Suicide is approximately midway between the others; the peak hours of Attempted Suicide do fall into the "after work" period of the day, suggesting that presence of other people was a factor. All four types of behavior fall off during the hours of 2:00 to 6:00 a.m.

b. *Day of Week.* The distribution of Suicide, Attempted Suicide, Homicide, and Aggravated Assault through the days of the week is shown in Table 3.21. These four distributions have then been correlated in all possible combinations, also shown in Table 3.21. It is seen that the weekly distributions for Homicide and Aggravated Assault show the astonishingly high correlation of .997; both tend to occur on weekends with a peak on Saturday. Attempted Suicide likewise is more frequent on weekends and shows some positive (though non-significant) correlation with Homicide and Assault. In this series Suicide is more common in the middle of the week, so that the relationship to the other behaviors is a negative one.

c. *Months.* The monthly distribution of Suicides, Attempted Suicides, Homicides, and Aggravated Assaults, for the same time intervals shown in Table 3.21, was tabulated and com-

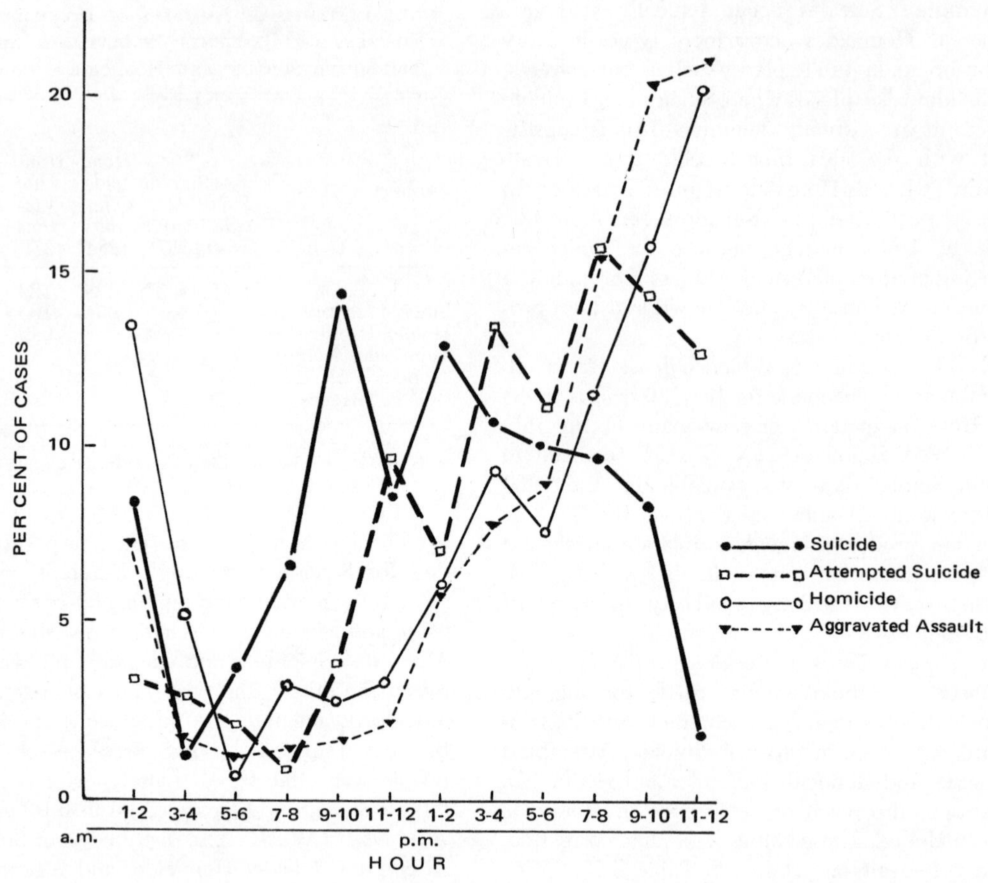

FIGURE: 3.1 HOUR OF OCCURRENCE: SUICIDE, ATTEMPTED SUICIDE, CRIMINAL HOMICIDE, AND AGGRAVATED ASSAULT.

pared. There were no striking monthly variations and no discernable trends or significant correlations.

d. *Quarters of Year.* The data for months were also grouped into four quarters of the year (January-March, April-June, etc.). Again there were no positive findings.

3. Persons

a. *Age, by Behavior Category.* The age distribution of persons involved in Suicide, Attempted Suicide, Criminal Homicide, and Aggravated Assault is shown in Table 3.22. One finding is that the age distribution for Homicide offenders and Aggravated Assault offenders is very similar. The age distribution for Attempted Suicide is similar, except that there is an even greater representation of the age 15-19 group. The age distribution for Suicide is quite different, involving relatively few individuals below 30 and many more in the 50 and over group.

To bring out this difference, the data for Suicide, Attempted Suicide, and Homicide are shown graphically in Figure 3.2. Note that the age groupings here are different, with larger intervals but with a further breakdown of the 50

TABLE 3.21

DISTRIBUTION OF SUICIDE, ATTEMPTED SUICIDE, HOMICIDE, AND AGGRAVATED ASSAULT THROUGH DAYS OF THE WEEK

Day of Week	*(1) Suicide (1960–1962)*	*(2) Attempted Suicide (1961–1962)*	*(3) Homicide (1955–1960)*	*(4) Aggravated Assault (1960)*
Sunday	35*	206	115	269
Monday ...	36	174	73	152
Tuesday ...	45	167	67	155
Wednesday..	46	151	63	128
Thursday ..	48	139	68	161
Friday	31	148	111	277
Saturday ...	31	178	190	472
Total	272	1163	687	1614

Pearson correlations between columns:

	(1)	(2)	(3)	(4)
(1)		–.482	–.764	–.754
(2)			.425	.380
(3)				.997
(4)				

*Data for this table is taken from Annual Reports, Houston Police Dept.

and over category. Here again Suicide shows up as distinctly different in age distribution; the other three groupings are very similar. Thus, in terms of age, Attempted Suicide seems to be more similar to Homicide and to Aggravated Assault than to Suicide.

b. *Age-Specific Rates.* In the preceding section, the values for age-groupings are given in percentages of the total number of cases of a given behavior (Suicide, Homicide, etc.). This was done to bring out how each behavior is distributed through the age periods.

Another way of handling age groupings is to derive age-specific rates. This brings out the frequency of a behavior in relation to the population at risk, as shown by the 1960 census. This has been done for the same data discussed in the preceding section, and the results are shown in Table 3.23. Because this complex table makes it difficult to compare the several behaviors, the data have also been graphed in Figure 3.2. It should be noted that three different scales have been used, to permit easy visual comparison. It is readily seen that the Suicide distribution is deviant, but that the other five distributions are very similar. Again Attempted Suicide resembles Homicide and Aggravated Assault more closely than it does Suicide.

c. *Race and Ethnic Group, by Behavior Category.* The race and ethnic membership of the persons involved in Criminal Homicide, Aggravated Assault, Suicide, and Attempted Suicide is shown in Table 3.24. The percentages of these groups within the general city population are also shown. The white group (called "Total

TABLE 3.22

AGE DISTRIBUTION OF PERSONS INVOLVED IN SUICIDE, ATTEMPTED SUICIDE, CRIMINAL HOMICIDE, AND AGGRAVATED ASSAULT

(Per cent of total)

	Suicide	*Attempted Suicide*	*Homicide Offender*	*Homicide Victim*	*Aggravated Assault Offender*	*Aggravated Assault Victim*	*Total City Population*
Total No. of Cases	320	400	416	425	1619	1619	938,219
age							
Under 15	0.0	0.3	1.1	5.7	1.2	1.9	33.4
15–19	3.8	14.5	8.2	4.8	8.6	9.0	6.5
20–24	5.9	16.2	14.8	13.2	11.7	14.1	6.5
25–29	5.9	17.3	17.6	16.9	14.3	19.8	7.4
30–34	8.8	14.3	13.0	17.4	13.9	16.0	8.2
35–39	10.0	15.9	12.6	9.6	10.1	13.8	7.9
40–44	13.1	8.2	8.4	8.9	7.0	9.7	6.5
45–49	12.5	4.5	7.5	8.2	4.0	5.5	5.9
50 and over	39.1	8.8	11.1	13.7	5.6	6.9	17.7
Unknown	0.9	0.0	5.7	1.6	23.6	3.3	0.0
Total (per cent) ..	100.0	100.0	100.0	100.0	100.0	100.0	100.0

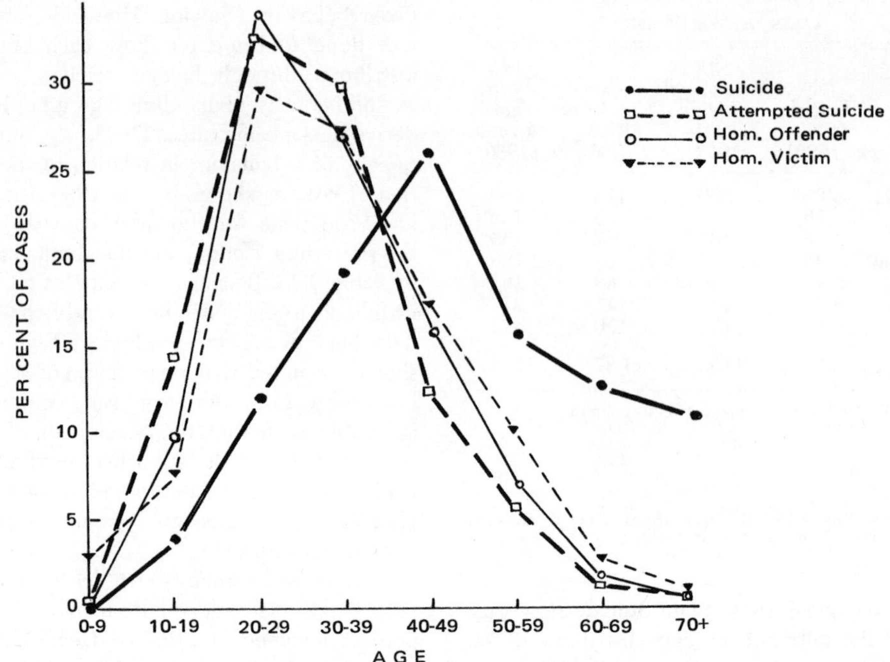

FIGURE 3.2. AGE DISTRIBUTION OF PERSONS INVOLVED IN SUICIDE, ATTEMPTED SUICIDE, AND CRIMINAL HOMICIDE.

TABLE 3.23

AGE-SPECIFIC RATES,* CITY OF HOUSTON, FOR PERSONS INVOLVED IN SUICIDE, ATTEMPTED SUICIDE, CRIMINAL HOMICIDE, AND AGGRAVATED ASSAULT

Age Group	*Suicide*	*Attempted Suicide*	*Homicide Offender*	*Homicide Victim*	*Aggravated Assault Offender*	*Aggravated Assault Victim*
Under 15	0.0	0.3	0.4	2.0	6.1	9.9
15–19	5.6	95.4	14.6	8.7	228.7	240.2
20–24	8.9	106.0	26.7	24.1	308.2	371.8
25–29	7.8	98.9	27.6	27.2	332.5	460.0
30–34	10.5	74.5	18.6	25.5	294.2	338.7
35-39	12.4	86.8	18.6	14.7	222.4	302.4
40–44	19.5	53.7	15.0	16.3	183.8	255.4
45–49	20.5	32.3	14.7	16.6	116.6	159.7
50 and over	21.5	21.0	7.3	9.2	54.7	67.3
Total	9.7	42.6	11.7	11.9	172.6	172.6

*All rates are per 100,000 persons per year.

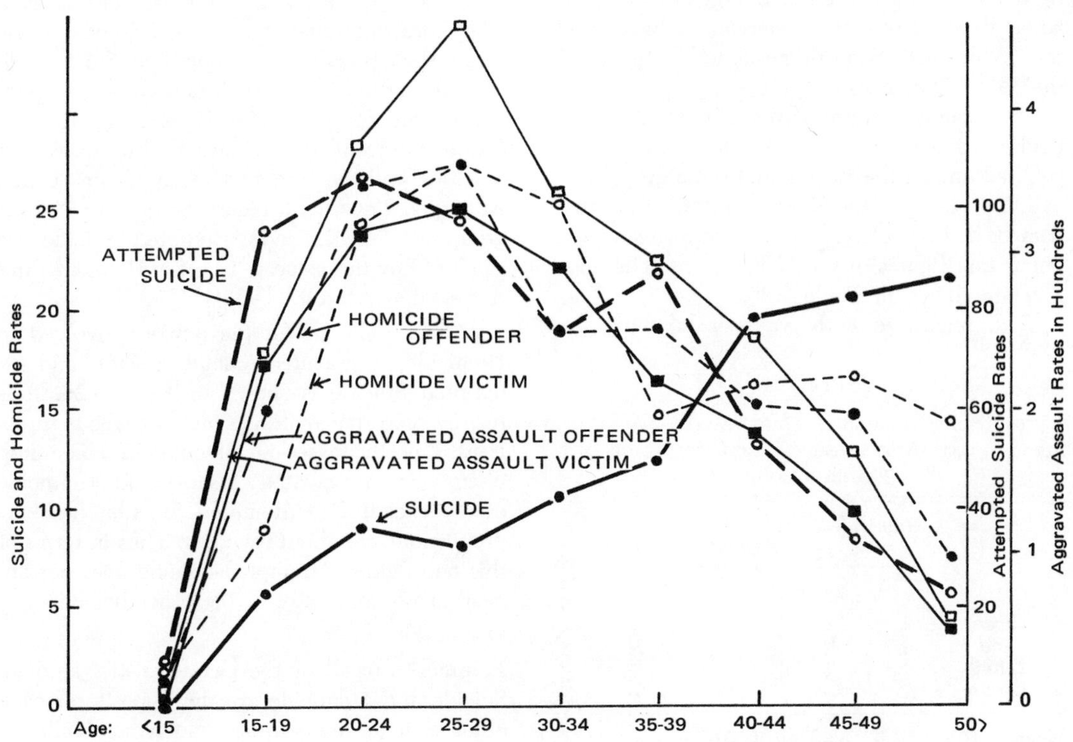

FIGURE 3.3. RATES FOR SUICIDE, ATTEMPTED SUICIDE, HOMICIDE, AND AGGRAVATED ASSAULT

TABLE 3.24

RACE AND ETHNIC GROUP OF PERSONS INVOLVED IN CRIMINAL HOMICIDE, AGGRAVATED ASSAULT, SUICIDE, AND ATTEMPTED SUICIDE
(Per cent of total)

	Homicide		*Aggravated Assault*				
Race and Ethic Group	*Offender*	*Victim*	*Offender*	*Victim*	*Suicide*	*Attempted Suicide*	*Total City Population*
Negro	61.4	61.9	66.1	68.2	8.8	7.2	22.9
Total White	35.3	37.6	29.1	31.7	90.6	92.8	76.8
Latin-American	7.4	6.8	9.0	9.1	1.2	5.0	6.8
Other white	27.9	30.8	20.1	22.6	89.4	87.8	70.0
Other	0.0	0.5	0.1	0.1	0.6	0.0	0.3
Unknown	3.3	0.0	4.7	0.0	0.0	0.0	0.0
Total	100.0 (416)	100.0 (425)	100.0 (1619)	100.0 (1619)	100.0 (320)	100.0 (400)	100.0 (938,219)

White") is subdivided into Latin-American and "Other White." For the percentage of city population listed after Latin-American, I have used the "White with Spanish surnames" category of the 1960 U.S. census.

The table is in terms of percentages of a particular behavior, to bring out how this is distributed among the Race and Ethnic groups.

d. *Race and Ethnic Groups, Rates.* The same data have been converted into rates, using the population figures of the 1960 census. The findings are shown in Table 3.25.

With regard to both ways of handling the Race and Ethnic groups data, it is apparent that Negroes are greatly overrepresented in the Homicide and Aggravated Assault columns, while being sharply underrepresented in the Suicide and Attempted Suicide columns. Just the opposite is true for the "Other White" group. The Latin-American group shows by far the fewest Suicides, and they are moderately low in Suicide Attempts. Thus, with regard to race and ethnic grouping, Suicide and Attempted Suicide are similar, and the same is true for Homicide and Aggravated Assault.

TABLE 3.25

RATES* OF HOMICIDE, AGGRAVATED ASSAULT, SUICIDE, AND ATTEMPTED SUICIDE BY RACE AND ETHNIC GROUP

Race and Ethnic Group	*Homicide*		*Aggravated Assault*			
	Offender	*Victim*	*Offender*	*Victim*	*Suicide*	*Attempted Suicide*
Negro	31.3	32.3	497.6	513.4	3.7	13.5
Total white ...	5.4	5.9	65.4	71.2	11.5	51.5
Latin-American ..	12.9	12.1	230.4	232.0	1.8	31.6
Other white ..	4.7	5.6	49.5	55.7	12.4	53.4
Total ...... (Including other and unknown race)	11.7	11.9	172.6	172.6	9.7	42.6

*All rates are per 100,000 persons per year.

e. *Sex.* The sex of the persons involved in Homicide, Aggravated Assault, Suicide, and Attempted Suicide is shown in Table 3.26. It is readily seen that males account for about three-fourths of the cases in all columns (including victims in Aggravated Assault and Homicide cases) except for Attempted Suicide; here the proportions are about reversed. Thus in terms of this one factor, Attempted Suicide does not appear to resemble any of the other behaviors.

DISCUSSION

In practically all of the characteristics studied, Suicide and Homicide are the opposite of each other. Suicide tends to occur at home, homicide away from home. The areas of residence of persons involved tend to be in different census tracts of the city. The hours of the day and days of the week are clearly different. The age distribution of the persons involved is distinctly different. Homicide is much more common in Negroes, whereas Suicide is much more common in Whites; in both cases, the Whites with Span-

TABLE 3.26

SEX OF PERSONS INVOLVED IN CRIMINAL HOMICIDE, AGGRAVATED ASSAULT, SUICIDE AND ATTEMPTED SUICIDE

(In per cent)

Sex	*Homicide*		*Aggravated Assault*				
	Offender	*Victim*	*Offender*	*Victim*	*Suicide*	*Attempted Suicide*	*Total City Population*
Male	73.7	80.2	68.6	75.8	73.1	28.0	48.8
Female	23.0	19.8	26.6	24.2	26.9	72.0	51.2
Unknown	3.3	0.0	4.8	0.0	0.0	0.0	0.0
Total	100.0 (430)	100.0 (425)	100.0 (1619)	100.0 (1619)	100.0 (320)	100.0 (400)	100.0 (938,219)

ish surnames are in an intermediate position. The only similarity of these behaviors in the characteristics examined is in the sex distribution: both are more common in males.

Thus most of the findings here support the view that these are polar opposites, rather than that they are directly related. At least this appears to be true of the groups as a whole. It may be that there exist subpopulations within these groups which would be similar; the Homicide-Suicide group might be one example. Durkheim[24] has suggested that his Egoistic Suicide is incompatible with Homicide, whereas his Altruistic and Anomic types may be compatible with it.

The view that Attempted Suicide is a class of behavior distinct from Suicide was supported in several facets of this study. The distribution in hour of occurrence is different, with Suicide highest in the morning and afternoon, whereas Attempted Suicide is most frequent in later afternoon and evening. The distribution in the days of the week is different. The distribution of ages is quite different, with Attempted Suicide commonest in the teens and twenties, whereas Suicide is infrequent before thirty and increases progressively with age. The proportions of the sexes are markedly different, in that 73% of Suicides are males and only 28% of Attempted Suicides are males.

The difference between Suicide and Attempted Suicide is not supported by the findings with regard to race, ethnic grouping, place of occurrence, and census tract location of home. Both Suicide and Attempted Suicide rates are low among Negroes, even lower in the Latin-American group, and relatively high in the "Other White" group. With regard to place, both Suicide and Attempted Suicide occur within the home in three-quarters of the instances. The persons involved tend to have lived in the same census tracts of the city.

By contrast, Criminal Homicide and Aggravated Assault seem to be similar in all of the analyses. They tend to occur in the same census tracts of the city. The distributions for the hour of the day and day of the week are remarkably similar. They have a very similar age distribution, with regard to both victims and offenders. The race and ethnic proportions in the two categories of offenses are quite similar. So is the representation of the sexes, in both victims and offenders. These findings suggest that Aggravated Assault and Criminal Homicide are basically the same category of behavior, and that it may be mainly a matter of chance that an assault becomes a homicide.

It should be acknowledged that the police data are probably not equally complete or representative for the four classes of behavior. They are likely to be the most complete for Homicide, since this major crime involves a death and is vigorously investigated. They are likely to be fairly complete in Suicide, since this involves a death. In cases of Assault, it is possible for the incident to go unreported, and this is even more true in case of Attempted Suicide where the attempt is not seriously life-threatening. It has already been mentioned that those Attempted Suicide cases reported to the Police are not investigated or reported as fully as Suicide cases, for obvious reasons.

How serious a problem is this presumed differential reporting in the data presented? It is my opinion that this is not a major problem, since socio-economic status is not being studied. The basic comparison is between four categories of violent behavior, in terms of objective items like sex, race, hour, day, etc., and these are unlikely to be seriously influenced by selective reporting.

Summary

1. Four types of human violence, Suicide, Attempted Suicide, Homicide, and Aggravated Assault, were compared to see if they arose in the same or different populations.

2. Data were obtained from Police records and tabulations, for all of such cases occurring in one city in periods ranging from one to five years, at or near the time of the 1960 census.

3. Comparisons were made in terms of type of place, census tract site of offense, census tract of home of persons involved, hour, day of week, month and quarter of year, age, race and ethnic group, and sex.

4. Suicide and Homicide differed from each

[24]Durkheim, *op. cit.*

other in all the comparisons except for sex; both were higher in males.

5. Suicide and Attempted Suicide were similar in place, race, and ethnic grouping, but differed in hour, day, age, and sex.

6. Homicide and Aggravated Assault were similar in all aspects studied, which suggests that these are basically the same category of behavior.

CHAPTER IV

Abnormal Sex Offenses

When the American public is informed of the commission of an abnormal sex offense they may react in a variety of ways. Among the most common responses are: "Crime is rampant in our society"; "It isn't safe for women and children to walk the city streets"; "Hundreds of thousands of sex fiends are loose and wandering about undetected"; Social service agencies are providing refuge and protection for perverts"; and, "Because of the complexities of legal interpretations, it is almost impossible to obtain convictions in the criminal courts." In many instances sex crimes are viewed with the same degree of disgust and anger as may be associated with a homicide.

Because the public has displayed such concern with this particular type of offense, it is not surprising that criminologists have devoted a good deal of the professional literature to the study of sex offenders. One such study, conducted in 1950 by the New Jersey Commission on the Habitual Sex Offender reported a number of fallacies regarding sex fiends. Among the most prevalent beliefs current at the time were the following:

1. There are tens of thousands of homicidal sex fiends abroad in the land. In fact the vast majority of the sex deviates are minor offenders, most of whom never come to official attention.
2. That sex offenders are usually recidivists. Sex offenders have one of the lowest rates as "repeaters" of all types of crime. Among serious crimes homicide alone has a lower rate of recidivism. Those who recidivate are characteristically minor offenders—such as peepers, ex-

hibitionists, homosexuals—rather than criminals of serious menace.

3. That the sex offender progresses to more serious types of sex crime. It is the consensus of opinion among psychiatrists, confirmed by crime statistics, that sex deviates persist in the type of behavior in which they have discovered satisfaction.
4. That it is possible to predict the danger of serious crimes being committed by sex deviates. Reports reveal a consensus that it is impossible to predict the occurrence of many serious crimes with much accuracy.
5. That "sex psychopathy" or sex deviation is a clinical entity. Two-thirds of the psychiatric authorities consulted by the writer pointed to the wide disagreement among psychiatrists as to the meaning of the term, sex psychopath.
6. That these individuals are oversexed. Most sex deviates are undersexed rather than hypergonadal types. A majority are passive or nonaggressive.[1]

The Commission went on to report that the authorities had to contend with considerable publicity given single instances of sex crimes, while the more objective studies were relegated to professional journals and scholarly monographs. Thus thousands of burglaries and auto thefts may be committed each week with very little time or space devoted by the news media to their reporting. But let one sex crime take place, and this single event may capture the headlines for several days. The public conscience is aroused, our citizens are horrified, and demands are made for new legislation capable of dealing with the problem.

Statistical evidence indicates that sexual deviance is distinctly a male offense. Females, with the possible exception of lesbians, are not involved (unless as victims) to any great extent in acts of exhibitionism, voyeurism, the selling, possessing, and displaying of pornographic literature, or any other abnormal sex offense. Forcible rape (not considered an abnormal sex offense, but nevertheless relevant to our discussion), by legal definition may be committed only by a male.

At this point it may be best to isolate and define the major sex offenses that must be dealt with in this country. Although the laws of our several jurisdictions vary according to their legal definitions of these deviant acts, I believe we may classify the several sex crimes by citing 11 distinct categories. These categories are:

1. Heterosexual pedophilia—sexual activity of any type with a female partner who has not started to show pubertal changes.

[1] "The Habitual Sex Offender" State of New Jersey, *Report and Recommendations of the Commission on the Habitual Sex Offender*, Paul W. Tappan, Technical consultant (Trenton, N.J., 1950), pp. 13–15.

2. Homosexual pedophilia—sexual activities of any type with a male partner who has not started to show pubertal changes.
3. Incest—sexual relations with a person who is a primary relative. (There is some variation among states in their definition of a primary relative. In some states it is limited to the immediate family—mother, father, and children; in other states this relationship may be extended to first cousins.)
4. Homosexuality—Lesbianism—sexual relations with a member of the same sex.
5. Exhibitionism—sexual pleasure derived from exposing oneself.
6. Sadism—pleasure derived from inflicting pain on others.
7. Masochism—pleasure derived from withstanding pain.
8. Voyeurism—pleasure derived from peeping.
9. Transvestism—excitement derived from dressing in clothing worn by members of the opposite sex.
10. Fetishism—urge to have contact with a possession (physical or personal) of a member of the opposite sex.
11. Bestiality—pleasure derived from sexual involvement with animals.

In the present chapter, the editor wished to explore the nature of sexual deviancy from several vantage points. The readings selected offer the student an opportunity to examine Stanton Wheeler's sociological critique on sex offenses, an analysis of the legal framework we must operate within, presented by Morris Ploscowe, and lastly, Maurice Leznoff and William A. Westley's description of the homosexual community as a specific case in point.

12.

Stanton Wheeler

SEX OFFENSES: A SOCIOLOGICAL CRITIQUE

INTRODUCTION

Issues raised by sex offender legislation cut across a number of problems that are of interest to law, psychiatry, and the social sciences. Three problems are selected for brief review in this paper. The first concerns the basis for deciding what types of sex relationships should be subject to legal restraint. Second, the paper will review objective evidence regarding social attitudes toward various forms of sex conduct between consenting partners. Problems posed by more serious sex offenders will be examined in the closing section, with special attention directed to sex psychopath statutes and to possible sociogenic factors in the development of sex offenders. For reasons of space, the special problems posed by prostitution are not considered. Since other contributions to this symposium deal with experience in other societies and with the special problems of juveniles, the concern in this article is limited primarily to social norms and laws relevant to adult sexual relationships in the United States.

I. PROBLEMS IN THE DEFINITION OF SEX OFFENSES[1]

A. Sex Relationships Subject to Legal Restraint

Most of our sex laws are designed to govern one or more of four aspects of sexual relationships. Strongest legal sanctions are directed to control of the *degree of consent* in the relationship, with many states allowing the death penalty for forcible rape. Other bodies of sex law place limits on the *nature of the object.* Currently, most states restrict legitimate objects to humans, of the opposite sex, of roughly the same age, and of a certain social distance in kinship terms. Thus, sodomy or bestiality statutes prohibit relations with animals, parts of the sodomy statutes prohibit relations with members of the same sex, statutory rape and indecent liberties or child-molestation statutes restrict the legitimate age range of the partner, and incest statutes prohibit relationships with relatives other than the spouse. In addition, many jurisdictions, through fornication and adultery laws, limit legitimate objects to marriage partners. Legal restrictions are also placed on the *nature of the sexual act.* Full legitimacy is restricted largely to acts of heterosexual intercourse. Even if the object is a legitimate sexual object, the act may be subject to severe legal sanction. Thus oral-genital contacts, digital manipulation, and common-law sodomy are legally deviant acts, although they may occur by consent between a married pair. Finally, the law attempts to control the *setting in which the act occurs.* Relationships that are otherwise subject to no restraints may become so when they occur publicly or when carried on in such a manner that the public may easily be aware of the relationship. States that do not punish single or even repetitive acts of fornication or adultery may do so if there is evidence of "notorious" show of public indecency. Public solicitation statutes as well as indecent exposure laws are likewise oriented to control of the setting, rather than the act itself.

[1]Statutes defining sex offenses have been reviewed in a number of publications and will not be discussed in detail here. Major sources on which this discussion is based include Robert V. Sherwin, *Sex and the Statutory Law* (1949); Morris Ploscowe, *Sex and the Law* (1951); Bensing, "A Comparative Study of American Sex Statutes," *Journal of Criminal Law, Criminology and Police Science,* Vol. 42 (1951), p. 57. See also Ploscowe, "Sex Offenses: The American Legal Context," *op. cit.,* pp. 217–24.

B. Aims of the Criminal Law

If there were an explicit and articulate rationale underlying the criminal law's attempts to control sex conduct, one might expect that the legal sanctions attached to the various relationships would show an orderly pattern. That nothing could be further from the case is a frequently-noted and often-condemned fact.[2] The wide disparity in definitions of sex offenses and in severity of sanctions reflects, in part, the differential judgment of the seriousness of all sex offenses. In addition, it reflects differing judgments of the *relative* seriousness of differing types of sex relationships. Some understanding of the sources of disparity emerges from consideration of the various and conflicting aims of the criminal law as it applies to sex offenses.

A traditional emphasis views the criminal law as reflecting the moral condemnation of the community. Émile Durkheim's discussion of the universal elements in crime stressed the feature of moral condemnation. Crimes "shock sentiments which, for a given social system, are found in all healthy consciences."[3] Crimes consist "in acts universally disapproved of by members of each society."[4] The image of a homogeneous community reacting through the collective conscience was forcefully presented as the characteristic reaction to crime. A vigorous statement of a similar position has recently been made from a legalistic perspective. Henry M. Hart has defined crime as "conduct which, if duly shown to have taken place, will incur the formal and solemn pronouncement of the moral condemnation of the community."[5] He has voiced the fear that this element may be lost in sentencing procedure, even if retained in the definition of crime, if corrective and rehabilitative emphases predominate.

The element of moral condemnation in sex laws is vividly portrayed in statutes defining "crimes against nature." The very use of such a vague and ill-defined concept is related to the revolting nature of the behavior. Ploscowe has noted a judge's ruling in such a case:[6]

> It was never the practice to describe the particular manner of the details of the commission of the crime, but the offense was treated in the indictment as the abominable crime not fit to be named among Christians. The existence of such an offense is a disgrace to human nature. The legislature has not seen fit to define it further than by the general term, and the records of the courts need not be defiled with the details of the different acts which may go to constitute it. A statement of the offense in the language of the statute is all that is required.

A different basis for the definition and grading of crimes is reflected in the conception that the criminal law should punish only those acts that are socially dangerous, independent of their moral character. The American Law Institute's Model Penal Code[7] and the Wolfenden Report[8] in England have been strongly influenced by this conception in the drafting of recommendations regarding sex offender laws. In recommending the restriction of the crime of fornication to open and notorious acts and those involving adoptive parents and children, the draftsmen of the Model Penal Code justify their position as follows:[9]

> The code does not attempt to use the power of the state to enforce purely moral or religious standards. We deem it inappropriate for the government to attempt to control behavior that has no substantial significance except as to the morality of the action.

Throughout the discussion of code provisions, emphasis is clearly placed on control of behavior that appears to show some immediate social harm, either through the use of violence, through the exploitation of children, or through the nuisance value of public indecency.

The Wolfenden Report reflects a similar concern. It has been noted that "the yardstick applied throughout was utilitarian. If it could

[2] Ploscowe, *op. cit.*, 136–55.

[3] Émile Durkheim, *On the Division of Labor in Society* 73 (George Simpson transl. 1933).

[4] *Ibid.*

[5] Henry M. Hart, Jr., "The Aims of the Criminal Law," *Law and Contemporary Problems*, Vol. 23 (1958), pp. 401, 405. Hart also has emphasized the obligations imposed by community life, although these obligations are only indirectly caught up in his formal definition. See *idem*, pp. 413, 426.

[6] Ploscowe, *op. cit.*, p. 197.

[7] *Model Penal Code*, art. 207 (Tent. Draft No. 4, 1955; Tent. Draft No. 9, 1959).

[8] Committee on Homosexual Offenses and Prostitution, *Report*, CMND No. 247 (1957).

[9] *Model Penal Code*, § 207.1, comment at 207 (Tent. Draft No. 4, 1955).

be proved that the behavior of an individual was socially injurious, he or she must be restrained."[10] Sex offenses are to be distinguished from sins and controlled in accordance with their objective social danger, rather than the degree of moral arousal they bring about.

A third criterion for the establishment of sex legislation has emerged during the past two decades. It is part of the growing influence of rehabilitative concerns on the administration of criminal law. This criterion reflects neither the moral condemnation nor the social danger of the offense; rather, the stress is on the degree of psychopathology characterizing the offender. The influence of this conception has been extended from sentencing and treatment considerations to the definition of antisocial acts. Some of the sex psychopath statutes have allowed commitment up to life for persons showing such characteristics as "emotional instability, impulsiveness, lack of good judgment, failure to see consequences of act, irresponsibility in sex matters. . . ."[11] Clearly, the emphasis is on personal qualities of the offender, rather than on the seriousness of any particular act.

Finally, there is increasing recognition of the important practical criterion of enforceability. The lack of visibility of most forms of sexual relations between consenting partners means that detection and arrest are nearly impossible for the vast number of cases. Such lack of enforceability may become another basis for judgment of selection of legal sanctions. Practical problems of enforcement are reflected in Model Penal Code recommendations concerning adultery and in discussion of the possible withdrawal of penal sanctions for deviate sexual intercourse between consenting adults.[12]

Current sex statutes reflect these varying aims of the criminal law. They do not fit a single dimension of social evaluation, but instead catch up in differing degrees the aims of expressing (a) the community's sense of moral condemnation or revulsion; (b) the degree of social harm resultant from the act; (c) the degree of psychopathology characterizing the offender; or (d) by omission, the practical problem of enforcement. Thus, it is no surprise that our sex laws are inconsistent and contradictory. A consistent criminal code for sex offenders is unlikely to emerge until there is agreement on the fundamental aims of the criminal law in this area.

C. Trends and Problems

The Model Penal Code and the Wolfenden Report give evidence of a movement toward a consistent framework for the criminal law regarding sex offenses. As noted, this framework places the social-danger criterion at the apex of the aims of the criminal law, assigns a lesser but important role to the aim of enforceability, and restricts the expression of the moral condemnation of the community to such cases as are also viewed as socially dangerous. This shift away from a moral emphasis presents some problems that deserve brief mention.

A chief difficulty in implementing a criterion of moral condemnation lies in the diversity of moral sentiment in modern communities. Durkheim's conception of a universal response to deviance was perhaps overdrawn, even for primitive communities. It seems particularly unrealistic in application to contemporary western societies. The very changes that were indexed by the growth of restitutive law have brought about also a change in the collective response to criminals. Increasing social differentiation makes it difficult to find acts that are universally condemned. To speak of moral condemnation of *the community* is to use the term community in a very loose sense. It may apply to certain acts of violence and to crimes against children. Beyond these areas are many actions where no single community opinion can be said to exist. Responses to gambling laws, to white-collar violations, or to sex offenses between consenting partners depend heavily on the cultural background of the offender or of the person making the judgment. These influences play upon processes of adjudi-

[10]Eustace Chesser, *Live and Let Live* (1958), p. 116.

[11]From a 1949 Indiana statute, as described in California Department of Mental Hygiene, *Final Report on California Sexual Deviation Research 45* (1954).

[12]*Model Penal Code*, 277–78 (Tent. Draft. No. 4, 1955).

cation and help to produce the great disparity in sentencing policies in different jurisdictions. Thus, the conception of a homogeneous community response, as implied by the moral condemnation argument, fails to square with contemporary life.[13]

In the face of these problems, the aim of limiting criminal sanctions to socially dangerous acts has great appeal. It purports to avoid the problem of differing moral judgments by establishing an objective standard of social danger; if acts surpass a certain minimal level, they are to be defined as crimes and graded as to severity according to the degree of danger involved.

The difficulties in working out such a formulation are evident in parliamentary response to the Wolfenden Report recommendations on homosexuality. There appeared to be general acceptance of the argument that conduct not injurious to society falls outside the legitimate concerns of the criminal law. But members of the House of Commons were uncertain that homosexuality between consenting adults was not injurious. There was fear that others might easily be corrupted if the act is not criminal—that persons will be willing to experiment with homosexual relations.[14] There was also the fear that removing the legal sanctions might imply condonation of homosexuality.[15]

Thus, even though there is no clear and present danger of bodily harm or corruption of morals in acts between consenting adults, there is always the possibility of long-term harmful consequences. Arguments to this effect can always be made and are hard to refute on empirical grounds, especially where the effects, if any, are likely to be subtle and only shown over a long time span. Although the history of legal control of sex conduct is largely one of failure,[16] this fact is a commentary on the problem of enforceability of the law; it does not, of itself, establish anything about the degree of social danger of the conduct. It is always possible to argue, as members of Parliament did, that conditions could be worse were the laws not on the books.[17]

This suggests something of the circular relationship likely to be maintained between social danger and moral condemnation as factors influencing public discussions and legislative decisions. The shift to an emphasis on the secular harms of various acts withdraws attention from their moral character. But in the absence of any clear-cut criterion of social danger, moral considerations will enter into and influence the perception of what is or is not socially dangerous. Until the consequences for society of various types of sex relationships are better known, changes in sex legislation will have to be based

---

[13]*Cf.* Fuller, "Morals and the Criminal Law," *Journal of Criminal Law and Criminology*, Vol. 32 (1942), p. 624. Evidence on variation in sentences comes from a variety of sources and is summarized in Glueck, "Predictive Devices and the Individualization of Justice," *Law and Contemporay Problems,* Vol. 23 (1958), p. 463.

[14]Murray, "Commons Debate on the Wolfenden Report," 122 *Justice.* p. 816 (1958).

[15]"Wolfenden Report in Parliament," 1959 *Criminal Law Review* (Eng.) 38. The recommendations of the Wolfenden Committee are discussed in greater detail elsewhere in this symposium. Hall Williams, *Sex Offenses: The British Experience, infra* pp. 334–60.

[16]All authorities are in agreement on the failures of legal controls, and the evidence is well known. Most states have almost no prosecutions under fornication, seduction, or adultery statutes. To quote Ploscowe, "Nowhere are the disparities between law in action and law on the books so great as in the control of sex crimes." Morris Ploscowe, *Sex and the Law* (1951), p. 155. Nor is this a recent phenomenon. Geoffrey May cites data for the town of Groton, Mass., showing extremely high rates of fornication during the height of puritanism in the colonies. Geoffrey May, *Social Control of Sex Expression* (1930), p. 254. When the Model Penal Code discussions review problems of enforceability, fairly good evidence for the claims is presented. When the discussions concern possible secular harms, claims are based largely on argument and opinion. See, *e.g.*, the discussion of adultery, *Model Penal Code,* §207.1, comment at 204–10 (Tent. Draft No. 4, 1955).

[17]A similar problem is evident in discussions about the effectiveness of correctional techniques. It is fashionable to think of the "new penology" as based on rational, scientific investigation; yet, there is little evidence that current techniques are any more effective than those used in the past. Increasingly, evaluative research is carried out to test the effectiveness of various programs. Even the best of the studies are subject to methodological weaknesses that make for ambiguity in results, so that interpretations may be made consistent with the ideology of the interpreter. See Cressey, "The Nature and Effectiveness of Correctional Techniques," *Law and Contemporary Problems,* Vol. 23 (1958), p. 754.

largely on changes in attitude and ideology, rather than on compelling evidence.

II. SOCIAL NORMS AND SEXUAL CONDUCT

The Kinsey volumes provided the first detailed account of sexual practices in the United States.[18] Public interest in the reports revealed the high degree of curiosity and anxiety aroused by the topic. But precisely because the subject of sex calls forth anxieties and fears, there has been a tendency for behavioral scientists to shy away from the systematic study of sexual attitudes and norms. No study of social norms regarding sexual conduct comes close to matching in quantitative detail the knowledge about sex acts contained in the Kinsey volumes. The result is that we have only meager evidence concerning the social evaluation of sexual conduct, as distinguished from the conduct itself.

Such evidence as is available comes from a variety of sources. The Roper Fortune Surveys have included a few items on sex attitudes in their national sample surveys over the past twenty-five years. Attitude questionnaires have been administered to select samples of individuals, primarily college students. Some case studies of particular communities or subcultures yield a modicum of data on normative patterns. Finally, inferences can be drawn from certain gross features of societal concern for sex relationships.

The data bear upon three questions frequently raised in discussions of sex mores: Is there evidence of a trend toward increasing permissiveness? Are there widespread subcultural differences in social norms regarding sexual conduct? Do the norms bear a close relationship to sexual behavior?

A. Trends in Values

Changes in American values during the twentieth century point to a widespread increase in sexual permissiveness, at least as gauged by the increasing freedom and lack of restraint in discussing sexual matters. Instead of the "Society for Sanitary and Moral Prophylaxis," the mid-twentieth century has a "Society for the Scientific Study of Sex." The pervasive influence of Freudian conceptions and the interest generated by the studies of Havelock Ellis are indicators of the same trend. The change has received support in modifications of obscene literature statutes, as brought forth most vividly in the recent case involving *Lady Chatterley's Lover*.[19] Although commentaries speaking darkly of a "sex revolution" pervading every aspect of social life seem highly overdrawn,[20] there is abundant evidence of increasing public attention and discussion of sexual codes.[21]

There is a vast difference, however, between the change in mores allowing greater freedom of discussion and a change reflecting either greater approval or a higher incidence of particular types of sex relationships. It is more difficult to find solid evidence for the latter type of change. Kinsey's data suggested, for instance, that the major change in rates of premarital intercourse for females occurred with those born between 1900 and 1910. Women born during the period from 1910 to 1930 had roughly the same pattern as those born during the first decade of the twentieth century.[22] And while younger-generation males had slightly higher rates of premarital intercourse with companions, the difference was largely offset by relatively more frequent contacts with prostitutes

[18] Alfred C. Kinsey, Wardell B. Pomeroy and Clyde E. Martin, *Sexual Behavior in the Human Male* (1948) [hereinafter cited as *Kinsey Male Report*]; Alfred C. Kinsey, Wardell B. Pomeroy, Clyde E. Martin and Paul H. Gebhard, *Sexual Behavior in the Human Female* (1953) [hereinafter cited as *Kinsey Female Report*].

[19] *Kingsley Int'l Picture Corp.* v. *Regents,* 360 U.S. 684 (1959).

[20] Pitirim A. Sorokin, *The American Sex Revolution* (1956).

[21] A major review of changes in American values shows increasing discussion of sex and a rising interest in extramarital relationships revealed in content analyses of best sellers. See Kluckhohn, "Have There Been Discernable Shifts in American Values during the Past Generation?", in Elting E. Morrison, *The American Style* (1958), p. 145. For changes of a similar sort during earlier decades, see Newcomb, "Recent Changes in Attitudes Toward Sex and Marriage," *American Sociological Review,* Vol. 2 (1937), p. 659. For interesting essays on the subject, see Abram Kardiner, *Sex and Morality* (1954).

[22] *Kinsey Female Report,* pp. 242–46.

TABLE 4.1

"DO YOU THINK IT IS ALL RIGHT FOR EITHER OR BOTH PARTIES TO A MARRIAGE TO HAVE HAD PREVIOUS SEXUAL INTERCOURSE?"

	1937	*1959*
All right for both	22%	22%
All right for men only	8%	8%
All right for neither	56%	54%
Don't know or refused to answer	14%	16%
	100%	100%

among the older-generation males.[23] The incidence of homosexuality and adultery also remained relatively constant, although suggesting slight intergenerational changes for different segments of the population.[24]

Caution must be used in interpreting these findings, for there are well-known methodological problems in the Kinsey volumes, the most important being the use of nonprobability sampling, volunteer subjects, problems of recall among the older respondents, and the possible differences between reported and actual behavior.[25] Within these limitations, the findings give no indication of significant changes in the gross features of sexual conduct since the 1920's.

Studies of the social evaluation of sexual conduct reveal a similar pattern. Impressionistic accounts of changes in the mores suggest that intercourse outside of marriage is increasingly viewed as an acceptable form of conduct. Unfortunately, there is no solid empirical evidence that can be used to evaluate this claim over a long time span, for objective methods of attitude and opinion assessment were not in use prior to the 1930's. The best available evidence for a more recent period consists in responses of national samples to an item asked in 1937 and again in 1959 by the Roper polling agency. If major changes in attitudes have occurred during the past twenty years, this fact should be revealed in the Roper data.

The question asked on both polls was: "Do you think it is all right for either or both parties to a marriage to have had previous sexual experience?"[26] Responses are indicated in Table 4.1. The results show a surprisingly stable pattern over the past two decades. When it is remembered that the period spanned included publication and widespread discussion of the two Kinsey volumes, it is apparent that the fears voiced in some quarters—that knowledge of the Kinsey results may have widespread effect on sexual standards—have not materialized.

It is, indeed, risky to base a conclusion on such limited evidence. Other interpretations than that of stability could be given. There may have been widespread shifts in opposite directions for different segments of the population, such that they cancel out in the summary findings. There may have been important changes of such a subtle nature that they are not reflected by a single item on an opinion poll. The results may be reliable, but may have caught the population at particular points in a cycle of sexual attitudes, thus giving a false appearance of stability. All of these interpretations are possible and cannot be refuted without

[23]*Kinsey Male Report,* pp. 411–13.

[24]*Ibid.,* pp. 413–17.

[25]An excellent review of the methodological problems in the Kinsey report on males is provided by William G. Cochran, Frederick Mosteller and John Tukey, *Statistical Problems of the Kinsey Report* (1954). These authors discuss the problem of establishing the stability of sexual patterns and caution against drawing more than tentative conclusions. *Ibid.,* p. 141.

[26]The 1937 data are from "The Fortune Quarterly Survey: VIII" *Fortune,* April 1937, pp. 111, 188–90. The 1959 results were supplied to the writer by Phillip K. Hastings, Director, The Roper Public Opinion Research Center, Williams College, Williamstown, Mass. Results from these surveys demonstrate the dangers in inferring trends from comparison of older and younger generations at a single point in time. In both surveys, the older generation were somewhat less approving. The trend data suggest that this is largely a function of age, rather than a changing climate of opinion.

further evidence. The simplest interpretation, however, is that there has been little over-all change in attitudes toward this form of sexual conduct over the period spanned by the studies.[27]

B. Socioeconomic Status and Sex Attitudes

One argument frequently raised in support of a change in legal controls is that communities are no longer homogeneous with respect to sexual standards—that the wide range of standards held in different segments of the population precludes application of universalistic legal standards. Kinsey's data are usually cited in support of this contention.[28] The most important of Kinsey's findings for present purposes are the variations in rates of premarital intercourse and in techniques of sexual arousal. Kinsey found that rates of premarital intercourse for males were highest at low educational levels and were considerably lower among the college-educated segment of his population.[29] At the same time he found that lower-level couples were likely to restrict their sexual contacts to the most direct form of sexual union, while upper-level couples employed a wide variety of coital techniques, mouth and breast stimulation, and manual and oral forms of genital stimulation. For example, oral stimulation of female genitalia was found in sixty per cent of the college-educated segment, but in only twenty and eleven per cent of the high-school and grade-school histories, respectively.[30] The direction of these relationships suggests that sex statutes limiting premarital intercourse are most frequently violated by lower-class members, while statutes defining various forms of heterosexual perversions are more likely to be violated by middle- and upper-level persons.

There is little systematic evidence to determine whether the normative patterns are consistent with the differential incidence rates for perversions. Kinsey suggests that his lower-level respondents viewed with disgust some of the petting and coital practices of middle- and upper-level persons, although systematic evidence is lacking. The pattern, if verified, is an interesting reversal of the usual view that legal standards of sexual conduct reflect a middle-class morality.

More evidence is available concerning the social evaluation of premarital intercourse at differing socioeconomic levels. Between 1939 and 1943, the Roper agency asked questions about sexual attitudes in three of their sample surveys.[31] Typical results are reported in Tables 4.2 and 4.3. The question for Table 4.2 was: "Do you consider it all right, unfortunate or wicked when young men (women) have sexual relations before marriage?" For Table 4.3, the question was: "Should men (women) require virginity in a girl (man) for marriage?" Variation in response by socioeconomic status is similar in both tables, although the strength of the relationships varies with the wording of the question.[32] The relationship is also found when occupation is used as the relevant variable.

---

[27]Studies of moral values among samples of college students provide some evidence of change over recent decades. One study compared the responses of students in 1939 and in 1956 on an instrument designed to assess the perceived importance of certain characteristics in the ideal marriage mate. It found a decline in the importance attributed to chasity consistent with an assumed change from traditional to romantic and companionship factors as bases for mate selection. McGinnis, "Campus Values in Mate Selection: A Repeat Study," *Social Forces,* Vol. 36 (1958), p. 368. A similar study, however, notes an increase in the severity of moral judgment regarding forms of promiscuity. See Rettig and Pasamanick, "Changes in Moral Values among College Students: A Factorial Study," *American Sociological Review,* Vol. 24 (1959), p. 24. While the increase in severity of judgment on three items dealing with sex was less than that for many other items, the values are still quite strong. For instance, "having illicit sex relations after marriage" was judged a more severe moral transgression than "nations at war using poison gas on the homes and cities of its enemy behind the lines"; or "a legislator, for a financial consideration, using his influence to secure the passage of a law known to be contrary to public interest."

[28]*Model Penal Code,* § 207.1, comment at 206–07 (Tent. Draft No. 4, 1955).

[29]*Kinsey Male Report,* p. 347.

[30]*Ibid.,* pp. 576–77.

[31]I wish to acknowledge the aid of the Roper Public Opinion Research Center in making the data available for analysis.

[32]The socioeconomic labels are interpreted from an index used by the Roper agency and may not match the distinctions made in other studies. These distributions probably fail to catch the extreme top and bottom of the socioeconomic scale, where different patterns might emerge. Data are for white respondents only.

TABLE 4.2

"Do You Consider It All Right, Unfortunate or Wicked When Young Men (Women) Have Sexual Relations Before Marriage?" (Women Only; N = 5220)

Socioeconomic Status	*Wicked for Men*	*Wicked for Women*
Upper	28%	36%
Upper-middle	34%	43%
Lower-middle	40%	50%
Lower	53%	62%

TABLE 4.3

"Should Men (Women) Require Virginity in a Girl (Man) for Marriage?" (Women Only; N = 2570)

Socioeconomic Status	*Men Should Require in Women*	*Women Should Require in Men*
Upper	64%	42%
Upper-middle	66%	47%
Lower-middle	71%	53%
Lower	72%	52%

Among males, the proportion who felt such activity was wicked increased from twenty-six per cent among white-collar and professional workers to thirty, thirty-five, and thirty-six per cent among blue-collar, unemployed, and farmers respectively.

What is surprising about the Roper results is not the degree of variation by social class, but its direction. Those in lower social strata are more likely to express disapproval of intercourse outside of marriage than are those in middle and upper positions. This is precisely the reverse of the direction for the behavioral record as found by Kinsey and others. The discrepancy could be due to such factors as a greater tendency among lower-class respondents to give what they perceive as socially desirable responses to middle-class interviewers, or the correlation of social class with religion or other variables. Certainly, the data are not strong enough to accept the finding as confirmed; yet, it does call into question the inference, frequently drawn by Kinsey's interpreters, that the social-class differences in rates are strongly supported by class differences in sex attitudes and values.[33]

There are reasons to believe that the relationship between overt sex acts and cultural values is much more complex than is usually presumed. Thus, a growing body of research has documented the higher degree of intolerance for deviant behavior among those of low education and socioeconomic position.[34] The response to sex may be part of the broader tendency to see the world in a good-evil dichotomy. The tendency is reinforced by the dogmatism of fundamentalist religious groups likely to flourish and have greatest appeal to those in lower social strata.[35] Class differentials in tolerance for sexual

[33] Kinsey's own interpretations frequently were based on this assumption. Other examples are included in Jerome Himelhoch and Sylvia Fava, *Sexual Behavior in American Society* (1955), pp. 175–205.

[34] Samuel A. Stouffer, *Communism, Conformity, and Civil Liberties* (1955), pp. 89–108; Lipset, "Democracy and Working Class Authoritarianism," *American Sociological Review*, Vol. 24 (1959), p. 482.

[35] See Liston Pope, *Millhands and Preachers* (1942).

expression are also indicated in recent studies of child-rearing patterns. Working-class mothers are found to be far less permissive and to use more punitive measures for preventing sexual exploration.[36] These findings would lead one to expect greater rather than less disapproval at lower socioeconomic levels.

At the same time, the objective life situation of lower socioeconomic groups may predispose them to greater pressure for engaging in the activity. Thus, studies of lower-class urban areas point to the frequency of female-based households in which if the mother is to have any normal sexual outlet, it becomes, by definition, adultery.[37] The greater amount of premarital intercourse among lower-class girls may reflect less a difference in stated values than the use of sex as a means of attracting males of higher status, in the absence of alternative qualities of attraction.[38] A related and important feature concerns differences in the use and effectiveness of social-control techniques. For example, the more punitive methods of child-rearing used in lower socioeconomic strata may be less effective in producing long-term internal controls, even though parental attitudes may be similar to those in other strata.

All of these features may operate to suppress the effect of cultural values on overt conduct. One of the reasons the relationships between socioeconomic status, sex attitudes, and sex behavior are not yet clearly understood is that they are probably quite complex, involving differential pressures for engaging in the behavior and different mechanisms of control. A particular pattern of conduct emerges from many social influences and is rarely a simple reflection of stated cultural values. These influences are frequently neglected in drawing conclusions from the Kinsey research.[39]

C. Other Structural Characteristics and Sex Attitudes

Considerable variation in sex attitudes is revealed when characteristics other than social class are studied. Even a single question on a public opinion poll reveals important differences in attitude by race. Where roughly fifteen per cent of the white females said that premarital intercourse for males was "all right," twenty-nine per cent of the Negro females gave that response. The differences in tolerance for women who engaged in the same behavior ranged from roughly five per cent for white respondents to seventeen per cent for Negroes.[40] Evidence on sex behavior leaves no doubt that the attitudinal differences are carried out in action. A study of army recruits located seven virgins among 500 Negro draftees.[41] Studies of illegitimate birth point to the extremely high rates for Negro girls in urban areas.

Kinsey's results revealed the influence of religious affiliation on sexual attitudes and behavior. Increasing rates of premarital intercourse are observed as one moves from Jewish to Catholic to Protestant groups. For each religious grouping, the proportion of women voicing regret for having premarital intercourse was greatest among the most active believers.[42]

---

[36] Robert R. Sears, Eleanor E. Maccoby and Harry Levin, *Patterns of Child Rearing* (1957), p. 428.

[37] See Miller, "Implications of Urban Lower-Class Culture for Social Work," *Social Service Review*, Vol. 23 (1959), p. 225; see also Allison Davis and John Dollard, *Children of Bondage* (1940), pp. 272–90.

[38] See Kanin and Howard, "Postmarital Consequences of Premarital Sex Adjustments," *American Sociological Review*, Vol. 23 (1958), p. 558; see also Ehrmann, "Influence of Comparative Social Class of Companion upon Premarital Heterosexual Behavior," *Marriage and Family Living*, Vol. 17 (1955), p. 48.

[39] A related point of misinterpretation hinges on Kinsey's use of an accumulative-incidence curve, which reflects single acts engaged in only during childhood, or perhaps on only one occasion as an adult. One can hardly assume that because an act has been committed at least once by the majority of the population, it is, therefore, regarded as culturally acceptable. Yet, this argument has apparently been used in court cases. See Himelhoch and Fava, *op. cit.*, pp. 244–50. On this basis, one would withdraw a large proportion of penal legislation, at least as it applies to males, including that governing tax evasion, malicious mischief, auto misdemeanors, disorderly conduct, and larceny. See Wallerstein and Wyle, "Our Law Abiding Law-Breakers," *Probation*, Vol. 25 (1947), p. 107.

[40] In response to the question reported in Table 4.2 *supra*.

[41] Hohman and Schaffner, "The Sex Lives of Unmarried Men," *American Journal of Sociology*, Vol. 52 (1947), p. 501.

[42] *Kinsey Female Report*, p. 319.

Regional and rural-urban differences are revealed in recent opinion poll results: permissive attitudes are highest in the urban Northeast (twenty-eight per cent), followed by the Far West (twenty-six per cent), the South (twenty-three per cent), and the Mid-west (fifteen per cent).[43] The same data also indicate that the double standard applies most clearly to Southern manhood. Thirteen per cent of the Southern respondents, compared to about five per cent in the other areas, say that premarital sex is "Okay for men only."

The above review of variation in social norms in differing sectors of society is probably a conservative statement of the actual variation, for it has been impossible to assess the combined effect of the several characteristics. At the same time, citation of percentages engaging in this or that conduct or holding particular attitudes tends to obscure the general lack of clarity of sex codes. With the exception of certain extremes found among particular ethnic or religious subcultures, it is probably fair to say that no single normative pattern is institutionalized in any large segment of the population, let alone the society as a whole. The wide variation in response to the Kinsey volumes gives abundant testimony to this fact.[44]

In part, the lack of clarity of sex codes is due to the specificity of sex attitudes. Whether premarital intercourse is viewed as acceptable or not depends on many features of the relationship between the couple. The sociologist William F. Whyte noted that Italian street-corner boys made a clear differentiation between "good girls," with whom intercourse was prohibited, and "lays" with whom it was highly desirable.[45] Studies of college students and middle-class sexual patterns suggest that intercourse is more acceptable to girls if part of a love relationship, while males are less likely to view it as acceptable under those conditions (although at any point, of course, premarital intercourse for males is considered more acceptable than for females).[46] Until recently, the social scientists' concern with sexual attitudes and conduct was limited largely to the gross features of such conduct as revealed by frequency counts and general opinion. The meaningful context of the behavior or attitude was seldom studied in detail. The growth of a body of knowledge about the meaning of the activity for participants should provide a more useful set of empirical findings on the social distribution of sex attitudes and behavior.[47]

A more pervasive influence is the lack of visibility of sex attitudes and behavior. To an important degree, no one knows what standards others are employing. Enough life remains in the puritan ethic to prevent persons from expressing their attitudes openly. This quite naturally produces a condition of pluralistic ignorance. Without this element, it would be hard to account for the amazing public interest in the Kinsey reports. And so long as the condition remains, it will be impossible to achieve any genuine normative consensus.

D. Homosexuality

Little can be said about attitudes toward other forms of sexual relations between consenting adults. While much has been written about the homosexual problem, there is almost no objective information on the degree of public tolerance for homosexuals or on conceptions of the desirability of penal sanctions as a means of control. Although mass responses are still shroud-

---

[43]From the 1959 Roper survey reported in Table 4.1, *supra*.

[44]See Palmore, "Published Reactions to the Kinsey Report," *Social Forces*, Vol. 31 (1952), p. 165.

[45]Whyte, "A Slum Sex Code," *American Journal of Sociology*, Vol. 49 (1943), p. 24.

[46]Ehrmann, "Premarital Sexual Behavior and Sex Codes of Conduct with Acquaintances, Friends and Lovers," *Social Forces*, Vol. 38 (1959), p. 158.

[47]One of the major complaints in popular literature about the Kinsey research was the overly biological orientation and lack of attention to love and affection as basis for sex relationships. Some of Kinsey's results as well as those of other investigators suggest, however, that where the abstinence standard no longer exists, the emerging standard permits coitus when part of a stable, affectionate relationship. See Reiss, "The Treatment of Pre-Marital Coitus in "Marriage and the Family" Texts," *Social Problems*, Vol. 4 (1957), p. 334. An interesting recent study finds a high degree of ego involvement in premarital sexual relationships, particularly among middle-class women, and suggests some of the conditions that encourage intimacies, for females in the middle and upper socioeconomic strata. See Vincent, "Ego-Involvement in Sexual Relations: Implications for Research on Illegitimacy," *American Journal of Sociology*, Vol. 65 (1959), p. 287.

ed in mystery and fear, the trend is surely toward a more enlightened, dispassionate perspective.[48]

Some inferences as to sources of changing perspectives can be drawn from other studies of tolerance toward deviance. As noted above, an increasing body of research suggests that tolerance toward nonconforming behavior may be a relatively general trait that may cut across many specific forms of deviation.[49] Tolerance is greatest among the younger generation and those with most education. The sociologist Samuel Stouffer's report on political nonconformity found tolerance also greater among community leaders.[50]

Whether these results hold for attitudes toward sexual nonconformity can only be determined by further study. The findings at least suggest the important sectors of the population that may be least resistive to changes of the type recommended by the Wolfenden Report in England. While such proposals are probably still in advance of public opinion, the forces making for greater tolerance are likely to remain and should be a sign of hope for supporters of more liberal legislation regarding homosexuals.[51]

E. Need for More Adequate Information

Review of objective data on social norms and sexual conduct reveals above all else the paucity of useful information. Aside from an occasional item in an opinion poll, a handful of studies of college students, and one or two anthropological accounts, there is nothing that even makes for intelligent speculation as to the sources and types of community reaction to sexual deviations between consenting adults. Such evidence as is available suggests that while there has been no great change in *standards* of sexual conduct at least over the past twenty years, there is a general trend toward greater *tolerance* of various forms of sexual relationships. Some of the more recent proposals for change in legislation invoke distinctions between mental illness, crime, and sin that major segments of the public are probably not yet prepared to understand or accept. Perhaps the single most important factor making for public recognition of these distinctions is the increase in average level of education.

The outstanding fact remains that no major study has been made of attitudes and norms regarding sex conduct. Any conclusions must be tempered by awareness of the flimsy evidence on which they are based. Within this arena of ignorance, the American Law Institute is attempting to design new legislation concerning sexual behavior. Important recommendations are being decided at least partially on the basis of guesses as to how the public or legislative officials will react.[52] Consideration of controversial proposals could benefit from

[48]Contributing to and reflecting this trend is an increasing willingness on the part of some homosexuals to make their problems a matter for public concern. See, *e.g.*, Peter Wildeblood, *Against the Law* (1956). And note the signs of incipient pressure-group formation in the following quotation from the trade journal, *One,* published in Los Angeles: "No American Politician regards as humorous a million votes. . . . Let's say the membership dues are . . . fifty cents a month . . . six dollars a year . . . multiply that by a million and you have the gigantic fighting strength . . . $6,000,000. . . . Nobody will care whose money it is . . . that of screaming pansies, delicate decorators or professional wrestlers. Nobody will give a damn because this is the U.S.A. and money talks. . . ." From the Sept. 1953 issue of *One,* as quoted in James M. Reinhardt, *Sex Perversions and Sex Crimes* (1957), p. 32.

[49]See authorities cited, note 34 *supra*. These results refer largely to response to behavior clearly defined as deviant. Whether a given pattern of behavior is recognized as deviant in the first place is a related, but separate, issue. At least in regard to mental illness, there is some evidence that lower-class persons with little education are less likely to recognize a particular behavior as that of a mentally-ill person than are more educated, middle-class persons. See August B. Hollinghead and F. C. Redlich, *Social Class and Mental Illness* (1958), pp. 171–93.

[50]Stouffer, *op. cit.*, pp. 26–57.

[51]Trends consistent with those noted above have been found for one item on sex criminals taken from a national survey. In response to the question: "What do you think is the best thing to do with sex criminals, send them to a hospital or a jail?," the younger and more educated were much more likely to choose the hospital. Significantly, a majority at all educational levels favored the hospital, as did a majority in all age groups up to age 45. See Woodward, "Changing Ideas on Mental Illness and Its Treatment," *American Sociological Review,* Vol. 16 (1951), p. 443.

[52]See the discussion of proposed changes in legislation regarding deviate sexual intercourse. *Model Penal Code,* § 207.5, comment at 276-81 (Tent. Draft No. 4, 1955).

more adequate information on public attitudes.[53]

III. THE SEX OFFENDER

Certain types of sex offenders are either a danger to the community or a nuisance that the community need not tolerate. Their offenses include rape, indecent liberties, exhibitionism, and incest, as well as a variety of related acts. The conception that sex offenders are different from any other types of law violators has led to legislation that results in a placement of sex offenders in a kind of limbo, somewhere between the criminal and the mentally ill. The remainder of this paper directs attention to the problems raised by sex offender legislation and to some possible sociocultural factors in the genesis of sex deviation.

A. History and Critique of Sex Offender Laws

Legislation defining sex psychopaths and establishing administrative procedures for their custody, treatment, and release was passed by some thirteen states between 1937 and 1950, and has been extended to other states since that time. Procedures leading up to the legislation were similar in the different jurisdictions. In a review of the development of sex psychopath laws, the late criminologist Edwin Sutherland noted a sequence characterized by (a) arousal in a community of a state of fear as a result of a few serious sex crimes, (b) agitated community response, leading to (c) the appointment of a committee that gathered information and made recommendations that generally were uncritically accepted by state legislatures.[54] The work of the committees proceeded largely in the absence of facts. Sutherland noted that the laws embodied a set of implicit assumptions that were explicit in much of the popular literature on sex offenses. These included the notion that all sex offenders were potentially dangerous, that they were very likely to repeat their offenses, that they can be accurately diagnosed and efficiently treated by psychiatrists. The laws were passed in the name of science, although there was little scientific evidence as to the validity of the assumptions underlying the statutes.

The act of passing the statutes set in motion the kind of data-gathering process that was needed to establish adequate legislation in the first place. Some of the legislation required study of the effectiveness of the statutes along with studies of sex offenders. These studies drew attention to the weaknesses of the legislation.

Many of the criticisms have been presented in reports prepared for state legislatures and will be mentioned only briefly here.[55] The label "sex psychopath" is so vague as to make administration of statutes unreliable.[56] Sex offenders are less likely to repeat their crimes than are other types of offenders.[57] Very few sex offenders present a grave social danger.[58] Current diag-

[53]To be sure, there are weaknesses and pitfalls in the gathering and interpretation of opinions on controversial issues. But these problems are well known to experts in opinion-research and are subject to increasing control. One need not suggest that public opinion replace legislative and judicial opinion in order to see the value that can come from knowledge of public attitudes, especially in areas where presumed public response is explicitly considered in making important decisions. For a recent study and discussion of the use of opinion surveys and their application to one area of legal concern, see Julius Cohen, Reginald A. H. Robson and Alan Bates, *Parental Authority: The Community and the Law* (1958). This is not to suggest that public opinion studies are the only or necessarily the most appropriate means of establishing the relationship of public opinion to legal process. The University of Chicago Jury Project is one instance of a much different approach that promises to reveal some of the areas of agreement and disagreement between the response of judge and of jury to certain types of offenses. See Broeder, "The University of Chicago Jury Project," *Nebraska Law Review*, Vol. 39 (1959), p. 744.

[54]Sutherland, "The Diffusion of Sexual Psychopath Laws," *American Journal of Sociology*, Vol. 56 (1950), p. 142.

[55]Reports with retailed analyses of sex offender statutes and experience in their use include Paul W. Tappan, *The Habitual Sex Offender* (1950) (prepared for the state of New Jersey); California Department of Mental Hygiene, *Final Report on California Sexual Deviation Research* (1954) [hereinafter cited as *California Report*]; Governor's Study Commission, *Report on the Deviated Criminal Sex Offender* (Michigan, 1951).

[56]Tappan, *op. cit.*, pp. 36–42; *California Report*, pp. 20–38.

[57]Tappan, *op. cit.*, pp. 22–25. Tappan cites a New York study that found that only 7% of convicted sex offenders were re-arrested for sex offenses over a 12-year period. A recent California study also found 7% sex recidivism among sex offenders. See Frisbie, "The Treated Sex Offender," *Federal Probation*, March 1958, p. 18.

[58]Tappan, *op. cit.*, pp. 20–22. See also Albert Ellis and Ralph Brancale, *The Psychology of Sex Offenders* (1956), p. 32.

nostic techniques are incapable of distinguishing reliably between the potentially dangerous and those that are not dangerous.[59] There has been no test of the assumption that treatment techniques are effective in rehabilitation of sex offenders.[60]

Given these findings, it is not surprising that members of the legal profession were reluctant to approve of the usual procedures for administration of the statutes. Significantly, the opposition was not along lines usually assumed to separate legal from psychiatric viewpoints: a free-will, punitive orientation *versus* deterministic, permissive orientation. Rather, the criticism has been directed to the possible denial of due process to offenders. Since the statutes typically called for commitment up to life, even for minor offenses, the usual safeguard of a maximum sentence was missing. In addition, the administrative procedure for release, frequently requiring certification that the offender was no longer a danger to the community, made release very difficult. Administrators were understandably reluctant to assert that the patient was cured.[61]

While these problems signify dissatisfaction with many of the procedures built into the earlier statutes, there is still no common agreement on the most appropriate solutions. Some states have dropped the label "sex psychopath" from their statutes, have restricted the scope of the statutes to more serious offenders, and have required that the offender be held no longer than the maximum sentence under traditional criminal provisions. One of the problems posed by these changes is illustrated by the experience in Massachusetts. Massachusetts revised its psychopathic personality statute in 1954. The new law discarded the term "psychopath" and included the requirement that an offender must be released at the expiration of his maximum sentence. The law was deemed inadequate after a double murder was committed by an offender whose release from the state reformatory could not be prevented by provisions of the 1954 act. The law was quickly amended to allow for indefinite commitment up to life for certain types of sex offenders.[62]

The case points to a familiar problem in the visibility of mistakes in the processing of offenders. Errors made in releasing men too early are publicly observable. Under a statute allowing commitment up to life, however, errors made in keeping men who may, in fact, be cured cannot be tested, because by the nature of the procedure, they are not given a chance either to succeed or to fail. While every failure of early release may come to public attention, errors of keeping men too long cannot be detected. Such errors may be quite frequent in the absence of accurate diagnostic procedures. There is always the danger of undue restriction of civil liberties in attempts to provide adequate protection to the community.

B. Development Careers of Sex Offenders

Perhaps the single most important outgrowth of recent experience with sex statutes is that we are now aware of how little reliable knowledge is available. Until recently, the major source of ideas about sex offenders stemmed from clinical reports on a wide variety of sex deviants. The case materials have filled most of the books written on sexual deviation.[63] Although the cases may enrich clinical understanding, they do not provide an adequate basis for the development of sound administrative procedures. The clinical interpretations stand logically not as fact, but as hypotheses requiring test.[64]

---

[59]For a beginning in this direction, see *California Report*, pp. 142–47.

[60]Tappan, *op. cit.*, pp. 15–16. Of course, a major problem has been that treatment has been almost totally lacking. Many states have passed laws requiring treatment without establishing treatment facilities. Beyond this, however, any treatment technique will have to be very effective if it is to reduce significantly the rate of recidivism, for the rate is already quite low.

[61]Tappan, *op. cit.*, p. 34.

[62]Edwin Powers, *The Basic Structure of the Administration of Criminal Justice in Massachusetts*, United Prison Association of Massachusetts, Res. Div. Rep. No. 5 (1957), pp. 15–17.

[63]Benjamin Karpman, *The Sexual Offender and His Offenses* (1954); Joseph Paul De River, *The Sexual Criminal* (1950); Reinhardt, *op. cit.*

[64]For a clear, concise statement of the needs and uses of controls in psychiatric research, see Committee on Research, Group for the Advancement of Psychiatry, Rep. No. 42, *Some Observations on Controls in Psychiatric Research* (1959). Neglect of the distinction between fact and hypothesis is illustrated in the following exchange in a discussion of a paper on sex psychopaths written by the psy-

Since the cases are drawn from an unknown population of offenders, there is no adequate basis for generalization. And since adequate control groups are not employed, any claims as to therapeutic effectiveness are claims, and no more. They remain untested.

The impetus to research provided by the sex psychopath statutes has resulted in knowledge that calls into question some of the earlier clinical findings. While the research is still at a descriptive rather than an experimental stage, it has been effective in casting doubt on assertions that all or almost all sex offenders are highly disturbed. Systematic study of 300 offenders committed to the diagnostic facility in New Jersey showed that on the basis of psychiatric diagnoses, fully forty-three per cent of the offenders were classified as normal or only mildly neurotic.[65] This raises the question of what distinguishes the psychiatrically normal from the abnormal sex offender. More broadly, are there systematic differences in the developmental careers of different types of sex offenders? Suggestions of such differences are apparent in recent research.

A distinction can be made between aggressive and passive offenders. The former usually commit offenses involving attempted or completed intercourse with a legitimate sexual object—*i.e.*, a person of the opposite sex beyond the age of puberty. Most rapes and sexual assaults fall in this category. The passive offenses include exhibitionism and noncoital sex play with children. In terms of physical danger, the former category presents the most serious social problem. The sex statutes were passed largely to control the violent acts of rape and sexual assault. Yet, available evidence suggests that as a group, such offenders are less likely to exhibit clear-cut pathological symptoms and may have more in common with nonsexual offenders than with the passive sex deviants.

The report on sex offenders processed through the New Jersey diagnostic center provides information on the characteristics of offenders classified by type of offense. Selected findings from the study are reproduced in Table 4.4 for the offense categories falling most clearly at the aggressive and passive poles.[66]

The aggressive offenders are more likely to be judged normal by psychiatric diagnosis. They are less inhibited sexually and tend to give fewer indications of severe emotional disturbance. Fewer of them are judged to have been exposed to severe emotional deprivation during childhood. Significantly, their prior arrest histories show few sexual offenses, but many nonsexual offenses. The ratio of nonsexual to sexual offenses is much higher for the aggressive than for the passive offenders. Finally, they are much more likely to show signs of hostility, a characteristic most common among property offenders from delinquent or criminal subcultures.[67]

Evidence from the California studies of sexual deviation supports the pattern noted above. Case descriptions of the most serious and aggressive sex offenses committed by delinquents in San Francisco revealed that over half of the cases were gang-motivated. Furthermore, of the thirty-seven serious offenders studied, half had previous records for nonsexual offenses, only three had previous sex arrests. Reading of the case descriptions further shows that the gang attacks were most frequently directed toward

chiatrist Benjamin Karpman. One of the discussants, Albert Ellis, suggested that Karpman's propositions should be regarded as hypotheses rather than facts, and that evidence for some of them was lacking; to which Karpman replied: "I deny these allegations in toto. All of my statements are based on *actual clinical material;* I do not have one bit of theory." Karpman, *op. cit.*, pp. 511–12, 525.

[65] Ellis and Brancale, *op. cit.*, p. 94.

[66] See *ibid.*, pp. 34, 38, 42, 46, 49, 56, 62. Two of the major categories excluded from the above review are statutory rape and incest. Ellis and Brancale provide convincing evidence of the essential normality of statutory rape offenders, and support the conclusions of Ploscowe and others that the age limit in such cases should be reduced. Evidence on incest cases suggests, as would be expected, that offenders are more like the aggressive than the passive offenders in terms of social and criminal background.

[67] The findings of the New Jersey study are, of course, subject to many weaknesses commonly found in sex offender research. As the authors of the study note, there is no way of knowing how their sample differs in background from sex offenders sentenced to state prisons or from those who are undetected. The number of cases is much too small, especially for the rapists, to place much confidence in the results. The characterizations of offenders, with the exception of prior arrest data, are undoubtedly colored by knowledge of which type of offense they committed.

TABLE 4.4

DIFFERENCES BETWEEN AGGRESSIVE AND PASSIVE SEX OFFENDERS ON SELECTED CHARACTERISTICS*

	Diagnosed Normal or Mildly Neurotic	*Commitable to Mental Institution*	*Over-inhibited*	*Severe Emotional Disturbance*
Aggressive offenders				
Sex assault	48	24	48	48
Forcible rape	38	25	50	63
Passive offenders				
Noncoital sex play with children	20	45	66	66
Exhibitionists	30	29	72	63

	Previous Arrest for Sex Offenses	*Previous Nonsex Arrests*	*Underlying Hostility*	*(No. of Subjects)*
Aggressive offenders				
Sex assault	14	48	72	21
Forcible rape	12	50	75	8
Passive offenders				
Noncoital sex play with children	51	43	35	51
Exhibitionists	34	23	25	89

*Each column contains the percentages of each type of offender characterized as indicated by column headings. Thus 30% of the exhibitionists were diagnosed normal or only mildly neurotic. Number of cases on which the percentages are based appear in the lower right column.

girls in middle or late adolescence, while the offenses against very young sexual objects were more likely to be committed by lone offenders.[68]

Ethnic differences in rates of sex offenses give further support to this pattern. The California research showed that Negroes and Mexicans were overrepresented in the rape category, underrepresented in offenses against children.[69] The New Jersey experience suggested that Negro sex offenders were less emotionally disturbed than their white counterparts.[70] Both of these findings are consistent with studies of racial differences in homicide rates and suggest the influence of cultural differences in restraints on the use of violence to resolve interpersonal affairs.[71]

The evidence thus suggests that the typical aggressive sex offender may be less "sick" than is usually supposed. Their backgrounds have much in common with nonsexual offenders who come from crime-inducing cultural settings. Instead of conceiving of their conduct as resulting from a highly specific and grossly deviant sexual motivation, it is perhaps more valid to view their offenses as part of a broader behavior system in which force may be used to attain their goals. It is the use of force, rather than any specifically deviant sexual motivation, that distinguishes these offenders from those who fall within the law.[72] Psychiatric study has revealed

[68]*California Report,* pp. 132–35.

[69]*Ibid.,* pp. 101–02.

[70]Ellis, Doorbar and Johnston, "Characteristics of Convicted Sex Offenders," *Journal of Social Psychology,* Vol. 40 (1954), p. 14.

[71]Marvin E. Wolfgang, *Patterns in Criminal Homicide* (1958), p. 329.

[72]The psychiatrist Richard L. Jenkins has observed that "the difference between the law-abiding man and the rapist lies typically not in a difference of sex impulse, but in a difference of inhibition and consideration for the personality of others." Jenkins, "The Making of a Sex Offender," in Clyde B. Vedder, Samuel Koenig and Robert E. Clark, *Criminology* (1953), pp. 293, 295. The above observations seem consistent with this view, but are at variance with psychiatric analyses, which see even statutory rape as fundamentally tied up with the oedipus complex, representing an unconscious attack upon the parent. See, *e.g.,* David Abrahamsen, *Who Are the Guilty?* (1952), pp. 184–85. Any theory that seeks to interpret sex aggression as a highly neurotic or psychopathic act must consider the prevalence of aggressive sexual acts among presumably normal populations of college students.

the frequency with which sexual motivations underlie such nonsexual crimes as arson and certain types of burglary. The suggestion here is that the reverse may hold for certain types of aggressive sex offenders. In a society stressing active mastery of the environment over passive acquiescence, perhaps it is not surprising that the aggressive sex offender who overresponds is judged less disturbed than the passive exhibitionist.[73]

Brief mention may be made of two additional points where sociological conceptions usually applied to nonsexual offenses may have bearing on deviant modes of sexual response. One of these points concerns the way in which the social structure exerts pressure on persons to use deviant means of achieving culturally acceptable goals. High rates of deviance are presumed to occur among those segments of the population that are least fortunately situated in terms of their abilities to achieve valued goals by legitimate means.[74] The same conception is applicable to the achievement of sexual gratification. Prisons are, of course, an extreme case of a structure that promotes deviant means of sexual outlet. But less extreme instances are in evidence as well. Thus, two studies note high rates of incest in rural populations, where the choice of alternatives to the wife, given dissatisfaction with her performance, is severely limited.[75] And prostitution flourishes in lumber and mining areas and in the central sectors of cities, where the sex ratio is abnormally high. These illustrations remind us that the availability of legitimate sexual outlets is itself socially-structured; resort to deviant outlets will reflect these structural features and need not be conceived solely as a result of faulty personality makeup.

Second, the dyadic character of many types of crime means that the victim may play more than a passive role. Wolfgang's recent study of Philadelphia homicides revealed that fully twenty-six per cent were victim-precipitated.[76] Similar findings might result from careful study of those convicted of rape, where the offense frequently follows an evening of drinking and mutual sexual arousal. Consideration of the victim's role means that the offense can be viewed as a product of a social situation; its explanation cannot easily be reduced to a search for the childhood emotional disorders of the party who becomes labeled the offender.[77]

These observations suggest some ways in which sociocultural and situational features may be related to deviant sexual behavior. Assumptions that direct attention solely to psychogenic factors may lead to an inaccurate conception of the causal processes involved, and hence to treatment programs that neglect important sources of the deviation. Specifically, further research may reveal that many aggressive sex offenders are responding to culturally learned patterns of aggression and to situational factors that are unlikely to be relieved by the usual methods of clinical psychotherapy. Patterns of cultural learning as well as psychogenic disorders may be reflected in their offenses. This may partially explain why such offenders are deemed generally less amenable to treatment than the less dangerous but more disturbed passive offenders.[78]

Sociological conceptions of crime are heavily

See Kanin, "Male Aggression in Dating-Courtship Relations," *American Journal of Sociology,* Vol. 63 (1957), p. 197. The Kanin article points to some of the factors that may prevent these cases from becoming officially labeled as felonious aggressions.

[73]The culture of prison inmates provides insight into the differences between aggressive and passive sex offenders. No special status is conferred on aggressive offenders or those convicted of statutory rape. In fact, the latter are viewed as having "bum beefs" as a result of "pick on your own size" laws designed to allow promiscuous teen-agers to get off the hook when they become pregnant. Offenders who engage in nonviolent sex acts with children, on the other hand, are relegated to the bottom of the social structure and referred to in derogatory terms as "rapos"—so afraid of women they had to pick on children.

[74]See Robert K. Merton, *Social Theory and Social Structure* (rev. ed. 1957), pp. 131–94.

[75]John Lewis Gillen, *The Wisconsin Prisoner* (1946), pp. 107–16; Reimer, "The Background of Incestuous Relationship," in Vedder, Koenig and Clark, *op. cit.*, p. 301.

[76]Wolfgang, *op. cit.*, p. 245.

[77]The Model Penal Code expresses recognition of these elements in suggesting that where a woman loses capacity to control her own conduct by voluntary use of intoxicants or drugs, any resulting intercourse cannot be charged as rape, although it can be under most existing statutes. *Model Penal Code,* § 207.4, comment at 248–49 (Tent. Draft No. 4, 1955).

[78]Ellis and Brancale, *op. cit.*, p. 78.

influenced by the sociologist's concern for the impact of culture and social organization. These elements are revealed most clearly in such types of offenses as professional crime, white-collar crime, and gang delinquency. Some of the evidence reviewed above suggests that there may be important sociogenic features in the development of certain types of sex offenders, and that further study could profit from an interdisciplinary approach to the problems posed by such offenders. The growing need for systematic knowledge should lead to research designed to reveal the combined influence of sociogenic and psychogenic sources of sexual deviation. Such research may suggest inadequacies in the conception that most sex offenders are a special breed of criminal requiring unique laws and administrative procedures for their control.

13.

MORRIS PLOSCOWE

SEX OFFENSES: THE AMERICAN LEGAL CONTEXT

A rational code of sex offense laws is long overdue in this country. Sex offense legislation presently on the books is largely unenforceable and much of this legislation does a great deal more harm than good. There are a number of fundamental reasons for this. In the first place, the prohibitions imposed by these laws are far too inclusive, covering far too many areas of sexual behavior. These laws make potential criminals of most of the adolescent and adult population, in that they proscribe every conceivable sexual act except a normal act of coitus between a man and a woman who are married to each other or an act of solitary masturbation. They, of course, prohibit not only the more innocuous kinds of sexual behavior engaged in by normal adults and adolescents, but also aberrant sexual behavior that may be dangerous. Thus, not only heavy necking, mutual masturbation, fornication, and adultery, but also forcible rape, forcible sodomy, incest, and the sexual abuse of small children are interdicted by these laws.

One goal of sex offense laws is to keep individuals chaste before marriage. Until then, individuals must not give overt expression to any sexual desires, except possibly through solitary masturbation; sex drives must be kept in check, under pain of incarceration.

After marriage, too, the law attempts to confine sexual activity. Thus, a married individual may not look for sexual liaison with other than his or her spouse, however embittered or distasteful their relations may have become. And should his or her spouse be in jail, in the country or overseas, or living separate and apart, a married individual must figuratively fasten on a chastity belt. Adultery may open the door to the penitentiary.

Nor is adultery the only invitation to sanctions for married individuals. Since time immemorial, men and women have engaged in what are politely called aberrant sex practices; nor are many of them—for example, oral-genital contacts—the exclusive usages of homosexuals and lesbians, but commonly may be indulged in a normal marital relationship. Indeed, most modern marriage manuals no longer view such practices with alarm as perversions, but rather consider them to be permissible preludes to normal coitus. The law, however, usually takes a different view and subjects participants in such acts to a possible felony conviction.

Reprinted with permission from a symposium, *Sex Offenses: The American Legal Context*, appearing in *Law and Contemporary Problems* (Vol. 25, No. 2, Spring 1960), published by the Duke University School of Law, Durham, North Carolina.

When American sex offense legislation is compared with the analogous law of Tudor England, one cannot but conclude that the modern American is considerably more naïve than were his English ancestors. Only a small part of the sexual behavior legally proscribed here today was prohibited by the criminal law of Tudor England. Forcible rape, sexual intercourse with a female under ten, the sexual corruption of children, lewd and indecent acts in public, bestiality, buggery, the maintenance of houses of prostitution, too, might be punishable under the old English criminal law; but large areas of sexual behavior—for example, fornication, adultery, incest, fellatio, cunnilingus, mutual masturbation—were beyond the reach of the law and were punishable only as sins or ecclesiastical offenses by the Church of England. Since the ecclesiastical courts were not received in this country, our laws, therefore, initially provided no institutionalized means for dealing with sexual behavior that had been ignored by the common law. But the lacunae did not long remain, for legislators, prodded by moralistic constituents, rushed to fill these gaps. And, as we have seen, they have succeeded only too well.

It was apparent to most serious observers long before the Kinsey studies[1] that our sex offense laws were honored more in the breach than in the observance. Few branches of the law have shown such a wide divergence between actual human behavior and stated legal norms. Nor should this be surprising. Sexuality simply cannot realistically be confined within present legal bounds. It does not mysteriously blossom when a man and a woman are united in holy matrimony; nor, despite legal prohibitions, is it thereafter restricted to conventional acts of coition between marital partners.

The wide-ranging character of the prohibitions of sex offense laws and the almost universal disregard that they are accorded elicited the following biting comment and criticism from Dr. Kinsey.[2]

All of these and still other types of sexual behavior are illicit activities, each performance of which is punishable as a crime under the law. The persons involved in these activities, taken as a whole, constitute more than 95 per cent of the total male population. Only a relatively small proportion of the males who are sent to penal institutions for sex offenses *have been involved in behavior which is materially different from the behavior of most of the males in the population.* But it is the *total 95 per cent* of the male population for which the judge or board of public safety, or church, or civic group demands *apprehension, arrest, and conviction,* when they call for a clean-up of the sex offenders in a community. It is, in fine, a *proposal that 5 per cent of the population should support the other 95 per cent in penal institutions.*

The writer has pointed out elsewhere[3] that this conclusion that ninety-five per cent of the male population could be jailed because of violations of sex offense laws is an exaggeration. It presupposes that such legislation is uniform throughout the country, that all sexual activity except solitary masturbation and normal marital intercourse is universally prohibited, and that these laws invariably prescribe jail and prison sentences for their violation. This, however, is not so. One of the most remarkable features of American sex offense laws is their wide disparity in types of sexual behavior prohibited and their extraordinary variation in penalties imposed for similar offenses.

Fornication, a common form of premarital sexual activity, is prohibited by a majority of state laws; but it is deemed only a meretricious transaction in many states[4] and is there beyond the reach of police, prosecuting attorneys, and jailers.[5] Where fornication is prohibited, penalties provided by law vary from a ten-dollar fine in Rhode Island[6] to a three-year prison sentence in Arizona.[7]

---

[1]Alfred C. Kinsey, Wardell B. Pomeroy and Clyde E. Martin, *Sexual Behavior in the Human Male* (1948); Alfred C. Kinsey, Wardell B. Pomeroy, Clyde E. Martin and Paul H. Gebhard, *Sexual Behavior in the Human Female* (1953).

[2]Alfred C. Kinsey, Wardell B. Pomeroy and Clyde E. Martin, *Sexual Behavior in the Human Male,* (1948), p. 392. (Emphasis added.)

[3]Morris Ploscowe, *Sex and the Law* (1951) p. 137.

[4]See, e.g., *Rachel* v. *State,* 71 Okla. Cr. 33, 107 P.2d 813 (1940).

[5]In at least 10 states—Louisiana, Michigan, Missouri, New Mexico, New York, Oklahoma, South Dakota, Tennessee, Vermont, and Washington—fornication is not statutorily proscribed.

[6]*R. I. Gen. Laws Ann.,* § 11-6-3 (1956).

[7]*Ariz. Rev. Stat. Ann.,* § 13–222 (1956). For a summary survey of the penalties imposed by the fornication statutes of the several states, see Robert Veit Sherwin, *Sex and the Statutory Law,* pt. 1, chart 5 (1949), p. 83.

Adultery is more widely prohibited than fornication, although the prohibition is by no means universal.[8] But among the states that do prohibit it, the same kinds of sexual misbehavior are not necessarily encompassed. In some states, a single act of coitus between a married individual and one who is not his or her spouse constitutes culpable adultery;[9] in others, however, the adultery must be "open and notorious" or "habitual" before the criminal statute is deemed violated.[10] In some states, an unmarried party to such a connection is deemed to be guilty of adultery;[11] in others, however, he or she would seem to be guilty of no more than fornication.

Generally, penalties for adultery are more severe than those for fornication, but they also vary considerably. Some states impose no penalties of imprisonment for adultery and make this offense punishable only by a fine;[12] in others, however, penalties of up to five years of imprisonment may be meted out for this offense.[13]

The crime of rape also differs greatly among the several states. In all states, it embraces much more than the forcible violation of the sexual integrity of a female, including as well conduct to which the female may have consented. In this latter connection, it should be noted that the age over which a female is regarded capable of consenting to coitus varies widely. The common-law age of consent of ten years has been discarded by modern statutes. An age limit of sixteen or eighteen years is now most common, although some states place it as low as twelve years,[14] and another, going to the other extreme, places it at twenty-one years.[15]

Other differences in the definition of rape and in the scope of its statutory prohibition may also be noted. In some states, the lack of chastity of an underage female may be a defense to the charge of rape;[16] in others, however, a conviction may still be had even if she was operating as a prostitute.[17] Some states, also, make allowance for the age of the male,[18] but most statutes are silent on this point. Moreover, in addition to such wide substantive differences as these among the several states as to what constitutes rape, there is also considerable disparity as to penalties. Death or life imprisonment may await a rapist in some states; other states, however, taking a more charitable view of his dereliction, may impose varying terms of imprisonment.[19]

Modern crime-against-nature and sodomy statutes and those interdicting lewd and lascivious behavior include most deviate sexual activity within the scope of their prohibitions. Nevertheless, there are differences here, too, among the several states, especially in the treatment of mutual male masturbation. This conduct is prohibited in many states, whether it occurs publicly or privately; in some, however, it is prohibited only if it occurs in a public place.[20] Penalties under sodomy and crime-against-nature statutes vary enormously as well. Thus, a consensual homosexual act between adults is only a misdemeanor in New York;[21] but it may be punishable by life imprisonment in some

[8]In at least five states—Arkansas, Louisiana, Nevada, New Mexico and Tennessee—adultery is not statutorily proscribed.

[9]See, e.g., *People* v. *Reed*, 246 App. Div. 895 (N.Y. 4th Dep't 1936).

[10]See e.g., *Warner* v. *State*, 202 Ind. 479, 483, 175 N.E. 661, 663 (1933): ". . . it is well settled that our present statute does not prohibit . . . acts 'of adulterous intercourse . . . of an occasional character, unaccompanied by any pretense of the parties living together.' . . . The design of this law is not to affix a penalty for the violation of the Seventh Commandment, but to punish those who, without lawful marriage, live together in the manner of husband and wife." *Cf. State* v. *Chandler*, 132 Mo. 155, 33 S.W. 797 (1896).

[11]E.g., *N.Y. Pen. Law*, § 100.

[12]These fines range from a minimum of $10 in Maryland, *Md. Ann. Code*, art. 27 § 4 (1957); to a possible maximum of $2,000 in Michigan. *Mich. Comp. Law*, §§ 750.30, 750.503 (1948).

[13]E.g., *Conn. Gen. Stat. Rev.*, § 53–218 (1958); *Me. Rev. Stat. Ann.*, ch. 134, § 1 (1954); *Okla. Stat.*, tit. 21, § 872 (1951); *S.D. Code*, § 3892 (1939); *Vt. Stat.* tit. 13, ch. 5, § 201 (1958). For a summary survey of the penalties imposed by the adultery statutes of the several states, see Sherwin, *op. cit.*, pt. 1, chart 7, p. 85.

[14]E.g., *Ala. Code* tit. 14, § 398 (1940); *La. Rev. Stat.* § 14:41 (1950).

[15]E.g., *Tenn. Code Ann.*, § 39–3706 (1955).

[16]E.g., *N.C. Gen. Stat.*, § 14–26 (1953); *Tenn. Code Ann.*, § 39–3706 (1955); *W. Va. Code*, ch. 61, art. 2, § 15 (1931).

[17]See, e.g., *State* v. *Snow*, 252 S.W. 629 (Mo. Sup. Ct. 1923).

[18]E.g., *N.Y. Pen. Law*, § 2010; *S.C. Code* § 1111 (1952).

[19]For a summary survey of the penalties imposed by the rape statutes of the several states, see Sherwin, *op. cit.*, pt. 1, chart 5, p. 85.

[20]E.g., *N.Y. Pen. Law*, § 722(8).

[21]*Ibid.*, § 690.

states,[22] a five-year minimum imprisonment in others,[23] and a five-year maximum imprisonment in still others.[24]

Even the age-old offense of prostitution shows considerable variation in treatment. Most statutes define prostitution as the indiscriminate offer by a female of her body for sexual intercourse or other lewdness, for the purpose of gain or hire; but in many states, indiscriminate and promiscuous sexual intercourse, even *without gain or hire,* may be prostitution.[25] Many states, moreover, make it possible to punish the customers of prostitutes, as well, either directly by specific statutory provisions[26] or indirectly by an extension of aiding-and-abetting statutes;[27] but other states refuse to punish customers, even though there can be no prostitution without them. While prostitutes are generally punishable by imprisonment of less than one year, there are notable exceptions, with maximum sentences running from thirty days[28] to five years.[29]

The fact that sex offender laws vary so widely among the several states and value judgments as to the danger of similar offenses differ so greatly (as reflected in the range of penalties imposed) is a compelling reason for framing a rational uniform code in this area. We are not a congeries of individual states, each isolated within a water-tight compartment. Modern means of transportation and communication have made state boundaries largely meaningless. American men and women are continually upon the move. They should not be exposed to the risk of being branded felons in one state for sexual behavior that may be legally innocuous in another. They should not be subjected to the possibility of long prison sentences or even death in some states for behavior that may be punishable by only fines or short jail sentences in others, or not even punishable at all. The time has come when the lawyers should attempt to bring some order out of the chaotic profusion and variety of sex offender laws that now obtain.

The revision of sex offender laws, however, will require much more than the mere elimination of disparities and differences among the several states; it must also consider the fact that many of the existing prohibitions, no matter how widespread, are inherently unenforceable and should be abandoned. Police and prosecuting officials may successfully investigate and prosecute criminal cases where a victim makes a complaint or where the criminal activity is more or less overt in character. But sexual activity is largely private. There is no victim to make a complaint in the ordinary case of fornication, adultery, or deviant heterosexual or homosexual activity. Despite criminal sanctions, therefore, sexual misbehavior of this sort, when carried on privately and discreetly, is practically never punished. It is only the rare unfortunate offender who comes to the attention of the authorities; and although he is no more guilty than the hundreds of thousands of others who have freely indulged in similar kinds of sexual activity, he is pilloried because he was caught. Should police and prosecuting officials be burdened with enforcing such laws against such offenders?

A rational code of sex offender laws would, moreover, basically revise some of our present concepts in this area. Thus, for example, although force, violence, and overpowering of the will of a female by violence, threat, or fear of bodily harm would continue to be the core of the crime of rape, it is to be hoped that the new formulation would not comprehend those cases where a man may have used considerable effort to persuade a woman to engage in coitus with

---

[22]E.g., *Nev. Rev. Stat.,* § 201.190 (1958); *Mich. Comp. Laws,* § 750.158 (1948).

[23]E.g., *Ariz. Rev. Stat. Ann.,* § 13–651 (1956); *Idaho Code Ann.,* § 18–6605 (1948); *Mont. Codes Rev. Ann.,* § 94–4118 (1947); *N.C. Gen. Stat.,* § 14–177 (1943); *Tenn. Code Ann.,* § 39–707 (1956).

[24]E.g., *Ky. Rev. Stat.,* § 436.050 (1955); *La. Rev. Stat.,* § 14:89 (1950); *N.H. Rev. Stat. Ann.,* § 579:9 (1955); *Wis. Stat.* § 944.17 (1957). For a summary survey of the penalties imposed by the sodomy statutes of the several states, see Sherwin, *op. cit.,* pt. 1, chart 4, p. 82.

[25]E.g., *Conn. Gen. Stat. Rev.,* § 53–226 (1958); *Del. Code Ann.,* tit. 11, § 731 (1953); *Fla. Stat.,* §796.07 (Supp. 1959); *N.C. Gen. Stat.,* § 14–203 (1953); *Tex. Pen. Code,* art. 607(20) (1948); *Wyo. Comp. Stat. Ann.,* § 9–508 (1945).

[26]E.g., *Conn. Gen. Stat. Rev.,* § 53–231 (1958); *Ill. Rev. Stat.,* ch. 38, § 162 (1957); *Ind. Ann. Stat.,* § 10–4219 (1956); *Wyo. Comp. Stat. Ann.,* § 9–517 (1945).

[27]*Cf. State* v. *Rayburn,* 170 Iowa 514, 153 N.W. 59 (1915).

[28]E.g., *Ind. Ann. Stat.,* § 10–4220 (1956); *Wyo. Comp. Stat. Ann.,* § 9–518 (1945).

[29]E.g., *Iowa Code,* § 724.1 (1958). For a summary survey of the penalties imposed by the prostitution statutes of the several states, see Sherwin, *op. cit.,* pt. 2, chart 4A, p. 68.

him, where this was the normal and expected outcome of their association together. Moreover, since most rape convictions involve consensual acts of coitus with young girls, with no element of force or violence, it has long been apparent that the legal age of consent must be reduced. Many girls of fifteen, sixteen, and seventeen years of age voluntarily enter sexual relations with men and boys. Each such sexual contact may technically be rape under some law and may subject the male involved to ferocious penalties, although except for the age of the girl involved, the act may be no different than fornication.

At common law, the lack of appreciation and understanding by a child under ten years of the nature and quality of the sexual act—and her consequent inability to consent to it—was justifiably assimilated to the force and violence and overpowering of the will in the traditional definition of the crime of rape. In our desire to shield young women from sexual experience, we have extended the age limits upward. It is absurd in our culture, however, to talk of young women of middle or late adolescence not having knowledge and appreciation of the sexual act. Such knowledge is usually acquired by the time of puberty. The law should, accordingly, take a more realistic view and fix the age of consent at fourteen years, instead of the higher limits that are more commonly found. Should the legislator wish to protect the morals of young women over fourteen years of age, this can be done by means other than branding as a rapist every male who may dally with them.

But whether or not the age of consent is reduced, it is imperative that the lack of chastity of the young woman be deemed a defense to a charge of statutory rape. It is ridiculous for the police to charge with rape every male who may have had sexual contact with a promiscuous young woman or a young prostitute. The law should, moreover, take into account the age of the male involved in defining this offense. Boys and girls of similar ages engage in many forms of sex activity, and if this leads to coitus, the boy should not necessarily be exposed to penal sanctions.

Also vitally essential in any revision of sex offender laws is a reconsideration of the evidentiary rules, so as to minimize the possibility of convicting innocent defendants. Complaints of sex offenses are easily made. They spring from a variety of motives and reasons. The psychiatrist and the psychoanalyst would have a field day were he to examine all complaints of rape, sexual tampering with children, incest, homosexual behavior with young boys, deviant sex behavior, etc., in any given community. He would find that complaints are too often made of sexual misbehavior that has occurred only in the overripe fantasies of the so-called victims. Frequently, the more or less unconscious wish for the sexual experience is converted into the experience itself. Sometimes, too, the so-called victim will charge not the one with whom he or she has had the sexual experience, but someone else who is entirely innocent. Prosecuting attorneys must continually be on guard for the charge of sex offense brought by the spurned female that has as its underlying basis a desire for revenge, or a blackmail or shakedown scheme.

Where the law permits, as it does with respect to many sex offenses, a conviction on the uncorroborated testimony of a complainant, it puts a premium on unfounded complaints. There is no barrier against convicting the innocent, except the good sense of prosecuting attorneys, courts, and jurors. But the moral indignation that is stirred up by a recital of dastardly behavior apparently often overrides good sense, and as a result, far too many men have been railroaded on sex offense charges. Accordingly, no conviction on a sex offense charge should be had where the testimony of the so-called victim is not corroborated by "other material evidence." It is true that such a requirement may result in guilty men escaping just punishment in cases where other evidence is not available. But the dangers involved to innocence where the law makes it possible to imprison a man on the uncorroborated testimony of a disturbed child or spiteful woman outweigh the necessity for obtaining convictions in sex offense cases.

Any revision of sex offender laws must also repeal much of the sexual psychopath legislation that is presently in force. These laws were passed to provide a means for dealing with dangerous, repetitive, mentally abnormal sex offenders. Unfortunately, the vagueness of the definition of sexual psychopaths contained in these statutes has obscured this basic underlying purpose. There are large numbers of sex offenders who engage in compulsive, repetitive sexual acts, which may be crimes, who may be mentally abnormal, but who are not dangerous. The transvestite, the exhibitionist, the frotteur, the homosexual who masturbates another either in the privacy of his bedroom or in a public toilet, the "peeping tom"—are typical of large numbers of sex offenders who are threatened with long-term incarceration by present sexual psychopath legislation. And what is even worse is that such legislation has not usually been implemented by facilities for treatment. The result is that many nuisance-type, nondangerous sex offenders have been imprisoned for long periods of time, without treatment, in those jurisdictions where such laws have been enforced. This is not to say that the compulsive nondangerous types of sex offenders should be immune from prosecution and punishment; but short sentences or probation are more than adequate to deal with these derelictions, unless better treatment facilities are provided.

In scooping up minor compulsive sex offenders, moreover, sight has been lost of the basic objective of sexual psychopath laws—namely to provide long-term incarceration for dangerous, repetitive sex offenders. Such offenders will be found primarily among those who show a pattern of using children as sexual objects and those whose sex offenses are marked by incidents of sadism and brutality. Such individuals can be dealt with just as effectively by traditional methods of law enforcement as under sexual psychopath laws. Obviously, the law should provide long-term prison sentences for dangerous sex offenders—up to life imprisonment, if necessary. It should permit such offenders to be paroled only on a showing of demonstrated improvement and rehabilitation. It should permit such offenders liberty only under the continued supervision of a parole officer and should facilitate their re-incarceration, if they exhibit signs of relapse into the kinds of sexual misbehavior that brought about their incarceration in the first instance.

These are but a few of the many problems that must be met in any revision of sex offender laws. Many have already been considered by the American Law Institute in its Model Penal Code project.[30] The specific recommendations that have eventuated cannot be analyzed here, but they deserve consideration by those interested in more rational sex offender legislation. The Institute is to be commended for undertaking so controversial a task that characteristically generates far too much heat, stirs entirely too much emotion. Radical departures from existing law in this area conceivably may imperil the acceptance of the Model Penal Code as a whole, and caution might have dictated the deletion of sex offenses from the agenda. Accordingly, it is to the credit of the Institute that it has met the challenge openly and is laying the basis for a more rational code of sex offender laws than is to be found on the statute books of any state.

[30] *Model Penal Code,* art. 207 (Tent. Draft. No. 4, 1955; Tent. Draft. No. 9, 1959).

14.

MAURICE LEZNOFF AND WILLIAM A. WESTLEY

THE HOMOSEXUAL COMMUNITY

The significance of homosexuality in our society has been minimized and obscured by the force of social taboo. Yet there is evidence that homosexuals are distributed throughout all geographical areas and socio-economic strata. Furthermore, the subjection of homosexuals to legal punishments and social condemnation has produced a complex structure of concealed social relations which merit sociological investigation. The psychological isolation of the homosexual from society, his dependence upon other deviants for the satisfaction of sexual needs and self-expression, the crystallization of social roles and behavior patterns within the deviant group, the reciprocal obligations and demands within the homosexual community, and their significance for the larger society in which they occur, are but a few of the areas of theoretical interest to the sociologist.

In this paper we shall confine our discussion to the social organization of one homosexual community and its constituent social groups: their function, etiology, and interrelationships.

The report is based upon an intensive study of 60 homosexuals in a large Canadian city. The data consist of four-hour interviews with 40 homosexuals and briefer interviews with 20 others.[1] In addition, the data include information based on the observation of many homosexual parties and gatherings in bars and restaurants, and a series of 30 letters written by one homosexual to another.

SOURCE: *Social Problems*, Vol. 3, No. 4 (April, 1956), pp. 257–63, The Society for the Study of Social Problems. Reprinted by permission of the authors and the journal.

The authors are indebted to the Canadian Social Science Research Council and to the McGill University Research Fund for grants in support of this study.

[1]Access to this homosexual community was obtained through a client at a social welfare agency.

FUNCTIONS OF HOMOSEXUAL GROUPS

The primary function of the homosexuai group is psychological in that it provides a social context within which the homosexual can find acceptance as a homosexual and collective support for his deviant tendencies. Most homosexuals fear detection and are often insecure and anxious because of this. The following statement illustrates this:

> The thought that you are "gay" is always with you and you know it's there even when other people don't. You also think to yourself that certain of your mannerisms and your ways of expression are liable to give you away. That means that there is always a certain amount of strain. I don't say that it's a relief to get away from normal people, but there isn't the liberty that you feel in a gay crowd. When I associate with normal people I prefer very small groups of them. I don't like large groups and I think I try to avoid them when I can. You know, the only time when I really forget I'm gay is when I'm in a gay crowd.

To relieve this anxiety the deviant seeks collective support and social acceptance. Since the homosexual group provides the only social context in which homosexuality is normal, deviant practices moral, and homosexual responses rewarded, the homosexual develops a deep emotional involvement with his group, tending toward a ready acceptance of its norms and dictates, and subjection to its behavior patterns. The regularity with which he seeks the company of his group is a clear expression of this dependency.

A prohibition against sexual relationships within the group, in a manner suggestive of the incest taboo, indicates the extent to which the group culture is oriented to this function. The quotation which follows is indicative of this taboo:

> As far as I know, people who hang around with each other don't have affairs. The people who are

friends don't sleep with each other. I can't tell you why that is, but they just don't. Unless you are married[2] you have sex with strangers mostly. I think if you have sex with a friend it will destroy the friendship. I think that in the inner mind we all respect high moral standards, and none of us want to feel low in the eyes of anybody else. It's always easier to get along with your gay friends if there has been no sex. Mind you, you might have sex with somebody you just met and then he might become your friend. But you won't have sex with him any more as soon as he joins the same gang you hang around with.

Within these groups the narration of sexual experiences and gossip about the sexual exploits of others is a major form of recreation. The narration of sexual experiences functions to allocate prestige among the members because of the high evaluation placed upon physical attraction and sexual prowess. Yet it creates hostility and sexual rivalry. The intense involvement of homosexuals in the results of this sexual competition is illustrated in the following statement which was overheard in a restaurant:

Who wouldn't blow up. That bitch is trying to get her[3] clutches into Richard. She can't leave anybody alone. I wouldn't be surprised if she ended up with a knife in her back. I don't mean to say I'm threatening her. But she's not going to get away with that stuff forever . . . playing kneesies under the table all night long. I had to get her away from Richard. That lousy bitch. From now on she better keep away from me.

An additional function is the provision of a social situation in which the members can dramatize their adherence to homosexual values. Thus, the gossip about sex, the adoption and exaggeration of feminine behavior, and the affectation of speech, represent a way of affirming that homosexuality is frankly accepted and has the collective support of the group. The extreme but not uncommon instance of this is the homosexual institution of the "drag" in which the members of the group dress and make themselves up as women. A good description of a drag is contained in the following letter:

Well, doll, last night was one to remember. Raymond of B. (city) gave me a letter of introduction to one of the local belles. He 'phoned yesterday and we arranged to go out in the evening. Met at my room and proceeded to the Frederick Hotel where I was introduced to my new acquaintances. It was decided to hold a party afterwards, Chez Norman, my new acquaintance. He told me they were supposed to be discontinued but we were going ahead in my honor. And in drag. One queen about 45-50 who is a window dresser brought some materials of fine nylon net, 2 yards wide and changing color across the width from yellow to flaming orange. There must have been about 25 yds. Well, he made his entrance wearing nothing but his shorts and this stuff wound around him and proceeded to do an exotic dance. Included in the costume was a blond wig from one of the store mannequins and artificial tropical fruits. It was something to see. It was very ludicrous to begin with and much more so when you realize that he is by no means graceful and has so much hair on him that I am smooth by comparison. Throughout the evening he kept on making variations of the costume—each becoming briefer until he was down to nothing. Really!

Another one, very slim, put on a pair of falsies, a turban hat to hide short hair, and a dress with a wide flair skirt. Other than hair on the chest which showed, the effect of femininity was so convincing (even his heels) that I promptly lost interest. Actually produced a beautiful effect—the kind of woman I would like if I could. Beautiful dancer, and performed all evening. Later borrowed some of the nylon net of the old queen and did a dance with flowing material and wearing *nothing*, but nothing else.

There were only three of us not in drag, including yrs. truly. But when it came time to leave (not alone, I might add) I couldn't resist flinging about my coat a fox fur which happened to be lying around. Really, my dear, it was quite an affair.

These functions reflect the common needs and problems which homosexuals face in hostile society.

ETIOLOGY: THE EVASION OF SOCIAL CONTROLS

In our society, homosexuality is defined both legally and socially as a criminal and depraved practice and the homosexual is threatened by powerful legal and social sanctions such as imprisonment, physical violence, social and occupational ostracism, and ridicule. Therefore, all

---

[2]A stable social and sexual relationship between two homosexuals is frequently referred to as "marriage."

[3]The substitution of the female for the male pronoun is a common practice within homosexual groups.

homosexuals face the problem of evading social controls. They do this in two predominant ways.

Some pass for heterosexuals on the job and in most of their social relationships. They mix regularly with heterosexuals for business, entertainment, and other social activities. They avoid situations and persons publicly recognized as homosexual for they fear that discovery will threaten their career and expose them to sanctions. This is illustrated in the following statement of a lawyer:

> I know a few people who don't care. They are really pitiful. They are either people who are in very insignificant positions or they are in good positions but are independent. I know of one who is in the retail business. He doesn't care. A lot of the artists don't care. For that reason I have never cultivated the friendship of artists. I just don't get along with anybody who doesn't care. That's why I really can't give you information about those who don't. It's just that I can't afford to get to know them very well, and I try to avoid them. Sometimes personal friends become this way. Then there is a mutual rejection of the friendship. From my point of view I am just no longer interested when they adopt that kind of attitude. From their point of view it means completely living outside of society and they are no longer interested in people who they consider hypocrites.

Others openly admit and practice homosexuality. They usually work in occupations where the homosexual is tolerated, withdraw from uncompromising heterosexual groups, and confine most of their social life to homosexual circles. This attitude is expressed in the following statement by a hairdresser:

> Rosenstein can go to hell as far as I care. She works you to the bone if she can get away with it. She told me I run around the place like a regular pansy. So I told her I am a pansy and if she doesn't like it she can get somebody else to do her dirty work for her. I knew she wouldn't fire me. All the ladies ask for me and I don't have to pretend to nobody.

While the problem of evasion is common to all homosexuals, the mechanisms of evasion present various alternatives. Most homosexuals find themselves compelled to conform outwardly to societal demands. They are conscious of their social position within society and seek such satisfactions as occupational mobility and prestige. They endeavor to retain intimate associations within the heterosexual community, and fear recognition as a status threat. Such homosexuals rely upon secrecy and the concealment of their deviant practices. They will therefore be referred to as "secret" homosexuals. A minority retreats from the demands of society and renounces societal goals. Such individuals will be referred to as "overt" homosexuals.

The mode of adaption is largely dependent upon the extent to which identification as a homosexual is a status threat. While economic status cannot be equated with social status, the individual's position within the work world represents the most significant single factor in the prestige scale. Therefore, the extent to which homosexuality is tolerated in various occupations determines to a great extent the mode of evasion chosen by the homosexual. Thus, there are many occupations, of which the professions are an obvious example, where homosexuals are not tolerated. In other areas, the particular occupation may have traditionally accepted homosexual linkages in the popular image or be of such low rank as to permit homosexuals to function on the job. The artist, the interior decorator, and the hairdresser exemplify the former type; such positions as counter man or bell-hop, the latter. Thus we find a rough relationship between form of evasion and occupation. The overt homosexual tends to fit into an occupation of low status rank; the secret homosexual into an occupation with a relatively high status rank. The relationship is shown in Table 4.5.

DISTINCTIONS BETWEEN THE SECRET AND OVERT GROUPS

The chief distinctions between homosexual groups correspond to the differences in the general modes of evading social controls which homosexuals have developed. Thus, secret and overt homosexuals form distinctive groups.

The distinctions between these groups are maintained by the secret homosexuals who fear identification and refuse to associate with overt homosexuals. This statement by a secret homosexual is illustrative:

> If someone who is gay wanted to be spiteful they could say something in the wrong quarter. Nobody who cared about himself would say anything. The

TABLE 4.5

OCCUPATION OF 40 SECRET AND OVERT HOMOSEXUALS*

*Occupation**	*Secret†*	*Overt*	*Total*
Professional and managerial	13	0	13
Clerical and sales	9	4	13
Craftsmen	2	1	3
Operatives	1	1	2
Service	0	6	6
Artists	0	3	3
Totals	25	15	40

*Except for artists the categories and ranking are those established by the National Opinion Research Center. (2) Artists have been listed as a separate category because they often represent a group which is apart from the status structure of the community.

†The secret homosexuals gave the following reasons for concealment: (a) desire to avoid social ridicule—22 cases; (b) fear of dismissal from the job, or where self-employed, inability to get clients—20 cases; (c) a desire to protect others such as family or friends—18 cases.

trouble is that some don't care. I make it a rule to avoid anybody who is perfectly open about himself. It's easy not to become friendly with those people but it's hard to avoid them entirely. You certainly don't want to snub them because that might make them antagonistic. You just don't call them or see them at social gatherings. But you do meet them at bars and that's where you can be introduced to them. If they remember you and continue to say hello to you on the street, you have to acknowledge them or they might feel that you are trying to snub them.

As a result of this social distance a certain amount of reciprocal hostility has developed between the members of secret and overt groups. This hostility helps maintain the social distance and distinctions between these groups. This is demonstrated in the following statements by an overt and a secret homosexual respectively:

I know some of them because sometimes they stoop down and have an affair with somebody from our gang. They even come to a party over at Robert's once in a while but they never hang around for very long and then you don't see them again. They go over to the Red Room sometimes but we don't have much to say to each other and the same thing happens when we go over to the Burning Flame.[4] We just might say hello. But sometimes they will cruise us and try to take someone home to bed. I think you could say we mix sexually but not socially.

There are some people who I don't like and I wish these people didn't know about me. Then there are the people I don't know too well: people who are obvious or what I uncharitably call the riff-raff. I have always attempted to avoid them and I avoid them now. It is inevitable that you bump into a lot of people you would rather not know. Homosexuals are very democratic people. To achieve their own ends they overlook a lot they wouldn't overlook in other fields. People are bound to each other like a link of a chain. You try to avoid being a link in this chain by carefully choosing.

This poses serious problems for the homosexual who is socially mobile. He is forced to change his primary group affiliations within the homosexual community.

The following statement by the manager of an appliance shop shows how the homosexual tends to change his orientation from "overt" to "secret" as he becomes upwardly mobile.

My promotions have made me more conscious of the gang I hang around with. You see, for the first time in my life I have a job that I would really like to keep and where I can have a pretty secure future. I realize that if word were to get around that I am gay I would probably lose my job. I don't see why that should be, because I know that I'm the same person gay or not. But still that's the way it works. I don't want to hang around with Robert[5] any more or any of the people who are like Robert. I don't mind seeing them once in a while at somebody's house, but I won't be seen with them on the street any more.

Both types of groups were identified and observed in the course of this research. Each group consisted of fourteen members. The descriptions which follow are based on the study of these groups.

SECRET GROUPS

The secret homosexuals form groups which consist of a loose amalgamation of small cliques. Interaction within the cliques is frequent, with members meeting at each other's homes and in bars and restaurants. The clique's structure is a product of the diverse interests and occupations and of the desire to limit homosexual contacts

[4]The Burning Flame refers to a bar which tended to draw its clientele from secret homosexuals; the Red Room was the acknowledged gathering place of overt homosexuals.

[5]Robert is the leader of an overt group of which the respondent was a member at the time he was contacted.

which characterize secret homosexuals. The clique unites its several members in common specialized interests apart from the larger group.

The following chart shows the clique structure and occupational composition of a secret homosexual group.

Clique A	*Clique B*
Lawyer	Clerk-bookkeeper
Personnel manager	Auditing clerk
University student	Assistant office manager
Economist	University student
	Secretary
Clique C	*Clique D*
Stenographer	Accountant
Store manager	Interior decorator
Manager of statistical dept.	

A secret homosexual group is generally characterized by: (a) informal standards of admission; (b) discretion in the manner in which homosexuality is practiced; (c) an attempt at concealment; (d) partial rather than complete involvement in the homosexual world.

Overt Groups

Overt homosexuals gather in cohesive social groups which become the dominant focus of their lives. These groups are openly homosexual in character. The members make little effort to conceal their deviation, spend almost all their free time with the group, and tend to regard their other activities as peripheral.

These groups generally draw their members from persons of low socio-economic status who have jobs where concealment is not a prerequisite. Table 4.6 presents the occupational composition of the overt group identified in this study.

The members of the group met daily either at a bar, a restaurant, or at the house of the acknowledged leader or "queen."[6] They spent their time in endless gossip about the sexual affairs of the members or other homosexuals known to them. Often they would go to bars and restaurants in the attempt to make a "pick-up," or spend the evening "cruising" individually or in groups of two's and three's.

TABLE 4.6

Occupational Composition of an Overt Homosexual Group

Occupation	*Frequency*
Manager of appliance shop*	1
School teacher	1
Hospital attendant	1
Hairdresser	4
Sales clerk	2
Foundry worker	1
Baker	1
Salesman	1
Waiter	1
Cashier	1
Total	14

*This individual had just been promoted and was beginning to leave the group. Both he and the school teacher retained for a time their affiliation with an overt group while at the same time concealing their homosexuality at work.

The queen seems to characterize only "overt" groups. Functionally, the role of the queen is very important in the life of these groups. He provides a place where the group may gather and where its individual members may have their "affairs." He helps finance members in distress, functions as an intermediary in making sexual contacts, partially controls the entrance of new members, and warns the members of hoodlums who would prey upon them. Generally the queen is an older homosexual who has had wide experience in the homosexual world.

The following statement about the queen by a member of the overt group provides insight into the functioning of the queen and tells something of the way in which the individuals relate to him.

> A queen really means the leader of the group. You see how that is in a small town where there are not many people who are gay and willing to admit it. She knows who's who and what's what. She will know every gay person in town and will arrange things just the way Roberta does.[7] The queen is always somebody pretty old and pretty much out of the game as far as getting anything for herself is concerned. But she doesn't have anything else to do, so she spends all her time on this. I don't know of any queen as commercial as Roberta.

[6]Our data with respect to the prevalence of this role are incomplete. However, homosexuals regularly refer to the queens of other cities, suggesting that the practice is widespread.

[7]The adoption of feminine names is a widespread practice among all homosexuals interviewed.

But that's because Roberta is so goddam crude. I know the queen in Hillsburg and she was a perfect lady if I ever saw one. She knows everything. She used to make quite a bit but it was always in the form of getting invitations for dinner or as a present. You feel grateful to somebody who does something for you and you pay off. It's like a debt.

Overt groups are characterized by: (a) no particular standards of admission; (b) unself-conscious and unrestrained practice of homosexuality; (c) little or no concealment; (d) high degree of social isolation with little involvement in heterosexual activities; (e) little concern with identification as a status threat or the sanctions of heterosexual society.

THE HOMOSEXUAL COMMUNITY

The diverse secret and overt homosexuals are linked together either through bonds of sex or of friendship. Within the primary group, the emphasis upon friendship rather than sex serves to eliminate excessive sexual competition and preserves group unity. However, this creates a sexual interdependency upon those outside the group with important social consequences.

In the first place, it forces the secret homosexual out into the open in an attempt to solicit sexual partners. He thus frequents the known homosexual meeting places within the city such as specific bars, hotel lobbies, street corners, and lavatories. These activities make him an increasingly familiar figure within the homosexual world.

Secondly, this solicitation leads to the interaction of secret and overt homosexuals on a sexual as opposed to a social basis. While these contacts occur in a spirit of anonymity, an approach to the other often requires an exchange of confidences.

Thirdly, this sexual interdependency increases the anxiety of secret homosexuals since it forces them to contact the overt ones whom they fear as a threat to their security.

Thus, it is the casual and promiscuous sexual contacts between the members of different categories of evasion (i.e., the secret and the overt) which weld the city's homosexuals into a community.

CONCLUSION

The homosexual community thus consists of a large number of distinctive groups within which friendship binds the members together in a strong and relatively enduring bond and between which the members are linked by tenuous but repeated sexual contacts. The result is that homosexuals within the city tend to know or know of each other, to recognize a number of common interests and common moral norms, and to interact on the basis of antagonistic cooperation. This community is in turn linked with other homosexual communities in Canada and the United States, chiefly through the geographical mobility of its members.[8]

[8]The queen of the overt group studied maintained an address book containing the names of approximately 3,000 homosexuals scattered across North America.

CHAPTER V

Drug Addiction

NARCOTIC ADDICTION has attracted considerable attention in the United States not only from the professional disciplines, but from journalists as well. Because of numerous research contributions published in scholarly journals and the mass of literature consumed by the lay population, questions pertaining to drug abuse have been placed in the public spotlight. We are now demanding answers to these questions, and for the answers we have turned to physicians, sociologists, psychologists, pharmacists, police officers, educators, attorneys, judges, and the ministry. Rather than charging one single discipline with this responsibility, an integrated approach is being attempted, for all have something of value to offer. Narcotic addiction is not only a medical problem—it is a social problem, a legal problem, and a moral problem.

If one would examine the physiological effects, he would note that drugs may be placed into two categories, the stimulants and the depressants. The stimulants, of course, will arouse and sustain the bodily activity of the person while the depressants work in the opposite direction, that is, decrease physical and mental activity. Not to be redundant, the following is only a capsule summary of the characteristics and effects of the major problem drugs.

Probably the best-known of the stimulants is cocaine. Although less frequently used than in the past, this drug is still of concern to customs authorities and other law enforcement agencies. In order to repeat the sensations produced by cocaine, additional doses must be taken at frequent intervals. Many adverse effects of prolonged usage have been noted—

among these are chronic nervousness, hallucinations, and profuse perspiration.

The amphetamines are central nervous system stimulants. Quite often amphetamines combined with barbiturates may be prescribed by a physician as a weight-reducing formula. Although barbiturates may be physically addictive, amphetamines taken by themselves will not produce physical withdrawal symptoms or dependence. Amphetamines are usually taken as pep pills to reduce fatigue and to generate a feeling of hyperperceptiveness. Negative effects include exhaustion and letdown as the drug wears off, and the unrealistic feeling by the user that he is capable of performing beyond his ability.

As noted above, if barbiturate consumption is abused by the user, this may well lead to psychological dependence and physiological addiction. It is well known that withdrawal from barbiturates can be more dangerous than from other drugs. Acting as a sedative, barbiturates have great medical value in that they calm the central nervous system. For those who suffer from certain mental disorders, nervous tension, and high blood pressure, this drug has significantly reduced the overt symptoms associated with the disease. However, if its use is abused it may lead to respiratory problems, coma, and even death.

The great majority of addicts in the United States are "hooked" on the depressant drugs. The most commonly used of these are the narcotic analgesics (pain killers), which include opium and its derivatives—morphine, codeine, and heroin. If the drug is taken regularly, the user will develop tolerance to the effects and physical dependence on the drug. Hence, withdrawal symptoms are quite severe. If the individual is well supplied with the drug, he may not even be recognized as an addict. However, if his supply stops he will manifest a number of symptoms that are easily recognized. Because of the severity of distress produced by withdrawal, this type of addict presents a most serious problem to society because he will do almost anything to replenish his supply.

Unlike the other stimulants and depressants mentioned above, marihuana has no medical use. This "cigarette" ("reefer," "joint") made from the leaves and stem of the hemp plant is not considered to be physically addictive. The most serious problem associated with marihuana is that prolonged use by juveniles may serve as a stepping-stone for eventual addiction to the "hard" drugs (morphine or heroin). The Federal Bureau of Investigation reported that the 60 percent increase in narcotic arrests between 1966 and 1967 was influenced primarily by marihuana arrests.

Among the hallucinogens, LSD-25, made from lycergic acid has received by far the most attention over the past few years. It is not yet clear just how LSD effects the body or what long-range consequences it might have. It is clear, however, that LSD expands the sensory perceptions of the individual and has a chemical effect upon the brain.

Selected Facts on Drug Abuse[1]

1. 71 percent of those placed on probation in 1963 for drug violations were rearrested.
2. 60 percent of those placed on parole were rearrested.
3. 29 percent of those persons charged with drug violations were acquitted or dismissed.
4. Between 1960 and 1967, arrests for those persons under 18 years of age for drug violations increased 773 percent for males and 806 percent for females.
5. Of the total number of persons arrested in 1967 on drug charges, 48.5 percent were under 21 years of age and 68.8 percent were under 25 years of age.
6. 86.2 percent of those arrested were male, 13.8 percent were female.
7. Of those arrested, 57,146 were white, 22,848 were Negro.

In the first selection, John A. O'Donnell examines the relationship between narcotic addiction and crime. Among the significant questions posed, Mr. O'Donnell asks, "What kind of crime is the addict most likely to commit, under what circumstances, and to what extent?" In the second selection, the President's Commission on Law Enforcement and Administration of Justice reports on the problems of addiction, the difficulties of arriving at satisfactory definitions, the psychological and physiological effects of various drugs, a brief summary of the narcotic statutes, and the difficult position of the physician when faced with the problem of prescribing drugs. In the next paper Charles Winick discusses the rather unique problem concerning physicians who have become addicted. Given the amount of professional knowledge these men have concerning drugs, why would they allow themslves to become addicted? In the final article, Julian B. Roebuck takes a close look at the Negro drug addict. Dr. Roebuck studied a sample of 50 addicts and 350 traditional criminal types in an attempt to gather the facts necessary for formulating a theory of the etiology of drug addiction.

[1]Based on 1967 statistics.

15.

John A. O'Donnell

NARCOTIC ADDICTION AND CRIME

It is generally agreed that narcotic addiction and crime are associated, but there is disagreement on the nature, extent, and significance of the association, and on its implications for public policy. This paper uses data collected in a follow-up study of addicts to examine the major questions debated in the literature.

Several ecological studies establish that some relationship exists between addiction and crime. The general findings are clear and consistent: high rates of addiction or drug use are associated with high rates of crime and delinquency. In New York City in the 1950's, and in Chicago about 1930 and again in the early 1950's, addiction was found to be concentrated in certain areas of the city in which other social problems, including adult crimes and juvenile delinquency, were also frequent.[1]

Other studies establish that histories of addiction and crime are frequently found in the same individuals. Most of these study a group of addicts in a prison, or in a hospital for the treatment of addiction, and demonstrate that some sizable percentage of these addicts have criminal records.[2] A few study a group of prisoners, and demonstrate that some appreciable percentage of them have a history of addiction.[3]

These studies establish that crime and addiction are associated. Disagreement begins when an attempt is made to explain the association, and particularly when a causal connection between them is postulated.

There is certainly a connection leading from crime to addiction. To become an addict one must have access to drugs, and outside of the health professions drugs are available mainly through contacts with criminals. Some prior contact with criminality is therefore a necessary condition of addiction for most addicts.[4]

Most authorities agree that there is also a causal connection in the opposite direction. At least three ways in which crime results from addiction have been suggested. First, drug addiction *per se* "causes a relentless destruction of character and releases criminal tendencies."[5] Others hold that it is the laws and attitudes of society which are responsible for the increase in crimes associated with addiction, first by defining as crime behavior which is part of addiction (e.g., possession of heroin), and second by making drugs expensive, so that addicts are forced by their need for money to commit crimes they would not have committed in a different social situation.[6]

Source: *Social Problems,* Vol. 13, No. 4 (Spring, 1966), pp. 374–85, The Society for the Study of Social Problems. Reprinted by permission of the author and the journal.

[1]Robert E. L. Faris and H. Warren Dunham, *Mental Disorders in Urban Areas* (Chicago: University of Chicago Press, 1939), p. 170; Bingham Dai, *Opium Addiction in Chicago* (Shanghai: The Commercial Press, 1937), pp. 88–89, 189; Harold Finestone, "Narcotics and Criminality," *Law and Contemporary Problems,* Vol. 22 (Winter, 1957), p. 72; Isidor Chein, Donald L. Gerard, Robert S. Lee, and Eva Rosenfeld, *The Road to H* (New York: Basic Books, 1964), pp. 11, 57–65.

[2]Alan S. Meyer (ed.), *Social and Psychological Factors in Opiate Addiction* (New York: Bureau of Applied Social Research, Columbia University, 1952), pp. 82–91. This annotated bibliography summarizes the findings of about 20 studies reporting empirical data on addiction and crime.

[3]H. J. Anslinger and William F. Tompkins, *The Traffic in Narcotics* (New York: Funk and Wagnalls Co., 1953), p. 194.

[4]William Butler Eldridge, *Narcotics and the Law* (New York: American Bar Foundation, 1962), p. 28.

[5]Anslinger and Tompkins, *op. cit.,* pp. 189–90.

[6]Alfred R. Lindesmith, *Opiate Addiction* (Bloomington, Ind.: Principia Press, 1947), pp. 192–93. See also *Drug Addiction: Crime or Disease?: Interim and Final Reports of the Joint Committee of the American Bar Association and the American Medical Association on Narcotic Drugs* (Bloomington, Ind.: Indiana University Press, 1961), pp. 45–50, 64–68; Alfred R. Lindesmith, *The Addict and the Law* (Bloomington, Ind.: Indiana University Press, 1965).

But the crimes committed by addicts might have been committed even if the offenders had not become addicted. Anslinger and Tompkins argue that many addicts were criminals before they become addicts, and imply that they would have continued to commit crimes whether or not they became addicts.[7] The studies which bear most directly on this point are those which date the beginning of addiction for individuals, and examine their criminal records before and after addiction.

Among such studies, Dai reports that of 1,047 addicts arrested in Chicago about 1930, 81 per cent had no criminal record before addiction.[8] By virtue of the way his sample was selected, all had such a record after addiction. Their post-addiction offenses were mainly violations of narcotic laws; offenses against property were frequent and crimes of violence infrequent. Pescor analyzed the records of 1,036 addicts hospitalized in Lexington in 1936–37, and reported that 75 per cent had no history of delinquency prior to addiction, but 86 per cent had a record of delinquency after addiction.[9] It is to be noted, however, that 82 per cent of his subjects were prisoners or probationers, so that the high percentage of post-addiction delinquency could again be due to the way the sample was selected.

Finestone studied 84 non-institutionalized young addicts in Chicago in the early 1950's. He does not report the percentage with official records of delinquency before and after addiction, but implies that most had committed delinquent acts before their addiction, and all had committed such acts after it. He sees both their criminality and use of narcotics as results of the same causes.

> It is irrelevant to ask whether the delinquency preceded the addiction or vice versa. Many of those who became addicted and were forced to engage in crime to support the high cost of their addiction would probably have gone on to engage in crime as adolescents regardless of whether or not they had become addicted.[10]

Chein studied 100 drug users under 20 years of age in New York in the early 1950's. They were chosen so that about half had delinquency records before drug use began and half had no such record, and it is not possible to estimate what percentage of drug users in New York had prior records. It is clear that all or almost all of them committed criminal acts after addiction, primarily crimes of profit, though the percentage with official records of arrests and sentences is not reported.[11]

In a recent 12-year follow-up of 100 New York City addicts treated at Lexington in 1952–53, it is reported that although many began drug use before age 18, "at least 57 per cent of our group were antisocial (chronically truant, dishonorably discharged, in juvenile court, or in reform school) prior to the use of drugs. . . . Although prior to Lexington only 46 per cent of the patients had been arrested, after leaving 92 per cent of the patients served time in jail."[12]

From the questions asked in these studies, and the ways in which their findings have been used, the statement that addiction causes crime can be rephrased as the hypothesis that those individuals who become addicts then begin to commit crimes, or more crimes than they would have committed if they had not become addicts. A test of the hypothesis logically requires that crimes after addiction be counted, and compared with the number of crimes expected if these persons had not become addicts. There are two difficulties with such a test.

The data available for testing the hypothesis include the number of arrests and sentences of addicts after the onset of addiction, but it is evident that these figures do not represent a full count of all criminal acts. In the analysis which follows it will be necessary to estimate the discrepancy between offenses which were officially recorded and offenses which were actually committed.

---

[7]Anslinger and Tompkins, *op. cit.*, pp. 268–70, 277.

[8]Dai, *op. cit.*, p. 67.

[9]Michael J. Pescor, "A Statistical Analysis of the Clinical Records of Hospitalized Drug Addicts," *Supplement No. 143, Public Health Reports* (Washington, D.C.: Government Printing Office, 1943), p. 25.

[10]Finestone, *op. cit.*, p. 76.

[11]Chein, *op. cit.*, p. 11.

[12]George E. Vaillant and Leon Brill, "A Twelve Year Follow-Up of New York City Addicts: I. The Relation of Treatment to Outcome," paper read at the American Psychiatric Association Annual Meeting, New York City, May 3, 1965.

The recorded offenses must be compared against the number of expected offenses. Criminology today does not provide as firm a basis for estimating expected offenses as do vital statistics, for example, for estimating expected deaths in a population, but criminal statistics on age of offenders do offer a basis for estimates accurate enough to test the hypothesis. The logic of these can be discussed when the estimates are made.

In looking for evidence of an increase in observed over expected crimes, attention must be given to the type of offense. The popular stereotype has been that addiction makes rapists and killers of addicts, but this is negated by most available data. Compared with other offenders, the criminal records of addicts show a preponderance of drug and property arrests and a low proportion of violent crimes.[13] Ecological correlations show that high drug rates are associated with profit-making, rather than violent crimes.[14] Finestone and Chein both report that after addiction their subjects committed more property offenses and fewer crimes of violence.[15] One pharmacological effect of the opiates has been said to be that they "change drunken, fighting psychopaths into sober, cowardly, nonaggressive idlers."[16] It may be, therefore, that crimes against the person will be reduced, and crimes for profit increased, after the onset of addiction.

In the following sections data are used from a study of 266 white addicts who had been residents of Kentucky at the time of their first admission to the United States Public Health Service Hospital in Lexington, Kentucky. Date of admission ranged from the opening of the hospital in 1935 to 1959, and follow-up data were collected in the years 1961 to 1963.[17] The data are organized, and compared with findings of the studies described above, in relation to three questions:

1. What proportion of addicts were criminals prior to their addiction?

2. Was addiction followed by more crimes than the addicts would have been expected to commit?

3. If there is an apparent increase in crimes after addiction, with what aspects of addiction is it associated?

FINDINGS

Table 5.1 shows that before they became addicted, 133 (63%) of the men had no arrests. Fifty-nine (28%) have a known number of arrests and in 20 cases the number is shown as unknown. In 4 of these 20 there was at least one arrest. Only 15 per cent of the men served a sentence before they became addicted. Four of the women had arrests prior to their addiction, and none served a sentence.

After they became addicted, the men show an increase in arrests and sentences. Only 80 (38%) had no arrests after addiction, and those arrested tend to have a large rather than a small number of arrests. More than half of the men, however, were not sentenced after addiction. Eighty-seven (41%) were sentenced, and about half of these had three or more sentences.

More women were also arrested and sentenced after addiction, but the pattern is much less marked than for the men. Forty (74%) of the women had no arrests, only four (7%) were sentenced, and these had only one or two sentences.

The table therefore indicates that prior to addiction this sample was not composed of known criminals. Addiction was followed by an increase in arrests and sentences for both sexes, but the increase was less marked for the women. It is to be noted, however, that even after addiction most of the women and over half of the men had no sentences.

Table 5.2 examines the criminal record of the male subjects before addiction in more detail. For this table, the arrests, sentences, and time served before addiction are combined into an index of criminal behavior by the following definitions:

1. None; no arrests or sentences before addiction—133 men.

2. Some; one or more arrests but no sen-

---

[13] Meyer, *op. cit., pp.* 82–91.

[14] Chein, *op. cit., pp.* 57–65.

[15] *Ibid.*, p. 11. Finestone, *op. cit.*, p. 76.

[16] Lawrence Kolb, "Drug Addiction in its Relation to Crime," *Mental Hygiene*, Vol. 9 (January, 1925), pp. 74–89.

[17] A description of the sample, and other data on it, may be found in the writer's "A Follow-up of Narcotic Addicts: Mortality, Relapse and Abstinence," *American Journal of Orthopsychiatry*, Vol. 34 (October, 1964), pp. 948–54.

TABLE 5.1

NUMBER OF SUBJECTS WITH SPECIFIED NUMBER OF ARRESTS AND SENTENCES, PRIOR TO AND AFTER ADDICTION, BY SEX

	Number of Subjects			
	Male		*Female*	
Number of Arrests	*Before Addiction*	*After Addiction*	*Before Addiction*	*After Addiction*
0	133	80	50	40
1 or 2	26	24	0	5
3 to 5	14	32	1	3
6 or more	19	56	—	4
Unknown	20	20	3	2
Total Cases	212	212	54	54
Number of Sentences				
0	180	122	54	50
1 or 2	23	41	—	4
3 to 5	8	29	—	—
6 or more	—	17	—	—
Unknown	1	3	—	—
Total Cases	212	212	54	54

TABLE 5.2

CRIME BEFORE ADDICTION RELATED TO YEAR OF ADDICTION AND AGE OF ADDICTION, MALE SUBJECTS (Percentages)

		Crime before Addiction			
1. Year of Addiction	*N*	*None*	*Some*	*More*	*Total*
Before 1920	20	95%	5	—	100%
1920–29	35	77%	20	3	100%
1930–39	62	65%	16	19	100%
1940–49	60	62%	30	8	100%
1950–59	19	53%	16	32	100%†
Total cases	196*	133	39	24	196
2. Age at Addiction					
Under 20	22	86%	9	5	100%
20–29	65	54%	25	22	100%†
30–39	54	67%	22	11	100%
40–49	35	74%	23	3	100%
50 or over	20	85%	5	10	100%
Total cases	196*	133	39	24	196

*Sixteen men not included because of insufficient data for classification on Crime before Addiction.
†Figures do not add to 100% due to rounding errors.

tences, or sentences totaling under 10 months—39 men.

3. More; one or more arrests, and one or more sentences totaling 10 months or more—24 men.

There were 20 men on whom the number of arrests before addiction is unknown. Four of these are known to have had sentences before addiction, and these are included in the table. The other 16 are omitted.

Table 5.2 shows a clear relationship between

crime before addiction and the year of addiction; the more recent the year of addiction, the more likely are the men to have a criminal record before their addiction. Further, except for a minor reversal in the 1940–49 decade, the more likely is this to be a more serious prior criminal record. The table indicates that over the past five decades addicts in Kentucky have increasingly been recruited from the ranks of criminals. Only 1 of the 20 men addicted before 1920 had had prior arrests, as compared with 9 of the 19 who became addicted in the 1950's.

The table also shows that crimes before addiction are inversely related to the age at which addiction began, with the exception of the group who became addicted before age 20. This is also the only age group for which there are specific reasons—statements by the subjects that they had stolen, or that their major income was from gambling—to believe that illegal acts were committed which did not lead to arrest, in the period prior to addiction. Taking this into consideration, it appears that the younger a man was at the onset of addiction the more likely he was to have committed criminal acts before addiction.

The two relationships shown in Table 5.2 are independent and additive. If either age or year of first addiction is controlled, the relationship of the other with crime before addiction holds. The increased probability that a man who became addicted after 1930 will have a prior criminal record is greatest for those who began in their twenties, next greatest for those in their thirties.

Table 5.3 uses the number of sentences imposed after addiction began as an index of post-addiction crime. A table using arrests rather than sentences, not included here, shows exactly the same associations described below.

TABLE 5.3

SENTENCES AFTER ADDICTION RELATED TO YEAR OF ADDICTION, AGE AT ADDICTION AND CRIMINAL RECORD BEFORE ADDICTION, MALE SUBJECTS
(Percentages)

		Number of Sentences after Addiction				
1. Year of Addiction	N	*0*	*1 or 2*	*3 to 5*	*6 or more*	*Total*
Before 1920	22	36%	27	27	9	100%‡
1920–29	38	47%	13	24	16	100%
1930–39	64	53%	27	9	11	100%
1940–49	65	75%	11	11	3	100%
1950–59	20	65%	30	5	—	100%
Total cases	209*	122	41	29	17	209
2. Age at Addiction						
Under 20	23	9%	30	26	35	100%
20–29	72	42%	24	22	12	100%
30–39	56	75%	14	11	—	100%
40–49	38	76%	21	3	—	100%
50 or older	20	95%	5	—	—	100%
Total cases	209*	122	41	29	17	209
3. Criminal Record before Addiction						
None	133	68%	13	11	8	100%
Some	38	45%	34	10	10	100%‡
More	23	17%	39	35	9	100%
Total cases	194†	112	39	26	17	194

*Three men not included; unknown on number of sentences.
†Sixteen men not included because of insufficient data for classification on Crime before Addiction.
‡Figures do not add to 100% due to rounding errors.

Table 5.3 shows that the men are more likely to have some sentences after addiction, and are more likely to have a large number of sentences: (1) the earlier the year of addiction; (2) the younger their age at addiction; and (3) the greater their criminal record prior to addiction.

Each of the three relationships holds when the other two variables are controlled. From the pattern of gamma and chi-square values in the partial tables it is clear that age at onset of addiction is the most powerful predictor of post-addiction sentences. Prior criminal record also determines the number of sentences, though its effect adds only a little for the younger men. The relationship of year of addiction with post-addiction sentences achieves statistical significance only when one or both of the other variables are also operating. But its effect is in the same direction under all conditions of controlling the other variables, so it may be regarded as having an independent, but weak, effect.

The relationship of age with post-addiction sentences may appear to be somewhat stronger than it actually is, since the younger men had longer life expectancies to accumulate a number of sentences. But this consideration would not explain away the fact that the proportion with zero sentences increases with age; all age groups had time to acquire at least one sentence.

OFFENSES

Table 5.4 examines the increase in crime after addiction in terms of the specific offenses committed. Arrests as well as sentences were coded as offenses, so the percentages in Table 5.4 do not coincide exactly with those in previous tables. Only three offenses before addiction, and three after, were coded per subject, so the full range of offenses is not included. The more serious and more frequent offenses were coded, and few subjects had committed more than

TABLE 5.4

PER CENT OF SUBJECTS WHO COMMITTED SPECIFIED OFFENSES BEFORE AND AFTER THEY BECAME ADDICTED

	Male		*Female*	
Offenses against Persons	*Before Addiction*	*After Addiction*	*Before Addiction*	*After Addiction*
Murder and homicide	3%	2%	—	—
Assault	2%	2%	2%	6%
Weapons	1%	1%	—	—
One or more of above	6%	5%	2%	6%
Robbery	2%	5%	—	—
Other offenses				
Burglary	6%	10%	—	—
Other theft	7%	22%	—	4%
Liquor laws (moonshining)	7%	7%	—	—
Sex offenses	*	—	4%	6%
Other	25%	38%	4%	11%
One or more of above	30%	47%	4%	15%
Drug Offenses				
Sale of narcotics	—	11%	—	—
Prescription forgery or fraud	—	14%	—	6%
Other narcotic offenses	—	18%	—	11%
Other drug offenses	—	2%	—	—
One or more of above	—	33%	—	15%
One or more offenses of any type	33%	60%	6%	24%

*Less than 1%.

three kinds of offense, so the practical effect of this restriction is negligible.

The offenses are grouped; the first includes offenses against the person, except that robbery, which is both an offense against the person and a money-producing crime, is listed separately. The next group includes mainly property offenses, or money-producing crimes, except for a few cases of vagrancy and drunkenness. The last is exclusively drug offenses.

The proportion of men with recorded offenses increased from 33 per cent before addiction to 60 per cent after addiction. The increases which occurred after addiction are in robbery and other income-producing crimes, burglary and other theft, and in drug offenses. Comparing the major groups of offenses, drug offenses are recorded for one-third of the men after addiction, against none before it. The miscellaneous group, mainly of income-producing crimes, increased from 30 to 47 per cent for the men. Crimes against the person did not increase. It may be inferred that the increase in robbery was related to the fact that it produced money, rather than to its status as a crime against the person.

The pattern for the women is generally the same, though less marked. It is perhaps worthy of special note that there is no significant decrease in any group of offenses after addiction, and no decrease in the frequency of any specific offense except homicide. Six men committed homicides before their addiction, and only four after addiction began.

While there is evidence of an increase in offenses after addiction, these are not recorded for all subjects. It may be asked why more subjects are not shown with offenses after addiction, and Table 5.5 presents a variable which provides a partial answer to this question. This is the source from which subjects obtained their narcotics. Subjects are grouped under five headings:

1. The first group, 45 subjects, obtained all their narcotics from one physician, or one at a time, by direct dispensing or on prescription. While the medical need for narcotics may have been questionable in some of these cases, the drugs were obtained legally, and the cost was not high. There would be little reason for such subjects to commit crimes unless drug use *per se* caused crimes, and 91 per cent of them had no sentences.
2. The second group, 22 subjects, obtained narcotics by "making" doctors—going to several physicians simultaneously to obtain prescriptions. Also included here are a few who used only exempt narcotics, those that can be bought in a pharmacy without a prescription. Technical violations of the law, mainly by giving false names and addresses, occurred in this group, but when these were detected the addict was usually pressured into seeking treatment, not prosecuted. The expense of

TABLE 5.5

Sentences After Addiction by Sources of Narcotics during History of Addiction, Male Subjects
(Percentages)

Sources of Narcotics	*N*	*Number of Sentences after Addiction* *0*	*1 or 2*	*3 to 5*	*6 or More*	*Total*
Doctors only, one at a time	45	91%	9	—	—	100%
Several doctors, and/or exempt narcotics ...	22	77%	—	18	5	100%
Mainly own supply ...	12	75%	8	8	8	100%*
Mainly medical, some illegal	29	62%	28	10	—	100%
Mostly or all illegal ..	82	28%	29	26	17	100%
	190†	57%	19	15	8	100%*

*Figures do not add to 100% due to rounding errors.
†Twenty-two men cannot be classified on Sources of Narcotics.

the drugs was little or no greater than for the first group, but the travel involved could approach a fulltime occupation, and make it difficult to hold a job. Some crimes, therefore, might be expected, and more are found than for the first group, but 77 per cent of these men avoided any sentences.

3. The third group consists of 12 physicians who used drugs from the supplies they acquired legitimately and cheaply. This involved a technical violation of the law, but again one which was more likely to lead to treatment than prosecution. The status of these subjects as physicians implies a number of factors which would make other offenses improbable and prosecution unlikely. It is therefore not surprising that 75 per cent of this group had no sentences.
4. The fourth group includes 29 subjects who obtained most of their narcotics from medical sources as in the first and second groups, but who also used at least some illicit narcotics. For them the proportion with no sentences drops to 62 per cent.
5. The last group of 82 subjects includes those who bought all or most of their drugs on the illicit market. Here the percentage with no sentences drops sharply, to 28 per cent, and the proportion with three or more sentences is much higher than in the other groups.

The pattern for the women is identical. Only four women had sentences. Of these, 1 came from the 8 women in the fourth group, and 3 from the 11 women in the fifth.

The percentage with sentences was higher after addiction, for each of the five groups, than the corresponding percentage with sentences prior to addiction. With respect to types of offenses committed, the following differences can be noted. The men in the fifth group slightly exceeded the others in the proportion who committed offenses against the person before addiction. The other four groups committed fewer such offenses after addiction. The fifth committed as many as before addiction, and they account for all of the increase in robbery. All five groups committed more income-producing offenses after addiction than before, but the increase was most marked for the fourth and fifth groups. Drug offenses were found for some members of each group after addiction. These were committed by only one or two persons in the first three groups, but by about one-fifth of the fourth group and one-third of the fifth—the illegal users.

DISCUSSION

The findings can be related to the studies summarized earlier on a number of points.

1. *What proportion of addicts were criminals prior to their addiction?*

Only one-third of the men in this sample and less than 10 per cent of the women had any arrests before they became addicted. The proportion with a prior record, however, increased steadily with the recency of addiction. Ninety-five per cent of the men addicted before 1920 had no prior record, and this percentage dropped to 53 for men who became addicted in the 1950's. The finding that the proportion with prior criminal records has changed over time is consistent with the low percentage of prior records reported by Dai and Pescor, whose samples were collected in about 1930 and 1936 respectively. It is equally consistent with the high percentage of prior delinquency indicated by Finestone, Chein, and Vaillant, whose samples were collected about 20 years later. These five studies, plus the one reported here, thus interlock to indicate that the degree to which addicts are recruited from criminals has been increasing. The Finestone, Chein, and Vaillant samples are of metropolitan addicts, who today greatly outnumber the type exemplified by the Kentucky subjects, and therefore justify the inference that for the past 15 years or more most new addicts have had prior criminal records.

2. *Was addiction followed by more crimes than the addicts would have been expected to commit?*

It is clear that in this sample there was an increase in the number of arrests and sentences after addiction, and in the proportion of subjects with arrests and sentences. With respect to criminal acts which were not recorded, there are specific reasons to believe these occurred, before addiction, only for about half of the men who became addicted before age 20—for about 5 per cent of the sample.

After addiction, it is probable that almost all subjects except those who received all of their drugs from one physician at a time were guilty of drug offenses (e.g., illegal possession of narcotics), so the percentage who committed drug offenses was closer to 75 for the men and 48 for the women than the figures of 33 and 15 per cent shown for drug offenses in Table 5.4. There are also specific reasons—in statements by subjects and other informants—to believe that the number of money-making offenses committed after addiction was appreciably greater than is shown in official records. These unrecorded offenses were attributed to those men for whom some offenses are recorded, rather than to those with no official record.

If, in short, information were available on all criminal acts committed but not recorded, it is probable almost to the point of certainty that they would add something to pre-addiction crimes, but more to post-addiction crimes. The increase in post-addiction over pre-addiction criminal acts would be even greater than the increase in arrests and sentences. But do these post-addiction arrests and sentences exceed what would have been expected in this sample?

Table 5.3 shows that the median age at addiction in the sample is slightly over 30; the exact figures are 31.3 years for the men, 30 for the women. Most of the sample, it has been shown, had had no arrests before addiction. Restricting the question to men, because most of the sample and most criminals are men, it can be rephrased to ask: What is the probability that men will reach the age of 31 with no history of arrests, and then acquire such a history? More specifically, what is this probability for those offenses in which increases were noted?

Glaser uses the *Uniform Crime Reports* to show that in 1962 the median age of persons arrested was 17.9 for burglaries, 17.5 for larceny, and 21.9 for robbery.[18] Since these medians are based on all arrests, and some of these would have been second or subsequent arrests, the median age at first arrest on these charges must be even lower than the figures cited. Such figures suggest, and it is the consensus of criminologists, that as men grow older the expectation that they will be arrested on such charges grows smaller rather than larger.[19]

That the observed number of post-addiction arrests exceeds the expected number, therefore, is suggested by two facts. First, the observed increase is in drug offenses and in money-producing crimes, and is greatest for those who used expensive illicit drugs. This makes it plausible that the increase is connected with the addiction. Second, the statistical expectation would have been a decrease from the number of arrests noted before age 30, approximately when addiction began, to the number after that age, rather than the increase which was in fact found.

The findings of this study thus repeat the findings of five previous studies, all of which report more crime after addiction than before. It differs from these studies in two ways which tend to give stronger support to the interpretation that the increase was greater than would have been expected.

The studies by Dai and Pescor selected samples from among persons who had been arrested recently; if there were addicts with no post-addiction criminal records they had no chance of being selected by Dai, and little of being selected by Pescor. In this study, on the other hand, only 47 of 212 men and 3 of 54 women were prisoners or probationers on their first hospital admission, the basis of sample selection. An absence of post-addiction offenses had a chance of being observed, and in fact was observed for a large proportion of the sample.

[18] Daniel Glaser, *The Effectiveness of a Prison and Parole System* (New York: Bobbs-Merrill Co., 1964), p. 469.

[19] *Ibid.*, p. 467–74. See also Donald R. Taft, *Criminology* (3rd ed.); New York: Macmillan Co., 1956), pp. 112–13; Marshall B. Clinard, *Sociology of Deviant Behavior* (New York: Rinehart, 1957), pp. 198–200; Ruth Shonle Cavan, *Criminology* (2nd ed.); New York: Thomas Y. Crowell, 1956), pp. 41–49. Almost any text on criminology makes the point, though none known to the writer makes it in terms of the probability of first arrest for given offenses at given ages. In this connection, it has also been stated "that drug addiction results in a large and permanent increase in the volume of crime" because the addiction constrains the addicts to continue in a criminal pattern which otherwise would have been abandoned with increasing maturity. See *Drug Addiction: Crime or Disease?*, *op. cit.*, pp. 66–67.

In the studies by Finestone, Chein, and Vaillant the majority of subjects had, before their drug use, committed offenses or acts which the investigators interpreted as predictive of later crimes. They were also in the age range for which most arrests are recorded. The post-addiction crimes they committed, therefore, must to some extent be regarded as a continuation of criminal patterns antedating addiction, and statistically expectable. In this study, on the other hand, only a minority of subjects had committed offenses before addiction, and in only part of this minority was there any indication of a stable criminal pattern which would be expected to continue. Further, their addiction began and then, for most, their first arrests occurred, after the age for which most first arrests are recorded. The increase in crime after addiction was not statistically expectable for them.

In passing, it might be noted that this study does not support the findings of previous studies that crimes against the person decrease after addiction. The decrease from 6 per cent of men who committed such crimes before addiction to 5 per cent after addiction is insignificant, and if robbery is counted with crimes against the person, as is usual, there was an insignificant increase in these crimes after addiction began.

The findings would be consistent with the hypothesis that increasing age and/or the direct effect of drug use reduce the probability of crimes against the person, while an indirect effect of drug use, through the way of life needed by users of illicit drugs to maintain the habit, is to increase the probability. The net effect, in this sample, is that the two opposed expectations cancel out, and for the sample as a whole there is no appreciable change in the number of crimes against the person.

The conclusion that addiction is followed by more crimes than would have been expected supports, though it alone is not enough to establish the inference that addiction causes crime. It is equally important, however, to note that crime is not a necessary consequence of addiction. More than half of the men in the sample had no sentences after addiction, and over one-third had no arrests. With respect to acts which could have led to arrests and sentences, there are good reasons to believe that no such acts were committed by about one-fifth of the men and about one-half of the women. For about another one-fifth of each sex, there are good reasons to believe that the only illegal acts committed were drug offenses, like illegal possession of drugs. (These statements represent the writer's evaluation of the case material on subjects, including his evaluation of the credibility of subjects and other informants.) This is an additional indication that there are distinct types of addicts, and that knowledge of addiction can be advanced by studying the differences among them.[20]

3. *What specific aspects of addiction cause the increase in crime?*

The data presented in Table 5.5 confirm the generally accepted conclusion that drug use *per se* does not cause crimes. The subjects who received drugs from a physician were using as much narcotics as others, and in recent years probably more, since their drugs were not diluted like illicit heroin or exempt narcotics. Yet only a few of them have a record of arrests, and there is much less indication for them than for others of undetected offenses.

The table shows that in this sample addicts with a stable legal source of narcotics were unlikely to acquire a criminal record, while those who bought most of their drugs on the illicit market were likely to acquire one. This is consistent with the fact that most metropolitan minority-group addicts, who normally use illicit heroin, acquire criminal records. It is equally consistent with the fact that "medical addicts," addicts in the 19th century, and addicts in countries where drugs are legally available are reported not to engage in crime.

The table implies that if stable and legal sources of narcotics had been available to more subjects in this sample, they would have committed fewer crimes. It does not justify an inference that if stable legal sources were opened

[20] John C. Ball, "Two Patterns of Narcotic Drug Addiction in the United States," *Journal of Criminal Law, Criminology and Police Science,* Vol. 56 (June, 1965), pp. 203–11.

to all users of illicit drugs these users would become non-criminals, because this sample is not representative of all users.[21]

SUMMARY

Data from a follow-up study of Kentucky addicts are related to other studies, and the combined findings interpreted as supporting two major conclusions. First, addicts have been more and more recruited from among persons with prior criminal records in recent decades, and today it is probable that most new addicts were criminals before their addiction. Second, they commit more crimes after their addiction than they would have been expected to commit. It is equally true, however, for this sample that many subjects did not have a criminal record either before or after addiction, and probable that a sizable minority never committed criminal acts.

A third finding of this study does not support the conclusions of others; here there was no evidence of a decrease in crimes of violence after addiction.

Evidence is presented that the increase in crime after addiction is not a direct effect of the drug use, but is due to the way of life which becomes necessary in many cases, but not in all, to obtain narcotics.

[21]Those who advocate making drugs available to addicts legally and cheaply to reduce their need to commit crimes, among other reasons, may reasonably regard the finding as support for their proposal; most addicts probably resemble those in this sample in that they would be less likely to steal money for expensive illicit drugs if cheap legal drugs were at hand. But the desirability of such a policy depends not only on its effect on crime, but also on its other probable effects, and of course on moral considerations. In the writer's opinion the probable ill effects of the policy outweigh the good to be expected from it.

16.

President's Commission on Law Enforcement and Administration of Justice

NARCOTICS AND DRUG ABUSE

In 1962 a White House Conference on Narcotic and Drug Abuse was convened in recognition of the fact that drug traffic and abuse were growing and critical national concerns. Large quantities of drugs were moving in illicit traffic despite the best efforts of law enforcement agencies. Addiction to the familiar opiates, especially in big-city ghettos, was widespread. New stimulant, depressant, and hallucinogenic drugs, many of them under loose legal controls, were coming into wide misuse, often by students. The informed public was becoming increasingly aware of the social and economic damage of illicit drug taking.

Organized criminals engaged in drug traffic were making high profits. Drug addicts, to support their habits, were stealing millions of dollars worth of property every year and contributing to the public's fear of robbery and burglary. The police, the courts, the jails and prisons, and social-service agencies of all kinds were devoting great amounts of time, money and manpower to attempts to control drug abuse. Worst of all, thousands of human lives were being wasted.

Some methods of medical treatment, at least for opiate-dependent persons, were being tried, but the results were generally impermanent; relapse was more frequent than cure. The established cycle for such persons was arrest, confine-

Source: A Report of the President's Commission on Law Enforcement and Administration of Justice, *The Challenge of Crime in a Free Society* (Washington, D.C., U.S. Government Printing Office, February, 1967), pp. 211–31.

ment with or without treatment, release, and then arrest again. And the cause of all this, the drug-prone personality and the drug-taking urge, lay hidden somewhere in the conditions of modern urban life and in the complexities of mental disorder.

Responsibility for the drug abuse problem was not at all clear. Was it a Federal or a State matter? Was it a police problem or a medical one? If, as seemed evident, it was a combination of all of these, which agencies or people should be doing what? The Conference did not answer these questions, but it did bring to them a sense of national importance and commitment.

The President's Advisory Commission on Narcotic and Drug Abuse was created in 1963 to translate this commitment into a program of action. The Commission's final report, issued in November of that year, set forth a strategy designed to improve the control of drug traffic and the treatment of drug users. The 25 recommendations of that report have been the basis for most of the subsequent Federal activity in this field. Many of them, notably those pertaining to civil commitment for narcotic addicts and the need for Federal controls on the distribution of nonnarcotic drugs, have been or are in the process of being implemented.

This Commission has not and could not have undertaken to duplicate the comprehensive study and report on drug abuse so recently completed by another Presidential Commission. Yet any study of law enforcement and the administration of criminal justice must of necessity include some reference to drug abuse and its associated problems. In the course of the discussion in this chapter, recommendations are made where they seem clearly advisable. In many instances these recommendations parallel ones made by the 1963 Commission.

There have been major innovations in legal procedures and medical techniques during the last few years. There are new Federal and State laws and programs designed to provide treatment both for narcotic addicts charged with or convicted of crime, and for those who come to the attention of public authorities without criminal charge. These laws and programs signify that the Nation's approach to narcotic addiction has changed fundamentally. They are a creative effort to treat the person who is dependent on drugs.

Careful implementation, evaluation, and coordination of the new programs, some of which are not yet in operation, will be absolutely essential. These are among today's first needs. New ideas are only a first step. Unless the programs they lead to are provided with sufficient money and manpower and are competently administered, no improvement in drug abuse problems can be expected. . . .

* * *

Addiction

There is no settled definition of addiction. Sociologists speak of "assimiliation into a special life style of drug taking." Doctors speak of "physical dependence," an alteration in the central nervous system that results in painful sickness when use of the drug is abruptly discontinued; of "psychological or psychic dependence," an emotional desire, craving or compulsion to obtain and experience the drug; and of "tolerance," a physical adjustment to the drug that results in successive doses producing smaller effects and, therefore, in a tendency to increase doses. Statutes speak of habitual use; of loss of the power of self-control respecting the drug; and of effects detrimental to the individual or potentially harmful to the public morals, safety, health or welfare.

Some drugs are addicting, and some persons are addicted, by one definition but not by another. The World Health Organization Expert Committee on Addiction-Producing Drugs has recommended that the term "drug dependence," with a modifying phrase linking it to a particular type of drug, be used in place of the term "addiction." But "addiction" seems too deeply imbedded in the popular vocabulary to be expunged. Most frequently, it connotes physical dependence, resulting from excessive use of certain drugs. However, it should be noted that one can become physically dependent on substances, notably alcohol, that are not considered part of the drug abuse problem. It should be noted also that psychic or emotional dependence can develop to any substances, not only drugs, that affect consciousness and that people use for escape, adjustment or simple pleasure.

NARCOTICS

The dictionary defines a "narcotic" as a substance that induces sleep, dulls the senses, or relieves pain. In law, however, it has been given an artificial meaning. It does not refer, as might be expected, to one class of drugs, each having similar chemical properties or pharmacological effects. It is applied rather to a number of different classes of drugs that have been grouped together for purposes of legal control. Under the Federal laws, narcotics include the opiates and cocaine. Under most State statutes, marihuana is also a narcotic.

The Opiates. These drugs have a highly technical legal definition, but . . . they may be taken to include opium, morphine, their derivatives and compounds and their synthetic equivalents. The opiates have great medical value. They differ widely in their uses, effects, and addiction potential. The most common are morphine and codeine. The former is a principal drug in the relief of pain, the latter in the treatment of cough. Many opiates are prescribed for use in approved medical settings. While the misuse or illicit use (drug "abuse" includes both) of some of these drugs has presented serious problems for State and Federal enforcement agencies, public concern as to the opiates is focused primarily on heroin, a morphine derivative. This is the chief drug of addiction in the United States.

The effect of any drug depends on many variables, not the least of which are the mood and expectation of the taker. Drug effects are therefore best expressed in terms of probable outcomes. The discussion here is selective rather than exhaustive. With these provisos, it may be said that heroin is a depressant. It relieves anxiety and tension and diminishes the sex, hunger, and other primary drives. It may also produce drowsiness and cause inability to concentrate, apathy, and lessened physical activity. It can impair mental and physical performance. Repeated and prolonged administration will certainly lead to tolerance and physical dependence.

This process is set in motion by the first dose. An overdose may lead to respiratory failure, coma and death. With dosages to which a person is tolerant, permanent organic damage does not occur. However, secondary effects, arising from the preoccupation of a person with the drug, may include personal neglect and malnutrition. The ritual of the American addict is to inject the drug intravenously with a needle, and infections and abscesses may be caused by the use of unsterile equipment. Euphoria is an effect often associated with heroin, often reflecting the relief a particular individual gets from chronic anxiety. Among the symptoms of the withdrawal sickness, which reaches peak intensity in 24–48 hours, are muscle aches, cramps, and nausea.

The Bureau of Narcotics maintains a name file of active opiate addicts. As of December 31, 1965, there were 52,793 heroin addicts (out of a total of 57,199 opiate addicts) listed. Most of the names in the file are of persons arrested by State and local police agencies and reported voluntarily to the Bureau on a form the Bureau provides for this purpose. Thus the inclusion of a person's name in the file depends in large measure on his coming to the attention of the police, being recognized and classified as an addict, and being reported. There is some uncertainty at each step. Moreover some police agencies, and many health and medical agencies, do not participate in the voluntary reporting system. There is also no place in the system for persons who use opiates without becoming addicted. For these reasons many people feel that the Bureau's file does not present a complete statistical picture of opiate use in this country. Indeed the Bureau makes no claims of infallibility for the reporting system. It is intended as a device for arriving at a workable estimate of the extent and concentration of opiate addiction. The Commissioner of Narcotics has testified numerous times that the Bureau's figures are only approximations. The State of California is another source for statistics on drug addiction; it maintains a file of addicts-users in the State.

It should also be noted that other estimates of the present addict population, some of which cite figures as high as 200,000, are without a solid statistical foundation.

More than one-half the known heroin addicts are in New York. Most of the others are in California, Illinois, Michigan, New Jersey, Maryland, Pennsylvania, Texas, and the District of Columbia. In the States where heroin addiction exists on a large scale, it is an urban problem. Within the cities it is largely found in areas with low average incomes, poor housing, and high delinquency. The addict himself is likely to be male, between the ages of 21 and 30, poorly educated and unskilled, and a member of a disadvantaged ethnic minority group.

The cost of heroin to the addict fluctuates over time and from place to place. So does the quality of the drug. Five dollars is a commonly reported price for a single "bag" or packet of heroin. The substance purchased ranges in purity from 1 to about 30 percent, the remainder consisting of natural impurities, and adulterants such as lactose and mannitol. Usually the addict does not know the strength of the doses he buys. Today, however, the drug available on the street is generally so far diluted that the typical addict does not develop profound physical dependence, and therefore does not suffer serious withdrawal symptoms.

The basic Federal control law, the Harrison Narcotic Act of 1914, is a tax statute. It is administered by the Bureau of Narcotics, an agency of the Treasury Department. The statute imposes a tax upon the manufacture or importation of all narcotic drugs. Payment of the tax is evidenced by stamps affixed to the drug containers. The statute authorizes transfers of narcotics in the original containers by and to persons who have registered with the Treasury Department and paid certain occupational taxes ranging from $1 to $24 a year. Official order forms must be used in completing these transactions. There is an exemption for the physician acting in the course of his professional practice. Unauthorized possession under the statute is a criminal offense, whether or not the drug is intended for personal use. Unauthorized sale or purchase is a criminal offense. Unauthorized importation is made punishable by a separate Federal statute. Unauthorized possession and sale are also criminal acts under the Uniform Narcotic Drug Act, the control statute in effect in most States.

Heroin occupies a special place in the narcotics laws. It is an illegal drug in the sense that it may not be lawfully imported or manufactured under any circumstances, and it is not available for use in medical practice. All the heroin that reaches the American user is smuggled into the country from abroad, the Middle East being the reputed primary point of origin. All heroin transactions, and any possession of heroin, are therefore criminal. This is not because heroin has evil properties not shared by the other opiates. Indeed, while it is more potent and somewhat more rapid in its action, heroin does not differ in any significant pharmacological effect from morphine. It would appear that heroin is outlawed because of its special attractiveness to addicts and because it serves no known medical purpose not served as well or better by other drugs.

Cocaine. This drug is included as a narcotic under Federal and other laws but, unlike the opiates, it is a powerful stimulant and does not create tolerance or physical dependence. It is derived from the leaves of the coca plant cultivated extensively in parts of South America. At present it is not the major drug of abuse that it once was.

Marihuana. This is a preparation made from the flowering tops of the female hemp plant. This plant often is found growing wild, or it can be cultivated, in any temperate or semitropical climate, including the United States. Most of the marihuana that reaches American users comes from Mexico. There it is cut, dried, and pulverized and then smuggled across the border, either loose or compressed in brick form. It is commonly converted into cigarettes and consumed by smoking. Other derivatives of the hemp plant, such as hashish, which are more potent than marihuana, are rarely found in the United States.

Marihuana has no established and certainly no indispensable medical use. Its effects are rather complicated, combining both stimulation and depression. Much of its effect depends on the personality of the user. The drug may induce exaltation, joyousness and hilarity, and disconnected ideas; or it may induce quietude or reveries. In the inexperienced taker it may induce panic. Or, one state may follow the other. Confused perceptions of space and time and hallucinations in sharp color may occur; the person's complex intellectual and motor functions may be impaired. These effects may follow within minutes of the time the drug is taken. The influence usually wears off within a few hours but may last much longer in the case of a toxic dose. The immediate physiological effects may include nausea and vomiting, but there are no lasting physical effects, and fatalities have not been noted. Tolerance is very slight if it develops at all. Physical dependence does not develop.

There is no reliable estimate of the prevalence of marihuana use. To the limited extent that police activity is an accurate measure, use appears to be increasing. Bulk seizures of marihuana by Federal enforcement authorities totaled 5,641 kilograms in 1965 as against 1,871 kilograms in 1960. Bureau of Narcotics arrests for marihuana offenses about doubled over the same period of time. So did the number of arrests by California authorities.

Marihuana use apparently cuts across a larger segment of the general population than does opiate use, but again, adequate studies are lacking. An impressionistic view, based on scattered reports, is that use is both frequent and increasing in depressed urban areas, academic and artistic communities, and among young professional persons. There are many reports of widespread use on campuses, but estimates that 20 percent or more of certain college populations have used the drug cannot be verified or refuted.

Marihuana is much cheaper than heroin. The director of the Vice Control Division, Chicago Police Department, testified in 1966 that the price of marihuana in Chicago was roughly 50 to 75 cents for a single cigarette, roughly $25 for a can the size of a tobacco tin, and from $85 to $125 a pound. Prices tend to be lower nearer the Mexican source.

The Federal law controlling marihuana is a tax statute enacted in 1937 and enforced by the Bureau of Narcotics. On its face the statute authorizes marihuana transactions between persons, such as importers, wholesalers, physicians, and others, who have paid certain occupational and transfer taxes. But in fact, since there is no accepted medical use of marihuana, only a handful of people are registered under the law, and for all practical purposes the drug is illegal. Unauthorized possession, which in this context means possession under almost any circumstance, is a criminal act under Federal tax law. Sale or purchase of marihuana are also criminal offenses under this statute. Importation is made punishable by a separate statute. Possession and sale are also offenses under the Uniform Narcotic Drug Act, which controls marihuana in most States.

Dangerous Drugs

The term "dangerous drugs" commonly refers to three classes of nonnarcotic drugs that are habit-forming or have a potential for abuse because of their stimulant, depressant or hallucinogenic effect. Central nervous system stimulants and depressants are widely used in medical practice and are not considered dangerous when taken in ordinary therapeutic doses under medical direction. They are available on prescription. Drugs in the hallucinogenic class have not yet been proven safe for medical purposes and are not legally available in drugstores. Their sole legitimate use at present is by qualified researchers in connection with investigations reported to and authorized by the Food and Drug Administration. There is an exception in the case of peyote, the use of which is authorized in connection with religious ceremonies of the Native American Church.

The Stimulants

The most widely used and abused of the stimulants are the amphetamines, which are known generally as "pep pills." They bear chemical names such as amphetamine sulfate or dextroamphetamine sulfate and particular nicknames such as "bennies" or "dexies" (after trade names of the two drugs). There are dozens of amphetamine preparations in the market. They are prescribed and apparently are medically effective for relief of fatigue, for control of overweight, and in the treatment of mental disorder.

The amphetamines cause wakefulness and have the capacity to elevate mood and to induce a state of well-being and elation. This is probably the basis of their medical value. It is also the likely reason for their abuse.

Tolerance develops with the use of amphetamines. This permits gradual and progressive increases in dosage. Too large a dose or too sudden an increase in dose, however, may produce bizarre mental effects such as delusions or hallucinations. These effects are more likely if the drug is injected intravenously in diluted powder form than if taken orally in tablet form. Nervousness and insomnia are milder symptoms of abuse. Physical dependence does not develop.

The Depressants

The most widely used and abused of the depressant drugs are the barbiturates. These are known generally as "goofballs." They have chemical names, such as pentobarbital sodium and secobarbital sodium, and particular nicknames, such as "nimbies" and "seccy" (after trade names of the two drugs). There are more than 25 barbiturates marketed for clinical use. They are apparently useful because of their sedative, hypnotic, or anesthetic actions and are most commonly prescribed to produce sleep and to relieve tension and anxiety.

A person can develop tolerance to barbiturates, enabling him to ingest increasing quantities of the drug up to a limit that varies with the individual. Chronic administration of amounts in excess of the ordinary daily dose will lead to physical dependence, resulting, upon withdrawal of the drug, in a sickness marked at peak intensity by convulsions and a delirium, resembling alcoholic delirium tremens or a major psychotic episode. Excessive doses may also result in impairment of judgment, loss of emotional control, staggering, slurred speech, tremor, and occasionally coma and death. Barbiturates are a major suicidal agent. They are also reported, like the amphetamines, to be implicated in assaultive acts and automobile accidents.

Among the other depressants involved in the drug abuse problem are a number of sedative and tranquilizing drugs, introduced since 1950, that are chemically unrelated to the barbiturates, but similar in effect. The best known of these are meprobamate (Miltown, Equanil), glutethimide (Doriden), ethinamate (Valmid), ethchlorvynol (Placidyl), methyprylon (Noludar), and chlordiazepoxide (Librium). There is strong evidence that abuse of these agents may lead to drug intoxication and physical dependence. Suicide by overdose, and deaths during withdrawal from some of the drugs, have also been reported.

The Hallucinogens

Hallucinogenic, or psychedelic, drugs and the controversy that surrounds them have recently aroused the attention of the mass media and the public. This is certainly due in part to the increasing incidence of their use on college campuses. It may also be due to the emergence of new substances, such as LSD, many times more potent than such older hallucinogens as peyote and mescaline. All these drugs have the capacity to produce altered states of consciousness. Generally they are taken orally.

LSD, the most potent of the hallucinogens, is a synthetic drug made by a chemical process; lysergic acid is the main component in the chemical conversion. Minute amounts of the drug are capable of producing extreme effects. It is usually deposited on sugar cubes in liquid form, although recently it has been found frequently in pill form. Swallowing such a cube or pill is called "taking a trip." A recent publication of the Medical Society of the County of New York described such a trip as follows:

> After the cubes, containing 100–600 mcg. [a microgram is one-millionth of a gram] each, are ingested a startling series of events occurs with marked individual variation. All senses appear sharpened and brightened; vivid panoramic visual hallucinations of fantastic brightness and depth are experienced as well as hyperacusis [abnormal acuteness of hearing]. Senses blend and become diffused so that sounds are felt, colors tasted; and fixed objects pulsate and breathe. Depersonalization also occurs frequently so that the individual loses ego identity; he feels he is living with his environment in a feeling of unity with other beings, animals, inanimate objects and the universe in general. The body image is often distorted so that faces, including the user's, assume bizarre proportions and the limbs may appear extraordinarily short or elongated. The user is enveloped by a sense of isolation and often is dominated by feelings of paranoia and fear. If large doses are ingested (over 700 mcg.) confusion and delirium frequently ensue. During LSD use, repressed material may be unmasked which is difficult for the individual to handle. Duration of the experience is usually 4 to 12 hours but it may last for days.

The same publication cited as dangers of LSD: (1) Prolonged psychosis; (2) acting out of character disorders and homosexual impulses; (3) suicidal inclinations; (4) activation of previously latent psychosis; and (5) reappearance of the drug's effects weeks or even months after use. It was reported that between March and

December of 1965 a total of 65 persons suffering from acute psychosis induced by LSD were admitted to Bellevue Hospital in New York.

The only legal producer of LSD ceased manufacture in April 1966, and turned over its entire supply of the drug to the Federal Government. A few closely monitored experimental projects involving LSD are still in progress.

Peyote is the hallucinogenic substance obtained from the button-shaped growths of a cactus plant found growing wild in the arid regions of Mexico. Mescaline is a natural alkaloid, which occurs in the same plant. These drugs have appeared in capsule and liquid form and as a powder that can be dissolved in water.

Psilocybin is a substance extracted from a mushroom fungus. It appears in liquid and powder form.

Different degrees of tolerance to the hallucinogens are reported. Physical dependence apparently does not develop.

There is no reliable statistical information on the prevalence of dangerous drug abuse. However, there are indications of widespread and increasing abuse. The former Commissioner of the Food and Drug Administration, for example, has testified that enough raw material was produced in 1962 to make over 9 billion doses of barbiturates and amphetamines combined, and he estimated that one-half of these ended up in the bootleg market. There is no similar estimate of the proportion of the more than 1 million pounds of tranquilizer drugs produced each year that fall into the hands of drug abusers, but the figure certainly is high. A spreading use of the hallucinogens has undoubtedly been caused in part by the activities and advertising of groups formed for the very purpose of promoting experience in these drugs. These groups, or cults, have made broad and appealing claims in regard to the capacity of the hallucinogens to expand the power of the mind to understand self, love, God, and the universe. They are likely to understate the dangers that line the route to such mystical experiences. Whatever the other causes, cases of dangerous drug abuse coming to the attention of school and medical authorities and police officials have been steadily increasing in number.

The prices of illicit dangerous drugs vary sharply in time and place. Some approximate ranges of reported price are from $0.10 to $1 for an amphetamine or barbiturate tablet, from $1 to $10 for a sugar cube saturated with LSD, and from $0.01 to $0.50 for a peyote button. All of these prices represent significant profits to the seller.

A series of Federal enactments that proved inadequate to deal with the traffic in dangerous drugs has given way to the Drug Abuse Control Amendments of 1965. The statute became effective February 1, 1966, and is now the principal Federal law in the field. It limits manufacture, sale, and distribution of any controlled drug to certain designated classes of persons, such as registered wholesale druggists and licensed physicians. It requires that inventories be taken and records of receipts and dispositions be maintained. It places restrictions on the refilling of prescriptions. Criminal penalties are provided for violations, including manufacture, sale, or distribution by unauthorized persons. The first offense is a misdemeanor; the second, a felony. Possession of drugs for personal use is not an offense under this statute.

All of the amphetamines and the barbiturates are controlled by specific language in the statute. In addition, any other drug with potential for abuse because of its depressant, stimulant, or hallucinogenic effect may be placed under control by designation. Some 22 other drugs have been so designated, including all of the hallucinogens and 3 of the tranquilizers discussed above. The statute is enforced by the Bureau of Drug Abuse Control, a newly created agency within the Food and Drug Administration.

Almost all States have some statutory scheme for controlling at least some of the dangerous drugs, but there is complete lack of uniformity in this legislation.

It is obvious that the increasing use of drugs, including particularly those like LSD with great potential for harm, presents a serious challenge to the Nation. . . .

DRUG ABUSE AND CRIME

Drug addicts are crime-prone persons. This fact is not open to serious dispute, but to determine its meaning is another matter. Analysis is best restricted to heroin because of the applicable laws, because of the information available, and because drugs with addiction liability present the clearest issues. In order to obtain an accurate idea of the drug-crime relationship, it is necessary to make a clear distinction between the drug offenses and the non-drug offenses committed by addicts.

Drug Offenses

Addiction itself is not a crime. It never has been under Federal law, and a State law making it one was struck down as unconstitutional by the 1962 decision of the Supreme Court in *Robinson v. California*. It does not follow, however, that a state of addiction can be maintained without running afoul of the criminal law. On the contrary, the involvement of an addict with the police is almost inevitable. By definition, an addict has a constant need for drugs, which obviously must be purchased and possessed before they can be consumed. Purchase and possession, with certain exceptions not relevant in the case of an addict, are criminal offenses under both Federal and State law. So is sale, to which many addicts turn to provide financial support for their habits. In many States, the nonmedical use of opiates is punishable, as is the possession of paraphernalia such as needles and syringes designed for such use. In other States, vagrancy statutes make it punishable for a known or convicted addict to consort with other known addicts or to be present in a place where illicit drugs are found.

Thus, the addict lives in almost perpetual violation of one or several criminal laws, and this gives him a special status not shared by other criminal offenders. Together with the fact that he must have continuous contact with other people in order to obtain drugs, it also gives him a special exposure to police action and arrest, and, in areas where the addiction rate is high, a special place in police statistics and crime rate computations.

Nondrug Offenses

The nondrug offenses in which the heroin addict typically becomes involved are of the fund-raising variety. Assaultive or violent acts, contrary to popular belief, are the exception rather than the rule for the heroin addict, whose drug has a calming and depressant effect.

Illicit drugs, as already noted, are expensive. Records compiled by the New York City police are sufficient proof of this. In May 1965, a total of 991 admitted users of heroin were arrested in New York City. The average daily cost of heroin to these users was $14.34. In December of that year, the 1,271 heroin users arrested spent a daily average of $14.04. The price of the drug is not uniform in time or place; it differs in New York and Los Angeles and fluctuates everywhere according to the supply available on the street. But it is never low enough to permit the typical addict to obtain it by lawful means. So he turns to crime, most commonly to the theft of property. Stolen property cannot be converted at full value, especially by an addict who needs to dispose of it quickly. It is said that between $3 and $5 in merchandise must be stolen to realize $1 in cash.

The mathematics of this are alarming. Assuming that each of the heroin addicts in New York City, whose names were on file with the Bureau of Narcotics at the end of 1965, spent $15 a day for his drug, and that in each case the $15 represented the net cash proceeds after conversion of stolen property worth $50, the addicts would be responsible each year for the theft of property valued at many millions of dollars in New York City alone. This amount would, of course, have to be adjusted to take into account the addicts who are in jail or hospitalized; those who obtain the price of heroin either through lawful means or by prostitution, selling of drugs, thefts of cash, or any other method which does not require the conversion of stolen property; and the addicts who are unknown to the authorities. The impact of these adjustments might be enormous but it cannot be accurately measured.

The projected totals are so impressive that they lead one into the easy assumption that addicts must be responsible for most crimes against property where addiction is widespread. But this assumption cannot so easily be verified.

Records compiled by the New York City Police Department indicate that 11.1 percent of those arrested in 1965 for those felonies against property most often committed by addicts were admitted drug (mostly heroin) users. The comparable figure for 1964 was 12.5 percent; for 1963 it was 11.7 percent. The involvement of admitted drug users in arrests for selected felonies against the person was much lower—on the order of 2 percent. The 1965 figure for the involvement of admitted drug users in arrests for petit larceny was 9.8 percent. It is impossible to judge what any of these figures might have been if they had reflected involvement in non-drug offenses of actual instead of admitted drug users.

For the fiscal years 1956-65 inclusive, an average of 8 percent of all persons committed to Federal prisons and other penal institutions had an admitted drug (again mostly heroin) use history. On the other hand, the New York City Department of Corrections reports that surveys taken of its average 1966 population (about 10,000 persons) show that almost 40 percent had an admitted history of drug use.

As of December 31, 1966, there were 4,385 persons identified as users of heroin in the FBI's "Careers in Crime Program"—a computerized record of criminal histories. This data is based on criminal fingerprint cards submitted by local and Federal agencies.

The 4,385 people who were identified as heroin users had an average criminal career (the span of years between the first and last arrest) of 12 years during which they averaged 10 arrests. Six of these arrests on an average were for offenses other than narcotics. Of the total arrests accumulated by heroin users in the property crime and violent crime categories, 26 percent were arrests for violent crimes and 74 percent arrests for property cimes. On the other hand, all criminal offenders in the program (over 150,000) averaged 23 percent arrests for violent crimes and 77 percent for property crimes. Seventy-two percent of all heroin users had an arrest for some other criminal act prior to their first narcotic arrest.

The simple truth is that the extent of the addict's or drug user's responsibilty for all non-drug offenses is unknown. Obviously it is great, particularly in New York City, with its heavy concentration of users; but there is no reliable data to assess properly the common assertion that drug users or addicts are responsible for 50 percent of all crime.

More broadly, the Commission's examination of the evidence on the causal connection between drug use and crime has not enabled it to make definitive estimates on this important issue. Since there is much crime in cities where drug use is not thought to be a major problem, to commit resources against abuse solely in the expectation of producing a dramatic reduction in crime may be to invite disappointment. While crime reduction is one result to be hoped for in eliminating drug abuse, its elimination and the treatment of its victims are humane and worthy social objectives in themselves. . . .

MEDICAL PRACTICE AND ADDICTION

What limits does the law set on the right of a physician to prescribe or administer narcotic drugs to a narcotic addict? This short question raises issues that have been warmly debated for a long time—issues that are not resolved by reference to the general proposition that the statutory and regulatory measures for the control of narcotic drugs are not intended to interfere with the administration of such drugs in legitimate medical practice. The important issues are: How and by whom is the concept of legitimate medical practice defined and given content? Does legitimate medical practice mean the same thing as that practice accepted and followed by a majority of doctors in the community or as that approved by official spokesmen of the medical profession? It so, and if adverse legal consequences attend any departure from legitimate medical practice, how can new medical ideas and techniques safely be developed? What allowance is made for the good faith of a doctor who departs from standard treatment procedures while acting in what he considers to be the best interests of his patient?

Some background is necessary to put these issues into perspective. The Harrison Narcotic Act of 1914 regulates the distribution of narcotics. It requires those whose usual business involves transactions in narcotic drugs (including physicians) to register and pay an occupational tax, and it imposes a commodity tax, evidenced by stamps, on all narcotics manufactured. It further requires that all narcotics be distributed and transferred in original stamped packages, pursuant to order forms provided by the Treasury Department. Failure to comply with these provisions is a criminal offense. Specifically exempted from the operations of the act, however, are prescriptions issued by a physician "for legitimate medical uses" and distribution of drugs to a patient "in the course of his professional practice only." The very obvious but very important point to note here is that the medical practice exemption is part of a criminal statute. A prescription of drugs that falls outside this exemption is much more than a professional mistake on the part of a doctor. It is a prosecutable offense.

The American Medical Association has adopted and issued several statements on the use of narcotics in medical practice. The most recent, which appeared in 1963, and is currently in the process of revision, was prepared in collaboration with the National Research Council of the National Academy of Sciences. It may be summarized as follows:

Continued administration of drugs for the maintenance of addiction is not a bona fide attempt at cure. In other words withdrawal of the drug must be accomplished before the rehabilitation phase of the treatment can begin.

Withdrawal is most easily carried out in a drug-free environment, in specialized wards or installations for narcotic addicts. Under certain circumstances withdrawal may be carried out in other institutional settings, such as psychiatric wards of general hospitals.

Withdrawal on an ambulatory basis (outside an institution) is, as a general matter, medically unsound and not recommended on the basis of present knowledge.

Ambulatory clinic plans (dispensing drugs to outpatient addicts through clinics established for that purpose) or any other form of ambulatory maintenance (giving stable doses to outpatient addicts) are also medically unsound on the basis of present knowledge.

It is proper ethical practice, after consultation and subject to keeping adequate records, to administer narcotics over a prolonged period to patients with chronic incurable and painful conditions, when reasonable alternate procedures have failed, or to maintain an aged or infirm addict, when withdrawal would be dangerous to life. Finally it is ethical to administer maintenance doses generally of methadone, a synthetic narcotic, to an addict who is awaiting admission to a narcotic facility, and to administer limited and diminishing doses to an addict during a process of withdrawal.

Research on the problems of narcotics addiction is absolutely necessary and present concepts are open to revision based on the results of such research. . . .

17.

CHARLES WINICK

PHYSICIAN NARCOTIC ADDICTS

This study was undertaken in order to explore what would appear to be the anomaly of the substantial incidence of drug addiction among physicians. It is an anomaly because addiction is generally perceived as a degraded and visibly pathological form of deviant behavior which is associated with the lower socioeconomic classes. In contrast, physicians are usually perceived as constituting one of the most prestigious and honored and wealthy occupations in our society.[1] A further anomaly is the extent to which

SOURCE: *Social Problems,* Vol. 9 (Fall, 1961), pp. 174–86, The Society for the Study of Social Problems. Reprinted by permission of the author and the journal.

[1]National Opinion Research Corporation, "Jobs and Occupations: A Popular Evaluation," *Opinion News,* Vol. 9 (September 1, 1947), pp. 3–13.

the physician is clearly a person who early learns to defer gratifications during his very lengthy training. In contrast, the addict's orality and need for his drug frequently make it very difficult for him to defer gratifications.

The incidence of opiate addiction among physicians has been estimated by the U.S. Commissioner of Narcotics as being about one addict among every 100 physicians, in contrast to a rate of one in 3,000 in the general population.[2] According to official records of the Federal Bureau of Narcotics, 1,012 physicians were reported as addicts and 659 were found guilty of illegal narcotics sales or prescription activity from 1942 through 1956. One report identified the dean of a university medical school and other well known physicians who became addicted.[3] The head of a leading state medical society became addicted and committed suicide. The number of physicians becoming addicted each year is roughly equivalent to the graduating class of a medical school. It is of course possible that there are physician addicts who are not known to the authorities, so that the incidence may be even higher.

A substantial incidence of addiction among physicians has been reported from several other countries, suggesting that there may be something about the physician's role independent of his nationality which is related to his use of narcotics. England has reported that physicians are the occupational group most heavily represented among addicts, accounting for 17 per cent of the country's addicts.[4] One authority, summarizing United Nations reports on the subject, has said that in England one physician in every 550 and in Germany one physician in every 95 was an addict.[5] Another study reported that addiction in the 1930's among German physicians was 100 times more frequent than in the general population, and that the typical physician addict used more drugs than other addicts.[6]

There have been two statistical studies of physician addicts, both conducted at the U.S. Public Health Service hospitals. One study of 47 addict physicians conducted 20 years ago at the U.S. Public Health Service Hospital at Fort Worth reported that the typical addict physician was a native-born, 52-year-old, white male, engaged in general practice in a small town.[7] He began using morphine at the age of 39 for the relief of a painful condition, and came from comfortable economic circumstances. He had sought a voluntary cure in sanitaria on three occasions and been in jail once. He was married and had two children. He had approximately the same prospects for cure as the average addict. A study of 457 consecutive admissions to the U.S. Public Health Service Hospital at Lexington for meperidine ("Demerol") addiction reported that 32.7 per cent of these cases of primary addiction were physicians and osteopaths.[8]

PROCEDURE

The purpose of this study was to explore the social and personality correlates of addiction in addict physicians. In order to explore these correlates, interviews were conducted in New York, Pennsylvania, Massachusetts, Rhode Island, New Jersey, and Connecticut, with 98 physicians who either were or had been opiate addicts. All the physicians had been addicts during a period of at least 10 years prior to the interview, and some may have been addicts at the time of the interview. Access to the physicians was obtained through a variety of non-law-enforcement sources. The physicians had previously been asked by an intermediary if they would consent to be interviewed about their use of opiates, and all those interviewed

[2] "Interview with Hon. Harry J. Anslinger," *Modern Medicine,* Vol. 25 (October 15, 1957), pp. 170–91.

[3] J. DeWitt Fox, "Narcotic Addiction among Physicians," *Journal of the Michigan State Medical Society,* Vol. 56 (February, 1957), pp. 214–17.

[4] Her Majesty's Government, *Report to the United Nations on the Working of the International Treaties on Narcotic Drugs* (London: HMSO, 1955).

[5] Lawrence Kolb, "The Drug Addiction Muddle," *Police,* Vol. 1 (January-February, 1957), pp. 57–62.

[6] Alfred R. Lindesmith, *Opiate Addiction* (Evanston: Principia Press, 1947), p. 60.

[7] Michael J. Pescor, "Physician Drug Addicts," *Diseases of the Nervous System,* Vol. 3 (June, 1942), pp. 173–74.

[8] Robert W. Rasor and H. James Crecraft, "Addiction to Meperidine," *Journal of the American Medical Association,* Vol. 157 (February 19, 1955), pp. 654–57.

had agreed to meet with the investigator who conducted the interviews.

The interviews were generally conducted in the office or home of the respondent and took an average of two hours. The format of the interview was simple: the respondent was asked to discuss his career, beginning with his first interest in medicine. If he did not mention his experience with opiates, he was asked to discuss it. Specific questions about the respondent's attitudes toward medicine and his early life were asked if he did not discuss these subjects in detail. He was asked about his youth, parents, career aspirations, health, and current family situation. The interviewer took notes on the physician's comments and these notes were content-analyzed into various content categories, which are summarized below.

Description of Interviewees

The physicians interviewed ranged in age from 28 to 78, with an average age of 44. There were 93 men and 5 women, 61 general practitioners and 37 specialists. All but one were married and 84 per cent had children.

The average age at which drug use began was 38. The average length of time since the addiction of the physicians interviewed had begun was six years. The range was 1 year to 22 years.

Of the physicians interviewed, 53 per cent had their practices in cities of over a million population, 33 per cent worked in communities of 250,000 to a million, and 12 per cent in communities of under 250,000. In contrast, 22 per cent were born in cities of over a million, 23 per cent in cities of 250,000 to a million and 55 per cent were born in communities of under 250,000.

Every physician interviewed was in private practice and had some kind of hospital affiliations. None had been involved in any official or institutional research project on narcotics. The physicians interviewed ranged from a few who were less successful than the average in their professional careers to some who were extraordinarily successful national figures. The typical physician interviewed was more successful than the average, in terms of income, honorific and institutional affiliations, and general professional activity. Most were useful and effective members of their community. For example, one physician was brought to a private hospital for treatment by the public prosecutor in his community in order to avoid charges being preferred against him by the prosecutor.

Eighty per cent of the subjects were meperidine ("Demerol") addicts, 9 per cent took dilaudid, 7 per cent used morphine, and 4 per cent took codeine. Every subject interviewed was an addict and not a user, in terms of the traditional addiction criterion of daily use of an opiate. Some of the physicians took as much as 50 or 100 cc of meperidine daily, which is several times the amount given a hospital patient in considerable pain. Some physicians (2 per cent) turned themselves in for treatment because they were almost saturated with meperidine and it was having less and less effect. One man who was taking 50 cc a day said, "It's like drinking four or five gallons of water a day."

Most (74 per cent) of the respondents said that their wives had known of their addiction. Many (61 per cent) said that their nurses knew of their addiction, although there were no cases of contamination of the wife or nurse by the physician.

There appeared to be no significant socioeconomic differences between the respondent who was a minimal addict, taking a small dosage daily, and the heavy user who took a large dosage. It is possible to speculate that the minimal addict may be "more" addicted than the heavy user, because he is taking so little of the drug that he might be able to stop it altogether—yet he cannot do so.

In New York, meperidine is often called "the doctor's drug." Its label clearly states that its use should be discontinued if euphoria is noted. In spite of this caveat, the drug was selected by so many physicians for a number of reasons. They thought it less addicting and less toxic than other opiates. It is relatively available. The users thought its effects would be less visible than those of other narcotics. Its medical connotations made it more acceptable. There was a feeling that it was somehow easier for a physician to cure himself of meperidine addiction than of addiction to other drugs. Its being a synthetic opiate made it more attractive to some.

Law Enforcement and the Physician

Eight of the interviewees had had their license to practice revoked, 38 were on probation, 51 had completed probation, and one had not received any formal punitive action.

A small proportion of the physicians interviewed (4 per cent) sought help for their condition before they were apprehended or before some official or government functionary discussed their drug use with them. The rest (96 per cent) of those who were in trouble with the law did not seek help until they were apprehended or could tell that they were just about to be apprehended.

The physicians who had run afoul of the law enforcement agencies were treated relatively kindly by the law. One reason for this was probably that none had attempted to prescribe drugs for other addicts. Every physician who was taking drugs could have been charged with a crime. Only one, however, actually had been so charged, and only a few were arrested. The reason for the leniency afforded these physicians was perhaps not only the feeling that they would be punished enough by having their licenses to practice suspended for varying periods of time. It was probably also the assumption that they could be salvaged for the community and not lose their years of training and preparation for their careers.

Once a physician has begun taking drugs himself, he is likely to have difficulties in concealing his activities for any considerable length of time. The pharmacists and nurses or wives who observe their activities may report the physicians to state or federal authorities, who may have already observed unusual prescription activity on the part of a physician. None of the physicians interviewed was reported by either a colleague or a patient.

The physicians exhibited considerable ingenuity in obtaining drugs illegally. The most frequent method was to write prescriptions in a real or imaginary patient's name and use the drug themselves. Others would give a patient a fraction of a dose and keep the rest for themselves. Some might order a standard 30 cc vial of meperidine for a patient in a hospital, give the patient a few cc, and keep the rest for themselves. Or they took what might be left from a hospital patient and withdrew it for "office use." Some might get drugs "in an emergency" from a friendly pharmacist without a prescription. Others might go to their hospital and feign having absentmindedly left their prescription pads at their offices. All of these procedures are, of course, illegal, and state and federal narcotics inspectors are on the alert for them.

A number of physicians (15 per cent) said that they were aware of the negative connotations of the way in which they got narcotics. "I've never done anything that has made me feel so degraded," said one respondent. "I went back to the hospital and told my nurse I had forgotten my prescription pad. She gave me some drugs and I took a shot. I knew it was wrong."

Federal or state narcotics law enforcement officials usually confront addict physicians with the evidence against them and turn them over to state licensing authorities who decide on the circumstances, if any, under which the physician will be able to practice. Some physicians were required to pay a fine and to demonstrate that they were not using drugs for a period of some years. Apprehended physicians are required to surrender their tax stamp which permits them to prescribe narcotics. The New York authorities have developed a procedure designed to protect the public against the addict physician while it assists the physician to rehabilitate himself. He usually has his license suspended and must demonstrate non-drug use for a year. He must agree to be treated by an approved physician and examined to check on his abstinence every three months for several years. A physician who has not demonstrated abstinence may have his license revoked.

Once confronted by state or federal authorities, the physicians usually said that they were relieved to be caught. They often said that they had been hoping someone would help them to stop drug use. No physician interviewed attempted to deny his use of narcotics once he had been caught.

Eighty-nine per cent of the physicians interviewed remained in the community in which they had been practicing, after being apprehended. There was practically no publicity about any of the cases. Where the physician had to leave his practice, he generally turned the practice over to a colleague and resumed it upon his return.

Physician Addicts and "Street" Addicts

The physician addicts interviewed differed in a number of ways from the typical "street" addict who buys drugs from a "pusher." The most obvious difference is that the age at which the physicians began to use drugs is just about the age that the typical addict stops using drugs, whether by "maturing out" or for other reasons. The "street" addict typically begins drug use in adolescence, while the physician begins when he is an established community and professional figure. The "street" addict takes heroin, while the typical physician addict took meperidine. The physician can get a pure quality of his drug, although it is not as strong as heroin. The "street" addict gets a diluted drug. He often starts with marijuana, although none of the physicians ever smoked marijuana.

The physician is usually discovered by the indirect evidence of a check of prescription records, while the "street" addict is usually arrested either because he has narcotics in his possession or has been observed making an illegal purchase. The physician is usually not arrested, while the typical "street" addict is arrested. Money to obtain drugs was not a problem for the physicians, as it usually is for the typical addict who must steal in order to obtain money to buy drugs illegally. The physicians could use their professional access to narcotics to obtain drugs without much money. Even if they paid, the legal prices of narcotic drugs are very low.

Most non-physician addicts associate with other addicts. In contrast, the physicians interviewed almost never associated with other physician addicts, or did not do so knowingly. They did not have any occasion for doing so, either for the purpose of getting drugs or for passing time, or for emotional support. They were solitary about their addiction. The "street" addict usually talks in a special jargon and often has a kind of wry insight into drug use, which stems from his extended discussions with his peers. The physicians did not talk in jargon and manifested very little insight into their drug use.

The typical "street" addict is not withdrawn in a medical setting. The physicians had almost all withdrawn in relatively comfortable medically supervised situations, so that there was little withdrawal distress. Seventy-four per cent had gone to a private hospital, usually under an assumed name; 11 per cent had gone to Lexington, and 15 per cent had made informal arrangements with friends and others.

"Street" addicts are likely to have been introduced to drugs by a contemporary. In contrast, none of the physicians interviewed had introduced anyone else to narcotic drugs or had "turned on" other physicians. It is possible to speculate that an addict physician, although he may not consciously wish to recruit addicts, may be unconsciously receptive to a patient who is especially eager for the physician to prescribe pain-killing drugs. He may identify with the patient's need and project his own need. Such a physician might possibly prescribe more drugs than the patient needs. It is possible, of course, that some addict physicians may be unusually sensitive to the possibility of patients becoming addicted and strive to prevent it. Twelve per cent of the respondents had come into contact with "street" addicts in hospitals. A typical reaction to such contact was, "I feel so degraded when I realize I'm like those people."

Factors Related to Drug Use

It took an average of two months of drug use for the physician to realize that he was addicted. The physician's professional knowledge of the qualities of opiates is certainly a factor in his using them himself, in terms of his knowledge of what effects they might have. His accessibility to drugs is not a complete explanation, because pharmacists are practically never addicted, even though they have much easier access to opiates than do physicians and can more easily manipulate their records.

It was possible to code several factors mentioned by the respondents as having been associated with their use of narcotics. In order of their incidence these themes could be categorized as overwork, physical ailments, self-concept, wives, level of aspiration, euphoric or depressing effect, liquor, insomnia, and age. A brief discussion of each theme follows, along with the proportion of respondents mentioning it. The total proportion of physicians interviewed who cited these themes came to 216 per cent, because many respondents mentioned more than one theme. Thus, the genesis of their drug use would appear to be multi-factorial.

Overwork (41 per cent). Almost all of these respondents had come from lower class homes in communities of under 250,000, and practiced in big cities. These physicians usually mentioned their feeling low and depressed as a result of their overwork, and there appeared to be an association in their thinking between fatigue and depression. "Demerol builds up my resistance when I am working hard so quickly it is tremendous," said one respondent. "If I take some dilaudid, I might do eight perfect operations under pressure instead of two," said another who had said that he was overworked.

Overwork may mean different things to different physicians. Some of those interviewed were working so hard that, as one said, they might "end up as the richest doctor in the cemetery." Those who become addicted may have had some reasons either for working hard or for leading themselves to think that they were working hard, and for using their heavy schedules as the rationale for their drug use. Some seem to have almost created a situation of overwork so that they could use the overwork as an excuse for narcotics use. "Anyone who worked as hard as I did was entitled to a half of a grain of morphine each day," said one. Most of these physicians seem to have had an unrealistic notion of how long they could take drugs without becoming addicted.

Some of the respondents who talked of working very hard conveyed a feeling of resignation that medicine was so demanding, and some expressed negative feelings about having entered the profession. "I wonder why I ever got into medicine at all," or "This is not a field I'd recommend to anyone," were comments typical of these respondents. A number of these respondents mentioned that a parent, usually the mother, had wanted them to be physicians.

Physical Ailment (36 per cent). Five-sixths of the physical ailments reported by the physicians who said that their drug use was related to the ailment was gastrointestinal disorders, like ulcers and colitis. The others reported a variety of ailments. The ailments were all chronic conditions. All but one of the physicians who had reported physical complaints were treating the ailments by themselves, although a few had undergone surgery. The drugs they took usually alleviated both their pain and symptoms. It is curious that practically none of the physicians with ailments commented on the unusualness of opiates alleviating the symptoms of the relatively serious ailments which they had.

Although none of these physicians discussed their addiction with physician colleagues, some (27 per cent) said that when they discussed their physical ailments with colleagues they mentioned the narcotics they were taking for pain relief. "I told a friend I was taking Demerol for my stomach," said one respondent. This kind of disclosure to a physician may have been one way in which the addict physician justified his regular use of narcotics to himself.

Self-Concept (32 per cent). About a third of those interviewed said that they were surprised at becoming addicted. "I felt I could take a shot when a crisis arose," "I felt I could stop at any time," and "I thought I'd toy with it because I knew enough about it to inhibit its reaction and control its use," were typical comments made by this group. "I thought I was above getting addicted," said another physician. Their professional familiarity with the effects of drugs appears to have provided a rationale for their semi-magical belief that the drugs would somehow have a different effect upon them than they had on non-physicians. Addicts other than physicians often believe that they can control the effects of drugs, or "take just one more shot," or reduce their intake. The physicians cited many of these rationalizations in clarifying their surprise at becoming addicted. The majority of these physicians believed that they were too smart to become "hooked."

Marital Problems (31 per cent). These physicians voiced a wide range of marital difficulties. The largest proportion of these respondents said that their wives were too aggressive and driving. A number said that they should have gotten a divorce, and some expressed other kinds of dissatisfaction with their wives. None of these physicians had taken any action toward a divorce or separation. A number of these physicians were also among those who reported physical ailments.

Level of Aspiration (24 per cent). These physicians generally had a history of disaffection toward and disagreement with their profession, usually coupled with a record of considerable achievement within the profession. They often were officers of their college pre-medical society, and tended to be good students in both college and medical school. Their level of aspiration and competitive spirit tended to be high.

For the physicians in this group who developed physical symptoms, the illness appeared to have been perceived as a very threatening interference with their fantasies about their success. The pain associated with their illness may have occasioned almost a panic in the physicians, and one way in which they may have coped with the panic was to begin taking drugs. The drugs they took were usually effective in the physicians' attempts to cope with their pain. This diminution of pain may have provided the physicians with a variety of further rationalizations for drug use.

It is possible to speculate that the high level of aspiration and competitive spirit of these physicians was so integral a part of their personality that it may have been very difficult for them to express their disaffection toward medicine because their medical career was the embodiment of their level of aspiration. The aggressiveness and disaffection may have thus been partially drained off by drug use.

Euphoric or Depressing Effect (21 per cent). These physicians specifically mentioned the drug's effect on their mood. Most of these physicians said that the drugs made them feel good and improved their work. "I realized that here was something I'd been looking for all my life, and the last piece of the jigsaw puzzle fell into place," said one.

There were others who said that the drug lost its stimulus effect after a while, and "I just took it to keep alive. It made me feel depressed and slow." These physicians tended to say that the continued use of opiates interfered with their work.

Liquor (17 per cent). These physicians said that they had been drinking fairly heavily before they began using drugs. Most of these respondents had been drinking by college and medical school days. Some began narcotics use because "You can't walk into an operation reeking of liquor on your breath." Two had switched from alcohol to barbiturates before using opiates. Others began because "Alcohol makes you fumble," and they could function with opiates but not with alcohol. Some began opiate use, either self-prescribed or prescribed by others, as one way of coping with hangovers from liquor. Whatever needs were met by alcohol were apparently also met by narcotics, since none of these physicians continued drinking after beginning narcotics use. None of the physicians who had been heavy drinkers before their addiction had returned to liquor after stopping drug use. Few of those who drank also reported somatic complaints. A number of the drinkers generally had negative things to say about their profession.

Insomnia (11 per cent). The physicians who were insomniacs were among the most intelligent interviewed. They seemed to have special difficulties in talking about their feelings. They were likely to report marital difficulties and disaffection toward medicine. Some of the physicians who cited their overwork said that they began drug use because they fell asleep more easily after taking a shot, and thus saved time in falling asleep and thus had more time available for their practice.

Age (3 per cent). A small number of the physicians interviewed were older men, in their 60's and 70's, who became addicted during World War II. These men said that they had retired or semi-retired and were called back to practice, over their objections, because of the wartime shortage of physicians. Most of them were from nonurban areas whose practices covered a fairly extended geographic area. They reported difficulties in meeting the increasing demands on them and in getting along with little sleep. They began taking a small dose of morphine in order to relieve fatigue and keep going. All of these physicians had ceased taking narcotics fairly soon after they returned to retirement, after the war.

Return to Drug Use

Over half the respondents had stopped drug use and then reverted, at least once. The circumstances of return to drug use varied. The physicians did not generally appear able to explain it. One said, "I got into a taxi to go to the hospital for an operation. Suddenly, as if it were another person inside me, I stopped the taxi at a pharmacy and got a shot." Another had gone to a ranch "cure" for three months, said he "felt great" there, and taken some drugs within an hour after his return to his office. Some physicians returned to drug use after a period of abstinence while in the middle of an investigation by an official agency, which could not help but uncover their reversion. One physician had been withdrawn and spent a month at a hospital, and went to a movie in a nearby city one afternoon. When he returned to the hospital that evening, he said that he had actually gone to his private office for the purpose of getting a shot. One physician returned to drug use after 19 years of abstinence. As in the case of non-physician addicts, logic did not appear to be very influential in assisting many of these physicians in remaining off drugs.

Of the respondents who had been to the U.S. Public Health Service Hospital at Lexington, most had remained off drugs. One said of the hospital: "Lexington cured me forever. It made me acutely aware of how sick I was, and I decided never again. I was so shaken that I never even got another narcotic tax stamp." One of the few Lexington patients who reverted said, "The hospital helped me. I realized I could get a shot in my vein that would be better than one in my arm."

Prognosis

The prognosis for many of these physicians can only be regarded as guarded. A licensed physician who has to engage in subterfuge to get drugs and who is aware of the implications of drug use, and who only seeks help when crisis or the law threatens, may not be a good risk for abstinence. "You have to fudge so much to get your drugs," as one physician said, that an addict physician who has been so willing to "fudge" may have difficulties in giving up narcotics. He has to do so many things that are destructive in order to get drugs that his addiction may be relatively salient.

However, it has been estimated by one student that 85 per cent of addicted physicians return to their practice and to a drug-free life, with the other 15 per cent deteriorating or committing suicide.[9] This high recovery rate is attributed to a considerable extent to the physician's recollection of the agreeable way of life that he enjoyed before addiction.

A variety of methods of abstinence was mentioned by the physicians who had stayed off drugs successfully for a period of several years. Most had had several periods of relapse, with the periods of time between reversion becoming longer and longer. Many took "milder" drugs like paregoric to ease the transition. Some adjusted their external schedules in order to minimize temptation: "I made up my mind to handle only the amount of practice I could handle without fatigue." Those in pain decided to be uncomfortable and live with pain rather than take drugs. Others had a version of the Coue method: "Every morning I make up my mind that nothing will make me take drugs today." A very few of the physicians had sought psychiatric help. Wives and colleagues did not seem to have much of a role in assisting the physician to get off drugs.

DISCUSSION

The established sociological theories of deviant behavior and of addiction do not completely explain the narcotics use of these physicians. The Mertonian theory of deviant behavior as a reflection of differences in the legitimate means of access to culturally prescribed goals does not appear to be relevant to these physicians, who had achieved such goals publicly and legiti-

[9]Edward R. Bloomquist. "The Doctor, The Nurse, and Narcotic Addiction." *General Practitioner,* Vol. 18 (November, 1958), pp. 124–29.

of a threat as non-achievement to some respondents. One said, "I was fighting to be top man for all those years, but when I reached the top, what did I have?" He began drug use because he felt that his victories were hollow, and there were no more conquests to make. No matter how successful such a man might be, his omnipotence would leave him restless. A number of these physicians began drug use when they had reached a stage in life at which they could begin to implement their omnipotence, and such implementation seemingly posed grave problems. Not one of the respondents reported any interest in drugs in the early stages of his career, even amidst the stress and demands of internship and the early stages of establishing a practice.

Effects of the Drug. One ultimate dimension of drug use by physicians is the drug's effect on its users. The effect of the opiate appears to be mediated by the personality of the physician user. Some users feel better and other users feel worse after taking opiates. The relationships between either the euphoric or depressing effect of the opiate and other factors related to its use are not clear.

Some combination of these factors of role strain, passivity, omnipotence, and effects of the drug, appear to underlie the narcotics use of the physicians interviewed. These factors may predispose physicians to addiction in a wide variety of external situations and environments. If these or similar factors are not present, the physician may not become addicted even in extremely taxing environments. No external situation, by itself, can be taxing enough to drive a physician to becoming addicted. Thus, there is not one recorded case of a Jewish physician who was in a Nazi concentration camp who became a drug addict during or after his incarceration. It would be difficult to imagine a more demanding situation than an experience in a concentration camp.

The external situations that faced the physician addicts interviewed, however, were perceived and experienced by the physicians themselves in a manner that gave rise to the deviant behavior of drug use. These physicians appear to have been addiction-prone through some combination of role strain, passivity, omnipotence, and effects of the drug. It is of course possible that the physicians interviewed are not typical of other addict physicians, or that they may be reflecting regional or other special factors.

18.

JULIAN B. ROEBUCK

THE NEGRO DRUG ADDICT AS AN OFFENDER TYPE

Several sociologists have demonstrated in research findings that incarcerated offenders share many personal and social characteristics. For the most part, however, the focus of attention has been on representative samples of delinquents and criminals in general. The relationships of these personal and social factors to offenders with different kinds of criminal behavior patterns have not been the subject of comprehensive and systematic study.[1] Robbers,

Reprinted by special permission of the *Journal of Criminal Law, Criminology and Police Science* (Northwestern University School of Law), Copyright © 1962, Vol. 53, No. 1.

[1]While in some studies certain offenders have been specified as ideal types, e.g., the alcoholic, drug addict, professional criminal, and sex offender, none of these studies have utilized categories of criminal behavior arrived at through the systematic sampling of large populations of offenders, nor have they specified clear-cut empirical criteria for the construction of such categories as might have been used.

housebreakers, narcotics offenders, and the rest usually have been treated as a single criminal category. The present paper differs from previous research in that it utilizes a typology of criminal categories which enables the researcher to isolate similarities and differences between types of offenders.[2] This is not the same thing as saying, "criminals in general have many personal and social characteristics in common"—a statement that has been made frequently enough. The use of the typology in the research reported in this paper permits a concentrated focus upon one relatively homogeneous group of offenders and a detailed empirical search for significant similarities and differences between this group, the narcotic drug laws offender, and other offenders.

The data so obtained supports the impressions of sociologists and psychiatrists who have long noted that the drug addict (opiate addict) as an offender type cannot be defined as a criminal in the traditional sense of a robber, auto thief, burglar, murderer, etc.[3] Generally, he is conceded to be a criminal only by virtue of a personal vice, no different than the alcoholic for example. Unlike the alcoholic, however, the addict's vice is a criminal act regardless of the social consequences. His behavior, as distinct from that of the traditional criminal, usually involves no victim, except, of course, the user himself. As has been noted by many observers, the drug addict is not a serious offender against person or property, nor is he to be found among the organized criminals, racketeers, or professional thieves.[4] The fact is that most crimes associated with drug addiction involve direct or indirect violations of state or federal narcotics acts and occasional unsophisticated thefts, burglaries, and forgeries.[5] The primary criminal motivation of this individual is neither gain nor the need to express aggression, but rather a physiological compulsion that demands satisfaction. In this his physical needs are little different from that of the diabetic, except that the latter will eventually die without insulin while the former will suffer extreme physiological discomfort without drugs. Thus, if the addict's motivation differs from that of the robber, the arsonist, or the professional thief, then it can be expected that he may possess social and psychological characteristics that distinguish him from the traditional criminal.

If a theory of the etiology of drug addiction is to be developed, the first requirement will be to find if there are significant differences between this offender and the traditional criminal. Until this step is taken, we do not know whether the differences that may be found between drug addicts and the law abiding may be a function of the arrest and incarceration process, rather than generic social or psychological differences. On the other hand, if there are no social or psychological differences between this offender and other offender types, it may well be that addiction has the same general etiology as other criminal behavior, only expressing itself in dissimilar ways. This paper reports the findings of a comparative study of 50 drug addicts and 350 traditional criminal types who comprised a sample group of 400 Negro inmates in the District of Columbia Reformatory.[6] The findings represent a tentative step in providing the needed

[2]For a survey of several attempts to construct criminal typologies see Gibbons & Garrity, "Some Suggestions for the Development of Etiological and Treatment Theory in Criminology," *Social Forces*, Vol. 38 (1959), p. 51.

[3]Reckless, *The Crime Problem* (2d ed., 1955), pp. 353–56; Pescor, *A Statistical Analysis of Clinical Records of Drug Addicts*, Supp. *Public Health Reports*, Vol. 145 (1938), p. 26; Karpman, "Laws That Cause Crime," *American Mercury*, Vol. 23 (1931), p. 74.

[4]Lindesmith, "Dope Fiend Mythology," *Journal of Criminal Law and Criminology*, Vol. 40 (1949), p. 199; Kolb, "The Drug Addiction Muddle," *Police*, Vol. 1 (1957), p. 57.

[5]Tappan, *Crime, Justice and Correction* (1960), pp. 165–67.

[6]The sample of 400 Negro felons was selected from 1,155 Negroes who entered the District of Columbia Reformatory, Lorton, Virginia, between the dates of January 5, 1954, and November 8, 1955. The Reformatory (actually a penitentiary) houses a heterogeneous group of felons serving sentences of various lengths ranging to life imprisonment. The findings on which this paper is based were drawn from an unpublished doctoral dissertation, "A Tentative Typology of 400 Negro Felons," completed at the University of Maryland, College Park, Maryland, August, 1958, by the writer. The research was one of several studies conducted under the auspices of the Institute for Criminological Research, Department of Corrections, Washington, D.C.

facts for a theory of the etiology of drug addiction.

A TENTATIVE CRIMINAL TYPOLOGY

The construction of a new typology was deemed necessary to provide the facts for a comparative study. Instead of using the conventional classification based on the offense for which the inmate was serving his sentence, a typology of criminal behavior based on the configuration of the total known arrests for the various criminal offenses of each inmate was devised.[7] It was assumed that an analysis of the official arrest histories of a sizable sample of offenders would reveal for some offenders a repetition of the same kind of criminal charges; and that for classification purposes it would be useful to examine these repetitions and establish the sequence of offenses found therein. It was expected that certain sequences of arrests by criminal charge would reveal the offender's criminal scheme of life. The pattern of criminal behavior shown in the arrest history seemed to offer a more valid basis for a typology of criminal behavior than one based upon the particular crime for which the inmate was presently serving his sentence. The arrest history reflects a period of time and hence is longitudinal; this improves the likelihood of its indicating a fixed behavior pattern of criminality.[8] The case of an offender whose official arrest history exhibits ten robbery charges out of twelve arrests may be cited as a hypothetical example of such a pattern. Similar sequences of arrests on other charges, e.g., assault, intoxication, housebreaking, etc., may be classified in this manner. This approach would make it possible to assign individual offenders to "criminal-pattern categories" on the basis of their past arrest histories. Obviously, some criminal histories would not disclose such a clear-cut criminal pattern. One would expect to find a variety of types.

It was assumed that criminals in their crime activities, as non-criminals in their legitimate activities, manifest a characteristic behavior pattern which becomes their identifying mark. Moreover, there is considerable justification for assuming that particular patterns of behavior in adult life are associated with particular social and personal background factors. The crux of the typology problem appears to center on the following:

1. The presence of criminal patterns in the offender's criminal record.
2. The association of certain social and personal background factors with the above patterns.

In the construction of the typology it was recognized that some criminals exhibit variation in their criminal activities. It was extremely difficult to develop mutually exclusive categories of criminal types. An inmate classified in one criminal category on the basis of the predominance of one criminal charge in his arrest history may also have been charged with other crimes, e.g., the robber, who, in addition to several charges for robbery, has in his arrest history one or two charges for petty larceny. To meet this problem, the most frequent charge or charges in the inmate's arrest history were used as a basis for classification, and the charges appearing in the later phases of the inmate's arrest history were given greater weight. It was reasoned that the

[7]In determining criminal patterns (arrest history patterns) a chronological arrest history on each of the four-hundred cases was derived from the official arrest records. Legal nomenclature was adhered to; the offense categories (*e.g.*, robbery, burglary, assault, etc.) found in the criminal codes of the District of Columbia (D.C. Code), of the United States (U.S. Code), and of the various states were followed. Two reasons prompted the use of legal labels: (1) the accessible official data concerned with the official criminal histories existed in terms of legal nomenclature, that is, arrests by criminal charge; (2) the criminal code, in the opinion of the writer, had established more definite substantive norms of behavior, and it contained a more clear-cut, specific, and detailed definition of criminal behavior for offenders, than had any other non-legal set of norms. See Tappan, "Who is the Criminal?," *American Sociological Review*, Vol. 12 (1947), p. 96.

[8]Of course, this index, as any other official record, does not account for all the crimes committed by the inmate in his crime career. No offender is apprehended and charged with the commission of every crime he commits. However, as Sutherland and others have noted, the further one gets from a criminal's arrest history, the more obscure and distorted become the facts of his criminal activities. Sutherland and Cressey, *Principles of Criminology* (5th ed.; 1955), p. 25–26.

later entries in an offender's arrest history would more accurately reflect his present criminal behavior pattern than those entries occurring in the earlier stages of his arrest history.[9]

An analysis of the 400 arrest histories based on the frequency of criminal charges occurring in each history permitted the grouping of all cases into four general classes:

1. *Single Pattern.* This label was attached to an arrest history which showed a high frequency of one kind of criminal charge. In order for an arrest history to be classified as a single pattern, it had to satisfy one of the following conditions:
   a) It had to show three or more arrests, *all* of which were for the same charge.
   b) An arrest history which contained at least four arrests for a given charge *and additional arrests for other charges* was divided into three chronological sections[10] and qualified for a single pattern:
      (1) If the four-or-more arrest charges appeared in the last section of the arrest history at least once; and,
      (2) If the charge constituted at least 33 per cent of those charges which occurred in the last two sections of the arrest history.
2. *Multiple Pattern.* An arrest history of two or more single patterns derived by the procedures set forth in Item 1(b), above.
3. *Mixed Pattern.* An arrest history of three or more arrests in which none of the charges form a frequency patters as defined above. ("Jack of all trades.")
4. *No Pattern.* An arrest history of fewer than three arrests. (This is a residual category of those offenders with insufficient arrests to warrant analysis.)

The final result was a typology of 13 criminal patterns, 11 of which include distinct legal categories.[11]

COMPARISON OF NARCOTICS OFFENDERS WITH OTHER CRIMINAL TYPES

On the basis of the frequency of criminal charges found in the arrest histories, 50 of our sample of 400 offenders were classified as narcotic drug laws offenders.[12] These men, comprising one-eighth of the sample, were compared with the remainder of the sample on a large number (42) of personal and social characteristics obtained on each offender from institutional records and

[9]In addition to frequency of charge, the role that time intervals between charges might play in determining patterning was taken into consideration. For instance, it would not be plausible to treat on equal footing two arrest histories, each of which showed four arrests for the same charge, if in one history the charges were equally spread over a thirty-year period, whereas in the other history, charges occurred within the same calendar year. Such extremes in the distribution of charges over time could have—methodologically speaking—introduced a serious weighting problem. Fortunately, a preliminary investigation of a large proportion of the study sample revealed a remarkable homogeneity in length of time intervals between charges. In fact, only 10 out of the total 400 arrest histories exhibited an interval of five or more years between arrests (omitting, of course, time spent in incarceration). This finding precluded another potentially troublesome problem in respect to time lapses between arrests—that of extreme variations between intervals *within the same history.*

[10]If the total number of arrests was divisible by three, the arrest history was divided into three equal sections. When the total number of arrests was indivisible by three, the latter section, or latter two sections were given more weight. "K" represents an *integral number* of arrests, *i.e.,* 1, 2, 3. . . . Therefore, an arrest history showing (3K + 1) arrests was divided into the three following sections: K, K, and K + 1, thus giving more weight to the last section. Similarly a history showing (3K + 2) arrests was divided into the three following sections: K, K + 1, and K + 1, thus giving more weight to the last two sections. The arrest histories containing four or more arrests were divided in accordance with one of these three schemes in preparation for analysis.

[11]
1. Single pattern of robbery (N32)
2. Single pattern of narcotic drug laws (N50)
3. Single pattern of gambling (N16)
4. Single pattern of burglary (N15)
5. Single pattern of sex offenses (N15)
6. Single pattern of confidence games (N10)
7. Single pattern of auto theft (N8)
8. Single pattern of check forgery (N4)
9. Triple pattern of drunkenness, assault, and larceny (N43)
10. Double pattern of larceny and burglary (N64)
11. Double pattern of assault and drunkenness (N40)
12. Mixed pattern (N71)
13. No pattern (N32)

[12]All 50 were heroin addicts as attested to by a medical examination conducted by a D.C. Department of Corrections physician.

interviews.[13] These characteristics, which covered much of the offender's life history, included family, neighborhood and school background, indices of personal disorganization, marital status, and indices of juvenile delinquency. These areas represent fields of investigation in which researchers have claimed to find marked differentials between offenders and non-offenders.[14]

The drug offenders were comparatively a young group (median age–25) of fairly literate offenders (S.A.T. grade median–8.6) of average intelligence (median I.Q.–100) who for the most part were reared in urban areas (94 per cent). (Remainder of sample: median age–33; S.A.T. grade median–5.0; I.Q. median–86; 65 per cent reared in urban areas.)

In many ways their early family, school, and community backgrounds and adjustments were more favorable than those of the other offenders. (See Table 5.6 below.) They were reared less frequently in slum neighborhoods. They were more often products of one home situation, and the home was less commonly marked by criminality, conflict, demoralization, and parental desertion. Less frequently were their mothers migrants from the South and domestic servants. More often they were products of families which enjoyed strong ties. As further evidence of this familial milieu, these drug addicts less frequently expressed hostility toward their fathers, and they were less often disciplinary problems either at home or in school. Additionally, fewer of them were school truants and "home run-aways." They worked less frequently at street trades during childhood and adolescence, and fewer of them had had delinquent companions. Furthermore they were less often found to be members of juvenile delinquent gangs; fewer of them had been adjudicated juvenile delinquents; and a smaller proportion of them had been picked up by police prior to their eighteenth birthdays. A higher proportion of them (86 per cent) had adult criminal companions as adolescents. This factor was probably quite significant in their becoming drug addicts, as these adult companions were, for the most part, themselves addicts.

TABLE 5.6

COMPARISON OF SINGLE PATTERN OF NARCOTIC DRUG LAWS OFFENDERS (N = 50) WITH ALL OTHER OFFENDERS (N = 350)
(Per Cent of Offenders Exhibiting Selected Social and Personal Attributes)

All Other Offenders—per cent	χ^2 *Level of Significance*	*Narcotics Offenders—per cent*	
44	=	12	Reared in more than one home
47	=	18	Mother fig. south. migrant
77	=	58	Mother fig. dom. servant
75	0	66	Dependent
39	=	8	Family broken by desertion
54	=	16	Demoralized family
47	=	12	Criminality in family
51	**	82	Mother figure dominant
73	**	98	Inad. superv. by father fig.
68	**	90	Inad. superv. by mother fig.
64	=	20	Conflict in family
46	=	18	Hostility to father fig.
20	0	14	Hostility to mother fig.
33	=	6	Disciplinary problem at home
50	=	16	Hist. running away from home
56	=	32	Weak parental fam. structure
75	=	36	No parental family ties
82	0	94	Reared in urban area
75	—	58	Reared in slum neighborhood
76	0	68	Living in slum area at arrest
54	=	24	History of school truancy
52	=	10	Disciplinary problem at school
53	=	32	Street trades as juvenile
70	0	82	No marital ties
62	=	34	Juv. del. companions
39	=	12	Member juv. del. gang
49	=	10	Adjudicated juv. del.
55	=	8	Committed as juv. del.
59	=	28	Police contact prior to age 18
34	**	86	Crim. companions as juv.

** Significantly above sample mean of all other offenders at .01 level
= Significantly below sample mean of all other offenders at .01 level
— Significantly below sample mean of all other offenders at .05 level
0 No significant difference

Probably the most important factor in the background of these offenders was maternal dominance. A higher proportion of them grew up in families where the mother was the dominant parental figure (82 per cent).[15] The father

[13] The records included social case workers' admission summaries and case recordings, and clinical psychologists' personality profiles based on clinical interviews and Minnesota Multiphasic Personality Inventories.

[14] Reckless, *op. cit.*, pp. 43–66.

[15] This difference and those noted in the immediately preceding paragraph were significant at the .01 level. The addicts were similar to the men in the remainder of the sample in that: a high pro-

figure seemed to have been quite indifferent to them, and in most cases he was dominated by the mother. Consequently, his presence and authority accounted for little in the family milieu. Quite frequently he spent long periods of time away from the home situation. As a typical addict commented:

> My old man was from nowhere, man. I seldom saw him. When he was home he sat in the corner and read the paper or something. Mama had to take care of things. She told us all what to do. . . . The old man walked the chalk too when she spoke. I don't know where he went. Probably out with some chick drinking or living it up.

From the inmates' comments during the interviews, the maternal figure appeared to be a strong-willed and mentally alert perfectionist who over-protected and over-indulged the offender at every turn. She often set high goals for the offender, who was usually her favorite child. During his formative years, she selected his limited number of playmates, many of whom were girls. This domination probably shielded the addict from the normal scuffles of boyhood. This is sharply portrayed by the following addict's comment:

> My mama man was a tight woman on me. She insisted I come home right after school. I wasn't allowed to run no streets, man. If I got in a fight, she raised hell. She didn't want me to play sports. Guess she was afraid I would get hurt. I didn't care much anyway. I enjoyed my spare time with her. She knew what was right for me.

Many of them stated that the mother encouraged them to participate in passive activities, e.g., reading, music, drawing, and art. As a consequence they spent a good share of their leisure time during childhood in the home isolated from neighborhood play groups. These remarks from one offender were typical:

> Mama didn't go for no rough stuff. She was hard, but she knew what was right. I got interested in music and art because she encouraged me. You know, she was refined. She wasn't like these hip bitches in the street.

It is likely that this maternal pattern accounted for the statistically significant infrequency of these men as disciplinary problems at school and at home when compared with the other men in the sample.

On the other hand, their adulthood maladjustment in all probability reflected their isolated status as drug addicts. At the time of their arrests they were, for the most part, slum dwellers cut loose from conjugal group ties. Only 9 had marital ties, though 49 had been married at one time or another.

Their remarks in the personal interviews demonstrated that heroin was the "prime mover" in their lives. They lived a hand to mouth existence in cheap rooming-houses where they were isolated from the majority of their former contacts with non-users, including their wives, children, and relatives (with the exception of the mother). This isolation was apparently self-imposed to allow escape from detection, proximity to drug sources and other addicts, and avoidance of the censure and reform attempts of relatives or other well wishers.

They had an excellent command of the criminal argot, and, as expected, they used the slang expressions generally identified with drug addicts. Though not closely identified with the organized underworld, their remarks indicated a greater criminal sophistication than possessed by others in the sample, with perhaps the exception of the professional gambler. While they were reluctant to discuss their criminal companions and their criminal activities, all of them admitted to the use of heroin with other drug addicts. They insisted that they engaged in theft and in the traffic of drugs in order to supply their drug needs. A typical quotation illustrates their attitude toward theft:

> My heart wasn't in it, but what could I do? I couldn't make $30.00 a day. If I didn't get drugs I got sick, so I hustled in some way. Usually I hustled alone.

All of them insisted that they were not "true" drug peddlers, and they showed marked bitterness at being so identified. As one addict stated:

---

portion of them grew up in economically dependent homes (66 per cent); generally they were living in slum areas when last arrested (68 per cent); most of them had no marital ties (82 per cent), In addition to the statistical findings reported above, considerable qualitative evidence was gathered from extensive interviews by the author to support and extend the quantitative study. This material is summarized below.

> By no stretch of the imagination am I a peddler. What the hell does the court treat me like one for? I was only trying to do a sick friend a favor when I copped the caps. I know how it is when I need to cop. You know you got to have it. Have you ever seen anybody sick? They punish me because I'm sick.

Approximately half of these men were jazz musicians who played in local night clubs. All of this group claimed that they were introduced to heroin by "fellow musicians," and they asserted that more than half of the musicians they knew used heroin or marijuana. As one fairly articulate musician commented:

> All the musicians I knew were well acquainted with drugs. Most of them used drugs in one form or the other . . . usually marijuana or heroin. A few cats didn't partake, but man they were regular fellows. I mean man they understand if the other cats "took off." The ones who didn't "cool it," drank the "hot stuff" (whiskey). It was more or less understood you had to get your "kicks" some way. Man, all musicians are sensitive and crazy. Playing long hours in clubs gets to be a drag. You need a kick to keep you cool. The trouble is when you get hooked you don't make enough money legit to buy the white stuff (heroin). You got to hustle.

Though their arrest histories were quite extensive (an average of nine arrests per man) few arrests were for offenses other than narcotic drug laws violations. Other violations were for non-violent property offenses, e.g., shop-lifting, petty larceny, and housebreaking. These acts apparently stemmed from their need to secure a personal supply of drugs. Forty-three of these offenders had never been arrested prior to their first use of drugs.

The District Attorney's Reports provided strong evidence that charges for the sale of narcotics were rarely motivated by gain per se. Frequently an addict became involved in a situation (technically defined in law as a sales situation) while acting as "contact man" between purchaser and the peddler from whom his own personal supply came. (The addict could be sure of at least a one-way cut!) This was the typical situation leading to a sales charge. In the few cases of sales charges where the offender actually possessed a supply for sale, they were found to be "small-time" street peddlers who sold drugs in order to earn money to support their own habits. They generally picked up a small supply of drugs at certain intervals. Usually they knew only the first name of the seller, and they had no idea of his drug source. The "pick-up" spots were frequently changed, and therefore they had difficulty in purchasing drugs. In short, they did not appear to be on the inside of a "true" peddler's organization. They were merely tools of the organized peddler in that they actually made street sales, and in so doing rendered themselves potential "fall guys." Five of the 50 men had tie-ups with a dope ring which imported heroin from outside the District of Columbia and distributed to street peddlers. Though professional in the sense that they lived from money made by selling drugs, they were not simon-pure drug wholesalers; they dispensed drugs to addicted street peddlers, and they personally transported drugs from other areas into Washington, D.C. Such obvious action does not attest to their status as "true" professionals.

As a group they had excellent verbal ability; their vocabularies were quite impressive in relation to their formal education. Soft spoken and non-aggressive in speech and general demeanor, they tended to intellectualize their problem of addiction. By and large they were introspective, passive and withdrawn, rarely expressing interest in active sports such as hunting, fishing, baseball, and boxing. On the other hand, they were generally interested in reading, movies, writing, and especially in listening to music. For this group of men the association of drugs and music constituted a way of life which for many other types of offenders was represented by an association of alcohol and women. As one addict commented:

> Man, I like to shoot a pill or two . . . then rear back and relax after I put on some of that crazy jazz like, say Sonny Stitt [well-known musician]. . . . Man . . . progressive jazz grooves me. Drugs and plenty crazy music was what I lived for.

Rarely did they speak of close friends, and when they did, their remarks suggested acquaintanceships rather than friendships. They voiced a preference for socializing with one or two male companions rather than with a larger group. Object relations to others appeared weak. A strong identification with the mother figure was expressed. They evinced affected, superior attitudes. Egocentric and lacking in self-criticism, they pretended to be quite satisfied with themselves as they were. They presented themselves in the interviews as victims of circumstances over which they had no control. One sensed a certain fatalism and resignation prevalent among them. They expressed very little interest in, or respect for, the opposite sex, with the exception of their mothers. Wives, girl friends, and former women companions were of no major concern. In movement and in speech they manifested what seemed to be a strong feminine component, though none was overtly homosexual.[16] Illustrative of their lack of sexual interest is this comment by one inmate:

> Man, women have never done too much for me. They are all the same anyway. When I was high—and man, I stayed high—I didn't want no woman. Course I have gone ahead with the thing if one insisted—you know, I was a man, but the kick from the drugs was the thing. Women want too much of your time. I had to hustle. Now if a broad could help me get some money or cop some drugs . . . well, you know, I went along with the happenings if I was able to. One way or the other I tried to satisfy the chick if she had some bread [money].

They abhorred violence of any kind, as exemplified by this characteristic statement:

> Man, these thugs are nothing. I wouldn't dirty my hands on them. You got to move people with your mouth. Just know what to say out of your mouth. Violence of any kind is for ignorant people. Only fools fight. Who wants to be a hero?

In summary, then, the addicts, unlike the other offenders, were criminals by virtue of their personal vice, drug addiction. As a group they were younger, more literate, and more intelligent than the offenders in the other patterns. They came less frequently from disorganized family backgrounds, and their childhood adjustments in school, at home, and in the community were such as to call less frequently for formal sanctions. They were less frequently involved in serious delinquencies which called for their adjudication as juvenile delinquents. On the other hand, they more frequently had adult criminal companions prior to their eighteenth birthdays. When engaged in delinquent or criminal activity they were more frequently "loners." They were reared by dominant mothers who kept them at home during their formative years, and who probably had much to do with rendering them what appeared to be "passive-dependent-dependent" personality types. During their adolescent and young adult years they were introduced to heroin by addict companions; and, for the most part they were not delinquent prior to their addiction. All of them stated that listening to jazz music was their chief means of recreation. Popular musicians who are known addicts were their heroes. Just what jazz music had to do with their addiction process is not known, but certainly there was a relationship. Other students of the addict have cited a relationship of drugs with jazz music.[17]

It may be that their personality type rendered them susceptible to the opiates. The state of euphoria produced by the opiate drugs is described in the literature as a peaceful, dreamy, and tranquil nirvana. This state is the antithesis of dynamic action. All these men abhorred alcohol, known to be somewhat of a personality irritant. The individual intoxicated on alcohol usually craves action and boisterous group entertainment. The drug addict, on the other hand, gets his "kicks" in a passive manner by listening to music or by daydreaming. Moreover, psychiatrists who have attempted therapy with both drug addicts and alcoholics have noted the difficulty involved in switching the drug addict to alcohol or the alcoholic to opiates.[18] During the research interviews the drug addicts expressed a great distaste for alcohol. Forty claimed they never had liked alcoholic beverages. Five claimed they had never used any. On the other hand, the "problem drinkers" expressed a similar distaste for opiates, although several stated they had experimented with heroin at one time or another.[19] These claimed it did nothing for them. The following

[16]These observations are based upon both the reports of the clinical psychologists found in each admission summary and the author's own interviews.

[17]Winick, "The Use of Drugs by Jazz Musicians," *Social Problems,* Vol. 7 (1959–60), p. 240.

[18]Meerloo, "Artificial Ecstacy," *Encyclopedia of Aberrations, A Psychiatric Handbook* (Podolsky ed. 1953), p. 201.

[19]Problem drinkers were included in another pattern of crime of the larger study. With the drug addicts excepted, the major recreational activities of all other criminal patterns revolved around alcohol, women, and gambling.

quotations from the interviews illustrate this point:

DRUG ADDICT: "Man, the joy-juice [alcohol] never did nothing for me. I never liked the stuff. I tried it a few times before getting hooked. That stuff makes you sick and wild. Why cats use that stuff I can't understand. It tears you up."

PROBLEM DRINKER: "Drugs! No. I don't go for the stuff. I shot a little H [heroin] once or twice along the way, but I got only sick and sleepy. I want something to make me feel peppy not something to knock you out. That stuff takes your nature away."

Be this as it may, pressed for the need of funds with which to purchase drugs, the addicts turned to illegal methods. Legitimate work did not pay enough to support their habits. In order to escape police detection and secure a ready supply of drugs, they isolated themselves in slum areas, away from relatives and "square" acquaintances, where they associated with addicts and petty criminals. Their possession and use of drugs and the petty offenses they engaged in to secure a ready supply of drugs rendered them vulnerable to police apprehension. Not one was found to be a racketeer or gangster. In short, they made up a group of petty, habitual offenders.

SUMMARY

The writer concludes that the present study demonstrates the utility of a typology based upon criminal careers as established by arrest history patterns. The use of this typology permitted the delineation of clear-cut and homogeneous offender categories. Of these the narcotic drug laws offender was selected for an intensive comparative study with the non-narcotic offender population. Such a comparative study of drug addicts and traditional criminal types is deemed to be an essential first step in any attempt to develop a satisfactory theory of the etiology of drug addition. The research reported here constitutes just such a first step. The empirical data, both quantitative and qualitative, clearly demonstrate that narcotic drug laws offenders differ from other criminal types in terms of theoretically relevant social and personal background factors.

CHAPTER VI

Alcoholism

MORE PERSONS are arrested each year in the United States for drunkenness than for any other criminal offense. In 1967, 1,396,280 arrests were made for this crime. Many individuals are arrested 5, 10, 20, or more times a year as a result of intoxication, and over a lifetime they may be rearrested several hundred times.

As a criminal category, drunkenness is not just a nuisance offense that the police must handle as a routine part of their work. In the case of violent personal crimes, intoxication has proven to be of some significance. In Wolfgang's study of criminal homicide discussed earlier (Chapter II), he concluded that there was a significant relationship between violent homicide and the presence of alcohol in the offender. Wolfgang stated that in approximately two-thirds of all cases, either the victim and/or the offender had been drinking immediately prior to the slaying. In another study dealing with patterns in aggravated assault (Chapter III), Pittman and Handy note that "alcohol ingestion was present in only slightly more than one-quarter . . . of all the cases [studied]." However, they conclude that "this may be a consequence of either the inability to detect the presence of prior alcohol ingestion or the failure to report it."

Another criminal category that must not be ignored is drunken driving. In 1967, the Federal Bureau of Investigation reported that 248,612 arrests were made for driving under the influence. Even though narcotics is included in the FBI definition of driving under the influence, it may be safely assumed that the great majority of those arrested were under the influence of alcohol. Some of these incidents involved accidents, serious injury or death. If this was the case, then the driver may very well be charged with a crime much more serious than drunken driving.

After alcohol is consumed it is disseminated in diluted form to every part of the body. Although a certain amount of alcohol is absorbed into the bloodstream the great bulk of it is carried to the small intestine. After consumption, alcohol will act as a depressant and an anesthetic. The prime effect will be its depressant action on the central nervous system. The behavior manifested by the user is the result of the part of the brain affected and the concentration of alcohol in the bloodstream. The effect of alcohol then is determined by the rate it is absorbed into the body. This is directly dependent upon the alcoholic content of the drink and the amount consumed by the user within a given period of time.

The influence of alcoholic beverages may be easily understood by a careful examination of the following table.

Selected Facts on Drunkenness[1]

1. Arrests for drunkenness totaled more than three times the arrests for the largest Index category (larceny-theft).
2. Between 1960 and 1967 arrests for drunkenness actually declined by 2.2 percent.
3. Male arrests outnumbered female arrests by more than 13 to 1.
4. Only 14.9 percent of those arrested for drunkenness were under 25 years of age.
5. Arrests for whites outnumbered arrests for Negroes by more than 3 to 1.
6. Only 17.4 percent of those arrested for driving under the influence were under 25 years of age.

In the first selection taken from the President's Task Force Report on Drunkenness, David J. Pittman discusses the characteristics of the alcoholic offender in the United States. Dr. Pittman examines the social and cultural forces acting upon the drinker along with his notion of the "deviancy reinforcement cycle—the revolving door." James R. MacKay then introduces the problem of drinking among juvenile delinquents. In this research report he is especially concerned with boys who have been classified as addictive drinkers. In order to classify boys as such, 11 standard questions dealing with drinking patterns were asked of each member of his sample at the Massachusetts Reception Center for Boys. In the next article Selden D. Bacon discusses the relationship between alcohol and criminal behavior. Dr. Bacon is concerned with degrees of drinking in American society and the types of deviants (criminals) most likely to exhibit signs of alcoholism. In the final selection, Albert D.

[1]Based on 1967 Statistics.

Ullman examines the sociocultural background of alcoholics. Dr. Ullman is concerned not only with amount of alcoholism, but also with the degree of deviation displayed by the drinker from the normal drinking patterns found in his culture.

TABLE 6.1

THE EFFECT OF ALCOHOLIC BEVERAGES

Amount of Beverage Consumed	*Concentration of Alcohol Attained in Blood*	*Effect*		*Time Required for All Alcohol to Leave the Body*
1 highball (1½ oz. whisky) or 1 cocktail (1½ oz. whisky) or 3½ oz. fortified wine or 5½ oz. ordinary wine or 2 bottles beer (24-oz.)	0.03%	No noticeable effects on behavior		2 hrs.
2 highballs or 2 cocktails or 7 oz. fortified wine or 11 oz. ordinary wine or 4 bottles beer	0.06%		Feeling of warmth—mental relaxation—slight decrease of fine skills—less concern with minor irritations and restraints	4 hrs.
3 highballs or 3 cocktails or 10½ oz. fortified wine or 16½ oz. (1 pt.) ordinary wine or 6 bottles beer	0.09%	Increasing effects with variation among individuals and in the same individuals at different times	Buoyancy—exaggerated emotion and behavior—talkative, noisy, or morose	6 hrs.
4 highballs or 4 cocktails or 14 oz. fortified wine or 22 oz. ordinary wine or 8 bottles (3 qts.) beer	0.12%		Impairment of fine coordination—clumsiness—slight to moderate unsteadiness in standing or walking	8 hrs.
5 highballs or 5 cocktails or (½ pt. whisky)	0.15%	Intoxication—unmistakable abnormality of gross bodily functions and mental facilities		10 hrs.

For those weighing considerably more or less than 150 pounds the amounts of beverage indicated above will be correspondingly greater or less. The effects indicated at each stage will diminish as the concentration of alcohol in the blood diminishes.

SOURCE: Leon A. Greenberg, "Intoxication and Alcoholism: Physiological Factors," *The Annals*, Vol. 315 (1958), p. 28. Reprinted by permission of the American Academy of Political and Social Science.

19.

David J. Pittman

PUBLIC INTOXICATION AND THE ALCOHOLIC OFFENDER IN AMERICAN SOCIETY

THE PROBLEM

Public intoxication is viewed as a crime in almost every jurisdiction in this country. Laws exist on State and municipal levels prohibiting public displays of drunkenness. And although disorderliness is a prerequisite for arrest under some such laws, the homeless, skid-row inebriate faces repeated arrest for disorderly and nondisorderly drunkenness.

Those who are most often arrested are likely to have the most serious drinking problem. Many are confirmed alcoholics. Yet treatment for alcoholism is clearly not part of the correctional regimen. The process of arresting inebriates, detaining them for a few hours or a few days and then re-arresting them has been called a revolving door. Some have been arrested 100 to 200 times and have served 10 to 20 years in jail on short-term sentences. The recidivism rates clearly indicate the futility of the present system in dealing with the underlying sociomedical problems involved. Further, the impact of such arrests—reportedly in excess of 2 million each year—is particularly great on the institutions of the criminal justice system. The police, the courts, and the correctional institutions allocate needed manpower and facilities to handle what most people recognize as a public health problem.

A related problem to the criminal justice system is the person who consumes large quantities of alcoholic beverages and commits crimes, from petty offenses to crimes of violence. The existence of mass drunkenness arrests, crimes of violence stemming from intoxication, and other social problems, including highway fatalities and marital difficulties, lead to one conclusion: A greater effort must be made to solve the alcoholic problem and truly rehabilitate the many who now violate existing laws.

DEVIANCY REINFORCEMENT CYCLE: THE REVOLVING DOOR

Chronic drunkenness offenders are generally excessive drinkers who may or may not be alcoholics, but whose drinking has involved them in difficulties with the police, the courts, and penal institutions. They are a group for whom the penal sanctions of society have failed and to whom existing community resources have not been applied. Although some of these men (very seldom women) are confirmed alcoholics, others are miscreants whose present use of alcohol is preliminary to alcoholism, and others are nonaddicted excessive drinkers who will never become alcoholics.

As yet no studies exist which clearly differentiate an alcoholic from a nonalcoholic in the chronic drunkenness offender group. The most widely accepted definition of alcoholism is one developed by the World Health Organization which states:

> Alcoholics are those excessive drinkers whose dependence upon alcohol has attained such a degree that it shows a noticeable mental disturbance or an interference with their bodily and mental health, their inter-personal relations, and their smooth social and economic functioning; or who show the prodromal signs of such development.[1]

From this definition it is obvious that a history of arrests for public intoxication is indicative of a drinking problem. Repeated arrests

Source: Task Force on Drunkenness, The President's Commission on Law Enforcement and Administration of Justice, *Task Force Report: Drunkenness* (Washington, D.C.: U.S. Government Printing Office, 1967), pp. 7–28.

[1] "Expert Committee on Mental Health, Alcoholism Subcommittee, Second Report," World Health Organization, Technical Report Series, No. 48, August, 1952.

for public intoxication are certainly a symptom of the disease of alcoholism. However, as a result of the paucity of scientific research and lack of funds at the Federal, State, and local governmental levels for research and treatment studies on alcoholism, there are few clear cut answers about this disease.

On the whole, Americans have a relatively tolerant orientation toward nonexcessive drinking of alcoholic beverages. On many occasions, however, it is socially permissible to drink to excess. These occasions are usually private or semiprivate, and range from fraternity "beer blasts" and debutante "coming-out parties" to office parties and conventions. However, when a person's drinking starts to interfere with his work or family life, certain negative sanctions are invoked by his friends. His wife may be ashamed to invite guests home, and, correspondingly, friends may be embarrassed to visit.

The alcoholic, as Jellinek has pointed out, "begins to drink in private . . . to conceal his drinking problem." Jellinek's description, however, applies to the middle class alcoholic. And the middle class alcoholic, as well as an excessive drinker in this class, is unlikely to come in contact with law-enforcement agencies since his behavior is concealed. The public is more likely to view him as an unfortunate, as someone who has a disease and as someone who should seek medical help, although these attitudes are intertwined with moralistic sentiments. Although the public labels these deviant middle class drinkers negatively, they do not invoke the same harsh sanctions against them as with lower class alcoholics.

On the other hand, the same public often considers lower class alcoholics and excessive drinkers as worthless derelicts and vagrants. It is highly undesirable to have men sleeping in alleys and doorways. But the present solution—using the criminal system—fails to correct the problem and is unjust. And the public's negative stereotype of the public intoxication offender is largely a result of this archaic and punitive policy.

* * *

Cultural Factors

Looking at Chart 6.1, the "Deviancy Reinforcement Cycle for Public Intoxication," we can see the ramifications of the last statement. Excessive drinking and alcoholism are considered in a moralistic and negative manner by the larger population. When the deviant behavior of excessive drinking is acted out in in public "B," the larger community's sanctions become greater, especially since these individuals are much more likely to be found in the lower socio-economic class.

Indeed, there seems to be a commonly accepted notion among therapists dealing with problem drinkers and alcoholics that there are two large sub-types. First, there is the person who has a disease and must be helped (middle and upper class alcoholics and problem drinkers). Secondly, there is the drunk or skid-rowite, who is hopeless and whom few professionals care to treat. Duff Gillespie evaluated 22 follow-up studies of treated alcoholics. It was found that the typical population in these public treatment facilities excluded lower-lower class whites and, especially, Negroes. The public drunkenness offender often does not expect to find tolerance even among professionals who are reputed to be among the more tolerant groups.

The lower class public drunkenness offenders are drawn from those who have difficulty in interpersonal relationships, are poorly educated, are frequently from an ethnic or racial minority and are typically dependent on institutionalized living arrangements (such as those found in the Armed Forces, the Merchant Marine, and the Salvation Army and kindred shelters). In short, they are at a disadvantage in competing with other persons for a productive role in our society.

After repeated arrests and incarcerations, the negative effects of the above sociological variables are reinforced ("D" and "E" on Chart 6.1). The constantly incarcerated individual finds it nearly impossible to maintain a meaningful marital and familial relationship; his ability to find employment is seriously jeopardized by his arrest record coupled with his poor education. By constantly being officially labeled by the police, the courts and correctional institutions as a public drunk, he begins to see himself as a public drunk; the jail becomes little more than a shelter to regain his physical strength. Be-

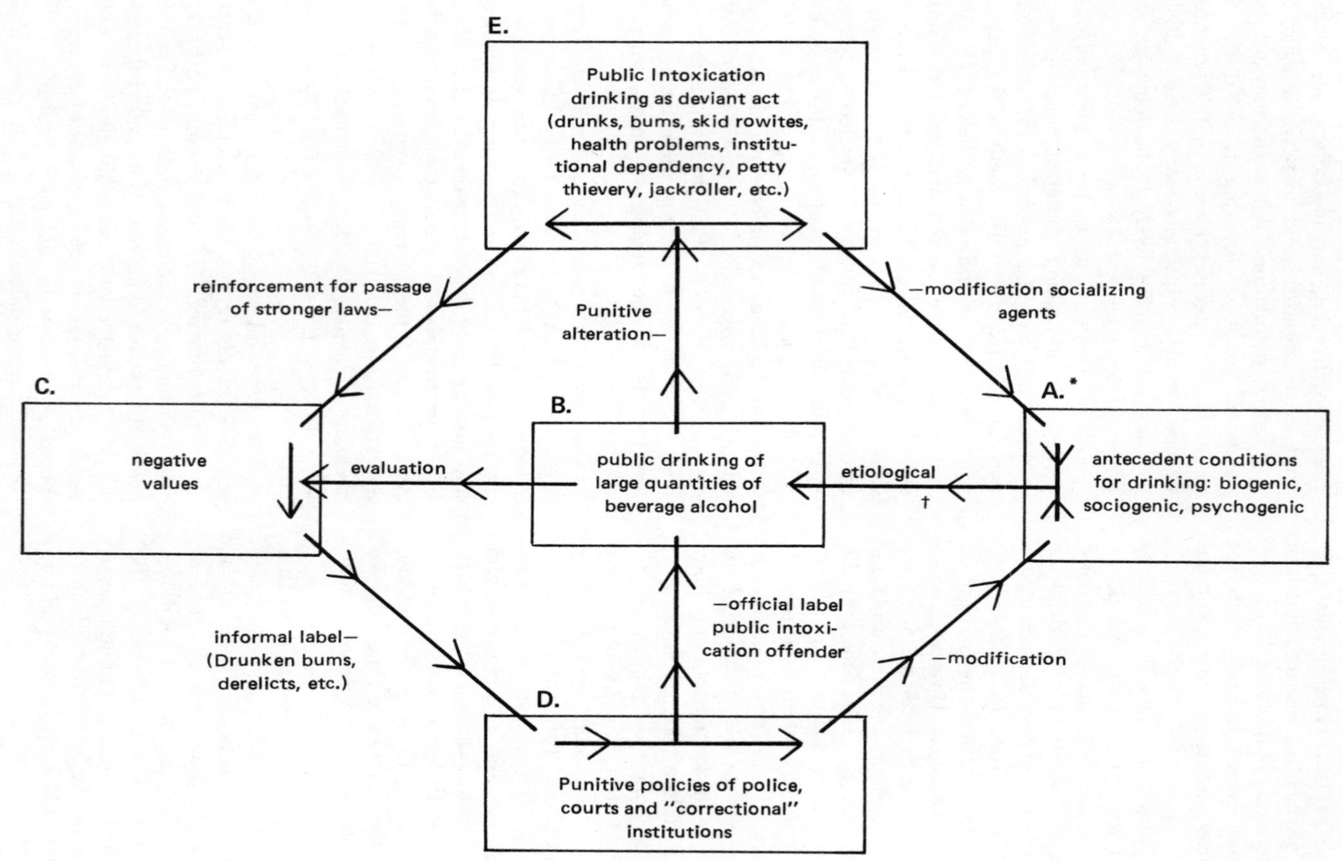

CHART 6.1

Model of the Deviancy Reinforcement Cycle for Public Intoxication

*Letters indicate theoretical sequency of events.
†Arrows indicate theoretical direction of influence.

cause the public intoxication offender is usually unable to support himself, he frequently turns to petty thievery. This is especially true if he is an alcoholic. The alcoholic will go to great lengths to maintain his supply of alcohol, and frequently he spends most of his nondrinking hours finding ways to obtain money for alcohol. As a result, the alcoholic public intoxication offender frequently presents a health problem, not only from diseases associated with an excessive intake of alcohol, but also from his indifference to caring for himself physically.

Social policy has its greatest negative effect on excessive drinkers who are not alcoholics. An excessive drinker who confines his drinking to weekend bouts (a pattern not uncommon in the middle classes), but who does not drink secretively, may find himself frequently arrested and perhaps incarcerated. If this happens often enough, he may be conditioned by the enforcement, the judicial, and the correctional processes in such a way as to contribute to his drinking problem. Where before he confined his drinking to weekends and managed to hold a job and be a breadwinner, he now finds these roles increasingly difficult and harder to maintain, and crises arrive which encourage his drinking. Instead of arresting his excessive drinking, the social policies have modified (relationships between "E"–"A," and "D"–"A," Chart 6.1) his deviant behavior and contributed to the development of a more serious deviancy—alcoholism. Thus, the public intoxication offender confronts the society with a serious social problem which involves the total community as well as the criminal justice system.

PSYCHOLOGICAL CHARACTERISTICS OF THE CHRONIC DRUNKENNESS OFFENDERS

The hard core of alcoholic offenders today is found in the 10 to 15 percent of the alcoholic population residing on skid rows. The term, skid row, appears to have originated in Seattle at the turn of the century. Yessler Street, which sloped to Puget Sound, was greased, and logs were skidded down into the water. Along this "skid road" were many taverns, amusement places, and hotels frequented by the men who came to Seattle during the log-shipping season. Yessler Street has formed the prototype of skid rows which include New York's famed Bowery, Chicago's West Madison Street, St. Louis' Chestnut and Market Streets, and similar areas in Copenhagen, Helsinki, Amsterdam and Paris.

Skid row is usually located near the city's central business district in what the urban sociologist calls the "zone of transition." It is an area characterized by severe physical deterioration—most of the commercial establishments and dwellings are substandard. Hotels and "flophouses," inexpensive restaurants, pawn shops and clothing stores, religious missions, men's service centers and bars are the usual establishments in the area.

Permanent Residents

The stereotype of the homeless man in the 1920's was the "hobo." During the depression of the 1930's homelessness and wandering were far from uncommon and indeed were the normal condition for a sizable portion of the poor.

Since then the skid row population has declined in number and is no longer the mobile group it used to be when the hobo was a familiar sight on the American landscape. A large proportion of the men are now permanent residents living impoverished, homeless lives in numerous missions, cheap hotels, and flophouses, and working when they can as casual laborers.

Though Donald J. Bogue, in his study of Chicago's Skid Row found that the majority of the men could not be defined as alcoholics, the incidence of "problem drinkers" is high in skid row.

Skid-row alcoholics compose the largest portion of the 2 million public drunkenness arrests made annually in the United States. A large number of these are the repeated arrests of the same men. These chronic drunks are arrested, convicted, sentenced, jailed, and released—only to be rearrested, often within hours or days. They are the men from skid row for whom the door of the jail is truly a "revolving door."

The Chronic Drunkenness Offender

The most systematic study of chronic drunkenness offenders completed in the United States is reported in Pittman and Gordon's *Revolving*

Door,[2] published in 1958. The findings were based upon an analysis of 187 case studies of a random sampling of all men who had been sentenced at least twice to a penal institution in New York State on a charge of public intoxication and who were incarcerated in the county jail when the investigation was conducted. The research was concerned with a group of excessive drinkers who may or may not have been alcoholics, but whose drinking had involved them in difficulties with the police, the courts, and penal institutions. They were a group for whom the penal sanctions of the society had failed along with existent community resources for rehabilitation.

The extensive case histories of the chronic intoxication offenders may be analyzed in terms of three major sets of factors which are crucial for the development of career patterns in public intoxication. These are: (1) sociocultural determinants; (2) socialization determinants; and (3) alcohol as the adaptive or adjustive mechanism in the life career.

Sociocultural Determinants

The chronic police case inebriate category consists of individuals with definable sociocultural traits as age, nationality background, race, marital status, religion, educational attainment, occupational skills and previous criminal record.

Age is one of the crucial attributes that differentiates these men from all other offender groups. Their age curve is skewed toward middle-age brackets, whereas commitments for such offenses as automobile theft, robbery, and burglary chiefly involve individuals under age 25. Their mean age of 47.7 years is higher than those of the general male population, of arrested inebriates, and of patients seen in the alcoholism clinics. The sample was one of the oldest problem drinking groups to be studied, in that 45 percent were over 50 years of age.

This sample was marked by a high proportion of Negroes (18 percent) in comparison to their representation in the general population of the county in which the jail is located (2 percent). Negro and white offenders were marked by age differentials: Two-thirds of the Negroes were under 45 years of age, compared to 30 percent of the whites. The Negroes were primarily from a rural or small-town, Southern, lower-class background and were having severe difficulties adjusting to the Northern urban pattern.

The most frequently represented nationality groupings were English and Irish. Irish ethnics composed 35 percent of the sample, but there was an increasing number of Irish with advancing age, especially after 45. Italians, although represented in significant number in the county's general population, composed only 2 percent of the sample.

In the related area of religious affiliation, the sample consisted of 42 percent Protestants, 40 percent Catholics, and 18 percent who professed no affiliation. There were no Jews. Religion, except in the case of groups such as the Jews who exhibit a specific culture pattern, appeared less important as an identifying sociocultural determinant of inebriation than nationality or ethnic status.

The marital status of these men was one of their most important attributes. Forty-one percent never married, 32 percent were separated, 19 percent were divorced, 6 percent widowed and 2 percent were living with their spouses before the current incarceration. Thus for these offenders, 96 percent of those who had married reported broken marriages, whereas the expectancy is only 11 percent, using the general male population of the county, corrected for age disparities.

The relationship which exists between marriage stability and problem drinking is a complex one. Many persons do not possess the competences in interpersonal relationships or in personality traits that are associated with entrance into marriage; or, once involved in marriage, these individuals do not possess requisite skills for continuing the marriage. Excessive drinking, which eventually causes severe disruptions in the individual's life, is destructive of the marriage relationship itself.

On the whole, the offenders were an educationally disadvantaged group. Seventy percent of the sample did not go beyond the eighth grade of school as compared to 40 percent of

---

[2] David J. Pittman and C. W. Gordon, *Revolving Door;* A study of the chronic police case inebriate (Glencoe, Ill.: The Free Press; and New Brunswick, N.J.: Rutgers Center of Alcohol Studies, 1958).

the county's general population. This educational impoverishment was reflected in their low order of primary occupational skills. Sixty-eight percent were unskilled workers, mainly laborers, 22 percent skilled workers, and 3 percent professional and allied workers, compared to 13, 46, and 22 percent, in the respective categories, in the general population.

Experience with the legal process in terms of arrests and incarcerations was another determinant of the career pattern in public intoxication. As a group, the inebriates exhibited a wide variety of criminal histories. The mean number of arrests for all causes was 16.5; the median was 10.2. For public intoxication only, the mean number of arrests was 12.8 and the median was 6.0. The "average" chronic drunkenness offender had experienced some 10 arrests on all charges, and the offender with 30, 40, or more arrests was atypical, though composing a sizable portion of the total.

The sample can be divided into three subgroups by previous criminal record: (a) 31 percent who had been arrested only for public intoxication; (b) 32 percent who had been arrested, in addition, on charges probably related to the excessive use of alcohol; and (c) 37 percent who had been involved in serious violations such as homicide, rape, robbery, or burglary. Men in the latter group showed a tendency to abandon the criminal career after the age of 33 or 40 with an intensified pattern of public intoxication thereafter.

Institutionalized living was a typical pattern of selective adaptation among the chronic police case inebriates. Tendencies toward dependency inherent in the experience of childhood, youth, and early adulthood were reinforced and supported through a selective adaptation to life in the semiprotective environments of the Civilian Conservation Corps, the Army, the railroad gang, the lake steamer, the jail, lumber and fruit camps, hospitals, Salvation Army and kindred shelters. The minimum requirements for living were met through institutional organizations which relieve the incumbents of individual responsibility to cope with food, housing, and related needs. They became habituated to dependent living which further limited their capacity to reestablish independent modes of life.

In summary, lower class individuals of Irish ethnic status and Negroes in the age bracket 40–49 with previous extensive arrest histories were most vulnerable to repeated arrests for drunkenness.

Socialization Determinants

Within this framework of sociocultural determinants are a series of socialization experiences which are conducive to the development of a career pattern in inebriation. The structural continuity of the family units was broken by death, divorce, or separation before the inebriate's 15th birthday in 39 percent of the cases. This seems to be an extremely high percentage of families whose structure collapsed.

On a more qualitative level, mother-son and father-son relationships evidenced a trend in the direction of serious deprivations for the inebriates in meeting their basic emotional, social, and psychological needs. Thus, the sense of belonging achieved by membership and acceptance in a social unit larger than the individual himself, such as the family primary group, was only partially attained by most of the inebriates.

An objective index to evaluate adolescent socialization experience and the significance of these situations for positive identity formation was constructed by the following criteria: (a) Participation in a clique or close friendship groups of boys; (b) heterosexual participation as reflected in an established dating pattern; (c) existence of goals and aspirations, whether middle class nature or not; (d) family integration as reflected in the individual's sense of belonging to the family unit; and (e) positive school adaptation as reflected in attendance and performance. If all these factors were found in a case, the socialization experience was scored as good or above average; the presence of four was scored adequate or average; and the presence of three or fewer was rated as poor or below what would be desired for adequate socialization. The results of these classifications indicated that the symptoms which warn of difficulties in assuming adult social roles are already present in these men at the end of the adolescent development era. By the index of the adolescent adjustment, 86 percent of our sample rated poor, only 10 percent could be rated adequate or average, and in 4 percent the index could not be applied because of incomplete data. In only one case were all five factors present.

Thus, the chronic police case inebriates were undersocialized, as determined by other quantitative and qualitative indexes for their original families and the adolescent sphere of development. This deficit was reflected in the adult inebriate career in his inability to perform two of the most demanding secondary task roles, i.e., occupational and marital roles.

Alcohol as the Adjustive Mechanism in the Life Career

The career of the chronic drunkenness offender was one in which drinking serves the socially handicapped individuals as a means of adapting to life conditions which are otherwise harsh, insecure, unrewarding, and unproductive of the essentials of human dignity. This type of career was, however, only one of the possible patterns of adjustment, given the combination of conditions in the early life of these men. Repeated incarceration for drunkenness was the terminal phase of a complex process in which the interplay of sociocultural and personality factors have combined to produce this long-run adaptation.

Using the age at which a man was committed the second time for public intoxication or a drinking-involved offense as a breakpoint, the study group fell into two types which we shall designate the "Early Skid" and the "Late Skid" careers.

The "Early Skid" career pattern involved approximately 50 percent of the offenders. In this group two-fifths of the men experienced their second incarceration in their twenties and the rest in their early thirties. Only a few had their second imprisonment in the age period 36–39.

The "Early Skid" career pattern was thus one in which the individual established his record of public intoxication in his twenties or early thirties. It represented serious social and/or psychiatric maladjustment to early adulthood which extended into middle adulthood. There was an absence of adult occupational adjustment independent of institutional living. The period of alcohol dependency formation was not associated with such stable marital adjustment as may be found in some of the "Late Skid" career pattern.

The "Late Skid" career pattern was defined by the postponement of the minimum record of two incarcerations for public intoxication until the forties or even fifties. The career type encompassed 50 percent of the men in the group if the age of 37 (for experiencing the second arrest) is used as the dividing point.

The period of alcohol dependency development was often marked by extended periods of occupational and family stability. Since this period was accompanied by drinking, it must be regarded as part of the conditioning period of alcohol dependency. More apparent in the "Late Skid" career was the physical decline of the man who experienced great difficulty in maintaining his economic needs through marginal types of employment. Younger men replaced him on the casual day-labor jobs. His drinking increased and finally his tolerance for alcohol declined.

In summary, the "Early Skid" career pattern was one in which drinking served as the primary means of adjustment to original social and/or psychiatric disability; whereas the "Late Skid" career pattern was secondary to failure in secondary role performance.

This study has shown the chronic drunkenness offender to be the product of a limited social environment and a man who has never attained more than a minimum of integration in society. He is and has always been at the bottom of the social and economic ladder; he is isolated, uprooted, unattached, disorganized, demoralized and homeless, and it is in this context that he drinks to excess. As such, admittedly through his own behavior, he is the least respected member of the community, and his treatment by the community has at best been negative and expedient. He has never attained, or has lost, the necessary respect and sense of human dignity on which any successful program of treatment and rehabilitation must be based. He is captive in a sequency of lack or loss of self-esteem producing behavior which causes him to be further disesteemed. Unless this cycle is partially reversed positive results in treatment will be difficult to attain.

ALCOHOLISM AND CRIME

Introduction

There are certain criminal categories that are intimately related to the use of alcoholic beverages. Most clearly involved are violations of public intoxication statutes and closely related charges of disorderly conduct, vagrancy, trespassing, and peace disturbance. These charges have been discussed in previous sections of this report.

Two major research approaches have characterized the investigation of the relationship of crime and alcohol use. First, what is the drinking behavior or status of the individual when he commits a crime? Second, what is the correlation between long-standing abuse of alcohol (alcoholism) and criminality?

The Commission of Crimes

In determining the drinking status of the individual at the commission of the crime, two research techniques have been used. Illustrative of one approach is Marvin E. Wolfgang's[3] study of homicides committed in Philadelphia in 1948–1952, composed of 588 victims (cases) and 621 offenders. He reports that "either or both the victim and offender had been drinking immediately prior to the slaying in nearly two-thirds of the cases."

A second, more accurate research technique is to analyze the blood or urine of the individual for alcohol content immediately after the commission of the crime. Illustrative of this approach is the program in Columbus, Ohio, where urine analysis for alcohol concentration was reported in a study by Shupe[4] on "882 persons picked up during or immediately after the commission of a felony" during the period March 1951 to March 1955. Shupe states:

> The figures show that crimes of physical violence are associated with intoxicated persons. Cuttings (11 to 1 under the influence of alcohol), the carrying of concealed weapons (8 to 1 under the influence of alcohol) and other assaults (10 to 1 under the influence of alcohol) are definitely crimes of alcohol influence, even crimes of true intoxication.[5]

Thus, the closest relationship between intoxication and criminal behavior (except for public intoxication) has been established for criminal categories involving assaultive behavior. This relationship is especially high for lower-lower class Negroes and whites. More than likely, aggression in these groups is weakly controlled and the drinking of alcoholic beverages serves as a triggering mechanism for the external release of aggression. There are certain types of key situations located in lower class life in which alcohol is a major factor in triggering assaultive behavior. A frequent locale is the lower class tavern which is an important social institution for this class group. Assaultive episodes are triggered during the drinking situation by quarrels that center around defaming personal honor, threats to masculinity, and questions about one's birth legitimacy. Personal quarrels between husband and wife, especially after the husband's drinking, frequently result in assaultive episodes, in the lower-lower class family.

Shupe's conclusion that 64 percent of his sample of 882 individuals were "under the influence of alcohol to such an extent that their inhibitions were reduced" is of major significance to American criminologists. Excessive drinking of alcoholic beverages is a significant fact in the commission of crimes. However, there are as yet no data that demonstrate that alcoholism is a significant factor in the commission of crimes.

Highway Accidents

The Congress currently is very concerned, as is the country, with reducing the horrible toll of deaths on the nation's highways. Unfortunately, very little attention has been directed by the Federal Government to a significant factor in vehicular accidents–drunkenness and alcoholism. Mr. Pyle, director of the National Safety Council, estimates that perhaps one-half of those involved in fatal automobile accidents

[3]Marvin E. Wolfgang, *Patterns of Criminal Homicide* (Philadelphia: University of Pennsylvania, 1958).

[4]Lloyd M. Shupe, "Alcohol and Crime: A Study of the Urine Alcohol Concentration Found in 882 Persons Arrested during or Immediately after the Commission of a Felony," *Journal of Criminal Law, Criminology and Police Science,* Vol. 44 (1954), pp. 661–64.

[5]*Ibid.*, p. 663.

are under the influence of alcohol. This can be confirmed by spot studies by scientists throughout this country. For example, of the first 43 individuals killed in motor vehicle accidents in St. Louis County, Mo., in 1966, 30 had alcohol-blood levels of 0.15 or higher, which is indicative of heavy intoxication. The *New York Times,* March 13, 1966, reports that in San Antonio in the last 9 years 61 percent of the drivers and pedestrians killed have been intoxicated. The blood alcohol levels were 0.15 or higher. The research of Selzer[6] in Michigan confirms that a sizable proportion, 40 percent of those drivers responsible for fatal motor vehicle accidents, can be diagnosed as alcoholics.

Correctional Institutions

Between 40 to 50 percent of those incarcerated in penal institutions for felonies in the United States have a drinking problem. The most systematic study of a prison population is one completed by a team of Washington University psychiatrists, headed by Sam Guze[7] who examined psychiatrically a series of 223 consecutive criminals, including probationers, parolees, and "flat-timers" at the Missouri State Penitentiary at Jefferson City. Although 48 percent of the sample were diagnosed as having no psychiatric disorder, 43 percent were diagnosed as alcoholics, the largest percentage by far in any psychiatric category.

Criminal Careers

Another relationship between intoxication and criminality is found in the factors associated with continuation of a criminal career. Previous criminological studies have indicated that the major variable correlated with drop-out from criminal activity is increasing age.

A recent study at the Institute of Criminology at the University of Copenhagen, Denmark, however, indicates that drop-out from criminal activity is correlated with increasing age, unless the individual has an alcoholic problem. If he has an alcoholic problem there is a strong tendency for the individual to maintain his criminal pattern in the middle years of life. Furthermore, as Pittman and Gordon have noted in *Revolving Door,* there is a tendency for certain criminals, who earlier in their criminal careers were involved in complex forms of crime, to become petty criminals with alcoholic complications in their middle and later years. These kind of criminals may be referred to as double failures since earlier in their life they used crime as a vehicle for social mobility, achievement and success but failed to make the grade in high level criminal activity. These are the men who do not become successful criminals. In later life they experience a second failure by being unsuccessful, petty criminals and frequently use a retreatist form of adaptation—chronic drunkenness.

---

[6]Melvin L. Selzer and Sue Weiss, "Alcoholism and Fatal Traffic Accidents—A Study in Futility," *The Municipal Court Review,* Vol. 5 (1965), p. 15–20.

[7]Samuel B. Guze, Vincent B. Tuason, Paul D. Gatfield, Mark A. Stuart and Bruce Picken, "Psychiatric Illness and Crime with Particular Reference to Alcoholism: A Study of 223 Criminals," *Journal of Nervous and Mental Disease,* Vol. 134 (1962), pp. 512–13.

20.

James R. MacKay

PROBLEM DRINKING AMONG JUVENILE DELINQUENTS*

The relationship of juvenile delinquency to the drinking of alcoholic beverages has caused a good deal of speculation and discussion among those responsible for the care of delinquents, but has, unfortunately, produced little systematic data on the subject. One aspect of it, however, has been studied by the Alcoholism Clinic of the Peter Bent Brigham Hospital, the Massachusetts Youth Service Board, and the Massachusetts State Division of Alcoholism. Several of us from these three agencies became concerned about youngsters who were committed to the Youth Service Board after being arrested for drunkenness or who were brought to the Detention Center drunk. Out of the concern about the serious drinking behavior described by these boys in interviews grew the research upon which this report is based.

The data under consideration pertain to those delinquents who were using alcohol pathologically or addictively and are based on a survey of 500 male delinquents admitted to the Massachusetts Youth Service Board Reception Center from February to October, 1960), a study of an additional 122 boys at the same facility, and a clinical research project involving 20 boys and girls referred for treatment by correctional authorities. These projects were designed to (1) provide basic statistical data on the use, nonuse, or misuse of alcohol among a representative group of delinquents, (2) categorize the group according to their use or nonuse of alcohol, (3) measure some significant aspects of their experience with alcohol, and (4) take a more intensive look into the meaning of their drinking experiences by considering personality characteristics and family backgrounds. This report will focus primarily on those boys classified as addictive drinkers.

SURVEY OF 500 MALE JUVENILE DELINQUENTS

The Reception Center for Boys receives all boys convicted in the courts of Massachusetts as delinquents for a period of diagnosis and classification. This affords an unusual opportunity for group research without restriction as to age, place of residence in the State, type of offense, intelligence or availability for interviewing. For a period of nine months, all admissions to the facility were interviewed until a total of 500 boys had been reached.

The ages of the group ranged from 7 to 20; the modal age was 15. Sixty-five per cent of the group were Roman Catholic, the rest were Protestant except for 2 who were Jewish and 5 who claimed no particular religious affiliation. The average boy had completed eight grades in school before coming to the Reception Center.

In over half of the cases studied, the parents were not living together at the time of the study. Sixty (12 per cent) of the boys' fathers had died and 26 (5.2 per cent) of the boys' mothers were deceased. The whereabouts of 21 fathers and 9 mothers was unknown to these sons. Divorces represented the largest reason for the parents' living apart (over 52 per cent); about one-fourth had been legally separated.[1]

Before beginning a detailed analysis of the problem of addictive drinkers, we should have a picture of the drinking experiences of the entire group. For the purposes of classification according to extent and seriousness of drinking, the following objective criteria were used:

Source: *Crime and Delinquency,* Vol. 9, No. 1 (January, 1963), pp. 29–38. Reprinted by permission of the author and the journal.

*Adapted from a paper presented at the Conference on Alcohol, Alcoholism and Crime, held in Chatham, Mass., June 6–8, 1962.

[1]James R. MacKay, Edward Blacker, Harold W. Demone, Jr., and Francis J. Kelly, "Delinquency and Drinking" (unpublished paper).

1. Do you drink whenever you get the chance?

2. About how many times have you felt "good," "high," or had "a glow on" from drinking? (Ten or more was required for a positive response.)

3. About how many times have you become drunk? (Six or more was required for a positive response.)

4. Have you ever done anything while drinking that you would not ordinarily do?

5. Have you ever done anything *after* drinking that you would not ordinarily do?

5a. Did you ever feel "high," "tight," or drunk while drinking alone?[2]

6. Did you ever drink before breakfast or instead of breakfast?

7. Did you ever have a fight when drinking?

8. Did you ever pass out while drinking?

9. Were you ever unable to remember what you were doing or where you were when you were drinking?

10. Have you ever been arrested for drinking?

11. Do you drink alone?

These eleven criteria were then applied to the data derived from the 500 boys and a number of categories were developed to pinpoint individual drinking behavior—abstainers, single drinking episode, mild drinkers who had experienced none of the eleven criteria, moderate drinkers (experienced one to four of the criteria), heavy drinkers (five to six of the criteria), problem or addictive drinkers (seven or more of the criteria). The following table shows the number of boys who fell into each category.

Categorization of 500 Boys According to Drinking Behavior

Category	*Number*	*Per Cent*
Abstainers	140	28.0%
Single drinking episode	42	8.4%
Mild drinkers	41	8.2%
Moderate drinkers	164	32.8%
Heavy drinkers	63	12.6%
Addictive drinkers	50	10.0%
Total	500	100.0%

THE ADDICTIVE DRINKERS

Fifty (or 10 per cent) of the total group were classified as addictive drinkers. The modal age of this group was sixteen, about a year older than the total delinquent population studied. Of the 50, 38 remembered taking their first drink of an alcoholic beverage at age thirteen or fourteen. The environment of the first drinking experience varied. Most reported that they drank with a male friend; a majority said they first drank because of curiosity. Most drank in alleys, playgrounds; many drank in autos; some drank at home unobserved by parents. Only 13 per cent of the boys reported that they were unaffected by their first drink. The majority said they became drunk or high or "dizzy." Of the 38 who recalled their first drink, 6 stole the alcohol, 7 had an adult buy it for them, 9 received it from a friend. The remainder used other methods which did not have parental sanction. One-fourth of the group drank again within a few days of their first drink; the others reported longer intervals.

Following the first drink, all of the boys reported that they routinely drank outside their home. For example, they drank in movies, cars, and alleys. In most instances, they took advantage of situations where parental regulation was absent. Most had not secured permission and did not think their parents were aware of their drinking.

Considerable evidence of severe drinking patterns was found. Over half the boys drank whenever they had the chance, and each of them reported being high or drunk on many occasions. In nearly all cases, the boys reported doing things when drinking that they would not ordinarily do; most reported assaultive behavior after drinking. Three-quarters of the group reported drinking alone, many of whom became high or drunk while doing so—thus indicating that their drinking was satisfying needs other than social. Almost half said that on occasion they drank before or instead of breakfast. Nearly all had passed out while drinking and had

[2]Question 5a was used in lieu of question 5 for the last 148 subjects of this study, at which time questions 4 and 5 were combined to make one question.

occasions of "blackouts" or periods when they were unable to recall anything that had happened while they were drinking; 32 had become sick because of drinking. Sources of supply of their alcohol ranged from stealing to having adult alcoholics buy it for them. Over half the boys had been arrested for drinking and a majority were arrested for offenses—mostly thefts—that were committed after they had been drinking. Yet, most of them felt that their drinking had nothing to do with their presence at the Youth Service Board Reception Center, did not consider themselves problem drinkers, and were not concerned about their drinking practices.[3]

SURVEY OF AN ADDITIONAL 122 BOYS

In order to arrive at some hypotheses as to why these boys were drinking to such a serious and extensive degree, a second study of an additional 122 consecutive admissions was conducted at the same facility.[4] Individually administered schedules rather than questionnaires were used as the sources of data. By the same objective criteria outlined above, 20 (or 16 per cent) of the 122 boys were found to be addictive drinkers—an even higher percentage than the original 500 boys—and to have had drinking experiences very similar to the group described above. Each boy in this group was interviewed individually (most of them on several occasions) by psychiatric social workers who focused on eliciting his opinions as to why he drank, his attitudes toward adults and toward his peers, and his attitudes in general as to why people drink.

The following background information, taken from a report on the subject, was gathered on this group of problem drinkers:

The average age of the 20 boys was 16, the range from 14 to 17, placing them all within the adolescent period. Sixteen of the group were Roman Catholic, 4 were Protestant, which is similar to the ratio in the facility. There was one Negro boy; the others were Caucasian. Eighteen of the boys were Massachusetts born and all lived within the State at the time of their commitment. Thirteen came from urban areas.

These 20 boys had appeared in court for a total of 94 offenses, about half of which were for some form of stealing. Only 5 of the boys had ever appeared in court for drunkenness (although 8 had arrests for drunkenness) and no boy appeared more than once on this charge. All of the boys had been in court for more than one kind of an offense and the majority had 3 or more combinations of offenses such as larceny, assault and truancy.

The young drinkers tended to be school problems. Seventeen were reported as truants and 17 were considered as having "poor scholarship" by school authorities. More than half were disciplinary problems while in school. Seven repeated more than one grade and the average grade placement at the time of commitment was the eighth.

Five of the boys were living with their natural parents. Seven were living with their mothers, one was living with his father. Four were living with relatives or adoptive parents and others were living with step-parents. Separations from one or both of the parents occurred for 12 of the youngsters at the age of 10 or before—for 8 at age 3 or before. Two were born out of wedlock. Separation from parents was caused by desertion, death, divorce, legal separation and imprisonment of parents. Court appearances of family members were frequent. There were some multiple marriages—4 of the boys had, as they grew up, 5 parental figures. Alcoholism was frequently noted in the histories of the parents. Two of the fathers died of diseases related to alcoholism.

In general, the families were poorly structured, the boys had experienced many instances of loss of one or more parents early in their lives. The all too familiar picture among delinquents of lack and loss was in evidence among these families.[5]

The answers given by the boys led the authors of this report to several tentative hypotheses regarding the boys' attitudes toward drinking:

1. The boys drank predominantly as a reaction to (or as a means of coping with) such personal emotional problems as sadness, anger, or a wish to forget an unpleasant situation.

2. The groups within which the boys drank provided the setting but not the motivation for their drinking. (Actually, some of the boys reported many solitary drinking experiences, although the majority usually drank in groups.)

3. The boys rarely appeared before the court on a drunkenness charge, so that the extent of their drinking was not revealed in their court

---

[3]MacKay, Blacker, Demone, and Kelly, *op. cit.*

[4]James R. MacKay, Andrew E. Murray, and Thomas Hagerty, "Problem Drinking among Delinquents" (unpublished).

[5]*Ibid.*

records. (All had been drinking extensively and had admitted committing delinquent acts while under the influence of alcohol.)

4. After drinking, the boys tended to lose control over their impulses, which, in turn, led them to commit delinquent acts or engage in violence. (At this time, however, the evidence is not sufficient to prove a causal relationship between their state of intoxication and the commission of delinquent acts.)

The boys' attitudes about drinking were interesting. They viewed moderate drinking as acceptable in both adults and in their peers, although abstinence among women was given special consideration and high approval. They did not approve of heavy drinking among adults, and related drunkenness among men to loss of control over their aggressions and, among women, to loss of sexual control. Yet their own drinking patterns contrasted sharply with what they defined as acceptable behavior for their age group.

Sower, in discussing teen-age drinking, outlined three types of problem drinking as an aid in planning research on the problem:

> 1. Drinking which leads to conflicts with other segments of society. Illustrations of conflicts are when drinking violates established law, or when it results in conflicts with school authorities. . . .
> 2. Drinking which leads to conflicts between the actions of an individual and his beliefs, sentiments, or values. . . .
> 3. Drinking which leads to detrimental consequences for the individual or for others, such as drinking which is followed by automobile driving, by illicit sexual relations, by failure to fulfill recognized social obligations, by group conflicts, and so forth.[6]

The groups of 500 and of 122 boys qualify in all three areas of problem drinking described by Sower. Both qualitatively and quantitatively, the findings suggest that those who were characterized as addictive drinkers drank differently, under different circumstances, and for different reasons than students studied in several high schools in this country. Indeed, the drinking behavior of these adolescents parallels that of the confirmed alcoholic seen in clinical practice, except that the teen-agers were still too young to have developed the physical debilitation that prolonged and excessive drinking causes. This group may also be distinguished from clinic alcoholics by the poor control they exercised over their impulses—a point that will be discussed in more detail later.

The data thus far have largely been confined to material outlining the extent and nature of the drinking practices of those groups of addictive drinkers who constituted 11 per cent of the populations (70 out of 622) studied at the Youth Service Board Reception Facility.

THE CLINICAL RESEARCH PROJECT

Pertinent to this inquiry and offering a framework for speculation as to the underlying causes of problem drinking are certain aspects of a previously published clinical observation of a group of 20 adolescent problem drinkers (17 boys and 3 girls).[7] Here again, the drinking experiences of the 20 members of this group were the same as for the two study groups described above. This particular group, however, was seen extensively in treatment, thus providing a much better opportunity to study each child and his family background in depth.

In every family studied, deprivation and neglect, both economic and emotional, were evident; in each, the father was an alcoholic and in some of the cases the mother was also. The recurring picture was that of an alcoholic father who was, by the time the youthful drinker reached adolescence, permanently out of the home by reason of death, desertion, separation, imprisonment, or hospitalization. Because of the instability of the breadwinner, the families were most often supported by public welfare and the boys were expected to take the place of their fathers as providers. Their earliest memories were of quarrels, inconsistencies, and frequent temporary separations from one or the other parent.

Pervasive personality disturbances resulting from these early conditioning experiences were found among the children studied, thus bearing

[6]Christopher Sower, "Teen-Age Drinking as Group Behavior," *Quarterly Journal of Studies on Alcohol*, September, 1959, p. 658.

[7]James R. MacKay, "Clinical Observations on Adolescent Problem Drinkers," *Quarterly Journal of Studies on Alcohol*, March, 1961, pp. 124–34.

out Myerson's findings[8] and the findings of several other clinicians who reported on the serious effect of neglect and deprivation on children.[9]

The 20 adolescents were viewed as having problems of hostility, impulsiveness, depression, and sexual confusion. Their hostility was particularly evident when they were under the influence of alcohol, which diminished their ability to control themselves. However, in no way was the resultant anger caused by drinking. Impulsiveness was apparent primarily in their poor control over their anger.

One youngster of 15 used to go to a dance armed with a bottle of liquor (much of which he had imbibed before arriving there), a pair of brass knuckles, a switchblade, and a bicycle chain. Although this boy was arrested for assault and battery, the seriousness of his drinking behavior did not become known until much later.

Another boy of 16, who was on parole from a training school, was being seen weekly at an outpatient clinic because of his problem with alcohol and an additional problem of being congenitally short and looking much younger than his age. Several times while he was on parole, he became drunk and attempted to assault the first police officer he found. Subsequently, he was returned to the training school as a parole violator.

In general, the boys gave the impression that it didn't matter what they did since there was no future for them—giving as a typical remark: "I don't care where I am. I've done time before and I can do it again." They attached no significance to their lack of self-control. Any appeal to them to think of their future was usually futile, since they were living for the "pleasure" of the present. (Parenthetically, I think one would have to look far for the pleasure they were enjoying.) Their attitude of "there's no tomorrow" at first appeared to be bravado and their claim of unconcern in their own future ("Why worry? I could walk out of here and get killed by a car on the street!") sounded contrived. Yet these remarks were not attempts at bravado or at shocking the listener. Rather, they were a clear demonstration of the boys' belief that they had little or no ability to exert self-control or to direct the future course of their lives.

Significantly, members of the group made great use of two psychological mechanisms—denial and projection. Denial, one of the simplest of emotional defenses, says, in effect, that something painful or anxiety-producing is not painful or anxiety-producing. The person who denies the fact that he has been or may be hurt or anxious seems outwardly detached or unconcerned about situations that would normally produce a great deal of concern. Thus, the anxiety which might help push a person toward psychotherapeutic help is missing.

The other commonly used defense is projection—a similar form of adaptation to stress except that the blame for a particular situation is shifted to another person. Thus, it is not at all unusual for members of this group to claim complete innocence and detachment from the situation or to place the blame on some other person, the environment, or both.

Just as the two defense mechanisms described are elemental, so is the depression suffered by these teen-agers. Many talked of suicide and some made overt attempts at it. At times, their drinking behavior itself approached self-destruction. One boy of 18 actually did die after drinking anti-freeze. Another boy, when he was drinking, would sit on a bridge and contemplate jumping into the water. Eventually, he became drunk and ran his car into a tree at 80 miles an hour, killing himself and another person. The group as a whole had more than their share of accidents. Members would hurt and disfigure themselves. Tattooing, for instance, was common among both boys and girls; one young girl stuck pins in herself and had to undergo surgery for the self-inflicted injury. These feelings of depression probably originated in the adolescents' formative years as an expression of the effect of emotional deprivation and as a response to early and repeated separation from one or both parents.

---

[8] D. J. Myerson, "Clinical Observations on a Group of Alcoholic Prisoners," *Quarterly Journal of Studies on Alcolohl*, September, 1959, pp. 555–72.

[9] *Ibid.* See also R. A. Spitz, "Anaclitic Depression: An Inquiry into the Genesis of Psychiatric Conditions in Early Childhood," *The Psychoanalytic Study of the Child*, Vol. 2 (New York: International Universities Press, 1956), pp 313–42, and J. Bowlby, *Maternal Care and Mental Health* (Geneva: World Health Organization, 1951), pp. 11–63.

Some investigators in the field have explained the alcoholic's sexual confusion in terms of his unconscious homosexual conflict;[10] others dispute this type of generalized explanation.[11] In the study under consideration, definite evidence was found of sexual confusion and of both overt and latent homosexual involvements. In practice, those who had participated in overt homosexual activity explained that they took a passive part or had become involved because they were drunk or needed the money. "I didn't do anything," said one boy, as he explained that the act had been performed on him and not by him.

From these three studies, we conclude that (1) a significant number (10 per cent) of juvenile delinquents are problem drinkers, (2) their excessive drinking conflicts with both their personal beliefs and the rules of the society in which they live, and (3) their drinking is caused by and is an attempt to cope with serious emotional problems.

* * *

[10] Israel Zwerling, "Psychiatric Findings in an Interdisciplinary Study of Forty-Six Alcoholic Patients," *Quarterly Journal of Studies on Alcohol*, Sept., 1959, pp. 543–54; S. Ferenczi, "Alkohol und Neurosen," *Jahrbuch für psychoanalytische und psychopathologische Forschungen*, 1912, pp. 853–57.

[11] J. V. Quaranta, "Alcoholism: A Study of Emotional Maturity and Homosexuality as Related Factors in Compulsive Drinkers" (master's thesis), Fordham University, 1947; C. Landis, "Theories of the Alcoholic Personality," *Alcohol, Science and Society* (New Haven: Quarterly Journal of Studies on Alcohol, 1945), pp. 129–38.

21.

Selden D. Bacon

ALCOHOL, ALCOHOLISM, AND CRIME

No single pattern of consumption of alcoholic beverages constitutes the norm for American society. Rather, there is a wide variety of expected and accepted patterns of drinking behavior. These can be described in terms of the person drinking, the type of beverage to be used, the frequency and quantity of its use, the person's drinking companions, the circumstances surrounding his drinking, and the explanation given for it. These behavior patterns can also be differentiated according to the drinking custom itself: how much importance is attached to it, its relationship to other customs, how it has been taught to the young, the severity of the penalties for deviation from it, who is responsible for maintaining the custom, and so on. Because there are so many drinking norms in our society, it follows that what may be acceptable to one group in one setting may be quite unacceptable to another group—a possibility greatly increased by two factors. The first is our urban and mobile way of life and the close relationship of drinking to our recreational activities outside the home, with the result that persons with strikingly different drinking habits come into frequent and close contact with each other. The second is the enormous diversity of drinking habits—from militant abstention, on the one hand, to practices that place a high value on frequent and wide use of distilled spirits, on the other. As a result, even if all norms were maintained at all times, there still would be extensive and clearly recognizable deviation throughout the nation.

This situation, which might be described as conflict of norms, is compounded by another condition which might be described as weakness of norms. For this type of characterization, drinking customs may be described in terms

Source: *Crime and Delinquency*, Vol. 9, No. 1 (January, 1963), pp. 1–14. Reprinted by permission of the author and the journal.

of a continuum. At one extreme are those patterns which are rigidly defined, which allow for little or almost no variation, which are implanted in a person with uniformity and emphasis, and which are attended by penalties for nonconformity—penalties expected to be quick and effective, possibly enacted by such formal, specialized agents as parents or police, but which would be exercised by almost any member of the group if the specialists were absent. In our society, I would say that human excretory practices form an obvious example of a rigidly defined cultural pattern. At the other extreme are the rather loosely defined patterns which allow for considerable individual variation, are not implanted in the new member of the group with certainty, regularity, and uniformity, and may in fact be characterized by uncertainty, irregularity, and even conflicting values. These patterns have weak penalties, which are neither always accepted by others nor always enacted, and the inhibiting agents are often uncertain, inconsistent, and perhaps at odds with each other. For many large segments of our population, I would say that drinking practices exemplify this end of the continuum. When deviations from the pattern are accompanied by deviations from other more rigidly defined patterns, the combination may lead to confusion in determining which sanctions are appropriate. For example, many persons feel that assault, obscenity, and property destruction are somewhat less blameworthy if the misbehavior took place "under the influence"; while others feel the misbehavior is *more* blameworthy if it took place "under the influence," as in the case of a driver getting into an accident.

ALCOHOL AND THE CENTRAL NERVOUS SYSTEM

American drinking customs are thus more productive of deviation than most of our other customs or most of the drinking customs of other societies, both because of the many conflicting norms and because of the weakness of so many of the normative structures. However, quite beyond the matters of cultural strength, integration, and uniformity or harmony, the use of alcoholic beverages is of particular interest to students of human deviation. Alcohol directly affects a person's central nervous system, his brain, temporarily altering its function so that he varies from his usual and expected pattern of response. Unless special circumstances or counterbalancing forces intervene, these variations in behavioral response are very likely to result in deviation. The impact of alcohol on a person's behavior temporarily diminishes the overall efficiency of three sorts of function: (1) sensitivity to outside stimuli, especially to what may be called cues to behavior; (2) learned habits and attitudes, especially those involving self-criticism and self-control; and (3) muscular coordination, reaction time, and balance. Their efficiency is reduced in proportion to the amount of alcohol in the central nervous system; but the amount of reduction should, of course, be judged in terms of the degree and quality of sensibility, learned controls, and muscular coordination already present in the person before he drinks. Since, however, the person imbibing alcohol does not function in a vacuum, he will not always manifest these effects even if he drinks the same amount over the same span of time. Furthermore, after he has ingested any alcohol, his behavior may be directly influenced by the presence of his wife, boss, or priest, by a sudden shock, by extreme fatigue, the raucous urging of friends, and so on.

For example, Mrs. Jones always expects her husband, Henry, to leave the Smiths' house by 11:15 P.M.; in fact, Henry himself has always made a point of not visiting with people later than that. This night, however, Henry has had two drinks more than usual and has "missed his cue." At 11:25 P.M. he glances at the clock and merely snickers, finally making it to the front door and putting on a wrestling exhibition while getting his coat. Since then, Henry has visited the Smiths many times and has had drinks, but the behavior he showed that night has not reoccurred. Although Henry's wife had been far from amused, I doubt that anyone at the Smiths' that fateful night thought a crime had been committed.

But let me add to the story. Henry drove home from the Smiths' house. To compensate for what was clearly a case of overindulgence, he drove along the extreme right-hand side of the road and didn't let the speedometer reach 30 mph even though he was allowed to go 40. Suddenly, a car containing a teen-age driver and his companion pulled out from a side road, over the speed limit and without stopping as required by law, into the main thoroughfare on which Henry was driving. Without alcohol, Henry would have been aware of the other car on the side road, its speed, the increasingly obvious chance that it would not stop at the intersection, and the consequent probability of a crash, and he could have done several things to avoid that eventuality. Please note that the youngsters were completely at fault, but also note that Henry had a clear chance to avoid the accident—at least, the normal or average or usual Henry would have had a clear chance. The Henry with a 0.12 per cent concentration of alcohol in his blood was just not up to meeting any situation requiring sensitivity, judgment, and quick response beyond the regularly expected course of events. I am not sure that we would all agree as to whether Henry was guilty of a crime in this automobile crash. Those who think he is should ask themselves whether they would also consider Henry guilty of a crime if no one had been on the road, if no crash took place, and if his cautious driving had merely resulted in his getting home a little later than usual.

Note that although Henry's sensitivity to cues was reduced, the reduction was quite uneven. He missed several cues at the Smiths' house and several cues just before the accident. On the other hand, he drove home slowly, keeping the speedometer needle below the 30 mph mark and keeping his car well to the right of the center white line; he was more sensitive than usual to those cues. However, his awareness of cues in general, especially his awareness of unusual cues or cues somewhat peripheral to his immediate activity, fell well below his usual average.

Alcohol also reduces what I will term overall intellectual production. Here, too, we should note that some intellectual functioning may actually improve. For example, a person given word association, synonym, or example tests before and after ingestion of alcohol will usually produce more associations of synonyms or illustrations after he has had a few drinks—perhaps four to six ounces of whiskey. Since the purpose of the tests was to produce these responses, there can be little doubt about the fact that he has performed "better" after whiskey. On the other hand, some of the associations or illustrations tend to be, shall we say, a little freer than the test-makers had anticipated. If the alcohol user is asked to list in forty seconds all the types of tree he knows, he may well list family tree, hat tree, tree of life, tree and tree make six, tree tops, and up a tree, as well as laburnum, oak, and cedar. What might be called judgmental control—thinking in proportion to the demands of the total situation—seems to be markedly reduced, even though a specific part of the whole might have been very well executed. Thus, as the amount of alcohol consumed increases, the person's response to the *overall* reality situation becomes more and more ill-balanced.

Another effect of alcohol on the person's learning is to lower his inhibitions; i.e., those behaviors which were learned as restrictions, especially on his immediate gratification. For example, some of the most difficult things for any member of a group to learn, and which every child goes through with great expenditure of energy (his own, his parents', and others'), are (1) taking turns, (2) sharing, (3) being unobtrusive, (4) being peaceful, (5) postponing immediate material gratification in order to achieve long-range goals, and so on. In this process of internalization of certain values, the person becomes, so to speak, his own policeman . . . With alcohol, however, the *efficiency* of this process is temporarily reduced.

Still another effect of alcohol has to do with reaction time and physical coordination, balance, and accuracy. Here, too, there is a loss of efficiency.

The reader should bear in mind that all these effects take place in a specific person—not in some abstract human being. One cannot expect two persons who have consumed the same amount of alcohol to behave in an identical manner—especially if one is highly sensitive, intensely socialized, and athletic, and the other insensitive, "loosely" socialized, obese, and unathletic. Immediate moods or particular physical status of the person just prior to or at the time of alcohol consumption enhance or lessen the expected impact of alcohol.

Another thing the reader should remember with regard to the effects of alcohol is the drinking situation itself. Some situations (such as driving a car on crowded highways) demand great sensitivity to cues, great capacity for use of learned socialization, and maximum use of intellectual and physical abilities. Other situations demand a minimum of all three—for example, a few men watching television at their bachelor friend's apartment. Then, too, special factors in the drinking situation may enhance or lessen the expected effect of alcohol—for example, the presence of one's teetotalist boss or the receipt of some very good or very shocking news.

* * *

DEVIATORS AND DEVIATIONS

The subject of the deviator and deviation in relation to use of alcohol in our society has been approached very slowly, perhaps some will feel even deviously. The reasons for this should be made clear. First, viewed from the level of the total society, there are so many different norms that *any* behavior, whether drinking or not drinking, pertinent to the subject can properly be termed deviant by some segments of the society, termed normal and acceptable by other segments, and termed deviant but excusable by still others. Second, deviation associated with alcohol is of two types: (a) deviation from a drinking custom *per se*—that is, drinking in "improper" fashion, at the wrong time, with the wrong people, or for the wrong reasons—and (b) from *other* behavior patterns while or after using alcohol, the deviation apparently being influenced by the alcohol. Third, since the dominant type of American drinking is recreational, rather than ritual or contractual in nature, many customs involve a reduction in controls and allow a flexibility in individual behavior which in other settings might frequently be deviation in and of itself. For this reason, the behavior in question must first be placed in its appropriate setting before one can determine whether or not it should be labeled deviant. This placement of behavior in proper context is highly complicated by two factors: (1) alcohol's control-reducing effect can persist beyond the limits of the drinking situation, and (2) in our congested and mobile society with its many different value systems, persons who are or just have been drinking are not well separated from those who have not. The use of the automobile illustrates how easily a person can move from an appropriate to an inappropriate context for drinking—a move whose impropriety, never too well delineated in our society, is even less discernible to the actor when there is some alcohol in his central nervous system. . . .

Listed below are four types of deviators, whose deviations are characteristically tied up with alcohol use. With one partial exception, they manifest not only deviations from the drinking customs of their particular social group but also deviations from other behavioral norms while drinking, after drinking, and, in some cases, just before drinking.

The first is a typically American type of alcoholic, a person with no noticeable signs of neurosis or social pathology who participates in groups in which rather frequent and heavy drinking is customary, and who gradually begins to use alcohol as much for relief of minor emotional and social tensions as for social jollification, positive gratification, and group expectancy. Increasingly, alcohol comes to mean more and drinking less. He deviates from the drinking custom. His deviations from other norms while drinking go beyond his group's tolerance. He starts drinking sooner and continues longer, even sneaks drinks, and occasionally lies about his intake. He gets into some troubles at home, with the police, perhaps on the job. He may go on the wagon for a while, may learn about "the hair of the dog," may find more relief for his ever increasing problems by drinking alone. He begins to feel isolated, resentful, guilty, unable to control his own fate—feelings which he resolves with more alcohol which, in turn, makes the feelings worse. In this type of drinker, the role of alcohol, situational pressures, and the tolerant or careless responses of associates are major causal factors. Deviations start in connection with the drinking and move out into wider and wider spheres. Although this statement admits that psychological problems may have made the development more likely, it places such problems in a secondary position so far as initiation of the condition is concerned.

The second type of person, also rather prevalent in America, is the converse of the first. Here, certain neurotic tendencies or developments were fairly evident to a good many people *before* any drinking pattern was established. Unless strong controls were placed on drinking, this person is, upon introduction to drinking, likely to become a chronic deviant. Depending on the situations, the surrounding people, and the presence of other satisfying ways of meeting his personality problem, this person also might spend several years before becoming an alcoholic. However, the role of alcohol and the force of current and continuing social pressures are less important in initiating the condition than they are for the first type of person.

A third type is the psychopath or early schizophrenic. Granted no immediate and strong counterbalance, this person in his earliest stages of alcohol use might show deviation comparable to that of the most advanced stage of alcoholism. It is doubtful that any adherence to a pattern of social drinking could be maintained.

A fourth type of chronic problem drinker is the Skid Row drunkard. He is the person who has *always* stood on the outer fringes of the lowest class rather than a person who has "drifted down" to Skid Row from the lower-middle or middle classes as a late step in an alcoholic career. Because of a rootless and undersocialized early life, he has developed few middle-class aspirations, fewer than average inhibitions, and has had too little training for more than minimal occupational achievement. Drunkenness or, preferably in the eyes of many as they get older, maintenance of a plateau of high alcohol concentration just short of drunkenness, is considered his natural goal. The degree of guilt, remorse, and self-pity generally considered characteristic of American alcoholics seen in clinics is far less pronounced in this type of person. His whole way of life, rather than alcohol or a specific psychic unbalance, is the more significant causal factor. Skid Row cases may form an exception to the rule that chronic problem drinkers deviate from drinking norms and also other norms; these men often adhere to a group pattern of alcohol use. However, these norms of drinking are so deviant from all other American drinking norms that the exception is special.

In all four of these types there remains the possibility that some yet unknown physiologic factor or complex may enhance a person's propensity toward alcohol addiction.

CRIME AND ALCOHOL

The word "crime" refers to (1) certain actions (occasionally, absence of an action) by a member or members of a society and (2) the socially accepted and expected response to that action in a purposeful and punitive or restraining fashion by government. Without *each* of these parts, there is no crime. A great many acts (or lack of action) are quite properly called deviations and are responded to restrictively or punitively by others; but they are not crimes unless the society realistically expects and accepts that *government* will be the punitive responder.

One means of classifying crimes particularly relevant for discussion of alcohol and crime is to divide them into three categories: (a) acts such as theft, assault, obscenity, which are in themselves directly painful or theatening to a member of the group and to which the government will respond with negative sanction; (b) acts which, while not in themselves directly painful to society, have been defined by government as being so likely to lead to acts in category (a) that they must be omitted or committed only in prescribed fashion, by license or permit; (c) acts directly affecting the government itself, such as restrictions on use of governmental property.

Because use of alcohol has for so many generations in this country been considered dangerous and because some sort of governmental control was considered essential in meeting the problems caused by its use, an enormous number of laws have been made—laws on production, storage, packaging, distribution, sales, and advertising of alcoholic beverages—to control acts of the second category (b). The government has gone even further than this and has enacted laws concerning what children shall be taught about alcohol or the distance to be maintained between churches and places where alcohol can be sold. A great deal of legislation has also been enacted concerning the third category of acts: alcoholic beverages have for some time been a source of governmental revenue and the use of alcohol has been prohibited everywhere on election days and in certain governmental territories and buildings.

This legislation emerged and persisted because the activities which were to be restricted or abolished were in fact occurring. By definition these acts are criminal.

Of this large and complicated area of alcohol and crime, only this will be said: the impact of alcohol on the central nervous system is irrelevant to the commission of either of these two types of crimes. This does not mean that the bootlegger, or the teacher failing to teach about alcohol as required by law, or the bartender serving to minors or serving after hours could not have had one or ten drinks before committing the crime; but drinking in these types of crimes would be unusual and unnecessary.

Ordinarily, the problem of alcohol and crime is based on activities of the first category. Usually, we become interested in the relationship between alcohol and crime when alcohol has, through its action on the central nervous system, affected the behavior of someone involved in the illegal act. Furthermore, our interest is usually directed toward the effect of alcohol on the offender's behavior, although the effect of alcohol on the victim may frequently be equally significant, as we shall see later. There are all sorts of crimes—larceny, rape, arson—but to clarify the effect of alcohol on deviators or their victims I shall first classify the offenders as professional, occasional or amateur, and neurotic. After noting the role alcohol might play with these offenders, I shall turn to some of the types of chronic problem drinkers and comment on *their* crimes.

The Professional Criminal. The class of behavior called professional crime may be distinguished from amateur, occasional, or neurotic crime in terms of the characteristics of those committing it: (1) they are usually skilled operators; (2) they learned their trade through contact with other professional criminals and through experiences calling for increased responsibility and "know-how"; (3) they recognize each other as "colleagues"; (4) they use a distinct occupational jargon; (5) they are aware of mistakes, bad luck, and the consequences of hysterical reactions; (6) they know how to capitalize on success as well as how to respond to apprehension or failure; (7) they have common enemies, common customers, common associates; (8) their criminal occupation is a regular way of life.

The impact of alcohol on the behavior of a professional criminal when he is at work will, in all probability, be very slight indeed. If it has any observable effect, he will surely tend to lose status with others who are important to him. Because his profession is always subject to attack by society, he has greater need for sensitivity, learned responses, and physical efficiency than professionals in socially accepted fields. Thus, alcohol and professional crime do not mix. This does not mean, however, that professional criminals never drink. They probably never drink to the extent that alcohol will reduce their efficiency during "business" hours.

But are there professional criminals who use alcohol beyond the limits tolerated by their group? Most likely there are, just as there are physicians, treasurers of large corporations, engineers, and lawyers who use alcohol excessively. The more important question, though, is whether use of alcohol will cause a person to lead the life of a professional criminal. For the most part, the answer to this question is "No." If alcohol usage reduced that person's efficiency, it would most likely keep him from entering this "occupational activity." Here, I wish to make a sharp distinction between drinking as a general practice and drinking which leads to inefficient behavior on the job. Perhaps 90 per cent of all thieves may drink, but stating that this practice can be causally correlated with their profession is about as sensible as attributing the cause of their criminality to their habit of wearing clothes.

The Amateur Thief. In some other types of crime, the role of alcohol may be more significant. For example, three boys in their late teens steal a car. They are not professional car thieves, but boys who wish to go joy-riding, show off, do something exciting. Not knowing how to turn the theft into a commercial venture, they plan to leave the car on a side street after the gasoline is used up or when their game or party is over. They may pick up anything of value in the car, even try to sell accessories to a junk dealer, but primarily they are stealing for use, not for profit. Let us say that the first of these three boys had stolen cars ten times, the second had stolen cars four times, and the third had never stolen a car—all without touching a drop of alcohol. But if we change the picture by adding that one or two or all of them had drunk about four ounces of whiskey in the preceding hour, we could reasonably assume that the desocializing or uninhibiting effect of alcohol may have made this car theft more possible for one or even all three of the boys. But stating that alcohol was the most significant cause of their action is going beyond reasonable interpretation.

To ask whether the alcohol affected the boys' behavior during the entire episode of the theft, however, is an entirely different matter. How was the driver of the car affected? Did the other two stimulate the driver differently because of the alcohol? The most likely answer is that as the amount of alcohol was increased to the point of intoxication, any poorly controlled, individualistic tendencies of an asocial or antisocial nature were allowed greater freedom.

The Physical Assaulter. Crimes of physical assault (from a kick in the shins to homicide) seem in most instances to require very little planning or preparation. For example, the three boys in the car-stealing episode may, on the spur of the moment, have been attracted to joy-riding merely by seeing a flashy sports car parked on the street corner. Most of the time, however, a certain amount of planning or searching must, of necessity, precede the theft itself. Most assault, however, is far less premeditated.

Alcohol by itself is not significant as a cause of assault; an enormous number of assaults occur without alcohol and an overwhelming majority of instances of alcohol use are *not* followed by assault. However, it is easy to see how the effects of alcohol—the lessening of sensitivity, inhibitions, self-control—on a particular person and in a particular situation could increase the possibility of an occurrence of assaultive behavior. In some social settings, physical aggression is more tolerated so that, as a result, some members of society will have lower barriers for alcohol to reduce. In other social settings, drinking may be expected to elicit greater expression of aggression than is usually allowed in most nondrinking situations, although this increase in aggressive behavior is usually verbal or symbolic in nature rather than physical.

Physical assault inevitably involves two people; often it involves many. Yet, even if only *one* of the two maintains his self-control, the assault may be avoided; either the insulter or the insulted can alter a touchy situation so that any deviant behavior will not advance to assault. Then, too, any number of people can intervene in an argument if physical assault seems imminent. Of course, the amount of alcohol in one or both of the quarrelers may reach the point where it will impair their physical dexterity, thereby reducing either offensive or defensive skills.

In our society, the assault considered most criminal is the assault resulting in death. Clearly, homicide is a violent and extreme deviation and almost always a violation of the cultural norm and the demands of socialization. It is probably the felony most highly correlated with alcohol use. Wolfgang's and Strohm's study of 588 homicides occurring over a five-year period in Philadelphia, an excellent presentation of the subject, revealed that alcohol was present, in either the offender or the victim or both, in 64 per cent (376) of the cases. In 14 per cent of these 376 cases alcohol was found in the victim; in 17 per cent it was found in the offender; and in 70 per cent in both the offender and his victim. The great majority of physical assault cases involved stabbing (228 cases), kicking, and beating by fists or a blunt instrument (128 cases)—a total of 356 cases, over 70 per cent of which involved alcohol. The remainder of the original sample of 588 was comprised of 194 cases of shooting and 38 cases of other types of assault; of these, only half involved the use of alcohol. These homicides bore no resemblance to the upper-class intrigue so characteristic of Anglo-American detective stories. Most of them were not assaults on strangers but rather the outcome of quarrels between members of the lowest social class groups over money or marital partners. An extraordinarily large percentage of them (about 66 per cent) occurred on Fridays, Saturdays, and Sundays.[1]

I am presenting Wolfgang's and Strohm's findings in this much detail in order to point out that even in these types of crimes most closely correlated with alcohol use, alcohol is unquestionably only *one* of many causative agents.

In addition to these crimes and criminal types are the three classes of problem drinkers mentioned earlier in this article: (1) the typical American alcoholic who commits a crime, (2) the psychopath who commits a crime during or after drinking, and (3) the drunkard of the lowest social class.

The Dominant American Alcoholic. The so-called dominant American type of alcoholic usually is a person who has gradually become dissocialized along with his chronic and excessive use of alcohol. At first his deviations are limited to the drinking situation but then become sufficiently marked so that two things occur: (1) he finds customary drinking situations too limited a way of ingesting alcohol, and (2) he begins to consume alcohol in nondrinking situations. If this process continues, depersonalization begins to set in so that a sort of psychopathology emerges. Alcohol becomes increasingly necessary as a kind of chemical comforter, thus leading to a vicious circle in which alcohol causes further social and personal disorganization which, in turn, results in still greater need for chemically provided relief. What is so peculiarly irritating to others is that this person can be acceptable and even attractive for days or weeks at a time and then unexpectedly show his deviancy.

The sort of criminal act that results seems to follow a pattern. Accompanying the person's deviation from customary drinking situations is his deviation from almost any pattern, so that very often he is picked up by the law for assault, disturbing the peace, or property damage. As his desocialization increases, his deviations seem to become more criminal. With this person, the total impact of alcoholism, rather than the specific occasion of alcohol ingestion, is significant. Although the alcohol in him is, of course, important, he probably did not commit that sort of offense five or ten years earlier when he was ingesting the same amounts.

The Psychopath. A psychopath is a person who is asocial, whose emotional responses to people, ideas, and situations seem uncertain and lacking in depth. His behavior and motives frequently appear bizarre and upsetting and may become dangerous when alcohol affects his central nervous system. The important distinction here is that this condition apparently has not been brought about by his drinking history or his current situation; rather, the problem is psychological in nature, and the alcohol acts only as an exacerbation. (It is quite possible that alcohol might also serve to diminish the strength of the deviant act.)

The Chronic Drunkenness Offender. Common drunks, or chronic drunkenness offenders, manifest a pattern almost antithetical to that of the dominant American alcoholic. In this group can be found the young person of low social-class background whose aggressive behavior—theft, vandalism, gang fighting, robbery—must frequently be deterred by the law through punishment, institutionalization, or rehabilitation. This person may have lacked a regular home life as a child, regular educational achievement, regular start in a job, and regular start in matrimony. He could, between the ages of thirteen and thirty, easily be called a criminal. He probably drank when he was young, although this would not have been a particularly salient aspect of his life. After reaching thirty years of age, however, his life seems to change: his behavior becomes less and less felonious and his use of alcohol more and more excessive. Resultant arrests for drunkenness become a more and more frequent occurrence.[2]

From an objective viewpoint, the behavior of this type of offender is properly labeled crim-

[1]Marvin E. Wolfgang and Rolf B. Strohm, "The Relationship between Alcohol and Criminal Homicide," *Quarterly Journal of Studies on Alcohol*, September, 1956, pp. 411–25.

[2]D. J. Pittman and C. W. Gordon, *Revolving Door* (Glencoe, Ill.: Free Press, 1958).

inal: after all, he is constantly being arrested, judged, and sentenced by the authorities. But *should* he be arrested, judged, and sentenced? If this man has, from childhood, been undersocialized, lacking in strong life goals, then he has no socially acceptable setting to which he can return and, even if he had, he lacks the assets needed for making such a trip. In other words, he would have to be "habilitated," rather than *re*-habilitated, to a new way of life.

Each of these last three types of chronic deviation accompanied by use of alcohol and resulting in crime is (1) quite different from the other two, (2) quite different from those deviations manifested occasionally by heavy social drinkers, and (3) quite different from the deviations of youngsters or beginning drinkers. This does not mean that they lack certain common factors. Rather, it means that education, evaluation, administration, and policy-making for meeting these types of crime will have to be more discriminating if they are to be effective. Simply stating that alcohol (or drunkenness or alcoholism) was a cause or, even worse, *the* cause of criminality is likely to increase misunderstanding and result in ineffective answers. This sort of over-simplification is on a par with the other single-cause explanations of crime: climate, ethnic background, poverty, lack of affection, boredom, overstimulation, or devils.

There are many relationships between alcohol and crime: Thousands of crimes involving alcohol are committed in which the action of alcohol on the central nervous system is utterly absent. Public drunkenness is, apart from motor vehicle violations, numerically the major crime in our society. Second, there are crimes related to alcoholism: Following use of alcohol, behavior that goes beyond social drinking convention and deviates from the norms may be criminal. And there are neurotic crimes, such as pyromania, which are highly correlated with alcohol use. The roles of alcohol are very different in each of these cases. We must never forget, however, that all these behaviors, excluding drunkenness, can occur without use of alcohol and that in the overwhelming majority of instances the use of alcohol is not followed by any crime at all.

22.

Albert D. Ullman

SOCIOCULTURAL BACKGROUNDS OF ALCOHOLISM

An obvious starting point in attempting to unravel the causes of any behavioral phenomenon is the consideration of the differences between those who demonstrate the behavior and those who do not. So it has been in the study of alcoholism. When alcoholism was considered a moral problem, those who dealt with it found differences in the moral fiber of normal and abnormal drinkers. While this approach to the problem has been abandoned in the recent surge of scientific interest in the causes of abnormal drinking, the process of comparing the problem with the "nonproblem" drinker goes on. The two groups have been compared in the way their systems metabolize alcohol and utilize sugar and in the hormonal and other physiological functioning.

These studies have been paralleled by others using the same comparative technique to investigate the personality of the problem drinker. Still others have dealt with his family situation.

One major flaw has been general: the problem drinker is usually compared with the normal drinker *after* he presents a problem. In the progression of addictive drinking, many things

Source: *The Annals,* Vol. 315 (January, 1958), pp. 48–54. Reprinted by permission of the author and the journal.

happen to the individual. Both personality and physical changes occur. To distinguish between cause and effect, we must know what the problem drinker was *before* his drinking became abnormal. In addition, we need to know the prevalence in the general population of items which are sometimes taken as characteristic of the problem drinker. For example, one reads that the alcoholic has a domineering mother and an autocratic father.[1] We do not know whether this condition applies to most people, only to alcoholics, or to alcoholics as well as other problem groups.

One set of comparisons that seems to have been productive of ideas on the causes of alcoholism has to do with deviations by individual drinkers from the typical drinking pattern of a given group. The need for this line of investigation has been highlighted by the tendency to define alcoholism in terms of departure from some typical mode of drinking. For example, the Alcoholism Subcommittee of the Expert Committee on Mental Health of the World Health Organization has in part defined alcoholism as ". . . any form of drinking which in its extent goes beyond the traditional and customary 'dietary' use, or the ordinary compliance with the social drinking customs of the whole community concerned, . . ."[2] Although there is not universal acceptance of this definition, general agreement does seem to hold that here we have a fruitful area for research. In our present state of knowledge, differences in rates of alcoholism cannot be explained in physiological or psychological terms alone. Some promising leads into understanding the pressures placed on the physiological and psychological processes are coming to us from investigations of the sociocultural terrain on which drinking occurs.

By and large, investigators have been interested in the differences among societies in the way alcoholic beverages are used as well as in attitudes toward drinking, drunkenness, and related aspects. One gain has been the discovery that differences in drinking customs exist not only between societies, but among subgroups of the same society; for example, subgroups differentiated on the basis of age, sex, or ethnic origin.

The challenge in the study of drinking customs is to be found in the possibility of correlating diverse customs with rates of alcoholism. Where customs differ and rates of alcoholism differ, we need to know whether these differences are functionally related. Of more general interest is the possibility that the student of this relationship may be making progress along lines that will be useful in other areas of mental health. Specifically, what the investigator in this field is trying to do is to discover how membership in a group sharing a certain culture predisposes one to a particular method of handling anxiety, whether "normal" or otherwise. He is working on the problem of symptom choice.

ALCOHOLISM RATES AND SPECIFIC ASPECTS OF DRINKING

For some groups or societies we have excellent descriptions of the use of alcohol but know nothing about the prevalence of alcoholism. In a few instances, particularly in civilized societies, we know something about the rates of alcoholism but have no adequate accounts of the drinking customs of those groups within the society which contribute most heavily to the alcoholic population.

What we need, then, is the following: descriptions of drinking customs, epidemiological information which tells who the alcoholics are and in what numbers, and information on enough societies and subgroups to tell whether the relationship between custom and alcoholism found in any group is significant or merely due to chance. We should be fortunate were we to find that some characteristic of the drinking custom is totally present or absent when alcoholism does or does not occur; however, this does not happen.

Another way of describing our task is to say we must discover in the drinking customs those independent variables upon which the presence of alcoholism is dependent. In doing this, it will be useful to look at some of the variables which have already been suggested as independent.

[1]Mary Phyllis Wittman, "Developmental Characteristics and Personalities of Chronic Alcoholics," *Journal of Abnormal and Social Psychology*, Vol. 34 (July, 1939), pp. 361–77.

[2]World Health Organization Technical Report Series, No. 42, 1951.

An example is frequency of drinking. We must note that we cannot compare alcoholics and normal drinkers in this regard. The finding that alcoholics drink more frequently than others tells us nothing, even if true, about frequent drinking as causative of alcoholism. However, if we should find that groups which use alcoholic beverages more frequently than others also have a higher rate of alcoholism, then we should have a useful relationship established.

The truth is that no such relationship is found. Numerous studies have shown that American Jews, particularly the Orthodox, and Italian-Americans are among those having extremely low rates of alcoholism accompanied by relatively high frequency of drinking. The evidence is sufficiently clear to cause us to abandon frequency of drinking as a cause of alcoholism.

If, instead of frequency of drinking, we examine frequency of drunkenness, we have a case that is not quite so clear cut but still convincing. Gerald D. Berreman's study of drinking patterns among the Aleuts, William Mangin's report of drinking among South American Indians, and Edwin M. Lemert's descriptions of the use of alcohol among Northwest Coast Indians all point out that in these instances drinking to get drunk is accompanied by low rates of alcoholism.[3] Thus, we cannot say that frequency of drunkenness is causally related to alcoholism.

Still another possibility is that the alcoholic content of the beverage is related to alcoholism. Here, again, we find no support for the hypothesis. An example of contrary evidence is found in Charles Snyder's studies of drinking among American Jews. He has shown that this low alcoholism group uses beverages ranging in potency from mild wine to strong spirits.[4] Also, evidence from primitive societies demonstrates that those who use native brewed or fermented beverages of low alcohol content show about as much alcoholism as those who have taken over the use of distilled beverages.

INTEGRATION OF DRINKING CUSTOMS

If we cannot find a simple mechanistic relationship between some aspect of drinking and alcoholism such as the variables examined above, we need either abandon the drinking custom as a field of research or go into the more complicated area of culturally produced attitudes toward drinking. We can readily see how the social environment is responsible for certain attitudes, but we still must ask if certain constellations of attitudes are more frequent among groups with high rates of alcoholism than among those with low rates.

The answer which will be supported here is that *in any group or society in which the drinking customs, values, and sanctions—together with the attitudes of all segments of the group or society—are well established, known to and agreed upon by all, and are consistent with the rest of the culture, the rate of alcoholism will be low.* Conformity to the drinking standards is supported by the total culture. However, under conditions in which the individual drinker does not know what is expected or when the expectation in one situation differs from that in another, it can be assumed that he will have ambivalent feelings about drinking. Thus, ambivalence is the psychological product of unintegrated drinking customs.

An excellent example of this situation is provided by Snyder's studies with the "purest" case of cultural consistency found among Orthodox Jews.[5] Members of this group start to use alcohol in childhood, they drink with relatively great frequency, exhibit little or no drunkenness, and have virtually no pathology associated with drinking. Because they have been introduced to alcohol so early, and because they use it in situations such as religious ritual where its func-

[3]See the following: Gerald D. Berreman, "Drinking Patterns of the Aleuts," *Quarterly Journal of Studies on Alcohol,* Vol. 17 (September, 1956), pp. 503–14. William Mangin, "Drinking among Andean Indians," *Quarterly Journal of Studies on Alcohol,* Vol. 18 (March, 1957), pp. 55–66. Edwin M. Lemert, *Alcohol and the Northwest Coast Indians,* University of California Publications in Culture and Society, Vol. 2, No. 6 (Berkeley and Los Angeles: University of California Press, 1954).

[4]There have been a series of articles by Charles R. Snyder published under the general title "Culture and Sobriety" in the *Quarterly Journal of Studies on Alcohol,* Vol. 16 (March, 1955), pp. 101–77; Vol. 16 (June, 1955), pp. 263–89; Vol. 16 (September, 1955), pp. 504–32; Vol. 16 (December, 1955), pp. 700–742; and Vol. 17 (March, 1956), pp. 124–43.

[5]*Ibid.*

tion is clear and where the situation itself is free from ambiguity, Jewish children see nothing unusual or immoral about the use of alcohol.

Giorgio Lolli and his collaborators as well as Phyllis H. Williams and Robert Straus have provided us with another example very much like the Orthodox Jews.[6] Reports on drinking by Italians and Italian-Americans show that they also begin drinking in childhood, drink frequently, exhibit little drunkenness and virtually no alcoholism. Perhaps the outstanding feature of the drinking patterns of the Italians (changing somewhat among Italian-Americans) is the use of wine with meals. As with the Jews, drinking occurs in clear-cut situations with no immoral connotations attached to the act. Everyone feels the same way about drinking, and there is no clash with other elements of the culture.

Still another example of a people with well-integrated drinking customs is to be found in Chinese society. Merrill Moore, Wesley LaBarre, and Milton L. Barnett all give the same picture of the use of alcohol in this group.[7] A statement by LaBarre is typical of their findings. He says,

> As for drinking, the Chinese indulge in it on all occasions of eating, and without the slightest discernible ambivalence, lacking the really very intricate attitudes that have been built up toward it in the West.[8]

Like Jews and Italians, Chinese begin using alcohol early, but, unlike them, quite frequently exhibit drunkenness. Barnett's description of celebrations in which drinking to a point of mild intoxication occurs is pertinent. His study is also useful in providing statistics of the low prevalence of pathological drinking among Chinese-Americans.[9]

It should be clear from the above that Orthodox Jews, Italians, and Chinese, among others, are free from ambivalence in the drinking situation precisely because their culture is so consistent in this regard. One should expect the opposite in cases of unintegrated drinking customs.

UNINTEGRATED DRINKING CUSTOMS

We can take as an example of lack of integration the description offered by Selden D. Bacon of drinking by a group he refers to as the "United States American of the Northeast quarter of the nation—Protestant, middle-class, urban, white, from Anglo-Saxon background of three or more generations in this country." Part of the description of the drinking customs and attitudes of this group is as follows:

> The social functions of drinking are rather vaguely and somewhat defensively described: they concern drawing people, both family members and also complete strangers, together, often for purposes of "fun," often to allow relaxation from . . . moral norms. . . . The rules and procedures are on occasion rather specific, but also show enormous variability so that a given individual may follow one set of rules with his family, another with business or professional associates, and the third on holiday occasions and show even different patterns when away from the home-town. . . . Sanctions for violations are extremely irregular. . . . Parents, employers, priests, physicians, and other agencies of sanction are most uncertain sources, both in formal statement and in actual behavior, many of them avoiding the issue whenever possible. . . . Sometimes the learning stems not from parents, ministers, physicians, elders, and teachers but from other adolescents, sometimes on trains, in cars or in commercial places. The custom is not significantly entwined with family and religious institutions. . . . There is great emotional feeling about the problem on the mass level as well as by individuals, feeling that has run rampant for generations. Activating the custom, especially by the young, is often attended with feelings of guilt, hostility, and exhibitionism and may occur as a

[6]Two series of articles on the Italian and Italian-American drinker have appeared in the *Quarterly Journal of Studies on Alcohol* between 1950 and 1954. The earlier group is by Phyllis H. Williams and Robert Straus, bearing in March and September, 1952, September, 1953, the general title, "Drinking Patterns of Italians in New Haven: Utilization of the Personal Diary as a Research Technique." Particular attention is called to those appearing in the March and December, 1950 issues. The articles by Giorgio Lolli and his associates to which the reader's attention is drawn appeared in December, 1954.

[7]See the following: Merrill Moore, "Chinese Wine: Some Notes on its Social Use," *Quarterly Journal of Studies on Alcohol*, Vol. 9 (September, 1948), pp. 270–79. Wesley LaBarre, "Some Observations of Character Structure in the Orient. II. The Chinese. Part Two," *Psychiatry*, Vol. 9 (November, 1946), pp. 375–95. Milton L. Barnett, "Alcoholism in the Cantonese of New York City; An Anthropological Study," in *Etiology of Chronic Alcoholism*, edited by Oskar Diethelm (Springfield, Ill.: Charles C Thomas, 1955).

[8]LaBarre, *ibid.*, p. 376.

[9]Barnett, *op. cit.*

secretive practice insofar as parents or employers or elders are concerned.[10]

The contrast between these drinking customs and associated attitudes and those of the Jews, Italians, and Chinese is clear. The difference in rates of alcoholism among the three groups mentioned and the one described by Bacon is also clear. The group Bacon portrays so vividly is probably above average in its contribution to the total population of alcoholics, while the other groups contribute very lightly.

We can now turn to a group which appears to contribute heavily to the population of alcoholics: the Irish-Americans. All studies of American ethnic groups show this one to be at or near the top in alcoholism rates; consequently its pattern of drinking is of particular interest. We are fortunate in having two excellent researches by Robert F. Bales and Donald D. Glad which compare drinking by Jewish-Americans with Irish-Americans.[11] The general findings are that Irish-American youths drink differently and hold vastly different attitudes toward the experience. In many respects, the situation for the Irish-American drinker is close to the Northeastern American described by Bacon, with some aspects seen in exaggerated form.

Unlike the Jewish drinker, says Glad, the Irish-American defines the drinking situation in terms of the "affective consequences, in which the physiological and psychological changes produced in the individual by alcohol per se are of primary importance."[12] This attitude leaves the drinking situation open to further definition on each separate occasion. While the purpose of drinking is to get drunk, and in this the Irish-American bears some resemblance to many primitive drinkers, the degree of intoxication often has to be handled quite delicately, unlike the primitive who will not be punished for his drunkenness. This is a very different situation from that of the Jewish, Italian, or Chinese drinker, most of whose drinking takes place under familiar, regulated circumstances. There is no need to manipulate the degree of intoxication achieved because ordinarily one does not drink to get drunk.

Some preliminary evidence gathered by the present writer supports this view. He found that the Irish-American tends to have his first drink under somewhat less protected circumstances than do members of many other groups. It may also be an emotionally significant experience, marked by some degree of intoxication, taking place in unusual places outside the home, and it may occur in the presence of companions who place pressure on the neophyte to "drink like a man."[13]

We may also suppose that the Irish-American has more frequent contact with alcoholism due to its relatively frequent appearance among friends, members of the family and of the families of contemporaries. Undoubtedly, this results in formal and informal sanctions against drinking. The person who violates these sanctions must enter the drinking situation with high ambivalence.

Somewhat different problems are faced by one of the most interesting categories of drinkers in our society. These are the Mormons who drink, thus directly violating their religious and familial training.[14] Proportionately, those Mormons who drink contribute more heavily to the number of problem drinkers than do other drinking groups. All of the factors we have indicated as associated with high rates of alcoholism are present when the Mormon drinks.

SEX DIFFERENCES

A clear difference in the rate of alcoholism between the sexes is found. In the United States, latest estimates show there are 11 male alcoholics for every 2 female.[15] Studies by Robert

[10]Selden D. Bacon, "Social Settings Conducive to Alcoholism: A Sociological Approach to a Medical Problem," *Journal of the American Medical Association*, Vol. 164 (May 11, 1957), p. 179 f.

[11]Robert F. Bales, "Cultural Differences in Rates of Alcoholism," *Quarterly Journal of Studies on Alcohol*, Vol. 6 (March, 1946), pp. 480–99. Also, Donald D. Glad, "Attitudes and Experiences of American-Jewish and American-Irish Male Youth as Related to Differences in Adult Rates of Inebriety," *Quarterly Journal of Studies on Alcohol*, Vol. 8 (December, 1947), pp. 406–72.

[12]Glad, *ibid.*, p. 461.

[13]Albert D. Ullman, "Ethnic Differences in the First Drinking Experience" (in preparation).

[14]See Bacon, *op. cit.*

[15]Mark Keller and Vera Efron, "The Prevalence of Alcoholism," *Quarterly Journal of Studies on Alcohol*, Vol. 16 (December, 1955), pp. 619–44.

Straus and Selden D. Bacon as well as by the present writer indicate that there are different expectations for the young man and young woman in the drinking situation.[16] There is less social pressure to drink and fewer kinds of situations in which drinking is expected of the girl. She does not have to "prove" her womanhood by drinking. There are hints that, in the case of the woman alcoholic, there is some confusion in her identification with the expected female role; that is, the woman alcoholic may feel pressures on her in the drinking situation which are typical of those felt by the man.

We have seen that the task of integrating drinking with the rest of one's activities and beliefs is made more or less difficult by virtue of one's ethnic group and sex membership. However, the culture is in large part transmitted through the medium of the small, face-to-face unit the sociologist calls the "primary group." There has been some work in this area which fits in with the theory that lack of cultural integration in the sphere of drinking activities and attitudes is directly related to higher rates of alcoholism. For example, Joan K. Jackson and Ralph Connor have shown that parents of alcoholics held inconsistent attitudes toward drinking. John L. Haer gives us evidence that the individual tends to drink more like his contemporaries than like the members of his childhood family.[17] For the people investigated, well-integrated attitudes toward drinking were impossible because the major primary group influence did not agree.

Probably no one comes into the drinking situation with more ambivalence than the child of an alcoholic. He has seen at first hand what can happen, yet he appears to be under extra compulsion to drink. In part, it may be because he is afraid of being a deviant or a "defective" person. We have here, in an exaggerated way, the situation of anyone who enters into drinking activity feeling that it is bad or dangerous. By the nature of things, if such a person drinks, his attitudes toward the act are conflicting.

ISOLATED GROUPS

It is not at all unusual to find someone who having been moved from his customary residence to an isolated group such as an army camp, lumber camp, foreign resort, or shipboard drinks less temperately than at home. Two comments are pertinent here. First, isolated groups such as the military or lumbermen are often strictly male. It follows that some of the pressures which have already been suggested as present when men drink are emphasized in an all-male society. Furthermore, the neutralizing effect of negative sanctions on drinking stemming from the presence of mother, sister, wife, daughter is absent in such communities. Second, removal from one's typical way of life may involve deprivations and usually does mean some anxiety. In these unusual circumstances, alcohol is useful in reducing anxiety. But we must keep clearly in mind that heavy drinking, particularly under temporary stress, is not the equivalent of compulsive or addictive drinking.

The picture of heavy drinking in the isolated group is further complicated by the fact that persons who are already having trouble with their drinking, meaning that they drink differently from their usual companions, seek out places where they can drink heavily without being unusual. The individual who first learns to drink in such circumstances as an army camp may represent a problem. He has no way of knowing that his teachers are deviant in their drinking, that their attitudes are not typical of the normal drinker.

Heavy drinking under circumstances such as those described above is not to be confused with that done by another category of drinkers: namely, those who have not taken on the value system of their society. These persons are spoken of as "unsocialized" or "undersocialized." Such individuals may drink immoderately, but they are not necessarily compulsive drinkers. Our

---

[16] Robert Straus and Selden D. Bacon, *Drinking in College* (New Haven, Conn.: Yale University Press, 1953). Also, Albert D. Ullman, "Sex Differences in the First Drinking Experience," *Quarterly Journal of Studies on Alcohol,* Vol. 18 (June, 1957), pp. 229–39.

[17] Joan K. Jackson and Ralph Connor, "Attitudes of the Parents of Alcoholics, Moderate Drinkers and Nondrinkers toward Drinking," *Quarterly Journal of Studies on Alcohol,* Vol. 14 (December, 1953), pp. 590–613. Also, John L. Haer, "Drinking Patterns and the Influence of Friends and Family," *Quarterly Journal of Studies on Alcohol,* Vol. 16 (March, 1955), pp. 178–85.

assumption is that many such persons drink because they want to avoid the responsibilities of sobriety, not because they are compulsively driven. . . .

A final word of caution is necessary. The amount of information available to us in the field is much less than necessary for validation of theories of causes of alcoholism. What has been described in this article represents a beginning in a kind of research that looks most promising. Intimate knowledge of the sociocultural factors which are conducive to alcoholism should help us to focus upon those physiological and psychological factors which are involved in establishing an addiction. Undoubtedly, additional information in all three areas will be needed before final answers are available.

CHAPTER VII

White-Collar Crime

White-collar crime may be defined as those offenses committed by persons acting in their occupational roles. The offenders in this case are middle- and upper class businessmen and members of the professions who have in the course of their everyday occupational activities violated the basic trust placed in them or acted in an unethical manner. In many cases these people are the "ideal" members of the community; physicians and lawyers dedicated to their work but overcome by conflict, because to survive in our competitive society they must adhere to the dictates and values of the "organization."

In this chapter the editor is unable to present valid statistics indicating how many white-collar crimes have been committed, what types of crime, and the arrest records of the law enforcement agencies. Because of the discreet nature of these business transactions and the honorable positions that their leaders enjoy, it is most difficult to make accusations, and at times impossible to bring formal charges. Even though white-collar criminal activities may take more money from the American people each year than all conventional property crimes combined, the Federal Bureau of Investigation has no way of reporting their volume in its *Uniform Crime Report*.

In the case of a white-collar offender, history has disclosed that if an infraction of the law is discovered, rather than appear before a criminal court judge, the accused will most likely be reprimanded by an administrative board or commission or take part in a civil trial.

For the sake of convenience, white-collar criminal activities may be divided into seven basic categories. These categories are:

1. Fraud—fraudulent activities by "respectable" businessmen. An example of this kind of activity may take the form of a misleading financial report distributed by a broker encouraging his clients to purchase a worthless stock or invest in a company which is not financially solvent. Individuals may also commit fraud by engaging in such acts as arson for the purpose of collecting insurance on homes or businesses destroyed by fire, false income tax reporting, or exaggeration of an injury received as a result of an accident. In the case of exaggerated injury the personal physician would have a significant role to play in the fraud.

2. Misrepresentation—in our consumer-minded American economy, federal agencies must constantly monitor the advertising claims of corporations and safeguard the rights of individuals to purchase exactly what they think they are purchasing. Thus, we must be concerned with false and misleading claims (advertising, labeling), in reference to what the product promises to do, and weights which might possibly deceive the consumer. (Example: By purchasing an economy-size package so labeled, the consumer may be paying more than if he were to buy two regular size cartons.)

3. Restraint of trade violations—again, federal agencies keep a continuous watch on corporations to be certain they are not violating any of our trade regulations, for if they are, ultimately the consumer will have to pay.

4. Rebates—buyers for large corporations may purchase huge quantities of a given product only if they receive a money payment from the seller once the product has been delivered. In this capacity the buyer may act on his own behalf or as a representative of the corporation. In order to meet this demand the producer may charge more for his product. If this is the case, the increase in price may again be passed on to the consumer.

5. Violations of trust—bank employees and accountants are especially susceptible to commission of acts falling into this category. Bank employees are charged with a good deal of responsibility in the handling and exchange of currency. "Mistakes" may be made of such great magnitude that it would be impossible to recover the losses. Accountants are primarily responsible for maintaining the records of businesses and financial institutions. Since most of these people are well-trained at our colleges and universities to be especially watchful for techniques used in manipulating funds and making false entries, they themselves may falsify the records and escape with a great deal of money before their activities are uncovered.

6. Misrepresentation by silence—just as we may have a case of overt misrepresentation, we may also have misrepresentation by silence. If a

shipment of cattle is diseased and the seller says nothing, this is just as serious as his claiming that the cattle are perfectly healthy.

7. White-collar bribery—(*a*) the bribery of public officials and (*b*) bribery to place products in stores and institutions. Although there may be specific criminal statutes dealing with this kind of activity, this act still can be classified as a white-collar offense. In the case of the bribery of public officials, the officials are considered just as guilty as the first party.

In the opening two selections the classic papers of Edwin H. Sutherland dealing with white-collar criminality are presented. In his first paper, Sutherland discusses the nature of white-collar crime and exposes specific instances of flagrant violations. In his second paper, Sutherland defends the concept of white-collar crime as an appropriate definition of the behavior patterns manifested by this type of offender. In the third article, Robert G. Caldwell reexamines the concept of white-collar crime, and considers its legal and sociological implications. He notes that there has been considerable controversy among sociologists and members of the legal profession regarding its usage. Dr. Caldwell considers the moral issues, the nature of a criminal act, legal definitions, and morality and ethics. In the fourth reading, Gilbert Geis reviews the definitions of white-collar crime developed by Sutherland, and then attempts "to point the way toward a more restricted and meaningful definition of the concept of white-collar crime." He notes that several leading sociologists are dissatisfied with the original definition and there is now a need for revision.

23.

Edwin H. Sutherland

WHITE-COLLAR CRIMINALITY

This paper[1] is concerned with crime in relation to business. The economists are well acquainted with business methods but not accustomed to consider them from the point of view of crime; many sociologists are well acquainted with crime but not accustomed to consider it as expressed in business. This paper is an attempt to integrate these two bodies of knowledge. More accurately stated, it is a comparison of crime in the upper or white-collar class, composed of respectable or at least respected business and professional men, and crime in the lower class, composed of persons of low socioeconomic status. This comparison is made for the purpose of developing the theories of criminal behavior, not for the purpose of muckraking or of reforming anything except criminology.

The criminal statistics show unequivocally that crime, *as popularly conceived and officially measured,* has a high incidence in the lower class and a low incidence in the upper class; less than 2 percent of the persons committed to prisons in a year belong to the upper class. These statistics refer to criminals handled by the police, the criminal and juvenile courts, and the prisons, and to such crimes as murder, assault, burglary, robbery, larceny, sex offenses, and drunkenness, but exclude traffic violations.

The criminologists have used the case histories and criminal statistics derived from these agencies of criminal justice as their principal data. From them, they have derived general theories of criminal behavior. These theories are that, since crime is concentrated in the lower class, it is caused by poverty or by personal and social characteristics believed to be associated statistically with poverty, including feeblemindedness, psychopathic deviations, slum neighborhoods, and "deteriorated" families. This statement, of course, does not do justice to the qualifications and variations in the conventional theories of criminal behavior, but it presents correctly their central tendency.

The thesis of this paper is that the conception and explanations of crime which have just been described are misleading and incorrect, that crime is in fact not closely correlated with poverty or with the psychopathic and sociopathic conditions associated with poverty, and that an adequate explanation of criminal behavior must proceed along quite different lines. The conventional explanations are invalid principally because they are derived from biased samples. The samples are biased in that they have not included vast areas of criminal behavior of persons not in the lower class. One of these neglected areas is the criminal behavior of business and professional men, which will be analyzed in this paper.

The "robber barons" of the last half of the nineteenth century were white-collar criminals, as practically everyone now agrees. Their attitudes are illustrated by these statements: Colonel Vanderbilt asked, "You don't suppose you can run a railroad in accordance with the statutes, do you?" A. B. Stickney, a railroad president, said to sixteen other railroad presidents in the home of J. P. Morgan in 1890, "I have the utmost respect for you gentlemen, individually, but as railroad presidents I wouldn't trust you with my watch out of my sight." Charles Francis Adams said, "The difficulty in railroad management . . . lies in the covetousness, want of good faith, and low moral tone of railway managers, in the complete absence of any high standard of commercial honesty."

Source: *American Sociological Review,* Vol. 5. No. 1 (February, 1940), pp. 1–12, American Sociological Association. Reprinted by permission of the journal.

[1]Thirty-fourth Annual Presidential Address delivered at Philadelphia, Pa., Dec. 27, 1939 in joint meeting with the American Economic Society (its Fifty-second) at which President Jacob Viner spoke on the relations of economic theory to the formulation of public policy.

The present-day white-collar criminals, who are more suave and deceptive than the "robber barons," are represented by Krueger, Stavisky, Whitney, Mitchell, Foshay, Insull, the Van Sweringens, Musica-Coster, Fall, Sinclair, and many other merchant princes and captains of finance and industry, and by a host of lesser followers. Their criminality has been demonstrated again and again in the investigations of land offices, railways, insurance, munitions, banking, public utilities, stock exchanges, the oil industry, real estate, reorganization committees, receiverships, bankruptcies, and politics. Individual cases of such criminality are reported frequently, and in many periods more important crime news may be found on the financial pages of newspapers than on the front pages. White-collar criminality is found in every occupation, as can be discovered readily in casual conversation with a representative of an occupation by asking him, "What crooked practices are found in your occupation?"

White-collar criminality in business is expressed most frequently in the form of misrepresentation in financial statements of corporations, manipulation in the stock exchange, commercial bribery, bribery of public officials directly or indirectly in order to secure favorable contracts and legislation, misrepresentation in advertising and salesmanship, embezzlement and misapplication of funds, short weights and measures and misgrading of commodities, tax frauds, misapplication of funds in receiverships and bankruptcies. These are what Al Capone called "the legitimate rackets." These and many others are found in abundance in the business world.

In the medical profession, which is here used as an example because it is probably less criminalistic than some other professions, are found illegal sale of alcohol and narcotics, abortion, illegal services to underworld criminals, fraudulent reports and testimony in accident cases, extreme cases of unnecessary treatment, fake specialists, restriction of competition, and fee-splitting. Fee-splitting is a violation of a specific law in many states and a violation of the conditions of admission to the practice of medicine in all. The physician who participates in fee-splitting tends to send his patients to the surgeon who will give him the largest fee rather than to the surgeon who will do the best work. It has been reported that two thirds of the surgeons in New York City split fees, and that more than one half of the physicians in a central western city who answered a questionnaire on this point favored fee-splitting.

These varied types of white-collar crimes in business and the professions consist principally of violation of delegated or implied trust, and many of them can be reduced to two categories: misrepresentation of asset values and duplicity in the manipulation of power. The first is approximately the same as fraud or swindling; the second is similar to the double-cross. The latter is illustrated by the corporation director who, acting on inside information, purchases land which the corporation will need and sells it at a fantastic profit to his corporation. The principle of this duplicity is that the offender holds two antagonistic positions, one of which is a position of trust, which is violated, generally by misapplication of funds, in the interest of the other position. A football coach, permitted to referee a game in which his own team was playing, would illustrate this antagonism of positions. Such situations cannot be completely avoided in a complicated business structure, but many concerns make a practice of assuming such antagonistic functions and regularly violating the trust thus delegated to them. When compelled by law to make a separation of their functions, they make a nominal separation and continue by subterfuge to maintain the two positions.

An accurate statistical comparison of the crimes of the two classes is not available. The most extensive evidence regarding the nature and prevalence of white-collar criminality is found in the reports of the larger investigations to which reference was made. Because of its scattered character, that evidence is assumed rather than summarized here. A few statements will be presented, as illustrations rather than as proof of the prevalence of this criminality.

The Federal Trade Commission in 1920 reported that commercial bribery was a prevalent and common practice in many industries. In certain chain stores, the net shortage in weights was sufficient to pay 3.4 percent on the investment in those commodities. Of the cans of ether sold to the Army in 1923–1925, 70 percent were rejected because of impurities. In Indiana, during the summer of 1934, 40 percent of the ice cream samples tested in a routine manner by the Division of Public Health were in violation of law. The Comptroller of the Currency in 1908 reported that violations of law were found in 75 percent of the banks examined in a three months' period. Lie detector tests of all employees in several Chicago banks, supported in almost all cases by confessions, showed that 20 percent of them had stolen bank property. A public accountant estimated, in the period prior to the Securities and Exchange Commission, that 80 percent of the financial statements of corporations were misleading. James M. Beck said, "Diogenes would have been hard put to it to find an honest man in the Wall Street which I knew as a corporation lawyer" (in 1916).

White-collar criminality in politics, which is generally recognized as fairly prevalent, has been used by some as a rough gauge by which to measure white-collar criminality in business. James A. Farley said, "The standards of conduct are as high among officeholders and politicians as they are in commercial life," and Cermak, while mayor of Chicago, said, "There is less graft in politics than in business." John Flynn wrote, "The average politician is the merest amateur in the gentle art of graft, compared with his brother in the field of business." And Walter Lippmann wrote, "Poor as they are, the standards of public life are so much more social than those of business that financiers who enter politics regard themselves as philanthropists."

These statements obviously do not give a precise measurement of the relative criminality of the white-collar class, but they are adequate evidence that crime is not so highly concentrated in the lower class as the usual statistics indicate. Also, these statements obviously do not mean that every business and professional man is a criminal, just as the usual theories do not mean that every man in the lower class is a criminal. On the other hand, the preceding statements refer in many cases to the leading corporations in America and are not restricted to the disreputable business and professional men who are called quacks, ambulance chasers, bucket-shop operators, dead-beats, and fly-by-night swindlers.[2]

The financial cost of white-collar crime is probably several times as great as the financial cost of all the crimes which are customarily regarded as the "crime problem." An officer of a chain grocery store in one year embezzled $600,000, which was six times as much as the annual losses from five hundred burglaries and robberies of the stores in that chain. Public enemies numbered one to six secured $130,000 by burglary and robbery in 1938, while the sum stolen by Krueger is estimated at $250,000,000, or nearly two thousand times as much. *The New York Times* in 1931 reported four cases of embezzlement in the United States with a loss of more than a million dollars each and a combined loss of nine million dollars. Although a million-dollar burglar or robber is practically unheard of, these million-dollar embezzlers are small-fry among white-collar criminals. The estimated loss to investors in one investment trust from 1929 to 1935 was $580,000,000, due primarily to the fact that 75 percent of the values in the portfolio were in securities of affiliated companies, although it advertised the importance of diversification in investments and its expert services in selecting safe securities. In Chicago, the claim was made six years ago that householders had lost $54,000,000 in two years during the administration of a city sealer who granted immunity from inspection to stores which provided Christmas baskets for his constituents.

The financial loss from white-collar crime, great as it is, is less important than the damage to social relations. White-collar crimes violate trust and therefore create distrust, which lowers

[2]Perhaps it should be repeated that "white-collar" (upper) and "lower" classes merely designate persons of high and low socioeconomic status. Income and amount of money involved in the crime are not the sole criteria. Many persons of "low" socioeconomic status are "white-collar" criminals in the sense that they are well-dressed, well-educated, and have high incomes, but "white-collar" as used in this paper means "respected," "socially accepted and approved," "looked up to." Some people in this class may not be well-dressed or well-educated, nor have high incomes, although the "upper" usually exceed the "lower" classes in these respects as well as in social status.

social morale and produces social disorganization on a large scale. Other crimes produce relatively little effect on social institutions or social organization.

White-collar crime is real crime. It is not ordinarily called crime, and calling it by this name does not make it worse, just as refraining from calling it crime does not make it better than it otherwise would be. It is called crime here in order to bring it within the scope of criminology, which is justified because it is in violation of the criminal law. The crucial question in this analysis is the criterion of violation of the criminal law. Conviction in the criminal court, which is sometimes suggested as the criterion, is not adequate, because a large proportion of those who commit crimes are not convicted in criminal courts. This criterion, therefore, needs to be supplemented. When it is supplemented, the criterion of the crimes of one class must be kept consistent in general terms with the criterion of the crimes of the other class. The definition should not be the spirit of the law for white-collar crimes and the letter of the law for other crimes, or in other respects be more liberal for one class than for the other. Since this discussion is concerned with the conventional theories of the criminologists, the criterion of white-collar crime must be justified in terms of the procedures of those criminologists in dealing with other crimes. The criterion of white-collar crimes, as here proposed, supplements convictions in the criminal courts in four respects, in each of which the extension is justified because the criminologists who present the conventional theories of criminal behavior make the same extension in principle.

First, other agencies than the criminal court must be included, for the criminal court is not the only agency which makes official decisions regarding violations of the criminal law. The juvenile court, dealing largely with offenses of the children of the poor, in many states is not under the criminal jurisdiction. The criminologists have made much use of case histories and statistics of juvenile delinquents in constructing their theories of criminal behavior. This justifies the inclusion of agencies other than the criminal court which deal with white-collar offenses. The most important of these agencies are the administrative boards, bureaus, or commissions, and much of their work, although certainly not all, consists of cases which are in violation of the criminal law. The Federal Trade Commission recently ordered several automobile companies to stop advertising their interest rate on installment purchases as 6 percent, since it was actually 11½ percent. Also it filed complaint against *Good Housekeeping*, one of the Hearst publications, charging that its seals led the public to believe that all products bearing these seals had been tested in their laboratories, which was contrary to fact. Each of these involves a charge of dishonesty, which might have been tried in a criminal court as fraud. A large proportion of the cases before these boards should be included in the data of the criminologists. Failure to do so is a principal reason for the bias in their samples and the errors in their generalizations.

Second, for both classes, behavior which would have a reasonable expectancy of conviction if tried in a criminal court or substitute agency should be defined as criminal. In this respect, convictability rather than actual conviction should be the criterion of criminality. The criminologists would not hesitate to accept as data a verified case history of a person who was a criminal but had never been convicted. Similarly, it is justifiable to include white-collar criminals who have not been convicted, provided reliable evidence is available. Evidence regarding such cases appears in many civil suits, such as stockholders' suits and patent-infringement suits. These cases might have been referred to the criminal court but they were referred to the civil court because the injured party was more interested in securing damages than in seeing punishment inflicted. This also happens in embezzlement cases, regarding which surety companies have much evidence. In a short consecutive series of embezzlements known to a surety company, 90 percent were not prosecuted because prosecution would interfere with restitution or salvage. The evidence in cases of embezzlement is generally conclusive, and would probably have been sufficient to justify conviction in all of the cases in this series.

Third, behavior should be defined as criminal if conviction is avoided merely because of pressure which is brought to bear on the court or substitute agency. Gangsters and racketeers have been relatively immune in many cities because of their pressure on prospective witnesses and public officials, and professional thieves, such as pickpockets and confidence men who do not use strong-arm methods, are even more frequently immune. The conventional criminologists do not hesitate to include the life histories of such criminals as data, because they understand the generic relation of the pressures to the failure to convict. Similarly, white-collar criminals are relatively immune because of the class bias of the courts and the power of their class to influence the implementation and administration of the law. This class bias affects not merely present-day courts but to a much greater degree affected the earlier courts which established the precedents and rules of procedure of the present-day courts. Consequently, it is justifiable to interpret the actual or potential failures of conviction in the light of known facts regarding the pressures brought to bear on the agencies which deal with offenders.

Fourth, persons who are accessory to a crime should be included among white-collar criminals as they are among other criminals. When the Federal Bureau of Investigation deals with a case of kidnapping, it is not content with catching the offenders who carried away the victim; they may catch and the court may convict twenty-five other persons who assisted by secreting the victim, negotiating the ransom, or putting the ransom money into circulation. On the other hand, the prosecution of white-collar criminals frequently stops with one offender. Political graft almost always involves collusion between politicians and businessmen but prosecutions are generally limited to the politicians. Judge Manton was found guilty of accepting $664,000 in bribes, but the six or eight important commercial concerns that paid the bribes have not been prosecuted. Pendergast, the late boss of Kansas City, was convicted for failure to report as a part of his income $315,000 received in bribes from insurance companies but the insurance companies which paid the bribes have not been prosecuted. In an investigation of an embezzlement by the president of a bank, at least a dozen other violations of law which were related to this embezzlement and involved most of the other officers of the bank and the officers of the clearing house, were discovered but none of the others was prosecuted.

This analysis of the criterion of white-collar criminality results in the conclusion that a description of white-collar criminality in general terms will be also a description of the criminality of the lower class. The respects in which the crimes of the two classes differ are the incidentals rather than the essentials of criminality. They differ principally in the implementation of the criminal laws which apply to them. The crimes of the lower class are handled by policemen, prosecutors, and judges, with penal sanctions in the form of fines, imprisonment, and death. The crimes of the upper class either result in no official action at all, or result in suits for damages in civil courts, or are handled by inspectors, and by administrative boards or commissions, with penal sanctions in the form of warnings, orders to cease and desist, occasionally the loss of a license, and only in extreme cases by fines or prison sentences. Thus, the white-collar criminals are segregated administratively from other criminals, and largely as a consequence of this are not regarded as real criminals by themselves, the general public, or the criminologists.

This difference in the implementation of the criminal law is due principally to the difference in the social position of the two types of offenders. Judge Woodward, when imposing sentence upon the officials of the H. O. Stone and Company, bankrupt real estate firm in Chicago, who had been convicted in 1933 of the use of the mails to defraud, said to them, "You are men of affairs, of experience, of refinement and culture, of excellent reputation and standing in the business and social world." That statement might be used as a general characterization of white-collar criminals for they are oriented basically to legitimate and respectable careers. Because of their social status they have a loud voice in determining what goes into the statutes and how the criminal law as it affects themselves is implemented and administered. This may be illustrated from the Pure Food and Drug Law. Between 1879 and 1906, 140 pure food and drug bills were presented in Congress and all failed because of the importance of the persons who would be affected. It took a highly dramatic performance by Dr. Wiley in 1906 to induce Congress to enact the law. That law, however, did not create a new crime, just as the federal Lindbergh kidnapping law did not create a new crime; it merely provided a more efficient implementation of a principle which had been formulated previously in state laws. When an amendment to this law, which would bring within the scope of its agents fraudulent statements made over the radio or in the press, was presented to Congress, the publishers and advertisers organized support and sent a lobby to Washington which successfully fought the amendment principally under the slogans of "freedom of the press" and "dangers of bureaucracy." This proposed amendment, also, would not have created a new crime, for the state laws already prohibited fraudulent statements over the radio or in the press; it would have implemented the law so it could have been enforced. Finally, the Administration has not been able to enforce the law as it has desired because of the pressures by the offenders against the law, sometimes brought to bear through the head of the Department of Agriculture, sometimes through congressmen who threaten cuts in the appropriation, and sometimes by others. The statement of Daniel Drew, a pious old fraud, describes the criminal law with some accuracy, "Law is like a cobweb; it's made for flies and the smaller kinds of insects, so to speak, but lets the big bumblebees break through. When technicalities of the law stood in my way, I have always been able to brush them aside easy as anything."

The preceding analysis should be regarded neither as an assertion that all efforts to influence legislation and its administration are reprehensible nor as a particularistic interpretation of the criminal law. It means only that the upper class has greater influence in moulding the criminal law and its administration to its own interests than does the lower class. The privileged position of white-collar criminals before the law results to a slight extent from bribery and political pressures, principally from the respect in which they are held and without special effort on their part. The most powerful group in medieval society secured relative immunity by "benefit of clergy," and now our most powerful groups secure relative immunity by "benefit of business or profession."

In contrast with the power of the white-collar criminals is the weakness of their victims. Consumers, investors, and stockholders are unorganized, lack technical knowledge, and cannot protect themselves. Daniel Drew, after taking a large sum of money by sharp practice from Vanderbilt in the Erie deal, concluded that it was a mistake to take money from a powerful man on the same level as himself and declared that in the future he would confine his efforts to outsiders, scattered all over the country, who wouldn't be able to organize and fight back. White-collar criminality flourishes at points where powerful business and professional men come in contact with persons who are weak. In this respect, it is similar to stealing candy from a baby. Many of the crimes of the lower class, on the other hand, are committed against persons of wealth and power in the form of burglary and robbery. Because of this difference in the comparative power of the victims, the white-collar criminals enjoy relative immunity.

Embezzlement is an interesting exception to white-collar criminality in this respect. Embezzlement is usually theft from an employer by an employee, and the employee is less capable of manipulating social and legal forces in his own interest than is the employer. As might have been expected, the laws regarding embezzlement were formulated long before laws for the protection of investors and consumers.

The theory that criminal behavior in general is due either to poverty or to the psychopathic and sociopathic conditions associated with poverty can now be shown to be invalid for three reasons. First, the generalization is based on a biased sample which omits almost entirely the behavior of white-collar criminals. The criminologists have restricted their data, for reasons of convenience and ignorance rather than of principle, largely to cases dealt with in criminal courts and juvenile courts, and these agencies are used principally for criminals from the lower economic strata. Consequently, their data are grossly biased from the point of view of the economic status of criminals and their generalization that criminality is closely associated with poverty is not justified.

Second, the generalization that criminality is closely associated with poverty obviously does not apply to white-collar criminals. With a small number of exceptions, they are not in poverty, were not reared in slums or badly deteriorated families, and are not feebleminded or psychopathic. They were seldom problem children in their earlier years and did not appear in juvenile courts or child guidance clinics. The proposition, derived from the data used by the conventional criminologists, that "the criminal of today was the problem child of yesterday" is seldom true of white-collar criminals. The idea that the causes of criminality are to be found almost exclusively in childhood similarly is fallacious. Even if poverty is extended to include the economic stresses which afflict business in a period of depression, it is not closely correlated with white-collar criminality. Probably at no time within fifty years have white-collar crimes in the field of investments and of corporate management been so extensive as during the boom period of the twenties.

Third, the conventional theories do not even explain lower class criminality. The sociopathic and psychopathic factors which have been emphasized doubtless have something to do with crime causation, but these factors have not been related to a general process which is found both in white-collar criminality and lower class criminality and therefore they do not explain the criminality of either class. They may explain the manner or method of crime—why lower class criminals commit burglary or robbery rather than false pretenses.

In view of these defects in the conventional theories, an hypothesis that will explain both white-collar criminality and lower class criminality is needed. For reasons of economy, simplicity, and logic, the hypothesis should apply to both classes, for this will make possible the analysis of causal factors freed from the encumbrances of the administrative devices which have led criminologists astray. Shaw and McKay and others, working exclusively in the field of lower class crime, have found the conventional theories inadequate to account for variations within the data of lower class crime and from that point of view have been working toward an explanation of crime in terms of a more general social process. Such efforts will be greatly aided by the procedure which has been described.

The hypothesis which is here suggested as a substitute for the conventional theories is that white-collar criminality, just as other systematic criminality, is learned; that it is learned in direct or indirect association with those who already practice the behavior; and that those who learn this criminal behavior are segregated from frequent and intimate contacts with law-abiding behavior. Whether a person becomes a criminal or not is determined largely by the comparative frequency and intimacy of his contacts with the two types of behavior. This may be called the process of differential association. It is a genetic explanation both of white-collar criminality and lower class criminality. Those who become white-collar criminals generally start their careers in good neighborhoods and good homes, graduate from colleges with some idealism, and with little selection on their part, get into particular business situations in which criminality is practically a folkway and are inducted into that system of behavior just as into any other folkway. The lower class criminals generally start their careers in deteriorated neighborhoods and families, find delinquents at hand from whom they acquire the attitudes toward, and techniques of, crime through association with delinquents and in partial segregation from law-abiding people. The essentials of the process are the same for the two classes of criminals. This is not entirely a process of assimilation, for inventions are frequently made, perhaps more frequently in white-collar crime than in lower class crime. The inventive geniuses for the lower class criminals are generally professional criminals, while the inventive geniuses for many kinds of white-collar crime are generally lawyers.

A second general process is social disorganization in the community. Differential association culminates in crime because the community is not organized solidly against that behavior. The law is pressing in one direction, and other forces are pressing in the opposite direction. In business, the "rules of the game" conflict with the legal rules. A businessman who wants to obey the law is driven by his competitors to adopt their methods. This is well illustrated by the persistence of commercial bribery in spite of the strenuous efforts of business organizations to eliminate it. Groups and individuals are individuated; they are more concerned with their specialized group or individual interests than with the larger welfare. Consequently, it is not possible for the community to present a solid front in opposition to crime. The Better Business Bureaus and Crime Commissions, composed of business and professional men, attack burglary, robbery, and cheap swindles, but overlook the crimes of their own members. The forces which impinge on the lower class are similarly in conflict. Social disorganization affects the two classes in similar ways.

I have presented a brief and general description of white-collar criminality on a framework of argument regarding theories of criminal behavior. That argument, stripped of the description, may be stated in the following propositions:

1. White-collar criminality is real criminality, being in all cases in violation of the criminal law.
2. White-collar criminality differs from lower class criminality principally in an implementation of the criminal law which segregates white-collar criminals administratively from other criminals.
3. The theories of the criminologists that crime is due to poverty or to psychopathic and sociopathic conditions statistically associated with poverty are invalid because, first, they are derived from samples which are grossly biased with respect to socioeconomic status; second, they do not apply to the white-collar criminals; and third, they do not even explain the criminality of the lower class, since the factors are not related to a general process characteristic of all criminality.
4. A theory of criminal behavior which will explain both white-collar criminality and lower class criminality is needed.
5. An hypothesis of this nature is suggested in terms of differential association and social disorganization.

24.

EDWIN H. SUTHERLAND

IS "WHITE-COLLAR CRIME" CRIME?

The argument has been made that business and professional men commit crimes which should be brought within the scope of the theories of criminal behavior.[1] In order to secure evidence as to the prevalence of such white-collar crimes, an analysis was made of the decisions by courts and commissions against the seventy largest industrial and mercantile corporations in the United States under four types of laws: namely, anti-trust, false advertising, National Labor Relations, and infringement of patents, copyrights, and trademarks. This resulted in the finding that 547

SOURCE: *American Sociological Review,* Vol. 10 (April, 1945), pp. 132–39, American Sociological Association. Reprinted by permission of the journal.

[1]Edwin H. Sutherland, "White-Collar Criminality," *American Sociological Review,* Vol. 5 (February, 1940), pp. 1–12; and "Crime and Business," *The Annals of the American Academy of Political and Social Science,* Vol. 217 (September, 1941), pp. 112–18.

such adverse decisions had been made, with an average of 7.8 decisions per corporation and with each corporation's having at least one.[2] Although all of these were decisions that the behavior was unlawful, only forty-nine, or 9 per cent, of the total were made by criminal courts and were *ipso facto* decisions that the behavior was criminal. Since not all unlawful behavior is criminal behavior, these decisions can be used as a measure of criminal behavior only if the other 498 decisions can be shown to be decisions that the behavior of the corporations was criminal.

This is a problem in the legal definition of crime and involves two types of questions: May the word "crime" be applied to the behavior regarding which these decisions were made? If so, why is it not generally applied and why have not the criminologists regarded white-collar crime as cognate with other crime? The first question involves semantics, the second interpretation or explanation.

A combination of two abstract criteria is generally regarded by legal scholars as necessary to define crime; namely, legal description of an act as socially injurious and legal provision of a penalty for the act.[3]

When the criterion of legally defined social injury is applied to these 547 decisions, the conclusion is reached that all of the classes of behaviors regarding which the decisions were made are legally defined as socially injurious. This can be readily determined by the words in the statutes—"crime" or "misdemeanor" in some, and "unfair," "discrimination," or "infringement" in all the others. The persons injured may be divided into two groups: first, a relatively small number of persons engaged in the same occupation as the offenders or in related occupations; and, second, the general public either as consumers or as constituents of the general social institutions which are affected by the violations of the laws. The antitrust laws are designed to protect competitors; they are also designed to protect the institution of free competition as the regulator of the economic system and thereby to protect consumers against arbitrary prices, as well as being designed to protect the institution of democracy against the dangers of great concentration of wealth in the hands of monopolies. Laws against false advertising are designed to protect competitors against unfair competition and also to protect consumers against fraud. The National Labor Relations Law is designed to protect employees against coercion by employers and also to protect the general public against interferences with commerce due to strikes and lockouts. The laws against infringements are designed to protect the owners of patents, copyrights, and trademarks against deprivation of their property and against unfair competition, and also to protect the institution of patents and copyrights which was established in order to "promote the progress of science and the useful arts." Violations of these laws are legally defined as injuries to the parties specified.

Each of these laws has a logical basis in the common law and is an adaptation of the common law to modern social organization. False advertising is related to common-law fraud, and infringement to larceny. The National Labor Relations Law, as an attempt to prevent coercion, is related to the common-law prohibition of restrictions on freedom in the form of assault, false imprisonment, and extortion. For at least two centuries prior to the enactment of the modern antitrust laws, the common law was moving against restraint of trade, monopoly, and unfair competition.

Each of the four laws provides a penal sanction and thus meets the second criterion in the definition of crime, and each of the adverse decisions under these four laws (except certain decisions under the infringement laws to be discussed later) is a decision that a crime was committed. This conclusion will be made more specific by analysis of the penal sanctions provided in the four laws.

The Sherman antitrust law states explicitly that a violation of the law is a misdemeanor. Three methods of enforcement of this law are provided, each of them involving procedures regarding misdemeanors. First, it may be enforced by the usual criminal prosecution, result-

[2] Cf., Edwin H. Sutherland, *White-Collar Crime* (New York: Dryden Press, 1949), pp. 15–182.

[3] The most thorough analysis of crime from the point of view of legal definition is Jerome Hall, *Principles of Criminal Law* (Indianapolis: Bobbs-Merrill, 1947).

ing in the imposition of fine or imprisonment. Second, the Attorney General of the United States and the several district attorneys are given the "duty" of "repressing and preventing" violations of the law by petitions for injunctions, and violations of the injunctions are punishable as contempt of court. This method of enforcing a criminal law was an invention and, as will be described later, is the key to the interpretation of the differential implementation of the criminal law as applied to white-collar criminals. Third, parties who are injured by violations of the law are authorized to sue for damages, with a mandatory provision that the damages awarded be three times the damages suffered. These damages in excess of reparation are penalties for violation of the law. They are payable to the injured party in order to induce him to take the initiative in the enforcement of the criminal law and in this respect are similar to the earlier methods of private prosecutions under the criminal law. All three of these methods of enforcement are based on decisions that a criminal law was violated and, therefore, that a crime was committed; the decisions of a civil court or a court of equity as to these violations are as good evidence of criminal behavior as is the decision of a criminal court.

The Sherman Antitrust Act has been amended by the Federal Trade Commission Law, the Clayton Law, and several other laws. Some of these amendments define violations as crimes and provide the conventional penalties, but most of the amendments do not make the criminality explicit. A large proportion of the cases which are dealt with under these amendments could be dealt with instead under the original Sherman Act, which is explicitly a criminal law. In practice, the amendments are under the jurisdiction of the Federal Trade Commission, which has authority to make official decisions as to violations. The commission has two principal sanctions under its control: the stipulation and the cease and desist order. The commission may, after the violation of the law has been proved, accept a stipulation from the corporation that it will not violate the law in the future. Such stipulations are customarily restricted to the minor or technical violations. If a stipulation is violated or if no stipulation is accepted, the commission may issue a cease and desist order; this is equivalent to a court's injunction except that violation is not punishable as contempt. If the commission's desist order is violated, the commission may apply to the court for an injunction, the violation of which is punishable as contempt. By an amendment to the Federal Trade Commission Law in the Wheeler-Lea Act of 1938, an order of the commission becomes "final" if not officially questioned within a specified time and thereafter its violation is punishable by a civil fine. Thus, although certain interim procedures may be used in the enforcement of the amendments to the antitrust law, fines or imprisonment for contempt are available if the interim procedures fail. In this respect, the interim procedures are similar to probation in ordinary criminal cases. An unlawful act is not defined as criminal by the fact that it is punished, but by the fact that it is punishable. Larceny is as truly a crime when the thief is placed on probation as when he is committed to prison. The argument may be made that punishment for contempt of court is not punishment for violation of the original law and that, therefore, the original law does not contain a penal sanction. This reasoning is specious, since the original law provides the injunction with its penalty as a part of the procedure for enforcement. Consequently, all of the decisions made under the amendments to the antitrust law are decisions that the corporations committed crimes.[4]

The laws regarding false advertising, as included in the decisions under consideration, are of two types. First, false advertising in the form of false labels is defined in the Pure Food and Drug Act as a misdemeanor and is punishable by a fine. Second, false advertising generally is defined in the Federal Trade Commission Act as unfair competition. Cases of the second type are under the jurisdiction of the Federal Trade Commission, which uses the same procedures as in antitrust cases. Penal sanctions are available in antitrust cases, as previously described, and

[4]Some of the antitrust decisions were made against meat packers under the Packers and Stockyards Act. The penal sanctions in this act are essentially the same as in the Federal Trade Commission Act.

are similarly available in these cases of false advertising. Thus, all of the decisions in false advertising cases are decisions that the corporations committed crimes.

The National Labor Relations Law of 1935 defines a violation as "unfair labor practice." The National Labor Relations Board is authorized to make official decisions as to violations of the law and, in case of violation, to issue desist orders and also to make certain remedial orders, such as reimbursement of employees who had been dismissed or demoted because of activities in collective bargaining. If an order is violated, the board may apply to the court for enforcement and a violation of the order of the court is punishable as contempt. Thus, all of the decisions under this law, which is enforceable by penal sanctions, are decisions that crimes were committed.

The methods for the repression of infringements vary. Infringements of a copyright or a patented design are defined as misdemeanors, punishable by fines. No case of this type has been discovered against the seventy corporations. Other infringements are not explicitly defined in the statutes on patents, copyrights, and trademarks as crimes, and agents of the state are not authorized by these statutes to initiate actions against violators of the law. Nevertheless, infringements may be punished in either of two ways: First, agents of the state may initiate action against infringers under the Federal Trade Commission Law as unfair competition and they do so, especially against infringers of copyrights and trademarks; these infringements are then punishable in the same sense as violations of the amendments to the antitrust laws. Second, the patent, copyright, and trademark statutes provide that the damages awarded to injured owners of those rights may be greater than (in one statute as much as threefold) the damages actually suffered. These additional damages are not mandatory, as in the Sherman Antitrust Law, but on the other hand they are not explicitly limited to wanton and malicious infringements. Three decisions against the seventy corporations under the patent law and one under the copyright law included awards of such additional damages and on that account were classified in the tabulation of decisions as evidence of criminal behavior of the corporations. The other decisions, seventy-four in number, in regard to infringements were classified as not conclusive evidence of criminal behavior and were discarded. However, in twenty of these seventy-four cases the decisions of the court contain evidence which would be sufficient to make a *prima facie* case in a criminal prosecution; evidence outside these decisions, which may be found in the general descriptions of practices regarding patents, copyrights, and trademarks, justifies a belief that a very large proportion of the seventy-four cases did, in fact, involve willful infringement of property rights and might well have resulted in the imposition of a penalty if the injured party and the court had approached the behavior from the point of view of crime.

In the preceding discussion, the penalties that are definitive of crime have been limited to fine, imprisonment, and punitive damages. In addition, the stipulation, the desist order, and the injunction, without references to punishment for contempt, have the attributes of punishment. This is evident both in that they result in some suffering on the part of the corporation against which they are issued and also in that they are designed by legislators and administrators to produce suffering. The suffering is in the form of public shame, as illustrated in more extreme form in the colonial penalty of sewing the letter *T* on the clothing of the thief. The design is shown in the sequence of sanctions used by the Federal Trade Commission. The stipulation involves the least publicity and the least discomfort, and it is for minor and technical violations. The desist order is used if the stipulation is violated and also if the violation of the law is appraised by the commission as willful and major. This involves more public shame; this shame is somewhat mitigated by the statements made by corporations, in exculpation, that such orders are merely the acts of bureaucrats. Still more shameful to the corporation is an injunction issued by a court. The shame resulting from this order is sometimes mitigated and the corporation's face saved by taking a consent decree.[5] The corpora-

[5]The consent decree may be taken for other reasons, especially because it cannot be used as evidence in other suits.

tion may insist that the consent decree is not an admission that it violated the law. For instance, the meat packers took a consent decree in an antitrust case in 1921, with the explanation that they had not knowingly violated any law and were consenting to the decree without attempting to defend themselves because they wished to cooperate with the government in every possible way. This patriotic motivation appeared questionable, however, after the packers fought during almost all of the next ten years for a modification of the decree. Although the sequence of stipulation, desist order, and injunction indicates that the variations in public shame are designed, these orders have other functions as well, especially a remedial function and the clarification of the law in a particular complex situation.

The conclusion in this semantic portion of the discussion is that 473 of the 547 decisions are decisions that crimes were committed. This conclusion may be questioned on the ground that the rules of proof and evidence used in reaching these decisions are not the same as those used in decisions regarding other crimes, especially that some of the agencies which rendered the decisions did not require proof of criminal intent and did not presume the accused to be innocent. These rules of criminal intent and presumption of innocence, however, are not required in all prosecutions under the regular penal code and the number of exceptions is increasing. In many states a person may be committed to prison without protection of one or both of these rules on charges of statutory rape, bigamy, adultery, passing bad checks, selling mortgaged property, defrauding a hotel keeper, and other offenses.[6] Consequently, the criteria that have been used in defining white-collar crimes are not categorically different from the criteria used in defining other crimes, for these rules are abrogated both in regard to white-collar crimes and other crimes, including some felonies. The proportion of decisions rendered against corporations without the protection of these rules is probably greater than the proportion rendered against other criminals, but a difference in proportions does not make the violations of law by corporations categorically different from the violations of law by other criminals. Moreover, the difference in proportion, as the procedures actually operate, is not great. On the one side, many of the defendants in usual criminal cases, being in relative poverty, do not get good defense and consequently secure little benefit from these rules; on the other hand, the commissions come close to observing these rules of proof and evidence although they are not required to do so. This is illustrated by the procedure of the Federal Trade Commission in regard to advertisements. Each year it examines several hundred thousand advertisements and appraises about 50,000 of them as probably false. From the 50,000 it selects about 1,500 as patently false. For instance, an advertisement of gum-wood furniture as "mahogany" would seldom be an accidental error and would generally result from a state of mind which deviated from honesty by more than the natural tendency of human beings to feel proud of their handiwork.

The preceding discussion has shown that these seventy corporations committed crimes according to 473 adverse decisions and has also shown that the criminality of their behavior was not made obvious by the conventional procedures of the criminal law, but was blurred and concealed by special procedures. This differential implementation of the law as applied to the crimes of corporations eliminates, or at least minimizes, the stigma of crime. This differential implementation of the law began with the Sherman Antitrust Law of 1890. As previously described, this law is explicitly a criminal law and a violation of the law is a misdemeanor no matter what procedure is used. The customary policy would have been to rely entirely on criminal prosecution as the method of enforcement. But a clever invention was made in the provision of an injunction to enforce a criminal law; this was not only an invention, but also a direct reversal of previous case law. Also, private parties were encouraged by treble damages to enforce a criminal law by suits in civil courts. In either case, the defendant did not appear in the criminal court, and the fact that he had committed a

[6]Livingston Hall, "Statutory Law of Crimes, 1887–1936," *Harvard Law Review*, Vol. 50 (February, 1937), pp. 616–53.

crime did not appear in the face of the proceedings.

The Sherman Antitrust Act, in this respect, became the model in practically all the subsequent procedures authorized to deal with the crimes of corporations. When the Federal Trade Commission Bill and the Clayton Bill were introduced in Congress, they contained the conventional criminal procedures; these were eliminated in committee discussions, and other procedures which did not carry the external symbols of criminal process were substituted. The violations of these laws are crimes, as has been shown above, but they are treated as though they were not crimes, with the effect and probably the intention of eliminating the stigma of crime.

This policy of eliminating the stigma of crime is illustrated in the following statement by Wendell Berge, at the time assistant to the head of the antitrust division of the Department of Justice, in a plea for abandonment of the criminal prosecution under the Sherman Antitrust Act and the authorization of civil procedures with civil fines as a substitute.

> While civil penalties may be as severe in their financial effects as criminal penalties, yet they do not involve the stigma that attends indictment and conviction. Most of the defendants in antitrust cases are not criminals in the usual sense. There is no inherent reason why antitrust enforcement requires branding them as such.[7]

If a civil fine were substituted for a criminal fine, a violation of the antitrust law would be as truly a crime as it is now. The thing which would be eliminated would be the stigma of crime. Consequently, the stigma of crime has become a penalty in itself, which may be imposed in connection with other penalties or withheld, just as it is possible to combine imprisonment with a fine or have a fine without imprisonment. A civil fine is a financial penalty without the additional penalty of stigma, while a criminal fine is a financial penalty with the additional penalty of stigma.

When the stigma of crime is imposed as a penalty, it places the defendant in the category of a criminal and he becomes one according to the popular stereotype of "the criminal." In primitive society "the criminal" was substantially the same as "the stranger,"[8] while in modern society "the criminal" is a person of less-esteemed cultural attainments. Seventy-five per cent of the persons committed to state prisons are probably not, aside from their unesteemed cultural attainments, "criminals in the usual sense of the word." It may be excellent policy to eliminate the stigma of crime in a large proportion of cases, but the question at hand is why the law has a different implementation for white-collar criminals than for others.

Three factors assist in explaining this differential implementation of the law: the status of the businessman, the trend away from punishment, and the relatively unorganized resentment of the public against white-collar criminals. Each of these will be described.

First, the methods used in the enforcement of any law are an adaption to the characteristics of the prospective violators of the law, as appraised by the legislators and the judicial and administrative personnel. The appraisals regarding businessmen, who are the prospective violators of the four laws under consideration, include a combination of fear and admiration. Those who are responsible for the system of criminal justice are afraid to antagonize businessmen; among other consequences, such antagonism may result in a reduction in contributions to the campaign funds needed to win the next election. Probably much more important is the cultural homogeneity of legislators, judges, and administrators with businessmen. Legislators admire and respect businessmen and cannot conceive of them as criminals; that is, businessmen do not conform to the popular stereotype of "the criminal." The legislators are confident that these businessmen will conform as a result of very mild pressures.

This interpretation meets with considerable opposition from persons who insist that this is an

[7]Wendell Berge, "Remedies Available to the Government under the Sherman Act," *Law and Contemporary Problems*, Vol. 7 (January, 1940), p. 111.

[8]On the role of the stranger in punitive justice, see Ellsworth Faris, "The Origin of Punishment," *International Journal of Ethics*, Vol. 25 (October, 1914), pp. 54–67; George H. Mead, "The Psychology of Punitive Justice," *American Journal of Sociology*, Vol. 23 (March, 1918), pp. 577–602.

egalitarian society in which all men are equal in the eyes of the law. It is not possible to give a complete demonstration of the validity of this interpretation but four types of evidence are presented in the following paragraphs as partial demonstration.

The Department of Justice is authorized to use both criminal prosecutions and petitions in equity to enforce the Sherman Antitrust Act. The department has selected the method of criminal prosecution in a larger proportion of cases against trade unions than of cases against corporations, although the law was enacted primarily because of fear of the corporations. From 1890 to 1929, the Department of Justice initiated 438 actions under this law with decisions favorable to the United States. Of the actions against business firms and associations of business firms, 27 per cent were criminal prosecutions; while of the actions against trade unions, 71 per cent were criminal prosecutions. This shows that the Department of Justice has been comparatively reluctant to use a method against business firms which carries with it the stigma of crime.

The method of criminal prosecution in enforcement of the Sherman Antitrust Act has varied from one presidential administration to another. It has seldom been used in the administrations of the presidents who are popularly appraised as friendly toward business; for example, McKinley, Harding, Coolidge, and Hoover.

Businessmen suffered their greatest loss of prestige in the Depression which began in 1929. It was precisely in this period of low status of businessmen that the most strenuous efforts were made to enforce the old laws and enact new laws for the regulation of businessmen. The appropriations for this purpose were multiplied several times and persons were selected for their vigor in administration of the laws. Of the 547 decisions against the seventy corporations during their life careers (which have averaged about forty years) 63 per cent were rendered in the period of 1935 to 1943, that is, during the period of the low status of businessmen.

The Federal Trade Commission Law states that a violation of the antitrust laws by a corporation shall be deemed to be, also, a violation by the officers and directors of the corporation. However, businessmen are practically never convicted as persons, and several cases have been reported (such as the "6 per cent case" against the automobile manufacturers) in which the corporation was convicted and the persons who direct the corporation were all acquitted.[9]

A second factor in the explanation of the differential implementation of the law as applied to white-collar criminals is the trend away from reliance on penal methods. This trend advanced more rapidly in the area of white-collar crime than of other crime because—due to the recency of the statutes—it is least bound by precedents and also because of the status of businessmen. This trend is seen in the almost complete abandonment of the most extreme penalties of death and physical torture; in the supplanting of conventional penal methods by nonpenal methods, such as probation and the case work methods which accompany probation. These decreases in penal methods are explained by a series of social changes: the increased power of the lower socioeconomic class upon which most of the penalties were previously inflicted; the inclusion within the scope of the penal laws of a large part of the upper socioeconomic class, as illustrated by traffic regulations; the increased social interaction among the classes, which has resulted in increased understanding and sympathy; the failure of penal methods to make substantial reductions in crime rates; and the weakening hold on the legal profession and others of the individualistic and hedonistic psychology, which had placed great emphasis on pain in the control of behavior. To some extent overlapping those just mentioned is the fact that punishment, which was previously the chief reliance for control in the home, the school, and the church, has tended to disappear from those institutions, leaving the state without cultural support for its own penal methods.[10]

[9]The question may be asked, "If businessmen are so influential, why did they not retain the protection of the rules of the criminal procedure?" The answer is that they lost this protection, despite their status, on the principle, "You can't eat your cake and have it, too."

[10]This trend away from penal methods suggests that the penal sanction may not be a completely adequate criterion in the definition of crime.

White-collar crime is similar to juvenile delinquency in respect to the differential implementation of the law. In both cases, the procedures of the criminal law are modified so that the stigma of crime will not attach to the offenders. The stigma of crime has been less completely eliminated from juvenile delinquents than from white-collar criminals because the procedures for the former are a less complete departure from conventional criminal procedures, since most juvenile delinquents come from a class with low social status, and because the juveniles have not organized to protect their good names. Because the juveniles have not been successfully freed from the stigma of crime, they have been generally held to be within the scope of the theories of criminology and, in fact, provide a large part of the data for criminology; because the external symbols have been more successfully eliminated from white-collar crimes, white-collar crimes have generally not been included within these theories.

A third factor in the differential implementation of the law is the difference in the relation between the law and the mores in the area of white-collar crime. The laws under consideration are recent and do not have a firm foundation in public ethics or business ethics; in fact, certain rules of business ethics, such as the contempt for the "price chiseler," are generally in conflict with the law. These crimes are not obvious, as is assault and battery, and can be appreciated readily only by persons who are expert in the occupations in which they occur. A corporation often violates a law for a decade or longer before the administrative agency becomes aware of the violation; in the meantime the violation may have become accepted practice in the industry. The effects of a white-collar crime upon the public are diffused over a long period of time and perhaps over millions of people, with no person's suffering much at a particular time. The public agencies of communication do not express and organize the moral sentiments of the community as to white-collar crimes in part because the crimes are complicated and not easily presented as news, but probably in greater part because these agencies of communication are owned or controlled by the businessmen who violate the laws and because these agencies are themselves frequently charged with violations of the same laws. Public opinion in regard to picking pockets would not be well organized if most of the information regarding this crime came to the public directly from the pick-pockets themselves.

This third factor, if properly limited, is a valid part of the explanation of the differential implementation of the law. It tends to be exaggerated and become the complete explanation in the form of a denial that white-collar crimes involve any moral culpability whatever. On that account it is desirable to state a few reasons why this factor is not the complete explanation.

The assertion is sometimes made that white-collar crimes are merely technical violations and involve no moral culpability (i.e., violation of the mores) whatever. In fact, these white-collar crimes, like other crimes, are distributed along a continuum in which the *mala in se* are at one extreme and the *mala prohibita* at the other.[11] None of the white-collar crimes is purely arbitrary, as is the regulation that one must drive on the right side of the street, which might equally well be that one must drive on the left side. The Sherman Antitrust Law, for instance, is regarded by many persons as an unwise law and it may well be that some other policy would be preferable. It is questioned principally by persons who believe in a more collectivistic economic system; namely, the communists and the leaders of big business, while its support comes largely from an emotional ideology in favor of free enterprise which is held by farmers, wage-earners, small businessmen, and professional men. Therefore, as appraised by the majority of the population it is necessary for the preservation of American institutions and its violation is a violation of strongly entrenched moral sentiments.

The sentimental reaction toward a particular white-collar crime is certainly different from that toward some other crimes. This difference is often exaggerated, especially as the reaction occurs in urban society. The characteristic reaction of the average citizen in the modern city

[11]An excellent discussion of this continuum is presented by Jerome Hall, "Prolegomena to a Science of Criminal Law," *University of Pennsylvania Law Review*, Vol. 89 (March, 1941), pp. 563–69.

toward burglary is apathy unless he or his immediate friends are victims or unless the case is very spectacular. The average citizen, reading in his morning paper that the home of an unknown person has been burglarized by another unknown person, has no appreciable increase in blood pressure. Fear and resentment develop in modern society primarily as the result of the accumulation of crimes as depicted in crime rates or in general descriptions, and this develops both as to white-collar crimes and other crimes.

Finally, although many laws have been enacted for the regulation of occupations other than business, such as agriculture or plumbing, the procedures used in the enforcement of those other laws are more nearly the same as the conventional criminal procedures, and law-violators in these other occupations are not so completely protected against the stigma of crime as are businessmen. The relation between the law and the mores tends to be circular. The mores are crystallized in the law and each act of enforcement of the laws tends to re-enforce the mores. The laws regarding white-collar crime, which conceal the criminality of the behavior, have been less effective than other laws in re-enforcement of the mores.

25.

Robert G. Caldwell

A REEXAMINATION OF THE CONCEPT OF WHITE-COLLAR CRIME

The concept of white-collar crime, which was originated by Professor Edwin H. Sutherland before World War II, is now widely used in sociological literature, and by many students it is considered to be a valuable contribution to the theory of criminal behavior. However, some sociologists and many members of the legal profession have been critical of its implications and have urged that it be more strictly defined or entirely discarded. It is the purpose of this article to reexamine the concept of white-collar crime, to consider its legal and sociological implications, and to analyze the controversy arising from its usage.

WHITE-COLLAR CRIME DEFINED

According to Sutherland's original definition, white-collar crime is "a violation of the criminal law by a person of the upper socioeconomic class in the course of his occupational activities."[1] To this he added the explanation that "the upper socioeconomic class is defined not only by its wealth but also by its respectability and prestige in the general society." By this definition, therefore, a fraud by a wealthy confidence man of the underworld or a murder by a businessman in a love triangle would not be a white-collar crime, but a fraud by a realtor in the sale of a house or a murder by a manufacturer in strike-breaking activities would be.

Most white-collar crimes involve a breach of trust which is usually accompanied and consummated by misrepresentation. This misrepresentation occurs, for example, in the financial statements of corporations, in advertising and other sales methods, in manipulations on the stock exchange, in short weights and measures, in embezzlement and misappropriation of funds, in

Source: *Federal Probation,* Vol. XXII, No. 1 (March, 1958), pp. 30–36. Reprinted by permission of the journal.

[1] Edwin H. Sutherland, "Crime and Business," *The Annals of the American Academy of Political and Social Science,* Vol. 217, September, 1941.

the bribery of public officials, in the violation of price regulations, in tax frauds, and in the misapplication of funds in receiverships and bankruptcies.

Sutherland, Clinard, Hartung, and other sociologists assert that white-collar crimes are very serious, persistent, and prevalent in American society. In order to support their views, they point to the conditions revealed by numerous governmental investigations and to their own independent research into various aspects of our economic system.[2] They insist not only that the financial losses resulting from white-collar crimes reach staggering proportions, but also that these losses are the least important of the consequences of such crimes. Ordinary crimes cause some inconvenience to the victims and, occasionally, if they involve serious bodily attacks, or are repeated in quick succession, they cause a general community disturbance. White-collar crimes, on the other hand, according to Sutherland and other sociologists, spread feelings of distrust, lower public morale, and produce social disorganization.[3]

The white-collar criminologists further contend that although white-collar crimes are very prevalent and very costly, few of the perpetrators are prosecuted or convicted in the criminal courts. This, they claim, is true because (1) the criminal courts are very lenient toward persons accused of white-collar crimes, (2) no effective method of dealing with offending corporations under the criminal law has as yet been devised, (3) efforts to make the criminal law more effective in cases involving corporations have been blocked by business interests, and (4) action in the civil courts and regulations by boards and commissions are widely relied upon to protect society against white-collar crimes.[4]

On the basis of this analysis, Sutherland and those who are in agreement with him conclude that those who commit white-collar crimes are relatively immune because of the class bias of the courts and the power of the upper classes to influence the implementation and administration of the law, and that therefore the difference in criminality between the lower and upper classes is made to appear greater in the record than it really is. This, in turn, in their opinion, has contributed to a distortion of the criminological theories of causation, since criminologists to a great extent have restricted their data to cases dealt with in criminal and juvenile courts, agencies which are used principally for offenders from the lower economic strata. In other words, they believe that the theory of causation which attributes criminal behavior in general either to poverty or to the psychopathic and sociopathic conditions associated with poverty is "based on a biased sample which omits almost entirely the behavior of white-collar criminals."[5]

The foregoing discussion indicates that there are two major issues involved in the controversy over the concept of white-collar crime, namely, (1) the moral issue and (2) the scientific issue. Each of these issues must be clearly identified and separately treated because although they are related, each requires a different kind of answer.

THE MORAL ISSUE

The moral issue has arisen from the contention that our criminal laws and their administration are biased and unfair, and that they tend to favor the rich and the influential and to discriminate against the poor and the friendless. Those that assume this point of view argue that many acts are the same, or nearly the same, as other acts that are now called criminal and should therefore be similarly labeled and condemned, even though the legislatures and the courts fail to do this. This is justified by some writers on the grounds that an act should be called criminal regardless of whether the pro-

[2]Edwin H. Sutherland, *White-Collar Crime* (New York: The Dryden Press, Inc., 1949), pp. 17–55; Marshall B. Clinard, *The Black Market* (New York: Rinehart and Co., Inc., 1952), pp. 28–50, 226–62; Frank E. Hartung, "White-Collar Offenses in the Wholesale Meat Industry in Detroit," *American Journal of Sociology*, July, 1950, pp. 25–34.

[3]Sutherland, "Crime and Business," *op. cit.*, p. 113. See also Sutherland, "White-Collar Criminality," *American Sociological Review*, February, 1940, p. 5.

[4]See, for example, Sutherland, "Crime and Business," *op. cit.*, pp. 114, 115.

[5]Sutherland, "White-Collar Criminality," *op. cit.*, p. 9.

visions concerning it are in the criminal law, the civil law, or governmental agency regulations, as long as it can meet these two requirements: (1) Is it proscribed or prescribed by a duly constituted legislative body? and (2) Has the legislative body declared it to be punishable and specified the sanctions to be imposed?[6]

Furthermore, it is urged by those who favor the concept of white-collar crime that we should stigmatize as white-collar criminals both those who are convicted in the criminal court and those who might have been so convicted but, instead, through pressure or influence, were able to avoid conviction or for various reasons were taken into a civil court or before an administrative board, bureau, or commission.[7] To a large extent, this point of view on the moral issue is a result of the strong influence exerted in American criminology by the Positive School, which focuses attention upon the criminal while ignoring the legal definition of crime.[8]

The foregoing arguments are seductive in their simplicity, but their limitations become apparent when a careful examination is made of the terms "crime" and "criminal." In our society the criminal law is a body of rules regarding human conduct which are prescribed, interpreted, and administered by our elected and appointed representatives and enforced by penalties imposed by governmental authority. A crime may be generally defined as the commission or omission of an act which the criminal law forbids or commands under pain of a punishment to be imposed by the state by a proceeding in its own name.[9]

It is obvious that not every act or failure to act could, or should, be regulated by the criminal law. Crimes are only those acts or failures to act that are considered to be so detrimental to the well-being of society, as judged by its prevailing standards, that action regarding them cannot be entrusted to private initiative, civil courts, or government agencies and bureaus but must be taken by organized society in accordance with especially devised procedures. In fact, even if the victim of a crime takes no action, opposes it, forgives the criminal, or tries to conceal the crime, the state can and may press the charges.

HOW DO WE KNOW A CRIME HAS BEEN COMMITTED?

On the basis of what has been said thus far it might appear that anyone who commits a crime is a criminal, but this definition immediately suggests an important question. How do we know that a person has committed a crime? Thus, in any particular case, it becomes clear that the definition of a criminal as one who violates the criminal law is not adequate. We must supplement it by establishing definite, exact, stable criteria to determine whether the accused actually committed a crime.

But why is it so important to have definite, exact, stable criteria to determine the guilt of the accused? The answer to this question can be found in the fact that a person's rights and reputation are involved. To apply the term "criminal" to a person is not only to lower his social status by publicly stigmatizing him, but also to declare that his guilt has been proved, that certain of his rights have been forfeited, and that he should be punished. The law, which defines the term "crime," is deeply aware of the serious implications of the term "criminal." Down through the years, it has carefully, and at times painfully, built up a definite procedure to determine the guilt of the accused and at the same time to protect his rights. By clearly defining terms, by precisely formulating methods, and by judiciously introducing changes, the law has promoted stability, dependability, and security of justice in its criminal procedure.[10]

In this procedure one of the important rules of evidence is that which requires proof of the

---

[6]Hartung, *op. cit.*, p. 25.

[7]Sutherland, "White-Collar Criminality," *op. cit.*, pp. 5–9.

[8]Jerome Hall, *General Principles of Criminal Law* (Indianapolis: The Bobbs-Merrill Co., 1947), pp. 542–51; Clarence R. Jeffery, "The Structure of American Criminological Thinking," *Journal of Criminal Law, Criminology and Police Science*, January-February, 1956, pp. 658–72, "Crime, Law and Social Structure," *ibid.*, November-December, 1956, pp. 423–35.

[9]Justin Miller, *Handbook of Criminal Law* (St. Paul, Minn.: West Publishing Co., 1934), p. 16.

[10]Paul W. Tappan, "Who Is the Criminal?" *American Sociological Review*, February, 1947, p. 100.

corpus delicti. This term defined literally means "the body of the offense" or "the substance of crime." Although in popular language it is used to describe the visible evidence of the crime, such as the dead body of a murdered person, it is properly applicable to any crime and relates particularly to the act element of criminality. This means that it must be proved that a certain prohibited act has been committed and that it was committed by a criminal human agency. Furthermore, in addition to establishing the corpus delicti in a particular case, the state must also prove beyond a reasonable doubt that the accused was the human agent who committed the act or procured it to be committed.[11]

When this has been accomplished according to the exacting regularities of legal procedure and due process,[12] the "accused" becomes the "convicted." Then, and not until then, does the "alleged criminal" become the "criminal." Anything short of this will often be inaccurate and unjust. Certainly, charges of crime by the press, the public, and the police do not meet the standard of rigorous precision that is required. Decisions by civil courts and administrative agencies, based as they may be upon a slight preponderance of evidence, and not upon proof beyond a reasonable doubt as convictions must be in the criminal court, "can show no more than civil wrong." And "evaluations of assorted deviations from social mores" by sociologists "are concerned with broader and looser constructs than crime."[13]

CRIME MUST BE DEFINED BY THE CRIMINAL LAW

Consequently, it must be insisted that no person is a white-collar criminal or any kind of criminal until he has been properly adjudicated as such in the criminal court. This is as true in the case of a corporation charged with some type of criminal behavior as is in the case of a person accused of murder. On this point Tappan states, "In studying the offender, there can be no presumption that arrested, arraigned, indicted, or prosecuted persons are criminals unless they also be held guilty beyond a reasonable doubt of a particular offense."[14]

This is not to deny that there are imperfections in the criminal law and its procedure. But the remedy for this is not to disregard the preventive devices that the law has created to shield the innocent. The correct approach to this problem lies in the improvement of the criminal law, in the stricter enforcement of its provisions, and in the vigorous, but unbiased and impartial prosecution of the accused.

Sutherland's original definition of white-collar crime, quoted above, had some merit inasmuch as it did not depart entirely from the principles of criminal law.[15] Since then, however, other definitions have appeared which make no attempt to do this. Clinard, in discussing the black market, defines white-collar crime as "a violation of the law committed primarily by groups such as businessmen, professional men, and politicians in connection with their occupations."[16] Hartung, using what he terms a narrower definition of the concept, defines white-collar crime as "a violation of law regulating business, which is committed for a firm by the firm or its agents in the conduct of its business."[17] Clinard, then,

[11]Miller, *op. cit.*, pp. 93, 94.

[12]"Due process of law in each particular case means such an exercise of the powers of the government as the settled maxims of law permit and sanction and under such safeguards for the protection of individual rights as those maxims prescribe for the class of cases to which the one in question belongs." *Black's Law Dictionary,* quoting Cooley, Const. Lim. 441 (3rd ed.; St. Paul, Minn.: West Publishing Co., 1933), p. 626.

[13]Paul W. Tappan, "Crime and the Criminal," *Federal Probation,* July-September, 1947, pp. 41–44. See also Tappan, "Who Is the Criminal?" *op. cit.*, pp. 100, 101.

[14]Tappan, "Who Is the Criminal?" *op cit.*, p. 100.

[15]In discussing his definition, Sutherland states: "White-collar crime is real crime. If it is not a violation of the criminal law, it is not white-collar crime or any other kind of crime." (Sutherland, "Crime and Business," *op. cit.*, p. 115).

[16]Marshall B. Clinard, *The Black Market* (New York: Rinehart and Co., Inc., 1952), p. 127. In presenting this definition, Clinard says, "Contrary to popular thinking, however, the use of a criminal sanction is not essential for a black market violation of law to be considered sociologically as a 'crime.'" (p. 127).

[17]Frank E. Hartung, "White-Collar Crime: Its Significance for Theory and Practice," *Federal Probation,* June, 1953, p. 31. See also his "White-Collar Offenses in the Wholesale Meat Industry in Detroit," *op. cit.*, pp. 25–34.

would make any businessman, professional man, or politician who engages in any illegal activity in connection with his occupation a white-collar criminal, while Hartung would confine the term to a firm or its agents that violate a law regulating business in the conduct of the firm's business. Like Sutherland, both Clinard and Hartung disregard the important element of conviction. Furthermore, it is quite clear that the criminal law is in no way concerned with much of the activity to which they refer since many illegal acts and violations of business regulations are not defined as crimes by the criminal law.

Even Sutherland abandoned his earlier position and later defined crime as any act which the law describes as socially injurious and for which it provides a penalty.[18] Thus, he made the violation of any law, civil or criminal, a crime when it is "socially injurious" and carries a penalty. But he did not stop with this. Later still, in writing of the dangers of white-collar criminality, he said, "Some of the offenses are not even a violation of the spirit of the law, for the parties concerned have been able by bribery and other means to prevent the enactment of laws to prohibit wrongful and injurious practices."[19] Here, then, the term "white-collar criminal" has deteriorated to the point where it can be used to refer to anyone who engages in what the observer considers to be unethical or immoral behavior. As Tappan says, white-collar crime becomes "the conduct of one who wears a white collar and who indulges in occupational behavior to which some particular criminologist takes exception."[20] Now, at last, the shrewd businessman, the inefficient workman, the immoral politician, the unethical doctor or lawyer—all can be condemned as criminals by a stroke of the pen. The result, states Tappan, may be "fine indoctrination or catharsis achieved through blustering broadsides against the 'existing system' [but] it is not criminology and it is not social science."[21]

[18]Edwin H. Sutherland, "Is 'White-Collar Crime' Crime?" *American Sociological Review*, April, 1945, p. 132. See also his *White-Collar Crime, op. cit.*, pp. 29–55.

[19]Edwin H. Sutherland, *Principles of Criminology* (4th ed.; Philadelphia: J. B. Lippincott Co., 1947), p. 37.

[20]Tappan, "Who Is the Criminal?" *op. cit.*, p. 99.

[21]*Ibid.*

MORALITY AND ETHICS NOT THE SAME AS LAW

However, what has been said here should not be regarded as an attempt to minimize the immoral and unethical practices of many American businessmen which have been exposed and justly condemned by a series of shocking investigations. The point is that morality and ethics are not the same as the law, and an immoral or unethical person is not necessarily a criminal. But should criminologists not study what they consider to be antisocial behavior with the view to having it defined as crime by the law? Yes, by all means, but until it has been so defined some terms other than "crime" and "criminal" should be used in describing it. Failure to do this can result only in the corruption of the terms "crime" and "criminal," the integrity of which the law has sought so vigilantly to preserve, and to open the door to endless confusion. That the danger of this is real is eloquently attested to above by the fact that the white-collar criminologists cannot agree among themselves as to the meaning of the terms "white-collar crime" and "white-collar criminal." Unless they can come to some agreement regarding these terms and define them according to the principles of criminal law, they should discard the concept of white-collar crime entirely because "vague omnibus concepts defining crime are a blight upon either a legal system or a system of sociology that strives to be objective."[22]

Furthermore, the legal profession is already entrusted by society with the responsibility of interpreting and administering the criminal law. In order to protect all parties concerned, the legal profession has always insisted upon a strict interpretation of the meaning of the term "crime" and has carefully constructed around it a technical procedure designed to reduce the possibility of injustice. It is not likely that the legal profession will change the meaning of the term "crime" at the mere suggestion of persons outside the profession. In fact, the expanded meaning of the word might actually tend to undermine the understanding and confidence

[22]*Ibid.*

between two professional groups whose increased cooperation is so important in the improvement of our laws and their administration.

DIFFICULTIES IN ESTIMATING THE EXTENT OF WHITE-COLLAR CRIME

As a result of the way in which the term "white-collar crime" is variously defined by different sociologists, there are major difficulties involved in any attempt to estimate the amount of this type of crime in the United States. For example, if we use Sutherland's original definition, we find these obstacles: (1) white-collar crime is a nonlegal term which refers to certain criminal acts, such as embezzlement and bribery, but does not specifically name the criminal acts to which it has reference; (2) it refers to a certain type of person, namely, a member of the upper socioeconomic class, but does not provide us with specific criteria by which to determine the social class of the person involved; and (3) the criminal law in defining acts that are usually referred to by the term "white-collar crime," with few exceptions, does not make any distinction regarding the social class of the offenders. Other definitions of white-collar crime present similar difficulties. It should be clear, therefore, why there are no official sources of criminal statistics by which to estimate the amount of white-collar crime.

If sociologists were to use the term "white-collar crime" to refer to acts that are defined as crimes by the law, official complications of white-collar offenses known to the police might then be included in the *Uniform Crime Reports*.[23] Although this arrangement would not provide a complete coverage of white-collar crimes, however defined, nor satisfy all the strict requirements set up by the white-collar criminologists, it would furnish official and highly reliable data that could be employed in a systematic and continuing revelation of the enormity of these crimes and in agitation for any necessary reforms in the criminal law and its administration.

All this, of course does not mean that we should forbid research and discussion regarding what *ought* to be called criminal. On the contrary, these activities should not only be conducted but should be encouraged. By such efforts the law can be brought more closely into line with the needs and desires of our people, and the justice of its administration can be more securely established. These goals can be achieved, however, only if the influence of public opinion is exerted through our legislatures and courts and not by mere attempts to change the meaning of the term "crime" through academic decree or fiat.

Jerome Hall has pointed out that there is a basic conflict in American criminology as a result of its failure to integrate the diverse streams of thought which have come to be known as the Classical and Positive Schools.[24] In the resolution of this conflict, both the crime and the criminal must be emphasized if the interests of the individual and those of society are to be balanced properly. "The criminal and his social relationships must be emphasized if we are to understand why he commits a crime and how his behavior may be modified. And crime as a legal concept must be emphasized if we are to understand how to protect society against the criminal and the defendant against his accusers and those who wield authority."[25]

THE SCIENTIFIC ISSUE

The scientific issue springs from the contention that those who commit white-collar crimes are relatively immune because of class bias of the criminal law and its administration, and that this in turn has led to a distortion of the criminological theories of causation since these theories have been based to a great extent on the official records of the criminal and juvenile courts and law-enforcement agencies. While this contention has merit, the remedy is to be found in the further development of an independent science

[23]Although in the strict sense of the word an act is not a crime until it has been properly adjudicated as such in the criminal court, *offenses known to the police,* as shown by the *Uniform Crime Reports,* are the best available index of crime in the United States.

[24]Hall, *op. cit.,* p. 542.

[25]Robert G. Caldwell, *Criminology* (New York: The Ronald Press Co., 1956), p. 24.

of human behavior and not in the mere tinkering with legal statistics as suggested by the white-collar criminologists.

The criminal law and the data about crimes and criminals accumulated during the law-enforcement process are useful in scientific research, but, as Thorsten Sellin has explained, "the application of scientific criteria to the selection and classification of these data independently of their *legal* form is essential to render them valuable to science." If the investigator in the field of criminology is to contribute to the science of human behavior, he must free himself from the concepts and terminology created by the criminal law. He must define his own terms and base them on the intrinsic character of his material so that they will designate properties in that material which are assumed to be universal. "The legislator and the administrator on the one hand, the scientist on the other, speak different languages, fundamentally irreconcilable. This is as it should be, for they are pursuing essentially different ends. . . . Confinement to the study of crime and criminals and the acceptance of the categories of specific forms of 'crime' and 'criminal' as laid down in law renders criminological research theoretically invalid from the point of view of science."[26]

The irreconcilable difference between the language of the criminal law and that of science can be no more sharply delineated than by a comparison of the meanings given the concept "cause" in these two fields. "By 'cause' science means the sufficient antecedent conditions necessary for the evocation of a given phenomenon. When these conditions are sufficient, the phenomenon appears; when they are insufficient, it does not. It refers, therefore, to a functional relationship between the phenomenon studied and the conditions necessary for its appearance. These conditions must be thought of in terms of their interaction in the total situation. Some exert more influence than others, but the functioning of all is necessary to produce the phenomenon, which would be different if there were the least modification in the total situation."[27]

[26]Thorsten Sellin, *Culture Conflict and Crime* (New York: Social Science Research Council, Bulletin 41, 1938), pp. 23, 24.

[27] Caldwell, *op. cit.*, p. 13.

The law, on the other hand, gives the concept "cause" a much more limited meaning. It recognizes that an act often has consequences that reach far and touch the lives of many persons, but the law does not hold a person responsible for every consequence of his act. "In a philosophical sense, the consequences of an act go forward to eternity and its causes extend back to the beginnings of time. But human responsibility cannot be measured by such standards. To do so would result in infinite liability for all wrongful acts, stir up boundless conflicts, and fill the courts with endless litigation."[28] Liability for the consequences of any act must be limited in terms of some idea of justice or social policy, which tends to be an expression of the dominant values of the group. In the light of what is considered to be justice in any society, a person's act is said to be the proximate or legal cause of the consequences, and if those constitute a crime and the requisite intent is present, he is held to be criminally responsible. But it is obvious that in any particular case this procedure may disregard certain factors that would be included by the application of the scientific concept of cause. The law, therefore, by its very nature and without necessarily being subject to any class bias or any unethical or immoral pressures or practices may produce official data which do not meet scientific standards. Thus, the psychiatrist in certain cases may find himself in conflict with the legal concept of insanity, which may serve socially defined ends as agreed upon by most of the members of all socio-economic classes but which does not square with the scientific concept of mental disease.

NEED OF INDEPENDENT SCIENTIFIC TERMINOLOGY

One more question needs to be examined. Why not strip the terms "crime" and "criminal" of their legal meanings in scientific research and give them a content which is acceptable to scientists? In answer to this question, it must be insisted that such a redefinition of terms, as in the case of the moral issue, would lead only to misunderstanding and confusion, and that every-

[28]*Ibid.*, p. 120.

thing that could be accomplished by it could be secured much more easily and effectively by the use of an independent scientific terminology. This is the course that has been followed by the psychiatrist who avoids the legal term "insanity" in his scientific research, even though he may agree that certain persons who have been declared insane by the law are mentally diseased and employs data regarding them which are taken from official legal sources. Sellin, while suggesting that criminologists study the violation of conduct norms in order to put criminology on a scientific basis, calls attention to the dangers involved in the loose usage of the term "crime." In his opinion it is wiser to retain this term for the violations of the norms that are embodied in the criminal law and to use the term "abnormal conduct" for violations of all norms whether legal or not.[29] Thus, he would study all deviations from conduct norms[30] as measured by concepts created by sociologists. To the extent that these deviations are already defined as crimes by the law, he would refer to them as such in his scientific investigation but, in his examination of the nature and causes of conduct deviations, he would in no way be restricted by the concepts of criminal law nor would he seek to alter its terminology. Naturally, this study of conduct deviations would involve not only the identification of conduct norms (both legal and nonlegal), but also the analysis of the sociohistorical setting in which these norms have developed.[31] The results achieved by such scientific research might then be utilized by the law in the modification of its own concepts and principles. In this way science and the law could work hand in hand while at the same time directing their efforts toward the attainment of their own goals.

[29]Sellin, *op. cit.*, p. 32.

[30]Other writers have used the term "deviant behavior" to refer to departures from the norms of a society. See, for example, Marshall B. Clinard, *Sociology of Deviant Behavior* (New York: Rinehart and Co., Inc., 1957).

ISOLATIONISM IN SOCIAL SCIENCE FIELD

Regardless of what our views may be on the subject of white-collar crime, in this controversy, as in so many others in the field of sociology, we are forcefully reminded of the immaturity of the social sciences. Since so little is known about the intricacies of normal behavior, we should not be overawed by any branch of science, any school of thought, or any type of methodology and thus neglect other promising leads. Instead, at present, we should use all available resources in every field of knowledge and organize them in a coordinated attack along all approaches to the study of human behavior. In this attack, teamwork by scholars in the social sciences and the law can do much to break down the isolationism that has so often characterized research in the field of criminology and contributed to unfortunate misunderstandings and needless disputes.

[31]See for example, Clarence R. Jeffery, "The Development of Crime in Early English Society," *Journal of Criminal Law, Criminology, and Police Science,* March-April, 1957, pp. 647–66.

26.

Gilbert Geis

TOWARD A DELINEATION OF WHITE-COLLAR OFFENSES

General Motors does not have an inferiority complex, United States Steel does not suffer from an unresolved Oedipus problem, and the Duponts do not desire to return to the womb, Edwin H. Sutherland noted sarcastically when he summarized the implications of his research into white-collar offenses.[1] It was a clever piece of invective, designed to decimate the position of clinical theorists in criminology. "The assumption that an offender may have some such pathological distortion of the intellect or the emotions seems to me absurd," Sutherland wrote, "and if it is absurd regarding the crimes of businessmen, it is equally absurd regarding the crimes of persons in the lower economic classes."[2] Having dealt with the presumptive opposition, correctly if not altogether logically,[3] Sutherland put forward his own hypothesis which, "for reasons of economy, simplicity, and logic" was to be used to explain both white-collar criminality and lower-class criminality. It was, of course, the theory of differential association: "Criminality is learned . . . in direct or indirect association with those who already practice the behavior . . ."[4] Since criminality is so learned, Sutherland maintained, it can be and is learned at all social levels in a society. Thus, for Sutherland, white-collar crime was as readily accounted for as the more traditional forms of criminal behavior.

The thesis of this paper is that Sutherland was led by his theoretical preconceptions into a number of intellectual traps which rendered the concept of white-collar crime, as it presently stands, of dubious utility for the study of criminal behavior. Having at hand a theoretical framework which could embrace virtually the entire range of human conduct, Sutherland felt no need to differentiate carefully among an extraordinarily wide range of offenses—criminal, ethical, and moral—engaged in by persons who were "respected" and "socially accepted and approved."[5] All would fit neatly into his interpretative scheme for white-collar crime in the same manner that professional crime, aggressive behavior following encephalitis, and a host of other highly divergent forms of behavior earlier had been "explained" by differential association.[6]

It is important to realize that no one, of course, had ever maintained that General Motors, or its management personnel, all suffered from an inferiority complex, any more than

Source: Originally published in Vol. 32, No. 2, of *Sociological Inquiry* (Spring, 1962), pp. 160–71. Reprinted by permission of the journal.

[1]Edwin H. Sutherland, "Crimes of Corporations," in Albert Cohen, Alfred Lindesmith, and Karl Schuessler (eds.), *The Sutherland Papers* (Bloomington, Ind.: Indiana University Press, 1956), p. 96.

[2]*Ibid.*

[3]That upper class criminals do not have pathological disturbances does not, of course, serve to disprove the proposition that lower class criminals may have such disturbances. It is not an illogical proposition, just an unlikely one. Sutherland does not overcome it, even with his questionable insistence that all criminals share similar explanatory concepts, since he does not demonstrate the absence of such disturbances in the individuals committing the corporate offenses.

[4]Edwin H. Sutherland, "White-Collar Criminality," *American Sociological Review*, Vol. 5 (February, 1940), p. 10. The theory of differential association is elaborated in Edwin H. Sutherland and Donald R. Cressey, *Principles of Criminology* (6th ed.; Philadelphia: Lippincott, 1960), pp. 74–80. Recent statements have concentrated on refining and shoring up the theory. See Donald R. Cressey, "Epidemiology and Individual Conduct: A Case from Criminology," *Pacific Sociological Review*, Vol. 3 (Fall, 1960), pp. 47–58, and Daniel Glaser, "The Differential-Association Theory of Crime," in Arnold M. Rose (ed.), *Human Behavior and Social Processes* (Boston: Houghton Mifflin, 1962), pp. 425–42. For a review of differential association's seeming merits and demerits see Herbert A. Bloch and Gilbert Geis, *Man, Crime, and Society* (New York: Random House, 1962), ch. 5.

[5]Sutherland, "White-Collar Criminality," *op. cit.*, p. 4, fn. 2.

[6]Sutherland and Cressey, *op. cit., passim.*

any serious scholar would have taken the position that all criminals, either lower or upper class, are driven by an unrequited yearning to return to the womb. Sutherland was obviously flailing a theoretical nonesuch. It was, in fact, Sutherland himself who, in one vital respect, came nearest to the theories he was belaboring, with his insistence that *all* criminals could, and should, be analyzed in terms of a single theoretical interpretation.

It was this commitment that inevitably tended to blur action distinctions for Sutherland. As Merton has noted, "the decision to encompass a great variety of behaviors under one heading naturally leads us to assume that it is what these behaviors have in common that is most relevant, and this assumption leads us to look for an all-encompassing set of propositions which will account for the entire range of behavior. This is not too remote," Merton points out, "from the assumption of a John Brown or a Benjamin Rush that there must be *a* theory of disease, rather than distinct theories of disease—of tuberculosis and of arthritis, of typhoid and syphilis—theories which are diverse rather than single."[7]

The present need in regard to the concept of white-collar criminality appears to be to separate out those types of activity which reasonably can be said to fall within the range of criminal statutes and then to gather together into less ubiquitous groupings those forms of behavior which analytically resemble one another both in their manifestation and in terms of the ingredients which appear to enter into their origin. This need is a common one for the field of criminology.[8] "[I]t should be abundantly clear the theories which treat crime as though it were a unitary concept are particularly prone to failure, and that the search for something which explains crime in general is the blind spot in criminology," Gibbs has written, while pointing out that "if our concern is with causal homogeneity, as it should be, we can ill afford to deal with broad categories of behavior; it is far better to look within these broad categories and delimit specific types of behavior for investigation."[9] Gibbons and Garrity have made the same point: "[T]he argument that crime is homogeneous only in that it is behavior which violates the criminal code is becoming increasingly popular. Consequently, there has been considerable concern for the development of classifications or typologies of criminals, in which no attempt is made to explain all crime, but rather, explanations are sought for different patterns of behavior viewed as homogeneous types of crime."[10] It is in terms of these theoretical dictates that the concept of white-collar crime must be re-examined.

CRIMES OF CORPORATIONS

One of the tightest definitions that Sutherland gave to "white-collar crime" was that it applied to criminal acts of corporations and individuals acting in their corporate capacity. This was not the only meaning accorded the concept for, as Tappan shows,[11] Sutherland altered his definition radically on different occasions, not as a matter of growth and refinement, but rather because, as we have seen, it was not important, given his theoretical approach, for him to be precise. Faced with the range of definitions, and granting the desirability of making a choice, it would appear most promising to concentrate on the corporation crimes that Sutherland discusses in *White Collar Crime,* his major work in this area. This book, which elaborates the thesis Sutherland first outlined ten years earlier in his presidential address to the American Sociological Society, is largely a recital of decisions rendered against the leading corporations in the United States for restraint of trade, infringement of patents, misrepresentation in ad-

[7]In Helen L. Witmer and Ruth Kotinsky (eds.), *New Perspectives for Research on Juvenile Delinquency,* Children's Bureau Publication No. 356 (1956), p. 27.

[8]On this point, see Gilbert Geis, "Sociology of Crime," in Joseph S. Roucek, *The Sociology of Crime* (New York: Philosophical Library, 1960), pp. 7–33.

[9]Jack Gibbs, "Needed: Analytical Typologies in Criminology," *Southwestern Social Science Quarterly,* Vol. 40 (March, 1960), p. 323.

[10]Don C. Gibbons and Donald L. Garrity, "Some Suggestions for the Development of Etiological and Treatment Theory in Criminology," *Social Forces,* Vol. 38 (October, 1959), p. 51.

[11]Paul W. Tappan, "Who Is the Criminal?" *American Sociological Review,* Vol. 12 (February, 1947), p. 98.

vertising, unfair labor practices, and similar acts. In the book, Sutherland stressed that the term white-collar crime "principally refers to business managers and executives."[12] Then within two pages of this pronouncement Sutherland illustrated white-collar crime by examples of thefts by employees in chain stores, over-charges by garage mechanics and watch-repair men, and fee-splitting by doctors. This testifies to the inconstancy of his formulation and/or to the dearth of illustrative materials. If the concept of white-collar crime is brought back and restricted to corporate offenses and highly cognate acts, however, it will have definitional integrity, fulfill the criteria of reasonable causal homogeneity, and provide a delimited area for significant criminological research.[13]

The major difficulty in *White Collar Crime* as criminological research lies in Sutherland's striking inability to differentiate between the corporations themselves and their executive and management personnel. When, in order to illustrate the possible development of white-collar offenses, Sutherland reproduced case-history documents of such non-corporate types as graduate students who work part-time as shoe salesmen, he was forced to grant that "the documents would not demonstrate the genesis of illegal practices by the managers of large industries" and to justify the inclusion of this peripheral case-study material on the ground that "unfortunately, similar documents, even of a scattered nature, are not available for the managers of large industries. No first-hand research from this point of view has ever been reported."[14] It is, then, this lack of relevant personal material which forced Sutherland to "humanize" the corporations themselves and which seduced him into taking literally the personifications and reifications that he himself created, and to treat them as he might treat their individual components.

Corporations are, of course, legal entities which can be and are subjected to criminal processes. There is today little restriction on the range of crimes for which a corporation may be held responsible, though it cannot, for obvious reasons, be imprisoned.[15] For the purpose of criminological analysis, however, corporations cannot be considered persons, except by recourse to the same type of extrapolatory fiction that once brought about the punishment of inanimate objects. Sutherland attempted to resolve this obvious dilemma by maintaining, not without some acerbity, that the crimes of corporations are precisely the crimes of their executives and managers. "The customary plea of the executives of the corporation is that they were ignorant of and not responsible for the action of the special department," Sutherland wrote. "This plea is akin to the alibi of the ordinary criminal and need not be taken seriously."[16]

Sutherland offered no proof for his categoric assertion. The empirical evidence, as we shall see, would seem to indicate that he was at best only partially correct. It should be stressed that the courts are willing to hold corporate officers personally responsible for blatant acts of administrative omission,[17] and to convict such officers when evidence indicates that they knowingly participated in violations of criminal statutes designed to control business operations. However, the courts are understandably reluctant to impose penalties for acts not supported by some

[12]Edwin H. Sutherland, *White Collar Crime* (New York: Dryden Press, 1949), p. 9, fn. 7.

[13]This is not meant to indicate that valuable studies cannot be made of crimes related to things such as the practice of medicine or the sale of used cars. Nor is it meant to indicate that worthwhile results cannot be had from examinations of the criminal behavior of individuals similarly situated in the class and occupational structure in order to learn how their position influences their adherence to criminal codes. It is meant to indicate that these studies cannot be grouped together as white-collar crime unless we wish to retain the present definitional anarchy.

[14]Sutherland, *White Collar Crime, op. cit.*, p. 240.

[15]See Glanville Williams, *Criminal Law—the General Part* (2d ed.; London, Stevens, 1961), ch. 22; R. S. Welsh, "The Criminal Liability of Corporations," *Law Quarterly Review*, Vol. 62 (October, 1946), pp. 345–65; Orvill C. Snyder, *Criminal Justice* (New York: Prentice-Hall, 1953), pp. 728–36.

[16]Sutherland, *White Collar Crime, op. cit.*, p. 54.

[17]Note, for instance, after the disastrous 1942 fire, the conviction for manslaughter of the owner of the Cocoanut Grove, Inc. for "intentional failure to take such care in disregard of the harmful possible consequences . . ." despite the fact that he was in the hospital at the time of the fire and claimed corporate, not personal, responsibility. *Commonwealth* v. *Welansky*, 316 Mass. 383, 55 N.E.2d 902 (1944).

reasonably probative evidence of individual culpability.[18]

Sutherland's anthropomorphic attitude toward corporations also on occasion led him into analogs which are as unnecessarily inflammatory as they are inaccurate and misleading. Thus, despite his repeated disclaimers that he was not interested in muckraking but only in criminal theory, Sutherland was impelled several times to compare corporations *per se* to habitual and professional criminals. Both, he pointed out, are about 45-years old (corporations presumably do not get the benefit of nonage principles) and both have violated the law more than four times during their lifetime.[19] As Emerson notes, Sutherland's approach was at times not far different from saying that the state of Rhode Island is criminalistic because a resident of Providence has violated the criminal law. Emerson also pointed out that the seventy corporations which Sutherland treated as single individuals were actually gigantic, rambling enterprises, often with hundreds of thousands of employees, and subject to hundreds of statutes and thousands of administrative regulations.[20] It is such diversionary tactics which left Sutherland open to charges that he was a "moralist"[21] and that the concept of white-collar crime was a "propagandist weapon, which under the meretricious guise of science is to be used for the establishment of a new order."[22] Neither of these strictures, of course, is germane to the theoretical integrity of Sutherland's position. However, such attacks have understandably tended to distract from the essential elements of Sutherland's position and to hinder its re-examination and the absorption of its more viable portions into the main body of criminological theory.

GENERAL ELECTRIC AND ANTITRUST CRIME

By restricting white-collar crime to the corporate setting, as is done in the main body of Sutherland's book and suggested in its introductory section, the concept can shed considerable light on a form of offenses accorded little attention by criminologists either before or after Sutherland's work. The recent involvement of manufacturers of heavy electric equipment in violations of the Sherman Antitrust Act provides a valuable lode of material. This case fills in some informational and personal document gaps whose existence Sutherland felt so keenly. Furthermore, this case allows closer scrutiny of a significant form of criminal activity, of the *individuals* who engage in such activity, and suggests fertile fields for further criminological cultivation.

The Sherman Antitrust Act is obviously a criminal statute.[23] It states that "every person who shall make any contract or engage in any combination or conspiracy declared [by the Act] to be illegal shall be guilty of a misdemeanor" and shall be punished by a fine or imprison-

[18]Acts of omission pose difficult problems both for criminologists and students of criminal jurisprudence, but it would seem desirable that some substantial doctrine of fault be attached to acts carrying criminal penalties. Note, in accord with this idea, Hall's emphasis on "some 'causal' relationship between the legally forbidden harms and the voluntary misconduct." Jerome Hall, *Principles of Criminal Law* (Indianapolis: Bobbs Merrill, 1947), p. 11. During 1962 or 1963, further clarification should be forthcoming regarding criminal responsibility of corporate officers under the Sherman Anti-trust Act. The Supreme Court accepted certiorari of *U.S.* v. *Wise,* a case bearing directly on this point, on December 18, 1961.

[19]Sutherland, *White Collar Crime, op. cit.,* pp. 25, 217–21.

[20]Thomas I. Emerson, Book Review, *Yale Law Journal,* Vol. 59 (February, 1950), pp. 581–85.

[21]Howard Jones, *Crime and the Penal System* (London: University Tutorial Press, 1956), pp. 6–8.

[22]Robert Caldwell, Book Review, *Journal of Criminal Law, Criminology, and Police Science,* Vol. 50 (September-October, 1959), p. 282.

[23]"The act . . . creates an offense, a crime, describing what the crime is." *U.S.* v. *Patterson,* 201 F. 697, 714 (Dist. Ct. Ohio 1912); "The Sherman act is primarily a criminal statute." *U.S.* v. *Swift,* 188 F. 92, 96 (Dist. Ct. Ill. 1911). Note the important observation that "The [Sherman] Act . . . prohibits conduct rather than status. . . . This is obvious from the fact that the statute carries criminal as well as civil sanctions." *U.S.* v. *E. I. du Pont de Nemours,* 118 F. Supp. 41 (1953). In the first Supreme Court decision since 1798 on whether a statute was penal, Chief Justice Warren in 1958 suggested that "the inquiry must be directed to substance" and that "a statute that prescribes the consequences that will befall one who fails to abide by these regulatory provisions is a penal law. . . . Even a clear legislative classification of a statute as non-penal would not alter the fundamental nature of a plainly penal statute," Warren wrote, *Trop* v. *Dulles,* 356 U. S. 86 (1958). It is a bit of judicial commonsense, important to bear in mind when laying out the boundaries of the criminological realm.

ment.[24] The Act, passed in 1890, did not create a novel form of liability, but was based upon long-standing common law principles of tort, crimes, and contracts.[25] By restricting white-collar analyses to it and cognate statutes, criminologists would respond to Tappan's legitimate observation that under present conditions "one seeks in vain for criteria to determine this white-collar criminality . . . for purposes of empirical research or objective description."[26] Here, among the violators of corporate criminal statutes, we do not have gathered together en masse "the shrewd businessman, the inefficient workman, the immoral politician, and the unethical doctor or lawyer" all of whom have been "condemned as criminals by the stroke of the pen" rather than by means of stringent legal procedure.[27] Instead, we have a discernible group of violators whose values and attitudes would seem to be reasonably similar and whose behavior, in regard to the criminal statutes involved, would be relatively homogeneous.

It has sometimes been alleged that the concept of white-collar crime is an inept designation because the individuals to whom it refers do not conceive of themselves as criminals. Ernest W. Burgess put forward this argument with the observation that a "criminal is a person who regards himself as a criminal and is so regarded by society."[28] George Vold has insisted, in the same vein, that "there is a basic incongruity involved in the proposition that a community's leaders and more responsible elements are also its criminals."[29] A reading of the testimony in the General Electric cases, however, clearly shows how inappropriate such objections can be for this type of offense, except in the most basic sense that they represent attacks on the use of that ill-defined term "criminal" to categorize a person.[30]

How did the men indicted and sentenced in the antitrust cases regard themselves? "There goes my whole life," a General Electric vice president said. "Who's going to want to hire a jail bird? What am I going to tell my family?"[31] A management official in the same company told the Senate subcommittee investigating fixed prices: "I went to great lengths to conceal my activities so that I wouldn't get caught."[32] The president of a smaller firm stated emphatically that "No one attending the gatherings was so stupid that he didn't know [they] were in violation of the law."[33] Again and again witnesses testified that their convictions had an effect upon their families and their position in the community.

The anti-trust offenders appeared to regard themselves as law violators both after and prior to their convictions. They employed code names, did their conspiratorial telephoning from public booths, held meetings at out-of-the-way places, and falsified expense accounts (making certain, in the last instance, to specify that they had gone to places within the radius of their actual meeting point. It would not do, of course, to cheat the company as well). Certainly their self-image was as "criminalistic" as that of amateur shoplifters who, as Mary Bess Cameron points out, do not consider themselves criminals until this interpretation of their behavior is pointedly impressed upon them by store detectives or

[24]15 U.S.C.A. section 7 (1951). The best and most comprehensive interpretation of American antitrust law is A. D. Neale, *Antitrust Laws of the United States* (Cambridge, Cambridge University Press, 1960).

[25]Eugene V. Rostow, *Planning for Freedom: The Public Law of American Capitalism* (New Haven, Conn.: Yale University Press, 1959), p. 276.

[26]Tappan, *op. cit.*, p. 98.

[27]Robert G. Caldwell, *Criminology* (New York: Ronald Press, 1956), p. 70.

[28]Ernest W. Burgess, Comment, *American Journal of Sociology*, Vol. 56 (July, 1950), p. 34.

[29]George B. Vold, *Theoretical Criminology* (New York: Oxford University Press, 1958), p. 253.

[30]When does a person become or stop being a criminal? Are misdemeanants criminals? Is everybody a criminal? The term is so vague and invidious as to be self-defeating for analytical purposes. "Criminals," it would seem, should be designated in terms of the offenses they have committed (e.g., murderers, rapists, anti-trust offenders), and grouped together (e.g., professional criminals, sex offenders, white-collar criminals) and then sub-divided only after a careful delineation of the types of acts and actors being denominated.

[31]Quoted in Richard Austin Smith, "The Incredible Electric Conspiracy," *Fortune*, Vol. 63 (April, 1961), p. 133.

[32]U.S. Senate Subcommittee on Antitrust and Monopoly, Committee of the Judiciary, 87th Cong., 2nd sess. (Washington, D.C.: U.S. Government Printing Office, 1961). "Administered Prices," *Hearings*, Pt. 27, p. 16683.

[33]Quoted by Senator Kefauver, *Hearings*, Pt. 27, p. 16511.

courts.[34] Then, and only then, like the anti-trust violators, the shoplifters appear to discontinue their illegal activities. No one has suggested that shoplifters, because of this, are not legitimate objects of criminological study. It would appear that variations in self-perception among different types of offenders, and variations of the community's reaction to such offenders, represents an important attribute to be studied by criminologists rather than a stricture against the study of any particular phase of criminal behavior.

By concentrating upon individual corporate offenders and their behavior rather than upon amorphous corporate entities, several of Sutherland's explanations of white-collar criminality find support. However, some of his interpretative comments seem to show telling flaws. There is evidence, for example, to support Sutherland's stress on intimate personal relations as an initiating factor into price-fixing (or into "stabilizing prices" as the officers almost invariably labeled it). A General Electric man noted: "I had no other alternative but to believe that this was the way that business was conducted and this was my job to try to do the best I could to make a profit and build up the sales for our company."[35] A second man, like many others, explained: "I found it this way when I was introduced to competitive discussions, and just drifted into it . . ."[36] On the other hand, a number of persons expressed, and their fellow workers attributed to them, strong repugnance toward meeting with competitors, but they did so because they believed that they had been ordered to engage in such practices. As one noted: "I thought the pressure was such that I would attend."[37]

In addition, there were large segments of the management corps in the same companies which never engaged in price-fixing discussions. Those production and sales divisions which did not fall prone to erratic price swings, the threat of cutthroat competition, and low prices saw no need to collaborate with rivals to set prices and to distribute among themselves a pre-arranged portion of the available market. It was, therefore, not only personal associations which were important in determining participation in the price-fixing schemes, but also the economic structure against which such participation occurred. Several times, as the market swung to a more favorable position, price discussions came to an end, with a "leprosy policy" prevailing in regard to competitors. Then the economic pendulum again swung and the talks were resumed.

It is intricate, interwoven items such as these which probably led Sutherland to place near the conclusion of *White Collar Crime* a statement, which he elsewhere appears to contradict, that "supplements" to the hypotheses of social disorganization and differential association were needed to explain "adequately" the phenomena of white-collar crime.[38] A supplement such as Glaser's "differential identification"[39] would seem, for instance, to offer a more promising avenue toward understanding the individual in the General Electric management bloc who categorically refused to go along with price-fixing discussions once he had signed, as all other personnel had signed—they hypocritically, he devoutly—the company edict forbidding such discussions. "[H]e was so religious," his colleagues explained, "that since he had signed this slip of paper saying that he would observe the policy . . . he would not talk with competitors . . . even when they came to his home."[40] The immediate superior of this man decided that he was not "broad enough to hold down the job." He was transferred, and eventually retired. Another employee wrote a letter to the chairman of the General Electric board of directors, protesting that price-fixing was occurring in his division. Analysis of this individual's behavior, however, is complicated by the fact that he was apparently emotionally disturbed, and that he soon thereafter suffered a mental break-

[34]Mary B. Cameron, "Department Store Shoplifting," Ph.D. Dissertation, Indiana University, 1953.

[35]*Hearings, op. cit.*, Pt. 27, p. 16633.

[36]*Ibid.*, p. 16668.

[37]*Ibid.*, p. 16867.

[38]Sutherland, *White Collar Crime, op. cit.*, p. 264.

[39]Daniel Glaser, "Criminological Theories and Behavioral Images," *American Journal of Sociology*, Vol. 61 (March, 1956), pp. 433–44.

[40]*Hearings, op. cit.*, Pt. 27, p. 16736; Smith, *op. cit.*, p. 137.

down.[41] But these are the kinds of data that bear upon criminal offenses within the corporate world. These items must be gathered together into an interpretative scheme by criminologists and other social analysts. It will not do merely to concentrate upon the gross record of decisions rendered against the corporate entities.

It is noteworthy that Sutherland's fundamental tenet that corporate violations represent interchangeably the criminal activities of corporate officers appears unwarranted when the anti-trust case material is examined. The law declares that directors and officers shall be guilty if they *authorize, order,* or *do* any of the acts constituting violations;[42] it requires, therefore, as Sutherland does not, that these persons commit some positive act. Few persons reading the hearings of the Senate subcommittee would likely doubt the innocence of some corporate officials who, on the face of the matter, might have been presumed to have been aware of and condoned the price-fixing offenses. The obvious lack of knowledge of one Westinghouse manager, in whose division price-fixing meetings were occurring, led a Senator to declare that he was nothing more than "a corporate eunuch."[43] The witness explained it more simply: He was an engineer, interested in the mechanics of plant operation, and took no cognizance of sales matters.[44] In the same vein, the president and inside counsel of General Electric promulgated directives against price-fixing on several occasions. At least at the highest levels of the corporate hierarchy it does not seem unreasonable to conclude that these directives were meant to be taken literally.[45] If true, such data illustrates the danger of assuming that a criminal record can be built up against individuals by a superficial tabulation of decisions against their corporations. Such an approach falls far short of providing essential data on the internal dynamics of the offenses and its use would seem to constitute a serious shortcoming in Sutherland's study of white-collar corporate crime.

41*Hearings, op. cit.,* Pt. 28, pp. 17274–17278.

4215 U.S.C.A. section 24 (1951).

43*Hearings, op. cit.,* Pt. 27, p. 16571.

44*Ibid.,* pp. 16539–16577.

45See *ibid.,* Pt. 28, pp. 17201–18290 (testimony of Robert Paxton), Pt. 28, pp. 17669–17772 (testimony of Ralph J. Cordiner).

WHITE-COLLAR CRIME: AN OVERVIEW

It has not been the object of this paper to attempt to offer theoretical interpretations of corporate criminality, but rather to point the way toward a more restricted and meaningful definition of the concept of white-collar crime. As it now exists, the concept can fairly be said to stand convicted of Vold's charge that it is "ambiguous, uncertain, and controversial"[46] and Allen's allegation that it is "among the least perceptive and satisfactory of [Sutherland's] many valuable contributions."[47]

It is noteworthy that Sutherland, by virtue of his position in American sociology, the attractiveness of his terminology, and the illustrations he used to support it, broadened the horizons of criminological research well beyond their traditional limits. This contribution should not be undervalued. Donald Cressey, in his introduction to the re-issue of *White Collar Crime,* observes that "the lasting merit of this book . . . is its demonstration that a pattern of crime can be found to exist outside both the focus of popular preoccupation with crime and the focus of scientific investigation of crime and criminality."[48] Donald Newman suggests that Sutherland's contribution may "possibly [be] the most significant recent development in criminology."[49]

It has been this expansion of the interest of criminologists, largely through the impetus of Sutherland's work, that has led to an array of important studies. Among the better-known works are Clinard's investigation of wartime price ceiling and related offenses,[50] Cressey's study of embezzlers,[51] Hartung's examination of

46Vold, *op. cit.,* p. 253.

47Francis Allen, "Criminal Justice, Legal Values and the Rehabilitative Ideal," *Journal of Criminal Law, Criminology, and Police Science,* Vol. 50 (September-October, 1959), p. 228.

48Donald R. Cressey, Foreword, *White Collar Crime* (New York: Holt, Rinehart, & Winston, 1961), p. xii.

49Donald J. Newman, "White-Collar Crime," *Law and Contemporary Problems,* Vol. 23 (Autumn, 1958), p. 735. Newman notes that studies of white-collar offenses have almost exclusively to-date concentrated on *crimes,* not *criminals,* in contrast to research into more traditional types of offenses. *Ibid.,* p. 742.

50Marshall B. Clinard, *The Black Market* (New York: Rinehart, 1952).

51Donald R. Cressey, *Other People's Money* (Glencoe, Ill.: The Free Press, 1953).

violations in the wholesale meat industry,[52] and Aubert's research into the behavior of lawyers.[53] Such studies, though intrinsically worthwhile, should not, however, indiscriminately be included within the framework of white-collar crime.[54] Efforts need to be made to determine their generic nature and, perhaps, to coin descriptive designations for those which prove to be criminologically kindred. Otherwise, in the manner described above by Merton,[55] the search for wide-sweeping causal linkage will lead to a continued emasculation of significant theory. In addition, partly because of its loose definitional framework, the term "white-collar crime" has been taken up by popular writers, who have employed it to lend academic legitimacy to diatribes against a wide range of violators of an even wider range of moral codes, legal statutes, administrative regulations, and even less clearly defined standards.[56]

It would seem desirable that studies of embezzlers, for instance, should be evaluated on their own merits (as Cressey generally did) rather than as investigations into a type of behavior similar to the crimes of corporate officials. Sutherland himself pointed out that "the ordinary case of embezzlement is a crime by a single individual in a subordinate position against a strong corporation,"[57] and Daniel Bell after declaring that Sutherland's *White Collar Crime* is "misleadingly entitled," goes on to remark that bank embezzlers, as a group, are not upper-class offenders, but middle-class individuals.[58] Embezzlers, to carry the point somewhat further, usually work alone, while anti-trust violators must work in compact with other individuals. The embezzler benefits himself directly, and harms his employer. On the other hand, the anti-trust violator, though he undoubtedly operates in terms of personal advantage, can rationalize his offense as contributing to the fiscal health of his employer. These may not be crucial variations, but it would seem desirable to examine offenses such as embezzling, tax evasion, corporate violations, and fee-splitting as distinct forms of crime which may be related to each other in some ways and to other offenses in different ways. It would also appear reasonable to concentrate initially on the elements of the criminal act itself for purposes of grouping rather than upon the social characteristics of the perpetrators of the acts, and to group behavior in terms of the latter item only for the most compelling pragmatic or interpretative reasons. The crimes of medical doctors, for instance, would appear to be susceptible to differentiation on more meaningful terms than the professional status of their perpetrators. The offenses of fee-splitting and abortion, both committed by doctors, seem about as related in most essential respects as the offenses of infanticide and adultery, both of which are committed by mothers.

It has been the aim of this paper, then, to suggest that the concept of white-collar crime be restricted to corporate violations of a reasonably homogeneous nature and to cognate criminal acts. The concept should be tied to the legal codes which state and define such offenses. Attention should be concentrated on the behavior of individuals within the corporate structure rather than upon the artificial construct of "corporate crime." The absence of relevant data in this area will undoubtedly continue to hamstring criminologists, as it has done, for instance, in the investigation of the criminals in organized crime.[59] Perhaps some day we may look for the Kinsey of the corporate world; in the interim, field studies into the illegal behavior of corporate officers would seem to offer an attractive form of criminological inquiry.

It is suggested, finally, that unless the concept

[52]Frank E. Hartung, "White-Collar Offenses in the Wholesale Meat Industry in Detroit," *American Journal of Sociology,* Vol. 56 (July, 1950), pp. 25–32.

[53]Vilhelm Aubert, "White Collar Crime and Social Structure," *American Journal of Sociology,* Vol. 58 (November, 1952), pp. 263–71.

[54]It is perhaps proper to indicate here that some of the foregoing strictures apply to chapter 14, "White-Collar Crime," in Bloch and Geis, *Man, Crime and Society, op. cit.,* so that the present paper is a self-critique as well as a critique of general tendencies in criminology.

[55]See text to footnote 8, *supra.*

[56]See, for instance, Frank Gibney, *The Operators* (New York: Harpers, 1960), and Norman Jaspan and Hillel Black, *The Thief in the White Collar* (New York: Lippincott, 1960).

[57]Sutherland, *White Collar Crime, op. cit.,* p. 231.

[58]Daniel Bell, *The End of Idealogy* (Glencoe, Ill.: The Free Press, 1960), p. 382, fn. 42.

[59]See Alfred Lindesmith, "Organized Crime," *The Annals,* Vol. 217 (September, 1941), pp. 76–83.

of white-collar crime is restricted, in line with the above or similar ideas, it will continue to remain prey to the legitimate criticisms of numerous scholars, some of whom have been quoted here, and it will continue to be so broad and indefinite as to fall into inevitable desuetude. Considering the potential value as well as the historical importance of this concept in the field of criminology, such a development would be unfortunate.

CHAPTER VIII

Professional Crime

IF ONE were to construct a status hierarchy of criminal offenders, the professional criminal would certainly be placed among those in the upper echelons. Along with leaders at the top levels of organized crime, and some white-collar criminals, the success of the professionals' career is dependent upon extraordinary skill, specialization, planning, and highly structured group activity.

The professional criminal is concerned with crimes of monetary gain. Professionals usually have a very high self-concept. They know their work is expert and tend to look down upon, disassociate themselves from, and generally ignore the amateur who is often sloppy, noncreative, and lacks the skill necessary to complete his job to perfection. Because of his superior skill, the professional is very likely to exploit the interests which will maximize his financial opportunities and minimize the possibility of apprehension. The stakes he goes after are generally high, and because he has enough money to "live in style," he may wait until conditions are strategically at their peak before he makes his move.

The professional criminal very often enters a life of crime directly from a legitimate and respected occupation. Instead of being recruited from delinquent gangs and lower level criminal groups and then taught new tricks, he continues doing what he knows how to do best—but rather than channel his efforts toward legitimate goals, he behaves in a deviant manner.

The criminal becomes a professional when he has won the respect of other professionals and develops his skills to the point of perfection.

The amateur offender is arrested and rearrested, thus indicating that he is not clever enough to avoid the clutches of the law. He will try several types of crimes, missing at some, hitting at others. The professional has developed a specialty. If he is a jewel thief, it is most unlikely that he will turn to confidence games or the passing of bad checks. The chances of his being expert in all three areas is remote; thus, in all probability he will continue with his specialty throughout the course of his criminal career.

The proper use of each member's ability in a professional group of criminals is most important. If a confidence game is being played, the member who is most appropriate for a given role will play that part, for in order to gain confidence a high degree of rapport must be established between the victim and the professional. For a jewel thief, a highly organized network must be developed between the professional, the fence, and the buyer, so that items taken may be disposed of quickly with the least amount of difficulty.

The first selection presented in this chapter is taken from the Task Force Report on Crime and its Impact—The President's Commission on Law Enforcement and Administration of Justice. The report examines the present-day nature of professional criminal activities in the United States, the extent of professional crime, and the characteristics of those involved. In the second reading, Robert L. Gasser provides a summary of the major characteristics of the confidence game. After "confidence" is defined, he discusses the role of the victim, illustrates types of games that may be played, establishes some rules of the game, and then concentrates on the members of the confidence team and their relations with other criminals, the law, and society. In the next article, Julian B. Roebuck and Ronald C. Johnson discuss the nature of the "short-con" man and the several games he may play. "Short con" as opposed to "big con" requires "fewer actors and props, less preparation, and less finesse and originality." In their paper, Roebuck and Johnson provide a description of the characteristics and activities of 10 Negro "short-con" men taken from a larger sample at the District of Columbia Reformatory. In the final selection, Edwin M. Lemert examines the behavior of the systematic check forger. In his study Dr. Lemert looks at forgery as a regular business, the role of planning prior to a forgery, technical skills required, the mobility patterns of the forger, and the associations he must maintain.

27.

President's Commission on Law Enforcement and Administration of Justice

PROFESSIONAL CRIME

Persons whose income is gained primarily from the fulltime pursuit of criminal activity account for a large proportion of certain crimes, particularly major thefts, and theft-related offenses, committed in the United States. No data are available on exactly how many crimes are committed by professionals nor how many criminals fall into the professional category, but both figures are undoubtedly substantial. Fuller understanding of the nature of professional crime could be a first step toward developing new techniques and approaches for control and prevention of this form of criminality.

Existing information about professional crime is fragmentary, and much of it may be outdated. A primary source is Edwin H. Sutherland's classic description of theft as a way of life, *The Professional Thief*, but that work, though helpful, was published in 1937 and describes the life of a thief in the period between 1905 and 1925. Other books published since have focused on particular types of criminal activity normally engaged in by professionals including confidence game operations,[1] pickpocketing,[2] professional robbery and burglary,[3] and receiving stolen goods.[4] These few studies provide the basic information on professional crime available in the literature. Although differences in emphasis and coverage exist among them, they present a reasonably coherent, though necessarily incomplete, description of certain types of professional criminal activity.

In order to supplement this material, the Commission sponsored a pilot field research study in four cities—Atlanta, Chicago, New York, and San Francisco—during the summer of 1966.[5] The study differed from previous research in that it used police and prosecutors as well as professional criminals as primary informants. Each consultant spent approximately half of his field time, or about 10 days, conferring with police and district attorneys on the problems of professional crime in their cities. In addition, some of the consultants observed the police in action and examined relevant materials in the files of special intelligence units. Law enforcement agents provided most of the leads to professional criminals.[6]

The consultants spent the balance of their time in the field (about 10 to 15 days each) locating and talking with professional criminals. The number of criminals interviewed varied from a low of eight in one city (Chicago) to 19 in another (San Francisco), with a total of 50 being interviewed. About two-thirds of the total number were in jail or prison at the time of their interviews. Although compared with prior studies the combined samples amounted to a relatively large number of informants, it is obvious that such a survey, conducted under such tight time limitations, could not result in a detailed comprehensive picture

SOURCE: Task Force on Assessment, The President's Commission on Law Enforcement and Administration of Justice, *Task Force Report: Crime and its Impact—An Assessment* (Washington, D.C.: U.S. Government Printing Office, 1967), pp. 96–101.

[1]D. W. Maurer, *The Big Con* (New York: Pocketbooks, Inc., 1949).

[2]D. W. Maurer, *Whiz Mob* (New Haven, Conn.: College and University Press, 1955).

[3]J. B. Martin, *My Life in Crime* (New York: Harper Brothers, 1952).

[4]See J. Hall, *Theft, Law, and Society* (2d ed., Indianapolis: Bobbs-Merrill, 1952).

[5]The Office of Law Enforcement Assistance, Justice Department, funded the project. Brandeis University administered the project grant. The project's coordinator was Prof. Leroy Gould of Yale University. Professor Gould was assisted by five field consultants, two advisors, and one research assistant.

[6]Some of those contacted through the police referred the staff to other professional criminals.

of professional crime in the United States. But the data collected are useful for obtaining some insights about professional criminals and the life they lead. . . .

For purposes of the Commission-sponsored study, professional crime was defined as: "Crime committed for personal economic gain by individuals whose major source of income is from criminal pursuits and who spend the majority of their working time in illegal enterprises." Organized crime and white-collar crime were specifically excluded. And while the definition was comprehensive enough to cover a variety of crimes such as killing or strong-arming for hire, professional arson and even prostitution, the principal emphasis of the Commission's study, following the pattern of earlier studies, was on essentially predatory crimes where the victim does not consent and where the actors usually function not as employees but as entrepreneurs. This approach tends to focus on theft and theft-related offenses, including such crimes as receiving stolen goods, shoplifting, pickpocketing, auto theft, burglary, forgery, confidence games, and various kinds of fraud.

This definition differs from traditional definitions in that it does not include any requirement that professionals have specially developed skills or that they have any particularly close association with other professionals. In Sutherland's classic study, the professional thief was described as having "a complex of abilities and skills . . . developed . . . by education" which "can be secured only in association with professional thieves."[7] Obviously this difference in definition affected the characteristics found to be associated with professional criminals. Thus prior studies found that professional criminals were often highly specialized, and that they tended to be quite loyal to members of their professional groups. The Commission-sponsored study, on the other hand, found that professional criminals tended to be generalists, to operate in a variety of loose associations with other professionals, and to exhibit no particular loyalty to their fellows. There is no way of knowing whether these different findings reflect only the difference in definition, or whether they reflect in addition changes in the character of professional crime. . . . It is obvious that any group which is engaged in criminal activity on a relatively full-time basis will be responsible for crime out of all proportion to its numbers. Moreover, unlike many occasional criminals, professionals typically make no significant contribution to society through legitimate activity. Their significance lies also in the fact that, compared to many of the criminal types dealt with in the Commission's report, professional criminals are a relatively rational and competent group of persons who are involved in crime because it is a profitable business. It would appear therefore that the traditional sanctions of the criminal law could be highly effective in dealing with many types of professional crime. But if law enforcement efforts are to succeed, more must be known about who professional criminals are and how they operate.

THE EXTENT OF PROFESSIONAL CRIME

There are no accurate statistics on the amount of professional crime. Published studies contain only estimates of career earnings of individual professional criminals, illustrative "touches," estimated average weekly earnings of various types of professional mobs, and other data of this order.[8]

The lack of accurate data on professional crime is in part a reflection of the general absence of adequate statistics on crime. . . . But there are particular difficulties in measuring professional crime. The professional and nonprofessional often engage in the same type of criminal activity. Even if crime reporting improves, it will still be difficult to distinguish the professional's work from that of the amateur. The task is complicated by the fact that the kinds

[7]E. H. Sutherland, *The Professional Thief* (Chicago: University of Chicago Press, 1937), pp. 197–98.

[8]For example, Martin's professional burglar estimated that he was in on $250,000 worth of thieving over a 4-year period. Martin, *op. cit.*, p. 139. This contrasts with the "scores" made by big con-men which during the 1920's were reported to run to $375,000. Mauer, *The Big Con, op. cit.*, pp. 26–30. At the other extreme, $15,000 is said to be a better than average income for a pickpocket, as of 1955. Maurer, *op. cit.*, p. 38.

of crimes committed by professionals change over a period of time.

Nevertheless, there is reason to believe that professional criminals are responsible for a large proportion of all property crimes committed and probably an even larger proportion of total property loss through such crimes. Available information indicates, for example, that there are a large number of professional criminals, all of whom, by definition, work at crime on a relatively full-time basis, and some of whom are reported to have very high incomes, sometimes exceeding $100,000. And it is apparent that thefts involving the loss of large amounts of valuable merchandise require the sorts of contacts with fences and commercial establishments that professionals develop.

There is evidence that the more successful professionals tend to spend substantial portions of their working time in developing lucrative opportunities and planning their criminal activity. A week, month, or even longer period may be spent in preparing for a particularly promising venture. As a result, "scores" tend to be good and the risk of apprehension low. The run-of-the-mill professional criminal, on the other hand, finds it necessary to spend more time in actual stealing to meet expenses and maintain himself at a comfortable and free-spending standard of living. Members of rackets, such as picking pockets and other forms of low-paying larceny, spend virtually all of their time this way.

The Commission's study produced some vivid descriptions of the day-to-day life of the typical professional, the flavor of which is captured by the term "hustling."[9] For the small-time professional criminal, hustling means moving around the bars and being seen; it means asking "what's up." It means "connecting" in the morning with two others who have a burglary set up for the evening, calling a man you know to see if he wants to buy 10 stolen alpaca sweaters at $5 each, and scouting the streets for an easy victim. It means being versatile: passing checks, rolling a drunk, driving for a stickup, boosting a car, burglarizing a store. It is a planless kind of existence, but with a purpose—to make as much money as can be made each day, no holds barred. While the more successful professional criminals hustle to some extent, they can afford to be much more purposeful and choosy in their criminal activities.

The Commission's study revealed that run-of-the-mill professionals regularly gather at certain bars and restaurants which in effect function as criminal job placement centers. These centers do for the professional criminal what want ads, employment offices, and businessmen's luncheons do for legitimate business. Through contact with other criminals, professionals learn of jobs to be pulled and of openings in groups planning to pull them. Contacts of this type also enable the professional to keep abreast of the latest techniques, and to gather information regarding criminal opportunities. These centers tend to attract the low-status professional criminal; apparently the successful practitioner in crime does not go to the employment office.

CHARACTERISTICS OF PROFESSIONAL CRIME

Skills

Sutherland drew a sharp distinction between the professional and the amateur thief based upon their relative skills. Under his classification, a person might steal as a full-time occupation, but he would not be a professional if he lacked the comprehensive complex of technical skills, personal contacts, and knowledge necessary in order to make a good living at crime in comparative safety. Sutherland's professional thief was contemptuous of the amateur's crude techniques, low income, and inability to avoid arrest. He therefore avoided association with amateurs and excluded them from the complex of reciprocal expectations and services which characterized his own way of life. But even under this definition, the professional criminal's skills vary significantly in kind[10] and degree. The big-time

[9]This term was often encountered in Atlanta and San Francisco where it is most likely to be used to describe the activities of run-of-the-mill professionals, rather than the more successful ones.

[10]A classification frequently encountered is the distinction between the "light" rackets in which stealing is accomplished by stealth or by manipulating the victim, and the "heavy" rackets in which force, or its threat, is used.

jewel thief and the "ropers" and "insidemen" who contrive to extract thousands of dollars from wealthy victims in the big con game are at one end of the spectrum. At the other are petty thieves, short con operators, and pickpockets who, though technically competent, lack the techniques needed to make big scores consistently.

Clearly there is an even greater range in skills when all persons who work at crime on a relatively full-time basis are classified as professionals. Nevertheless even this group is, as a whole, a relatively competent one. Many of its members possess, in addition to particular skills, the ability to plan and carry out detailed operations, to manipulate people, to analyze problems and implement solutions. It is clear that professional crime represents the loss to society of the potential contributions of a capable group of people, as well as the channeling of their energies into destructive activities.

Specialization

There is evidence that some individual professional criminals tend to specialize in a limited number of related rackets. Many exclude certain kinds of activities: thus some of the professional criminals who were interviewed in the course of the Commission's study said that they would not use violence. But in general the Commission's study indicated that professionals in the middle and lower status levels tend to be versatile.[11] Even the better professional criminal is not always free to follow his preferred line of work, since it may not be either profitable or safe at all times. Under these circumstances he may undertake activities at which he is not especially skilled.

Group Activity

Earlier studies described the relationship between professional criminals as relatively structured. Sutherland, in describing the professional thief of 40 years ago, and Maurer, in his treatment of professional confidence men and pickpockets, stressed the idea that professional criminals enjoy a sense of identity and solidarity and work within a set of well-defined norms and codes of loyalty, helpfulness, and honesty in dealing with one another.

The Commission-sponsored study, directed at a broader group of criminals, found that only the more successful members of this group could be so characterized. It found that the associations or gangs which run-of-the-mill professionals form to commit their crimes tend to be unstable, and that this instability results in part from the diversity of their activities. Different crimes require different kinds of personnel, amounts of financial backing, and types of fencing operations. Consequently, groupings and relations with loan sharks and fences may change from operation to operation. Even the few relatively stable groups which the consultants heard about brought in other professional criminals for certain jobs, and some members of the group might hire out from time to time on other jobs.

The shifting, transitory pattern of most professional criminals' working relationships was found to be accompanied by the absence of any strong ethical codes. Few of the professional criminals interviewed, for example, seemed to feel bound by any "no ratting" rule. Typically they appeared to take it for granted that others would do whatever necessary to protect themselves—to avoid imprisonment or reduce a sentence—and that they, therefore, should do likewise. As one professional criminal commented: "The one who gets his story told first gets the lightest sentence." There was little resentment expressed about this. It was treated like the weather—a fact of life. Further, criminals expected to be cheated by their colleagues, or by most colleagues. Many of those interviewed reported having been cheated by fences and even by their partners in a particular venture. Victimization of one professional group by another is apparently also fairly common, limited only by fear of reprisal.

There were exceptions to this general pattern, however. Some professional criminals stated that they had worked with certain individuals whom they trusted completely. And relative stability was found among the really successful professional criminals in New York and Chicago. In

[11]A notable exception are pickpockets who are relatively unsuccessful members of the professional crime group, and yet are highly specialized.

Chicago, for example, there is a group of between 50 and 200 "heavy" professional thieves who concentrate on such criminal activities as burglary, robbery, and cartage theft. It is said that this group, or at least the core members of the group, are quite stable and quite highly organized, and apparently they exert a considerable amount of control over their own regular members, as well as over persons who work with them only on occasional jobs.

CHANGING CRIMINAL OPPORTUNITIES

As conditions in society change, certain criminal occupations become relatively unprofitable, and other opportunities develop. The nature of crime will tend to change accordingly. Criminal activity like legitimate business activity may respond to the market, to supply and demand curves, and to technological developments. Professional crime, guided by the profit motive, can be expected to be particularly responsive to such factors. One example is the reported decline in safecracking. This is apparently due in part to such factors as increased law enforcement surveillance and mobility, and improvements in the design of safes. Undoubtedly the fact that safes no longer play as important a role has also contributed to the decline—modern economic transactions involve the transfer of credits much more than the transfer of cash. Thus it may have become both more difficult and riskier to rob safes, and also less profitable. At the same time, more promising opportunities for crime have arisen. One of these is check-passing. The Commission's study learned that nearly every burglar nowadays is also in the check business. One professional burglar said that in one period of several weeks between burglaries he passed over $20,000 of stolen checks. A generation ago burglars did not even look for checks to steal.

A good illustration of the effect of the development of a new market is auto theft and crimes relating to the automobile, such as auto stripping and auto "boosting" (stealing goods from parked cars), activities which are reported to be thriving in the cities surveyed. The Commission's study found also that there has been a rapid rise in recent years in home improvement and related frauds, a rise which corresponds roughly to the increase in privately owned homes. Some law enforcement officials think that in many cities these frauds currently constitute the most profitable source of income for professional criminals.

Professional criminals are also reported to be turning from robbing banks, picking pockets, and operating confidence games to other opportunities, but documentation for such new trends is scanty.

Careful research into changes in the general patterns of crimes committed by professionals and the factors that caused such changes would provide us with more insight into the nature of professional criminality and might provide a basis for designing better methods of crime prevention and control. It might also make it possible to begin to anticipate and plan for such changes.

KEY ASPECTS OF PROFESSIONAL CRIME

The services of the fence and the loan shark appear to be essential to the operations of many professional criminals. Since a great many professionals may depend on a very few such figures, they may constitute a particularly vulnerable aspect of professional crime. The "fix" appears to be of similar importance to the success of professional criminality.

The Fence

Nearly all professional theft is undertaken with the aim of selling the goods thereafter. Although the thief himself may retail his stolen merchandise,[12] he probably will prefer to sell to a fence. He thereby increases his safety by reducing the risk that he will be arrested with the goods in his possession, or that they will be stolen in turn from him. He also avoids the dangers associated with the disposal process itself. In addition, large quantities of goods which may be perishable or otherwise quickly lose their

---

[12]Most professional shoplifters are thought to bypass fences and sell directly to the public. See Mary B. Cameron, *The Booster and the Snitch* (Glencoe, Ill.: The Free Press, 1964), p. 57. Martin's burglar had considerable experience retailing the goods he had stolen (supra, note 3).

value, or for which there is a specialized demand, will require a division of labor and level of organization beyond the capacity of an individual thief operating as his own retailer. The professional thief thus needs a "middleman" in the same way and for some of the same reasons as the farmer, manufacturer, or other producer.

The types of thefts recorded by the Commission study staff in New York and Chicago suggest the presence of big-time fences who can handle large quantities of specialized goods. For example, in Chicago there recently occurred a cartage theft of $250,000 worth of merchandise and Green Stamps from a Sperry and Hutchinson warehouse and another cartage theft of copper metal valued at over $400,000. To dispose of such quantities of specialized goods requires connections with commercial firms. Most likely a highly accomplished fence served as a middleman between the thieves and the eventual buyers.[13]

As an illustration of the level of efficiency which may be attained by professionals working in cooperation with fences, the Commission's study learned from the New York City police that within the space of approximately 1 month following the recent increase in that city's cigarette sales tax, an entire system for distributing bootlegged cigarettes had been set up and was operating smoothly. The out-of-State suppliers, the truckers, and both the wholesale and retail distributors had been organized, and the system was operating on a scale capable of handling full truckloads of untaxed cigarettes shipped in from the South.

Some fences engage in fencing as a supplement to their legitimate businesses, often on a more or less regular basis. The consultants learned of clothing and appliance dealers who regularly serve as outlets for stolen goods. The major outlets for stolen jewels in one of the cities studied were reported to be legitimate jewelry merchants. Other fences deal primarily or wholly in stolen goods, and are therefore professional criminals themselves.

Some narcotics pushers act as fences, taking stolen goods instead of cash for narcotics. While dealing with addicts is generally regarded as more dangerous than dealing with nonaddicts, it is also more profitable. The addict in need of a "fix" does not bargain well.

Little research has been done on fencing,[14] despite its central role in professional crime. More information is needed about the nature of the market for illicit goods and the extent to which demand for various types of goods affects the incidence of theft. More should also be learned about the relationship of legitimate and illegitimate markets. Little is known about the pattern of distribution of stolen goods. When stolen automobiles are excluded, only a very small proportion of the total amount of goods stolen is returned to its owners. The redistribution of goods through theft and resale might constitute a significant subsidy to certain groups in our society; its curtailment might have significant side effects which should be explored. Finally, it would be desirable to have more information about the organization and operations of large-scale fencing operations, to aid in the development of better methods of law enforcement.

The Loan Shark

The loan shark also performs a key function by providing professional criminals with capital and emergency funds. The literature of professional crime contains few references to loan shark activity. Both Sutherland and Maurer[15] describe a practice whereby members of a professional criminal gang establish their own emergency fund. Each member of the gang contributes an equal share to the fund which he may receive back if he leaves the gang. If he is arrested while working with the gang, he has access to as much of the fund as he needs for a bail bond, legal fees, or related expenses. This sort of arrangement appears to be an extension of the natural interdependence of a closely knit group and tends to reinforce the solidarity of the group.

The loan shark functions quite differently. He

[13]See also John F. Lyons, "Lucrative Looting," *Wall Street Journal*, July 28, 1965, for an analysis of the role played by fences in the theft and distribution of large quantities of mercury and synthetic rubber.

[14]Jerome Hall's report, *op. cit.*, is the only systematic study of fencing published. Sutherland, Maurer, and Martin, however, provide some additional descriptive and analytic material (supra, notes 7, 1, and 3).

[15]Sutherland, *op. cit.*, pp. 31, 35–36, 111; Maurer, *Whiz Mob*, *op. cit.*, pp. 137–38.

may meet professional criminals' needs for cash in emergencies, but his activity often has secondary effects which tend to be detrimental to his clients.

Professional criminals may turn to the loan shark to finance crimes which require extra amounts of capital—to buy the tools, or whatever may be needed for the operation, or to bribe public officials. The professional criminal may be willing to pay usurious interest rates (sometimes reported to be as high as 100 percent per week for highly risky loans) if he expects his activities to be particularly lucrative. He may also need emergency financing when apprehended, to pay bail and legal costs. To repay the money borrowed plus interest upon his release, the criminal will often engage in further criminal activities, often more risky than those he ordinarily undertakes. If rearrested, he must post bond again and incur additional legal fees. This pattern may be repeated a number of times before he is finally brought to trial. The high interest charged by the loan shark may thus itself precipitate criminal activity.

The interaction between loan sharking and professional crime doubtless is far more complicated than was discovered during the course of the Commission's brief study. The study staff was told that some "legitimate" businessmen provide loans to criminals occasionally. And there was some evidence that professional criminals regard loan sharking as a relatively safe and profitable racket, and that those who make a big score or otherwise accumulate enough capital frequently set themselves up as loan sharks. But further study is needed on these as well as other facets of the relationship between professional crime and the loan shark.

The Fix

There is evidence that the professional criminal frequently bribes public officials to increase his security against law enforcement activity.[16] The fix may be applied in advance to forestall intervention by the police and thereby reduce a major occupational hazard of his profession. Or it may be used after the fact to alleviate the usual consequences of apprehension—to obtain reduced charges or a lighter sentence, or to arrange for preferential treatment. In some communities the professional must himself deal directly with the appropriate officials. In others there may be a local "fixer" who has connections with the party in power and who may be tied in with organized crime. Here the professional criminal need only deal with the fixer as a middleman.[17] Maurer reports that in some cities there are several fixers, each handling the fix for a different type of a racket. Specialization attaches even in the world of bribery.

Attorneys, bondsmen, politicians, and other ostensibly legitimate persons may be fixers. A fixer may also be a fence, the insideman in a big con game, or a member of organized crime. Cash is the usual commodity used to purchase immunity, but sometimes a case may be fixed for credit or as a favor.

The extent of fixing today is difficult to document. The Commission's study, which did not focus on this aspect of professional crime, encountered little evidence of the sort of fixing described here. The fact that police, judges, and prosecutors probably are better paid and trained today may mean that individually they are less susceptible to bribery. The increased bureaucratization of police operations and personnel practices may also make policemen less subject to corruption from above. And the decline of the big city political machine may have contributed to a decline in organized fixing. On the other hand, professional criminals still operate with considerable success, and it seems likely that they need some protection to do so.

RELATIONS WITH ORGANIZED CRIME

Professional crime may or may not be carried on in structured groups. In some ways it can be loosely analogized to legitimate business activity. But its essence is not business; it is outright theft or theft-related conduct. Organized crime, on the other hand, tends to bear a closer resemblance to the operations of business. It in-

[16] See generally, Maurer, *The Big Con*, *op. cit.*, pp. 216–51; Sutherland, *op. cit.*, pp. 118, 210–22.

[17] Martin's professional burglar found that: "With the exception of shooting the Mayor or the President, there isn't anything he can't straighten out. For money, lots of money." Martin, *op. cit.*, p. 247. However, it is also reported that "right towns" in which complete immunity can be purchased are becoming increasingly scarce.

volves thousands of criminals working in well-organized, highly structured operations engaged in activities involving the supplying of illegal goods and services—such as gambling, narcotics, and prostitution—to cooperative customers; it often involves infiltration into legitimate businesses and labor unions.

Regrettably, little is known of the nature and extent of the relationship between professional and organized crime. This is hardly surprising given the limited facts known about either activity. But it is apparent that a variety of working arrangements exist between professional criminals and organized crime, which are of substantial significance for both categories of crime. There is some evidence, for example, that the fences and loan sharks with whom professional criminals deal are frequently part of the organized crime operation. And there is some indication that organized crime exerts significant power and control over professional crime. The Commission's study staff was informed, for example, that in Chicago the syndicate occasionally provides the services of an arbitrator to settle disputes among the members of a large theft gang. And the syndicate apparently hires professional criminals, on occasion, to do particular jobs such as homicide. But organized crime may also be victimized by professionals. Martin's professional criminal frequently hijacked syndicate trucks and distilleries.

CONCLUSION

The professional criminal's energy and talents are devoted not merely to committing profitable crimes, but to avoiding the legal consequences of such activity. His methods range from simply taking full advantage of all rights accorded him by the system of criminal justice to actual corruption of the system. It is obvious that sophisticated methods of law enforcement are necessary to deal with the phenomenon of professional crime. A more sophisticated understanding of professional crime is a clear prerequisite.

Present knowledge about professional crime is clearly inadequate. The literature is limited in scope and may be outdated. The Commission's pilot study could obviously do little more than touch on issues deserving of further exploration. But even this brief study gave some indication of the potential that further research has for improved methods of law enforcement.

Some similarities, for example, have been noted between professional crime and ordinary business activity. Further study may lead to the application of the techniques of economic analysis, business and marketing to the problem of diverting and channeling professional criminal activity. More information about the direction of future change in the types of crimes professionals tend to commit would help planners to build crime prevention components into new business devices and law enforcement agencies to allocate their resources more efficiently. Greater concentration on key figures such as the loan shark or fence may provide a greater return per law enforcement dollar and greatly inhibit professional criminal activity. Further research may produce sufficient information to justify allocation of a larger proportion of law enforcement resources to dealing with professional crime.

28.

Robert Louis Gasser

THE CONFIDENCE GAME

Every year in the United States hundreds of thousands of dollars are taken from the victims of confidence schemes. We do not know how many people lose their money through such schemes nor do we have any idea how much money is lost. As a confidence man recently pointed out, there are at least two reasons for this: First, the victim does not realize he has been victimized, and second, his involvement is so direct or his humiliation so great that he fears any disclosure of the scheme.

Another reason for our lack of knowledge about the confidence game is that we do not know much about its nature. The popular conception of what constitutes a confidence game is hazy at best. Even our laws are not much help. Varying jurisdictions show wide variations in the way confidence is defined. Some jurisdictions regard the practice of a particular confidence game a misdemeanor, while others treat the same practice as a felony. Some state laws are specific in defining what constitutes confidence. Other state laws are omnibus regulations, lumping together such practices as fraud, embezzlement, gambling, forgery, and swindling, and designating them as "confidence." It is no wonder, then, that law-enforcement people have widely divergent views about the nature of confidence.

This confusion is perpetuated by newspaper accounts of so-called "confidence schemes" and by dramatic crime stories on radio and TV. Such confusion gives the professional "con folk" considerable advantage in carrying out their schemes.

CONFIDENCE DEFINED

What, then, is the nature of the practice of confidence? What distinguishes it from swindling or other types of fraud?

It is difficult to make a clear distinction between confidence games and other fraudulent practices; they seem to shade gradually into one another. There are, however, criteria which distinguish the practice of confidence from other types of fraud. The controlling factor in all true confidence schemes is the way in which the victim is involved. True confidence games always make use of the avarice and dishonesty of the victim. Their common element is showing the victim how to make money, or gain some other advantage, in a dishonest manner and then taking advantage of his dishonesty. A true confidence game leaves no innocent victim.

The practices of swindling and forgery and the perpetration of various fraudulent schemes which prey upon the victim's innocence, ignorance, or gullibility are not classified as confidence. Such schemes merely seek to cheat someone because of his ignorance or naïvete. Therefore, cheating little old ladies or amorous widows cannot be considered as confidence unless these ladies are led into some scheme they know to be dishonest—a scheme which they believe will help them achieve some gain. They, however, are "taken" themselves. The practice of confidence, then, is the manipulation of the victim through nonviolent methods into a situation of dishonesty in order to take advantage of the victim's dishonesty.

THE VICTIM AS AN ACCOMPLICE

Among the con folk there is a saying, "You can't cheat an honest man." By this they mean an honest man cannot be brought into a true confidence scheme. And, for their part, professional con players make sure the victim is willing to enter into a dishonest scheme. This affords them a de-

Source: *Federal Probation,* Vol. XXVII, No. 4 (December, 1963), pp. 47–54. Reprinted by permission of the journal.

gree of protection and makes the victim a partner in the proceedings.

One professional con man states, "It is hard to con an honest man, but there are so few truly honest men that the so-called con game can be successfully worked on the average person. A professional con man works on the assumption that 99 out of every 100 people are suckers."

Another says, "A thoroughly honest man doesn't expect to receive great profits at little cost."[1]

As pointed out, the victim of a con scheme must have some larceny in his heart. Since he agrees to be a party to a dishonest scheme, he becomes, in effect, the con man's accomplice. His dishonesty is what enables the confidence man to "take him." The confidence man believes he, himself, is no more guilty than his victim.

Nor do many victims consider themselves dishonest. They believe they have entered into a "business proposition," that they are in on the big end of a crooked deal. It is not cheap cynicism to say that a great many victims are worse crooks at heart than the con men.

Some victims do not even realize they have been cheated, for the scheme has been put to them so cleverly that they will attempt to get in on a sure thing again and again.

Even when the victim realizes he has been taken in, it is not often that he is willing to do very much about it. It he does, he will have to admit to the world that he participated in a dishonest scheme designed to cheat someone else but was himself cheated instead. Most victims of confidence schemes are not eager to talk about their experience or prosecute those guilty of "conning" them.

Confidence, then, is quite a different matter from a fraudulent or swindling scheme that cheats an innocent, unsuspecting victim. Most frauds or swindles merely misrepresent; the victim can make a protest with impunity. In a true con scheme, he cannot.

THE GAME ILLUSTRATED

The professional confidence man (or woman) is skilled in selecting his victim. Once he becomes acquainted with the "mark," he decides how best to appeal to his sense of dishonesty. In con parlance this is called "what the mark will go for," and may run the gamut from women to cards, from horses to stocks and bonds. The weakness, or the mark's "go for," is essential to the operation of the well-conducted confidence game for several reasons, not the least of which is control of the mark and limiting the number of players required to bring the game to a successful fruition.

This may be illustrated by the practice of a typical con team which operates successfully in many areas. The team is made up of a con man and his partner who poses as a "small-town" man. The con man elects an affluent victim and determines the most appealing way to bring him into the scheme. After he makes his acquaintance he tells him about the "small-town" man who recently came into a large sum of money. He points out that the "small-town" man is not too smart and suggests they might easily take him for what he's got. If the victim agrees, the con operator sets up a scheme designed to show the victim how the two of them can get the money. If the victim considers himself a good card player, for example, a card game is suggested.

When the three finally come together, the con operator and the "small-town" man act as if they are strangers. Eventually a card game is proposed. By prior arrangement, the con operator tips off the victim on the cards held by the "small-town" man. The "small-town" man loses his money consistently until it appears he has lost nearly all of it. By this time the victim is convinced he and the con operator can win all the money. The operator will make some irritating remark about the "small-town" man's ability as a player. The "small-town" man resents this and agrees to play one more hand. The operator gives the victim a signal which can be interpreted in more than one way. The betting begins to climb. The victim believes he cannot miss—that he and the operator have a good thing going.

With the final bets down, it turns out that the "small-town" man wins the hand, including all the money the victim was willing to bring into the game. The "small-town" man leaves the

[1] Robert L. Gasser, "The Confidence World as a Criminal Behavior System," doctoral dissertation. Washington, D.C.: The American University, 1955, p. 61.

game and the victim accuses the operator of giving him a wrong tip. The operator insists that the victim misread his signal.

This is a crucial moment in the operation of the confidence game. The con operator must be able to "cool the victim out." If he does this well, the victim often does not realize he has been taken, but believes the loss sustained resulted from misunderstanding. This "misunderstanding" is an integral part of all big-con games. Its function is twofold: First, it provides a plausible explanation of what happened; and, second, it is the first step in the "cooling-out" process which is designed to induce the mark not to complain or to prevent him from discovering that he is the victim of a con game. It sometimes happens that, in certain schemes, a victim is "cooled out" so expertly that he will come back time and again to the con man to try to get in on what he considers to be a good thing.

TYPES OF GAMES

Confidence games may be roughly divided into two types: short-con games and big-con games. Short-con games require only a short time to carry out and generally are limited to the amount of money the victim has on his person or can readily produce. Big-con games may take weeks or months to accomplish and usually involve the return of the victim to his home to get a large sum of money. In con parlance inducing the victim to return to his home is most often called "putting the mark on the send" and is always accompanied by the use of "trailers." "Trailers" are persons who follow or trail the mark to his destination to be sure that he gets there and that he does not go to a law-enforcement agency. Another reason for using the trailer is to see that another confidence group does not acquire the mark that the original group is playing for.

Short-confidence games usually require the services of two persons, although occasionally a scheme is used which may be performed by a lone player. The big-con games generally need the abilities of two or more confederates, the victim not included.

The late Edwin H. Sutherland has indicated the lengths to which the professional players will go to bring off a big-con game:

> The real artists in this field frequently spend from two to six months trailing their intended victim. They learn more of his business and family relations than he knows himself. If the sucker is a Mason, the con artists go through the entire course of training in the Masonic rites and are better equipped to discuss the most intimate details with the prospect than would be an authentic member of the order. The same applies, of course, to the Elks or any other organization. The buildup may require months and involves true finesse.[2]

It is possible to subscribe for agency services today that will furnish a con man a report on anyone, with information on his personal history, hobbies, clubs, lodges, habits, moral standards (as far as they are known), and even his mistress' name—all in 2 to 4 weeks. There is no need for today's con man to spend time getting this information on his own.

The artistry of the con man was brought up in a discussion with one of them. This particular operator said that to bring off a game properly, he had to put the right "touches" into it; otherwise, he might lose his "score." He related that he once had a woman ready to enter into a dishonest scheme which involved cheating an exclusive store out of an expensive fur coat. It meant, however, that the woman would have to go to the bank to withdraw her money. She decided not to do this because she was afraid of what her husband might say when he learned of it. The con man felt he had lost his score here, but kept talking to the woman while trying to think of a way to induce her to take her money out of the bank. While talking to her he remembered that he had first met her standing in front of a fur store admiring a coat. He took her to the store so that she might see the coat again. She wanted it so much that she went to the bank, withdrew her money, and gave it to the con man. He pointed out that this was what he meant by putting the right "touches" into the game—sometimes the difference between making a score or losing it.

Putting in the right "touches" is an integral part of the big-con game. It is also known as the

[2]Edwin H. Sutherland, *The Professional Thief* (Chicago: The University of Chicago Press, 1937), n. 15, p. 57.

"switch" or "offing the fly mark." The challenge is to keep the mark off balance and to confuse him if he insists on investigating any part of the game that will not bear severe scrutiny. The term "fly" refers to an alert individual.

The following is the usual chronological sequence of events and the terminology used in big-con games: (1) tying into the mark; (2) telling the mark the tale; (3) initial money gaff; (4) putting the mark on the send; (5) playing the mark against the store; (6) cooling out the mark; and (7) putting the mark in the door.

"Tying into the mark" is the method of meeting the victim. This is usually done through ropers or steerers, or through a purchase from a "moniker" file. A "moniker" file is a name file, usually supplied by other confidence men or, more often, by upright citizens who "sell" their friends to the con man for a stipulated price.

"Telling the mark the tale" is outlining the proposition to the victim, or explaining the scheme for the mark's benefit.

"Initial money gaff" is inducing the mark to give the confidence man an initial small amount of money. This money is used to involve the mark in the scheme.

"Putting the mark on the send" is sending the victim to the source of his funds.

"Playing the mark against the store" is actually taking off the score or relieving the mark of his money.

"Cooling out the mark" means preventing the mark from complaining to the law or even from realizing that he has been conned.

"Putting the mark in the door" refers to inducing the mark to leave; usually he is reluctant to do so.

SOME RULES OF THE GAME

Among con people there is a feeling that no one can really understand the con world unless he lives in it. Con men are amused at those who write of their own experiences and are not at all concerned about this, because only very little of the game and the feeling for it ever get into print. The games are never played in the same way more than once, because in each game the players improvise according to the situation at hand. This is why, when a con man writes about his experiences, there is no real revelation regarding the game.

Whenever possible, the con man will avoid the use of violence in carrying out a scheme, even if it means losing a score. It is generally felt that violence is beneath the dignity of the professional. It does occur, occasionally, but is as an exception rather than a general practice. Bodily harm may be done to the victim under certain circumstances. For example, if he attempts to run off with the initial winnings gained with money supplied by the con men themselves, or if he attempts to call in the police. As a rule, however, violence is rare in con games.

The con man's attitude is summed up in the words of one experienced operator: "Con is a game; if you lost, be a good sport and give the sucker a break. Let him go. You can't make all the money that you see . . . ."[3]

THE CON TEAM

In most con schemes, there are two essential operators. These players are called by various names, such as "outside-man" and "inside-man," "roper" or "steerer" and "spieler," "catchman" and "lickman," or any of a number of other designations. Each has his specific role to play.

The function of the outside-man, or roper, usually is to put a likely victim in touch with the inside-man, or spieler. The latter player then takes over the game and carries out the scheme. Some operators prefer, or are better equipped, to play one part than the other. Sometimes their talent for their special part in a game falls little short of genius. In short-con games, the roles are usually determined by which operator brings the mark into play; and, therefore, the outside-man and inside-man often change places from game to game. Though many con men can play either part well, especially in short-con games, it is rare for men to exchange roles with other members in a big-con game, in which more specialization is the rule.

Short-con groups seldom have bosses, in the normal sense of the word. However, it sometimes happens that the experienced man might take

[3] Gasser, *op. cit.*, p. 136.

charge of a game if one of the partners is weak in his role. The general consensus among these men is that the players work as a team, each having a particular role to play in attaining a common goal in which each will share equally in the gain, or according to the conditions of the particular game.

In the big-con games, the director or operator of the game is usually the man controlling the "store." Most confidence games of the big-con variety involve the use of rather elaborate props, such as a make-believe Western Union office, a false securities office, or a phony "betting establishment." Since such establishments require a degree of permanence or immobility, the same location is sometimes used for several types of establishments. Usually the owner of the "store" runs the game, or at least supplies the major direction of it. He also supplies "shills," or people who pretend to perform certain roles, such as clerks or bettors, so as to make the "store" appear genuine. "Playing the mark against the store" stems from such activities.

THE CODE WITHIN THE GROUP

Con men usually conceal their techniques from other con men who are not their partners or who are not within their own circle. There is a rule within professional con that prohibits the revelation of techniques to anyone. The con man must keep himself and his ideas secret. When he meets someone who knows how to keep things to himself, the con man might teach him some part of the game. If things go right, he is taught more, until he learns the ropes. After that, he must develop on his own.

There are reports that con men sometimes fleece other con men, but this does not happen frequently. The term used to denote a person who will stoop to this is "a niner." A common expression is "He'd nine ya' in a minute." Sanctions are invoked in such instances. However, as is the case in most other aspects of the confidence game operation, violence is avoided, so that these sanctions are largely economic in nature. The perpetrator is simply unable to secure the assistance of other operators or to find a "store" which will accept his play. The point here is that, if they value their reputations in the profession, con men are careful not to cheat their partners.

One con man has said that if a man were to cheat his partner, he could be killed for it. He himself follows the practice, when dividing a score with a partner, of seeing to it that his partner always receives a greater share than he takes for himself, even if it is only a few dollars. For him this is a safety device, as it is unlikely that his partner will be dissatisfied with his cut. This, he reported, is just his own way of doing things, because "there is always more to be taken from the suckers anyway, and why be greedy."

Generally, however, the score is divided evenly between the partners after the expenses of the operation have been met. It is important for a man in con to act honestly toward his partner because, if he does not, no one will want to work with him, and he may eventually be forced out of the group.

Con folk often go to the aid of each other in times of need. One old con man states that the esprit de corps is not what it was in years past, though. In the old days, he says, when a con man took a fall (was convicted of a criminal offense), his friends would get together at a party, or through solicitation, to contribute money to be used in meeting the con man's needs while in jail or prison and in trying to get him out. His closest friend would be given the money, and he would see to it that it got to the right places. It was not necessary that the con man pay this money back when he was released from prison, for in many cases he might not know all who had contributed to the fund or the amounts each gave. However, he would be expected to contribute to the needs of the next fellow who found himself in distress. Today, this man claims, such aid is not so frequently given because, as he puts it, "There are too many young fellows in the game who have no professional ethics."

Another old con man reports that this type of mutual assistance is still widely given today. He says that he himself has made many such contributions for the benefit of others and that, furthermore, he has even come out of "retirement" on several occasions to give another man "a day's work" to help put that man back on his feet financially.

COMMUNICATION WITHIN THE GROUP

Jargon is often used to identify con men among themselves, but it is never used if a potential victim is present. A true con man can be readily determined by the way he speaks and acts in the company of other professionals. There is some indication that signs are frequently used by con men among themselves. These signs convey certain meanings, such as warnings of impending danger; they are made in an inconspicuous manner and are understood only by the initiated.

Professional con men appear to be widely acquainted with other con men and make it their business to know who the operators are around the country. They know each other personally or by reputation and are able to meet operators in a strange town in various ways. Furthermore, many con men know who the professionals are in other countries. A professional knows where to inquire about anyone with whom he would like to make contact.

CON MEN AND THE UNDERWORLD

In the underworld the con men consider themselves as the elite; and they are, in turn, accorded this status by the underworld in general.

While con men seem to hold themselves aloof from the rest of the underworld, they often use the services of other underworld specialists. Gamblers sometimes give aid to con men, as do forgers or other operators having special talents. For a price, a con man can always get expert help.

David Maurer, a student of the language of the underworld, writes: "Some professional gamblers, often those employed by reputable gambling houses, double as confidence men during either short-con or big-con touches, which are laid in the gambling house either with or without the knowledge of the management."[4]

"Yellow Kid" Weil, a widely known con man, has written in great detail of using the services of an engraver to bring off many of his schemes. One of his lucrative ventures involved the doctoring of two hundred copies of a Sunday issue of *The Washington Post* so that a picture of the "Yellow Kid," his partner, Buckminster, and the German Ambassador to the United States, Franz von Papen, and an article concerning them, appeared on the front page. This was so cleverly done that no one but an expert would have been able to detect the fraud.

CON MEN AND THE LAW

Con teams sometimes have working agreements with the police. One con man, in discussing his relations with law-enforcement officers, reports that there are many cities and towns in the United States in which he is permitted to operate by the local officers for a fee so long as he does not trim the local residents. He reports, moreover, that in some cities he has been assigned by members of the police department a particular area in which to work. At times these arrangements are made directly with the police, but usually they are made through a lawyer or a person of influence in the town. Such arrangements may even include the removal of the con man's photo from the rogues' gallery.

It should be noted that the "fix" is not limited to the fixing of local law-enforcement officers. While this is very often the case, i.e., operating in an area in which "the clout is in," or what is also referred to as a "juice town," this is by no means the extent of fixing. The pay-off to police officers is minor compared to the expenses of bail bonds-men, attorneys, and, most important, newspaper reporters. Much of the confidence man's time is spent in determining what he will do when he is caught. Perhaps his most valuable ally is the newspaper reporter since the way the reporter writes his story will, unfortunately, influence public opinion.

Con men believe it is generally easier to set up a fix in foreign cities than it is in the United States. However, there is no such thing as an "air-tight" fix anywhere. The percentage paid for the fix varies according to the place and the situation. A fix usually goes bad because there is a leak somewhere. This generally happens when someone is dissatisfied with his cut.

---

[4]David W. Maurer, "The Argot of the Dice Gambler," *The Annals of the American Academy of Political and Social Science,* Vol. 269 (1950), p. 116.

Con men indicate that there are many in the con game who have felony conviction records for crimes other than con activity. Many times this is because, as previously pointed out, states are not uniform in their laws as to what constitutes confidence. There is a strong feeling among the con folk that, once a man is convicted of con activity, his conviction record from that point on is usually for this offense only.

While some professionals go through an entire life of con activity without going to prison, these appear to be the exception rather than the rule. Many serve short prison terms. But most of them have at least one long term, which is nearly always brought about by violating the postal regulations.

WHAT MAKES A CON MAN?

Con players come from all walks of life and may enter the practice at almost any age. They may come from any legitimate profession, provided they get to know a con man who will teach them the ropes. Their techniques are developed by apprenticeship training gained through association with professionals already operating. It is rare indeed for a man to become a professional in con by reading about it.

Very often, it appears, con men are recruited in prison. When a man gets into a discussion with a con man in jail or prison, he may indicate his interest in the game. The two men will talk of mutual acquaintances and, in time, become friendly. If the recruit is liked and found to be able to keep information to himself, he may be told something about the operation of the various games. When he gets out of prison, he may be given a small part to play in a game by a con man. If he does well, he may then be given other parts until he really learns the game.

In general, however, recruiting may go on anywhere; but it occurs only when the recruit gets to know someone who is already in the profession. Con men are probably more frequently recruited from the ranks of persons in closely allied rackets—among pickpockets or professional gamblers, for example—than from legitimate society. Usually the recruits begin in short-con games; then the most talented move up into the big-con operations. It is working in the short-con games that enables the confidence man to acquire the poise and polish necessary to bring off the big-con games. Some professional gamblers, because of their experience and ability, are able to operate almost immediately as outside-men in big-con games.

It is rare that con men train their own children in the game. Those who have children usually want something better than this type of activity for them.

Men with college educations are often found in professional con. One young man recently observed that there are many men in con activity who have attended college, but few who ever got through. However, con folk seem to agree that formal education is not necessary to con activity. Some feel it is not really necessary even to be able to read or write, but only to be specious; other feel that, while a formal education is not necessary, it helps one to put the right touches into his game.

For those engaged in it, con is a way of life, with traditions, codes of behavior based on recognized values and beliefs, and a system of techniques known only to the initiated. Con men believe that not just anyone can become a professional, but that this takes rigorous training and experience. They feel, too, that, once a person possesses the necessary skill in con, he never need worry again about having enough money.

In the con world it appears than one of the things that distinguishes a professional is his ability to move from team to team and to work effectively with all of them. The professional con man is always able to "fill in" in any team or group. In this way he is able to make more money and thus to enhance his professional standing within the group.

The confidence man engages in "fill-in" activity regularly. This might be compared to the salary portion of a salary-plus-commission job in normal, legitimate employment situations. The con man uses his "fill-in" assignments to carry him between scores.

Income is always important to a con man's professional standing; for often, among the con folk as in the legitimate professions, income is an indication of a person's ability. A man's standing in the profession really depends upon several factors, however: his income, his ability, acting like a gentleman, and, above all, how well he "goes along with the system."

For a professional con man to be successful, he must have what the con folk refer to as "larceny sense." Commenting on this, one con man said that con is a business, like any other business, and that, if a man works at it and develops himself, he will be successful. In con, a man thinks in a certain way, a way geared to making money in terms of the methods he knows, just as a legitimate businessman thinks in terms of making money by methods that are familiar to him. Each must have a "feel" for the possibilities of making money in every situation as it presents itself. For the con man, this is larceny sense; for the businessman, it is business sense. Actually, the con man doesn't see too much difference between his activities and those of other people. As another of them said, ". . . think back in your life and see if there is not one time or the other that you have not played con. It does not have to have been for money; it could have been for power. I don't think that there is a person that has not given someone some part of the game at one time or the other. . . ."[5]

PERSONAL LIFE OF THE CON MAN

While entrance into con may come at almost any age, it is rare for a man to become a professional in con before age 25. Some con men feel that a person has not had enough of life's experiences to become a professional in con as early as this.

It frequently happens that men remain active in con after age 60. Con men believe that the only things to prevent an old con man from active participation are losing his sight or losing his mind. About all that advancing age does to the con man is prevent him from traveling around as much as he once did, in which case he usually plays the inside-man for a roper or group of ropers who travel.

Some con folk maintain permanent places of residence, but this seems to depend upon methods of operation and the type of game involved. Most young con men, 25 to 30 years old, do not have permanent places of residence because this seems to hamper their work. They travel constantly and rely on "drops" to enable other con men to locate them. This is particularly true of men operating as ropers or locators of marks.

The older con men do maintain homes. Indeed, they must, for appearance's sake, when not engaged in the game itself, be above reproach! These older operators attempt to assume the role of Mr. Slightly-Above-Average-Citizen. One young con man reports that he has been a guest in the homes of con men, and that they generally put large amounts of money into their homes. When they have permanent homes, though, they usually do not operate in the city in which their home is located. It seems that the older a man is and the better established he is in the profession, the greater the likelihood that he will have a permanent place of residence.

When a con man decides to retire from activity, he generally does so for his own reasons, and is not generally looked down upon by others in the profession for doing so. Some men make enough money to set themselves up in a business; others become weary of trying to avoid detection and give up the practice; a few marry into wealth, save their money, or invest carefully and retire to a life of comfort.

Some con men believe that con folk never really retire. Many regard their ability at con as a gift that will always keep them supplied with money to meet their needs. Others regard the life work of any con man to be avoiding detection, and this is so complicated that it overshadows the actual technical practice of the profession. Many cannot stand the uncertainty, the possibility of being exposed, or the threat of confinement that constantly hangs over them; so they go into more legitimate kinds of activity.

RETROSPECT AND PROSPECT

Confidence games appear to be as old as recorded history. The earliest descriptions of the structure of the confidence system shows it to be

[5]Gasser, *op. cit.*, p. 142.

substantially the same as it is today; about all that differs is the name given to each position in the scheme. As we look back through history, it becomes apparent that, for more than 400 years, the art of confidence has had a continuing structure, organization, and tradition. This art seems to have been handed down from generation to generation, for it operates today in precisely the same way as it did in the 16th century, and with some of its argot surviving even to our day. In short, it has been a subculture in Western society.

If confidence operations are to be controlled, they must be more clearly understood by the public and the law. For, so long as people are eager to get something for nothing, so long as they are greedy or dishonest—willing to cheat others to gain an advantage—and so long as confidence is ill defined, confidence men will continue to flourish. Legislating against the inherent dishonesty of the victim is probably the only way in which the practice of con can be reduced, but such legislation would appear to be a difficult, if not an impossible, proposition.

29.

JULIAN B. ROEBUCK AND RONALD C. JOHNSON

THE "SHORT-CON" MAN

Though they do not always agree on his etiology, sociologists and psychologists generally consider the confidence man to be a professional criminal who has high prestige in the underworld.[1] Confidence men are described in the literature as smooth, adroit, convincing talkers who live by their wits and their ability to manipulate people. Their criminal activity, a form of "grift," is nonviolent. Victims give their money or property to con men voluntarily because of the confidence they place in them and their own desire to get something for nothing. The con man, in short, plays upon the gullibility and the latent larceny of his victim, who is generally willing to engage in an illegal act for profit. In Sutherland's *The Professional Thief,* Chic Conwell, the title's namesake, comments on the successful confidence man as follows:

> Not all persons can be good con men. They generally must have a winning personality, shrewdness, agility, like the good things of life, and be too lazy to work for them, and have great egotism. They must, first of all, be good actors. The whole con game is a matter of acting. . . . A confidence man must live by his wits.[2]

The elaborateness of the build-up, the period of time spent in "setting up" the victim and "trimming" him, the number of confidence operators involved in the swindle, and the amount of money taken from the victim determine whether a given confidence game or trick falls

SOURCE: *Crime and Delinquency,* Vol. 10, No. 3 (July, 1964), pp. 235–48. Reprinted by permission of the journal.

[1]H. A. Bloch and G. Geis, *Man, Crime, and Society* (New York: Random House, 1962), pp. 199–202; D. W. Mauer, *The Big Con: The Story of the Confidence Man and the Confidence Game* (Indianapolis: Bobbs-Merrill, 1940), p. 201; E. M. Schur, "Sociological Analysis of Confidence Swindling," *Journal of Criminal Law, Criminology and Police Science,* September-October, 1948, pp. 296–304; R. L. Jenkins, *Breaking Patterns of Defeat—The Effective Readjustment of the Sick Personality* (Philadelphia: J. B. Lippincott, 1954), pp. 148–58; E. Podalsky, "The Swindler: A Fascinating Sociopath," *Pakistan Medical Journal,* October, 1957, pp. 1–4; W. Bromberg and S. Keiser, "The Psychology of the Swindler," *American Journal of Psychiatry,* May, 1938, pp. 1441–58; W. C. Reckless, *The Crime Problem* (3rd ed., New York: Appleton-Century-Crofts, 1961), pp. 174–77.

[2]E. H. Sutherland (ed.), *The Professional Thief* (Chicago: University of Chicago Press, 1937), p. 3.

into the category of "big con" (sometimes called "long con") or "short con."[3] The "big-con" game includes numerous accomplices and props. Through pre-arranged stages, several operators (each one assuming a specific post) work at luring the victim into getting all the money he possesses or can command to put into a transaction they have devised. The proper build-up and subsequent "trimming" in the big-con game require weeks of planning and at least four contact positions. First in line is the "steerer" or "roper," an operator who selects the victim, introduces him to the scheme, and leads him to the second contact, the "buildup man." The latter gradually sounds out the victim regarding his resources, funds, and gullibility. The third contact stimulates his confidence. When the victim is ripe, the fourth contact relieves him of his money and "shakes him off." Together the contacts form an apparently casual chain of occurrences, but each gives some signal for an operator to appear and take his part in the conspiracy.[4] Often the victim of the big con is "cooled off" rather than "shaken off" in order to prevent him from making a complaint to the police. In the "shake off" the con man reminds the victim that if he reports the swindle he may also go to jail because of his own participation in an illegal act. He reminds him, in addition, that short of a jail sentence, the victim risks exposure, ridicule, and contempt from his friends and the police if he reports his loss. In the "cooling off" process, the con operator does not force the victim to realize he was just another "easy mark"; rather, he consoles him and attempts to redeem the ruse in a way that will make it easier for the victim to accept the inevitable and retain his self-respect. Cooling off represents a process of adjusting the victim to an impossible situation.[5]

Short-con games require fewer actors and props, less preparation, and less finesse and originality. They are geared toward smaller "scores" than the big-con games and the "take" is usually limited to the amount of money the mark has in his possession at the time. The method of operation is much quicker than in the big-con game; the operator must "hook the sucker and get rid of him fast." The short-con man usually works for brief periods in various cities, striking a location suddenly and then moving quickly in order to avoid contacts with his victim and the police.[6]

According to Maurer's researches, most of the long-con operators have been recruited from the short-con men. They entered the confidence game when young and had the benefit of early training from skilled operators.[7] Confidence men may be placed along a continuum ranging from the unsuccessful, bungling, frequently arrested short-con man (flimflammer), whose modus operandi is dated and pitched at a low level, to the highly successful, accomplished big-con man who is infrequently arrested and whose modus operandi is original and pitched at a high level.

While the highly successful long con, such as "Yellow Kid" Weil, has been dealt with in the literature,[8] little is known about the short cons, the smaller operators who work in every big city and probably make up the largest group of confidence men found in correctional institutions.[9] Maurer claims that not many long-con men are caught, very few are brought to trial, fewer are convicted, and fewer still ever serve time in a prison.[10]

This paper consists of a description of ten Negro short-con men who were part of a larger

[3]J. C. R. MacDonald, *Crime Is a Business: Buncos, Rackets, Confidence Schemes* (Stanford, Calif.: Stanford University Press, 1938), pp. 1–10. See also H. Soderman and J. J. O'Connell, *Modern Criminal Investigation* (New York: Funk and Wagnalls, 1951), pp. 380–88.

[4]For an overview of the *modus operandi* used in various con games, see: W. Dienstein, *Techniques for Crime Investigation* (Springfield, Ill.: Charles C Thomas, 1956), pp. 70–80; and C. E. O'Hara, *Fundamentals of Criminal Investigation* (Springfield, Ill.: Charles C Thomas, 1956), pp. 290–94.

[5]E. Goffman, "On Cooling the Mark Out: Some Aspects of Adaptation to Failure," *Psychiatry*, November, 1952, pp. 451–63. Also on cooling off the mark, see M. J. Fitzgerald, *Handbook of Criminal Investigation* (New York: Greenberg Publishers, 1951), pp. 173–90.

[6]MacDonald, *op. cit.*, pp. 2–3.

[7]Maurer, *op. cit.*, pp. 175–78.

[8]J. R. Weil and W. T. Brannon, *"Yellow Kid" Weil* (Chicago: Ziff-Davis, 1948).

[9]J. T. Barbash, "Compensation and the Crime of Pigeon Dropping," *Journal of Clinical Psychology*, October, 1951, pp. 92–94, reports a study of 25 "short-con" offenders in the Eastern State Penitentiary, Pennsylvania. He hypothesized an etiology based on compensation for feelings of inferiority.

[10]Maurer, *op. cit.*, p. 15.

sample of 400 offenders interviewed and tested at the District of Columbia Reformatory (actually a penitentiary) at Lorton, Va.[11] The 400 male prisoners were divided into offender types according to arrest history.[12] It was hypothesized that specific patterns of criminality result from rather specific sets of social and psychological background factors and that the background factors common to a particular pattern of criminality would be found to vary significantly from those common to other offender types. This appears to be the case.[13]

Previous comparisons of offender types involved statistical, quantitative measures.[14] So long as the frequency of offenders in any cell of the expected distribution is at least five, the background of the sample of 10 confidence men could be compared with that of the 390 other offenders by using such techniques as Chi Square. It was impossible to fulfill this requirement. Therefore, the description of these con men in comparison with other offenders is necessarily qualitative rather than quantitative.

CHARACTERISTICS OF THE CON MEN

The ten con men shared a number of characteristics.[15] They were of average ability (mean I.Q. 100) as compared with the general population and were considerably superior to the mean score of the remainder of the offender group (mean I.Q. 85). They had a median grade level of 6.4 on the Stanford Achievement Test, as compared with the 5.2 grade level of the remainder of the sample. They were older men, aged 30 and over (mean age 38), as compared with the remainder of the sample (mean age 30.4). At least eight of the ten were reared in slums in metropolitan areas (population 500,000 and over) and came from homes that were demoralized, criminalistic, in continuous conflict, dominated by the mother, or on relief. Not one was reared in a rural area. Their criminal tutelage started early. All had delinquent companions before age ten, and eight belonged, in a loose sort of way, to delinquent gangs. All had police contacts, and eight had criminal companions before reaching eighteen years of age. The major difference between the delinquencies of this group and those of most of the offenders in the rest of the sample was the avoidance of violence. The con men had not been involved in fighting at home, at school, or with neighborhood peer groups. They did not destroy property and did not participate in mugging or purse snatching. None carried weapons. Loitering on the street, gambling, running away from home, truancy, and petty sneak thefts from school lockers, stores, playgrounds, and private homes constituted their delinquency pattern in the community.

Probably the most significant factor in the development of these men was their early reliance, from four to eight years of age, on deceit as a major tool of life. As we shall soon see, their early childhood experiences approved and

[11] J. Roebuck, "A Tentative Criminal Typology of 400 Negro Felons," an unpublished study conducted in 1958 for the Institute for Criminological Research, District of Columbia Department of Corrections, Washington, D.C.

[12] An analysis of the configuration of each offender's total known arrests by criminal charge made it possible to assign individual offenders to criminal-pattern categories. The most frequent charge or charges in the inmates' arrest history were used as a basis for classification, and the charges appearing in the latter phases of the inmates' arrest history were given greater weight. For a complete description of the thirteen criminal pattern categories found, see Roebuck and Johnson, "The Negro Drinker and Assaulter as a Criminal Type," *Crime and Delinquency*, January, 1962, pp. 21–33.

[13] See J. Roebuck and M. L. Cadwallader, "The Negro Armed Robber as a Criminal Type: The Construction and Application of a Typology," *Pacific Sociological Review*, Spring, 1961, pp. 21–26; Roebuck and Johnson, "The Jack-of-All-Trades Offender," *Crime and Delinquency*, April, 1962, pp. 172–81; Roebuck, "The Drug Addict as an Offender Type," *The Journal of Criminal Law, Criminology and Police Science*, March, 1962, pp. 36–43.

[14] Eight of the 13 criminal pattern categories had enough cases for statistical comparison. Each of these eight, then, was compared with the remainder of the entire sample and with each of the remaining seven criminal patterns.

[15] In order to be included in the confidence game criminal category, the men had to have the following arrest record: four arrests throughout the arrest history had to be on confidence game charges; 33 per cent of all charges occurring in the last two-thirds of the arrest history had to be confidence game charges; at least one confidence game charge had to appear in the last third of the arrest history. The arrest histories of all of these 10 men demonstrated a clear-cut pattern of confidence game charges; in each case, the frequency of arrest for confidence game charges exceeded the minimum criteria employed.

rewarded deceit and made the practice of deception necessary.[16] The early necessity for and the practice, support, and reward of deceit were found much less frequently in the case histories of the remainder of the sample. When the 390 cases were broken down for comparison into twelve criminal pattern groups the findings were the same; i.e., the con men had a higher incidence of childhood training in deceit than any single subgroup.

Coupled with this early practice of deceit was the dictum that violence doesn't pay. Conflicts between the parents, between parents and children, and between brothers and sisters rarely resulted in physical violence as they did in the homes of most of the other cases (with the exception of 16 numbers men and 50 drug addicts) in the sample from which the con men were drawn.

Three of the men were reared in homes where, when their passive fathers were absent, the mothers would entertain paramours for money. In return for keeping these love affairs secret from the father, the sons would receive money or favors from the mothers, such as protection from truant officers or phony sick excuses to school administrators. To teachers visiting the home the mothers gave glowing and erroneous reports about their sons' accomplishments.

In three cases the mothers were small-time bootleggers who sold to clients in need of whiskey during hours when the liquor stores were closed. Their sons recruited buyers from the street and at times helped the mothers hide the liquor prior to a police raid. Occasionally, the police would interrogate them along with their mothers, and in the process they learned to lie and feign innocence early in life. In two of these three cases, the mothers also intermittently operated a poker game and the sons would serve drinks to the customers and help their mothers "cut the pot." As one of the two men commented:

I learned early that it was not always the man who held the best cards who won the pot. It was the man who could cheat and bluff . . . or the one who was in with my mother and could catch her signs fast enough to stay put, raise, or fold. Callers went to bed early in my house. Of course Mother didn't play. She just ran the game. She moved around and knew what everybody had. I never seen a successful gambler who was honest. She didn't allow no rough stuff either. She always told me the easy way is the best. Use your head. Any fool could fight—any fool could get bread with a gun. And get busted too.

In one of the cases the mother was a check passer and a shoplifter, and her son would accompany her in some of her illegal activities:

I learned from my mother that a good front and how you carry yourself is the main thing with the marks. She'd buy $10 worth of groceries and while I held them walk up to the man and give him a rubber check for $50. She talked fast, smooth, and bold. You know—like she had a million. Of course she always dressed the part. She had such a way about her that the clerks in stores where she stole dresses were afraid to question her though they had a good idea she had their "rags" under her coat. She always said, "Son, if you get in the life [life in the underworld] get a soft hustle. No rough stuff."

In two cases a pattern of stealing, lying, and disobedience at home and at school was evident at age eight. The dominant mothers in both cases were in conflict with their husbands and reacted to their son's behavior in a hostile fashion, frequently threatening corporal punishment. The two fathers, on the other hand, made light of the boys' behavior and repeatedly made restitution for their sons. In their talks with their sons' wives, teachers, school officials, and probation officers, the fathers evinced an unrealistic, overprotective attitude. They were unable or unwilling to set limits for their sons' behavior.

In the remaining case the mother was known in the community as the "root woman." She removed warts and treated headaches, rheumatism, and other somatic ills with magic words and the use of herbs. With the help of her son she also made sacred candles that were supposed to insure health and happiness in the homes in which they were lighted.

Not one of these ten men closed on pimping, bootlegging, gambling, check passing, shoplift-

[16]Jenkins, *op. cit.*, cites grift as an example of motivation behavior of a highly adaptive sort. He theorized that early childhood experiences which make deceit necessary and reward it make for a "budding grifter." Although he used illustrative cases of children whom he considered "budding grifters," he did not research the childhood experiences of known con men. The case histories of the 10 men under study definitely support his thesis.

ing, or fake healing as a criminal career. What they learned in childhood was not so much a set of criminal techniques but rather a principle —the principle of deceit and nonviolence.

COMPARISON WITH THE NUMBERS MAN

Though there were differences, the criminal offenses of the con men were most similar to the offenses of those involved in the numbers racket; both types of crime were nonviolent and required planning and organizational talent.[17] Despite other ostensible similarities—their high mental ability as compared with most other offenders under study and their distaste for violence—the numbers men and the con men were remarkably different in background and personality type. While the con men were upwardly mobile persons from slum environments who identified themselves with the underworld, the numbers men, despite their illegal activities, were products of, and identified with, the Negro middle class. Since the numbers game is condoned by many members of all classes in the Negro community, and con games are not, the numbers man may hold some claim to and gain some rewards of middle-class membership, while the con man is judged a criminal and lives a marginal existence. The numbers man was found to be a well-integrated personality, whereas the con man approximated the sociopath.[18] Thus, despite a certain similarity in the offenses of the con men and numbers men, quite different factors entered into their development and the consequences (in terms of influence on the life styles of the offenders) of these two varieties of offense were equally disparate.

The con men were most similar in social background to the least specialized and least competent of all groups, the "Jack-of-all-trades offender," in that both were products of the slums and were reared in economically and emotionally deprived homes.[19] The early practice of deceit, however, was not a factor in the developmental histories of the "Jack-of-all-trades offender." As a result of their deceitfulness, verbal ability, intelligence, egocentricity, nonviolence, and fastidiousness in dress as well as their "fast-buck," something-for-nothing approach to life, the con men managed to work their way up in the criminal hierarchy despite their poor backgrounds.[20] Their philosophy of life, as summed up by one of the ten con men, is as follows:

> There's a mark born every minute and a con man every hour. The con man is born to take care of the marks. Of course, I am a con man. There really are only two classes of people—marks and con men. I decided early in life that the angle boy gets the worm. I didn't make the rules. I just try to live by them. I'd rather be a con man than a mark.

Throughout their lives they were talkers, not fighters, and neatness ranked high among their values:

> I was no fighter, man. Heroes are stupid people —they are really marks. A smart stud gets what he wants without fighting. All you got to do is know what to say out of your month. I didn't want to get myself messed up. I wanted to be neat all the time. In my line of work you got to have front. You know, dress well. Of course, I always liked nice clothes anyway. I wore the best. You know, Bannister shoes at forty dollars a throw, twenty-dollar sport shirts, and silk suits if I could afford. You know, I wanted to go first class.

FINDING A "NICHE"

A well-dressed young man with a ready tongue, fair intelligence, and an aversion to foolish fighting might be expected to find a niche in society. These con men began seeking their

---

[17]See Roebuck, "The Negro Numbers Man as an Offender Type," *Journal of Criminal Law, Criminology and Police Science* (Vol. 54, No. 1, March, 1963, pp. 48–60), in which a group of 16 highly successful professional criminals is analyzed. This group of offenders constituted a part of the larger study of 400 Negro felons.

[18]An inspection of the Minnesota Multiphasic Personality Inventory profiles for the group of numbers men revealed no more deviation than one would find among profiles constituting the norm group.

[19]See Roebuck and Johnson, *op. cit.*, in which 71 criminals with long arrest histories that revealed no pattern or concentration on a specific variety of crime were analyzed. These offenders made up a marginal group of unsuccessful, frequently arrested, and frequently incarcerated habitual criminals.

[20]It has been established that different social types follow distinct patterns of crime. See E. M. Lemert, "An Isolation and Closure Theory of Naive Check Forgery," *Journal of Criminal Law, Criminology and Police Science,* September-October, 1953, pp. 296–307.

niches early in life. By the age of eight, each of them had begun a long career of running away. When they ran, they ran far, hitching rides up and down the Eastern seaboard, covering all of the Northeast coast while still in their teens. While on these expeditions, each of the offenders found his mentor, an experienced con man looking for an apprentice. A teamwork approach is required in most games rigged to con a mark. One man sets up the mark and the other "knocks him off." Thus, the experienced con man is benefited by having a bright young apprentice who is not in the position to demand an equal division of the loot. The apprentice is benefited by learning a trade that requires no hard work, can be profitable, is reasonably safe, and is never short of customers. The following typical remarks of one con man probably indicate the mechanism and criteria for recruitment into the racket:

> Well, when I traveled around the country from one big city to another I was always on the make for an easy dollar. I always dressed nice even if I didn't have enough to eat. I hustled alone at first—you know, at pool. Sometimes I pretended to be a pimp and collected a few bucks from guys dumb enough to give me money for broads they never saw. But I was on the look for some better con. I knew I was young. I had to learn from some smarter operator. You never learn nothing from hustlers at your own level. Well, if you act and talk right you get to meet pretty good con men who need a partner. You see con men go in pairs, two or more. They bust up now and then and get themselves new partners. That's the way I met Diamond Tooth Slim. His partner was busted and in the joint doing a bit. Slim needed himself a boy. I bumped into him at a quiet bar. We talked over a few toddies spread over a few days. He was sizing me up and I was sizing him up. We made a deal for the "high dice" game. Of course I didn't get much of a cut at first, but I was willing to write that off to learn. All those who get the call to be a con man don't get picked. Slim told me later he nearly passed me by, because he thought I talked a little too much at first. You know, I tried too hard to impress him. He thought I was a little bit of a Willie [country boy] who didn't know what was happening. It's not enough to have larceny in your heart. All people have that. You got to have the smooth, cool touch. And you got to be able to smell a mark.

And so each of the ten offenders entered an apprenticeship with an older con man, and after they learned their tutor's techniques, they moved out on their own:

> Well, I was doing O.K. with Long John, but then I got the urge to move on. I wanted to go a little faster and get some prestige for myself. After all, he was taking most of the big end of the string and I wanted to make my own money. He wasn't going to pull my coat any further than he would his own.

These men were not marked successes at their vocation. Even so, their reference group consisted only of con men. They had broken home ties early, were wanderers who had developed no permanent relationship with women, and had few if any close friends. They were acquainted with many other con men since, as noted above, many con games require cooperative efforts. Their favorite term for anyone who acted impulsively or who employed violence in the pursuit of money was "fool." All con men respect one another as not being fools. To be "smart" is to have a "rep" as an ingenious con man who has made much money and suffered few busts (arrests). Much jockeying for position occurred within the group as each told anecdotes of previous victories aimed at "putting down" his rivals and showing himself off as "smart." The true criterion of success was money, and all else was forgiven the "money man."

During the interviews they rationalized that their brand of criminal activity was acceptable behavior in this "dog-eat-dog society," but they were quick to criticize other types of criminal behavior as reprehensible:

> You know how it goes in this dog-eat-dog world. You got to take the other guy before he takes you. You know, the real sharpie outwits the marks. Of course, it all depends on how you get ahead. My way was no different from, say, a lawyer or businessman. You know, a lawyer has a license to steal. The cops should lay off con men. We don't hurt nobody. You can't con an honest man. The mark has more larceny in his heart than we do. The cops should do their job and clear the streets of the muggers, heist men, hop heads, and the rest. Why, it's dangerous for a decent man like me to walk down the street at night.

THE CON GAMES

Here are some of the more common games

used by these offenders in conning "marks":

High Dice

High Dice is a game based on the mark's desire to be recognized as an important person in his community, a man to whom others will look for advice and help. This bunko requires two operators.

A well-dressed and friendly stranger appears at a station prior to the arrival of an incoming train from the South. He selects as his victim a well-dressed Negro man or woman who appears to have resources. The operator enters into conversation with the victim by inquiring about hotels, names of persons, and the location of the Negro community.

While talking, both observe a Negro man (Operator 2) leaving the train in apparent bewilderment. He seems lost, and his dress and general demeanor classify him as a yokel. Operator 1 explains to the victim that he will talk to the stranger and see whether he can be of some help. He has a lengthy conversation with the yokel. He then walks back to the waiting victim and explains that the simple fellow is a farm laborer who has saved all of his last year's wages and has come to the big town to spend it on a good time. He wishes to meet an honest person who will give him lodging and take care of his money. He will pay well for this kind attention. The con man elaborates upon the evident simplicity of this yokel and how a smart person could obtain most of his money without great effort. He then suggests that the victim board this yokel at his home. Why should he not secure the yokel's money for himself? The victim agrees to meet the yokel and have a talk with him.

Operator 1 calls the yokel over to the victim, introduces them, explains that the victim has become interested in him and is willing to board him and show him the town. The yokel appears impressed by this kindness. He explains that he has $600, is frightened of the big city, and is afraid that city slickers will rob him of his hard-earned money. He shows his money to the victim, expressing a desire that the victim take care of it for him, and asks whether the victim knows how to handle big money. He desires some proof that the victim will be careful and not lose it. Has he (the victim) any money? If he has some money of his own, the yokel will gladly let him take care of his.

At this point, Operator 1 expresses amazement that anyone would carry so much money on his person. He turns to the victim and asks whether he would carry so much money on his person and also inquires where he keeps his money. Although the yokel has a fear of banks, he is willing to bank his money if the victim will withdraw his own and place it with his. Then the victim can place both lots in any safe place that he wishes. If the victim can take his money out of the bank, then the yokel is sure that his money will be safe.

Operator 1 pretends to be very much amused by the yokel's simplicity and fear of banks. He suggests that the victim make a withdrawal from his bank just to show this simple yokel that money can be withdrawn at any time. At this point the yokel suddenly becomes interested in some nearby vending machine and walks toward it—just far enough to be out of hearing.

Now Operator 1 suggests that the victim humor the yokel and not let all of that good money stray away from him. The yokel is too dumb to make a "kick" to the law and, after all, the victim will have continuous possession of his own money in addition to the yokel's roll. The victim weakens at this point and goes to the bank, accompanied by Operator 1, in order to prove to the yokel how easy it is to withdraw money. The yokel awaits their return. The victim, having been coached by Operator 1, shows his withdrawn money to the yokel. Although the yokel is surprised at the ease with which the victim can withdraw his money from the bank, he still is concerned about the way his money and the victim's ought to be wrapped for safety. He tries to describe the method used by his "boss man" and holds up his hands as if measuring small distances. Suddenly Operator 1 understands and says: "It's one of those large brown envelopes!" He leaves to obtain one. During his absence the yokel holds his money in his hands, giving the victim a "big eyeful" (generally a dummy roll). Operator 1 returns with a large brown envelope which the yokel recognizes as the kind used by his boss man. Operator 1 takes the yokel's money and places both rolls in the large brown envelope. As the yokel (Operator 2) engages the victim in animated conversation, Operator 1 deftly makes a switch, placing the envelope with the two rolls of money in his breast pocket and handing the victim a similar envelope containing folded paper. The yokel now expresses himself as fully satisfied. He wishes to know where the victim lives, is given the name and address, and promises to come to the victim's house within an hour or two. Each operator walks away in a different direction. The victim hurries away, his mind filled with the desire to open the package and look at his money.

The operators meet at a prearranged spot to divide the victim's money.

Pigeon Drop

Pigeon Drop is an ancient game whose exact origin is unknown. Reportedly introduced into this country by Chinese immigrants early in the nineteenth century, it was later adopted by whites and still later by Negroes predominantly. Endless varieties of this swindle prevail; but in all its modifications, certain basics must go into it, not the least of which is the "vic's" (victim's) own greed. Two players are active in this game (also known as "The Slip" and "The Drag"); sometimes—in a cruder form barely distinguishable from a polite robbery known simply as "stuff"—it is played by only one man.

The game consists of a story in three parts. The first part is enacted by the "catch man," who approaches the vic with a plausible but dramatic tale designed to win sympathy and show trust. The second part is executed by the "hit partner," who moves into the conversation on signal to report some "found money," usually described as a bookie's receipts. Through several ruses which may employ a "switch" (sleight-of-hand transference of the vic's money) or a direction to a fictional "boss," the money which the victim is asked to "show" as evidence of "good faith" or "financial responsibility" comes into the possession of the players. In the "blowoff," the third part of this bold drama, the vic is given some final instructions which allow the players to leave his presence before he discovers he has been mulcted.

Spanish Prisoner Game

Many variations of the *Spanish Prisoner Game* have evolved in the past thirty years. The props common to each consist of a worthless but impressive negotiable paper for a large sum of money, a purported smuggled letter from a dejected prisoner (customarily a Latin American), and a picture of the prisoner's "charming" daughter. For whatever arbitrary reason the operator may choose, the prisoner's letter promises the marked Galahad his daughter's hand and a sizable portion of his estate (or some secret treasure, or whatever else the mark has been prepared to find enticing), if a certain sum of money is given to a certain courier to effect his daughter's escape from "this villainous country." One may easily imagine the infinite variety of themes that may be used in this stock drama to fit the times and the breed of persons being tricked. The "Spanish Prisoner" is now occasionally the "American Prisoner," a wealthy businessman in jail for income tax evasion. But all the features of the game—the beautiful young daughter and hidden funds that require some bribery or "grease" before they can be brought into use (with the victim providing the grease)—remain substantially the same.

Three Card Monte

Three Card Monte, which requires two operators (one to rope in the mark and one to manipulate the cards) is, theoretically, a game of chance, requiring the use of three ordinary playing cards, two of a black suit and one of a red suit. The "sucker" is inveigled into believing how easy it would be to capitalize on the fantastic odds (purely illusory) and witlessness (equally imaginary) of the operator, who promises to double the bet if the sucker can put his finger on the "red card," which the operator deftly proceeds to manipulate in various positions face down.

The Greasy Pig

The Greasy Pig is worked in much the same fashion as Three Card Monte, except that three nut shells are used and a pea-shaped object becomes the elusive goal in the game to claim the stakes. The pea is shifted from one cover to another by a few quick movements of the hands and resides as often as not under the operator's fingernails instead of under the shell. No matter how devilishly simple these proposals may seem to the guileless person, once he gives in to the temptation to lay hold of this easy money, the fever to beat the confounding game is unrelenting. Never does it seem to occur to the mark's own larcenous bent of mind that a man's game rarely, if ever, gives away any odds other than to himself.

The ten con men also practiced, in addition to these games, the "Badger Game" (in which a prostitute lures a mark to her room and a con man, posing as a jealous husband, breaks in on them in the midst of their activities and is ultimately paid off by the mark) and the "Murphy Game" (in which the con man poses as a pimp, is paid by a mark to procure a prostitute, and then runs off with the money). "A long con man" would not usually resort to these low-level techniques.

LACK OF INGENUITY

Occasionally a con man would show ingenuity. One, for example, was proud of having sold two lions and an elephant to a remarkably gullible circus owner in Chicago via telephone, receiving a cashier's check for the not yet delivered, nonexistent animals. Most of the games, however, were old (the Spanish Prisoner Game can be traced back to the defeat of the Armada) and crude. Although the con man prides himself on being smart, these short cons were markedly lacking in creativity. They were not "money men"; their careers were full of short scores and many "busts." In manipulating their victims, they depended on sudden attack and speed and on quick exits from the city of their operations. They seldom used careful planning or long-con techniques such as "cooling off" the mark. Their failure as successful criminals may perhaps be explained by this obvious lack of finesse. Perhaps they broke away from their tutors in crime too soon. Perhaps a longer apprenticeship would have helped. Perhaps, too, they did not have what it takes—the self-discipline, study habits, perseverance, or personality—to make a big-con man. In any event, they showed little insight into the cause of their failures, but rather naïvely attributed failure to fate or, as they often put it, "Kismet":

> I could always set up a mark and I could always finish him off, but I just had a jinx for arrest. *Some* guys pull them off. I did, too, but somehow I took the falls—just one of those things.

They lived in cheap furnished rooms, waiting to make a score. When they did score, it was like this:

> You know, when I had a little bread, I lived it up. You know, a good hotel, good food, good drinks, and a few slick chicks. But when the bread was sliced too thin the holiday was over. Then I had to blow.

The con man would again return to a cheap rooming house and lead an impoverished life until he found a mark and made another score.

The arrest histories of these men were lengthy (mean arrests per man—18, and at least four workhouse sentences and two felonies in every arrest history) and the charges ranged from petty theft up to grand larceny. In most cases, however, once a confidence game charge is noted, the other types of charges rarely appear afterward. This lends some credence to their own belief (shared by the police): "Once a con man always a con man."[21] Charges for violent crimes against the person were practically nonexistent.

The district attorney's reports showed that these men operated at a rather low criminal level. Usually the marks were "set up" for a loss of not more than $250. Whether operating alone or in pairs, these con men did not have tight organization, leadership, timing, or careful planning. At times they were conned out of the take by their own confederates and various women companions. They, too, were marks. Yet, despite the fact that their stories and the institutional records show this to be the case, they were reluctant to admit being conned by others. As one of them remarked;

---

[21]Fitzgerald, *op. cit.*, p. 187, notes that the confidence man follows his trade despite the number of times he is arrested and he rarely engages in other types of crimes. Maurer makes the same point in *The Big Con, op. cit.*, p. 173.

> You know, I was conned by broads from time to time, but I didn't stay still long enough to be conned by no man. I guess we all are easy marks for women. What about you? You know how it goes.

The idea that "all you got to do is know what to say with your mouth" did not disappear as a result of getting "busted." Once inside the penitentiary the cons shifted operations and became "jail house lawyers," attempting to gain release through appeals. Nine of the ten mentioned technicalities in the law which they believed should have precluded their arrest. Eight of the ten were writing writs for fellow inmates for which they were "paid off" in cigarettes, although none of the writs composed during previous periods of incarceration had proven effective. Their attempts at "conning" were even less effective inside than outside the penitentiary.

As a group these men seemed in the interviews to be older than their chronological age. They had many different kinds of physical complaints and did not appear to be strong.[22] All of them reacted to the interviewer in an apparently friendly and cooperative manner. They spoke softly in a breezy, chatty way, and their verbal expression seemed to be better than their educational levels indicated. They were prone to "projection" in that they attempted to express their opinions as if they were the opinions of the interviewer. They expressed few warm ties of affection with others and seemed to be shrewd, calculating, and interested in others only for what they could get out of them. As one con man said:

> You know what a friend is? He is someone who wants something you can give him—something you got. I am a taker, not a giver.

A qualitative assessment of the personality characteristics of these Negro con men indicates a sociopathic trend.[23] They divided humanity into two groups, con men and marks. They definitely committed themselves to the ranks of the con men, felt superior to the marks, and rationalized their socially disapproved behavior by insisting that all people have larceny in their hearts and "you have to take others before they take you." Their interpersonal relationships were defective in that they expressed few if any emotional ties and evinced little interest in other people, except in terms of exploitation. When they did make a "score," they exhibited an inability to forgo immediate pleasures for future gains and long-range goals. Hedonistic, they lived in the present without consideration of the past or future. They demonstrated a lack of insight into the causes of their behavior, were unable to profit from their mistakes, and attributed failure to fate.

While certainly not among the most expert of con men, they had developed a rather high degree of proficiency as compared with most of the offenders in the remainder of the sample (390 cases).[24] Their reference group was that of con men, and they judged themselves (and others) according to the degree to which behavior was consonant with the values of con men. Since status depended on success, and they were in jail and thus seemingly unsuccessful, they blamed fate for their incarceration and continued to operate as con men in prison—in this case, attempting to con their way out to freedom. With this set of values, the con men's likelihood of making any marked change in their behavior patterns is questionable, but because of the small size of the sample and the type of data utilized, the findings are tentative and replications with larger samples are necessary.

---

[22]The medical records showed that two were organically sound, three were partially crippled in the legs, one had a stiff left arm, one suffered from myopia, one was a diabetic, and two had heart murmurs.

[23]The above personality assessment was in part validated by inspection of the MMPI scale 4 scores (Pd.), which showed that all of these con men had T scores above 75. No other criminal category scored higher on this scale with the exception of the armed robbers.

[24]The modus operandi of the 16 numbers men, organized professional criminals, was pitched at a much higher level than that of these 10 con men. The 15 men in the single pattern of burglary were also more proficient.

30.

Edwin M. Lemert

THE BEHAVIOR OF THE SYSTEMATIC CHECK FORGER

The concept of behavior systems in crime was first approximated in this country in Hall's analysis of several types of larceny in terms of their historical, legal, and social contexts. (15) Later the concept was made explicit and formulated into a typology by Sutherland and by Sutherland and Cressey. (32, 34, 21, 26, 14, 4, pp. 579–589). Although this has hitherto inspired only a few monographic studies, there seems to be a growing consensus that focusing attention on specific orders of crime or making behavior systems the unit of study holds considerable promise for criminological research. (27, p. 134)

Because this paper proposes to assess the usefulness of Sutherland's formulation of the behavior system in analyzing or understanding the behavior of the systematic check forger, the typology outlined in his study of the professional thief will be employed. The five elements of the behavior system of the thief are as follows: (1) stealing is made a regular business; (2) every act is carefully planned, including the use of the "fix"; (3) technical skills are used, chiefly those of manipulating people; this differentiates the thief from other professional criminals; (4) the thief is migratory but uses a specific city as a headquarters; (5) the thief has criminal associations involving acquaintances, congeniality, sympathy, understandings, rules, codes of behavior, and a special language. (31, 32, 6 pp. 256–262, 27, 5, Ch. V, 10, Ch. IV, 23, 37)

Altogether seventy-two persons currently serving sentences for check forgery and writing checks with insufficient funds were studied. Three additional check offenders were contacted and interviewed outside of prison. The sample included eight women and sixty-seven men, all of whom served time in California correctional institutions.

Thirty of the seventy-five check criminals could be classified as systematic in the sense that they (1) thought of themselves as check men; (2) had worked out or regularly employed a special technique of passing checks; (3) had more or less organized their lives around the exigencies or imperatives of living by means of fraudulent checks. The remaining forty-five cases represented a wide variety of contexts in which bogus check passing was interspersed with periods of stable employment and family life, or was simply an aspect of alcoholism, gambling, or one of a series of criminal offenses having little or no consistency.

FINDINGS

Projected against the typology of professional theft, the behavior of the persons falling into the systematic check forgery category qualified only in a very general way as professional crime. In other words, although it is possible to describe these forgeries as *systematic*, it is questionable whether more than a small portion of them can be subsumed as *professional* under the more general classification of professional theft. A point-by-point comparison will serve to bring out the numerous significant differences between systematic forgery and professional theft.

1. *Forgery As a "Regular Business."* It is questionable whether check men look upon their crimes as a "regular business" in the same way as do members of "other occupational groups" who "wish to make money in safety." (34, p. 240) In virtually all cases the motivation proved to be exceedingly complex. This fact was self-consciously recognized and expressed in different ways but all informants re-

Source: *Social Problems,* Vol. 6, No. 2 (Fall, 1958), pp. 141–49, The Society for the Study of Social Problems. Reprinted by permission of the author and the journal.

vealed an essential perplexity or conflict about their criminal behavior. The following statement may be taken as illustrative:

> Nine out of ten check men are lone wolves. Those men who work in gangs are not real check men. They do it for money; we do it for something else. It gives us something we need. Maybe we're crazy. . . .

The conflicts expressed involved not merely the rightness or wrongness of behavior; they also disclosed a confusion and uncertainty as to the possibility of living successfully or safely by issuing false checks. All of the cases, even the few who had a history of professional thieving, admitted that arrest and imprisonment are inevitable. None knew of exceptions to this, although one case speculated that "It might be done by an otherwise respected businessman who made one big spread and then quit and retired."

The case records of the systematic check forgers gave clear testimony of this. Generally they had but shortlived periods of freedom, ranging from a few months to a year or two at the most, followed by imprisonment. Many of the cases since beginning their forgery careers had spent less total time outside prisons than within, a fact corroborated by the various law-enforcement officers queried on the point.

Many of the check men depicted their periods of check writing as continuous sprees during which they lived "fast" and luxuriously. Many spoke of experiencing considerable tension during these periods, and two cases developed stomach ulcers which caused them to "lay off at resorts." A number gambled and drank heavily, assertedly to escape their internal stress and sense of inevitable arrest. A number spoke of gradual build-up of strain and a critical point just before their arrest at which they became demoralized and after which they "just didn't care any more" or "got tired of running." The arrests of several men having a very long experience with checks resulted from blunders in technique of which they were aware at the time they made them. Some of the men gave themselves up to detectives or FBI agents at this point.

In general the picture of the cool, calculating professional with prosaic, matter-of-fact attitudes towards his crimes as a trade or occupation supported by rationalizations of a subculture was not valid for the cases in question.

2. *Planning As an Aspect of Forgery.* In regard to the second element of professional theft—planning—the behavior of check forgers is again divergent. Actually the present techniques of check passing either preclude precise planning or make it unnecessary. Although systematic check passers undeniably pay careful attention to such things as banking hours, the places at which checks are presented, and the kinds of "fronts" they employ, these considerations serve only as generalized guides for their crimes. Most informants held that situations have to be *exploited as they arise,* with variation and flexibility being the key to success. What stands out in the behavior of systematic check forgers is the rapid tempo—almost impulsiveness—with which they work.

The cases seemed to agree that check forgers seldom attempt to use the "fix" in order to escape the consequences of their crimes. The reason for this is that although one or a small number of checks might be made good, the systematic forger has too many bad checks outstanding and too many victims to mollify by offering restitution. Although the forger may be prosecuted on the basis of only one or two checks, ordinarily the prosecuting attorney will have a choice of a large number of complaints upon which to act. About the best the check forger can hope for through fixing activities is a short sentence or a sentence to jail rather than to prison.

3. *Technical Skills.* Although the systematic check man relies upon technical skills—those of manipulating others—these are usually not of a high order, nor do they require a long learning period to master. From the standpoint of the appearance of the check or the behavior involved at the time of its passing, there need, of course, be no great difference between passing a bad check and passing a good check. This is particularly true of personal checks, which are at least as favored as payroll checks by check men.

When check men impersonate others or when

they assume fictitious roles, acting ability is required. To the extent that elaborate impersonations are relied upon by the forger, his check passing takes on qualities of a confidence game. Most of the check men showed strong preference, however, for simple, fast-moving techniques. A number expressed definite dislike for staged arrangements, such as that of the "out of town real estate buyer" or for setting up a fictitious business in a community, then waiting several weeks or a month before making a "spread" of checks. As they put it, they "dislike the slow build-up involved."

4. *Mobility.* Like the thief, the systematic forger is migratory. Only one check man interviewed spoke of identifying himself with one community, and even he was reluctant to call it a headquarters. Generally check men are migratory within regions.

5. *Associations.* The sharpest and most categorical difference between professional theft and systematic forgery lies in the realm of associations. In contrast to pickpockets, shoplifters, and con men, whose criminal techniques are implicitly cooperative, most check men with highly developed systems work alone, carefully avoiding contacts and interaction with other criminals. Moreover, their preference for solitude and their secretiveness gives every appearance of a highly generalized reaction; they avoid not only cooperative crime but also any other kinds of association with criminals. They are equally selective and cautious in their contacts and associations with the noncriminal population, preferring not to become involved in any enduring personal relationships.

A descriptive breakdown of the thirty check forgers classified as systematic bears out this point. Only four of the thirty had worked in check passing gangs. Two of these had acted as "fences" who organized the operations. Both were close to seventy years old and had long prison records, one having been a receiver of stolen property, the other having worked as a forger. Both had turned to using gangs of passers because they were too well known to detectives either to pass checks themselves or to permit their handwriting to appear on the checks. The other two forgers who had worked in gangs were female drug addicts who had teamed up with other female addicts.

Three other systematic check forgers did not work directly with other criminals but had criminal associations of a *contractual* nature. One oldtime forger familiar with the now little-used methods for forging signatures and raising checks usually sold checks to passers but never had uttered (passed) any of his own forgeries. Two men were passers who purchased either payroll checks from a "hot printer" or stolen checks from burglars. Apart from the minimal contacts necessary to sell or obtain a supply of checks, all three men were lone operators and very seclusive in their behavior.

Six of the thirty systematic forgers worked exclusively with one other person, usually a girl or "broad." The check men seemed to agree that working with a girl was equivalent to working alone. These pairs ordinarily consisted of the check man and some girl not ordinarily of criminal background with whom he had struck up a living arrangement and for whom he felt genuine affection. The girl was used either to make out the checks or to pass them. In some cases she was simply used as a front to distract attention. Some men picked up girls in bars or hotels and employed them as fronts without their knowledge.

The remaining seventeen of the thirty systematic check forgers operated on a solitary basis. The majority of these argued that contact with others is unnecessary to obtain and pass a supply of checks. Most of them uttered personal checks. However, even where they made use of payroll or corporation checks they contrived to manufacture or obtain them without resorting to interaction with criminal associates or intermediaries. For example, one Nisei check man arranged with a printer to make up checks for a fraternal organization of which he represented himself as secretary-treasurer. Another man frequented business offices at noon time, and when the clerk left the office, helped himself to a supply of company checks, in one instance stealing a check writing machine for his purposes.

It was difficult to find evidence of anything more than rudimentary congeniality, sympathy, understandings, and shared rules of behavior among the check forgers, including those who had worked in gangs. Rather the opposite seemed true, suspicion and distrust marking their relationships with one another. One organizer of a gang, for example, kept careful account of all the checks he issued to his passers and made them return torn off corners of checks in case they were in danger of arrest and had to get rid of them. Only two of the thirty forgers indicated that they had at times engaged in recreational activities with other criminals. Both of these men were lone wolves in their work. One other lone wolf stated that he had on occasion had dinner with another check man he happened to know well and that he had once or twice entered into a rivalry with him to see who could pass a check in the most difficult place.

The two men who had organized gangs of check passers worked with a set of rules, but they were largely improvised and laid down by the fence rather than voluntarily recognized and obeyed by the passers. The other check men with varying degrees of explicitness recognized rules for passing checks—rules learned almost entirely on an individual trial-and-error basis. The informants insisted that "you learn as you go" and that one of the rules was "never use another man's stunt."

Such special morality as was recognized proved to be largely functional in derivation. Thus attitudes toward drinking and toward picking up women for sexual purposes were pretty much the result of individual perceptions of what was likely to facilitate or hamper the passing of checks or lead to arrest. Many of the men stated that since they were dealing primarily with business, professional, and clerical persons, their appearance and behavior had to be acceptable to these people. "Middle class" is probably the best term to describe their morality in most areas.

Careful inquiries were made to discover the extent to which the check men were familiar with and spoke an argot. Findings proved meager. Many of the men had a superficial acquaintance with general prison slang, but only four men could measurably identify and reproduce the argot of check forgery or that of thieves. Three more could be presumed to have some familiarity with it. Only one of these spoke the argot in the prison setting. Another said that he never used the argot either in prison or on the outside, except years previously when once in a great while he had "let down at a thieves' party." There were only two men who spoke of themselves as being "on the scratch."

INTERPRETATION

How can these findings be reconciled with the specific statement of Sutherland's informant (31, p. 77) that "laying paper" is a form of professional theft most often worked in mobs? The answer to this apparent contradiction requires that a distinction be made between forgery of *the nineteenth and early twentieth centuries and that of the present day.* In the past forgery was a much more complex procedure in which a variety of false instruments such as bank notes, drafts, bills of exchange, letters of credit, registered bonds, and post office money orders as well as checks were manufactured or altered and foisted off. A knowledge of chemicals, papers, inks, engraving, etching, lithography, and penmanship as well as detailed knowledge of bank operations were prime requisites for success. The amounts of money sought were comparatively large, and often they had to be obtained through complex monetary transactions. (7) The technological characteristics of this kind of forgery made planning, timing, specialization, differentiation of roles, morale, and organization imperative. Capital was necessary for living expenses during the period when preparations for the forgeries were being made. (24, 25, pp. 338–441, 7) Intermediates between the skilled forger and the passers were necessary so that the latter could swear that the handwriting on the false negotiable instruments was not theirs and so that the forger himself was not exposed to arrest. A "shadow" was often used for protection against the passer's temptation to abscond with the money and in order to alert the others of trouble at the bank. "Fall" money was accumulated and supplied to assist the passer when arrested. Inasmuch as forgery gangs worked together for a considerable length of time, understandings, congeniality, and rules of behavior, especially with regard to the division of money, could and did develop. In short, professional forgery was based upon the technology of the period.

Although precise dating is difficult, the heyday of professional forgery in this country probably began after the Civil War and lasted through the 1920's. (29) It seems to have corresponded with the early phases of industrialization and commercial development before business and law-enforcement agencies developed methods and organization for preventing forgery and apprehending the offenders. Gradually technological developments in inks, papers, protectographs, and check-writing machines made the forging of signatures and the manufacture of false negotiable instruments more difficult. According to one source, for example, raised drafts have been virtually nonexistent since 1905. (29) Similarly, at the present time raising of checks is quite rare. The establishment of a protective committee by the American Bankers Association in 1894, related merchants' protective agencies, and improvements in police methods have made the risks of organized professional forgery exceedingly great. (24, 22)

Check gangs have always been vulnerable to arrest but this vulnerability has been multiplied many times by the large amounts of evidence left behind them in the form of countless payroll checks. Vulnerability is also heightened by the swiftness of communication today. If one person of a check-passing gang is arrested and identifies his associates, it becomes a relatively simple matter for police to secure their arrest. A sexually exploited and angered female companion may easily do the same to the check man. This goes far to explain the extreme seclusiveness of systematic check forgers and their almost abnormal fear of stool pigeons or of being "fingered." The type of persons who can be engaged as passers—unattached women, bar waitresses, drug addicts, alcoholics, petty thieves, and transient unemployed persons—also magnifies the probabilities that mistakes will be made and precludes the growth of a morale which might prevent informing to the police. These conditions also explain the fact that when the forger does work with someone it is likely to be one other person upon whom he feels he can rely with implicit confidence. Hence the man-woman teams in which the woman is in love with the man, or the case of the two homosexual girls, or of the two brothers mentioned previously.

Further evidence that organized forgery is a hazardous type of crime, difficult to professionalize under modern conditions, is indicated by the fact that the organizer or fence is apt to be an older criminal with a long record, whose handwriting methods are so well known that he has no choice other than to work through passers. Even then he does it with recognition that arrest is inevitable.

A factor of equal importance in explaining the decline of professional organized forgery has been the increasingly widespread use of business and payroll checks as well as personal checks. Whereas in the past the use of checks was confined to certain kinds of business transactions, mostly involving banks, today it is ubiquitous. Attitudes of business people and their clerical employees have undergone great change, and only the most perfunctory identification is necessary to cash many kinds of checks. Check men recognize this in frequent unsolicited comments that passing checks is "easy." Some argue that the form of the check is now relatively unimportant to passing it, that "you can pass a candy bar wrapper now days with the right front and story." It is for this reason that the systematic check man does not have to resort to criminal associates or employ the more complex professional procedures used in decades past.

These facts may also account for the presence among lone-wolf check forgers of occasional persons with the identification, orientation, skills, codes, and argot of the thief. Case histories as well as the observations of informants show that older professional criminals in recent decades have turned to check passing because they face long sentences for additional crimes or sentencing under habitual criminal legislation. They regard checks as an "easy racket" because in many states conviction makes them subject to jail sentences rather than imprisonment. Check passing may be a last resort for the older criminal.

The presence of the occasional older professional thief in the ranks of check forgers may actually token a general decline and slow disappearance of professional thieving. One professional thief turned check passer had this to say:

> I'm a thief—a burglar—but I turned to checks because it's getting too hard to operate. Police are a lot smarter now, and they have better methods. People are different nowadays too; they report things more. It's hard to trust anyone now. Once you could trust cab drivers; now you can't. We live in a different world today.

THE CHECK FORGER AS AN ISOLATE

The preference of many systematic check forgers for solitary lives and their avoidance of primary-group associations among criminals may also be explicable in terms of their educational characteristics and class origins. The history of forgery reveals that in medieval times it was considered to be the special crime of the clerical class, as indeed it had to be inasmuch as the members of this class monopolized writing skills. (36, pp. 5–31) It also seems to be true from the later history of the crime that it has held a special attraction for more highly educated persons, for those of higher socioeconomic status and those of "refined" or artistic tastes. The basic method of organized forgery is stated to have been invented and perfected in England, not by criminals but by a practicing barrister of established reputation in 1840. (28, 8) An early gang of forgers organized by a practicing physician is also described by Felstead. (11) A number of studies directed to the differentiating characteristics of check criminals point to an "above average" intelligence and formal education. This refers to the general population as well as to the criminal populations with which they have been compared. (3, 12, 17, p. 87, 18, p. 40)

All of this is not to say that less-educated persons do not frequently pass bad checks but rather that the persons who persist in the behavior and develop behavior systems of forgery seem much more likely than other criminals to be drawn from a segment of the population distinguished by a higher socieconomic status. Generally this was true of the systematic forgers in this study. Eight of the thirty had completed two or more years of college. Fourteen of the thirty had fathers who were or had been in the professions and business, including a juvenile court judge, a minister, a postmaster of a large city, and three very wealthy ranch owners. One woman came from a nationally famous family of farm implement manufacturers. Four others had siblings well established in business and the professions, one of whom was an attorney general in another state. Two of the men had been successful businessmen themselves before becoming check men.

The most important implication of these data is that systematic check forgers do not seem to have had criminal antecedents or early criminal associations. (19, 20) For this reason, as well as for technical reasons, they are not likely to seek out or to be comfortable in informal associations with other criminals who have been products of early and lengthy socialization and learning in a criminal subculture. It also follows that their morality and values remain essentially "middle" or "upper" class and that they seldom integrate these with the morality of the professional criminal. This is reflected in self-attitudes in which many refer to themselves as "black sheep" or as a kind of Dr. Jekyll-Mr. Hyde person. Further support for this interpretation comes from their status in prison where, according to observations of themselves and others, they are marginal so far as participation in the primary groups of the prison is concerned.

CONCLUSION

The cases and data presented suggest that present-day check forgery exists in systematic form but does not appear to be a professional behavior system acquired or maintained through associations with other criminals. The technical demands of contemporary check forgery preclude efficient operation on an organized, cooperative basis. In addition to these factors the class characteristics and backgrounds of systematic forgers incline them to avoid intimate association with other criminals.

REFERENCES

1. ADAM, H. L. *Oriental Crime* (London: T. Werner Laurie, 1908).
2. ADAM, H. L. *The Story of Crime* (London: T. Werner Laurie, 1908).
3. BERG, I. "A Comparative Study of Forgery," *Journal of Applied Psychology,* Vol. 28 (June, 1944), pp. 232–38.
4. BONGER, W. A. *Criminality and Economic Conditions* (Boston: Little, Brown, 1916).
5. CAVAN, R. S. *Criminology* (New York: Crowell, 1948).
6. CLINARD, M. B. *Sociology of Deviant Behavior* (New York: Rinehart, 1957).
7. DILNET, G. *The Bank of England Forgery* (New York: Scribners, 1929).
8. DILNET, G. *The Trial of Jim the Penman* (London: Geoffrey Bles, 1930).
9. EDWARDS, S. M. *Crime in India* (London: Oxford University Press, 1924).
10. ELLIOTT, M. *Crime in Modern Society* (New York: Harper and Bros., 1942).
11. FELSTEAD, T. S. in *Famous Criminals and Their Trials* (New York: Doran, 1926).
12. FOX, V. "Intelligence, Race and Age as Selective Factors in Crime," *Journal of Criminal Law and Criminology,* Vol. 37 (July-August, 1946), 141–52.
13. FREGIER, H. A. *Les Classes Dangereuses de la population dans les grandes villes* (Paris: Chex J. B. Ballière, 1840).
14. GRUHLE, H. W. and L. WETZEL (eds.). "Verbrechentype" in W. A. Bonger, *Criminality and Economic Conditions* (Boston: Little, Brown, 1916), p. 581.
15. HALL, JEROME. *Theft, Law and Society* (2d ed.; Indianapolis: Bobbs-Merril, 1952).
16. HARDLESS and HARDLESS. *Forgery in India* (Chunar: Sanctuary, 1920).
17. HOOTON, E. A. *The American Criminal,* Vol. 1 (Cambridge, Mass.: Harvard University Press, 1939).
18. LAWES, L. *Life and Death in Sing Sing* (New York: Sun Dial Press, 1938).
19. LEMERT, E. "An Isolation and Closure Theory of Naive Check Forgery," *Journal of Criminal Law and Criminology,* Vol. 44 (September-October, 1953), pp. 296–307.
20. LEMERT, E. "Generality and Specificity in Criminal Behavior: Check Forgery Considered," paper read before American Sociological Society, September, 1956.
21. LINDESMITH, A. R. & DUNHAM, H. W. "Some Principles of Criminal Typology," *Social Forces,* Vol. 19 (March, 1941), pp. 307–14.
22. MAURER, D. W. "The Argot of Check Forgery," *American Speech,* Vol. 16 (December, 1941), pp. 243–50.
23. MAURER, D. W. *Whiz Mob* (Gainesville, Fla.: American Dialect Society, No. 24, 1955).
24. PINKERTON, W. A. "Forgery," paper read before Annual Convention of the International Association of Chiefs of Police, Washington, D.C., 1905.
25. PINKERTON, W. A. *Thirty Years a Detective* (New York: G. W. Carleton, 1884).
26. PUIBARAUD, L. *Les Malfaiteurs de profession* (Paris: E. Flammarion, 1893).
27. RECKLESS, W. C. *The Crime Problem* (2d ed.; New York: Appleton Century, 1955).
28. RHODES, H. T. F. in *The Craft of Forgery* (London: J. Murray, 1934).
29. SPEARE, J. W. *Protecting the Nation's Money* (Rochester, N.Y.: Todd Protectograph Co., 1927).
30. STERNITSKY, J. L. *Forgery and Fictitious Checks* (Springfield, Ill.: Charles C. Thomas, 1955).
31. SUTHERLAND, E. H. *The Professional Thief* (Chicago: University of Chicago Press, 1937).
32. SUTHERLAND, E. H. "The Professional Thief," *Journal of Criminal Law and Criminology,* Vol. 28 (July-August, 1937), pp. 161–63.
33. SUTHERLAND, E. H. *Principles of Criminology* (rev. ed.; New York: Lippincott, 1947).
34. SUTHERLAND, E. H. & CRESSEY, D. *Principles of Criminology* (5th ed.; New York: Lippincott, 1955).
35. TEGG, T. *The Chronicles of Crime,* Vols. I, II (London: Camden Pelham, 1841).
36. TOUT, T. F. *Medieval Forgers and Forgeries,* Bulletin of the John Rylands Library, 5, 3, 4, 1919.
37. VON HENTIG, H. "The Pickpocket: Psychology, Tactics and Technique," *Journal of Criminal Law and Criminology,* Vol. 34 (May-June, 1943), pp. 11–16.

CHAPTER IX

Organized Crime

IT IS A MOST DIFFICULT TASK to write an authoritative statement on the nature of organized crime in the United States. Because we lack even the sometimes questionable statistics available when studying conventional property and personal offenses, it is only possible to estimate within a rather wide range the magnitude of organized criminal activities, trends in volume, yearly profits, types of illegal services rendered, number of victims who solicit these services, payoffs made to government officials, and legitimate business operations that have been infiltrated.

The primary goal of those involved in organized crime is financial gain. Through illegal channels they are able to provide their clients (victims) with goods and services which might otherwise be unavailable. A man who wants to place a bet on a horse but can't go to the racetrack must use the services of a bookmaker, a burglar with a bundle of stolen goods must find a reliable fence, the narcotics pusher must locate a dependable source, and the risky businessman who is in need of quick cash may have to rely on the loan shark. The common factor present in each of these examples is that the client sought the services of organized crime, the syndicate did not search out and attack the victim.

As indicated above, the activities of organized crime are extremely broad. They cover a wide range of services that are prohibited by law, but demanded by their customers. Many Americans knowingly seek these services while others may serve as innocent victims. The several activities (businesses) in which organized crime may engage are listed below, followed by a brief discussion of each.

1. Gambling
2. Narcotics
3. Loan sharking
4. Bootlegging
5. Fencing
6. Prostitution
7. Infiltration of legitimate business.

Gambling represents the most lucrative business activity of organized crime. Since there have been numerous estimates of the profits made through illegal gambling in this country it is impossible to offer an exact figure—however, many competent observers suggest that $20 billion per year would fall somewhere between a conservative judgment and gross exaggeration. Gambling now occupies the role once played by bootlegging during the period of prohibition, for it furnishes the basic lucrative support necessary to maintain other types of organized crime, thus broadening their scope of activity. Although horse-race betting is probably the most profitable form of gambling, business has branched out to include the numbers game (where odds are 1,000 to 1, but a winner will be paid only 500 to 1), and the recent mania to bet on sporting events such as boxing, basketball, baseball, football, and hockey. Of course gaming houses and casinos have been in existence for a long period of time. Organized crime is so powerful in the area of gambling that it would be virtually impossible for an independent bookmaker to remain in business if there was opposition from the syndicate.

Contraband drugs are smuggled into the United States through an intricate, well-organized, and highly effective system. By disguising shipments of goods and sometimes re-routing them, drugs are delivered to our major ports and then distributed throughout the country. Without the involvement of organized crime it would be impossible to import and distribute the quantities of drugs needed to support the habits of our countless addicts. As discussed in Chapter 5, narcotic addiction is not only a personal problem, it is also a most serious problem for society, for in order to support their habits, millions of dollars' worth of property is stolen each year, fenced, and then converted into cash so that the necessary drugs may be purchased.

The loan shark makes his services available to a variety of customers. The gambler who is in over his head and can't pay off on his debt, the businessman who needs quick cash but cannot justify his reasons to a financial institution, narcotic addicts who desperately need money (at any cost) to purchase drugs—these people are all dependent on the service provided. Loan sharking is probably the second largest source of income for organized crime. The interest rates a loan shark will charge may vary from 1 to 150 percent per week. As suggested in the first reading of this chapter, the rate is dependent upon the relationship established between the lender and borrower, the purpose of the loan, size of the loan, and plans for repayment. The most common loan will command an interest charge of 20 percent per week.

During the period of prohibition, bootlegging provided the major source of income for organized crime. But realistically, since the abolition of the 18th Amendment, this type of illegal activity is rather limited. However, the importance of bootlegging cannot be ignored historically, for when one studies the history of organized crime, it was during the era of prohibition that this highly structured criminal network was first tested.

Fencing is a service provided by organized crime to professional and amateur thieves alike who wish to quickly part with their stolen goods. Other than actual currency or items having the same value as currency, the thief wants to dispose of his articles as soon as possible. The fence will generally pay only a very small percentage of the actual value of the goods taken, but since this is the best the thief can do without risking the possibility of being caught "in possession," he must accept the price offered. Thus the fence provides a direct link between organized crime and the professional criminal.

Even though prostitution exists in nearly every major city in the United States today, and organized crime may well be involved in its operation, this is not a major moneymaking activity of the criminal syndicates. In the case of prostitution, it is most difficult to maintain discipline and keep at a safe distance from the law. Payoffs made to political officials and law enforcement officers for purposes of protection may prevent this from being a worthwhile financial venture. In addition to these factors, many high-priced call girls along with street and bar prostitutes work on an independent basis thereby providing a competitive element.

The most recent venture of organized crime has been the infiltration of legitimate business enterprises. In addition to the possible use of the business as a front for illegal activities, this has provided members of criminal syndicates with prestige and respectability in the community along with a legitimate source of income upon which to pay taxes. Given today's modern Internal Revenue Service, it is most important, if you are going to live high, to at least account for part of the money you are spending.

The first selection in this chapter is taken from the President's Commission on Law Enforcement and Administration of Justice. Organized crime is analyzed in terms of illegal activities, location of these activities, corruption of officials, membership in and organization of crime syndicates, and control of organized crime. In the second article, Thorsten Sellin presents a detailed account of how the numbers game is played in this country along with the personalities who take part. In the third selection, Gerard L. Goettel, a member of the New York State Bar Association discusses why it is most difficult for law enforcement agencies to move in on organized criminal syndicates and put an end to their sinister activities. Mr. Goettel reports his experiences as Deputy Chief of the Attorney General's Special Group on organized crime. His first-hand observations will confirm many of the assumptions appearing in contemporary reports on this subject. Finally, Daniel P. Moynihan offers a most interesting commentary on the private government of organized crime. Perhaps, in this concluding article, Dr. Moynihan sums up best what we have been attempting to understand in this chapter, namely that organized crime is invading nearly every sector of American society, and something must be done to rid ourselves of this infectious disease.

31.

President's Commission on Law Enforcement and Administration of Justice

ORGANIZED CRIME

Organized crime is a society that seeks to operate outside the control of the American people and their governments. It involves thousands of criminals, working within structures as complex as those of any large corporation, subject to laws more rigidly enforced than those of legitimate governments. Its actions are not impulsive but rather the result of intricate conspiracies, carried on over many years and aimed at gaining control over whole fields of activity in order to amass huge profits.

The core of organized crime activity is the supplying of illegal goods and services—gambling, loan sharking, narcotics, and other forms of vice—to countless numbers of citizen customers. But organized crime is also extensively and deeply involved in legitimate business and in labor unions. Here it employs illegitimate methods—monopolization, terrorism, extortion, tax evasion—to drive out or control lawful ownership and leadership and to exact illegal profits from the public. And to carry on its many activities secure from governmental interference, organized crime corrupts public officials.

Robert F. Kennedy, when he was Attorney General, illustrated its power simply and vividly. He testified before a Senate subcommittee in 1963 that the physical protection of witnesses who had cooperated with the Federal Government in organized crime cases often required that those witnesses change their appearances, change their names, or even leave the country. When the government of a powerful country is unable to protect its friends from its enemies by means less extreme than obliterating their identities, surely it is being seriously challenged, if not threatened.

SOURCE: A Report of the President's Commission on Law Enforcement and Administration of Justice, *The Challenge of Crime in a Free Society* (Washington, D.C.: U. S. Government Printing Office, February, 1967), pp. 187–200.

What organized crime wants is money and power. What makes it different from law-abiding organizations and individuals with those same objectives is that the ethical and moral standards the criminals adhere to, the laws and regulations they obey, the procedures they use, are private and secret ones that they devise themselves, change when they see fit, and administer summarily and invisibly. Organized crime affects the lives of millions of Americans, but because it desperately preserves its invisibility many, perhaps most, Americans are not aware how they are affected, or even that they are affected at all. The price of a loaf of bread may go up one cent as the result of an organized crime conspiracy, but a housewife has no way of knowing why she is paying more. If organized criminals paid income tax on every cent of their vast earnings everybody's tax bill would go down, but no one knows how much.

But to discuss the impact of organized crime in terms of whatever direct, personal, everyday effect it has on individuals is to miss most of the point. Most individuals are not affected, in this sense, very much. Much of the money organized crime accumulates comes from innumerable petty transactions: 50-cent bets, $3-a-month private garbage collection services, quarters dropped into racketeer-owned jukeboxes, or small price rises resulting from protection rackets. A one-cent-a-loaf rise in bread may annoy housewives, but it certainly does not impoverish them.

Sometimes organized crime's activities do not directly affect individuals at all. Smuggled cigarettes in a vending machine cost consumers no more than tax-paid cigarettes, but they enrich the leaders of organized crime. Sometimes these activities actually reduce prices for a short period of time, as can happen when organized crime, in an attempt to take over an industry, starts a price war against legitimate businessmen. Even when organized crime engages in a large transaction, individuals may not be directly affected. A large sum of money can be diverted from a union pension fund to finance a business venture without immediate and direct effect upon the individual members of the union.

It is organized crime's accumulation of money, not the individual transactions by which the money is accumulated, that has a great and threatening impact on America. A quarter in a jukebox means nothing and results in nothing. But millions of quarters in thousands of jukeboxes can provide both a strong motive for murder and the means to commit murder with impunity. Organized crime exists by virtue of the power it purchases with its money. The millions of dollars it can invest in narcotics or use for layoff money give it power over the lives of thousands of people and over the quality of life in whole neighborhoods. The millions of dollars it can throw into the legitimate economic system give it power to manipulate the price of shares on the stock market, to raise or lower the price of retail merchandise, to determine whether entire industries are union or nonunion, to make it easier or harder for businessmen to continue in business.

The millions of dollars it can spend on corrupting public officials may give it power to maim or murder people inside or outside the organization with impunity, to extort money from businessmen, to conduct businesses in such fields as liquor, meat, or drugs without regard to administrative regulations, to avoid payment of income taxes, or to secure public works contracts without competitive bidding.

The purpose of organized crime is not competition with visible, legal government but nullification of it. When organized crime places an official in public office, it nullifies the political process. When it bribes a police official, it nullifies law enforcement.

There is another, more subtle, way in which organized crime has an impact on American life. Consider the former way of life of Frank Costello, a man who has repeatedly been called a leader of organized crime. He lived in an expensive apartment on the corner of 72d Street and Central Park West in New York. He was often seen dining in well-known restaurants in the company of judges, public officials, and prominent businessmen. Every morning he was shaved in the barbershop of the Waldorf Astoria Hotel. On many weekends he played golf at a country club on the fashionable North Shore of Long Island. In short, though his reputation was common knowledge, he moved around New York conspicuously and unashamedly, perhaps ostracized by some people but more often accepted, greeted by journalists, recognized by children, accorded all the freedoms of a prosperous and successful man. On a society that treats such a man in such a manner, organized crime has had an impact.

And yet the public remains indifferent. Few Americans seem to comprehend how the phenomenon of organized crime affects their lives. They do not see how gambling with bookmakers, or borrowing money from loan sharks, forwards the interests of great criminal cartels. Businessmen looking for labor harmony or non-union status through irregular channels rationalize away any suspicions that organized crime is thereby spreading its influence. When an ambitious political candidate accepts substantial cash contributions from unknown sources, he suspects but dismisses the fact that organized crime will dictate some of his actions when he assumes office. . . .

THE TYPES OF ORGANIZED CRIMINAL ACTIVITIES

Catering to Public Demands

Organized criminal groups participate in any illegal activity that offers maximum profit at minimum risk of law enforcement interference. They offer goods and services that millions of Americans desire even though declared illegal by their legislatures.

Gambling. Law enforcement officials agree almost unanimously that gambling is the greatest source of revenue for organized crime. It ranges from lotteries, such as "numbers" or "bolita," to off-track horse betting, bets on sporting events, large dice games and illegal casinos. In large cities where organized criminal groups exist, very few of the gambling operators are independent of a large organization. Anyone whose independent operation becomes successful is likely to receive a visit from an organization representative who convinces the independent, through fear or promise of greater profit, to share his revenue with the organization.

Most large-city gambling is established or controlled by organized crime members through elaborate hierarchies. Money is filtered from the small operator who takes the customer's bet, through persons who pick up money and slips, to second-echelon figures in charge of particular districts, and then into one of several main offices. The profits that eventually accrue to organization leaders move through channels so complex that even persons who work in the betting operation do not know or cannot prove the identity of the leader. Increasing use of the telephone for lottery and sports betting has facilitated systems in which the bookmaker may not know the identity of the second-echelon person to whom he calls in the day's bets. Organization not only creates greater efficiency and enlarges markets, it also provides a systematized method of corrupting the law enforcement process by centralizing procedures for the payment of graft.

Organization is also necessary to prevent severe losses. More money may be bet on one horse or one number with a small operator than he could pay off if that horse or that number should win. The operator will have to hedge by betting some money himself on that horse or that number. This so-called "lay off" betting is accomplished through a network of local, regional, and national lay off men, who take bets from gambling operations.

There is no accurate way of ascertaining organized crime's gross revenue from gambling in the United States. Estimates of the annual intake have varied from $7 to $50 billion. Legal betting at racetracks reaches a gross annual figure of almost $5 billion, and most enforcement officials believe that illegal wagering on horse races, lotteries, and sporting events totals at least $20 billion each year. Analysis of organized criminal betting operations indicates that the profit is as high as one-third of gross revenue—or $6 to $7 billion each year. While the Commission cannot judge the accuracy of these figures, even the most conservative estimates place substantial capital in the hands of organized crime leaders.

Loan Sharking. In the view of most law enforcement officials loan sharking, the lending of money at higher rates than the legally prescribed limit, is the second largest source of revenue for organized crime. Gambling profits provide the initial capital for loan-shark operations.

No comprehensive analysis has ever been made of what kinds of customers loan sharks have, or of how much or how often each kind borrows. Enforcement officials and other investigators do have some information. Gamblers borrow to pay gambling losses; narcotics users borrow to purchase heroin. Some small businessmen borrow from loan sharks when legitimate credit channels are closed. The same men who take bets from employees in mass employment industries also serve at times as loan sharks, whose money enables the employees to pay off their gambling debts or meet household needs.

Interest rates vary from 1 to 150 percent a week, according to the relationship between the lender and borrower, the intended use of the money, the size of the loan, and the repayment potential. The classic "6-for-5" loan, 20 percent a week, is common with small borrowers. Payments may be due by a certain hour on a certain day and even a few minutes' default may result in a rise in interest rates. The lender is more interested in perpetuating interest payments than collecting principal; and force, or threats of force of the most brutal kind, are used to effect interest collection, eliminate protest when interest rates are raised, and prevent the beleaguered borrower from reporting the activity to enforcement officials. No reliable estimates exist of the gross revenue from organized loan sharking; but profit margins are higher than for gambling operations, and many officials classify the business in the multi-billion-dollar range.

Narcotics. The sale of narcotics is organized like a legitimate importing-wholesaling-retailing business. The distribution of heroin, for example, requires movement of the drug through four or five levels between the importer and the street peddler. Many enforcement officials believe that the severity of mandatory Federal narcotics penalties has caused organized criminals to restrict their activities to importing and wholesale distribution. They stay away from smaller-scale wholesale transactions or dealing at the retail level. Transactions with addicts are handled by independent narcotics pushers using drugs imported by organized crime.

The large amounts of cash and the international connections necessary for large, long-term heroin supplies can be provided only by organized crime. Conservative estimates of the number of addicts in the Nation and the average daily expenditure for heroin indicate that the gross heroin trade is $350 million annually, of which $21 million are probably profits to the importer and distributor. Most of this profit goes to organized crime groups in those few cities in which almost all heroin consumption occurs.

Other Goods and Services. Prostitution and bootlegging play a small and declining role in organized crime's operations. Production of illegal alcohol is a risky business. The destruction of stills and supplies by law enforcement officers during the initial stages means the loss of heavy initial investment capital. Prostitution is difficult to organize and discipline is hard to maintain. Several important convictions of organized crime figures in prostitution cases in the 1930's and 1940's made the criminal executives wary of further participation.

Business and Labor Interests

Infiltration of Legitimate Business. To have a legitimate business enables the racket executive to acquire respectability in the community and to establish a source of funds that appears legal and upon which just enough taxes can be paid to avoid income tax prosecution. Organized crime invests the profit it has made from illegal service activities in a variety of businesses throughout the country. To succeed in such ventures, it uses accountants, attorneys, and business consultants, who in some instances work exclusively on its affairs. Too often, because of the reciprocal benefits involved in organized crime's dealings with the business world, or because of fear, the legitimate sector of society helps the illegitimate sector. The Illinois Crime Commission, after investigating one service industry in Chicago, stated:

> There is a disturbing lack of interest on the part of some legitimate business concerns regarding the identity of the persons with whom they deal. This lackadaisical attitude is conducive to the perpetration of frauds and the infiltration and subversion of legitimate businesses by the organized criminal element.

Because business ownership is so easily concealed, it is difficult to determine all the types of businesses that organized crime has penetrated. Of the 75 or so racket leaders who met at Apalachin, N.Y., in 1957, at least 9 were in the coin-operated machine industry, 16 were in the garment industry, 10 owned grocery stores, 17 owned bars or restaurants, 11 were in the olive oil and cheese business, and 9 were in the construction business. Others were involved in automobile agencies, coal companies, entertainment, funeral homes, ownership of horses and race tracks, linen and laundry enterprises, trucking, waterfront activities, and bakeries.

Today, the kinds of production and service industries and businesses that organized crime controls or has invested in range from accounting firms to yeast manufacturing. One criminal syndicate alone has real estate interests with an estimated value of $300 million. In a few instances, racketeers control nationwide manufacturing and service industries with known and respected brand names.

Control of business concerns has usually been acquired through one of four methods: (1) investing concealed profits acquired from gambling and other illegal activities; (2) accepting business interests in payment of the owner's gambling debts; (3) foreclosing on usurious loans; and (4) using various forms of extortion.

Acquisition of legitimate businesses is also accomplished in more sophisticated ways. One organized crime group offered to lend money to a business on condition that a racketeer be appointed to the company's board of directors and that a nominee for the lenders be given first option to purchase if there were any outside sale of the company's stock. Control of certain brokerage houses was secured through foreclosure of usurious loans, and the businesses then used to promote the sale of fraudulent stock, involving losses of more than $2 million to the public.

Criminal groups also satisfy defaulted loans by taking over businesses, hiring professional arsonists to burn buildings and contents, and collecting on the fire insurance. Another tactic was illustrated in the recent bankruptcy of a meatpacking firm in which control was secured as payment for gambling debts. With the original owners remaining in nominal management positions, extensive product orders were placed through established lines of credit, and the goods were immediately sold at low prices before the suppliers were paid. The organized criminal group made a quick profit of three-quarters of a million dollars by pocketing the receipts from sale of the products ordered and placing the firm in bankruptcy without paying the suppliers.

Too little is known about the effects on the economy of organized crime's entry into the business world, but the examples above indicate the harm done to the public and at least suggest how criminal cartels can undermine free competition. The ordinary businessman is hard pressed to compete with a syndicate enterprise. From its gambling and other illegal revenue—on most of which no taxes are paid—the criminal group always has a ready source of cash with which to enter any business. Through union connections, the business run by organized crime either prevents unionization or secures "sweetheart" contracts from existing unions. These tactics are used effectively in combination. In one city, organized crime gained a monopoly in garbage collection by preserving the business's nonunion status and by using cash reserves to offset temporary losses incurred when the criminal group lowered prices to drive competitors out of business.

Strong-arm tactics are used to enforce unfair business policy and to obtain customers. A restaurant chain controlled by organized crime used the guise of "quality control" to insure that individual restaurant franchise holders bought products only from other syndicate-owned businesses. In one city, every business with a particular kind of waste product useful in another line of industry sold that product to a syndicate-controlled business at one-third the price offered by legitimate business.

The cumulative effect of the infiltration of legitimate business in American cannot be measured. Law enforcement officials agree that entry into legitimate business is continually increasing and that it has not decreased organized crime's control over gambling, usury and other profitable, low-risk criminal enterprises.

Labor Racketeering. Control of labor supply and infiltration of labor unions by organized crime prevent unionization of some industries, provide opportunities for stealing from union funds and extorting money by threats of possible labor strife, and provide funds from the enormous union pension and welfare systems for business ventures controlled by organized criminals. Union control also may enhance other illegal activities. Trucking, construction and waterfront shipping entrepreneurs, in return for assurance that business operations will not be interrupted by labor discord, countenance gambling, loan sharking and pilferage on company property. Organized criminals either direct these activities or grant "concessions" to others in return for a percentage of the profits.

Some of organized crime's effects on labor union affairs, particularly in the abuse of pension and welfare funds, were disclosed in investigations by Senator John McClellan's committee. In one case, almost immediately after receiving a license as an insurance broker, the son of a major organized crime figure in New York City was chosen as the broker for a number of such funds, with significant commissions to be earned and made available for distribution to "silent partners." The youthful broker's only explanation for his success was that he had advertised in the classified telephone directory.

In New York City, early in 1966, the head of one organized crime group was revealed to be a partner in a labor relations consulting firm. One client of the firm, a nationally prominent builder, said he did not oppose unions but that better and cheaper houses could be built without them. The question of why a legitimate businessman would seek the services of an untrained consultant with a criminal record to handle his labor relations was not answered.

LOCATION OF ORGANIZED CRIME ACTIVITIES

Organized criminal groups are known to operate in all sections of the Nation. In response to a Commission survey of 71 cities, the police departments in 80 percent of the cities with over 1 million residents, in 20 percent of the cities with a population between one-half million and a million, in 20 percent of the cities with between 250,000 and 500,000 population, and in over 50 percent of the cities between 100,000 and 250,000, indicated that organized criminal groups exist in their cities. In some instances Federal agency intelligence indicated the presence of organized crime where local reports denied it. Of the nine cities not responding to the Commission survey, six are known to Federal agencies to have extensive organized crime problems. Where the existence of organized crime was acknowledged, all police departments indicated that the criminal group would continue even though a top leader died or was incarcerated.

Organized crime in small cities is more difficult to assess. Law enforcement personnel are aware of many instances in which local racket figures controlled crime in a smaller city and received aid from and paid tribute to organized criminal groups located in a nearby large city. In one Eastern town, for example, the local racket figure combined with outside organized criminal groups to establish horse and numbers gambling grossing $1.3 million annually, an organized dice game drawing customers from four states and having an employee payroll of $350,000 annually, and a still capable of producing $4 million worth of alcohol each year. The town's population was less than 100,000. Organized crime cannot be seen as merely a big-city problem.

CORRUPTION OF THE ENFORCEMENT AND POLITICAL SYSTEMS

Today's corruption is less visible, more subtle and therefore more difficult to detect and assess than the corruption of the prohibition era. All available data indicate that organized crime flourishes only where it has corrupted local officials. As the scope and variety of organized crime's activities have expanded, its need to involve public officials at every level of local government has grown. And as government regulation expands into more and more areas of private and business activity, the power to corrupt likewise affords the corrupter more control over matters affecting the everyday life of each citizen.

Contrast, for example, the way governmental action in contract procurement or zoning functions today with the way it functioned only a few years ago. The potential harm of corruption is greater today if only because the scope of governmental activity is greater. In different places at different times, organized crime has corrupted police officials, prosecutors, legislators, judges, regulatory agency officials, mayors, councilmen, and other public officials, whose legitimate exercise of duties would block organized crime and whose illegal exercise of duties helps it.

Neutralizing local law enforcement is central to organized crime's operations. What can the public do if no one investigates the investigators, and the political figures are neutralized by their alliance with organized crime? Anyone reporting corrupt activities may merely be telling his story to the corrupted; in a recent "investigation" of widespread corruption, the prosecutor announced that any citizen coming forward with evidence of payments to public officials to secure government action would be prosecuted for participating in such unlawful conduct.

In recent years some local governments have been dominated by criminal groups. Today, no large city is completely controlled by organized crime, but in many there is a considerable degree of corruption.

Organized crime currently is directing its efforts to corrupt law enforcement at the chief or at least middle-level supervisory officials. The corrupt political executive who ties the hands of police officials who want to act against organized crime is even more effective for organized crime's purposes. To secure political power organized crime tries by bribes or political contributions to corrupt the nonoffice-holding political leaders to whom judges, mayors, prosecuting attorneys, and correctional officials may be responsive.

It is impossible to determine how extensive the corruption of public officials by organized crime has been. We do know that there must be more vigilance against such corruption, and we know that there must be better ways for the public to communicate information about corruption to appropriate governmental personnel.

MEMBERSHIP AND ORGANIZATION OF CRIMINAL CARTELS

Some law enforcement officials define organized crime as those groups engaged in gambling, or narcotics pushing, or loan sharking, or with illegal business or labor interests. This is useful to the extent that it eliminates certain other criminal groups from consideration, such as youth gangs, pickpocket rings, and professional criminal groups who may also commit many types of crimes, but whose groups are ad hoc. But when law enforcement officials focus exclusively on the crime instead of the organization, their target is likely to be the lowest-level criminals who commit the visible crimes. This has little effect on the organization.

The Commission believes that before a strategy to combat organized crime's threat to America can be developed, that threat must be assessed by a close examination of organized crime's distinctive characteristics and methods of operation.

National Scope of Organized Crime

In 1951 the Kefauver committee declared that a nationwide crime syndicate known as the Mafia operated in many large cities and that the leaders of the Mafia usually controlled the most lucrative rackets in their cities.

In 1957, 20 of organized crime's top leaders were convicted (later reversed on appeal) of a criminal charge arising from a meeting at Apalachin, N.Y. At the sentencing the judge stated that they had sought to corrupt and infiltrate the political mainstreams of the country, that they had led double lives of crime and respectability, and that their probation reports read "like a tale of horrors."

Today the core of organized crime in the United States consists of 24 groups operating as criminal cartels in large cities across the Nation. Their membership is exclusively Italian, they are in frequent communication with each other, and their smooth functioning is insured by a national body of overseers. To date, only the Federal Bureau of Investigation has been able to document fully the national scope of these groups, and FBI intelligence indicates that the organization as a whole has changed its name from the Mafia to La Cosa Nostra.

In 1966 J. Edgar Hoover told a House of Representatives Appropriations Subcommittee:

> La Cosa Nostra is the largest organization of the criminal underworld in this country, very closely organized and strictly disciplined. They have committed almost every crime under the sun . . .
>
> La Cosa Nostra is a criminal fraternity whose membership is Italian either by birth or national origin, and it has been found to control major racket activities in many of our larger metropolitan areas, often working in concert with criminals representing other ethnic backgrounds. It operates on a nationwide basis, with international implications, and until recent years it carried on its activities with almost complete secrecy. It functions as a criminal cartel, adhering to its own body of "law" and "justice" and, in so doing, thwarts and usurps the authority of legally constituted judicial bodies . . .

In individual cities, the local core group may also be known as the "outfit," the "syndicate," or the "mob." These 24 groups work with and control other racket groups, whose leaders are of various ethnic derivations. In addition, the thousands of employees who perform the street-level functions of organized crime's gambling, usury, and other illegal activities represent a cross section of the Nation's population groups.

The present confederation of organized crime groups arose after Prohibition, during which Italian, German, Irish, and Jewish groups had competed with one another in racket operations. The Italian groups were successful in switching their enterprises from prostitution and bootlegging to gambling, extortion, and other illegal activities. They consolidated their power through murder and violence. . . .

The scope and effect of their criminal operations and penetration of legitimate businesses vary from area to area. The wealthiest and most influential core groups operate in States including New York, New Jersey, Illinois, Florida, Louisiana, Nevada, Michigan, and Rhode Island. [There are] many States in which members of core groups control criminal activity even though they do not reside there. For example, a variety of illegal activities in New England is controlled from Rhode Island.

Recognition of the common ethnic tie of the 5,000 or more members of organized crime's core groups is essential to understanding the structure of these groups today. Some have been concerned that past identification of Cosa Nostra's ethnic character has reflected on Italian-Americans generally. This false implication was eloquently refuted by one of the Nation's outstanding experts on organized crime, Sgt. Ralph Salerno of the New York City Police Department. When an Italian-American racketeer complained to him, "Why does it have to be one of your own kind that hurts you?", Sgt. Salerno answered:

> I'm not your kind and you're not my kind. My manners, morals, and mores are not yours. The only thing we have in common is that we both spring from an Italian heritage and culture—and you are the traitor to that heritage and culture which I am proud to be part of.

Organized crime in its totality thus consists of these 24 groups allied with other racket enterprises to form a loose confederation operating in large and small cities. In the core groups, because of their permanency of form, strength of organization and ability to control other racketeer operations, resides the power that organized crime has in America today.

Internal Structure

Each of the 24 groups is known as a "family," with membership varying from as many as 700 men to as few as 20. Most cities with organized crime have only one family; New York City has five. Each family can participate in the full range of activities in which organized crime generally is known to engage. Family organization is rationally designed with an integrated set of positions geared to maximize profits. Like any large corporation, the organization functions regardless of personnel changes, and no individual—not even the leader—is indispensable. If he dies or goes to jail, business goes on.

The hierarchical structure of the families resembles that of the Mafia groups that have operated for almost a century on the island of Sicily. Each family is headed by one man, the "boss," whose primary functions are maintaining order and maximizing profits. Subject only to the possibility of being overruled by the national advisory group, which will be discussed below, his authority in all matters relating to his family is absolute.

Beneath each boss is an "underboss," the vice president or deputy director of the family. He collects information for the boss; he relays messages to him and passes his instructions down to his own underlings. In the absence of the boss, the underboss acts for him.

On the same level as the underboss, but operating in a staff capacity, is the *consigliere,* who is a counselor, or adviser. Often an elder member of the family who has partially retired from a career in crime, he gives advice to family members, including the boss and underboss, and thereby enjoys considerable influence and power.

Below the level of the underboss are the *caporegime,* some of whom serve as buffers between the top members of the family and the lower-echelon personnel. To maintain their insulation from the police, the leaders of the hierarchy (particularly the boss) avoid direct communication with the workers. All commands, information, complaints, and money flow back and forth through a trusted go-between. A *caporegima* fulfilling this buffer capacity, however, unlike the underboss, does not make decisions or assume any of the authority of his boss.

Other *caporegime* serve as chiefs of operating units. The number of men supervised in each unit varies with the size and activities of particular families. Often the *caporegima* has one or two associates who work closely with him, carrying orders, information, and money to the men who belong to his unit. From a business standpoint, the *caporegima* is analogous to plant supervisor or sales manager.

The lowest level "members" of a family are the *soldati,* the soldiers or "button" men who report to the *caporegime.* A soldier may operate a particular illicit enterprise (e.g., a loan-sharking operation, a dice game, a lottery, a bookmaking operation, a smuggling operation, or a vending machine company) on a commission basis, or he may "own" the enterprise and pay a portion of its profit to the organization, in return for the right to operate. Partnerships are common between two or more soldiers and between soldiers and men higher up in the hierarchy. Some soldiers and most upper-echelon family members have interests in more than one business.

Beneath the soldiers in the hierarchy are large numbers of employees and commission agents who are not members of the family and not necessarily of Italian descent. These are the people who do most of the actual work in the various enterprises. They have no buffers or other insulation from law enforcement. They take bets, drive trucks, answer telephones, sell narcotics, tend the stills, work in the legitimate businesses. For example, in a major lottery business that operated in Negro neighborhoods in Chicago, the workers were Negroes; the bankers for the lottery were Japanese-Americans; but the game, including the banking operation, was licensed, for a fee, by a family member.

The structure and activities of a typical family are shown in (Chart 9.1).

There are at least two aspects of organized crime that characterize it as a unique form of criminal activity. The first is the element of corruption. The second is the element of enforcement, which is necessary for the maintenance of both internal discipline and the regularity of business transactions. In the hierarchy of organized crime there are positions for people fulfilling both of these functions. But neither is essential to the long-term operation of other types of criminal groups. The members of a pickpocket troupe or check-passing ring, for example, are likely to take punitive action against any member who holds out more than his share of the spoils, or betrays the group to the police; but they do not recruit or train for a well-established position of "enforcer."

Organized crime groups, on the other hand, are believed to contain one or more fixed positions for "enforcers," whose duty it is to maintain organizational integrity by arranging for the maiming and killing of recalcitrant members. And there is a position for a "corrupter," whose function is to establish relationships with those public officials and other influential persons whose assistance is necessary to achieve the organization's goals. By including these positions within its organization, each criminal cartel, or "family," becomes a government as well as a business.

The highest ruling body of the 24 families is the "commission." This body serves as a combination legislature, supreme court, board of directors, and arbitration board; its principal functions are judicial. Family members look to the commission as the ultimate authority on organizational and jurisdictional disputes. It is composed of the bosses of the Nation's most powerful families but has authority over all 24. The composition of the commission varies from 9 to 12 men. According to current information, there are presently 9 families represented, 5 from New York City and 1 each from Philadelphia, Buffalo, Detroit, and Chicago.

The commission is not a representative legislative assembly or an elected judicial body. Members of this council do not regard each other as equals. Those with long tenure on the commission and those who head large families, or possess unusual wealth, exercise greater authority and receive utmost respect. The balance of power on this nationwide council rests with the leaders of New York's 5 families. They have always served on the commission and consider New York as at least the unofficial headquarters of the entire organization.

In recent years organized crime has become increasingly diversified and sophisticated. One consequence appears to be significant organizational restructuring. As in any organization, authority in organized crime may derive either from rank based on incumbency in a high position or from expertise based on possession of technical knowledge and skill. Traditionally, organized crime groups, like totalitarian governments, have maintained discipline through the

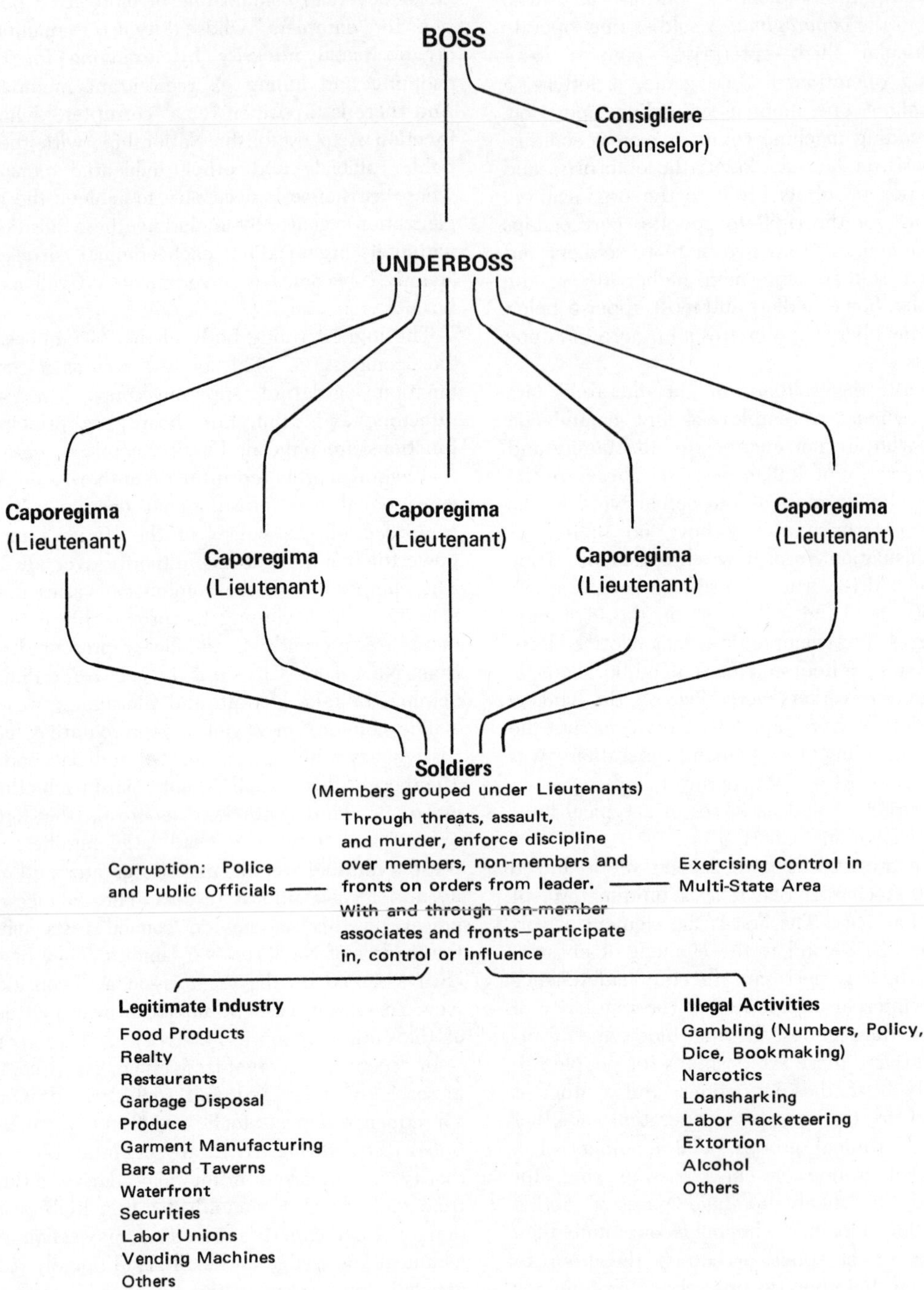

AN ORGANIZED CRIME FAMILY

unthinking acceptance of orders by underlings who have respected the rank of their superiors. However, since 1931, organized crime has gained power and respectability by moving out of bootlegging and prostitution and into gambling, usury, and control of legitimate business. Its need for expertise, based on technical knowledge and skill, has increased. Currently both the structure and operation of illicit enterprises reveal some indecision brought about by attempting to follow both patterns at the same time. Organized crime's "experts" are not fungible, or interchangeable, like the "soldiers" and street workers, and as experts are included within an organization, discipline and structure inevitably assume new forms. It may be awareness of these facts that is leading many family members to send their sons to universities to learn business administration skills.

As the bosses realize that they cannot handle the complicated problems of business and finance alone, their authority will be delegated. Decision making will be decentralized, and individual freedom of action will tend to increase. New problems of discipline and authority may occur if greater emphasis on expertise within the ranks denies unskilled members of the families an opportunity to rise to positions of leadership. The unthinking acceptance of rank authority may be difficult to maintain when experts are placed above long-term, loyal soldiers. Primarily because of fear of infiltration by law enforcement, many of the families have not admitted new members for several years. That fact plus the increasing employment of personnel with specialized and expert functions may blur the lines between membership and nonmembership. In organized crime, internal rebellion would not take the form of strikes and picketing. It would bring a new wave of internal violence.

Code of Conduct

The leaders of the various organized crime families acquire their positions of power and maintain them with the assistance of a code of conduct that, like the hierarchical structure of the families, is very similar to the Sicilian Mafia's code—and just as effective. The code stipulates that underlings should not interfere with the leaders' interests and should not seek protection from the police. They should be "standup guys" who go to prison in order that the bosses may amass fortunes. The code gives the leaders exploitative authoritarian power over everyone in the organization. Loyalty, honor, respect, absolute obedience—these are inculcated in family members through ritualistic initiation and customs within the organization, through material rewards, and through violence. Though underlings are forbidden to "inform" to the outside world, the family boss learns of deviance within the organization through an elaborate system of internal informants. Despite prescribed mechanisms for peaceful settlement of disputes between family members, the boss himself may order the execution of any family member for any reason.

The code not only preserves leadership authority but also makes it extremely difficult for law enforcement to cultivate informants and maintain them within the organization.

Need for Greater Knowledge of Organization and Structure

Although law enforcement has uncovered the skeletal organization of organized crime families, much greater knowledge is needed about the structure and operations of these organizations. For example, very little is known about the many functions performed by the men occupying the formally established positions in the organizations. In private business identifying a person as a "vice president" is meaningless unless one knows his duties. In addition to his formal obligations, the corporate officer may have important informal roles such as expediter or troubleshooter.

More successful law enforcement measures against the organized crime families will be possible only when the entire range of informal and formal roles for each position is ascertained. Answers to crucial questions must be found: While it is known that "money-movers" are employed to insure maximum use of family capital, how does money move from lower-echelon workers to top leaders? How is that money spread among illicit activities and into legitimate business? What are the specific methods by which public officials are corrupted? What roles do corrupted officials play? What informal roles have been devised for successful continuation of each of the illicit enterprises, such as gambling and usury? Only through the answers to questions such as these will society be able to understand precisely how organized crime maintains a coherent, efficient organization with a permanency of form that survives changes in working and leadership personnel.

THE NATION'S EFFORTS TO CONTROL ORGANIZED CRIME

Investigation and prosecution of organized criminal groups in the 20th century has seldom proceeded on a continuous, institutionalized basis. Public interest and demands for action have reached high levels sporadically, but, until recently, spurts of concentrated law enforcement activity have been followed by decreasing interest and application of resources.

Historical Background

The foothold that organized crime has gained in our society can be partly explained by the belated recognition on the part of the people and their governments of the need for specialized efforts in law enforcement to counter the enterprises and tactics of organized crime. A few law enforcement officials became concerned with the illicit enterprises of Mafia-type groups in the United States near the close of the 19th century. Sustained efforts at investigation were abruptly terminated by the murders of two police officers, one from New Orleans and one from New York City. The multimillion-dollar bootlegging business in the Prohibition era of the 1920's produced intensive investigations by the Treasury Department and the conviction of Chicago racket leader Al Capone.

In the 1930's, the special racket group of Thomas E. Dewey in New York City secured the conviction of several prominent racketeers, including the late Lucky Luciano, the syndicate leader whose organizational genius made him the father of today's confederation of organized crime families. In the early 1940's, FBI investigation of a million-dollar extortion plot in the moving picture industry resulted in the conviction of several racket leaders, including the Chicago family boss who was then a member of organized crime's national council.

After World War II there was little national interest in the problem until 1950, when the U.S. Attorney General convened a national conference on organized crime. This conference made several recommendations concerning investigative and prosecutive needs. Several weeks later the well-publicized hearings of the Senate Special Committee under Senator Kefauver began. The Kefauver committee heard over 800 witnesses from nearly every state and temporarily aroused the concern of many communities. There was a brief series of local investigations in cities where the Senate committee had exposed organized crime operations and public corruption, but law enforcement generally failed to develop the investigative and prosecutive units necessary to root out the activities of the criminal cartels.

In 1957 the discovery of the meeting in Apalachin, N.Y., of at least 75 criminal cartel leaders from every section of the Nation aroused national interest again. This interest was further stimulated by disclosures in the hearings of Senator McClellan's Select Senate Committee investigating organized crime's infiltration of labor and business. A concerted Federal enforcement response developed in the 1950's, and special, institutionalized efforts on the local level have been growing slowly since that time.

Federal Law Enforcement

Following the Kefauver hearings, the Department of Justice commenced a concerted drive against the leading racket figures identified in the hearings. Federal prosecutors throughout the Nation were encouraged to initiate investigations and prosecutions of such persons. As a result, a number of high level organized crime participants were convicted of Federal law violations. Under authority of the immigration statutes, the Department was successful in effecting the deportation of other racketeers. In 1954, the Justice Department formed an Organized Crime and Racketeering (OCR) Section to encourage the continuation of these prosecutive efforts. Efforts to institutionalize an antiracketeering intelligence program were hindered by a lack of coordination and interest by some Federal investigative agencies.

In 1958, after Apalachin, an Attorney General's Special Group on Organized Crime was created in the Department of Justice with regional offices from which intelligence information was gathered and grand jury proceedings conducted, concerning the Apalachin conferees. After trial and reversal of the convictions of 20 of these conferees for conspiring to obstruct justice, the group's functions were assumed by the existing OCR Section.

In September 1960, the Federal Bureau of Investigation began to supply the OCR Section with regular intelligence reports on 400 of the Nation's organized crime figures. But with only 17 attorneys and minimal intelligence information from other Federal agencies, the section could not adequately fulfill its functions, which included coordinating all Federal law enforcement activities against organized crime, accumulating and correlating all necessary data, initiating and supervising investigations, formulating general prosecutive policies, and assisting the Federal prosecuting attorneys throughout the country.

In 1961, the OCR Section expanded its organized crime program to unprecedented proportions. In the next 3 years, regular intelligence reports were secured from 26 separate Federal agencies, the number of attorneys was nearly quadrupled, and convictions increased. Indicative of the cooperation during this enforcement effort was the pooling of information from several Federal agencies for investigative leads in income tax cases. Over 60 percent of the convictions secured between 1961 and July 1965 resulted from tax investigations conducted by the Internal Revenue Service. Several high-level members of organized crime families in New York City were convicted through the efforts of the Federal Bureau of Narcotics.

The FBI was responsible for convictions of organized crime figures in New York City, Chicago, and elsewhere. Enactment of statutes giving the FBI jurisdiction in interstate gambling cases resulted in disruption, by investigation and prosecution, of major interstate gambling operations, including "lay off" betting, which is essential to the success of local gambling businesses.

In 1965, a number of factors slowed the momentum of the organized crime drive. A Senate committee uncovered a few isolated instances of wiretapping and electronic surveillance by Treasury Department agents, and some officials began to question whether special emphasis upon organized crime in tax enforcement was appropriate or fair. The Department of Justice was accused of extensively using illegal electronic surveillance in investigations of racketeer influence in Las Vegas casinos. Federal prosecutors in some large cities demanded independence from OCR Section attorneys and prosecutive policies. Attacks appeared in the press on the intensity and tactics of the Federal investigative and prosecutive efforts. A high rate of turnover among OCR Section attorneys meant discontinuity of effort and reduced personnel by nearly 25 percent.

This combination of adverse circumstances apparently led the OCR Section to believe that it could no longer expect the high degree of cooperation it had received from some Federal investigative agencies, and the intensity of its efforts diminished. In May 1966, however, President Johnson directed Federal enforcement officials to review the status of the national program against organized crime. He restated his determination to continue and accelerate the program. In a White House memorandum he called upon the appropriate agencies and departments to coordinate their activities and cooperate to the utmost with the Department of Justice.

State and Local Law Enforcement

The Commission made a survey of 71 cities to determine the extent of State and local law enforcement against organized crime. The survey revealed that only 12 of the 19 cities that acknowledged having organized crime have specialized units within the police department to investigate that activity. In only 6 of those 19 cities are prosecutors specially assigned to work on organized crime. Only 3 of the 43 police departments that answered that they had no organized crime in their area had created units to gather intelligence concerning the possibility of its existence. One of the three, Los Angeles, has a 55-man unit that gathers intelligence information to prevent the expansion of organized crime.

At present, well-developed organized crime

investigation units and effective intelligence programs exist within police and prosecutive agencies in only a handful of jurisdictions. There is, however, some evidence that local police and prosecutors are becoming more aware of the threat of organized crime. For example, in Philadelphia, both the police department and the prosecutor have created units to work exclusively in this area. In the Bronx County prosecutor's office responsibility for antiracketeering work has been centralized. The New England State Police Compact is a first step toward regional confrontations of organized crime. In addition to provisions for mutual assistance in a number of areas and for coordination of command training, the compact provides for a centralization of organized crime data to which all members contribute and from which all draw. This system should reduce current duplication and permit a better coordinated attack upon organized crime.

In 1956, the Law Enforcement Intelligence Unit was established in California. This was the first step toward the development of a network for the exchange of data concerning people active in organized crime. The LEIU has since expanded to more than 150 members throughout the Nation. It maintains a central file in California, and information is available to its members on request.

The effectiveness of these State and local efforts is difficult to assess. But only New York and California have developed continuing State programs that have produced a series of convictions against major figures in organized crime. Coordinated police activity has substantially aided this process. On the local level, Chicago and New York City, where the organized crime problem is the most severe, appear to be the only cities in which large, firmly established police intelligence units continue to develop major cases against members of the criminal cartels.

Public and Private Crime Commissions

Among the most effective vehicles for providing public information on organized crime are the crime investigating commissions, which exist in a number of States. When established without having to rely on continuing governmental financial support and the resulting potential political pressures, the private crime commission has frequently rendered major service in exposing organized crime and corruption and arousing public interest. The Chicago Crime Commission and the Metropolitan Crime Commission of New Orleans have played major roles in informing the citizens within their jurisdiction of the menace of organized crime and have fulfilled substantial educational, investigative, and legislative functions.

Where a governmentally sponsored nonpartisan crime commission is created, as with the New York State Temporary Commission on Investigation, significant benefits have resulted. Established shortly after the Apalachin meeting, it has through a series of public hearings exposed organized crime and corruption. Recent loan-shark hearings prompted legislative action to make prosecution of such offenders less difficult. The Illinois Crime Commission, through public hearings and the efforts of its own investigators, continually exposes organized criminal activity. A governmental commission in California detailed the operations of criminal cartels in that State in the early 1950's and recommended action that subsequently proved effective.

Limitations on Control Efforts

Efforts to curb the growth of organized crime in America have not been successful. It is helpful in devising a program for the future to examine the problems encountered in attempting to combat organized crime.

Difficulties in Obtaining Proof. As described above, criminal cartels have organized their groups and operations to insulate their higher echelon personnel from law enforcement and regulatory agencies. Every measure has been taken to insure that governmental investigation, no matter how intensive, will be unable to secure live witnesses, the sine qua non of prosecution. Street workers, who are not members of organized crime families, cannot prove the identities of the upper-level personnel. If workers are arrested for gambling or other illicit activities, the fear instilled in them by the code of nondisclosure prevents their telling even the little they may know. The organization provides money and food for families of incarcerated workers; this helps to keep the workers loyal. Lawyers provided by the cartels for arrested employees preserve the interests of the organization ahead of those of the particular defendant.

Usually, when a crime is committed, the public calls the police, but the police have to ferret out even the existence of organized crime. The many Americans who are compliant "victims" have no incentive to report the illicit operations. The millions of people who gamble illegally are willing customers who do not wish to see their supplier destroyed. Even the true victims of organized crime, such as those succumbing to extortion, are too afraid to inform law enforcement officials. Some misguided citizens think there is social stigma in the role of "informer," and this tends to prevent reporting and cooperating with police.

Law enforcement may be able to develop informants, but organized crime uses torture and murder to destroy the particular prosecution at hand and to deter others from cooperating with police agencies. Informants who do furnish intelligence to the police often wish to remain anonymous and are unwilling to testify publicly. Other informants are valuable on a long-range basis and cannot be used in public trials. Even when a prosecution witness testifies against family members, the criminal organization often tries, sometimes successfully, to bribe or threaten jury members or judges.

Documentary evidence is equally difficult to obtain. Bookmakers at the street level keep no detailed records. Main offices of gambling enterprises can be moved often enough to keep anyone from getting sufficient evidence for a search warrant for a particular location. Mechanical devices are used that prevent even the telephone company from knowing about telephone calls. And even if an enforcement agent has a search warrant, there are easy ways to destroy written material while the agent fulfills the legal requirements of knocking on the door, announcing his identity and purpose, and waiting a reasonable time for a response before breaking into the room.

Lack of Resources. No State or local law enforcement agency is adequately staffed to deal successfully with the problems of breaking down criminal organizations. Just one major organized crime case may take 2 to 3 years to develop and then several more years to complete through prosecution and appeal. Cases may require several man-years of investigative resources. The percentage of investigations that result in arrests is quite low. Requests for increased budgets in government are usually granted only upon a showing of success; i.e., a high number of arrests. An effective organized crime investigative effort may not be able to produce such statistics without years of intelligence gathering, and the drive for statistics may divert investigative energy to meaningless low-level gambling arrests that have little effect on the criminal organizations. Even with these known problems, the organized crime units of all but a few city police departments are staffed by less than 10 men, and only 6 prosecutors' offices have assigned assistants to work exclusively or particularly in organized crime cases.

Effective investigation and prosecution of organized crime require extensive experience. . . . Assistant prosecutors rarely stay in a district attorney's office for more than a few years, if that long. On the investigative level, with the exception of some Federal agencies, assignment to the organized crime intelligence unit may be only a step in an officer's career. The most proficient people are likely to be promoted out of the unit into supervisory positions, and their replacements must then start the difficult job of acquiring the skills for the peculiar demands of organized crime investigation. In addition, few units have any personnel with the necessary accounting and legal knowledge.

Lack of Coordination. Local police are hampered by their limited geographical jurisdiction, and law enforcement has not responded by developing sufficient coordination among the agencies. One gambling operation may range through several police jurisdictions; if only one agency is involved in the investigation, it may be unable to detect key elements of the illegal enterprise. The potential for Federal-local cooperation was illustrated in the past 3 years in Chicago. With search warrant affidavits signed by FBI agents and based on FBI information, Chicago police have arrested almost 1,000 gambling defendants and seized money and wagering paraphernalia valued at approximately $400,000. The monthly gross of gambling sites so raided exceeded $8½ million. Unfortunately, such instances of sustained intensity are extremely rare.

Agencies do not cooperate with each other in preparing cases, and they do not exchange information with each other. Enforcement officers do not trust each other for they are sensitive to organized crime's ability to corrupt law enforcement. Agencies have not developed strategies to overcome these problems and to insure that needed data can be effectively transferred.

Failure to Develop Strategic Intelligence. Intelligence deals with all of the things that should be known before initiating a course of action. In the context of organized crime there are two basic types of intelligence information: tactical and strategic. Tactical intelligence is the information obtained for specific organized crime prosecutions. Strategic intelligence is the information regarding the capabilities, intentions, and vulnerabilities of organized crime groups. For example, the body of knowledge built up by the FBI concerning the structure, membership, activities, and purposes of La Cosa Nostra represents significant strategic intelligence.

At present, most law enforcement agencies gather organized crime intelligence information with prosecution as the immediate objective. This tactical focus has not been accompanied by development of the full potential for strategic intelligence. That failure accounts for the gaps in knowledge, described above, concerning the ways in which criminal cartels organize and operate as a business. Prosecution based merely upon individual violations that come to the attention of law enforcement may result in someone's incarceration, but the criminal organization simply places someone else in the vacated position.

A body of strategic intelligence information would enable agencies to predict what directions organized crime might take, which industries it might try to penetrate, and how it might infiltrate. Law enforcement and regulatory agencies could then develop plans to destroy the organizational framework and coherence of the criminal cartels. Comprehensive strategic planning, however, even with an expanded intelligence effort, will not be possible until relevant disciplines, such as economics, political science, sociology, and operations research, begin to study organized crime intensively.

Failure to Use Available Sanctions. Gambling is the largest source of revenue for the criminal cartels, but the members of organized crime know they can operate free of significant punishment. Street workers have little reason to be deterred from joining the ranks of criminal organizations by fear of long jail sentences or large fines. Judges are reluctant to jail bookmakers and lottery operators. Even when offenders are convicted, the sentences are often very light. Fines are paid by the organization and considered a business expense.

And in other organized crime activity, when management level figures are convicted, too frequently the sentences imposed are not commensurate with the status of the offender.

Lack of Public and Political Commitment. The public demands action only sporadically, as intermittent, sensational disclosures reveal intolerable violence and corruption caused by organized crime. Without sustained public pressure, political office seekers and office holders have little incentive to address themselves to combatting organized crime. A drive against organized crime usually uncovers political corruption; this means that a crusading mayor or district attorney makes many political enemies. The vicious cycle perpetuates itself. Politicians will not act unless the public so demands; but much of the urban public wants the services provided by organized crime and does not wish to disrupt the system that provides those services. And much of the public does not see or understand the effects of organized crime in society.

32.

Thorsten Sellin

ORGANIZED CRIME: A BUSINESS ENTERPRISE

If we take a closer look at the term "organized crime," it becomes apparent that, as used today, it is not a very precise term. The word "crime" creates no difficulty, for it means, in this connection, conduct that violates the criminal law and can subject the offender to punishments prescribed by that law. It is the word "organized" that proves a stumbling block, because it could have more than one implication or interpretation. We assume that it does not describe the behavior of an individual, who carefully plots and carries out a crime, which is to bring him some personal gratification, without the aid or co-operation of others, no matter how systematically he may organize his plan of action. When he needs the co-operation of others to carry on his criminal activity and gain the benefits from it, we can begin to talk of "organization." A team of jewel thieves or pickpockets is one example; its members must have leadership and carry out specific and perhaps diverse tasks, stolen goods must be disposed of through a "fence," and, if they are caught, there may be an attorney, who knows them, who will handle their case. All these functions and relationships are parts of a pattern of organization.

This is not the kind of operation, however, that is covered by the term "organized crime" as it is commonly used today. It has come to be synonymous with economic enterprises organized for the purpose of conducting illegal activities and which, when they operate legitimate ventures, do so by illegal methods. They have arisen for the chief purpose of catering to our vices—gambling, drinking, sex, narcotics—which our laws do not tolerate, and they have found many other collateral ways of gaining illegitimate profits. Whatever form they take, financial profit is the goal, which they share with the entrepreneurs of legitimate business. Indeed, in their perverted way, they subscribe to the tenets of American entrepreneurship, in a system of free enterprise, as described by Sawyer:[1]

> individualism; competitive economic activity within an impersonal market; mobility, social and geographical; achieved as against ascribed status, with economic achievement the main ladder of advancement; emphasis on "success" in a competitive occupational system as the almost universally prescribed goal; money income as a primary reward and symbol of success; the institutionalization of innovation, risk-taking, change and growth.

These illegal enterprises also resemble the legal ones in other respects. An illegal liquor business, for instance, must own or have access to distilleries, means of transporting the wares, warehouses, outlets in saloons, clubs, restaurants, or private establishments. This requires capital, managerial personnel, and employees of various kinds. An illegal gambling enterprise faces the same problems of organization as a legitimate banking chain. The basic difference between the illegal enterprise and a legal one devoted to similar but approved functions is not in the hierarchical structure, the table of organization, or the distribution of the duties of its components, for they are essentially alike. It lies in the fact that the illegal nature of the business has created problems that have to be solved in ways that a legal firm does not have to employ. Both have in common a hope for continuity and survival. "Unlike most criminal groups but like most business enterprises, a

Source: *The Annals,* Vol. 347 (May, 1963), pp. 12–19. Reprinted by permission of the author and the journal.

[1]John E. Sawyer, "The Entrepreneur and the Social Order," Chap. 1 in William B. Miller (ed.), *Men in Business: Essays on the Historical Role of the Entrepreneur* (New York and Evanston: Harper & Row, 1962).

criminal organization contemplates a continuous life-span."[2]

THE NUMBERS BUSINESS

To illustrate the continuity just mentioned as well as the manner in which an illegal business must operate to survive, only one such business will be discussed, the one commonly referred to as the "numbers racket." Most people probably know what it consists of, for newspapers, magazines, and television have often described it. Briefly, "numbers" is an illegal lottery in which the player bets that a certain number or combination of numbers will win in a drawing. It is frequently assumed that it is of recent origin. "The origins of the game are somewhat obscure, but some believe that it was brought to this country from the Caribbean area early in this century and operated in various cities on a small-time basis"—according to an official New York report.[3] The same source calls the game either "policy" or "numbers," as though these words were interchangeable. In fact, they represent quite different ways of conducting the lottery, policy being an older form. The specific way of drawing the winners in numbers may not be very old and is bound up with the demise of legal lotteries in the United States, but the illegal lottery of which numbers is the most representative today may be nearly as old as the legal ones. It has survived all efforts to eliminate it, by law or law enforcement.

Evolution of the Genoese Lottery

The number lottery, or lotto, is said to have originated in Genoa early in the seventeenth century; it simulated the election of five political candidates from among a large number—rarely over 110 and finally fixed at 90—all identified by a number from 1 to 90. Printed lists of the names of the candidates and their numbers were distributed and bets were placed that one, two, or three of the numbers would appear among the five drawn in a public drawing from an urn. A bet on two numbers was called an *ambo,* on three a *terno.*

Lotteries based on the Genoese practice were organized in many American states during the last century. Although prohibited by law in New York in 1834, an author writing in 1868 claimed that New York City was the headquarters for lotteries in Kentucky and Missouri, where public drawings were held at noon and at night, respectively, the winning numbers being telegraphed to New York. These lotteries were known as ternary ones, based on numbers from 1 to 78, in which a lottery ticket with any three of the up to fourteen numbers drawn won the highest prize, and those with but two or one of the numbers won less.

It is a by-product of these lotteries, however, that is of special interest to us. According to Martin, writing in 1868:[4]

> Together with the sale of [lottery] tickets is carried on an extensive game of gambling known as "policy." To "policy" is to bet on certain numbers coming out in the [lottery] drawing, for either morning or evening. Thus, if I believe 4, 11, 44 will be drawn, I stake a dollar at the lottery office, or any sum I see fit, up to five hundred dollars, and if all three of the numbers make their appearance on the drawing, the liberal managers will give me two hundred dollars for my one . . . the three numbers taken are called a "gig"; two numbers a "saddle"; four numbers a "horse."

"Policy"—A Variation

Martin claimed that there were some 600 places in the city, known as exchanges, where lottery tickets could be bought and, presumably, "policy" played.

> The Negroes of the city are great "policy" players. . . . [One old woman] says she dreams her numbers. The sale of lottery dream-books is really immense. One firm on Ann Street sells several thousand a month of these books, wherein every possible dream is described and the proper "policy" attached to it.[5]

Essentially the same picture of "the lottery business, closely connected with which is 'policy dealing'," was described fourteen years later

[2]Earl Johnson, Jr., "Organized Crime: Challenge to the American Legal System, Part I," *Journal of Criminal Law, Criminology, and Police Science,* Vol. 53 (December, 1962), p. 401.

[3]Temporary Commission of Investigation of the State of New York, *An Investigation of Law Enforcement in Buffalo* (New York: January, 1961).

[4]Edward Winslow Martin, *The Secrets of the Great City* (Philadelphia, 1868), pp. 513–14.

[5]*Ibid.,* p. 517.

by McCabe[6] and in 1891 by Colonel Knox, who had this to say about it:[7]

"Playing policy" is a cheap way of gambling. . . . The play is upon numbers . . . drawn daily, usually in Kentucky or Louisiana, and sent by telegraph. The numbers are from 1 to 78; the room where the game is played is, like those of other cheap gambling dens, usually at the rear of a cigar store, barroom or other place, where it does not arouse suspicion if many persons are seen entering. A long counter extends the entire length of the room, and behind this counter, near its center, sits the man who keeps the game and is called the "writer." He is not the proprietor, but simply a clerk on salary, and his duties are to copy the slips handed up by the players, mark them with the amount paid, and watch to see that no fraud is practiced. There are twenty-five plays every morning and the same number in the evening at the regular shops, and they all get their winning numbers from a central office in Broad Street. Near the writer is an iron spike or hook on which are the policy slips; each slip contains the winning numbers and is placed face downwards so that nobody can see what it is.

A player, said Colonel Knox, might take a slip on the counter, write, let us say, five pairs of numbers and bet a sum on five "gigs." When the other players in the room have filed their bets, the writer picks up the top slip from the iron spike, writes the numbers he finds on it, in two columns of twelve each, on a slate and hangs it up for all to see. If the player has guessed two of the numbers in either column in one of the gigs he has won ten times the amount of his bet.[8]

Policy has survived and is still played in much the same manner as it was done a century ago. It flourishes in Chicago, according to recent descriptions. In 1945 Drake and Cayton wrote:[9]

Almost as numerous as the churches (and more evenly distributed) are Bronzeville's [Chicago's South Side Negro district] 500-odd "policy stations," in any one of which a person may place a bet that certain numbers will be announced as lucky by one of 15 or 16 "policy companies" . . . In order to keep up a semblance of respect for the law, about half the stations are "fronted" by legitimate businesses. Most of the others can be easily recognized by the initiated . . . by a sign on a window or door: "Open"–"4–11–44"–"Doing Business"—"All Books" . . . Winning numbers are listed three times daily, after selection at a public "drawing." The places where the drawings are made are known as "wheels" . . . scattered about the community. . . . The drawings are made from a small drum-shaped container in which 78 capsules or balls, numbered consecutively, are placed. After each turn of the drum, a ball is pulled and its number read aloud. As they are called, a printer sets the numbers into a special printing press. As soon as the last number is drawn, the press rolls out the policy slips, which are then distributed all over Bronzeville. . . . Indispensable for the inveterate policy player is his "dream book," valuable for translating both dreams and "significant" occurrences into "gigs." . . . The policy station is simply a brokerage office for the players. . . . Station owners are allowed to keep 25 per cent of the gross business they write, and so lucrative is the business that the 500 stations employ some 2000 porters, writers, and other employees. . . . Some legitimate businessmen have turned to it as their major enterprise and use their other business merely as a front. The station is simply the most visible expression of a complex machine employing over 5000 persons, which in 1938 had a weekly payroll of over twenty-five thousand dollars and an annual gross turnover of at least $18 million. This business is organized as a cartel with a syndicate of 15 men . . . in control of the game. On the syndicate payroll were 125 clerks, more than 100 pickup and delivery men, a dozen or so accountants, including several CPA's, and over 100 miscellaneous employees–doormen, floormen, janitors, stampers, bookkeepers, and "bouncers."

The Modern Numbers Game

In most of our large cities today, the old policy lottery has been displaced by or transformed into what people know as the numbers game. This has made it possible to dispense with public drawings, eliminate the paraphernalia and operations needed for them, and substitute an ingenious method of selecting the winning numbers, which enables the players to determine for themselves whether or not they have won at the end of the day, because newspapers will –inadvertently–give them the information. The

[6]James D. McCabe, *New York by Sunlight and Gaslight* (Philadelphia, 1882), p. 549.

[7]Helen Campbell, Thomas W. Knox, and Thomas Byrnes, *Darkness and Daylight; or Lights and Shadows of New York Life* (Hartford, Conn., 1891), p. 639.

[8]*Ibid.*, p. 640.

[9]Herbert L. Marx, Jr. (ed.), *Gambling in America* (New York: H. W. Wilson Co., 1952), pp. 74–77, quoting St. Clair Drake and Horace R. Cayton, *Black Metropolis* (New York: Harcourt Brace, 1945). A slightly more recent account, including illustrative photographs of the drum used in drawings and of a policy ticket, is found in W. T. Brannon's "Chicago–Penny Ante Paradise," *U.S. Crime*, Vol. 1 (December, 1951), pp. 76–83.

operation of this variant of the Genoese lottery has necessitated a change in the technique of betting. The player places a bet with a writer that, let us say, a certain number containing three digits, from 000 to 999, will be the winning one. He knows or is told how to find out the results of the "drawing." In some cities, the last figures in the number of (a) stocks that advanced, (b) stocks that declined, and (c) stocks that remained unchanged on the stock market would furnish the answer; in others, certain figures, perhaps the last three digits, in the total sum of money passing through the New York Clearinghouse; in still others, certain digits in the daily balance of the United States Treasury or in the total amount of money wagered by the pari-mutuel method on certain combinations of races at some predetermined track. Whoever invented the system, it is reasonable to believe that, when the Louisiana State Lottery collapsed in 1890 and Congress the same year prohibited the mailing of lottery tickets or material and, in 1895, the interstate transportation of tickets, somebody figured out this substitute for the ternary system that had relied on the results of the drawings in the southern lotteries as the source of the winning numbers. This may also explain the belief that numbers originated about the turn of the century.

THE BUFFALO INVESTIGATION

In 1959, as a result of prior extensive investigations made in Buffalo by the New York State Commission of Investigation, wholesale raids were made on numbers and other gambling operations. The raids and subsequent hearings provided much information about the nature of the illegal lotteries and the circumstances and conditions that permitted them to flourish. Thirteen numbers "banks" and "drops" (key collection points) were caught in the raids, which netted forty-six policy operators ("numbers" is still called "policy" in New York, in spite of the differences previously explained); they "included many key figures in the highest echelons of the policy racket, some of whom had never been arrested by the Buffalo Police Department, although they had operated for years. Voluminous books and records, policy slips, collectors' slips, bank tally sheets, and miscellaneous paraphernalia were seized."[10] The knowledge thus acquired by the Commission confirmed the belief that the numbers racket "is one of the most highly organized, fully staffed and disciplined of all underworld syndicated gambling operations."[11]

Organization and Operation

In Buffalo, bets could be placed with one of many hundreds of writers on the street or in many business establishments, even with some policemen. Investigators for the Commission made repeated bets in more than forty locations. The bets were recorded on specially printed slips called "B/R" slips or "Bond-Race" slips because they could be used either for bets on the outcome of New York Stock Exchange deals or on race-track wagering. The slips were made out in triplicate from bound pads, the original going to the bank and the copies retained by the writer and the player. The pads were supplied by the I. and M. Sufrin Company of Pittsburgh, Pennsylvania, whose records showed that in 1958 and 1959 some 200,000 pads had been shipped by common carrier to five "banks," or a total of five million sets of slips per year. In many instances, the supplier received payment in cash sent in packages by parcel post.

The bankers assigned specific territories to various members of their organizations in order to avoid conflict and to insure maximum efficiency.

> [Because] the nature of the operation requires that money and betting slips be deposited at the bank or in the hands of trusted members of the conspiracy prior to "post time" [at the race track] or the closing hour for wagers . . . control points known as "drops" were set up where writers turned in their slips and money. Pick-up men were employed to collect numbers and money from the drops and writers and to deposit them in the hands of controllers. From the drops, pick-up men and controllers would return winnings, if any, on the following day. All of these individuals, each essential to successful operation of the racket, were under the strictest discipline and control. Any deviation from fixed procedures or time deadlines could only

[10] *An Investigation of Law Enforcement in Buffalo*, *op. cit.*, p. 23.

[11] *Ibid.*, p. 38.

be authorized by the top banker himself . . . unflinching obedience to orders was required.[12]

The "banks" or headquarters . . ., where all management functions of the racket take place, in some instances were located in fully equipped offices containing furniture, telephones and calculating machines. A staff of clerical help assisted the bankers and controllers in the rapid calculations necessary to record and conduct the day's business.[13]

The Commission estimated, on the basis of information gained by the raids, that seven banks were managed by sixteen bankers. The net annual profits of these banks were estimated at close to two million dollars. This was achieved due to the favorable conditions under which the operations were carried on. One of the special investigators for the Commission

was directed by a uniformed Buffalo policeman to a location where numbers could be played . . .; this advice proved to be correct, as shortly after he actually placed numbers bets at the address. In many stores and business establishments in certain areas of Buffalo, numbers were played openly with slips and money freely displayed on store counters. Lines of people waiting to place their numbers bets were a common occurrence.[14]

The business was run quite openly.

The same pick-up men and controllers, using the same vehicles and generally following the same designated routes, made their rounds every day at almost exactly the same times in carrying out their functions without displaying any appreciable concern over the possibility that their activities were being observed.[15]

Law-enforcement Deficiences

In New York, persons who contrive a lottery or own, direct, and manage numbers operations are committing a felony, and persons found in possession of numbers slips are guilty of a misdemeanor. What, then, were the police of Buffalo doing about these violations under their very noses? Departmental instructions require police officers to make periodical reports of "suspected premises," but, during 1958, 1959, and the first two months of 1960, not a single such report was turned in concerning numbers operations. What of arrests? In the two years 1958–1959, a total of 195 persons were arrested for all kinds of gambling offenses, of which 131 were clearly identifiable as involving numbers.

Comparing the total policy arrests for 1959 with the total number of policy racket violators . . . again demonstrates the complete inadequacy of this performance. . . . Commission accountants have estimated that 3,560 persons were engaged in acts constituting policy misdemeanors and 182 persons . . . in acts constituting policy felonies, on any given day in 1959. Yet only 72 persons were arrested for policy violations during the entire year, *and all of them for policy misdemeanors.*[16]

What happened to those arrested? One served a jail sentence of thirty days, two received suspended sentences, and a total of 4,100 dollars was collected in fines from all those arrested.

During the hearing held by the Commission, a police captain with thirty years of service in the department expressed his belief that no gambler operated in his bailiwick, although some of the top racket figures in the city had been doing so for years. Other police officers testified that they knew that numbers operations existed and who directed them, but they failed to account for the lack of law enforcement. In other words, official tolerance of the illegal lotteries was, one might say, complete. How such tolerance was purchased is another matter. An illegal business, unlicensed because prohibited, is forced to resort to bribery and corruption of law-enforcement personnel and politicians in order to operate. Their illegal character also makes them vulnerable to extortion by persons who can in return offer immunity from arrest.

DEMAND AND SUPPLY

Buffalo has been used as an example, but its counterparts are numerous in all sections of the United States. It is claimed that, during the last decade or more, strong efforts by federal, state and some local governments—stimulated by the findings of highly publicized congressional investigations—to combat organized crime of all kinds have met with some success. However, so far as the illegal lottery business is concerned, history suggests that this particular business is not likely to suffer more than tem-

[12] *Ibid.*, p. 39.
[13] *Ibid.*, p. 37.
[14] *Ibid.*, p. 14.
[15] *Ibid.*, p. 37.
[16] *Ibid.*, p. 72.

porary reverses. Like other businesses, it has its ups and downs, its recessions and recoveries, but as long as it can count on a sizable market for its services, it will survive them all. In the last analysis, they continue to thrive because a large section of the population enjoys betting—betting on horses, football games, boxing matches, basketball games, and on numbers—sees no harm in it, and does not regard it as immoral even when it is illegal. As long as this public attitude persists and is shared by or exerts an influence on candidates for elective office or servants of the law, no effective enforcement of law is conceivable. We are, in fact, caught on the horns of a dilemma, for under these circumstances our gambling laws, passed in a noble hope that they would rescue the citizen from his own evil appetites or protect him against exploitation, have also inadvertently helped to create an entrenched source of bribery and political corruption, an undesired and undesirable effect of our high-mindedness.

33.

GERARD L. GOETTEL

WHY THE CRIME SYNDICATE CAN'T BE TOUCHED

The crime syndicate in America is one of today's stark realities. Though it would be soothing to dismiss such an assertion as a sinister—or even hysterical—myth, the evidence is incontrovertible.

In frightening contrast, our law-enforcement machinery is chaotic, fragmented, and totally unequal to a task which calls for a co-ordinated effort on the federal level.

These are the melancholy facts despite the acclaim which greeted the recent conspiracy conviction of the gangland leaders who met in November 1957 at the baronial home of Joseph Barbara in Apalachin (pronounced Ap-a-lā-kin), New York. Hailed as a crushing blow against organized crime, the government's legal "victory" was, in fact, Pyrrhic. Indeed, from the very outset the Apalachin affair dramatized the grotesque inadequacy of our defenses against the most malevolent enemies of our society.

The discovery of the meeting itself was sheer happenstance. New York State Police, while making a routine check at a local motel, came upon some suspicious characters. Next day they visited the Barbara estate where were assembled seventy-five men—all of Sicilian-Italian ancestry—who had come from many points in the United States and a few from Cuba and Italy. The group included many of the top echelon of the criminal world—along with an assortment of chauffeurs, bodyguards, friends, and helpers.

Rounded up despite their frantic efforts to escape, these "guests" had bizarre explanations for their presence. The gist was that this was merely a chance meeting of people who stopped by to visit a sick friend. This was, of course, patently absurd. No one believed that these influential and worldly men, with their common national and criminal backgrounds, living in distant places, would gather by chance on a rainy weekday morning at a spot that is hard to find even with explicit road-map directions.

While newspaper headlines screamed, the forces of law began to move. An investigation was launched at once by a Federal Grand Jury in New York City under the direction of U.S. Attorney Paul W. Williams, which had been investigating the operations of leading mobsters, including many of the Apalachin delegates.

Numerous state and county agencies started separate investigations, as did various federal bodies including the McClellan Committee (officially, the Senate Select Committee on Improper Activities in the Labor or Management Field). With such duplication of effort, federal agents tailing a suspect at times found themselves under surveillance by another agency.

Never before in this country had a suspected criminal gathering been so intensively investigated. But after five months little was known of the purpose or meaning of the meeting. This was not due to ineptitude. Investigations of Mafia-type organizations seldom get far. Whether or not a "Mafia" exists is an academic question. Whatever the Apalachin characters may call themselves, they match the deadly efficiency of the dreaded Black Hand. Though they may be too sophisticated for such fraternal tomfoolery as the "death kiss" and imprint of blood, they are still true to the historic Mafia tradition whose chief tenet is "*Omertà*," which means, in their terms, "noble silence." To these men the only heinous and unforgivable sin is testifying against their brothers in crime. Noble or not, the code of silence is effectively enforced in every major gang, from the mobsters of the New York garment industry to San Francisco's narcotics ring. The crime syndicates punish those who break their laws, and the death penalty carries no right of appeal.

SLEUTHS IN STRAIGHTJACKETS

Within the walls of *Omertà* the Apalachin mobsters found further refuge behind the Fifth Amendment. Meanwhile public and press clamored for action. But it was soon apparent that organized crime was everyone's concern and no one's responsibility. State and local groups had limited geographic jurisdictions—New York State could not even subpoena residents of other states.

Only the federal government could cope with the problem. Yet it was not set up to do so, because the jurisdiction of each investigatory agency was limited to specific federal crimes. Thus the law enforcers were required to identify the crime before they could even look for the criminal—a hopeless situation since no one would tell what crimes were being plotted at the remote hamlet of Apalachin. Syndicated crime operates in a law-enforcement vacuum.

What could be done? In April 1958, after five fruitless months, Lawrence Walsh, Deputy Attorney General of the United States, decided that the federal government must spearhead a unified attack on the criminal empire. To this end he inaugurated the "Attorney General's Special Group on Organized Crime" headed by Milton R. Wessel. I became its Deputy Chief.

We began work filled with the optimistic belief that we could defeat the forces of crime if we just tried hard enough. By the end of the year our group included more than twenty lawyers in four regional headquarters. However, we had no investigators—a serious handicap—forcing us to rely largely on facts gathered by past investigations. Unfortunately there are no centralized criminal intelligence files other than arrest and fingerprint records. We visited scores of federal, state, and local agencies, in the tedious task of collecting data. To cut red tape, we were often reduced to pirating information from the files of reluctant public officials.

It turned out that we were woefully wrong in assuming that various law-enforcement agencies would be eager to co-operate with us. We learned that in Washington there are Republicans, Democrats, and Bureaucrats, and while the first two come and go, the last are immutable. Bureaucratic opposition to our work—on grounds totally divorced from politics—proved our greatest stumbling block. Incredibly, in our battle against organized crime, the obstructionists were not merely the gangland leaders whom we sought to destroy, but also the public servants entrenched in the federal government, who disapproved of and mistrusted our crusade.

Typical was the attitude of a seasoned investigator of the otherwise helpful Immigration and Naturalization Service. Declining to work overtime on a case, he remarked, "I survived the Kefauver investigation and a couple of others like it, and I'll still be on the job long after you guys are back in your Wall Street law offices."

Similarly a field supervisor for the Food and Drug Administration refused to investigate a hoodlum's profitable scheme for adulterating olive oil. His budget, he said, was not even large enough to protect consumers from poisonous foods. Hence he could not waste valuable manpower on "cops and robbers capers."

The FBI was the coolest agency of all. J. Edgar Hoover at a national meeting of U.S. Attorneys decried the need for "special groups" to fight organized crime. The FBI viewed us as young "upstarts," whose mission was unclear and whose personnel were strangers. (This problem became even more acute with undercover groups such as the Narcotics Bureau.) The public was never told that the FBI gave us the cold shoulder. Indeed a recent magazine article attributed the ultimate success of the Apalachin trial to its fine investigative work. The author pointed to the fact that a preponderance of the government's exhibits were FBI reports. What he did not know was that the reports were not produced until the federal court, at trial, *directed* the FBI to do so.

This performance was consistent with the FBI's rigid policy of refusing to take on any case which does not clearly fall within its jurisdiction; nor will it investigate if another agency has already done so. (The best known example of this policy is reported in *The FBI Story* by Don Whitehead. In 1936 Roosevelt wanted "a broad intelligence picture" of Communist and Fascist activities. The FBI demurred on the ground that, under the terms of its appropriation, such a request must be made by the State Department which, in due course, was done.)

THE PIZZA PIE RUN

In the Apalachin case, the G-men did, in fact, quietly investigate every aspect of the meeting (an assignment they called the "Pizza Pie Run"). However, when it turned out that its criminal purpose could not be proved, they just as quietly shelved the reports. Everywhere we of the Attorney General's Special Group looked for evidence we found the Bureau had been there months earlier. But when we asked for copies of the reports, the G-men acted as if they had never heard of Apalachin. This aloofness was due in part to their mistrust of us. It also reflected an internal dilemma—the FBI has long taken the position officially that large criminal syndicates do not exist—or if they do, they are a state and local law-enforcement problem. In any event, Hoover seemed determined to stay clear of us, which was a certain way to avoid the stigma of failure.

Our operations, thus, were severely limited. We needed prima-facie proof (presumptive evidence) that a particular offense had been committed to force a federal agency to investigate. But we were hard-pressed to learn in what fields the leaders of organized crime were operating—let alone to establish the commission of a specific offense. And these offenses had to be *federal*, which—for example—the commoner forms of gambling, prostitution, and even murder are not.

Our predicament was incredibly frustrating. We traced a web of meetings and trips linking the men of Apalachin with a prominent Democratic politician and a wealthy Italian-American civic leader. Were we on the trail of the legendary "Mr. Big" of the Syndicate? Unfortunately, our tantalizing evidence did not warrant hauling in these prominent citizens for questioning, particularly in view of the political implications of an attempt by Republicans to connect prominent Democrats with the Mafia. When we requested a high-priority undercover investigation, various government agencies turned us down since there was not a prima-facie showing of crimes within their jurisdictions. And no federal agency is charged with investigating organized crime, as such.

For eight months we collected data which produced no indictments. So we resigned ourselves to the only approach left (which other agencies had found futile)—a Grand Jury investigation of the Apalachin meeting itself. We chose as our first witness, Joe Magliocco of Brooklyn, a beer distributor, who would risk losing his license if he claimed the Fifth Amendment. He testified that he had driven his brother-in-law, Joe Profaci, to Apalachin for an unknown purpose. He had remained outside in a parked car throughout the meeting. (He had given a similar explanation, some thirty years earlier, when he and Profaci were caught at a gangland convention in Cleveland.)

When I completed my examination of Magliocco and checked his testimony against other evidence and newly received reports, I found he had lied about remaining outside during the meeting and otherwise testified falsely. However the real core of his testimony—that he did not know the purpose of the meeting—could not be challenged under the strict federal perjury law, which requires direct, corroborated evidence.

Gradually I realized that we were on the wrong track in seeking individual indictments. A conspiracy was preventing us from learning its secrets—a conspiracy to obstruct justice. Hence I felt that our only chance lay in a sweeping conspiracy charge. Our attack need not be directed at the conspirators' "business" about which our knowledge was meager and inconclusive, but rather at their actions in thwarting the many investigations. Their very success might be the key to their undoing.

This idea at first seemed too simple and direct to be feasible. "How, without informers, do you prove the existence of the conspiracy?" my colleagues asked.

I contended that we could find proof in the testimony of the conspirators themselves. Most of the Apalachin delegates had made at least one statement—altogether there were several hundred. All agreed on three major points:

(1) The meeting was not planned and had no particular purpose.

(2) No one knew why the others, who had so much in common with them, were there.

(3) Nothing important took place and no criminal activities were discussed.

A wealth of circumstantial evidence contradicted these assertions: intricate hotel arrangements and travel plans showed prearrangement; the distances traveled and the odd time and place of the meeting betrayed a purpose; the delegates' panicky reaction to their discovery, and their brotherhood in crime, indicated that their purpose was not innocent.

In contrast with this unanimity there were amazing discrepancies on collateral issues on which conspirators would have had difficulty in prearranging harmonious testimony. For example, Joe Profaci claimed that the trip to Apalachin was Magliocco's idea, not his, directly contradicting the latter. Just as their agreement on a palpably false story bespoke conspiracy, the inconsistencies revealed the shoddy fabric of their alibi.

These theories of mine might still be in the debating stage had calamity not struck our investigation less than a year after our triumphal blast-off. An unfriendly Democratic Congress was using the purse strings as a noose. Coupled with this hostility was an increasing antagonism from the established law-enforcement agencies. Our report on the inadequacy of federal law enforcement was not made public when J. Edgar Hoover resented our implied criticism of the FBI's activities (or, more precisely, "inactivities") in the field of organized crime.

The brunt of these difficulties fell upon the Attorney General's office in Washington, which had the day-by-day problem of getting along with Congress and other branches of the government. The final blow was triggered by some ill-advised and unwarranted publicity for the Attorney General's Special Group.

From the start, we had tried to shun the limelight, both as a matter of ethics and to avoid public pressure for immediate and drastic action that we were not prepared to take. Unfortunately, this policy of secrecy whetted journalistic appetites to the point where anything that concerned the group was front-page news. When it became apparent that the report on which our chief, Milton Wessel, had relied heavily, was not to be endorsed and released publicly by the Department of Justice, the dam burst. Wessel's picture and opinions appeared in newspapers all over the country. *Life,* in a spread on the "Aces of Rackets and Their Stern Pursuers," described Wessel as "David Against the Goliaths." Such accolades, in contrast with our failure to produce tangible results, struck a rather sour note.

AIRBORNE INDICTMENT

Thus, by the end of February 1959 our group had become an albatross around the Attorney General's neck. It had to be quietly stuffed and mounted before it could cause further embarrassment. But against this background of failure we scored our one major accomplishment.

When told of the coming demise of the group, we were forced to reappraise our plans. We would have to forget our long-range probes of the nationwide gambling ring and racket-infested industries. With only four months left to us, the best hope seemed to lie in the Apalachin conspiracy indictment. From that point on, the entire group concentrated on creating a case out of the raw material of my theories and research.

In a little over two months we assembled a mass of evidence. We drafted and redrafted our indictment until there were no patent defects and it was limited to what could be clearly established. Then, with great trepidation, Wessel and I took the finished product to Washington, expecting opposition to such a sweeping attack, but hoping for approval.

The Department of Justice confronted us with the best legal talent of the Criminal Division. However we had prepared for every conceivable objection. To my amazement, our questioners gradually swung from skepticism to asking us why we had limited such an excellent approach to so few defendants. That night we boarded our plane exhausted but triumphant. We had the department's permission to seek a sealed indictment from the Grand Jury on the following morning against more than two dozen overlords of crime.

Our only remaining problem was to expand the indictment to include additional defendants. This Wessel and I did in the one-hour flight between Washington and New York. Crammed in the front seat of an airliner we struggled to hear each other over the roar of the engines—and so learned that in the government, things are done in one of two ways: after interminable study and consideration, or just off the cuff, on the spur of the moment.

When the indictment for conspiracy to obstruct justice was unsealed on May 21, 1959, it was headline news throughout the country. Ironically, the very agencies which had been so coy now rushed to share the credit. A Bureau of Narcotics field supervisor, for example, in a speech at Manhattan College, said that ten of his agents had been assigned to the Special Group and had made the arrests of the Apalachin leaders. Actually those ten men were assigned only *after* the indictment was voted by the Grand Jury.

The trial which followed was almost anticlimactic. The defendants stewed in their own juice as they listened to their fairy tales being read back to them. They had hired several dozen highly experienced defense lawyers. But their knotty objections were overruled by federal Judge Irving Kaufman. He dismissed the charge against one defendant but all the rest were found guilty by the jury. Most of the defendants were given the maximum sentence of five years and $10,000, and the others got substantial terms.

GRAY FLANNEL CAPONES

The overlords of Apalachin were brought to justice and will be out of circulation for some years, if the conviction stands up on appeal. But the basic problem remains. The Attorney General's Special Group was set up to combat organized crime on the national level—that group was disbanded on July 1, 1959. And no other national agency is charged with this task—a desperately urgent one made imperative by the changed techniques of crime in our time.

In bygone years, assorted and separate agencies could cope with the many varieties of lawlessness. But crime today has geared itself to a new era. The major criminals are far removed from direct conflict with the law. Narcotics worth thousands of dollars can be smuggled in by a pathetic refugee who is many levels away from contact with the head of a criminal syndicate. Industry rarely complains of labor abuses whose impact is oblique and can be passed on to the consumer, with economic gains accruing to all, so that management and unions often join in defending those who prey on them. The outright bribe is considered gauche. Matters are "fixed" through associations, connections, and political contributions. Worst of all, the captains of organized crime have acquired halos of respectability and culture. They have moved to residential communities far from the arena of their operations and the prying metropolitan police. Conservatively dressed suburbanites with lovely families, they head charity drives, nominate political candidates, receive accolades from churches and civic groups for their community services.

Gone is the flashy gang chief of the 'twenties with his fleet of rum runners and his diamond-studded moll. Glamorized by Hollywood and the tabloids, he was a kind of hero to a nation whose moral fiber had been corroded by Prohibition, which created a guilty affinity between the bootlegger and his customers. Revulsion became widespread only after the Wickersham Committee Report in 1931 spotlighted the enormity of the evil. A few years later, statutes were enacted to fight interstate crime. The FBI and other agencies caught up with such notorious characters as Machine Gun Kelly, John Dillinger, and Baby Face Nelson. The quiet accountants of the Internal Revenue Service wielded the income-tax laws as a weapon against Al Capone and his ilk. In New York, District Attorney Tom Dewey tracked down the thugs of Murder, Inc., and the king of vice, Lucky Luciano. The corrupt political empires of Pendergast in Kansas City and Jimmy Hines in New York were exposed.

But organized crime was not eradicated. Instead, the surviving leaders and their rising young followers had learned some important lessons:

Rule I: Crimes of violence, particularly against innocent victims or police officers, are dynamite, sure to arouse even the most complacent.

Rule II: The income from robberies and kidnapings is erratic and uncertain.

Rule III: Public notoriety and high living attract the unwelcome notice of ambitious prosecutors and investigators.

Rule IV: Violation of federal statutes exposes the criminal to attack by the G-men, whose facilities far outshine those of the local police.

With these truisms in mind, the overlords of crime began to focus their operations on legitimate businesses, selecting those which could most readily serve as fronts for vice or those in which corrupt labor unions had a foothold. This is a pattern revealed by a study of two hundred leading suspects which was made by the Attorney General's Special Group. Racketeers, we found, had infiltrated and corrupted an appalling number of fields. Coin-vending machines, for instance, provide a perfect base for gambling operations since they are an ideal cover for transportation of slot machines and "hot money"; visits to "bookie parlors" can be disguised as "servicing." Italian foods, such as huge wheels of cheese and drums of olive oil, have been used to smuggle narcotics into this country. The many restaurants, cabarets, motels, and hotels owned by racketeers are convenient rendezvous for them and sites for profitable gambling, prostitution, and bootlegging. Despite strict licensing laws in most states, a surprising number of racketeers are still plying their trade of Prohibition days as owners of respectable beer and liquor distributing concerns.

Corrupt union officials—often with the connivance of employers—have opened the door to hoodlums in a variety of industries, as disclosed in detail by the McClellan Committee. Criminals have made heavy inroads in the ladies' garment and garment-trucking industries where a small advantage in union rates and conditions can mean the difference between profits and bankruptcy. Other racket-ridden unions operate in the coin-vending machine industry, in restaurants, in garbage-carting services, laundry, and linen supply. The Apalachin delegates were an interesting sample of modern gangster vocations. Nineteen were involved in garment manufacturing, seven in trucking, and nine in the coin-machine business. Seventeen owned taverns or restaurants; eleven were olive oil and cheese importers. Others owned automobile agencies, coal companies, and funeral homes.

In the commoner areas of vice, the racketeers have found that local police and public officials, in most places, can be easily tamed. Minor gambling and prostitution, for instance, excite only sporadic moral indignation and once a policeman or politician has been "bought" for one purpose, he is easy to control for all. Violence becomes unnecessary when the businessman, union leader, and pimp are virtual partners of the racketeers. And it is possible for them to obtain competent legal advice *before* committing a crime.

Instead of publicly heading his ring, the new gang lord has become a sort of Chairman of the

Board, divorced from actual operations. He confers on finances and policy only with a small and trusted staff who see that his wishes are carried out. As a result the leaders of criminal syndicates have become immune to criminal prosecution. By operating in highly lucrative areas with limited possibilities of detection, they arouse no public ire and no one complains against them. On the rare occasions when their activities do run afoul of the law, their underlings pay the piper. The gangland leaders are so insulated by the many levels of their operations, the interstate scope of their activities, and the fine reputations they have created for themselves, that they rarely if ever become entangled in a criminal exposé.

The Apalachin delegates are splendid specimens for study. The sixty-three persons whose presence was established (another dozen are believed to have escaped) had among them 223 arrests and convictions, including such offenses as murder and narcotics peddling, and few were without criminal records. However, these records ran to a pattern: starting with thugster activities in the early 1920's they advanced into the prosperous commercial crimes (such as bootlegging and extortion) in the late 'twenties and early 'thirties, and disappeared thereafter—except for a few "respectable" charges such as income-tax violations. . . .

34.

DANIEL P. MOYNIHAN

THE PRIVATE GOVERNMENT OF CRIME

One of the largest and surely one of the most profitable industries in the United States is that unusual complex of skills and services known as organized crime. There is nothing secret about this modern big business. Tens of millions of Americans regularly come in contact with crime when they patronize a numbers runner, a bookmaker, or an after-hours drinking club, as well as when they become more than casually involved in any of the fifty-odd areas of racket infiltration, ranging alphabetically from advertising to transportation, that the Kefauver Committee uncovered.

Organized crime obviously has something to sell that many people want to buy. Yet always behind the pleasures of vice lie the ugliness of degradation and the terror of violence. It is pleasant to think of winning a lot of money, not so pleasant for an Irish tenement kid to stare at what is left of his father's face after the smiling bookies' psychotic "enforcers" have collected the hard way. We can all sympathize with the shame of parents who learn that their son in college has been paid off to shave the score of a basketball game, but most of us find it difficult even to imagine the feelings of Puerto Rican parents the first time their daughter comes down from the roof "high" on heroin.

But even thousands of personal tragedies like these may not be the worst by-products of organized crime in the United States. If any moderately determined amateur gambler can find a place to put down a bet nearly anywhere in this country, why can't the police find the same places? The question itself suggests to many people that law enforcement in this country is really phony, that the laws don't really mean what they say, and above all that government at many levels is controlled by massive and sinister commercial interests that the individual dare not defy.

The head of the Department of Justice's Spe-

SOURCE: *The Reporter,* Vol. 25, No. 1 (July 6, 1961), pp. 14–20. Reprinted by permission of the author and the journal.

cial Group on Organized Crime declared about a year ago: "The underworld gets about $9 billion of the estimated $47 billion spent annually on illegal gambling . . . Fully half of the syndicates' income from gambling is earmarked for protection money paid to police and politicians." Since the total salaries of the municipal police forces in the United States probably do not come to $1 billion a year, these figures would indicate that the American police receive more money from criminals than from taxpayers. Probably that is an exaggeration, but there is no question about the validity of the conclusion to which the figures point: corruption by organized crime is a normal condition of American local government and politics.

It is hardly surprising therefore that for the last quarter century organized crime has been a major political issue in the United States. It is, however, an issue that the voters by and large have recognized and responded to on their own rather than having it thrust upon them by the political parties, journalists, and academics who usually attempt to set the agenda for American politics. Those political leaders who have put themselves forward as challengers of the criminal hegemony have almost invariably found themselves the spokesmen for one of the most deeply rooted concerns of the American people.

The issue first appeared as a national rather than a purely local one about the time it became evident that organized crime had not gone away with the ending of Prohibition. Thomas E. Dewey became an aspirant for the Republican Presidential nomination in 1940 at the age of thirty-eight purely and simply on the basis of his record as a prosecutor of racketeering in New York City, a record that was highlighted by the conviction of Lucky Luciano and Jimmy Hines, the twin symbols of Italian mobster and Irish politician. In 1952 Estes Kefauver came to the Democratic convention with a vast national following and almost a majority of the delegates largely because of his Senate investigation of organized crime. More recently, John F. Kennedy made his first widespread impression on the American public through the hearings of the McClellan Committee, of which his brother Robert was chief counsel.

THE FALLACY OF THE NEW BROOM

As with many important popular undercurrents in American history, the reaction against organized crime has suffered both from a lack of effective leadership and from the too easy acceptance of simple solutions. The way most people think about crime has not advanced very far beyond the stage reached at the turn of the century, when Lincoln Steffens discovered that the Tammany chief of police ran crime in New York City—a matter of common knowledge to all of the police reporters. This revelation led to the notion that the major problem lay in the selection of police chiefs, and thence to the "throw-the-rascals-out" approach that has plagued most Good Government efforts ever since. It has been taken for granted that the installation of energetic and incorruptible public officials *of itself* would put an end to organized criminal activities carried on with official connivance. This has left reform leaders and their supporters woefully unprepared for the discovery that organized crime is a far more complex and persistent problem than they had imagined—that in effect organized crime constitutes a kind of private government whose power rivals and often supplants that of elected public government.

The quintessential experience in this regard is that of Thomas E. Dewey. Elected governor of New York in 1942 as a crime buster, Dewey promptly dropped the subject. During his first eight years in office his annual messages to the legislature were devoid of any reference to crime except for an occasional mention of juvenile delinquency or parole procedure.

When the Kefauver Committee began exposing organized criminal activities in New York City, Dewey was jubilant. In October, 1950, he told a campaign audience: "I have said before and I say again, that this could not happen were there not a definite link between the big-time gambling racketeer and those in high office. What we see revealed in New York City is what happens when crooked political bosses take control of a party and hand-pick their stooges. . . . The scandals in New York City could not happen if there were an aggressive, honest administration, owing nothing to the big party bosses. Tammany and 'Paving Block' Ed Flynn and their gang are responsible . . ."

Kefauver then moved his investigation to upstate New York—and found pretty much the same conditions he had found in the city. The "big-time gambling racketeer" was operating wide open in Saratoga, with liquor licenses provided by the state; all this was going on with the full knowledge of the state police—not to mention nearly everyone else in Albany. Kefauver then began asking why Dewey, who had put Lucky Luciano in jail in 1936, had seen fit to let him out of jail in 1946, ostensibly for helping in the war effort. Dewey did not answer. He went abroad.

It next developed that the Republican majority leader of the state senate had been visiting the racketeer Joey Fay in Sing Sing. Then it turned out that the Republican hierarchy (with the Democrats cut in) had been making fabulous profits out of harness-track franchises—involving just the same underworld characters Kefauver has turned up in New York City.

Dewey's last four years in office were devoted largely to the subject of crime commissions and harness-track czars, in a nearly frantic effort to clean up the mess that had suddenly been uncovered. But it was too late. In 1954 the Democratic gubernatorial candidate, Averell Harriman, made crime his principal campaign issue. "The story of the harness tracks," he declared, "has punctured for all time the myth about the integrity of the present-day leadership of the Republican Party of New York. For the first time, we see scandal reaching the Governor's closest and most intimate associates."

Harriman won, whereupon *his* administration promptly dropped the subject of crime. The issue was not mentioned in any of his first three annual messages. There was a flutter when it developed that the boys had tried to fix a parole-violation charge for one of Frank Costello's associates, "Socks" Lanza, but things were generally quiet until 1957, when the McClellan Committee began hearings on labor racketeering in New York connecting the Teamsters with the underworld. That summer, Albert Anastasia was executed in a New York barbershop, and on November 14 the state police arrested fifty-eight men at what was promptly labeled a "crime convention" near the upstate hamlet of Apalachin. At this point all hell broke loose, and Nelson Rockefeller did not fail to make the most of it in the 1958 state election.

The experience of the New York governors is not uncommon. Again and again across the country it has been demonstrated that electing a crime buster is not the same thing as busting crime. A fundamental reason is that while criminal jurisdiction has remained limited and local, crime has grown into a nation-wide operation.

A MANAGERIAL REVOLUTION

Rackets—a Hell's Kitchen term for big parties, to which local tradesmen were often "asked" to buy tickets—existed in a number of industries at the turn of the century, and there were loose associations of criminals at that time. But crime first got organized along modern business lines during Prohibition. This development has been clearly documented, although the reasons for it have been somewhat confused.

As an illicit industry, bootlegging tended to attract persons from marginal social groups, including a large number of Sicilian immigrants. This led to the notion—still the official theory of the U.S. Treasury Department—that the Sicilians brought organization over with them, in the form of the Mafia. But this is much too simple. Obviously the Southern Italians had qualities that made for successful organization men in this field: nerve, first of all, but also the peasant habit of group loyalty and a relative imperviousness to alcohol and narcotic addiction. Nor were they disheartened by the occasional necessity to settle disputes with violence. But the process by which crime became organized was essentially no different from that by which a score of small, fragmented industries have been gradually consolidated into ever larger units, tending always toward the commercial ideal of monopoly.

When Prohibition was abandoned, the new criminal groups turned to similar businesses, mainly gambling and, on a smaller scale, narcotics. The general corruption of local government that took place under Prohibition continued, making possible a great expansion of racketeering, in which threats of violence were used for commercial purposes. With law-enforcement agencies corrupted, the persons or corporations threatened had little recourse save to submit to the fiat of the private government that had usurped the publicly elected government's monopoly on the use of force. During the 1930's a good deal of hot money seems also to have gone into real estate, in which political connections are always useful.

These enterprises flourished, especially gambling. In the words of an American Bar Association report on organized crime, the operators of the illegal gambling industry in America "acquired control of an enterprise of fantastic proportions, with all the power that flows from the control of great wealth. The result has been a new type of criminal, living in luxury, flanked by expensive attorneys and advisors, able to cut deeper into our social structure by corrupting weak officials than he ever did by open defiance and violence."

WHERE STEFFENS STOPPED

For all its obvious importance, the subject of organized crime has rarely engaged the serious attention of American political scientists. In the decade of the 1950's, which began with the Kefauver hearings and ended with those of the McClellan Committee, not a single item on crime appeared in the *American Political Science Review*. There are, of course, formidable difficulties in collecting data on the subject. But the most likely explanation for the gap is simply ignorance.

In general, the academic view of crime remains that formulated by the muckrakers. Crime has been regarded as a governmental pathology that would not normally occur in a wholesome municipal atmosphere. Hence a half century of reform movements, which may have improved city government somewhat but have not bothered crime much at all.

The press has done no better, confining itself to periodic disapproval but rarely seeking adequate understanding. As a result, to the extent there is a consensus on what to do about organized crime, it consists of three very general, very old ideas: we must clean up the slums, which breed crime; we must break up the political machines, which tolerate crime; and we must keep a critical eye on the trade unions, which are generally associated with the dangerous assertion of raw power.

This ingenuous approach fails to take account of the changed meaning of the term "crime." At the turn of the century, protected crime generally involved only small, local operations: prostitution and some gambling as well as the traditional felonies such as burglary, which are estimated currently to account for only two per cent of the total "cost" of crime. There were few laws against drinking or narcotics ("Honey, have a whiff on me!"), and communications did not facilitate nation-wide betting. It was only with new prohibitions and new technology that a mass market was created for illicit goods and services. The executives who run these businesses are a different breed from the solitary pickpocket who relieved Steffens of his pay envelope under the benign surveillance of precinct detectives.

Thus it is probably too late to get at crime by cleaning up the slums: organized crime has moved to the suburbs and the underworld has become café society. The sociologist Lloyd E. Ohlin has suggested that this development may even account for the increase in juvenile violence. Traditionally, organized crime has offered one of the most attractive career opportunities open to the youth of the slums. This prospect, Ohlin notes, taught them "to curb overly aggressive and violent conduct. In the world of semiprofessional and organized crime there is no place for the impulsive, explosive, and undisciplined individual." Ohlin goes on to point out that "changes in criminal organization may be expected to have important consequences for delinquent youngsters in slum areas who aspire to an adult criminal career. Changing patterns of recruitment, in which skills such as accounting, public relations, legal and organizational ability are highly valued, may well lessen the appropriateness of delinquency as a training ground. . . . The encroachment of organized crime on legitimate business, such as trucking and the garment trades, appears likely to place recruitment of new personnel on a functional rather than a geographical basis." The delinquents will indeed be rebels without a cause when crime itself is closed to them.

As to the second part of the reformers' assumptions about the ways to wipe out crime, the effort to break up the political machines that tolerated and profited from crime has been largely successful. But far from having solved the problem of commercial crime, the elimination of the machines seems to have eliminated the one social force that was able to contain it. The decline of Tammany Hall since Steffens's time is a case in point. Over the years the New York police department has become steadily freer of politics, notably so during the Wagner administration. But this freedom has hardly been followed by an end of organized crime. The situation in policy offers an excellent example.

A MAJOR INDUSTRY IN HARLEM

Policy (from the Italian *pòlizza,* lottery ticket) is the most popular form of illegal gambling in New York City. It appears that some 1,500,000 New Yorkers—almost a third of the adult population—buy something to look forward to for a few hours by placing a small bet on the last three digits of pari-mutuel totals or the U.S. Treasury balance each day. It is a poor man's game and a sucker's game—the "split" is 60-40—but it flourishes, despite official disapproval. It is pre-eminently the type of crime that the Tammany of Lincoln Steffens's day would have controlled to the last nickel.

In 1958, when Congressman Adam Clayton Powell led a revolt against the Tammany leaders in Harlem, it was commonly agreed that much of his popular support came from the Negro numbers runners who were tired of working for white men who ran policy from outside Harlem. At the time, an N.A.A.C.P. official remarked that Carmine De Sapio's overstuffed officialdom didn't have a chance in competition with the runners turned poll workers, who, after all, called on the housewives of Harlem almost every day of the week. Just so. The regulars were clobbered and Powell's team took over. But two years later, Negroes still did not control policy.

Powell took to his pulpit to say that while he certainly did not approve of the numbers racket, he was "going to fight for the Negro having the same chance as an Italian." He also read into the *Congressional Record* a list of the names and addresses of the white gamblers who, he charged, were "pauperizing" Harlem. "Here we find a community lower in income than any other in the city and yet we spend $50,000,000 a year to support Italian and Jewish policy bankers."

In order to correct this situation, Powell called on the then Police Commissioner Stephen P. Kennedy to appoint a Negro deputy police chief. Kennedy was precisely the type of police chief Steffens dreamed of: he fought crime with a furious, consuming energy. Kennedy replied that Congressman Powell had only recently become a Tammany district leader and was perhaps on that account not fully aware that district leaders no longer made appointments to the New York City police force. A stirring retort. But was it not also a clear indication that no open and public institution, neither the police nor the party, could really claim to have any control over crime? The police commissioner was incorruptible, but the rackets flourished still—answerable only to themselves. Or, perhaps, they were answerable only to police officers further down the line.

THE SHAME OF OUR CITIES

Perhaps the single most important development in local government since Steffens' time has been the fragmentation of the political power formerly held by party machines, where they existed, into the complex of groups and individuals who influence events in the vast metropolises of today. Both the growth of the urban areas and the diminution of political power have lessened the ability of society to control a phenomenon such as organized crime. The criminal thrives. Here and there, from time to time, he actually dominates.

Take Kansas City. It appears that in Tom Pendergast's heyday ten per cent of the city police force had criminal records, and parts of the town were, of course, wide open. There was never any question about who was boss in Kansas City. But when the machine was broken and its leader sent to prison for income-tax evasion, the underworld, led by Charles Binaggio, moved in to fill the vacuum. Appropriately, Binaggio was shot down in his First Ward Democratic headquarters. Just recently a grand jury charged that a syndicate connected with the Mafia has for seven or eight years been operating a "criminal playground" in Kansas City under a pact with the police that has given organized crime free reign in its particular field in return for a pledge to refrain from major burglaries and similar crimes against property.

Take Schenectady, a city of enlightened capitalism and nonrevolutionary socialism, which has even had Walter Lippmann in its municipal employ. Some time after Assembly Speaker Oswald Heck, its leading citizen, denounced Harriman on the subject of crime, a pair of gamblers called on the Republican city manager and informed him that they wanted the chief of police dismissed from his post immediately. The chief did not wait to find out whether he would be fired. He resigned, fled, and has been in hiding ever since.

In neighboring Albany, where the O'Connell clan runs one of the last thriving urban Democratic machines in the nation, there is no shortage of bookmakers. But the mind boggles at the thought of what would happen to one such who tried to intimidate the chief of police!

In the past, crime tended to be associated first and foremost with the big Democratic cities. This may even then have been an exaggeration, but it is certainly true no longer. The rackets also flourish in Republican suburbs, and are well established in Republican cities and states. The New York State Commission of Investigation recently identified the Republican stronghold of Syracuse as the center of a vast bookmaking and policy network, a number of whose operatives were distinguished by the variety of police courtesy cards they carried. Despite Earl Warren's administration, Kefauver in 1951 found "Crime, vice, and corruption in California had a special flavor—exotic, overripe, and a little sickening." John Gunther reported of Missouri: "Kansas City is the heart of Democratic power . . . St. Louis the heart of Republican." Kefauver's chapters on these cities are entitled "Kansas City: Law of the Jungle," and "The St. Louis Area: Where Gambling Is Big Business." Thus the change of party which normally accompanies the election of a reform administration is rarely as much a blow to the criminal interests as it first appears —and as the reformers often innocently assume.

THE FATE OF JOHN ACROPOLIS

The third widely endorsed nostrum for controlling crime, that of keeping a sharp eye on the trade unions, might have had some effect had it taken the form of vigilant public support for legitimate trade-union leaders threatened by criminal incursion, but this has not generally been the case. The record of major industries actually employing criminals as labor-relations advisers is well known. Few industrialists can have felt much personal alarm to learn that a Jewish labor organizer had been stabbed to death in the garment district of New York or that a cargo net had been dropped on some Polish stevedore over in Jersey City. The alarm has normally only come later when the criminals have begun to make their new operation pay.

As Robert Kennedy made dramatically clear in the McClellan hearings, the activities of criminals in the labor movement are quite different from the *condottiere* operations of the 1930's, when racketeers offered their goon services to labor and management alike with fine impartiality. A typical example of the present situation is the garbage-removal business in the suburbs of New York. Robert Kennedy has written: "When there is a monopoly control, the refusal to remove garbage or waste can put a company out of business. . . . Because it is comparatively easy to gain and maintain control, gangsters and racketeers have been attracted to the multi-million-dollar industry. Important in their organization is a friendly labor union which can act as an enforcing arm." When John Acropolis, the Teamster official concerned with garbage in Westchester, defied the mob, he was simply murdered. The business was turned over to a local run by two hoodlums, Joe Parisi and Bernard Adelstein, and in short order the $50-

million business was being run at the direction of James Squillante, the *soi-disant* godson of Albert Anastasia. It is important to note that this is a new industry, created by the new shopping centers and new shifts in population, that Squillante is a new man—he was not sixteen years old when Prohibition came to an end.

MONEY TALKS

In some part at least, the persistence of criminal power can be accounted for by the general shift of attention, particularly of the special interests, away from local government. Crime remains as one of the few big commercial, cash-in-hand interests on the local scene. This is already obvious in the relatively small but significant area of campaign contributions. Alexander Heard, in his book on campaign finances, estimates that organized crime currently pays for fifteen per cent of campaign expenditures at state and local levels. In 1952 that would have been some $16 million—ten times the national contribution of organized labor. Heard quotes the remark of one mob official: "Show me a punk who wants to run for office, and I'll show you a man who can be had."

Judges, of course, are particularly important to organized crime. For a long time there have been indications that municipal benches and higher have been reached by criminals. As for most other types of public office, all the underworld requires of the incumbent in return for financial support is that he keep out of the way where crime is concerned. This is the point at which the problem extends beyond the existence of crime, bad as that may be. There was a wisecrack going around a few years ago that if a New York City official returned from lunch to find he'd had calls from the governor, the mayor, and Frank Costello—he would call Costello back first. For such officials, the problem of crime get priority, and other problems wait. As for what sort of officials the Costellos are likely to choose in the expectation that their calls will be returned first, the answer will be obvious to anyone with experience in American local government: stupid.

Crime has not only corrupted American government for its own purposes; it has also tended to immobilize government for many other purposes. The problems of the American city, to speak only of that level, are not going to be solved by the dimwits whose campaigns are financed by the syndicate. And is there any reason to suppose that the leaders of organized crime are incapable of perceiving that they will be better off if American municipal government remains fragmented, unco-ordinated, and in the hands, as much as possible, of incompetents? In some ways there are no more vigorous guardians of local government than these criminal states' righters.

WHAT ABOUT THE FBI?

The most common reaction to the seeming insolubility of the crime problem at the local level is to try to solve it at the state or Federal level. According to this argument, local governments are too small to resist corruption, they do not retain the services of capable officials long enough to accomplish anything, and since crime has become national in scale anyway, it must be fought by large units of government. It also is pointed out, quite correctly, that while corruption is practically the normal condition of American municipal police forces, the FBI and most state police organizations have maintained the highest standards of integrity.

This approach will be recognized as a variant of the original "get a new police chief" thesis. It is not to be discarded on that ground, but it must be pointed out that it involves the danger that in raising the level on which the fight against organized crime is waged, we may at the same time raise the level at which the corruption of organized crime takes place.

For whatever motives, it is quite clear that those law-enforcement organizations which have kept themselves free of corruption and infiltration by organized crime have done so by avoiding jurisdiction over the problem. The state troopers are what they are because they confine their attentions to traffic safety and crimes of passion. In the same pattern, the FBI has not hesitated to take on the toughest problems of national security but has successfully stayed away from organized crime.

Perhaps unintentionally, much of this success has stemmed from the presumption on the part of the public that the FBI is already fighting organized crime. The hundreds of thousands of men, women, and children who take the FBI tour at the Department of Justice each year are shown through a fantastic gallery of submachine guns, death masks, and ransom notes depicting an unceasing pursuit of the criminal all across the nation. One of the most popular features is the gallery of pictures of the Ten Most Wanted Fugitives of the moment. The free booklet *The Story of the Federal Bureau of Investigation* tells how crime met its match in 1934 when the FBI was given general jurisdiction over Federal crimes. John Dillinger, Pretty Boy Floyd, and Baby Face Nelson were dispatched, one-two-three. "The underworld finally realized that never again could it openly and brazenly flaunt justice and order." An accompanying pamphlet reassures law-abiding householders that the FBI has in its possession the fingerprints of 34,027,049 "Criminals and Suspects," illustrated by a sinister figure in a trench coat with smoking revolver and cigarette.

All this is quite overwhelming, but a closer look will make it clear that none of the criminals, or the offenses so dramatically illustrated on the tour, have any real connection with organized crime. Their post-office faces look out at you: the bewildered Middle Westerners who—once—tried bank robbing in the depression when farming failed, the idiot rapist, the sullen Negro auto thief, the rather seedy swindler by mail, the youth who blew up his Mom in an airplane. These are not the men of the syndicates who appoint judges, make police chiefs wealthy, or contribute $16 million a year to political campaigns.

"Crime is essentially a local matter," Hoover has written, and for thirty-seven years he has sought to avoid any assignment that would involve the FBI directly with problems that have often appeared to be insoluble. And he gets his way. The one significant bit of legislation that came out of the Kefauver period, the requirement that gamblers register with the Federal government and pay a fee, is enforced not by the FBI but by the Internal Revenue Service. In fact, the Treasury Department gets most dirty work of this kind. . . .

LEGALIZED GAMBLING?

Far from putting a stop to crime, some laws actually seem to promote its growth. When a government attempts to forbid certain activities that large numbers of citizens do not really disapprove of, it runs the risk of expanding rather than reducing the areas in which criminals find inviting opportunities to operate. It may be that a central difficulty with many of this nation's traditional notions about how to control crime is that they have often reflected the tastes as well as the morality of upper-middle-class persons who have not generally been attracted to the forms of entertainment—or vice, as you will—that criminals have found it profitable to purvey. At least not since Prohibition. Gambling, like the consumption of alcohol, is and always has been a universal phenomenon. As the sociologist Herbert A. Bloch observes, the volume of gambling has remained at a relatively high level so far this century, and no efforts to control it have succeeded.

Gambling provides the base on which other and far more ugly forms of organized crime can rise. This point was made just two years ago by a Brooklyn grand jury which declared: "Gambling is the very heartbeat of organized crime both on a local and national scale. Strangely enough, this vital finding, which should be apparent to everyone concerned with the problem of law enforcement, is recognized in theory but virtually ignored in practice. . . . Actually, if you scratch the professional operator of gambling ventures you find the narcotics peddler, the loan shark, the dice game operator, the white slaver and the murderer."

An increasing number of public officials faced with the impossible task of enforcing the betting laws have been coming forth with proposals for legal off-track betting, government lotteries, and so on. Such proposals, of course, inevitably run into strong, deeply felt opposition from the Protestant churches and their congregations. Protestant opinion does not appear to be solid on this subject, but a united front is maintained in deference to those groups for which gambling is an issue of urgent moral concern. There are certainly moral questions involved here. And one of them is whether it is better to leave gambling in the hands of the underworld or to bring it out into the open under public control.

THE NEXT STEP?

Past experience has certainly shown that no single solution can solve a problem as deep and complex as that of organized crime in America. What we have to reckon with is not only the existence of crime but also of a large, wealthy, and firmly entrenched criminal class. The end of Prohibition did not destroy this class, and it is not likely that the end of certain gambling restrictions would do so. So long as there are rules against something a lot of people really want, there are profits to be made in getting around them, and criminals will take advantage of that opportunity. The report of the American Bar Association on organized crime, which appeared during the Korean War, noted that gambling was by far the richest source of criminal revenue at that time, but that it could be expected that black-market revenues would soon exceed even those of gambling. Thus new strongholds are constantly being created for the barons of crime.

It is common enough to call for more light on any social problem, but organized crime is one that cries out both for understanding and for action. In the aftermath of the Apalachin meeting, of which so much has been said but so little proved, Edwin J. Lukas of the Society for the Prevention of Crime asked, without result, for "a thorough canvas of all the existing and known significant rackets that currently victimize the American community" and "an effort, in depth, to identify clearly the factors in our society which serve to cause and perpetuate rackets." More information is needed on this subject, and needed urgently.

The time of naïve faith in simple solutions is past. The private government of organized crime must be recognized as a national rather than a purely local problem. This does not mean that the no man's land in which city and state governments have shown they cannot wage war effectively must be occupied by the Federal government alone. The attack must be co-ordinated among all the various law-enforcement agencies. Only through this sort of co-operation can we avoid the dangers that may lie in the extension—and possible corruption—of Federal power, without leaving the job of fighting crime in the hands of the ill-sorted combination of various groups that prefer for both idealistic and practical reasons to maintain the present cozy relationship between outlaws and the law. But most important of all, we must realize that an enterprise that has become many-sided and national in scope can only be controlled by a many-sided and national effort.

This is a moment of rare opportunity. A vigorous Attorney General has pledged the full support of the national government to bring organized crime under control. The gambling fever of the postwar period, in which full employment coincided with a shortage of goods on which to spend the pay checks, seems to have abated somewhat, and there are no great commodity shortages to feed the black market. Crime, for the moment, is more vulnerable than it has been for some time.

The opportunity must be seized. In the words of the Attorney General, "If we do not on a national scale attack organized criminals with weapons and techniques as effective as their own, they will destroy us."

CHAPTER X

Property Offenses

THE GREAT BULK of the crime problem in this country consists of property offenses. The old notion that crime does not pay simply is not true. If one were to examine our criminal statistics he would find that by and large Americans are committing millions of property crimes and gaining very handsomely from them. The highest clearance by arrest record reported in the *Uniform Crime Reports* for 1967 was 30 percent for the crime of robbery, the low was 18 percent for larceny. The remaining two property offense categories of burglary and auto theft elicited 20 percent clearance records each. Thus, the majority of cases remain unsolved.

Robbery (as mentioned in Chapter 2) is both a violent crime and a property offense. This criminal category is defined by the FBI as "stealing or taking anything of value from the person by force or violence or by putting in fear, such as strong-arm robbery, stickups, armed robbery, assault to rob, and attempt to rob." In 1967, there were 202,050 robberies reported in the United States, up 27 percent over 1966. As can be seen in Chart 10.1 below, the number and rate of robberies has increased steadily since 1960.

The 1,605,701 burglaries committed in 1967 were the single greatest contributor to the crime index in the United States. Since the volume is so high in this category, a shift in the number of burglaries committed may have a significant influence on the total crime index. This offense is defined by the FBI as "housebreaking, safecracking, or any unlawful entry to commit a felony or a theft, even though no force was used to

CHART 10.1

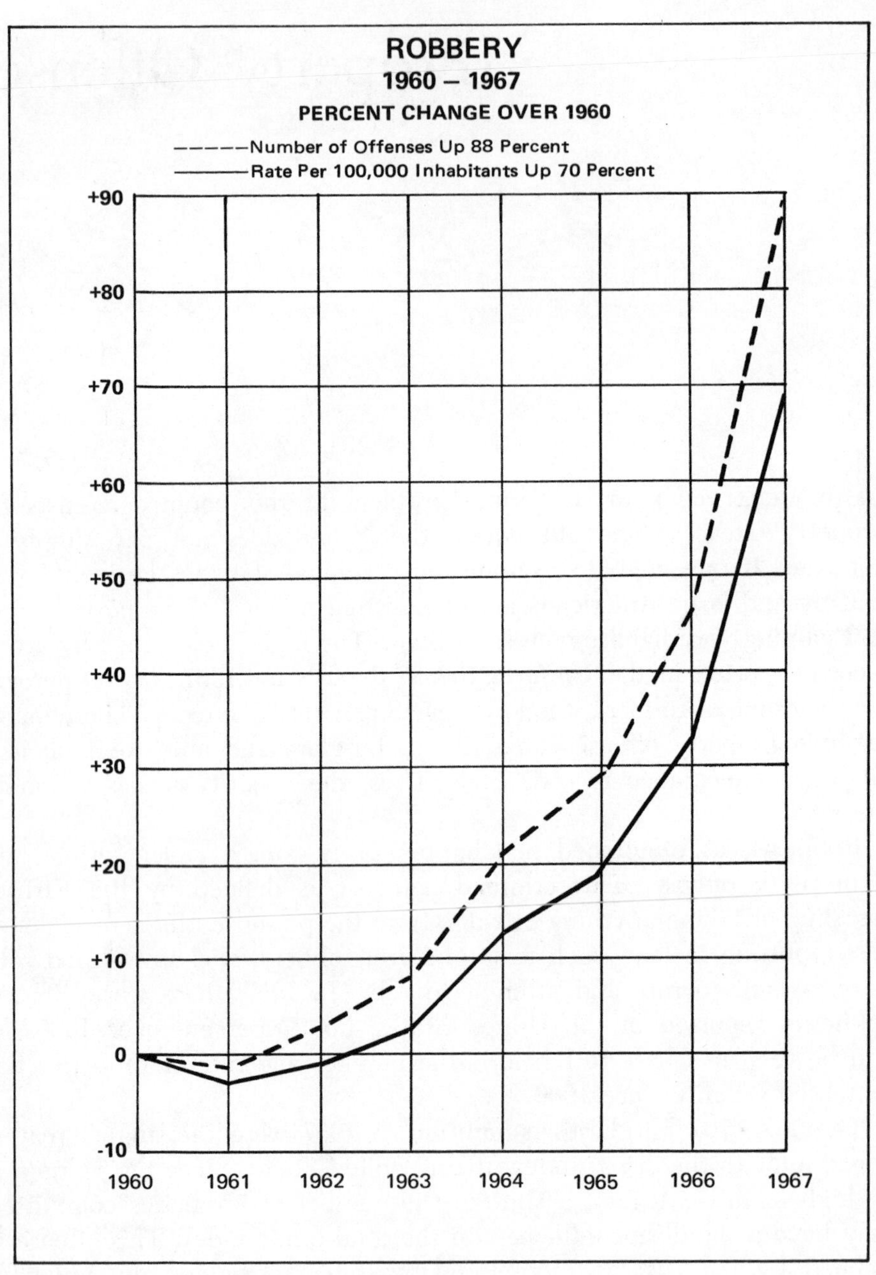

SOURCE: Federal Bureau of Investigation, U.S. Department of Justice, *1967 Uniform Crime Reports* (Washington, D.C.: U.S. Government Printing Office, 1968), p. 14.

gain entrance. . . ." Like other property crimes, burglaries are committed by professionals and amateurs alike. There is tremendous possibility for escape for one engaging in this type of crime since in most cases no contact has been made with victims who may possibly identify the offender. While four-fifths of the burglaries involved forcible entry, it is interesting to note that residence and nonresidential addresses were almost evenly divided when selection of a mark was made by the offender. As can be seen in Chart 10.2 below, like other property offenses, burglary has increased in volume significantly since 1960.

Larceny ($50 and over) is second in volume only to burglary as an index crime. In fact, the 1,047,085 larcenies committed in 1967 fell only about 550 cases short of the recorded burglaries. This offense category is defined by the FBI as "Thefts of bicycles, automobile accessories, shoplifting, pocket-picking, or any stealing of property or article of value which is not taken by force and violence or by fraud." Larceny is a most costly crime in terms of dollar loss to the victim. Unlike auto theft where 86 percent of the stolen vehicles were recovered, the return rate for larceny is considerably lower. This was reflected by the fact that the loss to victims in 1967 was in excess of $292,000,000. Since 1960, pocket-picking is up 55 percent, purse-snatching 145 percent, shoplifting 112 percent, thefts from autos 71 percent, theft of auto accessories 21 percent, and theft of bicycles 66 percent. The overall increase in number of larcenies between 1960 and 1967 may be seen in Chart 10.3 below.

Auto theft is primarily a problem in the metropolitan and suburban areas of the United States. This is reflected by the fact that in the Standard Metropolitan Statistical Areas the rate of auto theft was 439.8 per 100,000 inhabitants, as compared with 61.5 in our rural sections. Auto theft is defined by the FBI as "Stealing or driving away and abandoning a motor vehicle. Excludes taking for temporary use when actually returned by the taker or unauthorized use by those having lawful access to the vehicle." In 1967, 654,900 motor vehicles were reported stolen, this is an 18 percent increase in volume when compared with 1966. As indicated in the paragraph above, the police were able to recover 86 percent of the stolen vehicles, however, the remaining 14 percent represented a loss of over $93,000,000. Auto theft is an especially serious problem in the United States mainly because most of the persons arrested for this offense come from the young age groups. In fact, 80 percent of those arrested are under 21 years of age. Like the other property offenses, auto theft has also increased significantly over the past several years. As indicated in Chart 10.4 below, between 1960 and 1967 the number of offenses in this category is up 101 percent with the rate up 82 percent.

CHART 10.2

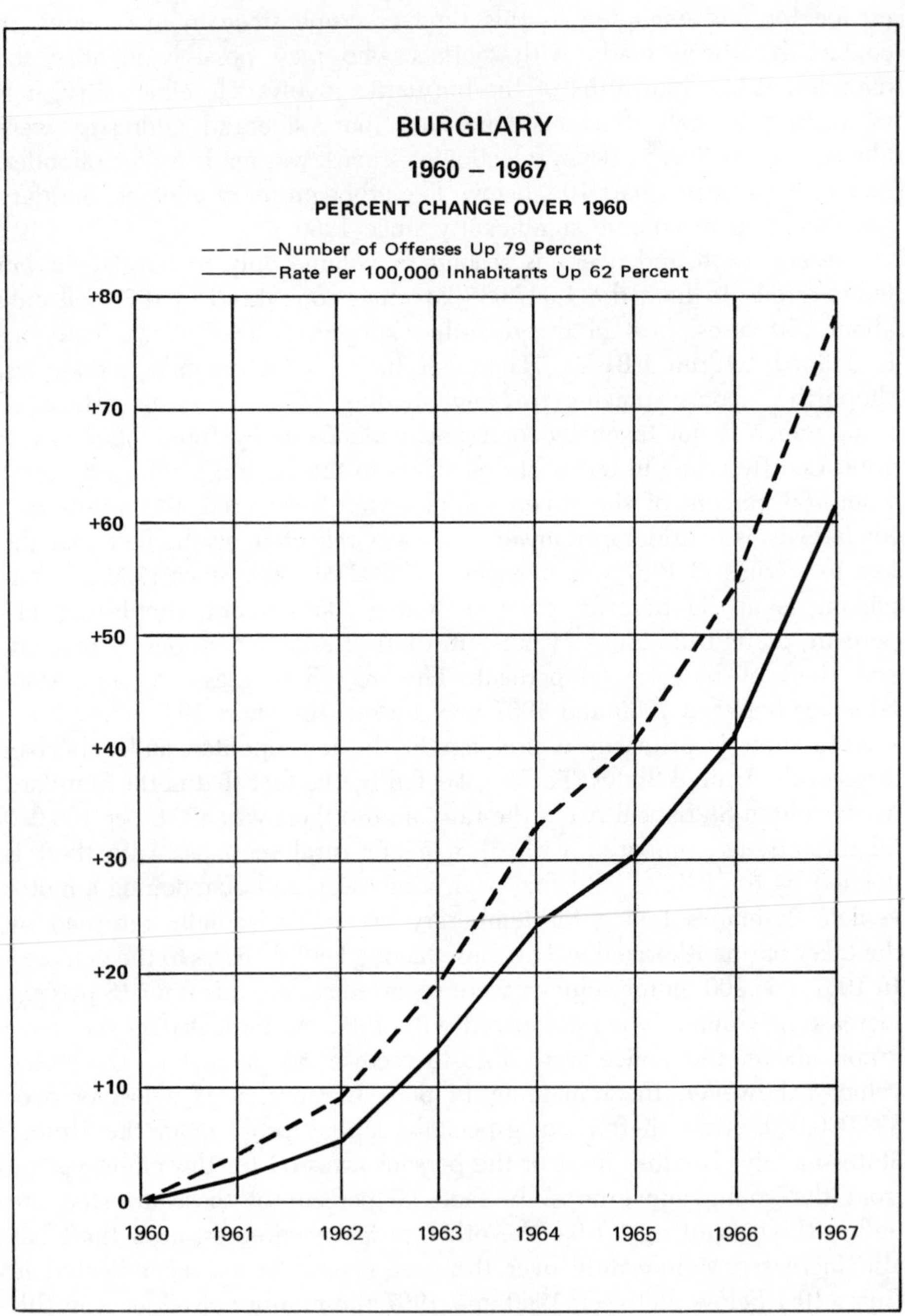

Source: Federal Bureau of Investigation, U.S. Department of Justice, *1967 Uniform Crime Reports* (Washington, D.C.: U.S. Government Printing Office, 1968), p. 20.

CHART 10.3

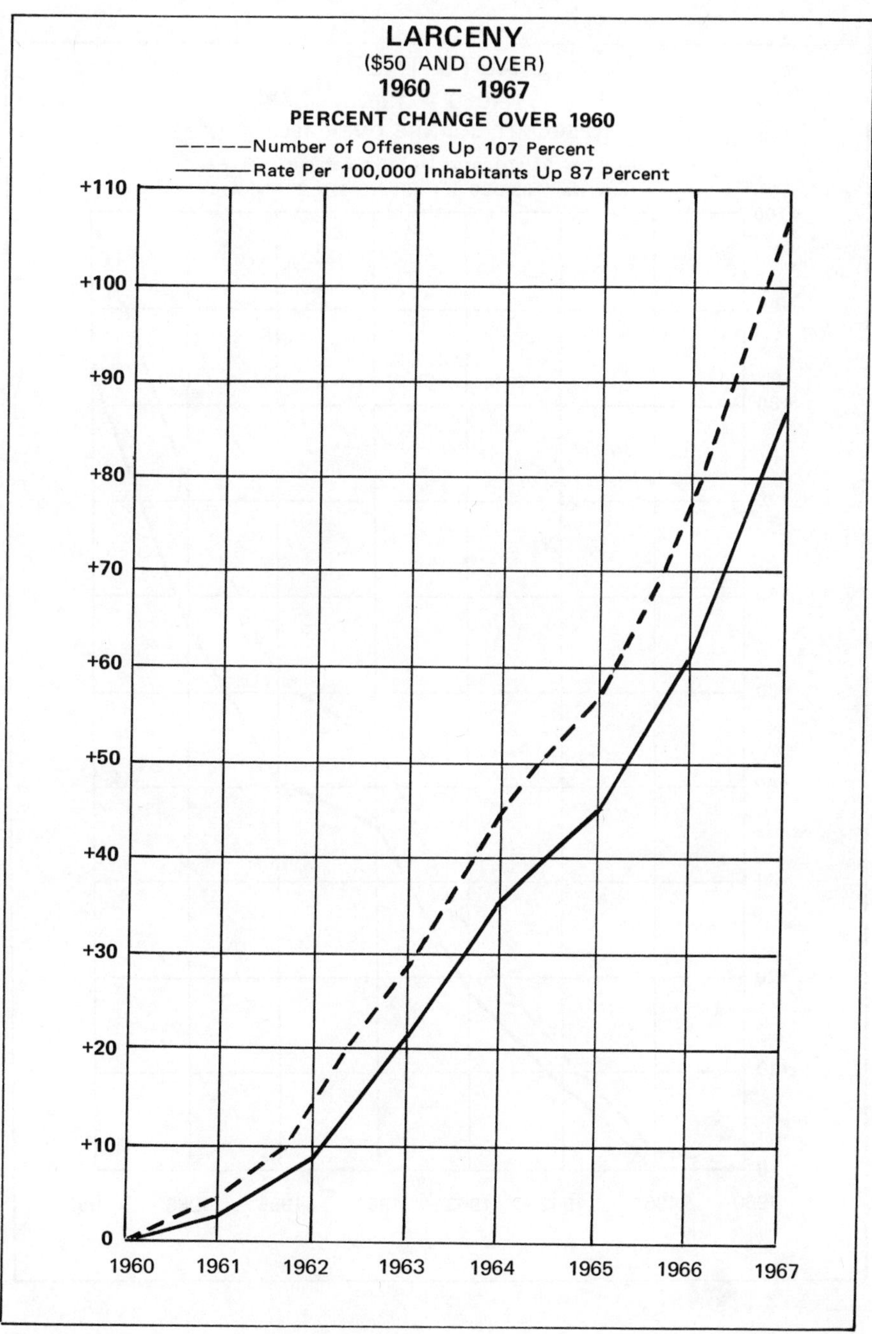

SOURCE: Federal Bureau of Investigation, U.S. Department of Justice, *1967 Uniform Crime Reports* (Washington, D.C.: U.S. Government Printing Office, 1968), p. 23.

CHART 10.4

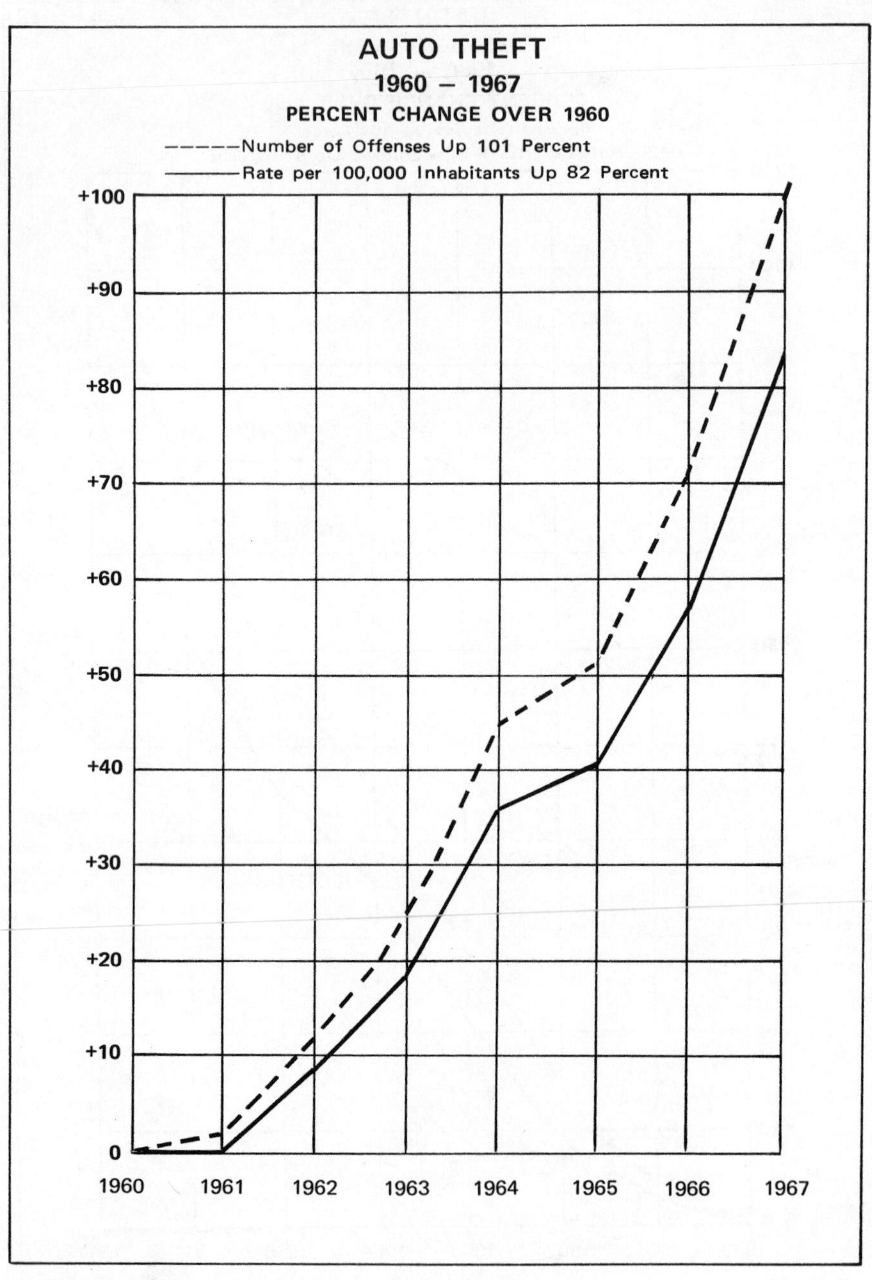

SOURCE: Federal Bureau of Investigation, U.S. Department of Justice, *1967 Uniform Crime Reports* (Washington, D.C.: U.S. Government Printing Office, 1968), p. 27.

Selected Facts on Property Offenses[1]

1. One robbery takes place every 2½ minutes.
2. One larceny ($50 and over) is committed every 30 seconds.
3. One auto theft takes place every 48 seconds.
4. One burglary is committed every 20 seconds.
5. Robbery makes up over 5 percent of the total crime index and represents about 41 percent of the violent crimes.
6. The heaviest volume of robbery occurred in the north central states (31 percent of the total).
7. Between 1960 and 1967, robbery increased 88 percent in volume.
8. Robbery rates in the larger cities were almost nine times as great as in suburban areas. (Robbery increases in proportion to density of population.)
9. 30 percent of the robberies committed were cleared by arrest.
10. Between 1960 and 1967, burglary increased by 79 percent in volume.
11. December was the peak month for burglary.
12. Persons under 25 years of age accounted for 82 percent of all arrests for burglary.
13. Burglary makes up 49 percent of the crime index.
14. 20 percent of all burglaries were cleared by arrest.
15. Between 1960 and 1967, larceny increased 107 percent in volume.
16. Larceny makes up 28 percent of the crime index.
17. Arrests of whites for larceny outnumbered Negroes by 2 to 1.
18. 45 percent of those charged with larceny were juveniles.
19. 20 percent of all larcenies were cleared by arrest.
20. Number of auto thefts increased 101 percent in volume between 1960 and 1967.
21. Volume of auto theft was greatest in the northeastern states.
22. October was the peak month for auto thefts.
23. Auto theft makes up 17 percent of the total crime index.
24. Police recovered 86 percent of the stolen motor vehicles.
25. 62 percent of all persons arrested for auto theft were under 18 years of age.
26. 20 percent of reported auto thefts were cleared by arrest.

The first selection in this chapter was contributed by Susan Black, a professional journalist, and reflects her observations of burglary in New York City. Miss Black combines humor and fact as she reports on methods used, techniques, and marks selected by burglars in New York. Included in this article are summaries of a number of cases that have been uncovered. The second selection was written by Mr. Everett DeBaun

[1]Based on 1967 statistics.

while he was serving time for armed robbery in an eastern state penitentiary. Mr. DeBaun discloses many of the techniques used and risks taken when selecting a mark and making the hit. He also discusses the responsibilities and difficulties involved in bringing together just the right combination of personalities who will successfully complete the armed robbery. In the final article, Gerald D. Robin discusses the patterns of department store shoplifting. In his study, which was conducted in the city of Philadelphia, Dr. Robin discusses the handling of shoplifters, age, sex, and race variables, disposition of the cases, and the role of aiders and abettors.

35.

SUSAN BLACK

A REPORTER AT LARGE, BURGLARY—I

* * *

As one might expect, New York City is in sheer numbers the most burglarious city in the country, though eighteen other big cities are ahead of it on a per-capita basis. Last year, burglaries occurred here at the rate of one every thirteen minutes, for a total of 40,568. Since burglary is the most common serious crime locally as well as nationally, it might be supposed that everybody would know precisely what it is; on the contrary, people nearly always mistake it for something else. Not long ago, an elderly lady returned from an evening's outing to her apartment in Manhattan and found her jewelry box empty. She telephoned the police at once and said, "I've been robbed. While I was out, somebody broke into my apartment and—" "That ain't a robbery, lady," the desk sergeant interrupted her wearily. "That's a burglary." Even the *News*, which has a reputation for being more knowledgeable about crime than elderly ladies are, uses "robbery" and "burglary" interchangeably almost every day. If burglary should not be confused with robbery, it should not be confused with larceny, either. The Penal Law of the State of New York defines robbery as "the unlawful taking of personal property from the person or in the presence of another, against his will, by means of force or violence," and goes on to mention the victim's "fear of injury, immediate or future . . ." A stickup is a robbery. Without force or fear—the elements essential to the crime of robbery—the unlawful taking of someone else's property is larceny. Picking a pocket is larceny. As for burglary, there are three degrees of it in New York State, the third degree being the least serious and the most common. "Burglary Three," as it is known in the trade, is defined in the Penal Law as the breaking and entering of a building "with intent to commit a crime therein." Apart from the building itself, there are three elements essential to burglary—the break, the entry, and the criminal intent—and learned articles devoted to each element have been published in law journals, because their meanings in burglary are a far cry from their ordinary meanings. In burglary, "breaking" does not necessarily imply force. The break may, of course, be effected by enormous physical effort (digging through a wall or jimmying a door), but it may also be effected by scant physical effort (opening an already partly opened door or window a little farther or turning a key and opening a door), or no physical effort at all (gaining admission by artifice, such as purporting to be a television repairman, or by collusion, with, say, an employee who is aware of the burglar's intention). In order to effect "entry," the burglar need not introduce all, or even a part, of his body into the premises; if he puts a hand, or an instrument held in the hand, through a window or other opening for an instant, the entry is just as complete as if the burglar had spent hours inside. In New York, the "building" that may be the subject of a burglary includes practically everything with four sides and a roof that comes quickly to mind, and some structures that don't. The Penal Law has a list of buildings that officially includes railroad cars, tents, house trailers, enclosed motor trucks, and enclosed ginseng gardens. (No one in the Police Department actually recalls a ginseng-garden burglary, but that may be explained partly by the fact that there are almost no Chinese burglars

---

SOURCE: *New Yorker*, December 7, 1963, pp. 63–128. Reprinted by permission;

"A Reporter at Large—Burglary I" is the first of a series of two articles.

and partly by the fact that there haven't been any ginseng gardens in the city for years.) The "intent to commit a crime" is usually inferred from what the burglar has done in the building or, if he is apprehended before he has succeeded in doing anything, from the circumstance of his being there without a legitimate reason. The crime intended in burglary is almost always larceny, but on occasion it may be rape, kidnapping, or murder. Hauptmann, for instance, committed burglary when he entered a window of the Lindbergh home. Although the intent to commit a crime at the time of breaking and entering is essential, there is no requirement that the intent be carried out (the burglar may be caught the minute he enters), or even attempted (he may change his mind), or that there was any possibility of its execution (the premises entered may be vacant and bare). It's still Burglary Three. And it's also Burglary Three if a person gets into a building without breaking, commits a crime therein, and then breaks out instead of in, but this is rarely the way it happens.

At common law, burglary has been defined as "breaking and entering the dwelling house of another in the nighttime with intent to commit a felony therein," but our individual states have modified this definition in a number of ways. In New York State not only needn't the violated premise be a dwelling house but a burglary may take place in the daytime, and the crime intended may be a misdemeanor. As burglary in New York State approaches the common-law definition, however, it becomes more serious. To be guilty of Burglary Two, the burglar must have entered a dwelling place in which there is a human being, and the definition of Burglary One, in addition to that requirement, states that the crime must be committed in the nighttime by a person who is armed with a dangerous weapon when he enters, or arms himself therein, or is assisted by a confederate actually present, or assaults someone in entering, committing the crime, or escaping. Most American states define burglary much as New York does, but England has kept the old common-law definition, and another crime—housebreaking—covers the daytime and applies to buildings other than dwelling houses.

In New York, Burglary Three is for a first offender punishable by a term of imprisonment not exceeding ten years, Burglary Two by a term not exceeding fifteen years, and Burglary One by a term not less than ten years or more than thirty. A burglar can also be punished separately for each collateral crime he commits on the premises. If, while he is burglarizing, he forces a door with a jimmy, breaks open a bureau, steals a watch, and strikes a tenant, he may be indicted not only for burglary but for possessing burglars' tools, for malicious mischief, for larceny, and for assault. The burglar will rarely be accused of assault, because he will rarely ("one time in a hundred," police estimate) enter a place that is occupied. The robber, to whom students of crime concede a certain amount of courage, steals from the victim in person—usually at the point of a knife or a gun. The burglar, who is generally held to be something of a coward, doesn't want the victim there; after all, the victim may pull a gun on *him*. Burglars rarely carry weapons themselves, and some are so gun-shy that, upon entering a house, they have been known to search for a gun (and, if they find one, to unload and hide it) before searching for loot. One Manhattan burglar who thought he'd broken into unoccupied premises was so flustered to find a lady at home that his only words were "If you make a noise, Madam, I'll scream." He then fled, as most burglars will who find themselves in occupied premises by mistake. The unexpected presence of rats has been known to give burglars the jitters; at the sound of scurrying feet in the woodwork, they may abandon loot they had already packed for removal. Even the one burglar in a hundred who knowingly invades occupied premises can generally be assumed to have no intention of harming anyone, but the most dangerous species of burglar is the nighttime burglar of residences, simply because he is either the bravest or the most desperate; he knows when he enters a residence that someone is probably there and that this someone may be not a frightened dowager but a policeman with a gun at his bedside.

Another reason that the burglar usually wants

the premises to himself is to preserve the great advantage he has over the robber, who "shows face," as a New York detective has put it, and thus makes it possible for the victim to give a description of him that may eventually lead to a trip up the river. Even if the robber is masked or wears a stocking over his face, the victim will certainly know whether he is tall or short, and probably whether he is Negro or white, old or young; the victim may also remember the sound of a voice or some physical characteristic that will mean something to the police. Pairs of robbers have slipped up by calling each other by their rightful names, or nicknames, during a holdup, and in Manhattan last May a young robber was caught as a result of a misspelling. He handed a drugstore owner a note reading, "I have a gun underneet my hat and get money and don't make any sound." The druggist gave the robber the money and then gave the police the note and a description. The police went to the home of a suspect who lived nearby. He was asked to write down some words, and "underneath" came out "underneet;" on being asked about this coincidence, the robber confessed. The victim of a burglary, on the other hand, hasn't any idea of the burglar's name, or how the burglar spells, or whether the burglar is a tall man or a short man—or, for that matter, a woman or a child. This accounts for the fact that the burglary-clearance rate is lower than the robbery-clearance rate. . . .

The burglar, having largely avoided danger to himself while he works as well as danger of later identification, enjoys, if he is caught, still another advantage over the robber—the advantage of nearly always being granted a greater measure of leniency in respect to his plea and, if he should be found guilty, to his sentence. In New York State, the penalties for Burglary One, Two, and Three are the same as those for Robbery One, Two, and Three, but a judge taking a plea and imposing a sentence is likely to be far more severe in the case of a robber, who is presumed to have endangered another person's life. Even if burglars are technically guilty of Burglary One or Two, they are usually allowed to plead to Burglary Three, and are rarely given the maximum sentences even for that. On the other hand, robbers, even if they are unarmed, are usually convicted of Robbery One or Two—a state of affairs that once prompted Richard G. Denzer, a former Assistant District Attorney in Manhattan, to puzzle, in verse, over Robbery Three, to wit:

Most robberies without knife or gun
  Are Robbery One or Robbery Two.
If two men rob, it's Robbery One,
  If only one, it's Robbery Two.

There's something else called Robbery Three,
  Which isn't Robbery One or Two.
I can't define this third degree,
  Except to say it's Robbery, too.

* * *

Nowadays, in most civilized parts of the world, burglary is punished by prison sentences, but when the death penalty for burglary is proclaimed, as it was by Fidel Castro in Cuba last March, burglars appear to be no more deflected from their calling than their predecessors were; the first Cuban execution for burglary took place in May, but, according to all indications, burglaries in Cuba are continuing at the usual rate. Nor has technological progress thwarted burglars. The art of burglary has kept up with all "improvements" in doors, windows, locks, and alarms. In fact, as technological progress makes life easier and more agreeable for the honest citizen, it makes it easier for the burglar, too. When a way was found to pivot the boulder at the mouth of a cave, the householder was saved the labor of rolling or pushing it aside, but then, so was the burglar; when locks came along, the doors to which they were attached became flimsier. ("The doors in many New York hotels are a joke," a successful New York burglar said last spring. "You could blow some of them down with a single breath.") As for the locks themselves, a detective has said, "The tug of war between the lock companies and the burglars has so far been won by the burglars."

Burglary has been prevalent in all societies, and as wealth in a given society becomes more abundant and more portable, burglary increases proportionately. A delightful book called *Brooklyn's Guardians,* published in 1887, deals with the police in Brooklyn's earliest days; the author, William E. S. Fales, writes that there were few offenses against person and property in Brooklyn around 1800:

> . . . probably from the fact that there was almost nothing to steal and neither place nor person to receive the booty after it had been secured. Wealth was quite evenly distributed, and consisted almost exclusively of real estate, live-stock and slaves. Marriage settlements were drawn as late as 1810, in which the jointure consists largely of farming land. There were no banks nor other means of investing money securely. Money itself was scarce. Nearly all the account books of both farmers and merchants of that time show that money transactions were infrequent and that barter was the basis of a large proportion of all the business done. It is not to be inferred that people were more honest then than now. They simply had no opportunities. The change from twenty-eight arrests in 1790 to thirty thousand in 1886 means not so much the increase of wrong-doers as it does the increase of portable wealth and of its concomitant temptations.

In the years since 1886, there has been an even greater increase in portable wealth and concomitant temptations; old-timers on the police force say that the amount of jewelry that New Yorkers have acquired in the last fifteen years is unprecedented, and that the amount of jewelry that has been stolen in New York in that period is also unprecedented. As our cities grew, burglars found them more attractive than small communities, where everyone was known to everyone else and a stranger stood out—well, like a burglar. Nearly two-thirds of our population now resides in or close to cities of over fifty thousand. . . .

As Mr. Fales would have understood, not only the number but the kinds of burglars and burglaries increase with opportunity. This is, moreover, notoriously an age of specialization, and our burglars are becoming as finicky in their specialties as doctors. Just as a heart specialist is apt to perform only a certain kind of heart operation (and, of course, never touches a kidney or lung), so a modern burglar usually limits himself to a certain well-defined area within the trade. Last year, police caught a burglar who specialized in stealing wigs, and this year the produce-market district has had a number of egg burglaries, the theatre district has been plagued with wardrobe burglaries, and several interstate trucking firms have complained that it is nearly impossible to ship a load of shrimp to New York City without the trucks' being burglarized. Whether a criminal is an embezzler or an auto thief or a burglar, he is likely to adhere to his specialty—or *modus operandi,* known familiarly to the police as "M.O." —with a fidelity that is unbelievable to a layman. The criminologists, Harry Söderman and John J. O'Connell have written:

> The ingenious and wise criminal is rarer than he is believed to be. Instead, the common burglar shows a marked narrowness of thought and a peculiar disability to vary his actions. Having once invented or learned a method, he believes it will do. . . . If he has started to enter houses by the roof, he will in all probability follow the same course throughout his career. If he has found it convenient to become familiar with the premises by making the acquaintance of servants, he will probably continue to do it as long as he is at liberty to follow a career of crime.

Some burglars are, naturally, more flexible than others (there are still a few general practitioners in medicine, too), but, as one police expert on burglary has said, "If we catch a guy burglarizing telephone coin boxes on the walls of rooming houses, this is the very thing—coin boxes, but *only* in rooming houses—that we'll look for him to go back to after he's served his sentence." (A few burglaries may even be said to bear the distinct trademark of the perpetrator. Police in Guildford, England, have been hunting for a two-trademark burglar who leaves drawings—a pair of feet with an arrow between them pointing toward the ceiling—on the dressing-table mirrors of the homes he burglarizes, and who also destroys bottles of gin whenever he comes across any.) The M.O. of today's burglar specialist consists of about a dozen elements, some of them overlapping or interdependent. They include the type of place he burglarizes, what he intends to steal, the technique he uses to gain entrance, his disguise or gimmick (if any), his planning of the job (again, if any), the time of day he prefers to work, how often he works, and whether he works alone or with a partner or partners. An M.O. depends on anything from local conditions to the burglar's nature, skill, appearance, and connections. Some burglars have a taste for office buildings; others prefer lofts, stores (or just store windows), rectories, or residences. The residence burglars, who were responsible for an estimated forty-three per cent of last year's jobs throughout the country and for about sixty per cent of those in Manhattan, can be subdivided into hotel, apartment, and private home burglars, and there is the acrobatic type that will invade nothing but penthouses. (Even more acrobatic are the "cat burglars," who climb up and down the drainpipes of buildings, and the so-called "human flies," who can scale the smooth brick faces of buildings.) Apartment burglars as a class can also be subdivided economically-*cum*-geographically, for one will work in a particular section of the city that another won't go near. As for non-residence burglaries, they can . . . be divided this way: about thirty-eight per cent were committed in retail stores, fifteen per cent in private business establishments and professional offices, fourteen per cent in gasoline or service stations, twelve per cent in public buildings, eleven per cent in warehouses, and eleven per cent in "others," such as private clubs and boxcars. Safes were attacked in only 2.5 per cent of all burglaries, and safe burglaries, unlike most, occurred more frequently in cities with a population of twenty-five thousand or less.

The estimated value of all the property stolen by burglars in the United States last year was a hundred and seventy-one million dollars, of which . . . thirty-eight per cent was cash, thirty per cent was personal property, twenty-five per cent was merchandise, and seven per cent was jewelry. Jewelry and cash are, of course, the first choice of most residence burglars (twenty-nine per cent of their loot was cash, fourteen per cent was jewelry, and the rest was personal property), but not of all. The bankbook specialist, who goes after bankbooks and some accompanying identification, often leaves cash behind, since the amount of money in the bank usually exceeds the amount lying around, and the cash might be missed before the burglar could use the bankbook. A couple of years ago, a bankbook burglar broke into an apartment in Manhattan and took a credit card with the victim's signature on it and a bankbook showing deposits of eighteen thousand dollars. He left six hundred dollars in cash in the drawer, and, sure enough, the victim needed some money the day after the burglary, took some of the cash there, and didn't notice the loss of his bankbook. Since that particular burglar did not have either a wife or a girl friend to serve as an accomplice, he had rented office space a few days earlier and put an ad in the newspaper for a secretary, offering a handsome salary. The first girl to apply was hired, and her first chore was to go to the bank and withdraw some money. The practiced bankbook burglar doesn't create a fuss by closing an account; he just taps it for a judicious fraction—in this instance, for fifty-two hundred and fifty of the eighteen thousand dollars. The burglar had the withdrawal slip made out—signature and all—and he gave it to the girl along with the bankbook. As the girl left the office, so did her new employer. When she stepped out of the bank, he just happened to be passing by. On learning that she had withdrawn the money, he thanked her, took the bankbook, the identification, and the fifty-two hundred and fifty dollars, and told her to go back to the office. He never went back himself.

Burglary changes with the times. Certain types that flourished only a few years ago are obsolete today. The transom burglar went out with transom doors; the dumbwaiter burglar, who rode up to his work, began to become obsolete when dumbwaiters began to become obsolete; and the skeleton-key burglar was in business only as long as the locks on most front doors were of a sort that could be opened by skeleton keys. The skylight burglar and the chimney burglar, the coal-slide burglar and the scuttle burglar are pretty much gone, and the next to go, at least in Manhattan, may be the so-called step-over burglar. People often lock windows that open onto fire escapes but don't lock the windows right next to them, so burglars long ago learned to step over from the fire escape to the ledge of the open window nearby. Unluckily for these specialists, most of the new buildings in Manhattan don't have exterior fire escapes. But if specific techniques come and go, basic techniques seem to develop slowly, and seldom change drastically. . . .

Police now divide burglars into four technical categories—the jimmy burglar, the pick burglar, the key burglar, and the celluloid burglar. The jimmy is a metal leverage tool sharpened at one end—common jimmies include crowbars, tire irons, and screwdrivers—and the burglar uses it to commit forcible entry. The three other technicians commit just the opposite, or what is known as "surreptitious entry," because they get in quickly, quietly, and without leaving any readily apparent marks to indicate how they managed it. Police in New York have noticed a sharp increase in surreptitious-entry burglaries over the last six or eight years.

The warded lock—the lock with the classic keyhole—was used on most doors in this country during the early part of the century. It offered poor security since it could be opened by a skeleton key on sale at the five-and-ten, or even by a piece of stiff wire. Thirty-five or forty years ago, the warded lock began to be replaced by the pin cylinder, a primitive version of which was invented in Egypt thousands of years ago. The pin cylinder is now used on the doors of almost all apartments and private dwellings, because it offers the best all-round protection. Still, there is no such thing, the ads of the lock companies notwithstanding, as a "burglarproof" lock. The pin cylinder can, of course, be opened with a key, and any lock that can be opened with a key can also be picked open. (A detective has somewhat guardedly defined a pick as a slender piece of metal with a curve at one end.) There is little defense against the pick burglar (though there are some pick-*resistant* pin cylinders that will slow him down); fortunately, picking requires a degree of technical ability that is beyond most burglars. An estimated thirty per cent of New York's increasingly numerous surreptitious entries are made by pick men.

A pin cylinder can also, needless to say, be opened with a key that is the duplicate of the owner's key, and, if the lock is part of a master system, with a master key. About ten per cent of New York's surreptitious entries are performed with keys. For some years after the pin cylinder came into general use, key burglaries in apartment houses were a comparatively minor problem for the police. Lately, however, the proliferation of new apartment buildings in Manhattan, coupled with the discovery that residence burglaries are an especially lucrative specialty, has led to a boom in stolen keys. Long before a new building is ready for occupancy, its locks are delivered to the construction site. In many instances, burglars have been able to steal two or more of these locks, and have then succeeded in making—or having made—a master key that will open every apartment in the building. The investment has generally proved to be a good one; some new buildings have had a dozen sizable burglaries during their first few months of occupancy. Other key burglaries in apartment houses occur when a burglar steals a master key from the superintendent or steals a purse in which he finds somebody's apartment key and address, or when he wangles a key from a maid or a building employee, or when the maid or the building employee performs the burglary.

The key burglary is, naturally, much more frequent in hotels, where keys are so much easier to get. Not long ago, a group of Canadians, five men and a woman, flew to New York and took up residence in a cheap hotel. Shortly after they arrived, one of their number phoned a good hotel and made a reservation for a Mr. and Mrs. Roger Gildersmith, from Akron, Ohio, whom the hotel was told to expect that afternoon. Presently, one of the men and the woman went to the hotel and registered as Mr. and Mrs. Roger Gildersmith. Mr. Gildersmith had in his possession a large suitcase, which was given ample weight by newspapers and magazines. A few minutes after he was shown to his room, he went down to the lobby and called his accomplices on a pay phone (he wanted no record of a phone call on his bill), in order to give them his room number. They arrived—one by one, so as not to attract attention—during the afternoon. A local lock expert, with whom previous arrangements had been made, also showed up. He removed the entire cylinder from the door, and within an hour had manufactured a key that would open a number of rooms in the hotel. (Some smaller hotels have a single master key for the entire building, but most have a sub-master key for every two to six floors or another pattern of sub-master keys.) The cylinder was then replaced. In the evening, when most of the other guests were out, the burglars let themselves into a couple of dozen rooms and gave them a thorough, but choosy, going over. By midnight, they were all back in their cheap hotel—all, that is, except Mr. and Mrs. Roger Gildersmith, who, when they checked out early the next morning with a suitcaseful of jewelry and cash, left behind many pounds of unread newspapers and magazines.

Burglars are seldom so methodical, but it often happens that a burglar will spend a night at a good hotel, "forget" to turn in the key to his room, and return to burglarize one of its future occupants. Or a burglar may stay in different rooms of a hotel over a period of time, until he has accumulated enough keys to give him a choice of rooms to burglarize. Actually, there's no need for a key burglar to go to the trouble and expense of staying at a hotel. In many of our better hotels, a burglar can often acquire a key by picking up one that happens to be lying on the counter at a busy time of day or by asking the desk clerk for the key to a specific room—914, say. If the desk clerk, because he is personally acquainted with the tenant of Room 914, or because the room is unoccupied, or because he is an unusually conscientious clerk, should ask the burglar his name, the burglar would give a false one and say that "Mrs. Miller" asked him to pick up something from her room. When the clerk says that Mrs. Miller doesn't live in Room 914, the burglar will say, "But I'm sure she said Room 914 at the St. Regis." The burglar will affect astonishment on learning that he is, in fact, at the Sherry-Netherland. Any number of other phony explanations can be used in a pinch (after all, it's no crime to ask for a hotel key), but in most cases the clerk will simply hand him the key. Some months ago, a female police detective assigned to the lobby of the Plaza saw a nice-looking young man walk in from the street. He checked his hat and coat at the entrance to the Oak Room, then walked through the lobby, went over to the desk, and picked up a pamphlet that was lying there. As he stood there leafing through it, two German businessmen came up to the desk to register. The young man was able to glance at their registrations, which gave him their room numbers and also the correct spelling of their names. He stepped away from the desk, walked around for a while, and then returned to ask for a key to the room of one of the German businessmen. No doubt he knew that there is more than one key for each room, because hotel keys are so frequently lost. The clerk gave him a key, and after a while he returned to the desk and collected a key to the second room from another clerk. Both rooms were on the fifteenth floor, and he took the elevator upstairs and listened at the doors. The two rooms were occupied; the men were unpacking. He went downstairs and had cocktails and dinner at the Oak Room, signing the name and room number of one of the men. He then went into the drugstore and bought a sun lamp and a large supply of toiletries, signing the other man's name; went down to the barbershop and treated himself to a haircut, a shave, and a manicure, signing again; and proceeded to the tobacco stand, where he made difficulty over the fact that the most expensive pipe on display cost a mere twenty-eight dollars. He bought it (that is, he signed for it) grumblingly, and returned to the Oak Room to check his "purchases" with his hat and coat. Then he went back to the lobby, where he picked up the house phone, rang the rooms, and discovered that both were now empty. He took the elevator up to the fifteenth floor, let himself into one of the rooms, and was engaged in burglarizing it when the female detective, who had been watching him all along, walked in and placed him under arrest. She had spotted him and tailed him because it was her feeling that most people who check their coats at the Oak Room go right into the Oak Room to eat. He hadn't.

Easy as it is to acquire hotel keys, most hotel burglars don't bother to, because most hotel doors are easily opened without them. So, for that matter, are many apartment doors and house doors. The lock set of which the pin cylinder is a part usually has a square dead bolt and a bevelled spring latch. If the dead bolt is activated, as it is if one turns one's key in the lock upon leaving, the only would-be surreptitious enterers one has to worry about are pick burglars and key burglars, but if the occupant simply slams the door behind him, he has activated nothing but the spring latch, and his door can be opened with a piece of celluloid. (Many people don't know that a door must be double-locked to afford adequate protection.) Sixty per cent of the surreptitious-entry burglaries in New York City are what are known as celluloid burglaries; the burglar introduces a piece of celluloid, called a "loid," between the door and the frame, a few inches above the lock, and brings it down until he hits an obstruction (the spring latch). He then works the loid up and down until he succeeds in pushing back the latch. It takes an experienced burglar only a few seconds to loid a door open. Among the loids frequently used by burglars are plastic-coated playing cards, the wallet-size calendars distributed by banks, the "This Seat Is Reserved" signs used on airplanes, and the "Light Coffee" and "Peanut Butter Sandwich 3 Nickels" placards to be found at the Automat. Ironically, hotels, many of which are particularly vulnerable to celluloid burglars because they have doors that can be double-locked from the inside of the room but not from the outside, are among the best providers of loids; burglars have stolen millions of dollars' worth of loot with laminated "Do Not Disturb" signs. . . .

Among those "one-in-a-hundred" burglars who will burglarize premises they know to be occupied, there are some who don't count on finding the door open. They count on somebody inside to open it for them. One of this rare breed was William (Milky) Hahn, who specialized in burglarizing fashionable East Side private houses in the nineteen-twenties, thirties, and forties—his working years. A pleasant-looking, bespectacled man, he would go up to the front door of a house at a time of day when he could expect only the maid to be home. When the maid answered the front door. Hahn would start to explain something to her in double-talk, making some distracting gestures with his left hand while, with his right, he pressed a button in the lock set, thus unlocking the door. The maid would be distressed at failing to understand his gibberish, but he would assure her that it was all right—that he'd come back later. She would return to her housework, and Hahn, as good as his word, after killing a little time, would go down into the areaway and ring the lower service-entrance doorbell. While the maid was on her way to answer, Hahn would dash back up the front stoop, open the front door, and run upstairs to the bedroom of the lady of the house, where the jewelry was sure to be. He took only money and jewelry—nothing bulky—and he got safely out of any number of houses. If a maid happened to see him leaving the premises, he would again double-talk his way out of the situation. Hahn is out of action now, and many of the private houses in Manhattan are gone, but there have been other burglars to take his place and to apply his technique to apartments. Recently, two children, a girl of twelve and a boy of nine, went around ringing doorbells in several apartment buildings on the East Side. They were dressed in Scout uniforms and said they were selling Scout cookies. Many people let them in, and while the girl was taking orders, the boy would ask for a drink of water, or a sharp pencil, or permission to use the telephone, and then a telephone directory—anything to get the cookie buyer out of sight—and while the victim was in the next room, the two of them would grab a wallet or whatever else was lying around. "They were only children," an adult victim said when they were caught. Nine and twelve *is* a little young (though a gang of child burglars in London is known to have included an infant of two), but burglary, like robbery and auto theft, is a crime of youth. . . .

Most burglars are "prowlers"—also known as "hit-or-miss" burglars—who go out to steal "on the blind." That is, while they may work in a particular section of town, or plan to try a certain building, they have no particular apartment or room in mind; . . . the young man in the Plaza didn't know who would be registering at the desk after he had checked his hat and coat at the Oak Room. But some burglars—including most of the better ones—choose their victims with care, knowing that while Apartment 6-C of a building might be occupied by a prosperous elderly couple, Apartment 6-D might have as its tenants five impoverished working girls.

Burglars plan ahead to establish both who has something worth taking and when he will be out. Even in this sort of "research" there is no end of specialization. Some burglars hunt for likely victims in restaurants and night clubs, learning their names from garrulous waiters; some sit in hotel lobbies and learn about likely victims from garrulous bellboys; some attend charity balls and get the names of likely victims from garrulous fellow-guests. Or a burglar may wait outside a garage at night until he spots a prosperous couple; he takes the license number of their car, writes to the Department of Motor Vehicles the next morning, and, by claiming that a car with that license plate sideswiped him and enclosing a fee of fifty cents, gets the name and address of the car's owner. Another burglar won't go anywhere; he'll sit at home and read the society columns, which tell him who is going to attend what luncheon and sometimes contain alluring pictures of jewelry attached to someone's neck, dress, ears, arms, and/or fingers. Some burglars subscribe to *Variety* or get access to the *Celebrity Bulletin*, which lets them in on which entertainers have come to town and where they are putting up, for burglars know that where there is a celebrity, there is conspicuous consumption, carelessness, and a group of hangers-on that is easy to become a part of. (Entertainers are considered such bad risks that many companies refuse to sell them burglary insurance.) Other burglars get hold of ships' passenger lists and raid the homes of passengers—first-class passengers, of course—while they are on their way to Europe. The "obituary" burglar will follow the death notices of the wealthy and burglarize an apartment while relatives of the deceased are attending the funeral (conservatively dressed, the burglar feels sure, and with all the good jewelry and furs left home), and the "wedding" burglar will study the notices of engagements of the rich and social, and burglarize the bride's family while everyone, including the devoted maid who raised the young bride, is at church. (Some of the good jewelry and furs will be in use at the happy event, perhaps, but all the wedding presents will be at home.)

Some of the burglars who believe in planning their jobs have their research done for them by confederates, who are known as "fingers." Some hotel employees live on the fringe of the underworld and, if they don't commit burglaries themselves, have no compunction about "fingering" a guest—tipping a burglar off to the fact that Mrs. Robinson, in Room 533, has especially nice jewelry. Florists and superintendents have often been in cahoots with burglars. Sometimes people serve as fingers unwittingly. A burglar in a bar may overhear an honest superintendent telling one of his drinking companions about an eccentric tenant who doesn't believe in locking her door, or a burglar's girl friend may go to a beauty parlor and hear another woman gossiping with the hairdresser about her next-door neighbor, Mrs. Jones, whose husband gave her a new sable coat, which she leaves casually reposing on the bed. One burglar worked with a man who sold wall safes to rich customers; eight or ten weeks after the safes were installed, each of the newly protected clients was burglarized. Fingers usually do more than provide the victim's name; they give information about when the victim is likely to be out and where the loot is probably to be found, and sometimes—especially in hotels—they turn over a key to the place. If a finger tells a burglar that Mrs. Smith goes out every day only from eleven to one, to do her shopping and air the baby, that is when she will be burglarized. If a burglar has to figure out for himself when the victim will be out, and how to get into the apartment, he will phone at different hours of the day over a period of days or weeks to determine when the apartment is most likely to be empty. . . .

Some years ago, certain prowlers worked in the morning or afternoon, while others worked in the early evening, and were known as "supper" burglars and "movie" burglars. Since the advent of television and TV dinners, fewer people seem to go out in the evening, and these categories of specialization are becoming extinct. Nowadays, residence burglars seem to prowl between eleven in the morning, when most apartment buildings have settled down for the day, and four in the afternoon, when people start coming home. They are unhindered by the servants that people no longer have, by the elevator men who were wiped out by automation, and by doormen who are often chasing cabs or attending to other duties besides the front door. Detectives call a number of new apartment buildings in the East Forties and Fifties "nine-to-five houses," because so many of the tenants are single people who work, or working couples with no children or grown children, that these buildings are practically deserted during the day. It is difficult to pinpoint the exact moment when a burglary occurred, because burglaries are almost always committed in premises that are unoccupied and the losses may not be immediately perceived, but the New York Police Department estimates that the bulk of residence burglaries occur during the daytime hours and the bulk of commercial burglaries during the night. Hotel burglars seem to favor the hours between seven and eleven in the evening; people may sit at home watching television back in Prairie du Chien, but when they come to New York they do the town by night as well as by day. Some hotel burglaries are accomplished between three and five in the morning, the advantage of the early-evening absence of the occupants being balanced by the early-morning presence of everything they have brought with them and the likelihood that they will be dead to the world after their carousing. This six-of-one, half-a-dozen-of-the-other principle also applies to working alone or working with a partner. If a burglar works alone, the entire proceeds of the burglary are his; he doesn't have to worry that the partner will spill the beans to a squealer in a drunken moment, and one man attracts less suspicion than a pair of men. On the other hand, most burglars are nervous when they work, and like to have someone along for company and reassurance; also, a second man can reduce the risk by serving as a lookout, but some burglars who have kept close to the front door have eventually learned that their partners, who went into the bedroom for the loot, put the good pieces of jewelry in their back pockets and divvied up only the so-so pieces, which they put into their side pockets. Detectives say that most burglars work in pairs, but that there are always quite a few who work alone—mostly those who have had unfortunate experiences with partners and those who are loners by nature. Some of the loners take along a silent partner who has no pockets and throws off suspicion nicely—a dog.

Police are in the habit of rating burglars on the basis of their M.O.s. They have great contempt for the "crude" burglar; they have little interest in the "run-of-the-mill" burglar; and they speak with grudging admiration of the "good" burglar, otherwise called "the real pro." Although the Police Department releases no statistics on burglars by race, honorably claiming that "crimes are committed by individuals," every experienced policeman knows that most crude burglars these days, especially in Manhattan, are from the less fortunate minority groups. Most of the crude burglars are narcotics addicts, whose appearance is such that they won't try to work in the better buildings and the better parts of the city; they say they "stick out" on Park Avenue, and consider it above their heads. Since the crude burglar works in the poorer parts of town (he often raids apartments that were visited by Welfare workers only hours earlier), he is prepared to steal whatever he sees, knowing in advance that it isn't likely to be much—old clothes, piggy banks, five-pound sacks of sugar, radios. Even if he should happen upon something more worthwhile, his fence, who can usually count on his being desperate for money for drugs, will give him five per cent—or, at best, ten per cent—of its value. Sometimes the burglar doesn't have a fence, and pawns his loot for even less, and sometimes he goes out to peddle the stolen merchandise by himself. One consequence of the crude burglar's hawking his loot is that he occasionally offers it to the victim. Last September, a musician was standing at a bar at 125th Street and Eighth Avenue, telling a friend that his favorite jacket had been stolen from his apartment. It was somewhere between brown and tan, with black stitching and slash pockets. Then a man came in, approached the musician, and said, "Hey, how'd you like to buy this jacket? You can have it for four bucks." The jacket was somewhere between brown and tan, with black stitching and slash pockets, and the musician said, "I'll buy it, I'll buy it. Wait here, I'll be back in a minute." He went outside and was back moments later—with a patrolman.

Since his gains are small, the crude burglar must burglarize often. Many crude burglars go out to work six or seven days a week and don't quit until they have scored. The crude burglar may have heard about celluloid and may carry a piece with him, but because the poor people he steals from are apt to be more careful than the rich, he generally finds their doors double-locked. He doesn't get their keys and he doesn't know how to pick, so he usually relies on a jimmy. The crude burglar is a messy worker; when he leaves an apartment, it looks as if a tornado had struck it. . . .

Police agree that while a burglar is generally content to remain a burglar, he sometimes proceeds to far worse crimes, if a burglary provides the occasion for them. A crude burglar who has entered what he thought were unoccupied premises may, on finding the premises occupied by a woman, decide to rape her. Last July, in Montclair, New Jersey, and last October, in Midland, Texas, burglars admitted they'd murdered women who surprised them while they were burglarizing their homes. Or a crude burglar who has got his hands on some loot that is too hot to be disposed of at that moment may commit a robbery in order to obtain some ready cash. At three-twenty on the morning of Thursday, June 20, 1963, a brick was thrown into the Fifth Avenue window of Van Cleef & Arpels, the jewellers. The store was protected by a Holmes burglar alarm, and when it went off, personnel from the Holmes Central Office, around the corner, came on the double, as did police from a nearby station. They didn't arrive in time to catch the burglar or burglars, who got away with seven pieces of platinum and diamond-studded jewelry—a bracelet, a watch, four diamond clips, and a pair of earrings—worth $34,100. On Friday, June 21, 1963, at three o'clock in the afternoon, a man walked into a jewelry store on Lexington Avenue at Forty-second Street, which was owned by an elderly couple. He pulled a knife out of his pocket and told the woman, "Let me have your money." She said she had none, and began to scream for her husband, who was in a back room. He ran to her aid, and the robber fled, the couple following him out of the store. A patrolman named Thomas Corbett heard the screams, spotted the man fleeing through the crowds in the Grand Central area, and yelled to him to halt. He didn't. Corbett ran after him, and as he was about to catch up with him, the robber turned and charged him, waving his knife. The two men grappled, and the patrolman felt the robber's knife nick his gun hand as he was working his service revolver free. Corbett, a veteran of seventeen years on the force, had never fired a shot in the line of duty. Now he killed the robber with one bullet. From papers found in his side packets, the dead man was promptly identified as Randolph Jackson. An hour later, when the police got around to searching his back pockets, the Van Cleef & Arpels burglary was solved. They found a manila envelope containing the bracelet, the watch, the clips, and the earrings that had been stolen thirty-six hours before. The burglar-robber, who had a record of thirteen arrests, including several for assault and burglary, had been released from a state prison in April after serving eight years for robbery.

On the top rung of the ladder of burglary, such as it is, police put the "good" burglar—the adjective representing a professional judgment, not a moral one. New York detectives say that today's good burglars tend to be Jewish or Italian, but that there are some good Canadian and Cuban burglars around. The good burglar goes after cash, traveller's checks, or money orders if he is a safe burglar, and after cash, jewelry, and furs if he is a residence burglar, as most good burglars are these days. Although a student who gets A's in English and Latin and C's in mathematics and chemistry will be well thought of by his English and Latin professors, he won't make the dean's list. In the same fashion, to be rated a good burglar by the police, a man must get an A not in two or three out of four subjects but in four out of four. These subjects are his appearance, his planning, his skill, and his fence.

The good burglar has the appearance to get into any of the best buildings in town, and he has the wherewithal to dress well—though in fact he usually chooses to dress rather flashily. If a good burglar is pointed out to the average citizen, the citizen's first reaction is bound to be "But he doesn't *look* like a burglar," which is precisely the point. . . .

The good burglar is almost never a narcotics addict, but he is almost always a gambler; therefore, with him everything is a matter of percentages. He plans all his jobs, either independently or with a finger; he knows that he may get the same jail sentence for stealing a hundred thousand dollars that he would get for stealing a hundred, so he goes after a big target every time. Furthermore, he knows that if the proceeds are always substantial, he won't have to work as often, and—percentages again—the less often he goes out to work, the less chance there is for him to be caught. Some good burglars work only once every three or four months. The good burglar either has the skill to pick a lock or has succeeded in getting a key to the premises. His fence gives him as much as thirty per cent of the value of whatever he steals.

The good burglar will enter surreptitiously, and he won't disturb anything while he is searching for treasure, because if it looks as if the best jewelry weren't at home, he will come back for it another time. The good burglar knows good jewelry, unlike the bungling burglar who takes a gold-plated pin and leaves a strand of priceless real pearls. The good burglar takes the good pieces and leaves the costume jewelry behind; sometimes he will take only the best of the good jewelry—pieces containing large stones that will be worth something on their own when they are removed from their settings—and won't bother with pieces that are valued as much for their workmanship as for their stones. . . .

The good burglar keeps his mind on his work and wants to get out as quickly as possible; he won't be sidetracked by tempting refreshments, or even by a pretty woman, Shakespeare's "Beauty provoketh thieves sooner than gold" notwithstanding. A good burglar once entered the apartment of a beautiful and well-known actress, believing it to be empty (she hadn't answered either his phone calls or his rings at the doorbell), and found her fast asleep on top of the bedclothes, without a stitch on. Coolly ignoring this agreeable apparition, the burglar took her jewelry and tiptoed out. This job was unusual chiefly in that the good burglar didn't leave *before* looking for the jewelry. If the average burglar will work in occupied premises one in a hundred times, the good burglar will do so only one in five hundred. . . .

The good burglar is a criminal, not a philanthropist, and if a victim is unusually persistent and harps on summoning the police, and the burglar sees a prison sentence staring him in the face, he will do whatever he thinks necessary to escape. If he does have to assault anyone, he tries his best not to do him serious harm. If police catch him in the middle of a job—what he calls being caught "dead bang right"— he will not resist arrest, or complain, but even if the arresting officer has arrested him before, he may not volunteer to tell the officer so much as his name until his lawyer comes. Good burglars con their victims; they are hardly ever conned by police. One police officer who has tried on many occasions to get good burglars to talk says, "One of the biggest distortions on television crime programs concerns the good burglar. I'm looking at the clock, knowing the show has to end in time for the last commercial, and there's this seasoned criminal denying a burglary or saying nothing at all. The police haven't got anything on him. Then some steadfast detective says, 'Think of your poor mother. Would she want you to be this way?' And out of the clear blue sky he confesses. It doesn't often happen with the average burglar, much less with the good burglar." And a professor of criminology recently wrote that good burglars "can in a high proportion of cases avoid arrest, prosecution, or prison sentence."

A burglar can be judged pretty well by the company he keeps. While a crude burglar will be familiar with only the criminals in his immediate neighborhood (dope pushers, fences, shoplifters, and, of course, other crude burglars), the good burglar will have intercity, interstate, and sometimes international connections. On the whole, both the good and the crude burglars associate only with other criminals, which isn't surprising, especially in a country like ours, where the first question asked of a stranger is apt to be "What do you do?" A burglar once confided to a reporter, "I've had a lot of friends, but the kind of people I go around with when I'm on the outside are naturally more or less criminals. It's pretty hard for me to have a friend who isn't a criminal, because when I have a friend I like to talk to them about everything, and if the friend wasn't a criminal, too, I couldn't talk about stealing and stuff like that. I strike up acquaintances in bars and places like that and have a good time for an evening or two talking to some dame or some guy, but you can't go very far with that without something about what you do for a living leaking out."

"Professional stealing is not organized crime," Edwin H. Sutherland wrote in 1937 in *The Professional Thief*, a book based on a series of interviews with one long-time professional thief and annotated by a large number of other professional thieves, who consented to read it in manuscript form. Pointing out that "there is no organized crime unless we are to call each mob, troupe, outfit, or combination which is grifting together an organization," Sutherland likens professional stealing to a business, much like any other business: "There is no underworld newspaper, but there is complete communication among the members, so that everyone knows everyone else in his particular part of the underworld." Even today, police do not have a legendary "ring" of organized burglars headed by a mastermind to cope with, though some of the best burglars do work together, and there are connections. For example, the good Canadian burglars exchange information with each other and with some good New York burglars on prospective victims, on residential layouts, and on market outlets. Good burglars meet in lawyers' offices, in certain bars, cafeterias, or other hangouts, through such business acquaintances as fences, and, on the rare occasions when they are imprisoned, in jail. Police who had obtained a court order for a wire tap heard a good Canadian burglar phone a good New York burglar and ask him for a certain type of safe technician; then they heard the good New York burglar telephone Miami to locate someone competent to do the job, and within ten minutes they heard him call the Canadian back to say the Miami man could be expected in Montreal the next day. . . . Years ago, a good burglar in Chicago or San Francisco might have stayed at home to work, but now, with jet planes, burglars come to New York after the lucrative targets, follow the sun and wealthy vacationers to resorts, and establish alibis for themselves in New York that cover them while they fly to Miami and back on a job. "Good burglars are always in transit," detectives say, with a touch of envy. "They take jets the way we take subways."

Between the crude burglar and the good burglar fall any number of more or less presentable, skilled, dangerous, experienced, and successful run-of-the-mill burglars. Most of them give up on an unyielding lock or door after a few minutes' effort, but others will work on it for an hour or so, if conditions permit. One pair of burglars showed a surprising amount of determination. Having opened the lock on an apartment door, they found the door had a chain; they'd forgotten to bring clippers with them, so one of them took a taxi home to fetch some while the other waited on the spot. . . . Most burglars, however, stick single-mindedly to burglary, and some are so attached to their M.O.s that they burglarize the same places or people again and again.

Unlike fishermen and hunters, burglars observe no season, though the burglary rate is a bit higher during the winter months than at other times. (Crimes of passion—forcible rape and aggravated assault—occur most frequently during the summer months.) Last year, January had the highest percentage of burglaries in New York City; March was second; and December was third. A burglar is apt to be highly superstitious, and to consider a particular day his "lucky day," but since each burglar has a different lucky day, and since many prowlers work a seven-day week, there is no substantial daily variation in the burglary rate. Weekends, however, when places of business are closed and families are likely to go on outings, have a slightly higher percentage of the week's burglaries than weekdays. . . .

Burglars are often tattooed (several have been found to have the legend "I Hate Cops" across their chests), and most of the ones who have been around a while have acquired aliases and nicknames. The Spook, Frank the Hotdog, Footsy, and Izzy the Eel are among the nicknames that contemporary burglars answer to. . . . Few burglars who get married stay married, but most burglars have a weakness for women and live, from time to time, with a mistress. Since burglars like to brag about their work, a burglar's lady friend usually knows exactly what line of work he's in. . . . Most burglars shoot craps or bet on the horses, and the more money they steal, the more they gamble, so even the successful ones have a tendency to be broke. There's no color line in the underworld, because a burglar feels that he has more in common with another burglar, regardless of his race, than with an honest citizen whose skin is the same shade as his own. A lot of white burglars have Negro girl friends, and a lot of Negro burglars have white girl friends. Burglars generally appreciate good publicity, and have been known to ask friends to save their newspaper clippings for them when they are in jail—not to the extent, however, that the burglary rate went down during the newspaper strike in New York in late 1962 and early 1963; on the contrary, it went up. New York burglars have a language of their own, just as Egyptian and Elizabethan burglars had, and just as advertising men, doctors, and other professional groups have now. At the moment, the proceeds of a burglary are usually known as "the score" (or "the take"), and the burglar's arrest is not an arrest but a "pinch" or a "collar." The vocabulary of the burglar—the good burglar included—is so liberally sprinkled with obscenities that it isn't easy for him to create an impression of refinement, even for the few minutes it takes him to con a victim. The vocabulary of the burglar is generally of such a narrow range that detectives making a collar some time ago were amazed to hear one burglar say to his partner, "We do the job, we're free and clear, and—lo and behold—the Philistines are upon us."

* * *

36.

EVERETT DEBAUN*

THE HEIST: THE THEORY AND PRACTICE OF ARMED ROBBERY

The holdup was a relatively rare form of crime forty or fifty years ago, though well publicized even then. It would be interesting to know the reasons for this sudden rise in popularity. No doubt the ever-increasing complexity of our way of life has had something to do with it. Psychologists declare that excessive discipline is likely to result in impulses of cruelty and destruction, and it seems probable that the innumerable social pressures to which the individual is subjected in our society give rise to aggressive feelings ultimately requiring outlets—certainly our preoccupation with bloodthirsty comics, movies, radio programs, and mystery and detective fiction is not accidental. And certainly the stickup is an aggressive action of classic directness and simplicity.

Such an explanation may account in part for the innumerable holdups of drug stores and filling stations, the frequent heists pulled with glass pistols, cap pistols, water pistols, air guns; the haberdasheries and cigar stores stuck up as Jesse James might have stuck up banks; the sadistic little jobs whose main purpose seems to be maltreatment of the victims: the Lovers Lane holdups, the cab-drivers robbed of fares and tips.

---

*At the time of original publication, the author, himself a heavy criminal, specializing in the heist before his arrest, was serving a sentence for robbery in a state penitentiary in the East.

Such holdups undoubtedly have a large emotional, or neurotic, component. Obviously, the motivation is not a rational weighing of risks against possible gain, for banks might be robbed almost as cheaply—not that bank robbery is lightly punished, but that we punish robbery of any type more severely than several varieties of murder. . . .

There are more tangible reasons for the emergence of the holdup as a *professional* technique, though here too emotional and social factors of course are present. Technological change occurs in the underworld, as elsewhere. During the past few generations several ancient and dishonorable professions have given way to others better suited to the times. In comparison with the burgeoning of the holdup, the decline of the box-busting racket is a case in point. Forty or fifty years ago, the safe-cracker was considered the prince of thieves. Though the best of the modern boxmen can open modern safes as efficiently as the petermen of half a century ago could open those of that day, the profession is fast on the down-grade. Cash simply is not kept in safes as it was. For the most part, business is carried on by check, and checks are worthless as loot. Similarly, securities are now seldom readily negotiable, stamps are giving way to postage meters, jewelry is a drug on the market—"slum," as it is familiarly called, brings but from 15 to 20 per cent of the replacement value at fence, while silver is hardly worth carrying off, and watches can be disposed of for no more than a portion of the value of the metal in the cases. Furthermore, that infallible source of cash in large amounts, the bank, is no longer vulnerable to the safe-cracker, thanks chiefly to the time lock, a device which may be set to jam the bolt mechanism for a period during which a vault may not be opened even by some one possessing the combination. Consequently, the Max Shinburnes, Leonidas Leslies, Chauncy Johnsons, Adam Worths, Bob Scotts, and Jimmy Hopes who during the last quarter of the past century burglarized banks of sums said to total close to a hundred million dollars—a number of the individual "scores" were for more than a million—have gone the way of the horse and buggy. Their present-day counterparts are top-grade holdup-men—"heist-men" in the underworld argot.

For technical reasons, chief among them the relative scarcity of readily convertible securities, holdups the size of the old-time bank burglaries are few and far between. Scores running into the hundreds of thousands are no rarity, but so far as I know there has been only one million-dollar holdup—that of a bank in Lincoln, Nebraska, in the early thirties. These big jobs are the work of what are probably the most highly skilled professional thieves in the world, but even on its lower levels the holdup in the hands of the professional has little but the name in common with the amateur, or neurotic, article. The almost invariable mark of the latter—called "cowboy-job" by the professional in derisive reference to the stagecoach holdups in Western movies—is recklessness. Planning is often non-existent; the simplest precautions may be ignored; victims may be unnecessarily maltreated; the robber is not infrequently caught in the act. A psychiatrist once said to me that the frequency with which holdup-men of this stamp manage to be caught on the job indicated to him a desire to *be* caught and punished—the social conscience at work. The idea is not as wild as it may sound. However, under our system punishments are so ferocious that the guilt-ridden culprit speedily becomes the aggrieved, free to work off his cholers without troublesome pangs of conscience. This state of mind, which may of course arise more often from causes other than imprisonment, is characteristic of the professional thief. Not very surprisingly, the earmarks of the professional holdups are careful planning and efficient execution.

A seventeenth-century cookbook advises those who would prepare jugged hare first to catch their hare. To pull a heist, first find your "mark." A mark may be any considerable sum of money or the equivalent in readily convertible swag. Professional heist-men judge marks in terms of the probable cash return relative to the risks involved.

Marks are either dug up or tipped off. When a heist-man says that he has dug one up, he means that he has found it himself. He may have sought it out, tailing ladies who appear in public festooned like Christmas trees with jewels, or armored cars making deliveries of payrolls, for instance. Or he may just have stumbled upon it, like one who was introduced by a casual resort acquaintance into a private poker game in which some $12,000 was in play, or another who noticed that the proprietor of a saloon where he occasionally stopped for a beer made a practice of cashing pay-checks for employees of a nearby refinery. Marks that have been tipped off are those that have been pointed out by others. One who tips off marks is called a finger-man or tipster; he may or may not be of the underworld. Sometimes pickpockets, gamblers, and other footloose grifters tip marks off to heistmen as a side-line. The standard remuneration for this service is 10 per cent of the gross score. A surprisingly large number of marks are tipped off by legit, or ostensibly honest, people, and no few are put up (whence, incidentally, the colloquial expression "put-up job") or prearranged: a truck driver would like a share of the value of the load of cigarettes or whiskey he will be carrying; a jeweler wants to beat his insurance company; a bank manager wishes to cover his embezzlements. As the police are well aware of this, many heist-men fight shy of such tips, for the legit citizen, having odd notions of honor by the thief's standards, is likely to break down under close questioning, and promises of immunity for himself, and finger his partners as thoroughly as he formerly fingered the mark.

Other things being equal, the cash mark is always preferable. There is nothing like a bank for cold cash in large amounts, and until recently the "jug" was beyond argument the best type of mark by professional criteria. It is true that for many years banks of any size have had what looks to be formidable protection, but in robbery as in warfare of other types the aggressor has a heavy advantage. Armed guards, vaults with walls of steel and concrete several feet in thickness, and elaborate alarm systems did not prevent heist-mobs from knocking over an average of about two banks a day during the early thirties. In 1934, however, Congress passed an act making bank robbery a federal offense and bringing it under the jurisdiction of the FBI, a police organization having almost unlimited funds and unique facilities, the most important of these being a corps of stool-pigeons probably as extensive as any outside Russia. . . . These additional risks require that others be at a minimum if a bank is to be marked nowadays, and the same is true of the mails.

There are numerous types of cash mark which do not involve federal heat, however. Of these, the payroll is probably the most popular. Although payrolls do not compare in size with banks as marks, they are far more numerous and, since their physical protection is usually comparatively light, are vulnerable to smaller mobs. Anyone working as a member of a three-handed mob scoring three $10,000 payrolls fares as well financially as if he had taken part in a five-handed bank robbery worth $50,000, at about one-tenth the risk.

Marks for swag, or loot readily convertible into cash, are still more numerous and usually even less well protected, but they have the considerable disadvantage that the take must be fenced, or sold. Since this involves a suicidal risk if undertaken through legitimate channels, swag is usually sold to a professional buyer of stolen goods. The fence not only helps himself to a whopping profit—he seldom pays more than 20 per cent even for gilt-edge swag—but often he is not reliable in the face of police pressure, and not uncommonly does business with police and politicians, or pays in money and information for tacit permission to operate. Sometimes, particularly when jewelry or securities are involved, it is possible to bypass the fence in favor of the company which has insured the loss. Settlement in such cases runs about 20 per cent of the insured amount, no questions asked. Several private detective agencies are widely known as specialists in negotiating such transactions, which also are often handled through attorneys. . . .

Given a mark, the next step is mobbing up, or getting together the men who will work the job. A working unit of underworld professionals of any type is called a mob. There are "single-o" heist-men, such as the one known in the papers as Slick Willie, who has robbed large and well-protected banks single-handed, but the vast majority of the brotherhood work in mobs. A heist-mob may comprise from two to six or eight members—the type of mark is usually the determining factor. Thus, the "same" mob—*i.e.*, several of a group of stickup-men who sometimes work together—may be five-handed for a jug-heist and three-handed for a payroll job. There are excellent reasons why the mob is generally of the minimum size compatible with efficient operation. One is selfish: "The smaller the mob, the bigger the cut." The other is protective: each additional member adds to the risk of a fall, paradoxical as this may seem. The answer is that the professional runs little danger of falling either *en flagrante* or, despite the highly imaginative information ladled out for popular consumption along this line, as a result of acute detective work. Almost always he is caught because of information given to police.

Eddie suddenly squares his debts and springs with a new car, for instance, or begins shooting high craps and buying drinks for the house, or buys a fur coat for Marge, who cannot resist throwing the needles to that catty Doris, who puts two and two together and confides the result to Nettie, whose husband Louie peddles dope or does a bit of pimping or wants to get City Hall's okay to book numbers or horses in his cigar store. In every city, police permit numerous Louies to operate in consideration for periodical cash donations, plus just such favors as the one Louie is now in a position to confer. If Eddie cannot stand up, . . . or if Marge knows who his partners are and can be talked or frightened into trading the information for a lighter sentence for him, the whole mob may fall.

Popular notions notwithstanding, the basic units of a heist-mob are not a "mastermind" and some servile morons who carry out his orders. As a matter of fact, among "heavy"[1] thieves no one gives orders for the good reason that no one takes them—the heavy is as independent a character as walks the earth. Within the mob, equality reigns. All share equally in risk and gain. All have equal authority. This is not to imply that the members of a mob simply behave as they please on the job. There a rather rigid discipline prevails, but all have had a voice in the plan being carried out and authority has been delegated willingly.

The true essentials of a heist-mob are a wheel-man and a rod-man. The former is a skilled driver, often a specialist who takes no other part (this is preferred practice). Yet if the mob is short-handed or somewhat slipshod in operation he may work the inside with the others. The rod-man's title is self-explanatory. A rod is a gun. Since most holdups involve the close control of a number of people during the course of the actual robbery, most mobs have two or more gun-wielding members. In special cases, a mob may use a man on the outside in addition to the man on the wheel. For example, the getaway route for a job located in the business section of a city may begin with a run down a narrow alley or a one-way street, in which case a tail, a car or truck which cuts in behind the getaway car and blocks the way long enough for the former to get a sufficient jump, may be used. But the great majority of heist-mobs work with a single man on the wheel and either two or three on the inside.

A mob forms rather casually. Eddie, let us say, has a promising mark. He decides that it can "go" three-handed. Thinking over the experienced men of his acquaintance who are out for action he fixes on Big Pete. This choice is based upon several considerations. Pete has a rep as a good man, which means that he is known to be trustworthy, dependable, and resourceful. When he makes a meet, or engagement, he keeps it. He has plenty of belly, or courage. He has shown that he is a sticker who will not panic and leave the others to shift for themselves in the event of trouble, and he has repeatedly stood up, or kept his mouth shut, under police questioning—American police question prisoners; only foreigners torture them. Furthermore, he will not burn, or cheat, his partners; he does not flash, or make a show of his money; and he has an air of calm authority which is valuable on the job: he can control a whole roomful of people without frightening them so that someone may do something foolish.

Eddie and Pete talk the job over—"cut it up," they say. If a tip is involved, Eddie lets

[1]Professional thieves fall into two categories. The "heavy" is primarily the rebel-without-a-cause; his attitudes are inflexibly anti-authoritarian; his techniques are based upon the use or threat of force. The "grifter" is essentially the businessman whose line happens to be illegal; his attitudes are closer to the conventional; his techniques feature superior dexterity or chicane.

Pete know that there will be a tipster's end (10 per cent) to come off the top, or before any deductions have been made, but without telling him who the tipster is, just as he will not tell the latter who will work the job, for by his code anyone who deals with him is entitled to full protection, and he considers them bound by the same standard. Other details are discussed. Yes, between them, the two can handle the inside without trouble. Probably they could handle the whole thing, but to be on the safe side they had better have a man on the wheel.

Since the mark is Eddie's, he is boss in this respect. He "owns" the job; it is therefore his right to select those who are to participate. Anyone who does not wish to work with any of the others may pull out, or withdraw. If one who pulls out should thereupon get his own mob together and take the job, Eddie would feel morally justified in shooting him, though if another mob working independently happened to beat Eddie to the job he would not consider himself wronged. If something happened to prevent him from taking part in the touch and Pete filled in another man and took it, Eddie would be entitled to half an end, or share, even though he was in prison when the job came off. . . .

The detailed planning and preparation which constitutes the next stage is the most important part of the heist. If this layout is done well, the mark is in the bag. The robbery itself becomes a simple transaction lasting but a few moments—sometimes less than thirty seconds.

Professionals agree that casing is far and away the most important part of laying out a heist. This word, which like many others of underworld origin is coming into popular use, is from the argot of faro, once as popular a betting game as craps is today. It originally referred to a record of the cards played as kept on an abacus-like contraption called a "case." As used in the underworld, the word means gathering information from observation.

Even when the tip includes detailed information, a good mob cases its marks with care. Tipsters often err. One mob, whose tipster worked in the place to be taken, was furnished with a layout-chart so complete that they did not bother casing the inside, to their subsequent sorrow, for the tipster had neglected to indicate that the partitions setting off the office they were to rob did not extend to the ceiling, and police were waiting for them when they came out.

Several matters are cased with particular care. The size of the score is checked in advance whenever possible—tipsters are likely to be very optimistic about the size of a prospective touch. If the mark is a bank, checking may involve little more than a glance at the quarterly statement, available at the local library or Chamber of Commerce, and the size of payrolls may be estimated satisfactorily from the number of employees, but most other kinds of mark are difficult to case accurately for size. A knowledge of the floor plan, arrangement of furniture, placement of doors and windows, and so forth, is essential to a fast, smooth piece of work.

On the theory that it helps to know where trouble is likely to come from, some heist-men like to get an advance look at the people on the inside as well. Impressionable young squirts who attend the movies too often and an occasional old towser who has had his job for thirty years—"heroes," the heist-man calls them sardonically—may, if not closely watched, rise in defense of the insurance company's stockholders, especially if women or big bosses are present. It is always well to know how many women must be dealt with, since they are an occupational hazard of the first order which I will describe later on. Armed guards are of course cased with care, though unless ensconced in a protective cage or turret they represent a threat more apparent than real, since they cannot go about with cocked pistols. A well-executed job takes so little time that alarm systems call for little or no attention, unless the mark is a bank. Bank heists usually take several minutes. . . .

Generally speaking, casing is the job of the inside-men. The wheel-man has work of his own. The procurement of the getaway car is one of his responsibilities. There are many car-thieves who will deliver to specifications of year and make for a moderate fee, but heist-men seldom patronize them for reasons of security. The simple job of stealing a car may be considerably complicated by the wheel-man's personal predilections. Most of them have strong convictions concerning various makes of car for this particular kind of service. Certain makes, widely known as "dogs on the get-out," which is to say that they accelerate slowly from a standing start, automatically are ruled out. In general, a small, fast car of common make is preferred for work in city traffic, but a heavy one where the getaway entails a long run over country roads. Having procured a suitable car, the wheel-man provides it with license plates which are not hot and plants it, or places it somewhere out of harm's way, until it is needed.

The wheel-man's other major responsibility is the layout of the get, or getaway route, a simple matter if the job is in a city and the mob intends to piece up there, but complicated if a run to another locality is in prospect, as is usually the case if the mark is located in a small community. . . .

There will be other details requiring attention. Perhaps the job is located in a town whose approaches may quickly be blocked off. If so, the mob may want to hide out in town until the heat has somewhat subsided, in which case a suitable plant, or hideout, will be required. There will have to be bags for the money—the paper shopping bags used by housewives are as good as any. And there is the matter of guns.

Mobs composed of men who often work together may have a small armory of weapons belonging to the mob as a whole, but as a general thing each man furnishes his own weapon, usually a pistol. Revolvers are preferred to automatics, for many of the Colt .45's circulating in the underworld came originally from army or other federal sources, and if one is used on a job the G-heat may assume it has been stolen and enter the case on that basis. Moreover, if the magazine clip of an automatic is kept loaded for a protracted time its spring may become "tired" and the gun may jam when used. The sub-machine guns so common in the movies are rarely used in real-life holdups. They are cumbersome, difficult to acquire, and at once bring the crime under federal jurisdiction. . . .

The job is ready to go when it has been cased and the other details have been attended to. The mob will have met several times to cut up, or talk things over, and to lay the job out, or make a detailed plan of action. The preparations in their entirety will have taken anywhere from a few hours to several weeks, depending upon the mark and the class, or quality, of the mob—the better the mob, the more thorough the layout.

As has been intimated, there is not much to the holdup itself if the layout has been well done. Each man knows just what to do on the job, when to do it, and what to expect of the others. Unforeseeable complications aside, the actual robbery is largely a matter of going through the motions on schedule. The term "schedule" is used advisedly, for the time element is important—so important that the time taken to "get in, get it, and get out" is a good measure of professional competence. It is not unusual for a class mob to carry out a run-of-the-mill holdup in half a minute.

The emphasis placed upon speed on the job probably owes less to fear of interference than to the hard-earned knowledge that surprise renders the average person incapable of comprehending what goes on about him with any accuracy, so that he is likely unconsciously to fill in from his imagination. . . .

In working a heist, the mob usually goes out from a meet, or appointment held a short time before the job is to go. Here the layout is gone over again, clothes are changed—if the mark is in a factory district the mob may work in coveralls, if in a business district in business suits; the idea is to remain as inconspicuous as possible —and other last-minute details are attended to. The members of the mob leave singly and go to the mark by separate routes in order to avoid the possibility of being seen together by coppers to whom they may be known. Possibly they do not rod up, or arm themselves, until they reach the job, just in case one of them might be stopped and searched. The wheel-man brings the guns in the car.

The mob meet the car a block or so from the mark and rod themselves up. They walk to the job; the wheel-man pulls ahead and parks near the entrance in such a way that he can swing out from the curb in a hurry. If possible, the inside-men work covered, or masked. This usually can be managed without difficulty unless the place must be entered directly from the street, and even then if scarves fastened with pins so that they may quickly be twitched up over the mouth and chin are used—the lower part of the face is the most easily identifiable.

Covered or bald, the mob enters as casually as any other visitors. Melodramatics are for the movies. One man does the talking: "All right, folks, stay where you're at! Keep quiet! Keep your hands where I can see them! Nobody but the insurance company is gonna get hurt, so take it easy." Generally this fellow stands near the door where he can keep the whole room under observation as well as intercept anyone who may come in while the robbery is in progress. He is an authoritative figure, the center of attention. Most witnesses hardly notice the other inside-men, who go about their job of collecting the score as quickly and with as little fuss as possible.

So far as may be, the mob are calm and polite on the job. "Cowboying," or the wild brandishing of pistols and shouting of orders in all directions is frowned upon—fear has made more heroes than courage ever has. People will not be gratuitously abused. The professional does not become so tensed up by fear and excitement that he strikes out blindly upon insignificant provocation. As one puts it: "When you're out on a heist you're out to get the dough and keep out of trouble. Halloween's the night for scaring people." However, courtesy on the job does not include softness or indecision. A holdup may easily become a shambles if the people under the gun think they detect nervousness or hesitation on the part of the man behind it.

The boys are particularly careful if women are present. Nobody can tell how women will react—at least, such is the considered opinion of the heist-men with whom I have cut up this situation. Looks tell nothing. One who has all the earmarks of a lady pipefitter may just roll up her eyes and swoon, while the little mouse who looks so scared a man itches to pat her on the head and say something soothing is really coolly examining the mob for warts or moles or counting the hairs on their knuckles as a means of future identification. Guns or no guns, some women will give out large pieces of their minds, and the less of this commodity they have to spare the more generous they appear to be with it. There are old ladies—one heist mob had a harrowing experience at the hands of a motherly soul who got into the middle of a loan-office heist before she realized what was going on. Then she was horrified and spoke severely to the mob. They should be ashamed, for she could tell that they were good boys at heart who had got off on the wrong foot. Since this was precisely what the boys secretly thought of themselves, they were moved; they ordered one of the clerks to destroy the record of the old lady's loan at once. This intended kindness only shocked her more, and she began to pray for them. The boys sweated copiously and might even have left if the manager, who had the combination of the safe, had not been due at that moment.

Let us not overlook the screamers, who are legend. The automatic yelper, who lets go involuntarily, from surprise, is not much of a problem. Her scream is little more than a species of exclamation. The aboriginal, or ritual, screamer is little more troublesome. Her scream is a notice to all males that a poor defenseless female is in distress, and what are they going to do about it? Still, heist-men find that this one need only be ordered sharply to shut up and she will subside. Then there is the smarty who puts the primitive, or come-and-get-poor-little-me, scream to more sophisticated uses. She lets out a shriek that can be heard over traffic for two blocks and then claps hand to mouth and gives with the big eyes as if to say: "Her didn't mean to, but her couldn't help it; gweat big you *fwightened* her so!" Actually a brontosaurus wouldn't scare her. She has been feeding that great-big-you line to voracious males so long and so successfully that she would spring it with confidence on the first lion she met walking down the street. What is on her mind at the moment are newspaper headlines: HEROINE OUTWITS DESPERATE BANDITS; PRETENDS HYSTERICS AND SUMMONS HELP, and she is just the cookie who will identify great big you with such dramatics that every man on the jury will yearn to see you hung and quartered, whether or not you happen to have been on that particular job. The consensus is that a good kick in the pants is what this number is asking for.

Worst of all screamers is the hysterical screamer. This one takes a kind of fit—clenches her eyes shut and lets loose at the top of her voice, and anything done to calm her is only likely to make her worse, if possible. Heist-men know of no formula for dealing with this kind of screamer, though isolated successes are spoken of. One says he stopped her cold by asking in the ordinary disgusted tone one might use to a bothersome child why she didn't quit that damn howling. . . .

Sometimes screamers can be a real hazard on the job, as when the mob must be inside for several minutes, but on the ordinary job they are more bothersome than dangerous and the mob ignores them. In some circumstances, as when there is a safe which must be opened, it may take the mob several minutes to get the score, but usually it is merely a matter of picking it up and carrying it out. The man on the door remains a few seconds to give the others time to get to the car, for despite his warning someone will probably throw up a window and begin yelling as soon as he leaves. As he comes out, the car already is inching ahead.

It is off the instant his foot touches the running board. Unless a policeman is where he cannot avoid responding to the cries coming from the window—policemen on a beat are seldom eager to careen along in chase of someone who may shoot back; they are not paid or very well trained for that kind of work and are likely to shoot their revolvers on double action, to the peril of spectators in upstairs windows—or unless some civilian in search of excitement gives chase, reckless driving is not indulged in. The car whisks around the first corner, takes several others in quick succession, then straightens out for a run of two or three blocks down a street having little traffic.

If no chase car shows up behind, the getaway car heads for wherever the front car—one legitimately owned by one of the mob—is parked. Meanwhile, the inside-men may have gotten into or out of coveralls and transferred the money into the receptacle provided: where there is no pedestrian traffic outside, the mob may not take time on the job to put the loot into bags but carry it out in a wastepaper basket or any other handy container. One of the mob takes the score and pistols in the front car to the place prearranged for the meet. The other inside-men may accompany him, or, if they want to play it safe all the way, go separately. The wheel-man continues in the getaway car to another part of the city, where, having wiped down the interior to remove fingerprints, he ditches it.

By the time he arrives at the meet, the money probably already has been pieced up into as many piles as there are members of the mob. "There she is," one of the others says. "Latch onto one."

37.

Gerald D. Robin*

PATTERNS OF DEPARTMENT STORE SHOPLIFTING

There are five large department stores in Philadelphia.[1] In one year's time, I had several interviews with each of the protection managers of these stores, who gave nonstandardized, highly descriptive accounts of shoplifting in general and in the store where each was working. These interviews revealed the manager's attitudes toward the prevention of shoplifting and toward the apprehension of suspected shoplifters, the procedure used in detecting and apprehending suspects, the store's treatment of those apprehended, and the factors influencing disposition of the case.

It is precisely because these interviews were informal and general in nature that I have relied upon them to provide a frame of reference for a more judicial analysis of the systematic and objective data later collected. Of special interest in these interviews was information relating to the procedural handling of suspects and to the definition of the term "shoplifting," without which valid comparisons between one store and another could not be made or, if made, could not be properly qualified.

HANDLING OF SHOPLIFTERS

All five department stores were highly uniform in their methods of apprehending and handling "suspected" shoplifters. They have thoroughly impressed on all their store detectives the possible consequences of apprehending an innocent customer. Each detective must absorb and put into practice the philosophy that it is better to let a hundred shoplifters escape than to apprehend one person falsely. He does not make an apprehension unless he is absolutely certain that the observed person is involved in shoplifting.[2] Once he is certain, the detective approaches the lifter as quietly and inconspicuously as possible, then places a firm hand on him and "suggests" that they go "upstairs." He makes every effort to avoid a scene. Most of the detecting is done by female detectives, with the male detectives nearby for "backing up" or lending a hand in the apprehension of persons who resist or become difficult to manage.

Once "upstairs" in the protection office, the suspect is searched and interrogated. Every store records a "case history" for each person involved in shoplifting. Although the amount and nature of information varied, almost all of the following items were recorded by all the stores: name and address of the person, occupation, marital status, age, sex, color, physical description, family situation, date of apprehension, retail value of the stolen merchandise in

---

*The author wishes to express his gratitude to Professor Marvin E. Wolfgang, of the University of Pennsylvania, for his guidance and assistance throughout this study. It is only the department stores' desire to remain anonymous that prevents the author from acknowledging the cooperation of the individual protection managers and other executive staff members.

Source: *Crime and Delinquency*, Vol. 9, No. 2 (April, 1963), pp. 163–72. Reprinted by permission of the author and the journal.

[1]Their estimated sales volume for the fiscal year 1959 ranged from $24,000,000 to $64,000,000. The minimum number of employees in each store ranged from approximately 1,600 to 3,800. The stores, which had from five to ten "selling" floors, occupied areas of from 850,000 to 1,600,000 square feet. Two of the stores each employed ten permanent full-time detectives; the number of detectives in the remaining three stores was not disclosed.

[2]Though almost nonexistent, cases of false apprehension have been recorded:

"In the office of one Fifth Avenue operative (detective) hangs a framed linen handkerchief, retailing for perhaps a dollar. Underneath it is written: 'This handkerchief is worth $2,000!' The woman arrested and accused of stealing it insisted she had bought it on a previous shopping trip. And in proof she pointed to a barely visible laundry mark. The store settled the claim of false arrest with a check for $2,000." Zeta Rothschild, "Why Shoplifters Get Caught," *Coronet*, August, 1950, p. 102.

the person's possession, and disposition of the case.

At some time during the interrogation the protection manager produces a confession form and asks the shoplifter to sign it. (Refusal to sign results automatically in prosecution.) The signed confession form constitutes an admission of guilt. Throughout the entire "interview" with the shoplifter, the protection manager attempts to determine the cause of his behavior and to make him recognize and admit the senselessness of his conduct. Sometimes the approach differs: the inherent wrongness of the act, the "disgrace to your family" theme, threats of legal punishment—any of these may be used. Regardless of approach, however, the message is always the same: "Crime doesn't pay!"

The last item of business is the disposition of the case. The following kinds of dispositions are used by the stores: juveniles are (1) released, (2) turned over to juvenile authorities for court action—i.e., arrest, or (3) turned over to juvenile authorities for remedial—i.e., unofficial—action. Adults are either released or prosecuted.

Although all five department stores were contacted, only three of them (hereafter referred to as Stores A, B, and C) made available any information concerning shoplifting in their stores in 1958. Stores A and B provided individual case information, which permitted an investigation of a number of relationships. Store C provided only "summary" information; e.g., the total number of males and females, whites and Negroes, juveniles and adults apprehended in 1958. Despite the differences in the amount and type of information supplied by Stores A, B, and C, the information received refers to every person apprehended for involvement in shoplifting in their stores in 1958. "Involvement in shoplifting" is defined as the involvement of any person not an employee of the store in the theft of merchandise during store hours.

In the present study, every person apprehended for shoplifting is considered guilty. This inference is justified because of (1) the extreme care exercised by the stores in apprehending persons and (2) the fact that each of the persons involved in the 1,584 shoplifting cases studied for Stores A, B, and C in 1958 signed a confession and none sued the store for false arrest.

DATA OBTAINED

A Popular Misconception

There appears to be a widespread belief—among storekeepers as well as laymen—that a suspected shoplifter cannot legally be apprehended until he has left the store or store premises with the stolen merchandise.[3] Only a few states have laws making such provisions, however.[4] For the most part, when a lifter carries an article 200 feet or more from the counter on which it was displayed, this is sufficient evidence to secure a conviction.[5] The states vary in specifying the conditions under which shoplifters may be apprehended. Only a few require that the apprehension take place *outside* the building within which the theft occurred. Illinois, for example, is quite explicit on this point, stating that it is not necessary to wait for the suspected shoplifter to leave the store with the merchandise before arresting him; it is only necessary to prove intent to steal.[6]

In several states, legislation concerning shoplifting permits, or at least does not prohibit, the apprehension of a suspect on the premises or within the store under reasonable conditions. West Virginia allows *any citizen* of its state to arrest a person discovered in the act of shoplifting.[7]

Nevertheless, although many merchants would like to have a suspect apprehended immediately, they have found through bitter experience that such action may provide the lifter with a number of defenses to the charge—he was looking

---

[3]Alex J. Arieff and Carol G. Bowie, "Some Psychiatric Aspects of Shoplifting," *Journal of Clinical Psychopathology*, January, 1947, p. 566.

[4]Ohio, for example, makes it unlawful to detain a suspected shoplifter until he has left the confines of the establishment but is still in the immediate vicinity. Ohio Revised Code Ann. tit. 29 § 2935.041 (1954).

[5]Stewart Sterling, "Stop That Shoplifter," *The Saturday Evening Post*, October 22, 1949, p. 66.

[6]Loren E. Edwards, *Shoplifting and Shrinkage Protection for Stores* (Springfield, Ill.: Charles C. Thomas, 1958), p. 16.

[7]Cumulative Supplement to the West Virginia Code of 1955 § 5990 (11).

for better light, for a salesperson to handle the transaction, and so on. The result is that a magistrate may discharge the defendant for lack of evidence.[8] In the absence of a statute clearly sanctioning apprehension within the store, the protection department will usually wait until the lifter has left the store before apprehending him—just to be on the safe side. This was the policy followed by all five department stores in Philadelphia prior to 1957, *but not because the law demanded it.* If the store detectives believed that a lifter who had stolen a great deal of merchandise would be "lost" on the outside, apprehension was made inside the store. In 1957, after Pennsylvania enacted a law providing for the apprehension and detention of suspected shoplifters by any merchant or merchant's employee under reasonable conditions, it became the rule to stop the lifter within the store—as evidenced by the fact that of all known shoplifters in Store B in 1958, 89 per cent were apprehended within the store.

Race, Sex, Age

Table 10.1 presents the race, sex, and age status of those in the shoplifting sample. A juvenile is defined as anyone under eighteen.

Of special significance is the finding that almost 40 per cent of persons apprehended in the three stores combined were male, contrary to many impressionistic statements that shoplifting is decidedly a female activity. In most of these statements females were believed to constitute 70 to 90 per cent of all shoplifters—with the edge given to the higher figure.[9]

Table 10.2 presents the age distribution of the shoplifting group for Stores A and B and the rates of apprehension based upon estimates of the population of Philadelphia for 1958.

In Store A, the shoplifters ranged from 6 to 87 years of age; in Store B they ranged from 13 to 78 years old. Those aged 14 through 17 made up 33 per cent of all shoplifters apprehended in Store A and 60 per cent of all shoplifters apprehended by Store B. In Store B the modal age was 15 years (180 cases), followed by age 16 (175 cases). Thus, 15- and 16-year-olds constituted 43 per cent of all shoplifters apprehended by Store B in 1958. In Store A the modal age was 16 years, followed by 15. This age distribution of shoplifters strongly indicates that this form of criminal activity is engaged in mainly by juveniles.

Size of Theft

The distribution for size of the theft, which refers to the total retail value of the merchandise recovered from the lifter, is presented in Table 10.3.

For Store A, juvenile thefts ranged in size from 60¢ to $41.95; adult thefts ranged from 90¢ to $1,302.98. Even if we omit the unusual $1,302.98 theft, the upper adult range would be $579.80. The median size of juvenile thefts was $5.98 compared with a median of $14 for adult shoplifters. Only one-seventh of the $6,152 worth of merchandise recovered from all shoplifters had been taken by juveniles.

For Store B, juvenile thefts ranged in size from $1 to $122, compared with an adult theft range of $1.98 to $268.46. The median for juvenile shoplifters was $8.97, compared with a median of $14.84 for adult shoplifters. Of the $12,172 worth of merchandise recovered from all shoplifters, one-third had been taken by juveniles—despite the fact that there were more juvenile than adult shoplifters. The data make it very clear, then, that juvenile shoplifting tends to be much more petty than adult shoplifting.

Disposition

For Stores A, B, and C combined, 14 per cent of the 1,579 cases *in which disposition* was known were prosecuted. This total figure, however, includes the juvenile shoplifters, whom Store B automatically turned over to the Juvenile Aid Division for disposition. If the Juvenile Aid Division recommended prosecution, the store became the complainant and invariably concurred with the decision of the juvenile authorities. Hence, if we wish to know the per-

[8]Ralph L. Woods, "Slick Fingers," *The Forum and Century*, July to December, 1939, p. 276.

[9]George C. Henderson, "Caught with the Goods," *The Pacific Monthly*, March, 1927, p. 40; Alvin F. Harlow, "When Lovely Woman Stoops to Steal," *Collier's*, August 22, 1925, p. 10; Clayton J. Ettinger, *The Problem of Crime* (New York: Ray Long and Richard R. Smith, Inc., 1932), p. 189; Charles Mercier, *Crime and Criminals* (New York: Henry Holt, 1919), p. 244.

TABLE 10.1*

RACE, SEX, AND AGE OF ALL PERSONS APPREHENDED FOR INVOLVEMENT IN SHOPLIFTING IN STORES A, B, AND C IN 1958

Store	*Race*					*Sex*					*Age Status*				
	White		*Negro*		*Total*	*Male*		*Female*		*Total*	*Juvenile*		*Adult*		*Total*
	No.	*%*	*No.*	*%*		*No.*	*%*	*No.*	*%*		*No.*	*%*	*No.*	*%*	
A	136	48.6	144	51.4	280	130	46.6	149	53.4	279	129	45.7	153	54.3	282
B	472	56.6	362	43.4	834	218	26.1	616	73.9	834	511	61.3	323	38.7	834
C	210	45.2	255	54.8	465	272	58.5	193	41.5	465	279	60.0	186	40.0	465
Total	818	51.8	761	48.2	1,579	620	39.3	958	60.7	1,578	919	58.1	662	41.9	1,581

*Although the total sample size for the three stores combined was 1,584 cases, bits of information were sometimes inadvertently omitted in the stores' records. For example, in Store A, 285 persons were apprehended for shoplifting but the race of 5 of them was not noted. Consequently the totals in this and the following tables may vary slightly from the total sample for each store.

TABLE 10.2

AGE DISTRIBUTION OF ALL PERSONS INVOLVED IN SHOPLIFTING IN STORES A AND B IN 1958 AND RATE OF APPREHENSION PER 100,000 ESTIMATED PHILADELPHIA POPULATION

Age	*Store A* No.	*Store A* %	*Store B* No.	*Store B* %	*A and B Combined* No.	*A and B Combined* %	*Rate per 100,000 Estimated Pop.**
5–9	7	2.49	—	—	7	.63	3.7
10–19	135	48.04	561	67.27	696	62.42	214.2
20–29	41	14.59	103	12.35	144	12.91	46.7
30–39	39	13.88	63	7.55	102	9.15	30.9
40–49	25	8.90	39	4.68	64	5.74	20.5
50–59	21	7.47	40	4.79	61	5.47	25.8
60–69	7	2.49	25	3.00	32	2.87	17.9
70 or over	6	2.14	3	.36	9	.81	7.4
Total	281	100.00	834	100.00	1,115	100.00	56.0

*Rates calculated from Philadelphia Public Health Department, Division of Statistics and Research, *Annual Statistical Report: 1958,* p. 6.

TABLE 10.3

SIZE OF THEFT DISTRIBUTION OF ALL PERSONS APPREHENDED FOR SHOPLIFTING IN STORES A AND B IN 1958

Size of Theft	*Store A* No.	*Store A* %	*Store B* No.	*Store B* %	*A and B Combined* No.	*A and B Combined* %
Below $5	60	28.04	109	16.39	169	19.23
$ 5– 9.99	48	22.43	185	27.82	233	26.51
$10–14.99	31	14.49	151	22.71	182	20.71
$15–19.99	16	7.48	77	11.58	93	10.58
$20–24.99	7	3.27	35	5.26	42	4.78
$25–29.99	11	5.14	25	3.76	36	4.09
$30–34.99	9	4.20	16	2.41	25	2.84
$35–39.99	7	3.27	15	2.26	22	2.50
$40–44.99	6	2.80	10	1.50	16	1.82
$45–49.99	4	1.87	7	1.05	11	1.25
$50 or over	15	7.01	35	5.26	50	5.69
Total	214*	100.00	665†	100.00	879	100.00

*Of the 285 persons involved in shoplifting in Store A, 265 could be identified according to their role in the crime: 30 were aiders and abettors and the remaining 235 were shoplifters proper. However, of the shoplifters proper, the exact retail value of their thefts was known in only *214* cases. The reason for this is that store records in group apprehensions would occasionally indicate only the *total* value of goods for both persons combined.

†Of the 834 persons involved in shoplifting in Store B, 169 were aiders and abettors and the remaining 665 were shoplifters proper.

centage of cases in which the *managers* of all the stores made the decision to prosecute or release, we should exclude the juvenile shoplifters in Store B from our figures. Such exclusion leaves 1,068 shoplifters whose disposition was known; of these, 19 per cent were prosecuted. Further analysis reveals that only 5.5 per cent of the juveniles involved in shoplifting were prosecuted, compared with 25.8 per cent of the adults.

These figures suggest that (1) the store managers (and the juvenile authorities[10]) were

[10]The Juvenile Aid Division, to whom Store B's 511 juvenile offenders were routinely turned over

extremely reluctant to "prosecute" juveniles but (2) were more willing to prosecute adults (one out of every four adults involved in shoplifting was prosecuted). This prosecution rate for adults is much higher than most estimates offered in the literature.

DISPOSITION AND SIZE OF THEFT

Because of the unwillingness of the store and juvenile authorities to prosecute juveniles, the restricted range of juvenile thefts, and the small number of juveniles actually prosecuted for shoplifting in Stores A and B, examination of the relationship between size of theft and disposition was confined to adult shoplifters.

Although all five protection managers stated that the single, overwhelmingly important determinant of the disposition of the case was the size of the theft, I decided to investigate the relationship between the two. A word, however, about certain procedures used in Store A and Store B is in order. Both stores checked with the Philadelphia Police Department to see whether the adult shoplifter had a criminal record. If he did, the store automatically prosecuted him regardless of the size of the theft. Since I did not know which adult shoplifters had a criminal history, any strong positive relationship between the size of theft and the prosecution may have resulted from the past records of these shoplifters and not from the size of their thefts. On the other hand, even if a substantial number of those prosecuted did have criminal records, they might have engaged in more costly thefts than the others. With these qualifications, I found that of the 299 persons who "lifted" goods worth less than $25 from Stores A and B combined, 26 (8.7 per cent) were prosecuted; of the 111 who "lifted" merchandise worth $25 or more, 78 (70.3 per cent) were prosecuted. Though the size of theft as a strong factor influencing disposition cannot be minimized, the reader should note that of those whose thefts amounted to $25 or more, there was a statistically significant difference (at the .05 level of confidence) between the prosecution of whites and Negroes; 62.1 per cent of the white shoplifters, compared with 79.2 per cent of the Negro shoplifters, were prosecuted.

The general relationship between size of theft and disposition is shown in Table 10.4.

TABLE 10.4

PROSECUTION OF ADULT SHOPLIFTERS BY SIZE OF THEFT

Size of Theft	*No. of Shoplifters*	*No. of Prosecutions*	*% of Prosecutions*
Below $20	280	17	6.07
$20–$29.99 ...	47	14	29.79
$30–$39.99 ...	30	22	73.33
$40–$59.99 ...	28	22	78.57
$60+	31	29	93.55
Total	416	104	25.00

Therefore, it seems that, other things being equal, if an adult pilfered merchandise whose total retail value was $30 or more, he would probably be prosecuted, his chances of prosecution increasing as the size of the theft increased.

APPREHENSION OF GROUPS

The social character of shoplifting by juveniles is sharply underscored by the fact that 75.3 per cent of them, compared with 23.3 per cent of the adults, were apprehended in groups. In other words, more than 7 out of every 10 juveniles were apprehended in groups, compared with 2 out of every 10 adults. The juvenile shoplifter, then, more often works as part of a team, whereas the adult is a solitary operator.

With respect to the size of the groups apprehended in Stores A and B combined, 75 per cent of the group apprehensions consisted of two persons, 21.5 per cent of three persons, and 3.5 per cent of four persons.

AIDERS AND ABETTORS

In Stores A and B persons involved in shoplifting were differentiated into two subgroups: (1) shoplifters—those who actually stole the merchandise; (2) aiders and abettors—those who

for disposition, recommended prosecution in 25, or 5 per cent, of the cases.

in some manner assisted in the shoplifting but did not directly steal the goods. Aiders and abettors act as "lookouts," attract attention to themselves while their companions escape with the goods, or receive the stolen merchandise from the lifter.

Aside from its group nature, juvenile shoplifting is also marked by the large number of aiders and abettors used—27.7 per cent of the 628 juveniles (compared with only 5.3 per cent of the 471 adult offenders) were aiders and abettors.

MONTHLY APPREHENSIONS

Inspection of Table 10.5 reveals that as Christmas approaches and people begin their Christmas shopping, the shoplifters begin their Christmas shoplifting. However, not all of the increase in apprehensions should be attributed to an actual increase in shoplifting during October, November, and December. As Christmas draws near, Stores A and B (as well as the other stores contacted) hire temporary store detectives who concentrate entirely upon detecting shoplifters. The mere fact that the store expects more shoplifting as Christmas approaches helps it find more, even though no more may really exist. This fact does not mean that shoplifting does *not* increase at this season, but rather that the true difference is probably not so large as the statistics suggest. Another extraneous factor likely to increase superficially the volume of Christmas shoplifting is that the stores remain open longer, thereby increasing the length of time during which shoplifting—and apprehension of shoplifters—is possible.

TABLE 10.5

MONTHLY APPREHENSIONS OF SHOPLIFTERS

Month	*Store A No.*	*Store B No.*	*A and B Combined No.*	*A and B Combined %*
Jan.	14	23	37	3.31
Feb.	12	28	40	3.57
March	28	26	54	4.83
April	23	54	77	6.88
May	25	63	88	7.86
June	14	63	77	6.88
July	16	50	66	5.90
Aug.	15	47	62	5.54
Sept.	15	54	69	6.17
Oct.	36	81	117	10.45
Nov.	33	112	145	12.96
Dec.	54	233	287	25.65
Total	285	834	1,119	100.00

Store managers single out the size of the detection staff as being of the utmost importance in accounting for increased apprehension during Christmas, for regardless of the number of hours the store remains open, shoplifters cannot be apprehended unless someone is there to apprehend them. For all practical purposes, the regular sales personnel play no significant part in apprehending shoplifters, for the following reasons: (1) they are not interested in apprehending shoplifters; (2) they are not qualified to apprehend shoplifters; (3) they are generally too busy, either working or chatting among themselves, to keep a suspicious person under surveillance; (4) their movements are restricted to their departmental area; and (5) they are instructed by the store not to apprehend a suspected shoplifter but to notify the protection department immediately. The entire burden of apprehending shoplifters falls to the protection personnel and consequently varies with changes in the size and policy of this group.

DISCUSSION

The picture of shoplifting presented above is one which the stores recorded themselves. Therefore, for any fact or pattern of shoplifting indicated by the statistics, a number of valid criticisms may be made. Shoplifting appears to be essentially a juvenile activity. But the store detective may pay special attention to all juveniles he notices, perhaps because he believes them less likely to be customers. Moreover, given equal observation of both juveniles and adults, a juvenile may be apprehended more readily than an adult for a number of reasons: The detective is able to handle the former more easily and is probably less concerned with the consequences of making a mistake. If an innocent juvenile were apprehended, the detective might claim that the juvenile was "disorderly" —an explanation difficult to substantiate in adult apprehensions. The detective may tend to apprehend juveniles immediately upon observing the theft of any merchandise, whereas he may wait for an adult to steal a second and a third article in order to be sure that he has a "strong case." If this is true it could explain much of the difference in the size of juvenile and adult thefts. Similarly, the preponderance of female shoplifters, especially among adults, may be more apparent than real. Since most of the detecting is done by females, it may be postulated that the observation and trailing of female suspects is much easier and less noticeable than is the surveillance of adult male suspects. In his modus operandi, the male lifter might utilize some areas in the store where the presence of a female detective (or any female) would be easily visible or downright embarrassing. Many female detectives may be afraid to apprehend certain men who are known to be shoplifters. Finally, we can only speculate what effect a totally white detective force has upon the apprehension of members of various racial groups.

Deciding which merchandise requires most protection is highly important. A limited staff makes it impossible to insure constant supervision of all the necessary goods. Protection may be heavily concentrated on women's articles —probably resulting in the apprehension of an all-female group—while protection of men's merchandise is sacrificed, thereby leading to an underestimation of male involvement.

The number of articles taken by the lifter may also serve to increase artificially one group's participation over another in shoplifting. Cameron reports that the probability of a shoplifter's being apprehended is related to the number of items he takes.[11] The store detectives interviewed by Cameron stated that if they are suspicious of a woman, they can carefully follow her, on the theory that she will probably steal additional items. In the case of a man, however, who presumably is more likely to be satisfied with one article, the suspicions of the detective could not be confirmed; hence, they would have no choice except to permit the male suspect to leave the store. If this condition prevailed in other department stores, it would tend to minimize the activity of male shoplifters in the stores' apprehension figures. Even the differences in the number of shoplifting cases apprehended in Stores A, B, and C must be partially explained by the differences in the size of the protection department, in the emphasis the protection manager places upon apprehension or prevention, and in the priority assigned to the shoplifting problem by the manager (control of merchandise is just one of the many functions which fall to the protection department). The store detectives' selective perception and the differences in policy and procedure among stores hinder the emergence of accurate, complete, and representative patterns of shoplifting.

---

[11]Mary B. Cameron, "Department Store Shoplifting" (unpublished Ph.D. dissertation, Department of Sociology, Indiana University), p. 74.

CHAPTER XI

Juvenile and Youthful Offenders

PERHAPS THE MOST FRUSTRATING PROBLEM related to the rate of criminality in the United States today is the number of young people involved in the commission of serious offenses. In its 1967 "Crime Capsule," the FBI reported that "arrests of juveniles for serious crimes increased 59 percent from 1960 to 1967, while the number of persons in the young age group (10–17), increased 22 percent." This same source goes on to report that 70 percent of the young offenders under 20 years of age released in 1963, repeated in crime. On the basis of this data one may conclude that we have failed many youngsters at two levels: (1) by providing too few legitimate alternatives through which he may channel his behavior and thus be turned away and discouraged from entering a life of crime, and (2) by failing to develop the kind of treatment facilities capable of resocializing the youngster and returning him as a productive member of society fully cognizant of his obligations and responsibilities.

The juvenile in the United States is encompassed by a vast array of legal codes. He must abide not only by all criminal statutes and ordinances governing adult behavior, but also to a second set of clauses applied to him because of his special status as a juvenile. The range of codes applicable to juveniles is too wide to review in this brief introduction, as he is subject to the laws of the 50 states, the federal government, District of Columbia, and our several possessions and territories. However, for the purpose of example I will list just a few. A young person may be considered delinquent if he:

1. Is habitually truant.
2. Is incorrigible.
3. Is growing up in idleness or crime.
4. Conducts himself immorally or indecently.
5. Habitually uses vile, obscene or vulgar language in a public place.
6. Habitually wanders about railroad yards or tracks.
7. Smokes cigarettes or uses tobacco in any form.
8. Makes indecent proposals.
9. Attempts to marry without consent in violation of the law.
10. Is given to sexual irregularities.

Although the maximum age of juvenile court jurisdiction may vary from state to state (and be different for boys and girls within the same state), I believe it is safe to use the age of 18 as the dividing line between juvenile and adult misconduct. In addition to this distinction, many jurisdictions have inserted the special age category of "youthful offender" between the juvenile delinquent and the adult criminal. The "youthful offender" is typically an individual between the ages of 18 and 23 years who has been convicted of a felony. He is customarily placed in a penal institution with other inmates in this age group and thus is segregated from the hard core adult criminal population. In the study of criminology we are especially concerned with the background characteristics of the "youthful offender" because of his disproportionate contribution to the crime problem in the United States. As can readily be noted in Table 11.1, young people under 25 years of age represented 75.3 percent of the total number of persons arrested for serious crimes in the United States in 1967. To professional criminologists and layman alike this rate is both alarming and frightful.

The readings selected for this chapter are intended to give the reader a broad view of the problems posed by juvenile and youthful offenders in the United States. In the first selection, The President's Commission on Law Enforcement and Administration of Justice considers not only the extent and volume of delinquency, but also the relationships existing between the juvenile and his family, the community, the school, and the job market. In the second article, Dr. William C. Kvaraceus explores the what's and why's of delinquency along with the possible roles that our social institutions might assume in combating the problem. Next, Walter B. Miller examines the characteristics of the lower class culture in an attempt to isolate the variables that may produce gang delinquency. Finally, Joseph W. Scott and Edmund W. Vaz direct our attention away from the slum neighborhood to explore the problems of delinquency among the rather well-to-do middle classes.

TABLE 11.1

Total Arrests of Persons Under 15, Under 18, Under 21, and Under 25 Years of Age, 1967
(4,566 agencies; 1967 estimated population 145,927,000)

Offense charged	Number of persons arrested					Percentage			
	Grand total all ages	*Under 15*	*Under 18*	*Under 21*	*Under 25*	*Under 15*	*Under 18*	*Under 21*	*Under 25*
TOTAL	5,518,420	527,141	1,339,578	2,015,338	2,613,887	9.6	24.3	36.5	47.4
Criminal homicide:									
(*a*) Murder and nonnegligent manslaughter	9,145	137	830	1,948	3,415	1.5	9.1	21.3	37.3
(*b*) Manslaughter by negligence	3,022	30	246	761	1,295	1.0	8.1	25.2	42.9
Forcible rape	12,659	475	2,515	5,418	8,133	3.8	19.9	42.8	64.2
Robbery	59,789	6,885	18,889	32,305	43,776	11.5	31.6	54.0	73.2
Aggravated assault	107,192	6,559	18,359	31,654	47,520	6.1	17.1	29.5	44.3
Burglary—breaking or entering	239,461	62,510	128,169	169,265	196,538	26.1	53.5	70.7	82.1
Larceny-theft	447,299	134,216	246,057	306,615	344,807	30.0	55.0	68.5	77.1
Auto theft	118,233	19,902	73,080	94,297	104,860	16.8	61.8	79.8	88.7
Subtotal for above offenses	996,800	230,714	488,145	642,263	750,344	23.1	49.0	64.4	75.3
Other assaults	229,928	14,837	37,849	65,822	101,073	6.5	16.5	28.6	44.0
Arson	8,058	3,768	5,236	5,953	6,495	46.8	65.0	73.9	80.6
Forgery and counterfeiting	33,462	806	3,918	9,783	16,572	2.4	11.7	29.2	49.5
Fraud	58,192	643	2,444	8,012	18,534	1.1	4.2	13.8	31.8
Embezzlement	6,073	53	256	810	1,863	.9	4.2	13.3	30.7
Stolen property; buying, receiving, possessing	28,620	3,542	9,901	15,247	19,502	12.4	34.6	53.3	68.1
Vandalism	109,299	54,782	83,571	93,053	98,357	50.1	76.5	85.1	90.0
Weapons: carrying, possessing, etc.	71,684	3,738	12,967	23,984	36,111	5.2	18.1	33.5	50.4
Prostitution and commercialized vice	39,744	97	848	6,729	21,017	.2	2.1	16.9	52.9
Sex offenses (except forcible rape and prostitution)	53,541	4,959	13,075	19,924	27,391	9.3	24.4	37.2	51.2
Narcotic drug laws	101,079	2,812	21,405	49,071	69,565	2.8	21.2	48.5	68.8
Gambling	84,772	343	2,143	5,735	12,865	.4	2.5	6.8	15.2
Offenses against family and children	56,137	264	860	6,435	15,829	.5	1.5	11.5	28.2
Driving under the influence	281,152	57	2,846	17,807	48,975	*	1.0	6.3	17.4
Liquor laws	209,741	4,924	63,587	154,897	169,228	2.3	30.3	73.9	80.7
Drunkenness	1,517,809	3,509	34,621	109,655	225,654	.2	2.3	7.2	14.9
Disorderly conduct	550,469	38,078	110,004	201,169	282,074	6.9	20.0	36.5	51.2
Vagrancy	106,747	1,646	9,777	28,155	41,455	1.5	9.2	26.4	38.8
All other offenses (except traffic)	654,915	76,082	189,921	282,299	364,765	11.6	29.0	43.1	55.7
Suspicion	95,794	5,674	21,800	44,131	61,814	5.9	22.8	46.1	64.5
Curfew and loitering law violations	94,872	23,794	94,872	94,872	94,872	25.1	100.0	100.0	100.0
Runaways	129,532	52,019	129,532	129,532	129,532	40.2	100.0	100.0	100.0

*Less than one-tenth of one percent.
Source: Federal Bureau of Investigation, U.S. Department of Justice, *1967 Uniform Crime Reports* (Washington, D.C.: U.S. Government Printing Office, 1968), Table 28, p. 123.

38.

President's Commission on Law Enforcement and Administration of Justice

JUVENILE DELINQUENCY AND YOUTH CRIME

America's best hope for reducing crime is to reduce juvenile delinquency and youth crime. In 1965 a majority of all arrests for major crimes against property were of people under 21, as were a substantial minority of arrests for major crimes against the person. The recidivism rates for young offenders are higher than those for any other age group. A substantial change in any of these figures would make a substantial change in the total crime figures for the Nation.

One of the difficulties of discussing the misconduct, criminal or not, of young people is that "juvenile" and "youth" are not precise definitions of categories of people. People are legally juveniles in most States until they pass their 18th birthdays, but in some States they stop being juveniles after they turn 16 or remain juveniles until they turn 21. The problems and behavior patterns of juveniles and youths often are similar.

FACTS ABOUT DELINQUENCY

To prevent and control delinquency, we must first know something about the nature of delinquency and the dimensions of the problem. We need to know how serious delinquency is. How much of it is there? How many of our youth are involved? What sorts of illegal acts do they commit? What have the trends in delinquency been in the past, and what can we expect in the future? We also need knowledge about the people who become delinquent—information such as where most delinquents live and under what economic conditions.

But we are severely limited in what we can learn today. The only juvenile statistics regularly gathered over the years on a national scale are the FBI's *Uniform Crime Reports,* based on arrest statistics, and the juvenile court statistics of the Children's Bureau of the U.S. Department of Health, Education, and Welfare, based on referrals of juveniles from a variety of agencies to a sample of juvenile courts. These reports can tell us nothing about the vast number of unsolved offenses, or about the many cases in which delinquents are dealt with informally instead of being arrested or referred to court. Supplementing this official picture of delinquency are self-report studies, which rely on asking selected individuals about their delinquent acts. While efforts are made to insure the validity of the results by such means as guaranteeing anonymity, and verifying results with official records and unofficial checks, such studies have been conducted only on a local and sporadic basis, and they vary greatly in quality.

Clearly, there is urgent need for more and better information. Nonetheless, enough is available to give some of the rough outlines of juvenile delinquency in the United States.

Seriousness of the Delinquency Problem

Volume. Enormous numbers of young people appear to be involved in delinquent acts. Indeed, self-report studies reveal that perhaps 90 percent of all young people have committed at least one act for which they could have been brought to juvenile court. Many of these offenses are relatively trivial—fighting, truancy, running away from home. Statutes often define juvenile delinquency so broadly as to make virtually all youngsters delinquent.

Even though most of these offenders are never arrested or referred to juvenile court, alarming numbers of young people are. Rough estimates by the Children's Bureau, supported by independent studies, indicate that one in every nine

Source: A Report of the President's Commission on Law Enforcement and Administration of Justice, *The Challenge of Crime in a Free Society* (Washington, D.C., U.S. Government Printing Office, February, 1967), pp. 55–89. Tables omitted.

youths—one in every six male youths—will be referred to juvenile court in connection with a delinquent act (excluding traffic offenses) before his 18th birthday.

Youth is apparently responsible for a substantial and disproportionate part of the national crime problem. Arrest statistics can give us only a rough picture—probably somewhat exaggerated since it is likely that juveniles are more easily apprehended than adults. In addition, it may be that juveniles act in groups more often than adults when committing crimes, thus producing numbers of juvenile arrests out of proportion with numbers of crimes committed. But even with these qualifications, the figures are striking. . . .

The picture looks even worse if attention is directed to certain relatively serious property crimes—burglary, larceny, and motor vehicle theft. The 11- to 17-year-old age group, representing 13.2 percent of the population, was responsible for half of the arrests for these offenses in 1965. The arrest rates for these offenses are much higher for the 15- to 17-year-olds than for any other age group in the population. But not all of the acts included within these categories are equally serious. Larceny includes thefts of less than $50, and most motor vehicle thefts are for the purpose of securing temporary transportation and do not involve permanent loss of the vehicle. Moreover, although juveniles account for more than their share of arrests for many serious crimes, these arrests are a small part of all juvenile arrests. Juveniles are most frequently arrested or referred to court for petty larceny, fighting, disorderly conduct, liquor-related offenses, and conduct not in violation of the criminal law such as curfew violation, truancy, incorrigibility, or running away from home.

It is an older age group—beyond the jurisdiction of almost all juvenile courts—that has the highest arrest rate for crimes of violence. The 18- to 24-year-old group, which represents only 10.2 percent of the population, accounts for 26.4 percent of the arrests for willful homicide, 44.6 percent of the arrests for rape, 39.5 percent of the arrests for robbery, and 26.5 percent of the arrests for aggravated assault.

Trends. In recent years the number of delinquency arrests has increased sharply in the United States, as it has in several Western European countries studied by the Commission. Between 1960 and 1965, arrests of persons under 18 years of age jumped 52 percent for willful homicide, rape, robbery, aggravated assault, larceny, burglary and motor vehicle theft. During the same period, arrests of persons 18 and over for these offenses rose only 20 percent. This is explained in large part by the disproportionate increase in the population under 18 and, in particular, the crime-prone part of that population—the 11- to 17-year-old age group.

Official figures may give a somewhat misleading picture of crime trends. Over the years there has been a tendency toward more formal records and actions, particularly in the treatment of juveniles. In addition, police efficiency may well have increased. But, considering other factors together with the official statistics, the Commission is of the opinion that juvenile delinquency has increased significantly in recent years.

The juvenile population has been rising, and at a faster rate than the adult population. And an increasing proportion of our society is living in the cities where delinquency rates have always been highest. These trends and the increase in the total volume of crime that they appear to foretell are testimony enough that programs for the prevention and control of delinquency deserve our full attention.

Who the Delinquents Are

Almost all youths commit acts for which they could be arrested and taken to court. But it is a much smaller group that ends up being defined officially as delinquent.

Official delinquents are predominantly male. In 1965 boys under 18 were arrested five times as often as girls. Four times as many boys as girls were referred to juvenile court.

Boys and girls commit quite different kinds of offenses. Children's Bureau statistics based on large-city court reports reveal that more than half of the girls referred to juvenile court in 1965 were referred for conduct that would not be criminal if committed by adults; only one-fifth of the boys were referred for such conduct. Boys were referred to court primarily for larceny, burglary, and motor vehicle theft, in order of frequency; girls for running away, ungovernable behavior, larceny, and sex offenses.

Delinquents are concentrated disproportionately in the cities, and particularly in the larger cities. Arrest rates are next highest in the suburbs, and lowest in rural areas.

Delinquency rates are high among children from broken homes. They are similarly high among children who have numerous siblings.

Delinquents tend to do badly in school. Their grades are below average. Large numbers have dropped one or more classes behind their classmates or dropped out of school entirely.

Delinquents tend to come from backgrounds of social and economic deprivation. Their families tend to have lower than average incomes and social status. But perhaps more important than the individual family's situation is the area in which a youth lives. One study has shown that a lower class youth has little chance of being classified as delinquent if he lives in an upper class neighborhood. Numerous studies have revealed the relationship between certain deprived areas—particularly the slums of large cities—and delinquency. . . .

Thus Negroes, who live in disproportionate numbers in slum neighborhoods, account for a disproportionate number of arrests. Numerous studies indicate that what matters is where in the city one is growing up, not religion or nationality or race. The studies by Shaw and McKay followed a number of different national groups—Germans, Irish, Poles, Italians—as they moved from the grim center of the city out to better neighborhoods. They found that for all groups the delinquency rates were highest in the center and lowest on the outskirts of the city.

There is no reason to expect a different story for Negroes. Indeed, McKay found Negro delinquency rates decreasing from the center of the city outward, just as they did for earlier migrant groups. And when delinquency rates of whites and Negroes are compared in areas of similar economic status, the differences between them are markedly reduced. But for Negroes, movement out of the inner city and absorption into America's middle class have been much slower and more difficult than for any other ethnic or racial group. Their attempts to move spatially, socially, economically have met much stiffer resistance. Rigid barriers of residential segregation have prevented them from moving to better neighborhoods as their desire and capacity to do so have developed, leading to great population density and to stifling overcrowding of housing, schools, recreation areas. Restricted access to jobs and limited upward mobility in those jobs that are available have slowed economic advance.

It is likely that the official picture exaggerates the role played by social and economic conditions, since slum offenders are more likely than suburban offenders to be arrested and referred to juvenile court. In fact, recent self-report studies reveal suburban and middle-class delinquency to be a more significant problem than was once assumed. But there is still no reason to doubt that delinquency, and especially the most serious delinquency, is committed disproportionately by slum and lower-class youth. . . .

* * *

One way of looking at delinquency is in the context of the "teenage culture" that has developed in America since the end of the Second World War. In America in the 1960's, to perhaps a greater extent than in any other place or time, adolescents live in a distinct society of their own. It is not an easy society to understand, to describe, or, for that matter, to live in. In some ways it is an intensely materialistic society; its members, perhaps in unconscious imitation of their elders, are preoccupied with physical objects like clothes and cars, and indeed have been encouraged in this preoccupation by manufacturers and merchants who have discovered how profitable the adolescent market is. In some ways it is an intensely sensual society; its members are preoccupied with the sensations they can obtain from surfing or drag racing or music or drugs. In some ways it is an intensely moralistic society; its members are preoccupied with independence and honesty and equality and courage. On the whole it is a rebellious, oppositional society, dedicated to the proposition that the grownup world is a sham. At the same time it is a conforming society; being inexperienced, unsure of themselves, and, in fact, relatively powerless as individuals, adolescents to a far greater extent than their elders conform to common standards of dress and hair style and speech, and act jointly, in groups—or gangs.

Adolescents everywhere, from every walk of life, are often dangerous to themselves and to others. It may be a short step from distrusting authority to taking the law into one's own hands, from self-absorption to contempt for the rights of others, from group loyalty to gang warfare, from getting "kicks" to rampaging through the streets, from coveting material goods to stealing them, from feelings of rebellion to acts of destruction. Every suburban parent knows of parties that have turned into near riots. Every doctor knows how many young unmarried girls become pregnant. Every insurance company executive knows how dangerously adolescent boys drive. Every high school principal is concerned about the use of marihuana or pep pills by his students. Every newspaper reader knows how often bands of young people of all kinds commit destructive and dangerous acts.

Other than that it appears to be increasing, little is known as yet about delinquency among the well to do. Its causes, to the extent that they are understood, are of a kind that is difficult to eliminate by any program of social action that has yet been devised. The weakening of the family as an agent of social control; the prolongation of education with its side effect of prolonging childhood; the increasing impersonality of a technological, corporate, bureaucratic society; the radical changes in moral standards in regard to such matters as sex and drug use—all these are phenomena with which the Nation has not yet found the means to cope.

Delinquency in the slums, which, as has been shown, is a disproportionately high percentage of all delinquency and includes a disproportionately high number of dangerous acts, is associated with these phenomena, of course. Both figures and observation clearly demonstrate, however, that it is also associated with undesirable conditions of life. Among the many compelling reasons for changing the circumstances of inner-city existence, one of the most compelling is that it will prevent crime.

The inner city has always been hard on whoever is living in it. The studies by Shaw and McKay show dramatically that it is in the inner city that delinquency rates have traditionally been highest, decade after decade and regardless of what population group is there. And besides delinquency rates, the other familiar statistical signs of trouble—truancy, high unemployment, mental disorder, infant mortality, tuberculosis, families on relief—are also highest in the inner city. Life is grim and uncompromising in the center of the city, better on the outskirts. As the members of each population group gain greater access to the city's legitimate social and economic opportunities and the group moves outward, rents are higher, more families own their own homes, the rates of disease and dependency—and delinquency—drop.

But in the inner city, now occupied by a different group, the rate of delinquency remains roughly the same, regardless of race, religion, or nationality. That strikingly persistent correlation, coupled with the fact, pointed out above, that the inner city is for its present Negro inhabitants more of a trap than a way station, emphasizes the urgency of intensifying efforts to improve in the inner city the institutions that elsewhere serve to prevent delinquency. . . .

The Family

Too frequently the combination of deprivation and hazard that characterizes the slums—a test by fire for the most cohesive of families—must be confronted in the slum by a family that lacks even minimal material and intangible supports.

The family is the first and most basic institution in our society for developing the child's potential, in all its many aspects: Emotional, intellectual, moral, and spiritual, as well as physical and social. Other influences do not even enter the child's life until after the first few highly formative years. It is within the family that the child must learn to curb his desires and to accept rules that define the time, place, and circumstances under which highly personal needs may be satisfied in socially acceptable ways. This early training—management of emotion, confrontation with rules and authority, development of responsiveness to others—has been repeatedly related to the presence or absence of delinquency in later years. But cause-and-effect relationships have proved bewilderingly complex, and require much more clinical experience and systematic research.

Research findings, however, while far from conclusive, point to the principle that whatever in the organization of the family, the contacts among its members, or its relationships to the surrounding community diminishes the moral and emotional authority of the family in the life of the young person also increases the likelihood of delinquency.

The following discussion draws upon the extensive—though not by any means exhaustive—work already done by numerous researchers.

Family Membership. If one parent (especially the father of a son) is absent, if there are many children, if a child is in the middle in age among several siblings—such family arrangements tend to reduce parental control and authority over children and consequently increase vulnerability to influences toward delinquent behavior.

Besides the basic membership of the family, relations among the members also appear significant in determining the strength of familial influence. It has been shown that deep unhappiness between parents increases the likelihood that the children will commit delinquent acts and that children reared in happy homes are less delinquent than those from unhappy homes. Apparently marital discord tends to expose the child to delinquent influences, perhaps by outright rejection or neglect or by undercutting his respect for his parents and so the force of their authority.

Discipline. The discipline associated with the loose organization and female focus that characterize many inner-city families has also been related by social scientists to the development of what has been termed "premature autonomy" and to consequent resentment of authority figures such as policemen and teachers. Often child-rearing practices are either very permissive or very stern—the latter reinforced physically. In the first instance, the child is on his own, in charge of his own affairs, from an early age. He becomes accustomed to making decisions for himself and reacts to the direction or demands of a teacher or other adult as to a challenge of his established independence. Strictness is not objectionable in itself, when it is seen as fairminded and well meant. But where strictness amounts simply to control by force, the child harbors resentment until the day when he can successfully assert physical mastery himself; rather than a learning and shaping process, discipline for him is a matter of muscle. . . .

Parental Affection or Rejection. More crucial even than mode of discipline is the degree of parental affection or rejection of the child. Perhaps the most important factor in the lives of many boys who become delinquent is their failure to win the affection of their fathers. It has been suggested that delinquency correlates more with the consistency of the affection the child receives from both parents than with the consistency of the discipline. It has also been found that a disproportionately large number of aggressive delinquents have been denied the opportunity to express their feelings of dependence on their parents.

Identification between Father and Son. Several recent studies focusing on identification between a boy and his father have tried to determine the conditions under which a boy is more likely to be attracted to his father, on the assumption that such attraction provides a basis upon which parental discipline can inculcate youthful self-control. Unemployment has been found to weaken a father's authority with his family, especially over adolescent children for whom he is unable to provide expected support. Children also appear less likely to identify with fathers if their discipline is perceived as unfair. The strong influence of the father over his son, for good or for ill, is also very significant. When father-son and mother-son relationships are compared, the father-son relationships appear more determinative in whether or not delinquent behavior develops.

Family Status in the Community. The capacity of parents to maintain moral authority over the conduct of their children is affected not only by the family's internal structure and operation but also by the relationships that the family maintains with the community and the role of the family itself in modern life. There seems to be a direct relationship between the prestige of the family in the community and the kind of bond that develops between father and son. Respected family status increases the strength of parental authority and seems to help insulate the child from delinquency.

In inner-city families one or more of the detrimental factors discussed above is particularly likely to be present. Many families are large. Many (over 40 percent according to some estimates) are fatherless, always or intermittently, or involve a marital relationship in which the parties have and communicate to their offspring but little sense of permanence. And the histories of delinquents frequently include a large lower class family broken in some way. . . .

Youth in the Community

The typical delinquent operates in the company of his peers, and delinquency thrives on group support. It has been estimated that between 60 and 90 percent of all delinquent acts are committed with companions. That fact alone makes youth groups of central concern in consideration of delinquency prevention.

It is clear that youth groups are playing a more and more important part in the transition between childhood and adulthood. For young people today that transition is a long period of waiting, during which they are expected to be seriously preparing themselves for participation at some future date in a society that meanwhile provides no role for them and withholds both the toleration accorded children and the responsibilities of adults. Some young people, however, lack the resources for becoming prepared; they see the goal but have not the means to reach it. Others are resentful and impatient with the failure of their stodgy elders to appreciate the contributions they feel ready to make. Many, slum dwellers and suburbanites both, feel victimized by the moral absolutes of the adult society—unexplained injunctions about right and wrong that seem to have little relevance in a complex world controlled by people employing multiple and shifting standards. Youth today accuse those ahead of them of phoniness and of failure to define how to live both honorably and successfully in a world that is changing too rapidly for anyone to comprehend.

The very rapidity of that change is making it ever more difficult for young people to envision the type of work they might wish to commit themselves to, more difficult for them to find stable adult models with whom to identify. To fill the vacuum, they turn increasingly to their own age mates. But the models of dress and ideal and behavior that youth subcultures furnish may lead them into conflict with their parents' values and efforts to assert control. It has been suggested that, besides being more dependent on each other, youth today are also more independent of adults; parents and their young adolescents increasingly seem to live in different and at times antagonistic worlds. That antagonism sometimes explodes in antisocial acts.

Most of the youngsters who rebel at home and at school seek security and recognition among their fellows on the street. Together they form tightly knit groups in the decisions of which they are able to participate and the authority of which they accept as virtually absolute. Their attitudes, dress, tastes, ambitions, behavior, pastimes are those of the group.

While the members are still young—before and during their early teens—such groups engage with apparent abandon and indifference in whatever seems like fun, delinquent and nondelinquent. Only some of what they do is seriously violent or destructive. Frequently, however, adults see even their minor misdeeds as malicious and defiant and label the actors troublemakers. The affixing of that label can be a momentous occurrence in a youngster's life. Thereafter he may be watched; he may be suspect; his every misstep may be seen as further evidence of his delinquent nature. He may be excluded more and more from legitimate activities and opportunities. Soon he may be designated and dealt with as a delinquent and will find it very difficult to move onto a law-abiding path even if he can overcome his own belligerent reaction and negative self-image and seeks to do so.

Being labeled a troublemaker is a danger of growing up in suburbia as well as in the slums, but the suburbs are more likely to provide parental intervention and psychiatrists, pastors, family counselors to help the youth abandon his undesirable identity. It is much harder for the inner-city youth to find alternatives to a rebel role. Thus it is in the slums that youth gangs are most likely to drift from minor and haphazard into serious, repeated, purposeful delinquency.

It is in the slums, too, that young people are most likely to be exposed to the example of the successful career criminal as a person of prestige in the community. To a population denied access to traditional positions of status and achievement, a successful criminal may be a highly visible model of power and affluence and a center of training and recruitment for criminal enterprise.

Delinquent gangs are commonly blamed for much of the street crime that presently alarms the Nation. In fact, however, according to a detailed 2-year study, recently completed, of the 700 members of 21 delinquent gangs, gang violence against persons is less frequent, less violent, and less uncontrolled than is generally believed. Only 17 percent of all the offenses recorded by observers included an element of violence, and about half of the violent offenses were committed against rival gang members. Much gang violence, in other words, appears to occur not against strangers but in attempts to achieve or preserve individual or gang status or territory. . . .

Delinquency and the School

The complex relationship between the school and the child varies greatly from one school system to another. The process of education is dramatically different in the slum than in the middle-class suburb. The child and the problems he brings to school are different. The support for learning that he receives at home and in his neighborhood is different. The school systems themselves are very different. The slum school faces the greatest obstacles with the least resources, the least qualified personnel, the least adequate capability for effective education.

The school, unlike the family, is a public instrument for training young people. It is, therefore, more directly accessible to change through the development of new resources and policies. And since it is the principal public institution for the development of a basic commitment by young people to the goals and values of our society, it is imperative that it be provided with the resources to compete with illegitimate attractions for young people's allegiance. Anything less would be a serious failure to discharge our Nation's responsibility to its youth.

The Commission recognizes that many in the field of education have identified the shortcomings of slum schools. The Commission recognizes too that in many places efforts are being made to improve various aspects of schools. But as a general matter our society has not yet been willing to devote resources sufficient for the radical changes necessary.

Recent research has related instances of delinquent conduct to the school-child relationship and to problems either created or complicated by schools themselves. First, in its own methods and practices, the school may simply be too passive to fulfill its obligations as one of the last social institutions with an opportunity to rescue the child from other forces, in himself and in his environment, which are pushing him toward delinquency. Second, there is considerable evidence that some schools may have an indirect effect on delinquency by the use of methods that create the conditions of failure for certain students. Mishandling by the school can lower the child's motivation to learn. It can aggravate his difficulty in accepting authority and generate or intensify hostility and alienation. It can sap the child's confidence, dampen his initiative, and lead him to negative definitions of himself as a failure or an "unacceptable" person.

Some schools, particularly in the poorest areas, are unable to deal with children who are neither ready nor able to learn. Asserting demands for performance that the child cannot meet, the frustrated teacher may become hostile and the child indifferent, apathetic, or hostile in turn. If the child is also rebelling at home, the effect is more immediate and the confrontation becomes intolerable to all. The too-usual result is that the child turns to other things that have nothing to do with academic learning, and the school finds a way to ignore him or push him out so the rest of its work can continue. . . .

School Response to Behavior Problems. Student misbehavior is a real and urgent problem in many slum schools. Much youthful obstreperousness is best understood as a process of "testing" those in authority and demonstrating—partly for the benefit of peers—one's toughness and masculinity. For many inner-city children, the teacher represents the first real challenge to their independence. While middle-class children, accustomed to the close supervision of parents or parent substitutes, defer almost automatically to the authority of the teacher, the slum child arrives at school in the habit of being his own master and is not about to surrender his autonomy upon demand.

The way in which the school responds to early signs of misbehavior may have a profound influence in either diverting the youngster from or propelling him along the path to a delinquent career. Not all teachers have trouble with "difficult" youngsters. Some, especially sensitive to what lies behind insolence and disobedience, adopt a firm but positive attitude that allows the task of learning to be carried on, if not always under placid conditions.

Other teachers simply submit, ignoring as best they can commotions and disruptions of classroom routine—an alternative that avoids head-on conflict with autonomy-seeking youth but at the same time deprives them of instruction even when they choose to accept it.

Many teachers, on the other hand, assume a right to unquestioning obedience. There results a sometimes ceaseless conflict between teacher and child. The child's assertions of autonomy are dealt with by the teacher, and eventually the school administration, as misbehavior, and sanctioned in a variety of ways. By labeling the youth a troublemaker and excluding him from legitimate activities and sources of achievement, the sanctions may reinforce his tendency to rebel and resist the school's authority. Nor is it easy for him to reform; grades lowered for misconduct, the stigma of assignment to a special class, and records of misbehavior passed on both formally and informally from teacher to teacher make his past difficult to live down. The conception he forms of himself as an outsider, a nonconformer, is of particular importance. With no other source of public recognition, such negative self-images become attractive to some young people, and they begin to adapt their behavior to fit the labels applied to them. A process of defining and communicating a public character occurs, and some young people in a sense cooperate in actually becoming the delinquents they are said to be. . . .

Delinquency and Employment

Growing up properly is difficult at best, but manageable with help at times of critical need. To become a fully functional adult male, one prerequisite is essential: a job. In our society a person's occupation determines more than anything else what life he will lead and how others will regard him. Of course other important factors—family, wealth, race, age—exert significant influence on his future. But for most young men, it is securing jobs consistent with their aspirations that is crucial, that provides a stake in the law-abiding world and a vestibule to an expanding series of opportunities: To marry, to raise a family, to participate in civic affairs, to advance economically and socially and intellectually. . . .

The Effect of Unemployment. It does not take the slum youth long to discover the gap between what he had hoped for and thought he was entitled to as an American and what actually awaits him; and it is a bitter as well as an oft repeated experience. So he looks for some other way out.

The career decisions of these youths, and the reasons for them, are varied; many are not really decisions at all. Some find their way back to school or into a job training program. Some drift among low paying jobs. Those who have good connections with organized criminal enterprises may feel few restraints against following a career that, although illegitimate, is relatively safe and lucrative; they have seen many others thrive on the proceeds of vice, and it will not be hard for them to persuade themselves that the steady demand for illicit goods and services justifies providing them. Others try theft; some become good enough at it to make it their regular livelihood; others lack aptitude or connections and become failures in the illegal as well as the legal world—habitués of our jails and prisons. Finally, there are those who give up, retreat from conventional society, and search for a better world in the private fantasies they can command from drink and drugs. . . .

CONCLUSION

Society's efforts to control and combat delinquency may be seen as operating at three levels.

The first and most basic—indeed, so basic that delinquency prevention is only one of the reasons for it—involves provision of a real opportunity for everyone to participate in the legitimate activities that in our society lead to or constitute a good life: education, recreation, employment, family life. It is to insure such opportunity that schools in the slums must be made as good as schools elsewhere; that discrimination and arbitrary or unnecessary restrictions must be eliminated from employment practices; that job training must be made available to everyone; that physical surroundings must be reclaimed from deterioration and barrenness; that the rights of a citizen must be exercisable without regard to creed or race.

The pursuit of these goals is not inconsistent with the need to strengthen the system of juvenile justice. Some young offenders are dangerous repeaters, responsible for holdups, muggings, aggravated assaults—the crimes that frighten people off the streets. Others, while less threatening, have already shown themselves resistant to noncoercive rehabilitating efforts. Dealing with these youths so as to protect society requires—at least at this point in our understanding of human behavior—custody, adjudication of fact, imposition of sanction. Those measures depend upon an effective, efficient system of juvenile justice. Swift apprehension, thorough investigation, prompt disposition—carried out by persons carefully selected and trained for their functions—should maximize the system's deterrent impact and the respect accorded the law it upholds. Insofar as the juvenile justice system does deal with delinquency, its dealings should be characterized by these attributes.

Further, the system should operate with all the procedural formality necessary to safeguard adequately the rights that any person has when he is subject to the application of coercive power. Juveniles should be represented by counsel; they should be able to confront those complaining of their conduct; their fate should not be determined by hearsay or gossip. They should not be unnecessarily detained.

Between these two aspects of delinquency control—the first relevant to all young people, the second reserved for those who appear to need the coercive authority of the court—there is a third: response to the special needs of youths with special problems. They may already have delinquency records. They may be delinquent but not seriously so. They may be law-abiding but alienated and uncooperative in making use of education or employment or other opportunities. They may be behavior or academic problems in school, or misfits among their peers, or disruptive in recreation groups. Whatever the nature or degree of the difficulty, today they are all too likely to be excluded by most agencies and institutions, which find these youngsters, whom ostensibly they exist to help, in fact more than their limited resources can manage. They may restrict the participation of such youths in extra-curricular school activities, keep them segregated from their fellows in special classes, eliminate them from recreation groups, rate them ineligible for certain sorts of therapy.

For such youths, it is imperative to furnish help that is particularized enough to deal with their individual needs but does not separate them from their peers and label them for life. Providing sufficiently specialized services while yet avoiding destructive labeling and stigma poses one of the central dilemmas in the delinquency prevention area. . . . Whatever the specific methods chosen, the problem must be attacked, for it is with these young people that most youth-serving agencies today are having the least success.

39.

William C. Kvaraceus

JUVENILE DELINQUENCY: A PROBLEM FOR THE MODERN WORLD

WHAT IS A JUVENILE DELINQUENT?

Almost every language in the world now yields a phrase labelling those youngsters of many nations whose behaviour or tastes are different enough to incite suspicion if not alarm. They are the "teddy boys" in England, the "nozem" in the Netherlands, the "raggare" in Sweden, the "blousons noirs" in France, the "tsotsis" in South Africa, the "bodgies" in Australia, the "halbstarken" in Austria and Germany, the "taipau" in Taiwan, the "mambo boys" or "taiyozuku" in Japan, the "tapkaroschi" in Yugoslavia, the "vitelloni" in Italy, the "hooligans" in Poland, and the "stiliagyi" in the U.S.S.R.

But it is not our right to assume that every "teddy boy" or every "blouson noir" is actively engaged in delinquency. These names often mislead people. It is unjust to assume automatically that a youngster who likes rock'n roll music or bizarre clothing is on his way to becoming a delinquent if he is not one already. Too often, the adult world has used the word "delinquent" to express anger or bewilderment at adolescent tastes.

Nor should every minor who breaks a rule or behaves offensively be considered a delinquent. The behaviour of young people rarely consistently conforms with the standards and expectations that adults have for them.

Variations on a Theme

What are the offences and what are penalties? The differences from country to country only indicate how divided the world is on who is a delinquent, who is not, and what should be done about it.

A widespread form of delinquency in Cairo is the collection of cigarette butts from the street. A recent survey in India, conducted in Lucknow and Kampur, indicated that the second most common juvenile offence was vagrancy. A few years ago in Hong Kong, juveniles brought before the magistrate's court reached the startling figure of more than 55,000 and yet over 90 percent of them had committed only technical breaches of the law such as hawking without a license. Information from Lagos, Nigeria, shows that a delinquent there is primarily an offender against the unwritten laws of the home: disrespect and disobedience are regarded as serious offences.

So we see that the numbers of children cited for delinquent acts can sometimes be misleading unless we are to know the nature of the offences and what particular law they violate.

Yet even when we take the most cautious attitude towards statistics on delinquency from all corners of the world, the evidence mounts. The offences are varied. They range from stealing, vandalism and property offenses, petty extortion and gambling to violent behaviour, rowdiness, truancy, immoral or indecent conduct, drinking, and drug addiction.

The Gang

In almost every city in the world where delinquency exists, so does the juvenile gang which looms up as a modern social institution. These gangs, innocent or evil, are an important element in the overall pattern of juvenile delinquency. Looking at delinquency in a worldwide context, one does not often see individual youngsters becoming delinquent each in his own fashion, but rather as a number of boys participating in joint activities that derive their meaning and pleasure from a set of common sentiments, loyalties, and rules.

Source: *Federal Probation,* Vol. XXVIII, No. 3 (September, 1964), pp. 12–18. Excerpts from *Juvenile Delinquency: A Problem for the Modern World* (UNESCO, 1964). Reprinted by permission of the author and the journal.

The majority of these gangs often engage in acts which do not always bring financial gains and to the rest of the world seem almost purposeless in their malice.

In Poland, teenage gangs have damaged railroad trains and molested passengers for no apparent reason. In Saskatchewan, Canada, groups of boys have entered private homes and mutilated expensive furnishings without attempting to steal a single object. In Chiengmai, Thailand, a band of male minors, with a symbol of a white eagle tattooed on their arms, found their greatest diversion in terrorizing or injuring outsiders. In Argentina, gangs of boys have gathered in cafés or bars to insult or humiliate customers.

Some juvenile delinquents, however, have clearer goals in mind. Racketeering or petty extortion are good examples. A gang in Detroit, Michigan, which was composed of 15 boys from 13 to 16 years of age, organized a racket in which all the smaller children of the neighbourhood were forced to pay 5 cents for the insurance of not being molested on the way to and from the local cinema. A report from India indicates that gangs of young boys and girls have learned to be highly successful smugglers of illicit liquor and drugs.

The Hidden Delinquent

In the past, tabulations on the backgrounds of a cross section of the juvenile delinquents always seemed to indicate that these children were reared in poor living conditions. A recent United Nations report, however, points to a strong change in this tendency. There are numerous and increasing indications that children from the higher-income brackets are becoming delinquents. In France, the expression "blousons dorés" (jackets of gold) is a somewhat sarcastic reference to delinquents from richer families than those of the "blousons noirs."

In the United States, a recent survey revealed that a relatively large number of teenage boys admitted that they had committed serious acts of delinquency which had never become a matter of court record. These were sons of middle- and upper-income families.

One of the richest collections of twentieth century myths surrounds the subject of delinquency. Usually, they are oversimplified versions of what causes delinquency. But generalizations are useless. Such explanations as slum living, "broken" homes, films, and deprivation fail to provide us with universal and realistic reasons. Sometimes, each of these may be one among many factors that shape a child's life but no factor can be accepted as the single overall reason for the thousands and thousands of delinquent cases.

To begin to understand the problem, we must realize that delinquents often do the same thing for vastly different reasons and to achieve vastly different results.

Three Case Histories

To illustrate these differences—as far as reasons and results go—here are examples of boys each of whom might be considered a juvenile delinquent.

A 15-year-old American, John G., from Los Angeles, California, is one of 12 members of a street gang called the "Sharks." The gang has an inflexible code of values, standards, and morals. All the members have sworn allegiance to this peculiar code and, for John G. it is the most serious and important emotional commitment of his life. Last summer, he and four other gang boys stole a car that was parked in the neighbourhood. They abandoned the car, a mile and a half away, the next morning around 4 a.m. When John G. was questioned by a juvenile court he did not feel anxious to explain why he had done it and there was not the slightest attempt to show he was sorry. He had previously been in trouble for breaking windows and slashing the roofs of convertible cars with a razor.

His background showed that both parents worked and their combined incomes were meagre. Their apartment was too small for the five members of the family. John G.'s record in school was dismal and his teachers resented his pose of boredom and contempt. His attitude, in school and outside, was spiteful and malicious, yet a psychiatric examination revealed no pronounced emotional disturbances and a normal intelligence.

By conventional standards, John G. might be considered a disgrace to his law-abiding parents, a failure by his school, and a threat by his community. And yet there is a telling logic in what he does. All of this delinquent's most offensive acts won the approval and respect of the people he most admires: gang members of the "Sharks." His conduct is right by the standards of his own street-corner subculture, although it happens to be wrong to the outside world.

A 13-year-old English boy, Basil P. comes from a prosperous family in London. Basil does not do well in school, much to the distress of his father who also studied there and achieved a reputation as a student. Basil's most conspicuous difficulty is poor reading; in any subject requiring much effort in reading he is apt to become distracted or lazy. He might have remained an anonymous or inadequate student, but for the fact that several of his teachers and many of his classmates know that Basil has "a habit of taking things."

The child makes no attempt to deny it. For a long period of time he has been pilfering objects from other boys, stealing both valuable and trifling things. Basil does not hoard them but often gives them away to classmates, consciously increasing the risk that the original owner will see his possession and claim it. Once, in London on a holiday, Basil stole three gramophone records from a music store. He says he is "sorry" he steals, he does not know why he does it, and he wishes he could stop. A psychiatric examination revealed that on a deep symbolical level the objects Basil stole stand for or substitute for something unconsciously desired but somehow forbidden or unattainable. It was recommended, and agreed, that he would receive psychiatric help and treatment.

A 17-year-old African, Pierre N., travelled from his home village on the Ivory Coast to try to find a job in the nearest city. He hoped to be employed in a hotel. Pierre N. could read and write, speak two languages, and was a bright youngster. In the city he was caught by a clerk when trying to steal a shirt from a store. To the judge of a court Pierre explained that his own clothes were shabby, he had no money, and he hoped a new shirt would make a better impression when he looked for a job.

The considerable differences between these three case histories give only some indication of the hazards of lumping all adolescent trangressions under the label of juvenile delinquency.

WHY DELINQUENCY EXISTS

Delinquent behavior, which stems from so many combinations of factors, cannot be treated or controlled until several scientifically evolved theories about the individual offender have been checked. The boy must be considered apart from his conspirators. His life at home, his problems at school, his relationships with his parents, his own self-image, and his personality must all be carefully revealed and evaluated.

One theory says that delinquency results from severe frustrations suffered by a growing child. Another, that it is an expression of rebellion. Yet another theory suggests that juvenile delinquency is perhaps the failure of a young male to be able to identify himself with what is professionally referred to as a "male authority figure." This naturally means the child's father, the dominating and consistent male influence in his life. If there is no father, if he is rarely at home, or even if he is a dim or withdrawn figure in the child's life, a small boy may come to feel a very deep insecurity about his own image of himself as a man.

In some families the child does not lack a "male authority figure"—there is a father and an assertive one. But what happens when the mother derides the father and constantly reminds the child of his faults? The child comes to understand that to be loved and accepted he must somehow be different from the man who is his father—the one man it is most natural for him to idealize. It is more than possible that a youngster in this situation will have the same fears about himself as the child who lacks a father.

Aggressiveness—Reaction of the Unsure

In the broadest sense, any adolescent who is unsure of himself can appease his worries—or will try to—by being aggressive. Here is where one of the rare positive statements about all delinquent behaviour can be made: it is remarkably aggressive. Aggression may be verbal, it may consist of destructive acts, it may be sexual. Aggression may be directed toward one's self, towards the world, or both.

A very simple illustration of how some boys dispel their doubts about their own masculinity by extremely aggressive behaviour—stealing of cars—is contained in a report from Sweden: "A phrase often heard is: 'If you've got a car, you'll get a girl.' At the same time one is struck by the extreme inadequacy of this category of car thieves in their dealings with girls. A great many of them cannot dance, even though they are of the 'dancing age.' This means they lack not only the skill to dance, but also have no way with girls and are completely without confidence in their own manliness."

A deep questioning in the child's mind about his own value as a human being can cripple him so that he is almost unable to make any honest or lasting attachment with other people. For if his parents have not loved and accepted him and admitted him, how can a child believe that someone else will? Children who feel they are not loved or wanted can be very severely damaged by such deprivation—real or imaginary. Maladjusted adolescents are usually those youngsters who have suffered from these feelings.

In Quest of an Identity

Sometimes even genuine love is not enough. In the case of a family where the mother is the head of the house, the provider, and the voice of authority, a rebellion may occur. Young boys wishing to become young men must break from this world of feminine rule, even if it means defying the mother, and assert themselves as males. When there is no man around the house on a permanent basis this becomes difficult. The boy is under a peculiar sort of stress. It is possible that because of this stress he will try to take on attributes which will symbolize to him, and to the world, an unassailable masculinity. There are a number of activities and even possessions which symbolize clear-cut and irreproachable masculinity. For example, there is ability in combat, ownership of a car or motorcycle, techniques in violence or sadism, or even a vocabulary. There are forms of dress. One has only to think of the much-publicized American juvenile delinquent who owns a motorcycle and wears a black leather jacket and blue jeans.

In most societies it is accepted and understood that adolescence is the period when a youngster forms his own identity, usually by a meaningful conflict with his parents or the older generation. Nothing in this world causes as much concern to the adolescent as this question of his own identity: how he sees himself and how he feels the rest of the world sees him. Even a negative identity—and more than one habitual delinquent child has described himself as "plain mean"—can be satisfying.

Young people usually want and need parental models either to imitate or reject. Few children might actively complain about the increasing tolerance and permissiveness of their parents, but their behaviour often reflects their own inner confusion. Where there are no clear boundaries in a child's life, when the "rules" are never defined, when neither his father nor his mother represents certain values and certain commitments to life, it becomes harder for the child to discover a true image of himself and to set limits of behaviour.

The Outside World

So much for the interior forces that may shape the child so crucially at the beginning of his life. There is also the outside world which begins to intrude upon his thoughts and feelings when he is very young.

For example, a young person who grows up in a deprived area learns certain kinds of behaviour as naturally and normally as the middle-class boy learns exactly the opposite. A middle-class child might be taught to fear poor marks in school, fighting, cursing, and being rude to his teacher. But the slum child, conversely, might fear doing well in school and being friendly with his teacher, for this would set him apart from the other children and possibly evoke their anger or ridicule. All too often he learns that the best way to express his aggressions is with his fists.

It cannot be assumed that all deprived areas are jungles of violence. What is clearly shown in many scientific research projects is that while they are never the one and only cause for delinquency, they can provide a different set of traditions which are unfamiliar to outsiders. Many children who are exposed to values which almost encourage delinquency do not automatically become delinquents. Others prove more vulnerable.

The child who lives in an underprivileged neighbourhood may often resent the limits that he feels society has imposed. This may be illustrated through hundreds of case histories. One example could be the boy who knows he will never make enough money to buy the car he wants. Another is the child who knows that it is impossible for him to attend college. These are frustrations that society creates and they can often be as disturbing as the frustrations that are emotionally aroused by a lack of inner security.

Industrialization and Changing Society

Many complex problems in human behaviour have been traced to intense industrialization. Sociologists have remarked very often about the type of work that absorbs years of men's lives when their entire working day consists only of pressing buttons and pulling levers or switches. The assembly line hardly offers a man a sense of joy or fulfilment in his work. He has no commitment, no sense of achievement, no pride in craftmanship, and no sense of social purpose. For a young boy who can look forward only to many years of this sort of monotony, delinquency can often serve as the best and most exciting sort of protest against a dreary and unacceptable future.

Added to this, there is a frightening freedom for people who live in big cities, divorced from the traditional values and familiar standards that shaped their lives. Very often, they are anonymous and alone, cut off from the smaller society from which they came.

When normal values and traditions break down, and cannot be so easily replaced, it is often the adolescents who feel the most stress. It has been said that the social problem of one generation is a psychological problem for the next. In the case of societies undergoing modernization, it is often the rate—the degree of acceleration—of these changes much more than the changes themselves that must be considered.

There are many conclusions to be drawn from understanding and appreciating the viewpoints of the specialists on the subject of juvenile delinquency. One conclusion must always be remembered. There is not one cause for delinquency but rather a sequence of interlocking factors in the child's life that can result in delinquency. Different factors sometimes can result in the same type of delinquent behaviour; on the other hand, different kinds of delinquent behavior are often caused by the same factors.

Juvenile Delinquency: What a Community Can Do

What emerges clearly from many studies and reports and surveys is that delinquent behaviour must be the concern of the entire community, not just dismissed as a problem to be handled by local schools, police courts, or professional agencies. Professionals will always be needed but the impetus must come from the community itself.

The Role of the Schools

One of the most crucial forces, if we consider only the number of years during which it exerts an influence over the child, is the school. Together with the home it provides the basic learning experience for all children. The teacher, who is a trained observer, can detect evidence or incipient signs of personal or social problems that are affecting the child and perhaps offer the pupils some form of help and relief. He can do much to make the child aware of his own basic values and teach him how to develop them.

Ideally, specialized professional personnel are needed to reinforce and augment the assistance a teacher can give to a pupil. Through timely and skilful use of auxiliary services, the school can often help a child from becoming a failure. The visiting teacher who can establish a close contact with a child's parents, the school social worker, or the psychiatric worker are all trained to evaluate and relieve the pressures that often contribute to a child's defeat in the classroom.

Many educators have expressed the opinion that far too many schools adhere too rigidly to a curriculum that has no significance or value to every pupil. If we agree that the child who might become a good mechanic is not to be considered a human being inferior to the child with an interest in medicine, then we must also acknowledge that a single school should accommodate and benefit both of them. Pouring all students into a single academic mould causes many children who might be vulnerable to delinquency to come a good deal closer to it. What can and should be considered by the authorities and the community is the establishment of different types of school experiences for children who cannot benefit by a standard academic education or those children who, for any number of reasons, cannot hold their own in the regular classroom.

Some large cities have attempted to diminish their delinquency problems among other objectives by establishing separate vocational or technical high schools, and through work-study programmes. The programmes of these schools are realistically connected both to the employment situation and to the requirements of the apprentice system in various trades.

Every community will not be able to establish a vocational high school. But there are other possibilities. Some schools have adopted the system of an optional period during the week: there is a class in vocational training for those who elect it, other pupils can study foreign languages. In other places, schools and local industries have developed cooperative work-study programmes for selected youngsters.

Help for the Family

Delinquents, for a variety of reasons, frequently do not have an accepting or reassuring relationship with their parents. Any education programme or any counselling that the community makes available to parents, provided it is wisely presented, can often be a turning point.

Many things can be meant by parent education. It is not always helpful to tell a mother outright to be a better mother, but, sometimes, by relieving her of economic or health worries she is freer to love and consider her children.

In many instances, the very parents of the children most exposed to delinquency have very little concept of what it means to be a member of a community and belong to an organization. They may react suspiciously or resent the visit of an outsider wishing to advise them on their family problems. Very often, hostility can be overcome if the parents are contacted, not with a reproachful or condescending attitude by others, but with an invitation to contribute something to the life of the community. The larger the number of adults from all backgrounds that one community can interest in belonging to some type of stable and enduring organization, the easier it will be to reach them as parents and possibly direct them.

Some city communities have established neighbourhood centres where informal educational activities are conducted. These activities include parent discussion groups. Through these neighbourhood centres, people of all backgrounds who have a natural ability for different kinds of leadership can be found and involved in committee or recreational work.

The Police

The importance of the police in a community with delinquency can hardly be overrated since they often represent the first official contact between the young offender and the law. The policeman or juvenile officer is the one who must frequently decide whether to let the child off with a reprimand or to refer him to a juvenile court or some other agency set up to deal with such children.

In some countries the evolution of the work of the police has given rise to more definite forms of action of a preventive nature. In Liverpool, since 1949, there has been developed a city police programme known as the Juvenile Liaison Scheme. Its object is to deal with youngsters under 17 years of age who manifest some behaviour disorders or who have already committed petty offenses. The police officials try, after an interview with a child, to secure the cooperation of the individual family and school. Then they often contact appropriate services such as youth clubs, probation officers, and family service units in order to provide suitable help.

The liaison officer visits the child and parents often. He tries to advise and assist them in various ways. What is most significant about the Liverpool plan is that it improves the relations between the police and the public in general. It is claimed that this special operation was a contributory factor to diminishing the figures of juvenile delinquency in Liverpool, a city with the unhappy distinction of once having the highest delinquency rate in England.

Very often a separate division or bureau in the police department, specially for juvenile aid, can accomplish much. A juvenile aid bureau generally handles all the cases of youngsters who are picked up either by the regular police force or by a juvenile squad. The staff also may carry on research concerning any local youth problems; they can assume a good share of the responsibility for enforcing child labour laws, supervising children in street trades and checking on those local danger spots which often foster delinquent behaviour.

The Real World of Work

If there are a number of boys who have left school in one particular neighbourhood with a high incidence of delinquency most people would hope that they would find jobs instead of loitering on street corners. But it is not enough to find them jobs—any job—just to keep them out of trouble. What has to be done is to make youngsters who are vulnerable to delinquent behaviour *more* employable in addition to creating new employment opportunities for them.

One possible remedy, especially in poorer neighbourhoods, is a community-organized youth jobs centre, the function of which would be to help the young person enter the world of work. Such a centre could offer guidance and counselling, placement service, and help redirect the youngster to a training programme. The aim should be to make the boy more employable by improving his social, academic, and job skills.

New Outlooks: Involving the Delinquent

In the long run, only the delinquent can solve the delinquency problem. In the past, many agencies working with the delinquent encouraged him to be passive. The professional workers tended to moralize over him, scold him, threaten him, study him, relocate him, and treat him. Today, hopefully, the emphasis in many parts of the world is to encourage the delinquent to play a much more active and decisive role in the solution of his own problems.

This must be done with considerable skill and patience. Very often, he will refuse to cooperate and refuse to help himself. Involving the delinquent can mean a multitude of things. Here is a very simple example of how one community approached it. At the suggestion of a team of professionals, a group of 34 delinquents who had previously been gang members were divided into three squads, according to age. They were encouraged to suggest or consider certain projects for their particular group with an adult adviser. A feeling of mild competition between the three squads was encouraged.

During a 2-month period, each squad carried out a certain programme. One squad was busy cleaning up an empty lot to use as a recreational area. Another squad operated a darts booth and a lemonade stand at a neighbourhood fund-raising carnival in order to make enough money for a summer camping trip. The third squad was engaged in repainting a wing of a local hospital; what money they made went into a fund. In each squad, there was a strong esprit de corps; individual and group performance was encouraged; special citations were awarded by community groups—such as a chamber of commerce—for programmes that genuinely benefited the community as a whole. The leader of each squad had the responsibility of seeing that each project was carried out within a time limit.

The ideal result of such a project is not to convert every delinquent into a civic-minded prude. It is to show the young delinquents that conformity need not be stifling, and that they themselves are capable of choosing and reaching socially acceptable goals.

In trying to involve the delinquent in his own re-education, one thing must be remembered. He already knows failure to an exceptional degree. Therefore, caution must be taken not to involve him in an adult plan or set up such difficult expectations that he would face still another failure. Neither should he be so protected and supervised that he is not permitted to make mistakes in judgment.

40.

WALTER B. MILLER

LOWER CLASS CULTURE AS A GENERATING MILIEU OF GANG DELINQUENCY

The etiology of delinquency has long been a controversial issue, and is particularly so at present. As new frames of reference for explaining human behavior have been added to traditional theories, some authors have adopted the practice of citing the major postulates of each school of thought as they pertain to delinquency, and going on to state that causality must be conceived in terms of the dynamic interaction of a complex combination of variables on many levels. The major sets of etiological factors currently adduced to explain delinquency are, in simplified terms, the physiological (delinquency results from organic pathology), the psychodynamic (delinquency is a "behavioral disorder" resulting primarily from emotional disturbance generated by a defective mother-child relationship), and the environmental (delinquency is the product of disruptive forces, "disorganization," in the actor's physical or social environment).

This paper selects one particular kind of "delinquency"[1]—law-violating acts committed by members of adolescent street corner groups in lower class communities—and attempts to show that the dominant component of motivation underlying these acts consists in a directed attempt by the actor to adhere to forms of behavior, and to achieve standards of value as they are defined within that community. It takes as a premise that the motivation of behavior in this situation can be approached most productively by attempting to understand the nature of cultural forces impinging on the acting individual as they are perceived *by the actor himself*—although by no means only that segment of these forces of which the actor is consciously aware—rather than as they are perceived and evaluated from the reference position of another cultural system. In the case of "gang" delinquency, the cultural system which exerts the most direct influence on behavior is that of the lower class community itself—a long-established, distinctively patterned tradition with an integrity of its own—rather than a so-called "delinquent subculture" which has arisen through conflict with middle class culture and is oriented to the deliberate violation of middle class norms.

The bulk of the substantive data on which the following material is based was collected in connection with a service-research project in the control of gang delinquency. During the service aspect of the project, which lasted for three years, seven trained social workers maintained contact with twenty-one corner group units in a "slum" district of a large eastern city for periods of time ranging from ten to thirty months. Groups were Negro and white, male and female, and in early, middle, and late adolescence. Over eight thousand pages of direct observational data on behavior patterns of group members and other community residents were collected; almost daily contact was maintained for a total time period of about thirteen worker years. Data include workers' contact reports, participant observation reports by the writer—a cultural anthropologist—and direct tape recordings of group activities and discussions.[2]

SOURCE: *The Journal of Social Issues.* Vol. XIV, No. 3 (1958), pp. 5–19.

[1]The complex issues involved in deriving a definition of "delinquency" cannot be discussed here. The term "delinquent" is used in this paper to characterize behavior or acts committed by individuals within specified age limits which if known to official authorities could result in legal action. The concept of a "delinquent" individual has little or no utility in the approach used here; rather, specified types of *acts* which may be committed rarely or frequently by few or many individuals are characterized as "delinquent."

[2]A three year research project is being financed

FOCAL CONCERNS OF LOWER CLASS CULTURE

There is a substantial segment of present-day American society whose way of life, values, and characteristic patterns of behavior are the product of a distinctive cultural system which may be termed "lower class." Evidence indicates that this cultural system is becoming increasingly distinctive, and that the size of the group which shares this tradition is increasing.[3] The lower class way of life, in common with that of all distinctive cultural groups, is characterized by a set of focal concerns—areas or issues which command widespread and persistent attention and a high degree of emotional involvement. The specific concerns cited here, while by no means confined to the American lower classes, constitute a distinctive *patterning* of concerns which differs significantly, both in rank order and weighting from that of American middle class culture. Chart 11.1 presents a highly schematic and simplified listing of six of the major concerns of lower class culture. Each is conceived as a "dimension" within which a fairly wide and varied range of alternative behavior patterns may be followed by different individuals under different situations. They are listed roughly in order of the degree of *explicit* attention accorded each, and, in this sense represent a weighted ranking of concerns. The "perceived alternatives" represent polar positions which define certain parameters within each dimension. As will be explained in more detail, it is necessary in relating the influence of these "concerns" to the motivation of delinquent behavior to specify *which* of its aspects is oriented to, whether orientation is *overt* or *covert*, *positive* (conforming to or seeking the aspect), or *negative* (rejecting or seeking to avoid the aspect).

The concept "focal concern" is used here in preference to the concept "value" for several interrelated reasons: (1) It is more readily derivable from direct field observation. (2) It is descriptively neutral—permitting independent consideration of positive and negative valences as varying under different conditions, whereas "value" carries a built-in positive valence. (3) It makes possible more refined analysis of subcultural differences, since it reflects actual behavior, whereas "value" tends to wash out intracultural differences since it is colored by notions of the "official" ideal.

Trouble. Concern over "trouble" is a dominant feature of lower class culture. The concept has various shades of meaning; "trouble" in one of its aspects represents a situation or a kind of behavior which results in unwelcome or complicating involvement with official authorities or agencies of middle class society. "Getting into trouble" and "staying out of trouble" represent major issues for male and female, adults and children. For men, "trouble" frequently involves fighting or sexual adventures while drinking; for women, sexual involvement with disadvantageous consequences. Expressed desire to avoid behavior which violates moral or legal norms is often based less on an explicit commitment to "official" moral or legal standards than on a desire to avoid "getting into trouble," e.g., the complicating consequences of the action.

The dominant concern over "trouble" involves a distinction of critical importance for the

---

under National Institutes of Health Grant M–1414, and administered through the Boston University School of Social Work. The primary research effort has subjected all collected material to a uniform data-coding process. All information bearing on some 70 areas of behavior (behavior in reference to school, police, theft, assault, sex, collective athletics, etc.) is extracted from the records, recorded on coded data cards, and filed under relevant categories. Analysis of these data aims to ascertain the actual nature of customary behavior in these areas, and the extent to which the social work effort was able to effect behavioral changes.

[3]Between 40 and 60 per cent of all Americans are directly influenced by lower class culture, with about 15 per cent, or 25 million, comprising the "hard core" lower class group—defined primarily by its use of the "female-based" household as the basic form of child-rearing unit and of the "serial monogamy" mating pattern as the primary form of marriage. The term "lower class culture" as used here refers most specifically to the way of life of the "hard core" group; systematic research in this area would probably reveal at least four to six major subtypes of lower class culture, for some of which the "concerns" presented here would be differently weighted, especially for those subtypes in which "law-abiding" behavior has a high overt valuation. It is impossible within the compass of this short paper to make the finer intracultural distinctions which a more accurate presentation would require.

CHART 11.1

FOCAL CONCERNS OF LOWER CLASS CULTURE

Area	*Perceived Alternatives (State, Quality, Condition)*	
1. *Trouble:*	law-abiding behavior	law-violating behavior
2. *Toughness:*	physical prowess, skill; "masculinity"; fearlessness, bravery, daring	weakness, ineptitude; effeminacy; timidity, cowardice, caution
3. *Smartness:*	ability to outsmart, dupe, "con"; gaining money by "wits"; shrewdness, adroitness in repartee	gullibility, "con-ability"; gaining money by hard work; slowness, dull-wittedness, verbal maladroitness
4. *Excitement:*	thrill; risk, danger; change, activity	boredom; "deafness," safeness; sameness, passivity
5. *Fate:*	favored by fortune, being "lucky"	ill-omened, being "unlucky"
6. *Autonomy:*	freedom from external constraint; freedom from superordinate authority; independence	presence of external constraint; presence of strong authority; dependency, being "cared for"

lower class community—that between "law-abiding" and "non-law-abiding" behavior. There is a high degree of sensitivity as to where each person stands in relation to these two classes of activity. Whereas in the middle class community a major dimension for evaluating a person's status is "achievement" and its external symbols, in the lower class, personal status is very frequently gauged along the law-abiding-non-law-abiding dimension. A mother will evaluate the suitability of her daughter's boyfriend less on the basis of his achievement potential than on the basis of his innate "trouble" potential. This sensitive awareness of the opposition of "trouble-producing" and "non-trouble-producing" behavior represents both a major basis for deriving status distinctions, and an internalized conflict potential for the individual.

As in the case of other focal concerns, which of two perceived alternatives—"law-abiding" or "non-law-abiding"—is valued varies according to the individual and the circumstances; in many instances there is an overt commitment to the "law-abiding" alternative, but a covert commitment to the "non-law-abiding." In certain situations, "getting into trouble" is overtly recognized as prestige-conferring; for example, membership in certain adult and adolescent primary groupings ("gangs") is contingent on having demonstrated an explicit commitment to the law-violating alternative. It is most important to note that the choice between "law-abiding" and "non-law-abiding" behavior is still a choice *within* lower class culture; the distinction between the policeman and the criminal, the outlaw and the sheriff, involves primarily this one dimension; in other respects they have a high community of interests. Not infrequently brothers raised in an identical cultural milieu will become police and criminals respectively.

For a substantial segment of the lower class population "getting into trouble" is not in itself overtly defined as prestige-conferring, but is implicitly recognized as a means to other valued ends, e.g., the covertly valued desire to be "cared for" and subject to external constraint, or the overtly valued state of excitement or risk. Very frequently "getting into trouble" is multifunctional, and achieves several sets of valued ends.

Toughness. The concept of "toughness" in lower class culture represents a compound combination of qualities or states. Among its most important components are physical prowess, evidenced both by demonstrated possession of strength and endurance and athletic skill; "masculinity," symbolized by a distinctive complex of acts and avoidances (bodily tatooing; absence of sentimentality; non-concern with "art," "literature," conceptualization of women as conquest objects, etc.); and bravery in the face of physical threat. The model for the "tough guy" —hard, fearless, undemonstrative, skilled in physical combat—is represented by the movie gangster of the thirties, the "private eye," and the movie cowboy.

The genesis of the intense concern over "toughness" in lower class culture is probably related to the fact that a significant proportion of lower class males are reared in a predominantly female household, and lack a consistently present male figure with whom to identify and from whom to learn essential components of a "male" role. Since women serve as a primary object of identification during pre-adolescent years, the almost obsessive lower class concern with "masculinity" probably resembles a type of compulsive reaction-formation. A concern over homosexuality runs like a persistent thread through lower class culture. This is manifested by the institutionalized practice of baiting "queers," often accompanied by violent physical attacks, an expressed contempt for "softness" or frills, and the use of the local term for "homosexual" as a generalized pejorative epithet (e.g., higher class individuals or upwardly mobile peers are frequently characterized as "fags" or "queers"). The distinction between "overt" and "covert" orientation to aspects of an area of concern is especially important in regard to "toughness." A positive overt evaluation of behavior defined as "effeminate" would be out of the question for a lower class male; however, built into lower class culture is a range of devices which permit men to adopt behaviors and concerns which in other cultural milieux fall within the province of women, and at the same time to be defined as "tough" and manly. For example, lower class men can be professional short-order cooks in a diner and still be regarded as "tough." The highly intimate circumstances of the street corner gang involve the recurrent expression of strongly affectionate feelings towards other men. Such expressions, however, are disguised as their opposite, taking the form of ostensibly aggressive verbal and physical interaction (kidding, "ranking," roughhousing, etc.).

Smartness. "Smartness," as conceptualized in lower class culture, involves the capacity to outsmart, outfox, outwit, dupe, "take," "con" another or others, and the concomitant capacity to avoid being outwitted, "taken," or duped oneself. In its essence, smartness involves the capacity to achieve a valued entity—material goods, personal status—through a maximum use of mental agility and a minimum use of physical effort. This capacity has an extremely long tradition in lower class culture, and is highly valued. Lower class culture can be characterized as "non-intellectual" only if intellectualism is defined specifically in terms of control over a particular body of formally learned knowledge involving "culture" (art, literature, "good" music, etc.), a generalized perspective on the past and present conditions of our own and other societies, and other areas of knowledge imparted by formal educational institutions. This particular type of mental attainment is, in general, overtly disvalued and frequently associated with effeminancy; "smartness" in the lower class sense, however, is highly valued.

The lower class child learns and practices the use of this skill in the street corner situation. Individuals continually practice duping and outwitting one another through recurrent card games and other forms of gambling, mutual exchanges of insults, and "testing" for mutual "conability." Those who demonstrate competence in this skill are accorded considerable prestige. Leadership roles in the corner group are frequently allocated according to demonstrated capacity in the two areas of "smartness" and "toughness"; the ideal leader combines both, but the "smart" leader is often accorded more prestige than the "tough" one—reflecting a general lower class respect for "brains" in the "smartness" sense.[4]

[4]The "brains-brawn" set of capacities are often paired in lower class folk lore or accounts of lower class life, e.g., "Brer Fox" and "Brer Bear" in the Uncle Remus stories, or George and Lennie in *Of Mice and Men.*

The model of the "smart" person is represented in popular media by the card shark, the professional gambler, the "con" artist, the promoter. A conceptual distinction is made between two kinds of people: "suckers," easy marks, "lushes," dupes, who work for their money and are legitimate targets of exploitation; and sharp operators, the "brainy" ones, who live by their wits and "getting" from the suckers by mental adroitness.

Involved in the syndrome of capacities related to "smartness" is a dominant emphasis in lower class culture on ingenious aggressive repartee. This skill, learned and practiced in the context of the corner group, ranges in form from the widely prevalent semi-ritualized teasing, kidding, razzing, "ranking," so characteristic of male peer group interaction, to the highly ritualized type of mutual insult interchange known as "the dirty dozens," "the dozens," "playing house," and other terms. This highly patterned cultural form is practiced on its most advanced level in adult male Negro society, but less polished variants are found throughout lower class culture—practiced, for example, by white children, male and female, as young as four or five. In essence, "doin' the dozens" involves two antagonists who vie with each other in the exchange of increasingly inflammatory insults, with incestuous and perverted sexual relations with the mother a dominant theme. In this form of insult interchange, as well as on other less ritualized occasions for joking, semi-serious, and serious mutual invective, a very high premium is placed on ingenuity, hair-trigger responsiveness, inventiveness, and the acute exercise of mental faculties.

Excitement. For many lower class individuals the rhythm of life fluctuates between periods of relatively routine or repetitive activity and sought situations of great emotional stimulation. Many of the most characteristic features of lower class life are related to the search for excitement or "thrill." Involved here are the highly prevalent use of alcohol by both sexes and the widespread use of gambling of all kinds—playing the numbers, betting on horse races, dice, cards. The quest for excitement finds what is perhaps its most vivid expression in the highly patterned practice of the recurrent "night on the town." This practice, designated by various terms in different areas ("honky-tonkin' "; "goin' out on the town"; "bar hoppin' "), involves a patterned set of activities in which alcohol, music, and sexual adventuring are major components. A group or individual sets out to "make the rounds" of various bars or night clubs. Drinking continues progressively throughout the evening. Men seek to "pick up" women, and women play the risky game of entertaining sexual advances. Fights between men involving women, gambling, and claims of physical prowess, in various combinations, are frequent consequences of a night of making the rounds. The explosive potential of this type of adventuring with sex and aggression, frequently leading to "trouble," is semi-explicitly sought by the individual. Since there is always a good likelihood that being out on the town will eventuate in fights, etc., the practice involves elements of sought risk and desired danger.

Counterbalancing the "flirting with danger" aspect of the "excitement" concern is the prevalence in lower class culture of other well established patterns of activity which involve long periods of relative inaction, or passivity. The term "hanging out" in lower class culture refers to extended periods of standing around, often with peer mates, doing what is defined as "nothing," "shooting the breeze," etc. A definite periodicity exists in the pattern of activity relating to the two aspects of the "excitement" dimension. For many lower class individuals the venture into the high risk world of alcohol, sex, and fighting occurs regularly once a week, with interim periods devoted to accommodating to possible consequences of these periods, along with recurrent resolves not to become so involved again.

Fate. Related to the quest for excitement is the concern with fate, fortune, or luck. Here also a distinction is made between two states—being "lucky" or "in luck," and being unlucky or jinxed. Many lower class individuals feel that their lives are subject to a set of forces over which they have relatively little control. These are not directly equated with the supernatural forces of formally organized religion, but relate more to a concept of "destiny," or man as a pawn of magical powers. Not infrequently this often implicit world view is associated with a conception of the ultimate futility of directed effort towards a goal: if the cards are right, or the dice good to you, or if your lucky number comes up, things will go your way; if luck is against you, it's not worth trying. The concept of performing semi-magical rituals so that one's "luck will change" is prevalent; one hopes that as a result he will move from the state of being "unlucky" to that of being "lucky." The element of fantasy plays an important part in this area. Related to and complementing the notion that "only suckers work" (smartness) is the idea that once things start going your way, relatively independent of your own effort, all good things will come to you. Achieving great material rewards (big cars, big houses, a roll of cash to flash in a fancy night club), valued in lower class as well as in other parts of American culture, is a recurrent theme in lower class fantasy and folk lore; the cocaine dreams of Willie the Weeper or Minnie the Moocher present the components of this fantasy in vivid detail.

The prevalence in the lower class community of many forms of gambling, mentioned in connection with the "excitement" dimension, is also relevant here. Through cards and pool which involve skill, and thus both "toughness" and "smartness"; or through race horse betting, involving "smartness"; or through playing the numbers, involving predominantly "luck," one may make a big killing with a minimum of directed and persistent effort within conventional occupational channels. Gambling in its many forms illustrates the fact that many of the persistent features of lower class culture are multi-functional—serving a range of desired ends at the same time. Describing some of the incentives behind gambling has involved mention of all of the focal concerns cited so far—Toughness, Smartness, and Excitement, in addition to Fate.

Autonomy. The extent and nature of control over the behavior of the individual—an important concern in most cultures—has a special significance and is distinctively patterned in lower class culture. The discrepancy between what is overtly valued and what is covertly sought is particularly striking in this area. On the overt level there is a strong and frequently expressed resentment of the idea of external controls, restrictions on behavior, and unjust or coercive authority. "No one's gonna push *me* around," or "I'm gonna tell him he can take the job and shove it. . . ." are commonly expressed sentiments. Similar explicit attitudes are maintained to systems of behavior-restricting rules, insofar as these are perceived as representing the injunctions, and bearing the sanctions of superordinate authority. In addition, in lower class culture a close conceptional connection is made between "authority" and "nurturance." To be restrictively or firmly controlled is to be cared for. Thus the overtly negative evaluation of superordinate authority frequently extends as well to nurturance, care, or protection. The desire for personal independence is often expressed in such terms as "I don't need *nobody* to take care of me. I can take care of myself!" Actual patterns of behavior, however, reveal a marked discrepancy between expressed sentiment and what is covertly valued. Many lower class people appear to seek out highly restrictive social environments wherein stringent external controls are maintained over their behavior. Such institutions as the armed forces, the mental hospital, the disciplinary school, the prison or correctional institution, provide environments which incorporate a strict and detailed set of rules defining and limiting behavior, and enforced by an authority system which controls and applies coercive sanctions for deviance from these rules. While under the jurisdiction of such systems, the lower class person generally expresses to his peers continual resentment of the coercive, unjust, and arbitrary exercise of authority. Having been released, or having escaped from these milieux, however, he will often act in such a way as to insure recommitment, or choose recommitment voluntarily after a temporary period of "freedom."

Lower class patients in mental hospitals will exercise considerable ingenuity to insure continued commitment while voicing the desire to get out; delinquent boys will frequently "run" from a correctional institution to activate efforts to return them; to be caught and returned means that one is cared for. Since "being controlled" is equated with "being cared for," attempts are frequently made to "test" the severity or strictness of superordinate authority to see if it remains firm. If intended or executed rebellion produces swift and firm punitive sanctions, the individual is reassured, at the same time that he is complaining bitterly at the injustice of being caught and punished. Some environmental milieux, having been tested in this fashion for the "firmness" of their coercive sanctions, are rejected, ostensibly for being too strict, actually for not being strict enough. This is frequently so in the case of "problematic" behavior by lower class youngsters in the public schools, which generally cannot command the coercive controls implicitly sought by the individual.

A similar discrepancy between what is overtly and covertly desired is found in the area of dependence-independence. The pose of tough rebellious independence often assumed by the lower class person frequently conceals powerful dependency cravings. These are manifested primarily by obliquely expressed resentment when "care" is not forthcoming rather than by expressed satisfaction when it is. The concern over autonomy-dependency is related both to "trouble" and "fate." Insofar as the lower class individual feels that his behavior is controlled by forces which often propel him into "trouble" in the face of an explicit determination to avoid it, there is an implied appeal to "save me from myself." A solution appears to lie in arranging things so that his behavior will be coercively restricted by an externally imposed set of controls strong enough to forcibly restrain his inexplicable inclination to get in trouble. The periodicity observed in connection with the "excitement" dimension is also relevant here; after involvement in trouble-producing behavior (assault, sexual adventure, a "drunk"), the individual will actively seek a locus of imposed control (his wife, prison, a restrictive job); after a given period of subjection to this control, resentment against it mounts, leading to a "break away" and a search for involvement in further "trouble."

FOCAL CONCERNS OF THE LOWER CLASS ADOLESCENT STREET CORNER GROUP

The one-sex peer group is a highly prevalent and significant structural form in the lower class community. There is a strong probability that the prevalence and stability of this type of unit is directly related to the prevalence of a stabilized type of lower class child-rearing unit—the "female-based" household. This is a nuclear kin unit in which a male parent is either absent from the household, present only sporadically, or, when present, only minimally or inconsistently involved in the support and rearing of children. This unit usually consists of one or more females of child-bearing age and their offspring. The females are frequently related to one another by blood or marriage ties, and the unit often includes two or more generations of women, e.g., the mother and/or aunt of the principal child-bearing female.

The nature of social groupings in the lower class community may be clarified if we make the assumption that it is the *one-sex peer unit* rather than the two-parent family unit which represents the most significant relational unit for both sexes in lower class communities. Lower class society may be pictured as comprising a set of age-graded one-sex groups which constitute the major psychic focus and reference group for those over twelve or thirteen. Men and women of mating age leave these groups periodically to form temporary marital alliances, but these lack stability, and after varying periods of "trying out" the two-sex family arrangement, gravitate back to the more "comfortable" one-sex grouping, whose members exert strong pressure on the individual *not* to disrupt the group by adopting a two-sex household pattern of life.[5] Membership in a stable and solidary peer unit is vital to the lower class individual precisely to the extent to which a range of essential functions—psychological, educational, and others, are not provided by the "family" unit.

The adolescent street corner group represents the adolescent variant of this lower class structural form. What has been called the "delinquent gang" is one subtype of this form, defined on

[5]Further data on the female-based household unit (estimated as comprising about 15 per cent of all American "families") and the role of one-sex groupings in lower class culture are contained in Walter B. Miller, "Implications of Urban Lower Class Culture for Social Work," *Social Service Review*, Vol. 33, No. 3 (1959).

the basis of frequency of participation in law-violating activity; this subtype should not be considered a legitimate unit of study per se, but rather as one particular variant of the adolescent street corner group. The "hanging" peer group is a unit of particular importance for the adolescent male. In many cases it is the most stable and solidary primary group he has ever belonged to; for boys reared in female-based households the corner group provides the first real opportunity to learn essential aspects of the male role in the context of peers facing similar problems of sex-role identification.

The form and functions of the adolescent corner group operate as a selective mechanism in recruiting members. The activity patterns of the group require a high level of intra-group solidarity; individual members must possess a good capacity for subordinating individual desires to general group interests as well as the capacity for intimate and persisting interaction. Thus highly "disturbed" individuals, or those who cannot tolerate consistently imposed sanctions on "deviant" behavior cannot remain accepted members; the group itself will extrude those whose behavior exceeds limits defined as "normal." This selective process produces a type of group whose members possess to an unusually high degree both the *capacity* and *motivation* to conform to perceived cultural norms, so that the nature of the system of norms and values oriented to is a particularly influential component of motivation.

Focal concerns of the male adolescent corner group are those of the general cultural milieu in which it functions. As would be expected, the relative weighting and importance of these concerns pattern somewhat differently for adolescents than for adults. The nature of this patterning centers around two additional "concerns" of particular importance to this group—concern with "belonging," and with "status." These may be conceptualized as being on a higher level of abstraction than concerns previously cited, since "status" and "belonging" are achieved *via* cited concern areas of Toughness, etc.

Belonging. Since the corner group fulfills essential functions for the individual, being a member in good standing of the group is of vital importance for its members. A continuing concern over who is "in" and who is not involves the citation and detailed discussion of highly refined criteria for "in-group" membership. The phrase "he hangs with us" means "he is accepted as a member in good standing by current consensus"; conversely, "he don't hang with us" means he is not so accepted. One achieves "belonging" primarily by demonstrating knowledge of and a determination to adhere to the system of standards and valued qualities defined by the group. One maintains membership by acting in conformity with valued aspects of Toughness, Smartness, Autonomy, etc. In those instances where conforming to norms of this reference group at the same time violates norms of other reference groups (e.g., middle class adults, institutional "officials"), immediate reference group norms are much more compelling since violation risks invoking the group's most powerful sanction: exclusion.

Status. In common with most adolescents in American society, the lower class corner group manifests a dominant concern with "status." What differentiates this type of group from others, however, is the particular set of criteria and weighting thereof by which "status" is defined. In general, status is achieved and maintained by demonstrated possession of the valued qualities of lower class culture—Toughness, Smartness, expressed resistance to authority, daring, etc. It is important to stress once more that the individual orients to these concerns *as they are defined within lower class society;* e.g., the status-conferring potential of "smartness" in the sense of scholastic achievement generally ranges from negligible to negative.

The concern with "status" is manifested in a variety of ways. Intragroup status is a continued concern, and is derived and tested constantly by means of a set of status-ranking activities; the intra-group "pecking order" is constantly at issue. One gains status within the group by demonstrated superiority in Toughness (physical prowess, bravery, skill in athletics and games such as pool and cards), Smartness (skill in repartee, capacity to "dupe" fellow group members), and the like. The term "ranking," used to refer to the pattern of intra-group aggressive repartee, indicates awareness of the fact that this is one device for establishing the intra-group status hierarchy.

The concern over status in the adolescent corner group involves in particular the component of "adultness," the intense desire to be seen as "grown up," and a corresponding aversion to "kid stuff." "Adult" status is defined less in terms of the assumption of "adult" responsibility than in terms of certain external symbols of adult status—a car, ready cash, and, in particular, a perceived "freedom" to drink, smoke, and gamble as one wishes and to come and go without external restrictions. The desire to be seen as "adult" is often a more significant component of much involvement in illegal drinking, gambling, and automobile driving than the explicit enjoyment of these acts as such.

The intensity of the corner group member's desire to be seen as "adult" is sufficiently great that he feels called upon to demonstrate qualities associated with adultness (Toughness, Smartness, Autonomy) to a much greater degree than a lower class adult. This means that he will seek out and utilize those avenues to these qualities which he perceives as available with greater intensity than an adult and less regard for their "legitimacy." In this sense the adolescent variant of lower class culture represents a maximization or an intensified manifestation of many of its most characteristic features.

Concern over status is also manifested in reference to other street corner groups. The term "rep" used in this regard is especially significant, and has broad connotations. In its most frequent and explicit connotation, "rep" refers to the "toughness" of the corner group as a whole relative to that of other groups; a "pecking order" also exists among the several corner groups in a given interactional area, and there is a common perception that the safety or security of the group and all its members depends on maintaining a solid "rep" for toughness vis-à-vis other groups. This motive is most frequently advanced as a reason for involvement in gang fights: "We *can't* chicken out on this fight; our rep would be shot!"; this implies that the group would be relegated to the bottom of the status ladder and become a helpless and recurrent target of external attack.

On the other hand, there is implicit in the concept of "rep" the recognition that "rep" has or may have a dual basis—corresponding to the two aspects of the "trouble" dimension. It is recognized that group as well as individual status can be based on both "law-abiding" and "law-violating" behavior. The situational resolution of the persisting conflict between the "law-abiding" and "law-violating" bases of status comprises a vital set of dynamics in determining whether a "delinquent" mode of behavior will be adopted by a group, under what circumstances, and how persistently. The determinants of this choice are evidently highly complex and fluid, and rest on a range of factors including the presence and perceptual immediacy of different community reference-group loci (e.g., professional criminals, police, clergy, teachers, settlement house workers), the personality structures and "needs" of group members, the presence in the community of social work, recreation, or educational programs which can facilitate utilization of the "law-abiding" basis of status, and so on.

What remains constant is the critical importance of "status" both for the members of the group as individuals and for the group as a whole insofar as members perceive their individual destinies as linked to the destiny of the group, and the fact that action geared to attain status is much more acutely oriented to the fact of status itself than to the legality or illegality, morality or immorality of the means used to achieve it.

LOWER CLASS CULTURE AND THE MOTIVATION OF DELINQUENT BEHAVIOR

The customary set of activities of the adolescent street corner group includes activities which are in violation of laws and ordinances of the legal code. Most of these center around assault and theft of various types (the gang fight; auto theft; assault on an individual; petty pilfering and shoplifting; "mugging"; pocketbook theft). Members of street corner gangs are well aware of the law-violating nature of these acts; they are not psychopaths, nor physically or mentally "defective"; in fact, since the corner group supports and enforces a rigorous set of standards which demand a high degree of fitness and personal competence, it tends to recruit from the most "able" members of the community.

Why, then, is the commission of crimes a customary feature of gang activity? The most general answer is that the commission of crimes by members of adolescent street corner groups is motivated primarily by the attempt to achieve ends, states, or conditions which are valued, and to avoid those that are disvalued within their most meaningful cultural milieu, through those culturally available avenues which appear as the most feasible means of attaining those ends.

The operation of these influences is well illustrated by the gang fight—a prevalent and characteristic type of corner group delinquency. This type of activity comprises a highly stylized and culturally patterned set of sequences. Although details vary under different circumstances, the following events are generally included. A member or several members of group A "trespass" on the claimed territory of group B. While there they commit an act or acts which group B defines as a violation of its rightful privileges, an affront to their honor, or a challenge to their "rep." Frequently this act involves advances to a girl associated with group B; it may occur at a dance or party; sometimes the mere act of "trespass" is seen as deliberate provocation. Members of group B then assault members of group A, if they are caught while still in B's territory. Assaulted members of group A return to their "home" territory and recount to members of their group details of the incident, stressing the insufficient nature of the provocation ("I just *looked* at her! Hardly even said anything!"), and the unfair circumstances of the assault ("About *twenty* guys jumped just the *two* of us!"). The highly colored account is acutely inflammatory; group A, perceiving its honor violated and its "rep" threatened, feels obligated to retaliate in force. Sessions of detailed planning now occur; allies are recruited if the size of group A and its potential allies appears to necessitate larger numbers; strategy is plotted, and messengers dispatched. Since the prospect of a gang fight is frightening to even the "toughest" group members, a constant rehearsal of the provocative incident or incidents and the essentially evil nature of the opponents accompanies the planning process to bolster possibly weakening motivation to fight. The excursion into "enemy" territory sometimes results in a full scale fight; more often group B cannot be found, or the police appear and stop the fight, "tipped off" by an anonymous informant. When this occurs, group members express disgust and disappointment; secretly there is much relief; their honor has been avenged without incurring injury; often the anonymous tipster is a member of one of the involved groups.

The basic elements of this type of delinquency are sufficiently stabilized and recurrent as to constitute an essentially ritualized pattern, resembling both in structure and expressed motives for action classic forms such as the European "duel," the American Indian tribal war, and the Celtic clan feud. Although the arousing and "acting out" of individual aggressive emotions are inevitably involved in the gang fight, neither its form nor motivational dynamics can be adequately handled within a predominantly personality-focused frame of reference.

It would be possible to develop in considerable detail the processes by which the commission of a range of illegal acts is either explicitly supported by, implicitly demanded by, or not materially inhibited by factors relating to the focal concerns of lower class culture. In place of such a development, the following three statements condense in general terms the operation of these processes:

1. *Following cultural practices which comprise essential elements of the total life pattern of lower class culture automatically violates certain legal norms.*
2. *In instances where alternate avenues to similar objectives are available, the non-law-abiding avenue frequently provides a relatively greater and more immediate return for a relatively smaller investment of energy.*
3. *The "demanded" response to certain situations recurrently engendered within lower class culture involves the commission of illegal acts.*

The primary thesis of this paper is that the dominant component of the motivation of "delinquent" behavior engaged in by members of lower class corner groups involves a positive effort to achieve states, conditions, or qualities valued within the actor's most significant cultural milieu. If "conformity to immediate reference group values" is the major component of motivation of "delinquent" behavior by gang members, why is such behavior frequently referred to as negativistic, malicious, or rebellious? Albert Cohen, for example, in *Delinquent Boys* (Glencoe: Free Press, 1955) describes behavior which violates school rules as comprising elements of "active spite and malice, contempt and ridicule, challenge and defiance." He ascribes to the gang "keen delight in terrorizing 'good' children, and in general making themselves obnoxious to the virtuous." A recent national conference on social work with "hard-to-reach" groups characterized lower class corner groups as "youth groups in conflict with the culture of their *(sic)* communities." Such characterizations are obviously the result of taking the middle class community and its institutions as an implicit point of reference.

A large body of systematically interrelated attitudes, practices, behaviors, and values characteristic of lower class culture are designed to support and maintain the basic features of the lower class way of life. In areas where these differ from features of middle class culture, action oriented to the achievement and maintenance of the lower class system may violate norms of middle class culture and be perceived as deliberately non-conforming or malicious by an observer strongly cathected to middle class norms. This does not mean, however, that violation of the middle class norm is the dominant component of motivation; it is a by-product of action primarily oriented to the lower class system. The standards of lower class culture cannot be seen merely as a reverse function of middle class culture—as middle class standards "turned upside down"; lower class culture is a distinctive tradition many centuries old with an integrity of its own.

From the viewpoint of the acting individual, functioning within a field of well-structured cultural forces, the relative impact of "conforming" and "rejective" elements in the motivation of gang delinquency is weighted preponderantly on the conforming side. Rejective or rebellious elements are inevitably involved, but their influence during the actual commission of delinquent acts is relatively small compared to the influence of pressures to achieve what is valued by the actor's most immediate reference groups. Expressed awareness by the actor of the element of rebellion often represents only that aspect of motivation of which he is explicitly conscious; the deepest and most compelling components of motivation—adherence to highly meaningful group standards of Toughness, Smartness, Excitement, etc.—are often unconsciously patterned. No cultural pattern as well-established as the practice of illegal acts by members of lower class corner groups could persist if buttressed primarily by negative, hostile, or rejective motives; its principal motivational support, as in the case of any persisting cultural tradition, derives from a positive effort to achieve what is valued within that tradition, and to conform to its explicit and implicit norms.

41.

Joseph W. Scott and
Edmund W. Vaz

A PERSPECTIVE ON MIDDLE-CLASS DELINQUENCY

Most literature on juvenile delinquency describes it as essentially a product of the lower socio-economic classes. While there has been some speculation over the incidence and quality of middle-class delinquency, what evidence exists is largely impressionistic. Nevertheless, the prevailing view is that delinquency among middle-class youth has increased in recent years. The present paper seeks a sociological and theoretical perspective to help account for the dominant forms of juvenile delinquency among middle-class youth. It attempts also to explain the emergence and the particular qualities of middle-class delinquency as a consequence of structural changes taking place in the larger society.

Accounting for middle-class delinquency in North America requires an understanding of the dominant culture of middle-class youth. Structural changes in society over the last half-century have produced opportunities for extensive adolescent peer-group participation and the emergence of a mass youth culture. During the growth of this youth culture, in which the majority of middle-class teenagers participate, there have emerged, jointly, both delinquent and non-delinquent patterns of behaviour. It is the thesis of this paper that the bulk of middle-class delinquency occurs in the course of *customary, non-delinquent* activities and falls within the limits of adolescent group norms. Moreover the knowledge of both delinquent and non-delinquent patterns in the youth culture is widely shared among middle-class teenagers. Thus, in order to account for middle-class delinquency one need not look for a separate "delinquent subculture."

Source: *The Canadian Journal of Economics and Political Science,* Vol. 29, No. 3 (August, 1963), pp. 324–35. Reprinted by permission of the authors and the journal.

Any explanation of the emergence and growth of the contemporary middle-class youth culture must first consider the changes which have occurred in society over the past seventy-five years. The social and economic structure has undergone vast transformation. The first half of the period was an era of rapid expansion, of untempered competition, with increasing opportunities for the accumulation of wealth, vertical mobility, and employment based on technical skills. The economy had an almost limitless capacity for absorbing unskilled and semi-skilled labour, and it was viewed as a mine of opportunities and rewards for men of "good character." David Riesman has suggested that the old middle class was ideologically equipped to exploit such opportunities.[1] Imbued with the importance of integrity, self-discipline, and hard work, and the conviction that what it was doing was morally right, it possessed the resiliency and enterprise necessary for confronting and overcoming the challenges of the economy. It can truthfully be said to have striven with self-reliant and dedicated individualism.

To inculcate the energy, determination, and moral fortitude to meet the widening frontier of economic and occupational opportunity, considerable attention was given in the home to the formal character training of children. It soon became an integral part of the education of the child, and parental demands for conformity at this time were for "characterological fitness and self-discipline." At the same time, because of their diligence and effort at work, fathers often cut themselves off from friends and family. Indeed the middle-class father, instilled with industry and frugality, was preoccupied with production, self-help, and the "character-

[1] David Riesman, Nathan Glazer, and Reuel Denney, *The Lonely Crowd* (New York, 1955), pp. 30 ff.

conditioned need to test and discipline himself." For these reasons he was largely incapable of casual relationships even with his own children. However, with the expansion of the occupational structure, the father's absorption in his work pointed up clear-cut goals for his children; thus they were not only motivated, but also shown the way to get ahead.

While parents emphasized the "building" of character and moral principles in the upbringing of their children, the formal educational system concentrated upon the teaching of ideas and the disciplined pursuit of learning. As Riesman writes, this procedure "affirms to the child that what matters is what he can *accomplish* and not how nice is his smile or how cooperative his attitude."[2] Formal education was prized and the significance of university training was reflected in hours of rigorous self-application. In school the teacher held undisputed authority, discipline was harsh, and scholarship was encouraged. The whole system neatly fitted the child for the emerging needs of a growing economy.

Home life precluded the development of extensive peer-group relationships. Parental emphasis upon ambition and achievement, and character-forming behaviour patterns such as "saving for college" and "working after school," modelled after parental patterns of "hard work and hard saving," served to keep middle-class youth occupied, indoors, and off the streets. Playmates were usually brothers and sisters. Peer-group associations were time-consuming and often costly, and middle-class youth were disinclined to waste either time or money.

It seems clear that on all fronts the middle-class boy was prevented from forming a "street-corner society." His diurnal round of activities, his duties in the home, his role as student and the expectations associated with it, besides the consumption of his time, all tended to divert him from peer-group affiliations. Such activities as "vandalism," gambling, widespread drinking, "partying," and sex activities on a large scale would have conflicted with his daily routine.

After the First World War the American economy underwent significant change. Of great importance was the growth of technology and technological efficiency. Coupled with a declining demand for unskilled and semi-skilled labour was a decline in the number of proprietors, and the massive centralization of industry. More and more people were corralled into large-scale organizations. C. Wright Mills writes: "In 1939, 1 per cent of all firms in the country—27,000 giants—engaged over half of all the people working in business."[3] This structural upheaval severely restricted upward mobility for the lower-placed worker. With an increase in life expectancy and a decrease in the birth rate, the population pyramid soon showed an increase of persons in the productive years of life. Furthermore, the levelling of income and social resources favoured the mass production of educated and specialized personnel for the labour market. Concomitantly industry could afford to become highly selective in its choice of personnel[4] which meant that the criteria for recruitment and promotion underwent change, and factors other than technical expertise became crucial. William H. Whyte quotes excerpts from his research: "We used to look primarily for brilliance," said one president. "Now . . . we don't care if you're a Phi Beta Kappa or a Tau Beta Phi. We want a well-rounded person who can handle well-rounded people."[5] Thus conformity to the norms of the Protestant ethic became impracticable and gave way to the structurally generated social skills and social values of a new morality—the social ethic.

Under changing social and economic conditions there occurred, also, a gradual transformation in the make-up of the nuclear family, family patterns, and child-rearing practices. The traditional, patriarchically-controlled family soon gave way to the more "democratic" unit in which parents and children shared in the decision-making process. Standards guiding parent-child relationships became blurred, and the family atmosphere became increasingly "permissive." In contrast to the acquisition of technical skills and ethical values for the

[2]*Ibid.*, p. 79.

[3]C. Wright Mills, *White Collar* (New York, 1956), p. 24.

[4]See William H. Whyte, Jr., *The Organization Man* (New York, 1957).

[5]*Ibid.*, p. 150.

achievement of goals, the institutionalized means for "getting ahead" and for gaining prestige are, under such circumstances, elusive, subtle, and difficult to teach. "The loss of old certainties in the spheres of work and social relations is accompanied by doubt as to how to bring up children."[6] Under such circumstances parents can hardly be expected to instruct their offspring in the adolescent role. Thus, the definition of the adolescent role is vague, and standards of behaviour, moral prescriptions, and the traditional distinctions between right and wrong are necessarily soft-pedalled.[7]

The school, meanwhile, has not remained unchanged. The new requirements of corporate business and industry have made themselves felt. The hallmarks of the modern educational process are "group adjustment," success, and controlled individuality. Moreover, there has been a shift in power from teachers to pupils, a move in the direction of adult deference to the inclinations and interests of the pupils.[8] Gradually, "the school . . . begins to parallel the career pattern of the adult, particularly that of the male, in that it now absorbs more and more of the personality of the child."[9] This change in focus of the school has been noted by Seeley in the study of Crestwood Heights: "The educational system of Crestwood Heights is becoming, to a greater and greater degree, responsible for the successful 'adjustment' of the child, as a person, to the culture in which he lives."[10] The school, in socializing the "whole" child, neatly prepares him to meet the newly developing requirements of large-scale business and industry. In emphasizing the "socially adjusted," effective personality, the contemporary school system satisfies the "Organization's" needs for a "well-rounded person who can handle well-rounded people."

Under such circumstances the school becomes noticeably more "permissive," fixed standards of performance are abandoned on the grounds that they "straitjacket the child," and the whole learning experience, slowly but ineluctably, becomes a "painless process."[11] With drastically relaxed academic expectations, schoolwork for the teenager becomes routine, and, since household chores have become minimal, the middle-class adolescent has little work to absorb his time throughout the day or evening. With leisure time, peers become available and the emergence of peer-groups possible. In fact, there gradually emerges a middle-class street-corner society. The teenager, reared witness to the daily significance of social standing and the peer-group mentality of the parents, is also peer-group oriented. Furthermore, parental emphasis on group-belonging soon becomes a moral imperative, and prevailing teaching encourages dependence on adolescent peer-group affiliation for social prestige and recognition.[12]

The adolescent conspicuously lacks an exact definition of the expectations and obligations attached to his role in society and he is left to define for himself what is "right" conduct. However, the peer-group begins to exercise an inexorable influence upon the teenager and to substitute for the ambiguity in family relationships. But the peer-group cannot state explicitly what "ought to be," that is, what the content of the general normative system is, and each individual must learn to conform to whatever behaviour patterns happen to prevail. In contrast to an earlier era of individual initiative, there is now little justification for non-conformity, and the violation of group norms becomes a serious offence.

To understand the development and maintenance of the middle-class youth culture it is necessary to examine the functions of the contemporary high school. In a rapidly changing, highly industrialized society like ours, the high school has become the principal social setting for a system of informal relationships and a fabric of social norms which help knit teenagers together. Besides providing the opportunity for formal learning, the modern high school acts as

[6]Riesman *et al., op. cit.*, p. 67.

[7]Edgar Z. Friedenberg, *The Vanishing Adolescent* (Boston, 1959), pp. 1–38.

[8]Albert K. Cohen, "Teachers vs. Students: Changing Power Relations in the Secondary Schools." A public lecture at the University of California, Berkeley, Aug. 22, 1961. See also Whyte, *op. cit.*, pp. 425 ff.

[9]John R. Seeley, R. Alexander Sim, and Elizabeth W. Loosley, *Crestwood Heights* (Toronto, 1956), p. 236.

[10]*Ibid.*, p. 245.

[11]Whyte, *op. cit.*, p. 426.

[12]*Ibid.*, p. 434. See also Seeley, *op. cit.*, p. 116.

a central agency in the socialization process, and in the informal distribution of satisfactions for the teenager. The setting apart of adolescents in schools (which constantly take on more functions, more extracurricular activities) for an ever-increasing period of training has a singular impact on a youth.[13] He is divorced from the remainder of society, and more or less compelled to carry out his whole social life with others of his own age, that is, within his peer-group.

It is within the peer-group that the teenager first feels his independence, tries out new ideas, and shares secret emotions. Here, for example, he can pry and probe with impunity into the much tabooed secrets of sex while the nagging, if uncertain, intervention of adults is absent. So important is the peer-group for the middle-class teenager that his success and failure in the classroom cannot be explained irrespective of his peer-group affiliations.[14] Conformity to peer-group norms is rigidly required, and the norms decry scholastic effort. Thus, nowadays, it is almost a commonplace that there is in the schoolroom restriction of scholastic output.[15] The old refrain, "I never crack a book," and the opprobrium attached to the "damned average raiser" are classic testimony to the informal system in operation.

It is abundantly clear that peer-group attachment confers social approbation on the teenager and gives notice (to peers and parents alike) that the teenager is socially adjusted. Thus Coleman writes, "even the rewards a child gains from his parents may help reinforce the values of the adolescent culture . . . because parents want their children to be successful and esteemed by their peers."[16] More significant, however, is the increase in social status derived from conformity to peer-group expectations. Peer-group membership offers the adolescent access to teenage parties, "high-ranking" girls, "big dates," the latest style, esteemed events, and other "social objects." Conversely the student who persists in conforming to other standards, through concern for studies and good grades, is seldom sought after by the opposite sex. In the contemporary high school it is the "active" student, the boy or girl who engages in social affairs, extra-curricular activities, and athletics, who ranks highest within the adolescent culture and, often, among the teachers as well.

It is precisely because they symbolize membership and prestige in the peer groups that such events and activities as parties, dances, dates, and "socials" become especially instrumental for the middle-class teenager. In familiar fashion, an increase in prestige elicits greater social approval from the group which, in turn, evokes further status-rewarding opportunities, activities, and relationships within the youth culture. Moreover, because teenage participation in social activities is rewarded, conformity to peer-group expectations assures a stable group status. Under these conditions deviance becomes costly and cannot be tolerated since it might result in the loss of social honour and the downfall of the group. The maintenance of social status depends, therefore, upon the continuation of conformity to group norms and expectations.

MIDDLE-CLASS DELINQUENCY[17]

While adolescent conduct within the middle-class youth culture seems to be infinite in variety, dominant themes include "joy-riding," "drag-racing," "partying" (which means late hours), drinking, gambling, and variations of sex behaviour. Such activities usually involve both sexes and present adolescents with the opportunity for status gain and social success among their peers. If such behaviour were altogether

[13]James S. Coleman, *Social Climates in High Schools* (Washington: U.S. Department of Health, Education, and Welfare, 1961), pp. 3 ff.

[14]James S. Coleman, "Academic Achievement and the Structure of Competition," *Harvard Educational Review,* Vol. XXIX (Fall, 1959), pp. 339-51.

[15]See James S. Coleman, *The Adolescent Society* (Glencoe, Ill., 1961), pp. 244 ff.

[16]*Ibid.,* p. 34.

[17]For some recent alternative views on middle-class delinquency, see Robert H. Bohlke, "Social Mobility, Stratification Inconsistency and Middle Class Delinquency," *Social Problems,* Vol. VIII, No. 4 (Spring, 1961); Albert K. Cohen, *Delinquent Boys* (Glencoe, Ill., 1955); Albert K. Cohen, "Middle-Class Delinquency and the Social Structure," a paper read at the annual meeting of the American Sociological Society, 1957; Albert K. Cohen and James Short, "Research in Delinquent Subcultures," *Social Issues,* Vol. XIV, No. 3 (1958).

unacceptable to the group, adolescents would be unlikely to participate for fear of lowering the group's status. In fact, however, teenagers who engage in these activities are neither rebuked for their acts nor especially condemned by the group.

Since conformity is the keynote within the youth culture, the question of change and cultural variation arises. From our perspective delinquent behaviour evolves from such non-delinquent, legitimate activities as dating, parties, dances, and possession of an automobile, within the adolescent youth culture. We have already noted the gradual transformation—the democratization of family relations, the ambiguity in traditional distinctions between right and wrong, and the concomitant undermining of parental authority and teaching—in the make-up of the nuclear family. We have also suggested that parental behaviour indicates the need to acquire social skills and competence and the importance of the responses of others in determining one's behaviour. Under these circumstances "operating inventions"[18] (behavioural innovation) among adolescents become probable. Indeed the pursuit of scarce desired goals among adolescents makes innovation likely, since it is socially rewarded so long as it meets the expectations and demands of peer-group members. And it is precisely because peer-group expectations *are* middle-class that innovating behaviour must not transgress the adolescent, middle-class value system. Thus, whatever deviation emerges must not jeopardize group status, and is tolerated by group members only within the limits of socially acceptable youth culture activities. So we find that violence, armed robbery, and the carrying of lethal weapons fall outside the prescribed boundaries, but "joy-riding," drunkenness, and sexual intercourse are variations on conduct patterns which fall within the limits.

In the course of legitimate, everyday activities and relationships within the middle-class youth culture, "veiled competition" for status leads to varying efforts at innovation. Such innovation covers a wide range of exploratory acts and is likely to be tentative, uncertain, and ambiguous. Yet because there is "mutual exploration and joint elaboration" of behaviour among adolescents, such small, almost unobtrusive, acts gradually lead to unanticipated elaboration beyond the limits of legitimacy—into the realm of delinquency and the illegitimate. But since each succeeding exploratory act is so small an increment to the previously acceptable pattern, at no stage in the process need the behaviour be perceived as "delinquent."[19] Once these patterns develop and are socially rewarded they generate their own morality, norms, standards, and rewards. It is in this manner that delinquent behaviour gradually emerges from socially acceptable, non-delinquent, activities among adolescents within the middle-class youth culture.

At this point we address ourselves to some of the socially acceptable activities among middle-class adolescents and attempt to show how delinquent behaviour arises from respectable behaviour.

In the larger middle-class society the party is a prominent, socially structured situation for learning particular attitudes and forms of behaviour. Similarly, within the youth culture the party is a group event where the learning and transmission of conduct patterns occur. Such behaviour habitually is first taught in the home where, at an early age, the child is introduced to the vignettes of culturally approved conduct. By acting as "junior host" and "helping out" at adult gatherings the youngster soon learns the appropriate behaviour, skills, and demeanour for such occasions. At the same time he also learns the "party games," and the "party drinks" which are served at such times. With the added significance given adolescent participation in social activities, the increase in adolescent prerogative, and the tacit approval given to "having a taste" or "spiking" the party punch, drinking becomes acceptable. The phrase, "a glass of beer won't hurt him," reflects the approval given by parents to teenage drinking in the home on special occasions. As the drinking pattern develops among adolescents it generates its own morality, its special game rules, standards, and its particular

[18]Robert Dubin, "Deviant Behaviour and Social Structure: Continuities in Social Theory," *American Sociological Review*, Vol. XXIV (April, 1959), p. 152.

[19]The basic idea is taken from Cohen, *op. cit.*, p. 60.

rewards. Among older adolescents, informal drinking bouts to test one's capacity for alcoholic beverages are certainly not alien to the youth culture. Indeed the approval given to the adolescent who can "hold his liquor" follows adult lines, and reflects such practices and games among middle-class teenagers. And adolescent intoxication is not altogether disapproved since it simply represents an unsuccessful attempt to conform to the rules of the game.

The possession of an automobile is one of the crowning symbols of distinction among teenagers. It is a core cultural element and gives meaning to social events and practices integral to the youth culture. "Without a car a boy must be chauffeured to movies, sports events, and—most embarrassing of all—to dates."[20] Highly visible, easily presented, the automobile is a unique means of self-distinction and an extension of one's self-image. Indeed the possession of a car is often the accolade of social status among both male and female teenagers. While changes in clothing styles among adolescents often mirror changes in self-conception and the silent struggle for status,[21] so too, the presentation of car and its manipulation along the highway undergo change. Here behavioural innovation varies from the initial efforts at "dressing" the automobile to sporting "duals or Hollywood mufflers," "joy-riding,"[22] "drag-racing," and ultimately, to "playing chicken" at a hundred miles an hour. This form of marginal differentiation reflects the effort for prestige among such adolescents. While some of the practices are functionally related to the masculine, middle-class value of courage and "daring," others are linked to the equally important value of possessing a "social personality." Such conspicuous, yet limited, innovation is significant evidence of the "antagonistic co-operation" for social recognition among middle-class adolescents.

That dating is a socially rewarding activity in the middle-class youth culture cannot be gainsaid. Moreover, dating and varying degrees of "friendship" between sexes are encouraged by parents and teachers alike as respectable, "healthy," "normal" activities for adolescents. Furthermore, restricted forms of physical contact between sexes are approved. Thus, holding hands, dancing, good-night kisses and, under certain conditions such as "going steady," initial stages of "necking" are condoned as indications of "social maturity," and part of "growing up."

Delinquent sex behavior among middle-class adolescents emerges from culturally approved activity, and can be explained as a variation on the encouraged patterns of dating. In this regard girls face a dilemma in having to use sex appeal and glamour as the chief way of attracting and holding the opposite sex, yet simultaneously endeavouring to maintain their reputation. In the absence of firmly established moral rules and clearly defined role patterns, rules and norms develop in the course of resolving the dilemma which help govern the sex game among adolescents. The value of these game rules is illuminated by Coleman's remarks: "In very early adolescence, before courtship has begun in earnest, kisses flow freely at party games. They have not yet become currency in the competition for status and control. Later, the girls who once played post office with abandon now dispense their kisses much more strategically."[23] No less than in other areas, innovating and exploratory behaviour emerges from the dating relationship. Under these conditions it is likely that succeeding degrees of physical intimacy can be correlated with succeeding stages in the "romantic" attachment. For each stage there may come to exist a corresponding normative expectation of physical intimacy. If the good-night kiss is correlated with the "first date," "going steady" may be expected to result in efforts at sexual intercourse. Moreover, whatever factors tip the scales in favour or rejection of sexual intercourse

---

[20]Coleman, *op. cit.*, p. 23.

[21]C. Wayne Gordon, *The Social System of the High School* (Glencoe, Ill., 1957), pp. 119–22.

[22]Some of the terms used by middle-class adolescents seem to serve as a convenient technique of immunization actually inhibiting the development of a delinquent self-conception. The innocuous term "joy-riding" seems simply to define the use to which the car is put and mirror the motives of the boys. Furthermore, the automobile offers multiple functionally related services for the middle-class adolescent. A status symbol, it enhances the success of dating and also presents easily taken opportunities for engaging in sex behaviour.

[23]Coleman, *op. cit.*, p. 121.

among adolescents must also be normatively influenced. The give-and-take between sexes, the degree of intimacy, types of kissing, the extent of physical contact and, eventually, the sex act gradually become circumscribed by game rules.

While both boys and girls engage in the dominant behaviour patterns and activities in the youth culture, in the daily course of events there are recurrent situations in which only boys participate. Here rules and forms of social control applicable only to boys are likely to develop and different role-expectations and behavioural configurations emerge. Yet the veiled quest for social recognition is no less important. Here we should expect behavioural innovation to take another form, conceivably of less "sophisticated," more "masculine" quality. Thus, groups of boys "hanging about" at night, returning from a football match, or simply wasting time "roughhousing," often engage in acts of destruction such as "stomping" on the hoods and roofs of automobiles, letting air from tires, ripping antennae from automobiles, and breaking streetlights. However, "muggings," "rolling drunks," and "breaking and entering" rarely occur among middle-class boys. Such behaviour of a violent nature usually undertaken to steal money reflects values foreign to the middle-class culture. This type of activity is noticeably absent from the daily routine of middle-class teenagers, and roundly condemned within the middle-class youth culture.

The learning of delinquent behaviour is an insufficient condition to insure its performance. There must be an opportunity to carry out the learned activity. That is, the structure of opportunity—the particular form of social organization—must support the actual role performance.[24] In this case it is the opportunity structure for *legitimate* behaviour which is necessary for the performance of illegitimate, disapproved conduct.

If the daily round of activities of middle-class adolescents includes delinquent patterns of behaviour, the more a middle-class adolescent is immersed in the youth culture the more likely he is to become involved in juvenile delinquency. Some adolescents will have greater opportunities for delinquency than others. The question now is: under what circumstances is the middle-class teenager most likely to become involved in delinquent behaviour?

One condition for delinquent conduct among middle-class adolescents is access to the requisite physical objects for participating in the teenage youth culture. We have suggested that prominent behaviour patterns among middle-class teenagers spotlight such "things" as the possession of a car, accessibility to teenage girls, alcoholic beverages, pocket money, the latest style, and so forth. Therefore, access to one or all of these "social objects" is extremely important for participation in the middle-class adolescent culture. Indeed it is difficult to conceive of an adolescent's becoming part of the middle-class teenage crowd if he has neither control over nor access to some of these "objects." For example, dating is a highly valued experience within the youth culture, and the possession of an automobile is a symbol of social rank; thus the youth who owns or has access to a car has an obvious advantage in dating. To the extent that the means of participation in teenage activities are not equally available to all, participation in the youth culture and involvement in juvenile delinquency will likely be unevenly distributed.

A second contingency is a receptive attitude towards youth cultural activities on the part of the individual adolescent. Since participation in the prevailing network of legitimate activities within the youth culture results in favourable responses from his peers, the adolescent will likely derive social and emotional satisfaction from it, and define it as "normal" or as "having fun." But what aspect of participation he stresses is important. Thus we find that some teenagers believe that "stirring up a little excitement"[25] is crucial for participation in the teenage crowd. Others accept the car as the only "right" way to be "in with the crowd." Physical attractiveness, "personality" characteristics, and athletics are also significant for success in the middle-class youth culture. So also,

[24] Richard A. Cloward and Lloyd W. Ohlin, *New Perspectives on Juvenile Delinquency* (New York: Columbia University School of Social Work, 1959), mimeo.

[25] Coleman, *op. cit.*, p. 124.

for others, are "sociability," or sex activity with girls, or money, or clothes, or a "flashy appeal." In brief, to the degree that an adolescent favours all or various combinations of such characteristics and activities as means of participating in the youth culture he is likely to become involved in delinquent behaviour.

The social organization and "cultural flavour" of the "big city" differ greatly from the semi-rural and "main street" atmosphere of the small town. The presence of night-clubs, jazz-dens, "bohemian" coffee-houses, bars, "artistic" restaurants, theatres and the like in a metropolis serve as organized opportunities for middle-class adolescents to engage in a wide variety of "sophisticated" and novel behaviour with members of the opposite sex. If a teenager resides in a rural area, his choice of activities will be restricted.

Finally, the price for non-participation in the contemporary youth culture is likely to be inordinately high for the average middle-class adolescent. Today it is not easy, if it is possible at all, to shrug off the responses of others and the judgements and respect of our peers and schoolmates. Hence Gordon tells us that "an 'isolate' views her lack of clique membership as the major failure of her high school career."[26] Is it any wonder, then, that the teenager who is in a social setting where he must engage in youth culture events or else lose access to desirable, satisfying experiences, will have little choice but to act in a delinquent manner if such opportunities arise in the *routine* course of events?

If we are correct, the opportunities which exist for the middle-class adolescent to engage in legitimate, approved activities will greatly influence the probability of his becoming involved in illegitimate, disapproved behaviour. Easy access to the means for participation in the youth culture, highly desirable physical and "personality" qualities, the appropriate psychological definition of youth culture activities, residence in or near a metropolitan area, and active participation in the middle-class youth culture—all are important conditions determining the opportunities for the individual adolescent to engage in middle-class delinquency.

INTEGRATION AND STABILITY OF THE YOUTH CULTURE

As the emerging network of contacts and relationships becomes established over time, culturally approved patterns of behaviour and norms arise, the youth culture takes shape, and tends to persist irrespective of the initial forces giving rise to it. Although the variables "causing" its appearance remain and help maintain the cultural system in operation, other variables are recognizable which contribute to its stability.

By continuously pointing up the importance of internal group relations and morale, the adult community alerts the adolescent to the significance of peer-group membership and conformity to youth culture activities. The schools have been quick to underline conformity and adjustment to the peer-group as characteristics of adolescent growth. With heavy emphasis on the pragmatic and the social, the concept of "adjustment" soon becomes the over-arching criterion in evaluating the student's maturity. More specifically, profound parent-teacher concern over teenagers who do not "mix with the others" imposes on adolescents the moral obligation to engage in youth culture events. Under such circumstances, "the child who tends to be withdrawn is given special attention."[27] Furthermore, the deeply felt importance of sustaining "high morale" among "our children" underscores the necessity of peer-group association.

In a limited, yet significant, way the adult community creates structured opportunities for adolescents to engage in youth culture activities, that is, in "wholesome" recreation. Organized dances, high school "formals" and informal "hops," church "socials," and athletic events reflect this structural link between the youth culture and the adult community, and reveal especially cherished values and expectations sustained by adults.

The age-sex roles of adolescents are equally

[26]Gordon, *op. cit.*, pp. 113–14.

[27]Whyte, *op. cit.*, p. 425.

important for understanding the increasing stability and permanence of the middle-class youth culture. Adult expectations of middle-class teenage behaviour involve a growing concern for contact and interaction with members of the opposite sex. At a very early age a network of organized events begins to surround the child, activities *formerly* associated with an older age group. Dating, parties, dances, "socials," and kissing games begin at eleven or twelve years of age, and sometimes earlier. While parents might not always approve of all such activities, they are nevertheless "committed to the notion that both sexes should learn to adjust to each other by boy-girl participation" in social activities.[28] Indeed, in pre-teen years, steps are taken to develop in the child qualities which are considered prerequisite for social success later on. Once adolescence has been reached, increased participation in dating and other social events involving both sexes and the use of "dad's car" are culturally recommended. With the increase in leisure time and the greater possibility of spending this time together, stable conduct patterns among adolescents become entrenched. In this way adolescent adaptation to structured, age-graded expectations is a major contributory link towards increased stability of the middle-class youth culture.

The conditions which give rise to the adolescent youth culture are typically urban and most teenagers in metropolitan areas are exposed to the youth culture. Merely by association with the multiplicity of cultural sources and social groups, middle-class youngsters, at an early age, become influenced by, sensitive to, and later recruited into the adolescent youth culture. For example, teenagers have become increasingly active consumers. The increased spending power of the teenager over the past fifty years or so is likely to govern the nature, organization and prosperity of certain types of small and large businesses. Furthermore, the teenage youth culture has contributed to the birth and popularity of a variety of new occupations and associations in society, such as counseling and guidance officers, recreation "leaders," "disc jockeys," and "Little League" sports. This widespread transformation has made the youth culture conspicuously important and a full-fledged institution of the society. It has become an approved and encouraged segment of the community and cannot escape the recognition of the mass media of communication. The popularity of the adolescent market, and the dissemination of information about the teenage youth culture, publicize its existence and call the attention of the adolescent community to the prominence and rewards of membership therein.

A major implication of this paper is that a special set of motives need not be recruited to explain delinquent behaviour within the middle-class youth culture. At no time does the middle-class teenager turn from legitimate to illegitimate means in order to attain his ends. In terms of a means-end schema, this can only make sense if there has been neither a rejection of cultural goals nor frustration in the employment of legitimate means. The seeds of middle-class delinquency reside in the prominent, culturally esteemed patterns themselves. Therefore, delinquent behaviour can best be understood through knowledge of the structure and content of the *legitimate* youth culture and its structural connections to the community within the larger historical transformation taking place.

---

[28]Seeley, *op. cit.*, p. 99.

CHAPTER XII

Civil Disorders

OVER THE PAST SEVERAL YEARS, the United States has been afflicted by a considerable amount of social unrest and civil disorder. Members of various minority groups led by both militant and nonmilitant leaders have protested their conditions in several of our major cities. Watts, Harlem, Newark, and Detroit are only a few of the metropolitan areas that have been hard hit. Perhaps the most important question one might ask is why? Why is it happening today? To answer this question properly we must carefully examine the nature of our society. We are living amidst great material abundance. The gross national product is at an all-time high, consumer goods are being produced by the millions—yet several minority groups, Blacks in particular, have not even approached the minimal standards of living most middle-class Americans would accept for themselves. These people are tired of being treated as second-class citizens and are now making the demands heard that they have carried with them for generations. They have reached their breaking point and will no longer tolerate the fact that they were pushed into a restricted economic and social corner of society and expected to remain there.

The other part of the civil disorder picture concerns the activities of groups opposed to the war in Viet Nam and U.S. intervention in the domestic affairs of other nations; groups in favor of more academic freedom and a greater student voice in the administration of our colleges and universities; others who are throwing their support to one political candidate and rejecting another; and still more who are concerned with the civil rights issue, open housing, and countless other causes. For the most part they are young people between the ages of 18 and 30. Some are hippies, yippies, and beats, while others are average Ivy League or Midwest college students who simply have taken an interest and are fighting for a cause.

The articles selected for this chapter deal with the major problem areas producing civil disorder in our country today. In the first selection, Lee Rainwater writes an open letter on white justice and the riots. Dr. Rainwater discusses the nature of riots, causes, and incidents growing out of a riot. He examines the police problem, our caste system, Negro deprivation, and the lack of understanding. The second article was taken from the *Report* of the National Advisory Commission on Civil Disorders and deals with the relationship between the news media and the disorders. The basic question asked was "What effect do the mass media have on the riots?" In this report emphasis was placed on the nature of news reporting during their coverage of the civil disorders in the summer of 1967. In relation to television and newspaper reporting questions were answered regarding accuracy of the coverage, ghetto reactions to the mass media, and conduct of press representatives. The next reading was taken from the report submitted by Daniel Walker, Director of the Chicago Study Team, to the National Commission on the Causes and Prevention of Violence. The report concerns itself with the disturbances that took place during the 1968 Democratic National Convention in Chicago. Mr. Walker concentrates on the actions and reactions of the demonstrators and the police in an attempt to get to the root of the problem. What took place at this convention may have an impact on American politics for several years to come, thus it is most important that we understand the behavior of all participants. For the final selection I have turned to the Report of the Fact-Finding Commission Appointed to Investigate the Disturbances at Columbia University in April and May, 1968. The authors identify the general characteristics of the present generation of university students along with their attitudes and concerns. Columbia is but one of several great American universities where disturbances have occurred. Even though the specific problems may differ, the major issues have a good deal in common.

42.

Lee Rainwater

OPEN LETTER ON WHITE JUSTICE AND THE RIOTS

A great deal of the difficulty in understanding what causes riots and what might be done about them comes from a misunderstanding of exactly what their nature is. A riot seems almost always to begin with an incident in which the police make an effort at enforcing one or another law—whether the culprits involved be a tipsy driver, a traffic law violator, or the operators and patrons of a blind pig. In other words, riots grow out of efforts at social control where society's officials move in on behavior which the informal social controls of the community do not prove sufficient to contain.

As the police go about their business, a curious crowd gathers. The crowd watches what is going on and reflects on it, and some members come to deny the legitimacy of what the police are doing. Rather than responding with satisfaction to the smooth functioning of the social control forces, the crowd members respond with anger and resentment; they identify with the culprits rather than with the law. This identification often takes the form of a belief either that the culprits are innocent, or that they're being treated more roughly than is warranted or just.

The riot develops from this initial incident as the people in the crowd begin to express their anger in response to the situation—they throw rocks at the police, or make attempts to rescue the prisoners. Here they are only acting out the strong and unpleasant emotions stimulated by what they see and the meanings they assign to it. But as this process continues and people talk to each other about what has happened, the matter becomes more ideological—that is, the events are interpreted in an increasingly larger context. The incident becomes an example of a society in which whites do as they please, while Negroes are held accountable for every minor infraction, even those infractions involving behavior that is not really voluntary. For example, a man may get drunk because he is depressed and discouraged about his situation, or he may spend his time on the streets and get in trouble there because he has given up looking for a job. The fury of the rioters is probably exacerbated by their weariness at trying to manage their lives in such a way that they can avoid the attentive ministrations of the social control agents (and these include truant officers, welfare investigators, and personnel officers, as well as the police).

By now the guilt or innocence of the culprits, and the manner in which the police treat them, are no longer that central. Instead, the focus is on the crowd members' general feelings that they live in a world in which they are constantly held accountable to standards of justice which are not applied to others. They feel that the merchants with whom they deal cheat them, that employers are either indifferent or exploiting toward them, that the police are disrespectful and suspicious of them. Therefore, they feel that the police (as representatives of the society at large) are perpetrating the greater evil—an evil by comparison with which the minor peccadillos of the drunken driver, traffic violator, the blind-pig patron are, in human terms, irrelevant.

Further, as incidents like this multiply, and as sophistication about Negro victimization rises in the ghetto community, it becomes increasingly possible to generalize this process without a particular incident. Following the news of the Newark, Detroit, and East Harlem riots in July, a group of Negro teenagers went on a rampage after a rock and roll concert, smashing and looting several of New York's Fifth Avenue stores. They did not need the provocation of an actual

---

Source: *Trans*-action, Vol. 4, No. 9 (September, 1967), pp. 22–32.

encounter with the police to touch off this vivid rejection of legal authority.

A riot is a social event which provides different opportunities to different participants. It is a short-lived "opportunity structure." Of all the aspects of the riot, this is the least well understood. There is no single "rioter," but rather many kinds of activities, each contributing a little bit to make up the total event. We know almost nothing about who takes each of the possible roles in the rioting—looter, sniper, police attacker, sympathetic bystander, ideological interpreter, and so on. It does seem that the most popular category is that of looter. This makes sense; what the rioters are saying, more than anything else, is "we haven't gotten our share." On Detroit's East and West sides the furniture and appliance stores seemed the hardest hit. "Big ticket" items are the proof of the affluent society and the looters knew exactly where to find them. In this respect the riots become a kind of primitive effort at an income redistribution which the society refuses to support in any lawful and regularized way.

The snipers, on the other hand, we can only vaguely understand. Indeed, the evidence seems to suggest that snipers are more often phantom than real; a very few snipers (perhaps none at all) are necessary to legitimate the belief of police and National Guardsmen that they are "at war" and that the danger is so great that they may fire with impunity into the rioting community. In Detroit, one such phantom sniper was apparently responsible for the National Guard machine-gunning a "white" motel near the General Motors building and inadvertently hitting an out-of-town woman staying there.

Riots are difficult to control precisely because of this voluntary division of labor among the participants. Because their many different sorts of activities require different sorts of responses, the riot becomes a highly complex event that can be brought under control only by a mass show of force (or perhaps by a show of no force at all). This, plus the fact that once the riot gets under way there is almost total denial of legitimacy to the police, means that the area must be *occupied* to be controlled—a process that calls ever further into question the legitimacy of the total society and its laws. The riots elicit from the official world exactly the kind of behavior that confirms the ghetto's estimate of white justice. The trigger-happy behavior of the National Guard and the police and the haphazard way in which arrests are or are not made deepens the conviction that being accorded justice depends more on luck than on the rule of law. The rising hysteria of the fatigued and frightened men in uniform seems to release all of their latent hostility to Negroes. In New Jersey, Los Angeles, and numerous smaller cities the civilian officials have hardly behaved better; it is to the credit of Detroit's Mayor Cavanaugh and his cabinet that no hint of such prejudice and bitterness has been apparent there.

Riots, then, provide different kinds of ghetto dwellers with different opportunities to pursue highly varied goals. The larger the riots get, the easier for individuals to become participants, and probably the more varied the goals they pursue.

In this context, it's quite clear from the data on the social characteristics of those arrested and convicted in Watts that the rioters are probably *not* exclusively "young hoodlums." For example, over half of those arrested in Watts were twenty-five years of age and over and as many as 40 percent were over thirty. Further, about two-thirds of those arrested and convicted were employed. It is certainly true that those arrested were very familiar with the law; less than 30 percent of them had no prior arrest. This, however, is not evidence that they are criminals, but only that they live in the ghetto. (Note, for example, that half of those arrested had never been convicted.) We would need more precise data to know what differences there might be between those who form some kind of active core of the rioters and those who take part more casually, by minor looting and the like. It might well be that the active core is more youthful and more solidly involved in delinquent activity than the others. But the most important fact here is that one could not make a riot of any size with the dominant proportion of the participants composed only of "young hoodlums."

There should be no mistake on this point. A very large proportion of the able-bodied members of any lower class Negro ghetto are potential participants in a riot. And, the riot has an ideological meaning for them; it is not simply a diversion which allows for criminal activity. The man who steals a six-pack of beer or breaks a store window does it not out of "criminal" motivation (it would hardly be worth his while), but because he is expressing some important feelings about his world and trying to put these feelings "on the record." If in the process he can derive some material benefit, like a television set or a new G.E. range, that is all to the good because it makes his point even clearer. Everyone in America knows that money talks. The greater the damage in terms of the financial cost of the looting and burning, the more effectively the point has been made.

But just as a riot provides a wide range of opportunities, it also involves a wide range of costs—primarily those of being killed, arrested, or burned out. It is probably true that stable working class Negroes (who are often as much prisoners of the ghetto as lower class people) are much less interested in the opportunities of riots and more concerned about the costs. They often share the feeling that legal authority is neither just nor fair, but they also have material possessions and social positions to protect. They don't want their homes burned by rioters or strafed by the National Guard. And they are concerned that their children will become involved in the riot—that they will be treated as, and may come to think of themselves as, the "young hoodlums."

Because this more stable working class in the ghetto usually supplies its "community leaders," there is real danger that any investigating committee will be misled into believing that the riots represent the feelings of only a small minority. These "respectable" spokesmen for the area must not be allowed (no matter how honest their personal views might be) to mislead an investigating group in its analysis of the nature of riot participation.

There is always deep conflict and ambivalence in the ghetto over the issue of police protection versus police harassment. The ghetto is a dangerous place for its inhabitants, and they would like to have firm and competent police surveillance. On the other hand, that very surveillance carries with it the danger of unjust and unseemly behavior by the police. Police rationality dictates that anyone in the ghetto is more suspect of crime than anyone in a white middle class neighborhood. From the police point of view, then, ghetto residents should be more willing to cooperate by answering questions and accepting arrest. The conflict built into this kind of situation can perhaps be somewhat ameliorated by more integrated police forces, and by vigorous supervision of the police to see that they are not impolite or overly aggressive. But that is no real solution to the problem.

Further, riots may well become more frequent and larger as time goes on due to the diffusion of knowledge, almost technical in nature, about how a riot is carried on. It is not too fanciful to say that anyone who watches television and reads the newspapers learns from the coverage of Watts, Hough, Newark, Harlem, and Detroit how to participate in a riot. Therefore, *without any organization at all* in the sense of a command structure, people in all parts of the nation know what to do and what roles one might take should a riot opportunity present itself. Millions of Americans today could, on request, fashion Molotov cocktails, who a year or two ago would not have known the meaning of the term. Similarly, millions of Americans now know that many rioters are not arrested and that snipers are seldom caught. There is no way of preventing the diffusion of this knowledge; we can only try to prevent the need and willingness to use it.

Finally, the particular quality of the riots reflects the Negro cultural emphasis on expressivity over instrumentality—practical, goal-directed action. A WASP riot under similar conditions would probably be a much more hard-nosed and certainly much more bloody and violent event. The "carnival atmosphere" noted by observers at all major riots is probably a direct reflection of the expressive emphasis in all group activity among Negroes, whether it be church participation, the blues, a rock and roll concert, or street corner banter.

This is perhaps also part of the key to why the riots seem to be relatively unorganized, both locally and nationally. Discussion of an organized national conspiracy is probably a white projection. Whites find it very difficult to understand why Negroes aren't more efficient in their rebellion—why there is no national cadre, no command structure, no greater efficiency in doing damage. A good part of this may be because this is not the Negroes' preferred way of going about things. Rather, in the midst of an ineffable group solidarity, a kind of free enterprise prevails in which each individual works for himself, perhaps cooperating for short periods of time with others to accomplish some immediate goals, but in the main doing things his own way as an expression of his own feelings. The expressive focus may be very important in formulating an ideology, and thus ultimately have a strong effect on the frequency and nature of rioting. But, that effect is achieved not by *organization,* but rather through *communication* of a developing social doctrine.

Negro expressiveness may also account for the tremendous disjunction between the verbal communication of supposedly violent groups such as RAM and spokesmen for violence like H. Rap Brown, and the fact that organized paramilitary action seems to be virtually absent from the riots. They behave as if they were designed more for display to the white press and titillated or scandalized Negro audiences than for actual committed revolutionary action. I don't think this point about Negro expressive life style is particularly important in understanding or accounting for the riots except to the extent that it helps us understand and get behind the myths that some whites (particularly Senators Eastland and McClellan, the press, and law enforcement agencies) and some Negroes (like Carmichael in Havana) are putting forth.

When we seek the basic causes of the riots the central question is: Why are there so many Negroes for whom riots provide an opportunity for meaningful self-expression and gain? Further, why are the opportunities sought in such situations so destructive of social order? We know that in other situations which provide technical opportunity, for example, blackouts, nothing of the sort happens, although the authorities always fear that it might.

Much of the popular interpretation of riots has turned on an understanding of the really desperate situation of the worst off in the ghettos, of those who make up the "underclass," which may include anywhere between one-third and one-half of the ghetto population. Again, however, the figures on the Watts arrestees are instructive. Two-thirds of the men arrested and convicted were employed and perhaps as many as one-third of them were earning over $300 a month. Forty percent (or over half of those who had ever been married) were living with their spouses. Thus, when a riot takes place, a significant portion even of those above the poverty line may well be drawn into participation. This should alert us to the fact that rioting is not exclusively a problem of poverty as currently defined.

One may talk about two major kinds of causative factors—one involving *class* (by which is meant simply economic deprivation and all of the cultural and social consequences that flow from it) and the other involving the inferior *caste* position of Negroes to whites. This latter factor is most directly expressed in ghetto hostility toward the police, but it is also involved in the attack the riots come to represent on the total white-dominated society. Even the Negro who is well off in class terms may feel a strong pull toward participation if he has had the experience of being interrogated and perhaps arrested in a ghetto area simply because his face is black. Where men have little to protect and where their experience of hostility and indifference from the white world is even more pervasive, as in the case of the lower class, the resistance to participation will be even less.

The fact that even a significant minority of the participants are members of seemingly stable families earning above poverty level incomes tells us something about what is involved in exclusion from ordinary American society in a city as prosperous as Detroit or Los Angeles. Whatever poverty as minimum subsistence may mean, it is quite clear that people with incomes as high as $5,000 a year are really not able to feel that they participate in the broad spectrum of average American affluence and satisfaction. A community in which the great majority of the families must exist on significantly less than the median family income for the nation is a community of failures. Inclusion in such a community, compounded as it is by belonging to a historically excluded group and the knowledge that there is a connection between racial exclusion and economic exclusion, is undesirable to those who live within its confines as well as to those outside.

Thus, the ghetto community has few informal social controls; people tend to minimize trouble by avoiding each other more than by building up informal social networks which ensure observance of common group standards. Everybody does pretty much what he wants as long as he can stay out of the clutches of the authorities. Thus, the individual has few effective sanctions available at the informal level. Even those who disapprove of rioting are powerless to do much about it by informally punishing those who participate. Any influence they might have is vitiated by the common perception of all that the authorities are just about as unjust as the law-breakers. Ghetto residents will, in desperation, call upon officialdom to punish those of their fellows who are directly making trouble for them, but they do it in much the same way that one might pay the neighborhood bully to discipline an enemy. The bully is called upon because of his power, not because of any legitimate authority.

The riots bring into high relief the ever present schism in the Negro community between those who feel they have nothing to lose, and those who want to protect what they have—while the former riot, the latter deluge the police and mayor's office with telephone calls demanding that the riot be put down before their homes are burned, their community destroyed. The physical contrast in Detroit is particularly striking. Not three blocks from the 12th Street riot area are substantial homes on well-maintained tree-lined streets. Their residents, like other stable working and middle class Negro Detroiters, wanted the riots put down with all possible dispatch; the potential cost of getting even with Whitey was too great.

And then there are the Negro businessmen in the ghetto—the "soul brothers." Detroit's Grand River Boulevard, where the riot-damaged buildings string out for miles, has a great many soul brothers (and one soul mother) whose quickly inscribed signs protected them from damage while on either side the looting or burning seemed complete. But, one can't count the "soul brother" signs that are no longer there because the glass was broken; and an occasional sign is still observable when only one broken show window in a soul brother's store was required to accomplish the looting. The signs obviously provided some protection, but exactly how much they lower the risk is a moot point. If the protection is very high, it would suggest that the hostility of the more prosperous and respectable Negroes is not returned by the rioters; if protection is low the rioters might be saying, as those in Bedford-Stuyvesant are reported to have taunted Negro policemen, "Take off your black masks so we can see your white faces."

Summing up: (1) the root cause of the riots lies in a caste system deeply imbedded in our society that has created a situation in which (a) a very large proportion of Negroes are denied the opportunity to achieve an average American standard of living, and (b) even those Negroes who do, by dint of their own efforts, manage to come reasonably close to an average American standard are still subjected to special disabilities and insults because of their confinement to a ghetto community. (2) From the immediate point of view of the rioters, the most pervasive factor which prevents their achieving some sense of a decent life is that of living in poverty or near-poverty (as a rough rule from, say, having incomes less than one-half to two-thirds that of the median family income for the nation). This economic exclusion affects almost everything they do—their ability to purchase all those elements that make up the "standard package" that most American families deem their right. And the inability to earn more than this kind of poverty or near-poverty income affects the respect they are able to elicit from their own family members, members of their immediate community, and from the society at large.

It seems likely that the starting mechanisms for a riot are fairly dependent on the existence of pronounced poverty coupled with very high rates of unemployment. This, at least, would seem to be important to the extent that young men (say men under twenty-five) have a disproportionate influence on getting a riot going. This group is excluded not only from the availability of something like an average American life, but is excluded even within its own community. The older men do tend to be employed and to earn incomes reasonably close to the poverty line. It is the younger men in the ghetto who are most completely and dramatically excluded from any participation in the conventional rewards of the society.

If this diagnosis is correct—that the direct cause of participation in the riots (as opposed to the precipitating incidents) is economic marginality—it should put us on notice that no "community action" programs, whether they involve better police-community relations or rapprochement with the new black militant leaders, will prevent riots. Rather, the necessary condition for any permanent solution to the riot problem will be to provide a reasonable approximation of the "average American standard of living" for every family. This means managing the society so that poverty and near-poverty are eliminated. Only then can those who now participate in and support the riots find themselves in situations where rioting has become a meaningless, useless activity. This "income strategy" has two principal elements.

The more important of these is creating work. The demand for goods and services must be manipulated in such a way that private and public employers have more jobs which they are willing to offer to relatively unskilled and "undesirable" employees because they need these employees to satisfy the demands for their products. This is the aggregate demand solution to poverty argued by James Tobin, Hyman Minsky, and others. Such a solution has the advantage that it makes maximum use of what is already our main technique for distributing goods and services to families—that is, employment. A further advantage is that an aggregate demand, full employment situation tends to upgrade wages in low wage industries and thus alleviate the problem of near-poverty and poverty among employed workers.

An integral part of this strategy will probably have to be some direct planning by the government to make demand for unskilled workers roughly equal to that for more skilled workers. The most promising suggestions in this area involve the "new careers for the poor" proposals which create new kinds of jobs and avenues for advancement in public service activities. But it is very important that these programs not be developed as programs of "last resort employment," but rather as permanent programs which are productive for the entire society.

It might be well to design crash programs, as well as possible subsidized employment in private industry, for young workers. Such crash programs would be a dead end, however, unless they were part of an overall aggregate demand plus special-programs-for-unskilled-workers strategy.

It follows that the government agencies who should be responsible for solving the problems of the riots are not so much HEW, Labor, and OEO, as they are the Treasury Department, Council of Economic Advisors, and the Federal Reserve Board. OEO-type programs such as the Job Corps, which are designed only to train a small number of lower class individuals to compete more successfully within a system that offers them little or no opportunity as long as they remain unskilled, cannot hope to solve the massive income problems of the whole disadvantaged sector. Unless the power and skills of those agencies which set basic fiscal and economic policy are brought to bear (and backed, of course, by a committed President) it is very difficult to believe that we can solve the problem of rioting—or the more general problem of poverty, and the racial caste system it supports.

The second aspect of the income strategy will involve some form of guaranteed minimum income. We now know that the various particular plans that have been suggested—negative income tax, family allowance, upgraded welfare systems, and the like—all represent variations on a common system of income redistribution (see Christopher Green, *Negative Taxes and the Poverty Problem,* The Brookings Institution, 1967). The important issue is not so much which of these plans is best as what the guaranteed minimum is to be and what the tax rate on the subsidy is to be. Given the amount of current research activity on income maintenance, the basic technical issues involved in a guaranteed income program will be resolved in the next two or three years. The real question is how we are to muster the political goodwill to put a program into effect.

A guaranteed minimum income program will be crucial for two reasons. First of all, there will always be families for whom the economy cannot provide a reasonable income on a regular and secure basis. Perhaps more important from a political point of view, a national commitment to a guaranteed minimum income will spur the government to maintain employment as fully as possible so that the maximum number of people will derive the maximum proportion of their incomes from their own earnings and not from the national dole. The political vulnerability of any group which over a long period of time derives a significant proportion of its income from government transfers will always be great. Therefore, income maintenance plans can only be a form of family insurance and national political insurance, not a major way of channeling income to families.

A solution to the Negro income problem is thus the sine qua non for a permanent solution to the problem of rioting. With this achieved, tremendous pressure will be generated to move out of the ghetto. I would guess that only a small minority of current ghetto residents would prefer to stay, given a choice. This pressure will itself facilitate the development of desegregated housing; but the government must also facilitate the dispersion of ghetto residents to a more integrated life away from the central city ghettos. That dispersion would to some extent be aided by fair housing laws, but perhaps more important would be the development of government-supported programs for the expansion of middle and lower middle income housing. This would maximize the range of choice available to anyone seeking a better place to live.

It is my belief that it will prove impossible to solve the many other problems of the ghetto until the income problem is solved. Further, I believe that these other problems—education, health, political participation, and the like—would be amenable to very different and much simpler solutions if the Negro families involved had decent incomes.

The ideological developments of the past ten years in connection with the situation of the Negro American pose a challenge to the government and to white society generally. Depending on how this challenge is met, we will move more slowly or more quickly toward the basic economic solutions offered above. I see the vague and often contradictory militant civil rights ideology which has developed over the past few years as a result of two factors. First, as the nation has become more prosperous, it has become increasingly obvious that it is not necessary to have a deprived and excluded group in our midst. The dynamics of affluence themselves call into question the old caste-like racial arrangements. As some Negroes participate in that prosperity, and as they look on the tremendous affluence of white society, there is a strong push in the direction of forcing the society to accord Negroes their share. This factor was perhaps the dominant influence in the early period of the new civil rights consciousness that started in the early '60's—suddenly it seemed ridiculous to most Americans that anyone should be excluded when we have so much.

Second, and more recently, has come a new wave of black populism. The common theme running through many of the ideas of the new black militants is that Negroes have a right to their own future and their own place in the sun, not just in economic terms but as full men in society. The emphasis on blackness is a reaction to the price that white society seems to want to exact for economic payoffs, a price that seems to involve a denial of oneself as Negro and to require a tame imitation of whatever the going definition of the proper white person is. Now there is a lot of nonsense these days about what Negro culture involves and what black autonomy might mean. But, at the core of the black populist movement is a denial of the right of whites to define who the Negro is and what he may become. This is not only healthy, but much more realistic than the earlier, simple-minded integrationist myth that dominated civil rights activity for so long.

There are now, and will probably continue to be for some time, conflicts between moving toward the economic goals of the civil rights movement and the black populist goals. The political challenge for white society is to thread its way through these conflicts without denying the validity of either factor, and to select those areas in which the government can further the Negro goals (to my mind, principally the economic area) and those areas in which the main effort at constructing a new social reality will have to be made primarily by Negroes themselves.

The danger here is that the reaction to the black populist goals on the part of the government and whites generally will be so hostile that Negro leaders who emphasize such aims will be progressively alienated and provoked into activities destructive to both sets of goals. In the main, however, the mutual alienation and viciousness that has tended to dominate the civil rights-white power structure dialogue for the past two years is more a result of the government's unwillingness to make major economic commitments than it is of any inherent tendencies in the black populist movement.

In short, the government cannot give Negroes a black culture or a black consciousness, but it can manage the society in such a way as to give them a "black affluence." If the government does not do what it can do, then we can only expect the courageous and the committed in the Negro community to become more aggressive and more destructive toward the larger society which has the necessary means, but refuses to use them.

43.

THE NATIONAL ADVISORY COMMISSION ON CIVIL DISORDERS

THE NEWS MEDIA AND THE DISORDERS

INTRODUCTION

The President's charge to the Commission asked specifically: "What effect do the mass media have on the riots?"

The question is far reaching and a sure answer is beyond the range of presently available scientific techniques. Our conclusions and recommendations are based upon subjective as well as objective factors; interviews as well as statistics; isolated examples as well as general trends.

Freedom of the press is not the issue. A free press is indispensable to the preservation of the other freedoms this nation cherishes. The recommendations in this chapter have thus been developed under the strong conviction that only a press unhindered by government can contribute to freedom.

To answer the President's question, the Commission:

Directed its field survey teams to question government officials, law enforcement agents, media personnel, and ordinary citizens about their attitudes and reactions to reporting of the riots;

Arranged for interviews of media representatives about their coverage of the riots;

Conducted special interviews with ghetto residents about their response to coverage;

Arranged for a quantitative analysis of the content of television programs and newspaper reporting in 15 riot cities during the period of the disorder and the days immediately before and after;

From November 10-12, 1967, sponsored and participated in a conference of representatives from all levels of the newspaper, news magazine, and broadcasting industries at Poughkeepsie, New York.

Finally, of course, the Commissioners read newspapers, listened to the radio, watched television, and thus formed their own impressions of media coverage. All of these data, impressions, and attitudes provide the foundation for our conclusions.

The Commission also determined, very early, that the answer to the President's question did not lie solely in the performance of the press

---

SOURCE: *Report* of the National Advisory Commission on Civil Disorders, Governor Otto Kerner, Chairman, Chapter 15, 1968.

and broadcasters in reporting the riots proper. Our analysis had to consider also the overall treatment by the media of the Negro ghettos, community relations, racial attitudes, urban and rural poverty—day by day and month by month, year in and year out.

On this basis, we have reached three conclusions:

First, that despite incidents of sensationalism, inaccuracies, and distortions, newspapers, radio and television, on the whole, made a real effort to give a balanced, factual account of the 1967 disorders.

Second, despite this effort, the portrayal of the violence that occurred last summer failed to reflect accurately its scale and character. The overall effect was, we believe, an exaggeration of both mood and event.

Third, and ultimately most important, we believe that the media have thus far failed to report adequately on the causes and consequences of civil disorders and the underlying problems of race relations.

With these comments as a perspective, we discuss first the coverage of last summer's disturbances. We will then summarize our concerns with overall coverage of race relations.

Coverage of the 1967 Disturbances

We have found a significant imbalance between what actually happened in our cities and what the newspaper, radio, and television coverage of the riots told us happened. The Commission, in studying last summer's disturbances, visited many of the cities and interviewed participants and observers. We found that the disorders, as serious as they were, were less destructive, less widespread, and less a black-white confrontation than most people believed.

Lacking other sources of information, we formed our original impressions and beliefs from what we saw on television, heard on the radio, and read in newspapers and magazines. We are deeply concerned that millions of other Americans, who must rely on the mass media, likewise formed incorrect impressions and judgments about what went on in many American cities last summer.

As we started to probe the reasons for this imbalance between reality and impression, we first believed that the media had sensationalized the disturbances, consistently overplaying violence and giving disproportionate amounts of time to emotional events and "militant" leaders. To test this theory, we commissioned a systematic, quantitative analysis, covering the content of newspaper and television reporting in 15 cities where disorders occurred. The results of this analysis do not support our early belief. Of 955 television sequences of riot and racial news examined, 837 could be classified for predominant atmosphere as either "emotional," "calm," or "normal." Of these, 494 were classified as calm, 262 as emotional, and 81 as normal. Only a small proportion of all scenes analyzed showed actual mob action, people looting, sniping, setting fires, or being injured, or killed. Moderate Negro leaders were shown more frequently than militant leaders on television news broadcasts.

Of 3,779 newspaper articles analyzed, more focused on legislation which should be sought and planning which should be done to control ongoing riots and prevent future riots than on any other topic. . . . They make it clear that the imbalance between actual events and the portrayal of those events in the press and on the air cannot be attributed solely to sensationalism in reporting and presentation.

We have, however, identified several factors which, it seems to us, did work to create incorrect and exaggerated impressions about the scope and intensity of the disorders.

First, despite the overall statistical picture, there were instances of gross flaws in presenting news of the 1967 riots. Some newspapers printed "scare" headlines unsupported by the mild stories that followed. All media reported rumors that had no basis in fact. Some newsmen staged "riot" events for the cameras. . . .

Second, the press obtained much factual information about the scale of the disorders—property damage, personal injury, and deaths—from local officials, who often were inexperienced in dealing with civil disorders and not always able to sort out fact from rumor in the confusion. At the height of the Detroit riot, some news reports of property damage put the figure in excess of $500 million.[1] Subsequent

[1]As recently as February 9, 1968, an Associated

investigation shows it to be $40 to $45 million.[2]

The initial estimates were not the independent judgment of reporters or editors. They came from beleaguered government officials. But the news media gave currency to these errors. Reporters uncritically accepted, and editors uncritically published, the inflated figures, leaving an indelible impression of damage up to more than ten times greater than actually occurred.

Third, the coverage of the disorders—particularly on television—tended to define the events as black-white confrontations. In fact almost all of the deaths, injuries and property damage occurred in all-Negro neighborhoods, and thus the disorders were not "race riots" as that term is generally understood.

Closely linked to these problems is the phenomenon of cumulative effect. As the summer of 1967 progressed, we think Americans often began to associate more or less neutral sights and sounds (like a squad car with flashing red lights, a burning building, a suspect in police custody) with racial disorders, so that the appearance of any particular item, itself hardly inflammatory, set off a whole sequence of association with riot events. Moreover, the summer's news was not seen and heard in isolation. Events of these past few years—the Watts riot, other disorders, and the growing momentum of the civil rights movement—conditioned the responses of readers and viewers and heightened their reactions. What the public saw and read last summer thus produced emotional reactions and left vivid impressions not wholly attributable to the material itself.

Fear and apprehension of racial unrest and violence are deeply rooted in American society. They color and intensify reactions to news of racial trouble and threats of racial conflict. Those who report and disseminate news must be conscious of the background of anxieties and apprehension against which their stories are projected. This does not mean that the media should manage the news or tell less than the truth. Indeed, we believe that it would be imprudent and even dangerous to down-play coverage in the hope that censored reporting of inflammatory incidents somehow will diminish violence. Once a disturbance occurs, the word will spread independently of newspapers and television. To attempt to ignore these events or portray them as something other than what they are, can only diminish confidence in the media and increase the effectiveness of those who monger rumors and the fears of those who listen.

But to be complete, the coverage must be representative. We suggest that the main failure of the media last summer was that the totality of its coverage was not as representative as it should have been to be accurate. We believe that to live up to their own professed standards, the media simply must exercise a higher degree of care and a greater level of sophistication than they have yet shown in this area—higher, perhaps, than the level ordinarily acceptable with other stories.

This is not "just another story." It should not be treated like one. Admittedly, some of what disturbs us about riot coverage last summer stems from circumstances beyond media control. But many of the inaccuracies of fact, tone and mood were due to the failure of reporters and editors to ask tough enough questions about official reports, and to apply the most rigorous standards possible in evaluating and presenting the news. Reporters and editors must be sure that descriptions and pictures of violence, and emotional or inflammatory sequences or articles, even though "true" in isolation, are really representative and do not convey an impression at odds with the overall reality of events. The media too often did not achieve this level of sophisticated, skeptical, careful news judgment during last summer's riots.

The Media and Race Relations

Our second and fundamental criticism is that the news media have failed to analyze and report adequately on racial problems in the United States and, as a related matter, to meet the Negro's legitimate expectations in journalism. By and large, news organizations have failed to communicate to both their black and

---

Press dispatch from Philadelphia said "damage exceeded $1 billion" in Detroit.

[2]Michigan State Insurance Commission Estimate, December, 1967. See also *Meeting the Insurance Crisis of Our Cities*, a Report by the President's National Advisory Panel on Insurance in Riot-Affected Areas, January, 1968.

white audiences a sense of the problems America faces and the sources of potential solutions. The media report and write from the standpoint of a white man's world. The ills of the ghetto, the difficulties of life there, the Negro's burning sense of grievance, are seldom conveyed. Slights and indignities are part of the Negro's daily life, and many of them come from what he now calls "the white press"—a press that repeatedly, if unconsciously, reflects the biases, the paternalism, the indifference of white America. This may be understandable, but it is not excusable in an institution that has the mission to inform and educate the whole of our society.

* * *

I. NEWS COVERAGE OF CIVIL DISORDERS—SUMMER 1967

The Method of Analysis

As noted, the Commission has been surveying both the reporting of disorders last summer and the broader field of race relations coverage. With respect to the reporting of disorders, we were trying to get a sense of content, accuracy, tone, and bias. We sought to find out how people reacted to it and how reporters conducted themselves while carrying out their assignments. The Commission used a number of techniques to probe these matters and to provide cross checks on data and impressions.

To obtain an objective source of data, the Commission arranged for a systematic, quantitative analysis of the content of newspapers, local television, and network coverage in 15 cities for a period from three days before to three days after the disorder in each city.[3]

The cities were chosen to provide a cross-section in terms of the location and scale of the disorders and the dates of their occurrence.

Within each city, for the period specified, the study was comprehensive. Every daily newspaper and all network and local television news films were analyzed, and scripts and logs were examined. In all, 955 network and local television sequences and 3,779 newspaper articles dealing with riot and race relations news were analyzed. Each separate analysis was coded and the cards were cross-tabulated by computer to provide results and comparisons for use by the Commission. The material was measured to determine the amount of space devoted to news of riot activity; the nature of the display given compared with other news coverage; and the types of stories, articles, and television programming presented. We sought specific statistical information on such matters as the amount of space or time devoted to different kinds of riot stories, the types and identities of persons most often depicted or interviewed, the frequency with which race relations problems were mentioned in riot stories or identified as the cause of riot activity.

The survey was designed to be objective and statistical. Within its terms of reference, the Commission was looking for broad characterizations of media tone and content.

The Commission is aware of the inherent limitations of content analysis techniques. They cannot measure the emotional impact of a particular story or television sequence. By themselves, they provide no basis for conclusions as to the accuracy of what was reported. Particular examples of good or bad journalistic conduct, which may be important in themselves, are submerged in a statistical average. The Commission therefore sought through staff interviews and personal contact with members of the press and the public to obtain direct evidence of the effects of riot coverage and the performance of the media during last summer's disturbances.

Conclusions About Content[4]

Television

1. Content analysis of television film footage shows that the tone of the coverage studied was more calm and "factual" than "emotional" and rumor-laden. Researchers viewed every one of 955 television sequences and found that twice as many "calm" sequences as "emotional" ones

[3]Detroit, Michigan; Milwaukee, Wisconsin; Cincinnati, Ohio; Dayton, Ohio; Tampa, Florida; Newark, New Jersey; Plainfield, New Jersey; Elizabeth, New Jersey; Jersey City, New Jersey; East Orange, New Jersey; Paterson, New Jersey; New Brunswick, New Jersey; Englewood, New Jersey; New Haven, Connecticut; Rochester, New York.

[4]What follows is a summary of the major conclusions drawn from the content analysis conducted for the Commission.

were shown. The amount and location of coverage were relatively limited, considering the magnitude of the events. The analysis reveals a dominant, positive emphasis on control of the riot and on activities in the aftermath of the riot (53.8 percent of all scenes broadcast) rather than on scenes of actual mob action, or people looting, sniping, setting fires, or being injured or killed (4.8 percent of scenes shown). However, according to participants in our Poughkeepsie conference, coverage frequently was of the postriot or interview variety because newsmen arrived at the scene after the actual violence had subsided. Overall, both network and local television coverage was cautious and restrained.

2. Television newscasts during the periods of actual disorder in 1967 tended to emphasize law enforcement activities, thereby overshadowing underlying grievances and tensions. This conclusion is based on the relatively high frequency with which television showed and described law enforcement agents, police, national guardsmen, and army troops performing control functions.

Television coverage tended to give the impression that the riots were confrontations between Negroes and whites rather than responses by Negroes to underlying slum problems. The control agents were predominantly white. The ratio of white male adults[5] to Negro male adults shown on television is high (1:2) considering that the riots took place in predominantly Negro neighborhoods. And some interviews with whites involved landlords or proprietors who had lost property or suffered business losses because of the disturbances and thus held strongly antagonistic attitudes.

The content analysis shows that by far the most frequent "actor" appearances on television were Negro male adults, white male adults, law enforcement agents, and public officials. We cannot tell from a content analysis whether there was any preconceived editorial policy of portraying the riots as racial confrontations requiring the intervention of enforcement agents. But the content analysis does present a visual three-way alignment of Negroes, white bystanders, and public officials or enforcement agents. This alignment tended to create an impression that the riots were predominantly racial confrontations between black and white citizens.

3. About one-third of all riot-related sequences for network and local television appeared on the first day following the outbreak of rioting, regardless of the course of development of the riot itself. After the first day there was, except in Detroit, a very sharp decline in the amount of television time devoted to the disturbance. In Detroit, where the riot started slowly and did not flare out of control until the evening of July 24, 48 hours after it started, the number of riot-related sequences shown increased until July 26, and then showed the same sharp drop-off as noted after the first day of rioting in the other cities.[6] These findings tend to controvert the impression that the riot intensifies television coverage, thus in turn intensifying the riot. The content analysis indicates that whether or not the riot was getting worse, television coverage of the riot decreased sharply after the first day.

4. The Commission made a special effort to analyze television coverage of Negro leaders. To do this, Negro leaders were divided into three categories: (a) celebrities or public figures, who did not claim any organizational following (e.g., social scientist Dr. Kenneth B. Clark, comedian Dick Gregory); (b) "moderate" Negro leaders, who claim a political or organizational following; and (c) "militant" Negro leaders who claim a political or organizational following. During the riot periods surveyed, Negro leaders appeared infrequently on network news broadcasts and were about equally divided among celebrity or public figures, moderate leaders, and militant leaders. On local television, Negro leaders appeared more often. Of the three categories, "moderate" Negro leaders were shown on local stations more than twice as often as Negro leaders identified primarily as celebrities or public figures, and three times more frequently than militant leaders.

---

[5]The white male adult category in this computation does *not* include law enforcement agents or public officials.

[6]Detroit news outlets substantially refrained from publicizing the riot during the early part of Sunday, the first day of rioting.

Newspapers

1. Like television coverage, newspaper coverage of civil disturbances in the summer of 1967 was more calm, factual and restrained than outwardly emotional or inflammatory. During the period of the riot there were many stories dealing exclusively with nonriot racial news. Considering the magnitude of the events, the amount of coverage was limited. Most stories were played down or put on inside pages. Researchers found that almost all the articles analyzed (3,045 of 3,770) tended to focus on one of 16 identifiable subjects. Of this group, 502 articles (16.5 percent) focused primarily on legislation which should be sought and planning which could be done to control ongoing riots and prevent future riots. The second largest category consisted of 471 articles (15.5 percent) focusing on containment or control of riot action. Newspaper coverage of the disorders reflects efforts at caution and restraint.

2. Newspapers tended to characterize and portray last summer's riots in national terms rather than as local phenomena and problems, especially when rioting was taking place in the newspaper's own city. During the actual disorders, the newspapers in each city studied tended to print many stories dealing with disorders or racial troubles in other cities. About 40 percent of the riot or racial stories in each local newspaper during the period of rioting in that city came from the wire services. Most newspaper editors appear to have given more headline attention to riots occurring elsewhere than to those at home during the time of trouble in their own cities.

Accuracy of the Coverage

We have tested the accuracy of coverage by means of interviews with local media representatives, city and police officials, and residents of the ghettos. To provide a broad base, we used three separate sources for interview data: the Commission's field survey teams, special field teams, and the findings of a special research study.

As is to be expected, almost everyone had his own version of "the truth," but it is noteworthy that some editors and reporters themselves, in retrospect, have expressed concern about the accuracy of their own coverage. For example, one newspaper editor said at the Commission's Poughkeepsie conference:

> We used things in our leads and headlines during the riot I wish we could have back now, because they were wrong and they were bad mistakes . . . We used the words "sniper kings" and "nests of snipers." We found out when we were able to get our people into those areas and get them out from under the cars that these sniper kings and these nests of snipers were the constituted authorities shooting at each other, most of them. There was just one confirmed sniper in the entire eight-day riot and he was . . . drunk and he had a pistol, and he was firing from a window.

Television industry representatives at the conference stressed their concern about "live" coverage of disorders and said they try, whenever possible, to view and edit taped or filmed sequences before broadcasting them. Conference participants admitted that live television coverage via helicopter of the 1965 Watts riot had been inflammatory, and network news executives expressed doubts that television would ever again present live coverage of a civil disorder.

Most errors involved mistakes of fact, exaggeration of events, overplaying of particular stories, or prominently displayed speculation about unfounded rumors of potential trouble. This is not only a local problem; because of the wire services and networks, it is a national one. An experienced riot reporter told the Commission that initial wire service reports of a disturbance tend to be inflated. The reason, he said, is that they are written by local bureau men who in most cases have not seen a civil disorder before. When out-of-town reporters with knowledge in the field, or the wire services' own riot specialists arrive on the scene, the situation is put into a more accurate context.

Some examples of exaggeration and mistakes about facts are catalogued here. These examples are by no means exhaustive. They represent only a few of the incidents discovered by the Commission and, no doubt, are but a small part of the total number of such inaccuracies. But the Commission believes that they are representative of the kinds of errors likely to occur when, in addition to the confusion inherent in civil disorder situations, reporters are rushed and harried or editors are superficial and careless. We present these as examples of mistakes that we hope will be avoided in the future.

In particular, we believe newsmen should be wary of how they play rumors of impending trouble. Whether a rumor is reliable and significant enough to deserve coverage is an editorial decision. But the failure of many headlined rumors to be borne out last summer suggests that these editorial decisions often are not as carefully made as the sensitivity of the subject requires.

In Tampa, Florida, a deputy sheriff died in the early stages of the disturbance, and both national wire services immediately bulletined the news that the man had been killed by rioters. About 30 minutes later, reporters discovered that the man had suffered a fatal heart attack.

In Detroit, a radio station broadcast a rumor, based on a telephone tip, that Negroes planned to invade suburbia one night later; if plans existed, they never materialized.

In Cincinnati, several outlets ran a story about white youths arrested for possessing a bazooka; only a few reports mentioned that the weapon was inoperable.

In Tampa a newspaper repeatedly indulged in speculation about impending trouble. When the state attorney ruled the fatal shooting of a Negro youth justifiable homicide, the paper's news columns reported: "There were fears today that the ruling would stir new race problems for Tampa tonight." The day before, the paper quoted one "top lawman" as telling reporters "he now fears that Negro residents in the Central Avenue Project and in the West Tampa trouble spots feel they are in competition, and are trying to see which can cause the most unrest—which area can become the center of attraction."

A West Coast newspaper put out an edition headlined: "Rioting Erupts in Washington, D.C. / Negroes Hurl Bottles, Rocks at Police Near White House." The story did not support the headline. It reported what was actually the fact: that a number of teenage Negroes broke store windows and threw bottles and stones at police and firemen near downtown Washington, a mile or more from the White House. On the other hand, the same paper did not report unfounded local rumors of sniping when other news media did.

Television presents a different problem with respect to accuracy. In contrast to what some of its critics have charged, television sometimes may have leaned over too far backward in seeking balance and restraint. By stressing interviews, many with whites in predominantly Negro neighborhoods, and by emphasizing control scenes rather than riotous action, television news broadcasts may have given a distorted picture of what the disorders were all about.

The media—especially television—also have failed to present and analyze to a sufficient extent the basic reasons for the disorders. There have, after the disorders, been some brilliant exceptions.[7] As the content analysis findings suggest, however, coverage during the riot period itself gives far more emphasis to control of rioters and black-white confrontation than to the underlying causes of the disturbances.

Ghetto Reactions to the Media Coverage

The Commission was particularly interested in public reaction to media coverage; specifically, what people in the ghetto look at and read and how it affects them. The Commission has drawn upon reports from special teams of researchers who visited various cities where outbreaks occurred last summer. Members of these teams interviewed ghetto dwellers and middle-class Negroes on their responses to news media. In addition, we have used information from a statistical study of the mass media in the Negro ghetto in Pittsburgh.[8]

These interviews and surveys, though by no means a complete study of the subject, lead to four broad conclusions about ghetto, and to a lesser degree middle-class Negro, reactions to the media.

Most Negroes distrust what they refer to as the "white press." As one interviewer reported:

> The average black person couldn't give less of a damn about what the media say. The intelligent black person is resentful at what he considers to be a totally false portrayal of what goes on in the ghetto. Most black people see the newspapers as mouthpieces of the "power structure."

These comments are echoed in most interview

[7]As examples, less than a month after the Detroit riot, the Detroit *Free Press* published the results of a landmark survey of local Negro attitudes and grievances. *Newsweek* Magazine's November 20, 1967 special issue on "The Negro American—What Must Be Done" made a significant contribution to public understanding.

[8]The Commission is indebted, in this regard, to M. Thomas Allen for his document on *Mass Media Use Patterns and Functions in the Negro Ghetto in Pittsburgh.*

reports the Commission has read. Distrust and dislike of the media among ghetto Negroes encompass *all* the media, though in general, the newspapers are mistrusted more than the television. This is not because television is thought to be more sensitive or responsive to Negro needs and aspirations, but because ghetto residents believe that television at least lets them see the actual events for themselves. Even so, many Negroes, particularly teenagers, told researchers that they noted a pronounced discrepancy between what they saw in the riots and what television broadcast.

Persons interviewed offered three chief reasons for their attitude. First, they believed, as suggested in the quotation above, that the media are instruments of the white power structure. They thought that these white interests guide the entire white community, from the journalists' friends and neighbors to city officials, police officers, and department store owners. Publishers and editors, if not white reporters, supported and defended these interests with enthusiasm and dedication.

Second, many people in the ghettos apparently believe that newsmen rely on the police for most of their information about what is happening during a disorder and tend to report much more of what the officials are doing and saying than what Negro citizens or leaders in the city are doing and saying. Editors and reporters at the Poughkeepsie conference acknowledged that the police and city officials are their main—and sometimes their only—source of information. It was also noted that most reporters who cover civil disturbances tend to arrive with the police and stay close to them—often for safety, and often because they learn where the action is at the same time as the authorities—and thus buttress the ghetto impression that police and press work together and toward the same ends (an impression that may come as a surprise to many within the ranks of police and press).

Third, Negro residents in several cities surveyed cited as specific examples of media unfairness what they considered the failure of the media:

To report the many examples of Negroes helping law enforcement officers and assisting in the treatment of the wounded during disorders;

To report adequately about false arrests;

To report instances of excessive force by the National Guard;

To explore and interpret the background conditions leading to disturbances;

To expose, except in Detroit, what they regarded as instances of police brutality;

To report on white vigilante groups which allegedly came into some disorder areas and molested innocent Negro residents.

Some of these problems are insoluble. But more first-hand reporting in the diffuse and fragmented riot area should temper easy reliance on police information and announcements. There is a special need for news media to cover "positive" news stories in the ghetto before and after riots with concern and enthusiasm.

A multitude of news and information sources other than the established news media are relied upon in the ghetto. One of our studies found that 79 percent of a total of 567 ghetto residents interviewed in seven cities[9] first heard about the outbreak in their own city by word of mouth. Telephone and word of mouth exchanges on the streets, in churches, stores, pool halls, and bars, provide more information—and rumors—about events of direct concern to ghetto residents than the more conventional news media.

Among the established media, television and radio are far more popular in the ghetto than newspapers. Radios there, apparently, are ordinarily listened to less for news than for music and other programs. One survey showed that an overwhelmingly large number of Negro children and teenagers (like their white counterparts) listen to the radio for music alone, interspersed by disc jockey chatter. In other age groups, the response of most people about what they listen to on the radio was "anything," leading to the conclusion that radio in the ghetto is basically a background accompaniment.

But the fact that radio is such a constant background accompaniment can make it an important influence on people's attitudes, and perhaps on their actions once trouble develops. This is true for several reasons. News presented on local "rock" stations seldom constitutes much

[9]Detroit, Newark, Atlanta, Tampa, New Haven, Cincinnati, Milwaukee.

more than terse headline items which may startle or frighten but seldom inform. Radio disc jockeys and those who preside over the popular "talk shows" keep a steady patter of information going over the air. When a city is beset by civil strife, this patter can both inform transistor radio-carrying young people where the action is, and terrify their elders and much of the white community. "Burn, baby, burn," the slogan of the Watts riot, was inadvertently originated by a radio disc jockey.

Thus, radio can be an instrument of trouble and tension in a community threatened or inundated with civil disorder. It can also do much to minimize fear by putting fast-paced events into proper perspective. We have found commendable instances, for example, in Detroit, Milwaukee, and New Brunswick, of radio stations and personalities using their air time and influence to try to calm potential rioters. . . .

Television is the formal news source most relied upon in the ghetto. According to one report, more than 75 percent of the sample turned to television for national and international news, and a larger percentage of the sample (86 percent) regularly watched television from 5 to 7 p.m., the dinner hours when the evening news programs are broadcast.

The significance of broadcasting in news dissemination is seen in Census Bureau estimates that in June 1967, 87.7 percent of nonwhite households and 94.8 percent of white households had television sets.

When ghetto residents do turn to newspapers, most read tabloids, if available, far more frequently than standard size newspapers and rely on the tabloids primarily for light features, racing charts, comic strips, fashion news and display advertising.

Conduct of Press Representatives

Most newsmen appear to be aware and concerned that their very physical presence can exacerbate a small disturbance, but some have conducted themselves with a startling lack of common sense. News organizations, particularly television networks, have taken substantial steps to minimize the effect of the physical presence of their employees at a news event. Networks have issued internal instructions calling for use of unmarked cars and small cameras and tape recorders, and most stations instruct their cameramen to film without artificial light whenever possible. Still, some newsmen have done things "for the sake of the story" that could have contributed to tension.

Reports have come to the Commission's attention of individual newsmen staging events, coaxing youths to throw rocks and interrupt traffic, and otherwise acting irresponsibly at the incipient stages of a disturbance. Such acts are the responsibility of the news organization as well as of its individual reporter.

Two examples occurred in Newark. Television cameramen, according to officials, crowded into and in front of police headquarters, interfering with law enforcement operations and "making a general nuisance of themselves." In a separate incident, a New York newspaper photographer covering the Newark riot repeatedly urged and finally convinced a Negro boy to throw a rock for the camera. Pushing and crowding may be unavoidable, but deliberate staging of events is not.

We believe every effort should be made to eliminate this sort of conduct. This requires the implementation of thoughtful, stringent staff guidelines for reporters and editors. Such guidelines, carefully formulated, widely disseminated, and strictly enforced, underlie the self-policing activities of some news organizations already, but they must be universally adopted if they are to be effective in curbing journalistic irresponsibility.

The Commission has studied the internal guidelines in use last summer at the Associated Press, United Press International, the Washington Post, and the Columbia Broadcasting System. Many other news organizations, large and small, have similar guidelines. In general, the guidelines urge extreme care to ensure that reporting is thorough and balanced and that words and statistics used are appropriate and accurate. The AP guidelines call for broad investigation into the immediate and underlying causes of an incident. The CBS guidelines demand as much caution as possible to avoid the danger of camera equipment and lights exacerbating the disturbance.

Internal guidelines can, and all those studied

do, go beyond problems of physical presence at a disturbance to the substantive aspects of searching out, reporting, and writing the story. But the content of the guidelines is probably less important than the fact that the subject has been thoughtfully considered and hammered out within the organization, and an approach developed that is designed to meet the organization's particular needs and solve its particular problems.

We recommend that every news organization that does not now have some form of guidelines—or suspects that those it has are not working effectively—designate top editors to (a) meet with its reporters who have covered or might be assigned to riots, (b) discuss in detail the problems and procedures which exist or are expected and (c) formulate and disseminate directives based on the discussions. Regardless of the specific provisions, the vital step is for every news-gathering organization to adopt and implement at least some minimal form of internal control.

44.

National Commission on the Causes and Prevention of Violence

VIOLENCE AT THE BANDSHELL

* * *

By 2:15 p.m. the Secret Service estimated 1,000 persons were in the bandshell area, but before the afternoon was over, the crowd had swelled to an estimated 8,000 to 10,000. The makeup of the crowd was mixed: there were a lot of hippies, but there were also some conventionally dressed persons, young and old, and even some infants. A law student states that he saw "about 100 people scattered throughout the crowd" armed with such weapons as sticks with nails, knives and bags of human waste. Other witnesses saw small pieces of floor tile being handed out "as weapons" and rocks and bottles were in evidence.

Some of the persons present, however, can only be described as curious onlookers. Among them, for example, was a woman who lives in a luxurious lakefront high-rise apartment building and who, after lunching at a downtown hotel with several delegates' wives, led the ladies to the bandshell on the hunch that "it might be interesting to listen to hippie speeches." A number of "Viet Veterans for Peace" hats could be seen in the crowd.

There was another element in the crowd, as well. A witness recalls seeing two "clean-cut looking" men with guns sticking out from under their coats. He took them to be "poorly disguised" police undercover men. A Chicago attorney says he saw "roving bands of plainclothes policemen 'disguised' as hippies. . . . They fooled nobody. . . . They seemed to think that if they put on dark glasses, did not shave that morning, and wore a sport shirt and jacket they would be one of the crowd. What concerned me was their manner of traveling in a pack and constantly barging through groups of protesters, bumping into them, making cracks and achieving, if nothing else, the escalation of tempers and hostility."

Intelligence reports indicate that there were at least ten plainclothes policemen dressed in business suits in the bandshell area, but their commanding lieutenant denied that his men at any time "provoked any incident." One of the undercover agents said he arrived at the bandshell about 1 p.m. and joined the parade mar-

---

Source: A report submitted by Daniel Walker, Director of the Chicago Study Team, to the National Commission on the Causes and Prevention of Violence.

shal training. He said black armbands were passed out signifying marshals and the unsanctioned march to be held after the rally was discussed. . . .

Two witnesses who had come to the rally from Lincoln Park with a group of about 200 "young, Yippie-type" demonstrators recall that "a lot of literature was passed out among the crowd, urging all varieties of action from passive resistance to violent overthrow." Jutting from the crowd were standards bearing Viet Cong and red and black flags and protest signs. A Viet Cong flag hung from the loud-speaker stand west of the bandshell.

The Police

Meanwhile, the police set up lines along the west side of Lake Shore Drive, which flanks the east edge of the park; the west (and occasionally the east) side of Columbus Drive, a north-south thoroughfare which divides the park and runs west of the bandshell area; and the north side of the park's southern boundary, Roosevelt Drive. In effect, this boxed the rally in on three sides, while still allowing access to the bandshell area from the north. Reserve groups of police, numbering in total about 100 men, were assembled among a few small, scattered trees north and west behind the bandshell, out of sight to most of the crowd.

A young law student reports that as he and a friend passed near the officers en route to the bandshell, "We were jeered by large groups of police." Some persons, anticipating trouble, brought along wet face cloths in case of tear gas.

More than a dozen police officers kept busy handing out thousands of flyers informing the demonstrators, who sat on the bandshell's open-air benches or on the grass, that the rally was legal and would be "protected" because of the permit. A witness states that many of the officers were Negroes and that they joshed good naturedly with the demonstrators. A minister attending the rally as a medical aide says he thought "the police were working hard to communicate with the crowd."

However, the flyers, which were signed by Chicago's Police Superintendent, warned that no rally would be permitted near the Amphitheatre and that no march or parade outside the park had been sanctioned. "Each and every participant" in any march, the flyers warned, would be arrested. "We earnestly request your cooperation so that rights of dissent and protest will be properly safeguarded as well as the rights of all others including those delegates at the Democratic National Convention," the notice said.

The Speeches

There is no question that the leaders wanted and urged a march on the Amphitheatre, and many persons in the crowd were similarly determined. A Lutheran theology student, who arrived near the start of the rally to observe it for the American Friends Service Committee, recalls overhearing a group of demonstrators discussing a march on the Amphitheatre. "They said they expected violence but were determined to march anyway. They were talking about the fact that medics would be on hand. I also heard [demonstrator] marshals in different areas planning the oncoming march." A march was also endorsed—"whether it is legal or not"—by the rally's various speakers.

Among others appearing during the afternoon were Dick Gregory, William Burroughs ("You are doing something workable about an unworkable system"), Norman Mailer and Vietnam veterans who told of killing civilians and described cooperation of the Vietnamese with the Viet Cong. One young black speaker, a member of the Boston draft resisters group and wearing a red college sweatshirt, burned what he alleged was his draft delinquency notice. To facilitate the rally, says Dellinger's son, David, who was acting as his bodyguard, the park district provided a technician to operate the shell's sound equipment and police stood guard at the rear of the shell to keep unauthorized persons off the stage.

Announcements were made that peanut butter and jelly sandwiches were available and that "Peace" buttons were on sale down front. Ice cream vendors did a brisk business, and occasionally members of the audience with transistor radios would shout out reports on the convention's debate of the Vietnam peace plank. Someone on stage issued a plea for anyone knowing the whereabouts of a teenage girl missing since Monday to contact one of the demonstration marshals. Pigasus, the pig candidate for president, also "spoke"—he was held to the microphone and emitted a stirring "Oink."

* * *

The crowd was so vast (about 10,000 by this time) that rarely was there a central focus of events. Some people ignored the stage completely to nap or read newspapers. Others huddled in groups, talking among themselves or chanting "Ho, Ho, Ho Chi Minh." Some led small parades or waved the many red, black and Viet Cong flags in the audience. Some on the edge of the crowd are reported by one student witness to have spent their time baiting and spitting upon three young men who appeared costumed as "The Spirit of 1776" to protest the protesters.

Through all this, it appears, the uniformed police remained outside the bandshell area. They gathered in units of strength around the park perimeter; police vans and squad cars lined park roadways; one and possibly two helicopters criss-crossed above the crowd and National Guard troops were clearly visible on the roof of museum buildings at the south end of the park near the Soldier Field post and were stationed, with tear gas, along Roosevelt Drive. Some demonstrators who wandered over to the museums during the rally chanted for the Guardsmen to "Jump, jump!" Others booed the men. The Guardsmen, it was reported, just smiled.

The Flag Lowering

Then at about 3:30 or 4 p.m., the first violence erupted near the bandshell. Because of the enormous size of the crowd and the great confusion that followed, it is difficult now to reconstruct a precise chronology of what happened, but the evidence suggests the following sequence of events.

While a speech opposing the draft was being given, a young man wearing an army helmet shinnied up the base of a slim flagpole to the left of the bandshell stage, climbed onto the pole's braces, from which he could reach the halyard, and began to lower the American flag. A police sergeant says the crowd hollered, "Tear down the flag!" But a young postal worker, in the park as an onlooker and sitting near the pole, says, "People started to yell to lower it to half-mast."

Another witness says that several persons on the bandshell stage shouted to the youth to leave the flag alone, and that one left the stage to tell him personally to get down.

According to a police lieutenant, Dellinger took the microphone and announced to the pole climber that the flag should not be taken down but should be flown at half-mast in honor of the "wounded, loyal demonstrators." Other witnesses say the crowd wanted the boy to leave the flag at half-mast as a symbol that democracy at the Democratic covention was dead.

While the youth was still on the pole, recalls the postal employee, "a white-shirted police officer [on the Chicago force, white shirts denote lieutenants and above] came through the crowd and tried to grab the demonstrator who had climbed the pole." According to one witness, the youth tied the flag at half-mast and began to climb down; he was grabbed by the white-shirted officer and two blue-shirted officers. Two plainclothes men then came up to help. A police lieutenant present at the rally states that the youth was not mistreated "in any manner, shape or form" and that no excessive force was used in making the arrest. But another witness asserts, "They began clubbing the hippie with their nightsticks all over his body. . . ."

A roar of protest rose from the audience: "Pigs! . . . Pigs!" The police sergeant quoted earlier heard the shout, "Kill the pigs!" A marshal at the rally states that while the arrest was being made, another young demonstrator attempted to incite the crowd with "Look at what they are doing to your brother; are you going to let those lousy pigs do that to your brother?"

People in the crowd began throwing things at the retreating police. A demonstration marshal claims that the crowd threw "balloons, paper and flowers at the police." Other witnesses remember it differently. One states: "They were tossing anything they could lay their hands on—heavy chunks of concrete, sticks, cans, bags of what looked like paint." The sergeant recalls, "I was hit in the stomach with a large brick and also on the ankle and back of the head with thrown objects. I suffered a large bruise on my right side from a thrown brick." The lieutenant quoted above was struck by a brick on his leg and a chunk of concrete, ripping his trousers and inflicting a painful injury that caused him to limp for three days. Among the objects he saw flying through the air at police were asbestos, metal and clay floor tiles; placards and placard sticks; balloons filled both with paint and urine; bricks; concrete chunks; tree branches; "all types of stones"; eggs; tomatoes and "many other items." After the officer placed the flag-lowering youth in the squad car, he returned to the police line, was hit by a 5″ by 4″ piece of concrete. Other officers state they were hit with sticks, rocks, soda cans, tomatoes, tiles and pieces of park bench.

A *Denver Post* reporter relates that someone on the stage yelled into the microphone, "Stop throwing things! This is worthless! You're hitting your own people! Stop throwing things." The chant, "Sit down, sit down" was taken up by some of the crowd. One youth heaved a large piece of concrete shotput style and the missile fell short, crumpling a demonstrator several feet in front of him.

Suddenly, a half dozen burly young men from the crowd gathered around the pole, untied the flag rope and lowered the flag to the base. As they removed it, one witness remembers, "a few older ladies in the crowd started crying." A Catholic priest who was there on the east side of the bandshell adds: "The feeling of the crowd, especially around me, was nonapproval. Most people felt lowering the flag to half-mast was symbolic, a form of protesting the actions in and outside of the convention. But to take the flag down was not acceptable." Quickly the youths at the flagpole tied an object to the rope and hoisted it to full height. Just what this object was is not known, despite published accounts that describe it variously as "a black flag of anarchy," "a red flag of anarchy," "a red flag of revolution," and a "Viet Cong flag." Some witnesses contend it was a knotted pair of red long underwear, others a red arm band or rag. But on films of the incident, it appears more likely to have been a knotted red cloth or a girl's bright red slip.

Some of those present claim that the actual flag lowering was the work of police undercover agents. The *Chicago Tribune* reported that Robert L. Pierson, who as "Big Bob" Lavin served in an undercover capacity as Jerry Rubin's bodyguard, was "in the group which lowered an American flag in Grant Park." Pierson has said, however, that he had no part in lowering the flag.

At this point six or eight policemen from the group assembled among the trees north and west of the bandshell charged the flagpole area. "I thought it was insane to send eight men into a group of 15,000," a *New York Times* reporter who had been on the scene said in his statement. "If the crowd had meant business, it would have killed these men."

On their heels now came perhaps 15 others, pushing into the flagpole area in an effort to nab the youth who had raised the red cloth. As they came, Rennie Davis shouted over the loudspeaker, "Here come the blue bonnets." The blue-helmeted police were surrounded by demonstrators who attempted to prevent or interfere with the arrests. Chants of "F--- the pigs" and "Dirty pigs" drowned out exhortations from the speaker's stand to "Sit down." One demonstrator waved a placard at the police. It pictured a young man burning his draft card and was captioned, "F--- the draft." The officers swung their batons freely. The officers also were hit with all kinds of material. Someone tried to grab an officer's gun as he fell. Another officer was struck with a liquid which burned a hole in his pants.

"Many people around me panicked and ran," says a law student. "A girl trying to get away was severely beaten over the head and back by the police. She cried hysterically. At this time I noticed that the shell was surrounded by police."

According to some witnesses, Rennie Davis went into the flagpole crowd in an effort to quiet the demonstrators. "The police yelled 'Get Davis!'" recalls one reporter. "They hit him a couple of times." A few minutes later, another witness says Davis appeared on the bandshell platform "with blood all over his face and shirt."

Eventually officers in the flagpole area extricated at least some of the so-called "flag" raisers from the crowd. Then they pulled down the red object but never restored the American flag. The crowd around the flagpole began to pelt them with stones, bricks, planks, chunks of concrete, cans, bottles and some smoking and flaming objects that may have been rags and firecrackers. A second demonstrator was also taken into custody. Several demonstrators crowded around and as the prisoners were being led away to a squad car, a witness relates, "Two girls—one black, and one white, casually dressed—tackled the police officer with the white shirt to try to free the hippie in his custody. They knocked the officer down and then began to run back toward their seats. Several policemen followed them into the seats and held them down. They clubbed them on their stomachs, backs and legs. Then they dragged them away." Later under arrest in a squad car, the Negro girl is alleged to have bitten a policeman on the neck. (The police lieutenant mentions nothing about these girls in his statement and believes the arrest of the lone demonstrator to have been entirely peaceful.) A police officer shouted to news photographers, "Take a picture of those bastards. Show people what they're doing." An Assistant U.S. Attorney was hit with one plastic bag containing urine, another indelible ink.

The Police Reaction

Police in the area fell back for cover. A line of approximately 50 policemen formed facing the crowd, and the rain of missiles continued with such intensity that the police again had to fall back. Sticks, firecrackers, shoes, clods of earth, empty fruit juice cans, bottles, flaming rags and other objects including a plastic "baggie" filled with what appeared to be a bloody sanitary napkin, showered the lawmen.

A short while earlier, an unmarked police car had pulled into a position between the flagpole and the trees where most of the officers were assembled; and some demonstrators started to pelt the car with, the sergeant recalls, "red paint or dye and cellophane bags of human excrement."

Police huddled inside the unmarked car fled the vehicle, and demonstrators swarmed around it, smashing the windows, pounding on the roof and hood and screaming, "Rock it! Rock it!" One policeman, disregarding the shouted warnings of his fellow officers, ran back to the edge of the mob to get the car and drove it in reverse out of the area under a barrage of missiles.

On stage, Dellinger, the afternoon's master of ceremonies, was trying futilely to quiet the crowd. Many in the audience had climbed onto the benches or were trying to join the unruly mob around the flagpole. "Sit down!" people present remember Dellinger shouting through a microphone. "There's much more of the program to come. Be calm! Don't be violent!"

Around a refreshment stand south of the main crowd, however, two witnesses claim they noticed several persons filling Coke bottles with gravel and breaking benches for "sticks to use as clubs." One boy, they say, had a four-foot piece of inch-square wood with a switch-blade knife taped to one end. Films taken at the rally show another youth armed with a stick to which a can opener had been nailed, and some demonstrators testing strong branches against a park bench.

Someone shouted, "We have two more days to burn Chicago!"

By now it was clear that the demonstration marshals were seeking to regain control over their demonstrators. Leaders linked hands to push their own people back. The priest quoted earlier says Dellinger ordered the marshals to line up between the flagpole demonstrators and those still in the bandshell's bench area, apparently in an effort to segregate the flagpole incident.

A minister's wife entering the area about this time with her husband and several college students noticed a policeman out of range of the crowd nervously rubbing his nightstick. As she passed him, she says, he called to her: "This one's for you, baby!" A young McCarthy worker walking into the park with his girlfriend was urged by a man with a walkie talkie (he thinks possibly a plainclothes man) to turn back because the police were "putting on helmets and gas masks, and you might get hurt." The matron quoted earlier "being a cautious person," hurried up to a policeman near the bandshell and "inquired if they expected any difficulty." One responded, "If I were you, I'd get the hell out of here before we bash their heads in!"

A representative of the police has said that profanity and spitting did not have the same effect on the police that incidents involving the flag did. He feels that abuse or misuse of the flag deeply affected the police.

"At precisely that moment," the McCarthy worker remembers, "I saw tear gas exploding in the center of the crowd." Witnesses were uncertain as to exactly what was exploding. They described it variously as a smoke grenade, a stink bomb, a canister of nausea gas, and "a black object about the size and shape of a softball" that released tear gas. A few believed the object was thrown first from the crowd and hurled back by the police.

Subsequent police statements, however, reveal that the sergeant quoted earlier felt himself jeopardized by the ensuing crowd assaults and took a smoke bomb from a squad car and hurled it into the mass of missile throwers in an attempt to disperse them.

A teen-ager wearing heat-resistant gloves snatched up the smoking grenade and lobbed it back among the police, who by now were forming a double line west of the bandshell. The police, who were not wearing gas masks, scattered as the bomb landed in their midst. The crowd applauded. An officer threw it back. Then the police quickly regrouped and several more smoke bombs were hurled. Their front rank stood with nightsticks held at the standard horizontal position. An attorney in the park overheard a plainclothes man say to another, "Let's teach them a lesson."

"Marshals to the point! Everyone else sit down!" came a voice over the loudspeaker.

The police paused for a moment, adjusting helmets and visors and taking test swipes with their clubs, as a chorus of shouts began rising from those in the crowd nearest them. "You're provoking this," someone shouted over the microphone at the police. . . .

The marshals, at least one of whom was a girl, were still struggling with the crowd and had locked arms and were facing the police who stood about 50 feet away. One of the marshals, asked later how he imagined the police might have viewed this marshal line, said, "They probably thought we were going to charge," and said they were "wrestling to keep the crowd from moving on the police." In fact, the films show it was the police who rushed forward. While this is not entirely clear, it is possible to conclude from the films that, with the exception of occasional missile throwing, the crowd had now disengaged from the police and that relative calm prevailed in the bandshell area. It is also possible that the police who now advanced into the bandshell were not the same officers who had taken down the red "flag."

They came first in a relatively straight line. Then as the line of marshals broke in the face of the police advance, the officers waded into the crowd individually.

"At first," according to the statement given by a correspondent from the St. Louis paper, "the police stepped forward in unison, jabbing in an upward motion with their nightsticks with each step and [looking] like a well-drilled marching unit. . . . Suddenly they stopped the unison and began flailing with their clubs in all directions. . . . People scattered. . . . Some went down, screaming and cursing and moaning. I saw a number of women . . . literally run over. In the wink of an eye, the police appeared to have lost all control." As the police moved into the crowd, benches were piled in front of and behind them. The demonstrators hurled pieces of concrete at them and one officer had his radio taken from him. Three demonstrators tried to hurl a park bench at the police line.

Another observer (not a demonstrator) states: "Persons who had done no more than listen to speakers were beaten by clubs or shoved backward in chairs." The matron quoted earlier reports "indiscriminate beating of large numbers of people." A woman who was on the stage claims "some medics were hit even though they were plainly marked in white coats and red armbands." Some demonstrators, she says, piled benches in a barricade in an effort to escape the police. "The police," says a young attorney who was standing at the rear of the bandshell area, "hit and shoved whoever was in their path—men, women, clergymen, newsmen. . . . Some were beaten and clubbed while on the ground."

"A number of people fell in the stampede to escape," says the young law student quoted earlier. "One young boy just two rows in front of me had fallen over a bench and was being slugged and kicked in his back by a policeman." In a crowd of more than 10,000, "it was very hard to move fast enough," recalls a girl who was trying desperately to avoid the swinging clubs. "People were stepping on one another. I looked behind me and caught a glimpse of the face of one of the policemen. I became terrified. The expression was like he wanted to kill."

A young seminary student reports police shoving and clubbing a young man of 19 or 20, four or five times in the shoulders. The boy was dressed in a sport coat and had short blond hair. An officer, on being shown a picture published in *The Chicago Daily Defender* showing several police "beating" a prone demonstrator stated that, in fact, the demonstrator had refused to come with the police and had to be carried away. The officer said the picture actually showed the police trying to pick him up.

As police broke ranks and carried out individual actions, one began hitting an older lady. A marshal jumped on his back and was "clubbed off by another policeman." Demonstrators made barricades with the benches and a marshal threw papers under it and lighted them. Other demonstrators put the fires out. The marshal then prepared newspaper torches with alcohol supplied by the medic teams) and prepared to throw them if the police entered the crowd again.

All this, from the first sighting of the boy on the flagpole to the end of the melee, took place in less than 20 minutes—the longer estimate made by those who state that the film shows that the crowd had become calm before the final police entry. By the time the police had made their way to the center of the seating area, the crowd had scrambled out and the officers stood alone among the jumbled benches, a few bleeding demonstrators moaning on the ground around them, while the dust settled from the air. Medics hurried up to treat head wounds; someone called an ambulance; and crowd marshals darted among the demonstrators urging "Sit, sit! Save your rocks!" and passed out vaseline, instructing demonstrators to smear it on their faces as protection against mace or gas burns; the police walked back to the grove of trees north and west of the bandshell. . . .

A total of 30 policemen were injured at the bandshell incident, according to police reports. Injuries included cuts and contusions on the body as well as head wounds. There is no available count of the demonstrators injured.

After the crowd quieted down, bearded poet Allen Ginsberg, claiming that a sore throat handicapped his appearance, led the throng in a humming of "om-om-om-om," his crowd-calming sound.

* * *

THE ATTEMPTED MARCH TO THE AMPHITHEATRE

The Speeches

At about 4:30 p.m., Dellinger took the microphone and announced that there was going to be an attempt to march nonviolently to the Amphitheatre. A secretary who had come to the rally from her Loop office remembers: "He stressed that 'If you are looking for trouble, don't come with us. We don't want violence.' He then went on to suggest that a second group, primarily the people with families and children, should disperse [or, some witnesses say, "remain in silent vigil at the bandshell"]. He indicated there would be three groups in all: the group that wanted to march, the one that would disperse and one that was 'going to the streets.' . . ."

The sound films reveal a speaker telling those who want violence, or who will at least not abide by the nonviolent principle of the march, to "break up into small groups and do your own thing in the Loop."

A UPI correspondent who was on the scene says that Dellinger "was interrupted while speaking, and asked the crowd to wait a minute." There was then a short conference with the man who had interrupted him, after which Dellinger said, "I am told by some that there is a group which intends to break out of the park and that will be violent. Anyone who wishes to go with that group may, but the group I'm leading will be nonviolent." A young medical student remembers hearing "repeated messages" concerning the march to the effect,

"If you want to do violence, that's your thing; but get away from this group."

* * *

Many of the more normally dressed persons drifted off or remained in their seats, returning eventually to their cars or walking north out of the area. The crowd at the bandshell had, on the whole, been made up of young people. Those who joined the line of march were almost all young.

At the Columbus statue, continues the secretary, "Dellinger had a bullhorn and kept saying over and over again that this would be a nonviolent march. He said this at least 12 times. He added that if anyone was looking for trouble, he should leave the area now."

Although the speakers had made no reference to the fact that a city permit had not been issued for the Amphitheatre march, as the police flyers had noted, Dellinger now announced it. "We will try to negotiate for a permit when we get out into the street," the secretary remembers his saying. "Anyone afraid," he added, "should leave before any possible confrontation, because there is a chance there might be trouble."

Another witness, a young McCarthy worker from New York, saw demonstrators putting on helmets and bullet-proof vests. A college student remembers the crowd being told to abandon placards on sticks, for fear the sticks might be provocative. Some of the marchers had broken boards from park benches and were waving them in the air.

The March Negotiations

"We began to assemble into a marching formaation," the secretary says. "They told us to line up in lines of eight, boys on the outside, girls on the inside. I was in the middle of one of these lines fairly close to the front."

National Guardsmen were stationed along the south end of the park at 12th Street and at a footbridge leading west from the park to 11th Street; the heavy traffic of Lake Shore Drive swept along the east edge; and police were to the west. The marchers moved north.

A young female college student recalls: "There was a tremendous feeling that what we were doing was right, and there was a great feeling of being close to the people around you even though you didn't know them. People were tearing up cloth and wetting it to use in case of tear gas. Other people were passing out vaseline to use in case of mace."

"We marched up the Columbus Drive sidewalk," says the secretary, "where we met a column of police. Consequently, we stopped."

The marchers, 5,000 to 6,000 strong by Secret Service estimate, had come to a line of about 40 police who blocked their path at the intersection of Columbus and Balbo Drive. The senior police officer told Dellinger: "On orders of the Chicago Police Department, there will be no march today."

When the marchers sat down on the sidewalk to await developments, the police commander on the scene announced that they were in violation of the law. No arrests were made, however. The commander explains that he held off any arrests pending the completion of the negotiations or orders from his superiors.

Discussions were opened between the marchers and the police. The conferees were a deputy superintendent of police (the police commander on the scene), a city legal aide and Sidney Peck of the National Mobilization Committee. Dellinger had appointed Peck as a conferee when police asked to meet with a responsible member of his group. The bulk of the negotiations were held in a shanty and in a Park District building near 9th Street, with Peck running back now and then to confer with Dellinger.

Peck essentially restated Dellinger's position: He intended to hold a brief rally in a parking lot a mile from the Amphitheatre, and march back to the Loop.

At about 4:30 p.m., the police made announcements from a squad car equipped with a loudspeaker that all those remaining on the east side of Columbus were in violation of the law and that anyone not wanting to be arrested should move to the west side of Columbus. The police estimate that about 2,000 people then crossed Columbus, seeking a way to get out of the park and over to Michigan Avenue. A sound car also warned photographers and newsmen to leave the park. After this announcement, a line of police moved east across Balbo and severed the line of march into several parts.

A police commander states that one of the march leaders said: "Don't create any trouble here, we're in their ball park. Break up into groups of ten and 20, and go into stores, theaters and the like and create trouble." He also states that at this point the southernmost end of the line of march crossed Columbus and moved diagonally across the park's ball fields towards the Balbo bridge and Michigan Avenue.

At about 5 p.m. during the negotiations between police and marchers, a convoy of Guardsmen of the 2/129th Infantry moved south from the staging area near the Field Museum to the intersection and took up positions blocking passage north across Balbo. They then formed a perimeter at the intersection of Balbo and Columbus.

During this period a witness in front of the Hilton saw numerous things dropped from the hotel falling in the middle of the street. A bag of urine landed on a policeman's helmet.

The demonstrators at Columbus and Balbo did little but sit and wait. Allen Ginsberg provided some diversion by wandering through the crowd clutching a bouquet of daisies and leading another "om" experience. Sometimes the crowd chanted: "More pay for cops!" and "Let the people pass." The UPI correspondent says that some persons were smoking marijuana, although this was mentioned by no other witness.

"Periodically," says a woman in the crowd, "one or two guys would run through the crowd telling everyone to get up and take to the streets. Many people were getting restless, but the crowd did not react to these few would-be inciters. On the other hand, many people sitting on the sidewalk told these guys to sit down. Most of the people around me totally ignored them. During this lull we could see that more police and various news media people were being moved in."

At one point in the waiting, a squad car equipped with a loud-speaker drove backwards on Columbus advising the marchers again that the march was illegal, that they were subject to arrest if they attempted to leave the park as a group and that anyone who did not want to face arrest should pass over to the west side of the drive. Few people in the line of march accepted this offer. Persons in the crowd with loudspeakers, meanwhile, continued to exhort their marchers to "keep your cool."

A crowd marshal states that at one point he took a megaphone, announced that plainclothes men were in the crowd and urged the group not to try to confront them. One of the detectives pointed to him, the marshal claims, and said to his companions, "Don't bring him out walking." But no arrest or assault was actually attempted.

While the negotiators were in session, a Chicago police beat reporter strolled back to the bandshell area. There, he says, he saw a group of demonstrators driving nails into the end of snow fence stakes. On the ground were three or four sticks with four-inch spikes in the end. These, he learned, had been taken from Park District employees whose job it was to pick up litter. While they were fashioning their weapons, the reporter recounts, the demonstrators threatened, "We'll get these f----- pigs with these."

In the negotiations, which dragged on for about an hour, the deputy superintendent of police held firm. He later said he "clearly explained" to Peck that since no permit to march had been given, the demonstrators would not be permitted to march. He said they could move as individuals but that any effort to act in concert would meet with arrest.

When Peck asked what alternatives the group had, the deputy said he named three: One was to stay in Grant Park all night if they wished to demonstrate there; the second was to go to Lincoln Park and demonstrate, and the third was to go to the area of Grant Park east of the Conrad Hilton where the crowd had been on Tuesday night.

45.

Report of the Fact-Finding Commission Appointed to Investigate the Disturbances at Columbia University

STUDENT UNREST AT COLUMBIA

STUDENT ATTITUDES AND CONCERNS

General Characteristics

1. The present generation of young people in our universities is the best informed, the most intelligent, and the most idealistic this country has ever known. This is the experience of teachers everywhere.

It is also the most sensitive to public issues and the most sophisticated in political tactics. Perhaps because they enjoy the affluence to support their ideals, today's undergraduate and graduate students exhibit, as a group, a higher level of social conscience than preceding generations.

The ability, social consciousness and conscience, political sensitivity, and honest realism of today's students are a prime cause of student disturbances. As one student observed during our investigation, today's students take seriously the ideals taught in schools and churches, and often at home, and then they see a system that denies its ideals in its actual life. Racial injustice and the war in Vietnam stand out as prime illustrations of our society's deviation from its professed ideals and of the slowness with which the system reforms itself. That they seemingly can do so little to correct the wrongs through conventional political discourse tends to produce in the most idealistic and energetic students a strong sense of frustration.

Many of these idealists have developed with considerable sophistication the thesis that these flaws are endemic in the workings of American democracy. They argue that their form of pressure—direct action, confrontations, sit-ins, and (in some cases) physical violence—applied at points of institutional weakness, is a legitimate political tool comparable to the other forms of pressure—large political contributions, covert lobbying, favoritism, and the like—effectively applied by those who would lead society astray.

For some of these students their universities have become surrogates for society. The university administration is close at hand. One can bedevil and strike out at it. If the frustrated activist cannot beat the system, he can at least insist that his own university should not lend itself to evil. There are a smaller number who see the university as a place of shelter untouched by the evils of society. They suffer profound shock when they find that the university, and therefore they as parts of it, are not so far removed. In their view this makes them guilty of complicity in profound social and moral evil.

2. Six thousand years ago an Egyptian priest carved on a stone the lament: "Our earth is degenerate . . . children no longer obey their parents." Impatience and antipathy for authority have always been hallmarks of youth, yet today one encounters the irony that this most promising of all student generations appears unusually antagonistic to all forms of restraint and peculiarly violent in social or political protest.

May not the fault lie with the older generation? Unless we are prepared to concede that ours is a sick society too corrupt to be saved, we must acknowledge that we have failed to transmit to many of the ablest young men and women either a sense of the values of reason, order, and civility or an appreciation of the fact that freedom depends upon voluntary restraint. We have managed to convey the idea that, because some of the values we upheld are outdated and others were always wrong, the remainder must also lack merit.

The sources of this shortcoming are not easily identified. One source may be our actual or

---

Source: Excerpts from the Report of the Fact-Finding Commission Appointed to Investigate the Disturbances at Columbia University in April and May 1968.

seeming slowness and resistance to change where change is plainly required. Others may be inherent in our current civilization. The insight of the social sciences and the honesty of the arts have taught us to look at ourselves stripped of our pretense, and what we see is unlovely. We have the honesty and courage to see ourselves as we are, but perhaps, as Archibald MacLeish suggests, we lack the greater Hellenic courage to see man stumble and fall, yet avow his nobler capacity. It became unfashionable among forward-looking intellectuals 30 to 40 years ago to speak of progress, virtue, and wisdom, or to examine the supports on which they rest. . . .

When decisions are made largely on the basis of who has the most power, especially when power is concentrated in a formal authoritarian structure, more and more people within the institution will be dissatisfied. When the decisions are made after full and frank discussion of the various issues involved, and with all opinions being taken into consideration, cohesion develops and effective teaching about the ways in which a democracy should operate is possible—in fact, an actual demonstration takes place. The radical demonstrations for "student power" illustrate what can occur when thoughtful groups trained to criticize and dissent are forced into the tactics of manipulation instead of the rational correction of defects in education and research.

3. During the years in which the present university students were in secondary school the gap between the generations was widened by marked changes in speech, conduct, dress, and manners. Although older people generally disapproved the changes, the more exaggerated the new styles became the more they were promoted by entertainers and influential mass media. The cycle became self-sustaining. Inflated rhetoric and violence began to spread through contemporary society—again largely because the mass media give them the greatest attention. Among the young, inflated rhetoric and bizarre personal appearance have become symbolic behavior indicating disapproval of the "Establishment" and the older generation. As the number of late adolescents and young adults increased in relation to older people, the young became increasingly aware of their power if only they were willing to reject conventional restraints.

The conflicts of style and removal of customary restraints breed antagonisms and even distrust; thus, they increase the tendency to resolve problems by strongly emotional and often intolerant lines of action. And, to a degree, even violent obstruction (as in April) becomes a form of generational self-expression.

4. The size and complexity of the large universities in an urban society increase the alienation of students and, as we shall see, there is too little at Columbia to offset the feeling. One form of response, which must be mentioned among the causes of violent demonstrations, is the romantic reaction against complexity, rationality, and restraint, which has become a small but pervasive thread in student life.

In philosophy, it is illustrated by the popularity of Anarchism.

In politics, the appeal of rigid doctrine with simple explanations becomes irresistible. A simplistic demonology purportedly describing the "Establishment" that controls "the system" comes to explain all the hardships and injustices resulting from the complex cross-currents of a technological society and the selfishness and blundering awkwardness of man. . . .

At Columbia more than a few students saw the barricading of the buildings in April as the moment when they began meaningful lives. They lived gloriously like revolutionary citizens of Paris. They liberated buildings and flew the Red flag. Men and women shared alike without restraint. The marriage ceremony performed in a liberated building by a chaplain attached to the University symbolized the glorious moments of truth. Later, a graduate student, asked to explain to us why he had joined in the seizure, replied that, although he had participated in civil rights activities and every possible peace demonstration, all had come to nothing, but in April, in the buildings, he and others knew that at last they were taking effective action for things worthwhile. The mixture of political and social romanticism varied widely from individual to individual. Many took part without political motivation.

* * *

SOCIAL ATTITUDES TOWARD DISRUPTIVE DEMONSTRATIONS

The forms in which student protests find expression are normally affected, in marked degree, by the social and moral judgments of a wider community. For even if those judgments were wholly rejected by most students—and they are not—still they would be operative facts with which the student leaders must deal as a matter of tactics. Thus, one of the conditions contributing to the April disturbances at Columbia was the prevalent moral uncertainty over the acceptability of the seizure of buildings as a means of influencing reform.

The past decade has seen a marked change in attitudes toward the acceptability of disobedience, harassment, and physical obstruction as methods of influencing social and political action. Tactics that would have been so widely condemned 10 or 15 years ago as to be self-defeating are now accepted and approved in many quarters as moral endeavors to achieve worthy ends. This is especially true among political liberals and youth. The spreading use of such tactics and the much, much wider spirit of tolerance toward their use not only increased the likelihood of resort to physical seizure and occupation of buildings but enabled the rebels to escape unanimous condemnation and gain widespread support among students and faculty once the seizure occurred.

We need scarcely recall the national events in the civil rights movement that spread tolerance for passive disobedience of unjust laws, then for deliberate confrontation with officials enforcing arguably unconstitutional restrictions upon freedom of expression, and finally for the tactics of physical obstruction and harassment as means of influencing policy. The sequence began with the bus boycott in Montgomery, Alabama. It spread next to the sit-in demonstrations at segregated lunch counters and restaurants. Later, there were instances of plain physical obstruction such as completely blocking the entrances to restaurants or crowding into libraries. Student activists gained first-hand experience with such tactics when they went into the south, and later into the northern urban ghettos, to work for racial equality. They could not fail to observe the effectiveness of the tactics, both in dramatizing a cause and in compelling concessions. Any moral or legal scruples were overwhelmed by the morality of the objective. There was virtually no condemnation of their action in segments of the community interested in reform.

Disruption, harassment, and physical obstruction then became common tactics in the peace movement, in which student leaders everywhere played dedicated roles. Again, although more doubts were expressed, there was no general outcry that the tactic was intolerable regardless of its goal.

Thus, the use of disruptive indoor demonstrations and sit-ins as methods of student protest against university policy—at least in relation to the black community or the war in Vietnam—resulted from the progressive extension of tactics encouraged by many moral and political leaders. Careful thought makes it plain that distinctions can, and probably should, be drawn. The Montgomery bus boycott involved neither physical obstruction nor disobedience to law. The sit-ins, at least where there was no physical interference with other patrons, involved the bona fide claim of a constitutional right to service in the lunch counter or restaurant. Both are a far cry from the seizure of buildings as a way of forcing action upon other issues, and from physical harassment or obstruction of others' activities as a means of compelling concessions. But the distinctions, vital as they are, were usually overlooked and the tactics lumped loosely under such heads as "civil disobedience," "non-violence," and "direct action." No one should be greatly surprised, therefore, that students, accustomed to the acceptability of one, should move gradually into the other. Nor is it altogether strange, in this milieu, that the crowded occupation of a college building by 250 protesting students was spontaneously converted into a sit-down, and then a seizure with barricaded doors.

It seems quite plain that, in April, there was no consensus on the Columbia campus that condemned the tactics of disruptive demonstrations. Columbia has a proud tradition of freedom of expression. Even as the demonstrations grew more strident and then more obstructive during 1966 and 1967, the Administration itself usually leaned toward tolerance (although once or twice it sought to draw a tighter line). Other members of the University community in position to have strong influence on its standards of acceptable conduct provided social and moral support. During the April disturbances, a clergyman attached to the Columbia community married two students in Fayerweather Hall during the period of student occupation. The support of this religious counselor and another contributed to the escalation and duration of the disorders by conferring an appearance of moral legitimacy. The Ad Hoc Faculty Group (AHFG) not only offered to disrupt the University by calling a faculty strike as a substitute for the students' physical occupation of the buildings; it also resolved to enforce its will by physical obstruction in the event that the Administration chose to clear the building by the normal processes of law. The threat was repeated in modified language in an effort to induce the Administration to accept the AHFG proposals for settlement. Nice distinctions can be drawn and subtleties of meaning were doubtless intended. Nevertheless, such incidents both reveal and help to create a climate in which even the physical seizure and occupancy of buildings is not seen as an intolerable offense against the entire University community.

To observe the climate is not to approve it. . . . We are convinced that any resort to physical harassment or obstruction as means of influencing the policies and specific decisions of a university is as intolerable as the attitude that policies affecting the public stance of a university are not the concern of faculty or students.

Nor do we suggest that the acceptance of physical harassment and obstruction as a permissible expression of dissent was the unanimous, or even the majority, view of either faculty or students. The point is simply that the largely accidental conversion of a disruptive demonstration into the physical occupancy and barricading of buildings by more than 750 students was made markedly easier, and their refusal to leave voluntarily was stiffened, by the failure of many high-minded liberals to develop the necessary distinctions among the kinds of conduct often too loosely lumped together as "direct action" or "civil disobedience."

Our judgment that such conduct is unacceptable in a free university may provoke the debate. We appreciate the need for rethinking a question that has been thrown into confusion by the strong forces of social reform. The essence of our finding is that one of the causes of the April disturbances was the failure of the academic community to think out the implication of many current forms of political demonstration and to build a firm consensus of moral opinion concerning the limits upon morally acceptable methods of expressing dissent.

CHAPTER XIII

The Victim

ONLY RECENTLY have criminologists turned their attentions to the study of "victimology." In traditional criminological research, the role played by the victim was often ignored, with the major emphasis being placed on the behavior of the offender. However, because of the established importance of the victim-offender relationship, especially after sentencing, the courts and correctional officials, along with parole and probation officers must be thoroughly acquainted with it. The victim and/or offender must both be protected if it is judged that their continued interactions may produce another crime. This has aroused the curiosity of many criminologists who in the past few years have begun turning out an increasing number of articles dealing with the role of the victim at the time of the offense.

Le Roy G. Schultz cites four ways in which a victim may contribute to an offense and facilitate its execution. These are: "(1) By provoking or initiating a hostile reaction in the offender; e.g., during a heated argument one party hands the other a gun and, knowing full well the other's hostile mood, accuses him of not having 'the guts to shoot.' (2) By direct invitation or incitation; e.g., a female engages in heavy petting and mutual sexual preludes and, at the last moment, begins to resist the man's advances that are, by that time, uncontrollable. (3) By omission of normal preventive measures; e.g., the auto-theft victim parks his car unlocked with the engine running while he does some shopping. (4) By unconsciously inviting the offense through his emotional pathology;

e.g., a wife has masochistic needs that are gratified by her assaultive husband."[1]

The first selection in this chapter was taken from the President's Commission on Law Enforcement and Administration of Justice and deals with the victims of crime. Discussed are victim-offender relationships in crimes of violence, places where victimization occurs, compensation to victims, commercial establishments and organizations as victims of crime, and crimes against public organizations and utilities. In the second article, J. Ll. J. Edwards discusses the problems involved in compensating victims of violent crimes. Dr. Edwards examines the nature of the criminal act, the behavior of the victim as a contributing factor, the basis of compensation awardable, amount of compensation payable, characteristics of the victims, procedures that may be used, and the possibility of recovery from the offender. In the third article, Marvin E. Wolfgang examines the problem of victim-precipitated criminal homicide. Data for Dr. Wolfgang's study were collected from the files of the Philadelphia Police Department between January, 1948 and December, 1952. In this article Dr. Wolfgang investigates a number of variables related to victim-precipitated homicide. Included are: race, sex, age, methods used, place and motive, victim-offender relationships, presence of alcohol, and previous arrest record. The final reading, written by Michael Fooner, is focused on victim-induced criminality. Dr. Fooner deals with a number of issues that must be examined if an adequate, functional system of victim compensation is to be created. Among the issues cited are: Should the victim's behavior at the time of the offense be considered when determining compensation? Must an offender be found guilty prior to a victim's receiving compensation? What effect will victim compensation laws have on the temptation of a victim to be abused?

[1]Le Roy G. Schultz, "The Victim-Offender Relationship," *Crime and Delinquency*, Vol. 14, No. 2 (April, 1968), p. 137.

46.

President's Commission on Law Enforcement and Administration of Justice

THE VICTIMS OF CRIME

TASK FORCE ON ASSESSMENT

One of the most neglected subjects in the study of crime is its victims: the persons, households, and businesses that bear the brunt of crime in the United States. Both the part the victim can play in the criminal act and the part he could have played in preventing it are often overlooked. If it could be determined with sufficient specificity that people or businesses with certain characteristics are more likely than others to be crime victims, and that crime is more likely to occur in some places than in others, efforts to control and prevent crime would be more productive. Then the public could be told where and when the risks of crime are greatest. Measures such as preventive police patrol and installation of burglar alarms and special locks could then be pursued more efficiently and effectively. Individuals could then substitute objective estimation of risk for the general apprehensiveness that today restricts—perhaps unnecessarily and at best haphazardly—their enjoyment of parks and their freedom of movement on the streets after dark.

Although information about victims and their relationships to offenders is recorded in the case files of the police and other criminal justice agencies, it is rarely used for systematic study of those relationships or the risks of victimization. To discover variations in victimization rates among different age, sex, race, and income groupings in the population, the Task Force analyzed information on these items obtained in the national survey by NORC.

Rather striking variations in the risk of victimization for different types of crime appear among different income levels in the population. The results shown in Table 13.1 indicate that the highest rates of victimization occur in the lower income groups when all index offenses except homicide are considered together. The risks of victimization from forcible rape, robbery, and burglary, are clearly concentrated in the lowest income group and decrease steadily at higher income levels. The picture is somewhat more erratic for the offenses of aggravated assault, larceny of $50 and over, and vehicle theft. Victimization for larceny increases sharply in the highest income group.

National figures on rates of victimization also show sharp differences between whites and nonwhites. (Table 13.2) Nonwhites are victimized disproportionately by all Index crimes except larceny $50 and over.

The rates for victimization shown for Index offenses against men (Table 13.3) are almost three times as great as those for women, but the higher rates of burglary, larceny and auto theft against men are in large measure an artifact of the survey procedure of assigning offenses against the household to the head of the household.

The victimization rate for women is highest in the 20 to 29 age group. In fact the victimization rates for women for all the Index offenses reported, with the exception of larceny, are greatest in this age group. The concentration of offenses against women in this age group is particularly noticeable for forcible rape and robbery and much less apparent in aggravated assault and the property crimes.

For men the highest Index total rate falls in the 30–39 age category, a result heavily influenced by the burglaries assigned to men as heads of households. Actually, all the Index property offenses against men show peak rates in the older age categories. This is probably due

Source: Task Force on Assessment, The President's Commission on Law Enforcement and Administration of Justice, *Task Force Report: Crime and Its Impact—An Assessment* (Washington, D.C.: U.S. Government Printing Office, 1967), pp. 80–84.

TABLE 13.1

VICTIMIZATION BY INCOME

(Rates per 100,000 Population)

Offenses	*Income*			
	$0 to $2,999	*$3,000 to $5,999*	*$6,000 to $9,999*	*Above $10,000*
Total	2,369	2,331	1,820	2,237
Forcible rape	76	49	10	17
Robbery	172	121	48	34
Aggravated assault	229	316	144	252
Burglary	1,319	1,020	867	790
Larceny ($50 and over)	420	619	549	925
Motor vehicle theft	153	206	202	219
Number of respondents	(5,232)	(8,238)	(10,382)	(5,946)

SOURCE: Philip H. Ennis, "Criminal Victimization in the United States: A Report of a National Survey." (Field Survey II, President's Commission on Law Enforcement and Administration of Justice [Washington, D.C.: U.S. Government Printing Office, 1967], adapted from Table 14, p. 31.) Hereinafter referred to as the NORC study.

TABLE 13.2

VICTIMIZATION BY RACE

(Rates per 100,000 Population)

Offenses	*White*	*Non-White*
Total	1,860	2,592
Forcible rape	22	82
Robbery	58	204
Aggravated assault	186	347
Burglary	822	1,306
Larceny ($50 and over)	608	367
Motor vehicle theft	164	286
Number of respondents	(27,484)	(4,902)

SOURCE: NORC study, adapted from Table 16, p. 33.

not only to their role as household heads but also to the fact that at older ages they are likely to possess more property to be stolen. Crimes against the person, such as aggravated assault and robbery, are committed relatively more often against men who are from 20 to 29 years of age.

Thus, the findings from the national survey show that the risk of victimization is highest among the lower income groups for all Index offenses except homicide, larceny, and vehicle theft; it weighs most heavily on the non-whites for all Index offenses except larceny; it is borne by men more often than women, except, of course, for forcible rape; and the risk is greatest for the age category 20 to 29, except for larceny against women, and burglary, larceny, and vehicle theft against men.

VICTIM-OFFENDER RELATIONSHIPS IN CRIMES OF VIOLENCE

The relations and interactions of victims and offenders prior to and during the criminal act

TABLE 13.3

VICTIMIZATION BY AGE AND SEX

(Rates per 100,000 Population)

Offense	*10–19*	*20-29*	*30–39*	*40–49*	*50-59*	*60 plus*	*All Ages*
	Male						
Total	951	5,924	6,231	5,150	4,231	3,465	3,091
Robbery	61	257	112	210	181	98	112
Aggravated assault	399	824	337	263	181	146	287
Burglary	123	2,782	3,649	2,365	2,297	2,343	1,583
Larceny ($50 and over)	337	1,546	1,628	1,839	967	683	841
Motor vehicle theft	31	515	505	473	605	195	268
	Female						
Total	334	2,424	1,514	1,908	1,132	1,052	1,059
Forcible rape	91	238	104	48	0	0	83
Robbery	0	238	157	96	60	81	77
Aggravated assault	91	333	52	286	119	40	118
Burglary	30	665	574	524	298	445	314
Larceny ($50 and over)	122	570	470	620	536	405	337
Motor vehicle theft	0	380	157	334	119	81	130

SOURCE: NORC study, adapted from Table 17, pp. 34–35.

are important facts to know for understanding and controlling crime and assessing personal risks more accurately. The relationships most often studied have been those involving crimes of violence against the person, especially homicide and forcible rape. Typical of the findings of these inquiries are the results of an analysis of criminal homicides in Philadelphia between 1948 and 1952.[1] This study clearly demonstrated that it is not the marauding stranger who poses the greatest threat as a murderer. Only 12.2 percent of the murders were committed by strangers. In 28.2 percent of the cases studied, the murderer was a relative or a close friend. In 24.7 percent he was a member of the family. The murderer was an acquaintance of the victim in 13.5 percent of the cases.

These findings are very similar to those reported nationally in the *UCR*.

> In 1965 killings within the family made up 31 percent of all murders. Over one-half of these involved spouse killing spouse and 16 percent parents killing children. Murder outside the family unit, usually the result of altercations among acquaintances, made up 48 percent of the willful killings. In the latter category romantic triangles or lovers' quarrels comprised 21 percent and killings resulting from drinking situations 17 percent. Felony murder, which is defined in this program as those killings resulting from robberies, sex motives, gangland slayings, and other felonious activities, made up 16 percent of these offenses. In another 5 percent of the total police were unable to identify the reasons for the killings; however, the circumstances were such as to suspect felony murder.[2]

Unfortunately, no national statistics are available on relationships between victims and offenders in crimes other than criminal homicide. However, the District of Columbia Crime Commission surveyed a number of other crimes. Its findings on victim-offender relationships in

[1]Marvin E. Wolfgang, *Patterns of Criminal Homicide* (Philadelphia: University of Pennsylvania Press, 1958). See also Menachem Amir, "Patterns of Rape and the Female Victim" (unpublished Ph. D. thesis, The University of Pennsylvania, 1965); Albert J. Reiss, Jr., "Studies in Crime and Law Enforcement in Major Metropolitan Areas," Field Surveys III, President's Commission on Law Enforcement and Administration of Justice (Washington, D. C.: U.S. Government Printing Office, 1967), Vol. 1, Sec. 1, Table 6, p. 35. Hereinafter referred to as the Reiss studies.

[2]*UCR, 1965*, pp. 6–7.

rape and aggravated assault closely resemble those for murder:

Almost two-thirds of the 151 [rape] victims surveyed were attacked by persons with whom they were at least casually acquainted. Only 36 percent of the 224 assailants about whom some identifying information was obtained were complete strangers to their victims: 16 (7 percent) of the attackers were known to the victim by sight, although there had been no previous contact. Thirty-one (14 percent) of the 224 assailants were relatives, family friends or boyfriends of the victims, and 88 (39 percent) were either acquaintances or neighbors.[3]

And among 131 aggravated assault victims, only 25 (19 percent) were not acquainted with their assailants:

Fourteen (11 percent) of the victims were attacked by their spouses, 13 (10 percent) were attacked by other relatives, and 79 (60 percent) were assaulted by persons with whom they were at least casually acquainted.[4]

Again, as in murder, a substantial number (20 percent) of the aggravated assaults surveyed by the District of Columbia Crime Commission involved a victim and offender who had had trouble with each other before.[5]

Another source of the concern about crime, in addition to its violence and its frequency, is the extent to which it is assumed to involve interracial attacks. Therefore a key question in any assessment of the crime problem is to what extent men or women of one racial group victimize those of another. For evidence on the way in which the race and sex of victims and offenders might affect the probability of criminal assault, the Commission, with the cooperation of the Chicago Police Department, studied 13,713 cases of assaultive crimes against the person, other than homicide.[6]

As shown in Table 13.4, it is Negro males and females who are most likely to be victimized in crimes against the person. A Negro man in Chicago runs the risk of being a victim nearly six times as often as a white man, a Negro woman nearly eight times as often as a white woman.

The most striking fact in the data is the extent of the correlation in race between victim and offender. Table 13.4 shows that Negroes are most likely to assault Negroes, whites most likely to assault whites. Thus, while Negro males account for two-thirds of all assaults, the offender who victimizes a white person is most likely also to be white.

The President's Commission on Crime in the District of Columbia discovered similar racial relationships in its 1966 survey of a number of serious crimes. Only 12 of 172 murders were interracial.[7] Eighty-eight percent of rapes involved persons of the same race.[8] Among 121 aggravated assaults for which identification of race was available, only 9 percent were interracial.[9] Auto theft offenders in the District are three-fourths Negroes, their victims two-thirds Negroes.[10] Robbery, the only crime of violence in which whites were victiminized more often than Negroes, is also the only one that is predominantly interracial: in 56 percent of the robberies committed by Negroes in the District of Columbia, the victims are white.[11]

The high proportions of both acquaintance between victim and offender and the intraracial character of offenses are further borne out by the findings of another study developed for the Commission. Analyzing data obtained from the Seattle Police Department, this study compared the census tract where the crime occurred with the tract (or other place) in which the offender lived. It found that a relatively large percentage of crimes against persons, as contrasted with crimes against property, had been committed in the offender's home tract—an area likely to be racially homogeneous and in which he is most likely to be known at least by sight.[12]

This analysis shows that a failure to collect adequate data on victim-offender relationships

---

[3]"Report of the President's Commission on Crime in the District of Columbia" (Washington, D.C.: U.S. Government Printing Office, 1966). Hereinafter referred to as the D.C. Crime Commission Report. Further detail is contained in a study by Irving A. Wallach, "A Description of Active Juvenile Offenders and Convicted Adult Felons in the District of Columbia—Vol. 2: Adult Felon," in appendix volume, D.C. Crime Commission Report, pp. 452–645.

[4]*Ibid.*, p. 76.

[5]*Ibid.*

[6]Reiss, *op. cit.*, Vol. 1, Sec. 1, pp. 38–72.

[7]D.C. Crime Commission Report, *op. cit.*, at p. 42.

[8]*Ibid.*, at p. 54.

[9]*Ibid.*, p. 76.

[10]*Ibid.*, p. 101.

[11]*Ibid.*, p. 56.

[12]Reiss studies, *op. cit.*, pp. 203–16.

TABLE 13.4

VICTIM-OFFENDER RELATIONSHIPS BY RACE AND SEX IN ASSAULTIVE CRIMES AGAINST THE PERSON (EXCEPT HOMICIDE)

	Offenses attributable to–				
	White offenders		*Negro offenders*		*All types of offenders*
	Male	*Female*	*Male*	*Female*	
Victim rate for each 100,000:*					
White males	201	9	129	4	342
White females	108	14	46	6	175
Negro males	58	3	1,636	256	1,953
Negro females	21	3	1,202	157	1,382
Total population*	130	10	350	45	535

*The rates are based only on persons 14 years of age or older in each race-sex category. The "total population" category in addition excludes persons from racial groups other than Negro or white.

SOURCE: Special tabulation from Chicago Police Department, Data Systems Division, for period September 1965 to March 1966, reported in Reiss studies, supra note 1, vol. 1, section 1, adapted from Table 6, pp. 35–36.

may lead to a miscalculation of the source and nature of the risk of victimization. At present the Nation's view of the crime problem is shaped largely by official statistics which in turn are based on offenses known to the police and statistics concerning arrested offenders; they include very little about victims.

PLACE WHERE VICTIMIZATION OCCURS

Crime is more likely to occur in some places than in others, just as some persons are more likely than others to be the victims of criminal offenders. The police often distribute their preventive patrols according to spot maps that locate the time and place of occurrence of different types of crimes. Such information, however, has not been developed well enough to inform the public of the places it should avoid.

A well-designed information system should also provide crime rate figures for different types of business premises in different areas of the city. Victimization rates based upon the number of drugstores, cleaning establishments, gas stations, taxicabs, banks, supermarkets, taverns, and other businesses in a neighborhood would furnish better indicators of the likelihood of crime in that neighborhood than exist at present. Determining such rates would require enumerating premises of different types and locating them by area. This information would help to test the effectiveness of control measures and to identify the nature of increases in crime by making it possible to detect changes in the pattern of risk for various businesses. It would also permit more refined calculations of risk for insurance purposes and guide the placement of alarm systems and other crime prevention devices.

The study of victimization of individuals carried out in cooperation with the Chicago Police Department recorded the types of premises for all major crimes against the person except homicide.[13] Table 13.5 classifies victims by sex in relation to the place where the offense occurred. For assaultive crimes against the person, the street and the home are by far the most common places of occurrence. Men are more likely to be victimized on the street, and women are more likely to be victimized in residences.

The findings in general are closely related to the characteristic patterns of interaction among men and women in our society. Men are more likely to meet one another outside the home. A substantial portion of assaults arises from drinking—the tavern is the third most common setting for men to be victims of assault and battery—and some of the conflicts among drunks later erupt into street fights. Men and women more frequently engage in conflicts with each other in domestic settings.

[13] *Ibid.*, pp. 123–69.

TABLE 13.5

VICTIMIZATION BY SEX AND PLACE OF OCCURRENCE FOR MAJOR CRIMES (EXCEPT HOMICIDE) AGAINST THE PERSON

(In Percent)

Place of Occurrence	*Victims of Major Crimes against Person*	
	Male	*Female*
School property	3.2	2.4
Residence	20.5	46.1
Transport property	1.4	.4
Taxis and delivery trucks	2.6	....
Businesses	3.2	1.1
Taverns and liquor stores	5.7	2.8
Street	46.8	30.7
Parks	.8	.5
All other premises	16.0	16.0
Total percent	100.0	100.0
Total number	(8,047)	(5,666)

SOURCE: Special tabulation from Chicago Police Department, Data Systems Division, for period September 1965 to March 1966, adapted from Reiss studies, supra note 1, Vol. 1, section 1, Table 34, p. 149.

COMPENSATION TO VICTIMS OF CRIME

Programs granting public compensation to victims for physical injuries from violent crimes have aroused increased interest in recent years. The community has evidenced concern for the plight of victims of muggings, stabbings, and other violence. In the absence of such programs victims generally suffer losses that are not compensated in any way. Their civil remedies are most likely to be unsuccessful because of the poor financial condition and prospects of most offenders. And the criminal law generally makes no effort to use its sanctions to insure restitution to the victim. Indeed it often aggravates the vicim's problem by incarcerating the offender, thus preventing him from earning money to make restitution.

Two philosophies underlie the recent movements for victim compensation. The first argues that the government is responsible for preventing crime and therefore should be made responsible for compensating the victims of the crimes it fails to prevent. The second approach, an extension of welfare doctrines, rests on the belief that people in need, especially those in need because they have been victimized by events they could not avoid, are entitled to public aid.[14]

The first modern victim-compensation programs were established in New Zealand and Great Britain in 1964. California's program, which became effective in the beginning of 1966, was the first in the United States. Only victims with limited financial resources qualify for compensation under this program. New York's victim-compensation bill, enacted in 1966, also provides compensation only for those who would suffer "serious financial hardship" as a result of the crime. . . .

The Commission has been impressed by the consensus among legislators and law enforcement officials that some kind of State compensation for victims of violent crime is desirable. Recent public opinion polls indicate that a considerable majority of the public is in favor of victim compensation.[15] The Commission believes

[14]Gilbert Geis, "State Aid to Victims of Violent Crime," published in appendix B of President's Commission on Law Enforcement and Administration of Justice.

[15]See the Gallup poll, Oct. 29, 1965, where 62 percent of the public were in favor of compensation for the victims of crime. Also, the national survey conducted by NORC for the Commission indicated

that the general principle of victim compensation, especially to persons who suffer injury in violent crime, is sound and that the experiments now being conducted with different types of compensation programs are valuable.

COMMERCIAL ESTABLISHMENTS AND ORGANIZATIONS AS VICTIMS OF CRIME

It is very difficult to discover the exact extent to which businesses and organizations are the victims of crime. Few attempts are made to keep systematic records or report such crimes to any central place. Police agencies do not ordinarily separate the crimes against individuals from those against organizations. It was not possible in the short time available to the Commission to undertake a systematic census of victimization of different types of industrial, business, professional, religious, or civic organizations throughout the Nation. This task ought to be undertaken, and some assessment procedure developed, using reports, special sample surveys or similar devices.

The Commission was able to make a pilot survey, however, of a sample of neighborhood businesses and organizations in eight police precincts in Chicago, Washington, and Boston. The objective was to discover through interviews what types of victimization businesses and organizations had experienced from crimes such as burglary, robbery, shoplifting, passing of fraudulent checks, and employee theft.

Burglary and Robbery. Reports to the *Uniform Crime Reports* indicate that nationally about half of all burglaries in 1965 were nonresidential, and that the average worth of the property stolen in such burglaries was about $225.[16] In the Commission survey almost one of every five businesses and organizations in the eight neighborhood police precincts surveyed was burglarized at least once during the one-year period covered by the survey. Considering only those that were burglarized, 62 percent had from two to seven burglaries.[17]

In both Chicago and Washington, but for some reason not in Boston, the burglary victimization rates were highest in the districts where the overall crime rates were highest. Precinct 13 in the District of Columbia, for example, had a victimization rate of 51.8 per 100 organizations—nearly twice that of the precinct with the fewest burglaries—and a third of all the businesses and organizations sampled in that area had been victimized.[18]

Nationally, reports to the *UCR* indicate that in 1965 9 percent of all robberies were of service stations or chain-stores, almost 1 percent were of banks, and more than 20 percent were of other types of commercial establishments. The average value of the property reported stolen varies from $109 for service station robberies to $3,789 for bank robberies.[19]

In the Commission survey the picture that emerges for victimization by robbery is similar to that for burglary, which occurs more frequently. Among the organizations that were robbed, 80 percent reported only one robbery but 2 percent had as many as five.[20] While any business in a high crime rate area is obviously in danger, it appears that some businesses, like some people, are more likely than others to be victimized by crime. Clearly, the reasons for the differences need investigation as guides in prevention. The findings of the President's Commission on Crime in the District of Columbia with respect to the circumstances of housebreaking are suggestive of the way risks vary:

> In 21 (7 percent) of the 313 commercial burglaries surveyed housebreakers entered through unlocked doors and in 70 instances (22 percent) through unlocked windows. In 111 instances the housebreakers broke windows to gain entry, and locks were forced in 95. A total of 105 of the commercial establishments victimized were reported to have had burglar-resistant locks; 65 of these establishments, however, were entered other than by tampering with the lock. Sixty-four percent of the burglarized com-

that 56 percent of the sample interviewed were in favor of compensation for victims. See NORC study, supra, source note Table 13.1, p. 69.

[16]The data for the 1965 arrest rates were derived from "Uniform Crime Reports for the United States, 1965" (Washington, D.C.: U.S. Department of Justice, Federal Bureau of Investigation, 1966), pp. 107–45.

[17]Reiss studies, *op. cit.*, pp. 99, 100, 103.

[18]*Ibid.*

[19]"*UCR., 1965*" *op. cit.*, p. 11.

[20]Reiss studies, *op. cit.*, pp. 99, 100, 103.

mercial establishments were located on the first floor.[21]

Shoplifting. Shoplifting usually involves the theft of relatively small and inexpensive articles, although the professional shoplifter may steal expensive furs, clothes, and jewelry. It is heaviest in the chainstores and other larger stores which do the most retail business. However, it is the smaller establishments, particularly those that operate on a low margin of profit, to which shoplifting may make the difference between success and failure.

In the Commission survey, 35 percent of the neighborhood wholesale and retail establishments surprisingly reported no problem with shoplifting, while sizable percentages of other types of businesses, such as construction companies (30 percent), manufacturers of nondurables (33 percent), finance, insurance, and real estate firms (25 percent), which might not be expected to have any problem, reported some shoplifting difficulties. The average amount of shoplifting experienced by the nontrade establishments was considerably less than that for retail establishments.[22]

As one might expect, the highest rates of shoplifting were reported in the high crime rate districts. The most common items carried off by shoplifters were food, liquor or beer, clothing and footwear, and miscellaneous small items worth less than $10.[23] However, it is the total volume, rather than individual acts, that makes shoplifting a serious problem for most commercial enterprises.

Nationally most large retail businesses estimate their overall inventory shrinkage due to shoplifting, employee theft, and accounting errors at between 1 and 2 percent of total inventory. Experts in industrial and commercial security estimate that 75 to 80 percent of the inventory shrinkage is probably attributable to some type of dishonesty.[24] Among the 47 percent of neighborhood businesses found by the Commission survey to have high rates of shoplifting, 60 percent placed their losses at less than 2 percent of total inventory; another 28 percent estimated they had lost between 2 and 6 percent. Surprisingly, 23 percent of all businesses in the survey were unable to give any estimate at all of the amount of their losses that might be due to shoplifting.[25]

Employee Theft. According to security experts for retail and other commercial establishments, theft by employees accounts for a considerably larger volume of theft than shoplifting.[26] Theft of merchandise or equipment by employees is particularly hard to control because detection is so difficult. Employees have opportunities for theft every working day, whereas the shoplifting customer cannot steal merchandise regularly from the same establishment without arousing suspicion.

Employee theft is also a problem in many industrial concerns. A recent survey by the National Industrial Conference Board of 473 companies indicated that 20 percent of all companies and nearly 30 percent of those with more than 1,000 employees had a serious problem with employee theft of tools, equipment, materials or company products. More than half of the companies with a problem of employee theft indicated trouble with both white and blue collar workers.[27]

In neighborhood establishments surveyed by the Commission only 14 percent reported the discovery of any employee dishonesty. Among those, 40 percent estimated losses at no more than $50 a year. Most managers or owners surveyed attempted to establish the honesty of employees before hiring them. Nearly one-third made an effort to check references or to clear the employee with the local police department but 74 percent did not report to the police the discovery of theft by their own employees, preferring to discharge the employee or handle the matter in some other way by themselves.[28]

---

[21] D.C. Crime Commission Report, *op. cit.*, p. 86.

[22] Reiss studies, *op. cit.*

[23] *Ibid.*

[24] See chapter 3, "The Economic Impact of Crime."

[25] Reiss studies, *op. cit.*

[26] "The Economic Impact of Crime," *op.cit.*

[27] National Industrial Conference Board, Division of Personnel Administration, "Personnel Practices in Factory and Office" (New York: National Industrial Conference Board, Inc., 1964), p. 140.

[28] Albert J. Reiss, Jr., "Employee Honesty in Businesses and Organizations in Eight Police Precincts of Three Cities." A report to the President's Commission on Law Enforcement and the Administration of Justice, 1966 (mimeo).

CRIME AGAINST PUBLIC ORGANIZATIONS AND UTILITIES

Public organizations and utilities are repeatedly victimized by crime. While some of the crime committed against these organizations is reported to the police, it is not clear just how much goes unreported and how widespread it is.

To obtain some estimation, the Commission surveyed 48 such organizations in Boston, Chicago, and Washington with special attention to the police districts in which other surveys were being conducted.[29]

The most prevalent and persistent problem reported was vandalism of buildings and equipment. Telephone companies, electric companies, schools, libraries, traffic and highway departments, parks, public transportation, and housing all are victims. Estimates of damage ranging up to $200,000 a year were quoted for such facilities as public housing, transportation, public parks, and recreation facilities in schools. The public school system in Washington, D.C., for example, provided data for 1965 showing a total of 26,500 window panes broken and replaced at a cost of $118,000. A similar report was received in Boston.

Larceny was also a frequently mentioned problem, involving such thefts as stealing loose equipment and personal possessions, theft from coin meters, and breaking and entering. Some organizations make a distinction between amateur and professional theft. For example, the telephone companies distinguished between the organized coinbox larceny using forged keys and the amateur forcible entry involving damage to the equipment. Employee theft was not reported as a serious problem except in hospitals where it represents the most common reason for the apprehension and discharge of employees.

Many public facilities reported problems with various forms of violence within their boundaries. Assaults and child molestation occur in parks, libraries, and schools. Emergency rooms of hospitals cited disturbances by drunken and disorderly persons. The threat of violent behavior or the presence of disorderly persons was reported to affect markedly the patronage of parks, libraries and after-school activities, especially in areas with high crime rates.

[29]Stephen Cutler and Albert J. Reiss, Jr., "Crimes Against Public and Quasi-Public Organizations in Boston, Chicago, and Washington, D.C." A report to the President's Commission on Law Enforcement and the Administration of Justice, 1966 (mimeo).

47.

J. Ll. J. Edwards

COMPENSATION TO VICTIMS OF CRIMES OF PERSONAL VIOLENCE

In its first report to Parliament, tabled in October 1965, the British Criminal Injuries Compensation Board declared:[1] "The need in the modern state for a scheme for the compensation of victims of crimes of violence has been well shown even during the few months of the running of this scheme. It is true that many of the applications submitted relate to comparatively minor injuries and the compensation paid is correspondingly small. But no one who is called to deal with those cases in which a blameless victim has been seriously disabled, sometimes for life, or with those cases in which the elderly and infirm have suffered injury and shock, can

Source: *Federal Probation,* Vol. XXX, No. 2 (June, 1966), pp. 3–10. Reprinted by permission of the author and the journal.

[1]Cmnd. 2782, p. 7.

fail to feel deeply what a worthwhile part is played in the full administration of justice by the power to award compensation."

This emphasis on the humanitarian features of the British scheme may surprise those who tend to view the question of crime compensation as basically an economic problem. Critics of the principle of victim compensation by the state have maintained that it constitutes an unwarranted incursion into the private insurance field and that it represents a disturbing dilution of the concept of sturdy individualism.[2] Every adult member of society, it is argued, should be regarded as capable of making adequate provision from his own resources to meet any eventuality that might affect his future economic status in society. State interference is looked upon as the perennial bogey that weakens the national character, and in doing so the plight of the underprivileged and the poor is often overlooked. Insofar as there exists, however, in every society a substantial proportion of its members who are unable to make provision for themselves or their families to meet the hazards that can befall any citizen there appears to be a strong prima-facie case in favour of the state assuming this responsibility. . . .

The current surge of concern for the innocent victim of a violent crime, which is evident in the various studies that have been set in motion in recent months in New York, New Jersey, Michigan, Pennsylvania, Maryland and other parts of the United States is, in itself, an interesting phenomenon. Not for the first time in the field of social legislation, New Zealand has shown the way and provided the necessary leadership by drawing attention to the yawning gap in the law of nearly every civilised country so far as providing some form of compensation for the victims of crime is concerned. In some ways our Anglo-Saxon forbears were more advanced in their laws than our modern criminal legislation, providing as they did appropriate forms of sanction for wrongdoing by the exaction of *bot* and *wergild* in the form of monetary compensation to the victim or his family.[3] Hebrew law, as reflected in the Book of Exodus,[4] and the Salic law of the Franks,[5] provide additional testimony as to the wide resort in early Western culture to the notion of crime compensation.

Basic to each of these early precedents was the requirement that the offender himself should make reparation to the victim of his misdeeds, a principle that modern states have been all too prone to ignore in the development of their penal systems. Such a requirement represents one of the more notable differences between the British and New Zealand schemes as originally formulated. It is significant, however, that in the British Government's most recent White Paper on "The Adult Offender"[6] the view is reiterated that an eventual solution to the problem of providing work for prisoners "may be a system under which prisoners received normal wages, out of which they contribute to their own support and that of their families, and perhaps also to the cost of compensating their victims."

The administrative difficulties in translating this Utopian philosophy into a realistic set of operational principles are fully recognised but a scheme that is designed to achieve these aims has already been examined by the prison department of the British Home Office.[7] Such an innovation, if successfully implemented, would surely have wide repercussions not only with respect to the training of offenders but also in the observance and enforcement of the criminal law. We might then even begin to see developed a better integration of the attitudes and efforts of the judiciary, law enforcement, and correctional agencies in place of the present conflict of philosophies that does little to enhance respect for the criminal law or to im-

[2]For the most comprehensive examination of the problem, in which each of the conventional schools of thought is clearly spelt out, see G.O.W. Mueller, *et al., Minnesota Law Review,* Vol. 50 (1965), pp. 121–310.

[3]See C. S. Kenny, *Outlines of Criminal Law* (15th ed.) pp. 23–24, citing Pollock and Maitland's *History of English Law,* Vol. 1, p. 26, Vol. 2, p. 448.

[4]21 *Exodus* 18, 19.

[5]Marvin E. Wolfgang, *Minnesota Law Review,* Vol. 50 (1965), p. 226, quoting J. L. Gillin, *Criminology and Penology* (3rd ed., 1945), p. 338. Prof. Wolfgang's examination of the development of the principle of victim compensation in primitive cultures and in early civilised countries is particularly worthy of attention.

[6]Cmnd. 2852, presented to Parliament in December, 1965.

[7]See *The Times,* October 11, 1965.

prove the chances of controlling the level of criminal activities.

The accumulative body of experience that has been gained in Britain and New Zealand in administering their respective schemes may be of value to those states which are contemplating a similar development in their own jurisdictions. It is proposed, therefore, to consider the important issues underlying a state system of victim compensation by examining the statutory and administrative principles applied in these two countries and adopted by any other jurisdictions that have revealed their own legislative proposals.

1. Boundaries of Criminal Acts Within Which Compensation May Be Awarded

Although much of the theoretical discussion in the United States during the past few years has centred on the astronomical costs of compensating victims for damage to *property*, it is important to note that neither of the existing schemes in New Zealand and Britain makes any provision for reparation in such circumstances. Two notable aspects, however, distinguish the approach adopted by the respective countries. First, New Zealand law provides for compensation in the event of a person being killed by any act or omission of another person which falls within a list of crimes enumerated in a schedule to the Criminal Injuries Compensation Act, 1963. The British scheme is more flexible and makes no reference to any specified crimes. Instead, it provides the simple criterion that compensation is recoverable where personal injury is directly attributable to a criminal offence. Secondly, the British scheme makes an important extension to the customary doctrine of victim compensation by also providing reparation to any person who suffers personal injury (1) in the course of arresting or attempting to arrest a suspected offender, (2) in the course of preventing or attempting to prevent an offence from being committed, or (3) in giving help to a police officer who is engaged in arresting an offender or in preventing the commission of an offence.[8] No power exists to reward a public spirited citizen simply for assisting the police, but if he is injured in doing so then the state assumes an obligation to compensate him for any loss that he might sustain as a result of his volunteering help to maintain law and order. . . .

2. Relevance of the Victim's Own Behavior in Contributing to the Injuries Inflicted Upon Him

The extent to which victims of crimes of violence contribute to the situation by their own actions or words has already proved to be a fruitful area of criminological research. Recognition of this kind of situation, by no means unknown to the criminal courts, is made explicit in both schemes. Thus, the New Zealand statute requires its Compensation Tribunal, when determining whether to make an order and also in deciding the amount to be awarded, to have regard to any behaviour of the victim which directly or indirectly contributed to his injury or death. The British scheme adopts the same approach and requires the Board to reduce the amount of compensation, or to reject the claim altogether, in accordance with its assessment of the degree of responsibility attributable to the victim.

The civil law of contributory negligence provides a ready precedent for this sensible principle. Special attention must be paid, according to the British system, to applications in respect of sexual offences or other offences arising out of a sexual relationship. These are scrutinised with particular care in order to determine whether the victim provoked the assault. If, however, the circumstances have been immediately reported to the police, the Compensation Board is authorised to entertain applications for compensation arising out of rape and sexual assaults, both in respect of pain, suffering and shock and also loss of earnings due to pregnancy

[8]This principle has a lineage in English statute law dating back to 1826. Under the Criminal Law Act of that year, sections 28–30, provision is made for the payment of compensation (1) to persons, whether injured or not, who have been active in the apprehension of certain offenders, and (2) to the families of persons killed trying to apprehend an offender. In contrast to the present scheme, the former law did not permit compensation to be paid where a citizen intervened to prevent the commission of an offence. The 1826 legislation, moreover, was rarely invoked—there are records of payments to only 26 persons during the years 1950–59.

resulting from rape. Compensation is not payable for the maintenance of any child born as a result of sexual offence committed in Britain.

3. Basis of the Compensation Awardable

A criticism often levelled against the introduction of a system of crime compensation is the alleged dangers that would arise if the victim, or his next of kin, were to become not only an aggrieved party but also someone who has a financial stake in the conviction of the defendant. Were this in fact to be the case it would undoubtedly be a matter of concern, though it is doubtful how much weight should be attached to the element of private greed when viewed in the light of the safeguards inherent in the adversary system of criminal trials.

The British scheme, it is important to notice, enables the Compensation Board to make an award to a victim whether or not the offender has been brought to justice. What is required is that the circumstances of the injury shall have been reported to the police without delay or have been the subject of criminal proceedings in the courts. The award of compensation is not made dependent on a finding of guilt. This is surely right, if only in view of the technicalities of the criminal law and the underlying philosophy of the entire scheme which is to compensate for the injury suffered provided the bona fide nature of the claim is established. An additional safeguard is the requirement that an applicant must be prepared to submit to such medical examination as the Compensation Board may require. Apart from these general safeguards the only prerequisite condition is the necessity of establishing that the degree of injury suffered was "appreciable." This is interpreted to mean an injury that results in at least 3 weeks' loss of earnings or an injury for which $150 would be the minimum amount of compensation.

The New Zealand Criminal Injuries Compensation Act, 1963, follows much the same lines. In particular, section 17(6) states that the Tribunal may make an award "whether or not any person is prosecuted for, or convicted of, any offence arising out of the [criminal] act or omission." The standard of proof in establishing that the injury resulted from a criminal act is the "balance of probabilities" criterion, familiar to litigants who bring their cases before the civil courts. Unlike the British scheme, the New Zealand legislation spells out the matters which are compensatable. These include: (a) expenses actually and reasonably incurred, (b) pecuniary loss to the victim as a result of total or partial incapacity for work, or pecuniary loss to the dependants of a victim who is killed, (c) pain and suffering, and (d) any other expenses which, in the opinion of the Tribunal, it is reasonable to incur.[9]

4. Amount of Compensation Payable

It is interesting to note that upper limits of compensation are laid down in the New Zealand legislation, in sharp contrast to the British scheme which places no restrictions on the discretionary powers of the Compensation Board. There is already accumulating, however, a substantial body of experience which permits some interesting comparisons to be drawn between the levels of compensation available in the two countries for those who are victims of crimes of violence. . . .

During the first year's operation of the New Zealand legislation seven applications only were received by the Crimes Compensation Tribunal. Of these, three cases concerned women who were attacked by an intruder when alone at home, the remainder being male victims of criminal attacks. The total amount awarded as compensation for the first full year was $9,600 composed, in each case, of lump payments.[10] This mode of payment is discretionary, the other procedure envisaged by the New Zealand Act, where there has been total or partial incapacity for work, is the making of periodical payments up to a maximum period of 6 years. Additional sums are provided for the wife of a victim and any dependent children up to 18 years who are engaged in a full-time course of education or training. For any other pecuniary loss or expenses the ceiling is set at

[9]Act No. 134 of 1963, s. 18.

[10]Only the briefest summary of the Tribunal's work is given in the 1964–65 *Annual Report of the New Zealand Department of Justice*, p. 14.

$3,000, and up to an additional $1,500 may be awarded for pain and suffering.[11]

Compensation, under the British scheme, is expressly assessed on the basis of common law damages for personal injuries and, other than in exceptional circumstances, a lump sum payment is made. The principle of a periodical pension, as provided for in the New Zealand system, is not recognised in Britain, but more than one payment may be made, for example, where only a provisional medical assessment can be given at the time of the original application. Any element of punitive or exemplary damages in the form of compensation is totally excluded, and likewise with respect to loss of expectation of happiness. Furthermore, where the victim is alive, or in the case of a fatal injury the standard of reparation for loss of earnings, is not to exceed twice the average of industrial earnings at the time that the injury was sustained.[12] What then has been the actual experience in administering the British scheme of victim compensation?

The first report of the British Criminal Injuries Compensation Board contains a great deal of interesting information on the working of the experimental scheme, which has already established itself as an essential part of the country's machinery of criminal justice. Preceding its introduction, it may be well to remember, was the same kind of foreboding that presently marks much of the public debate and literature on the subject in the United States. "So far" says the Report "we have had very few claims indeed which give rise to a suspicion of fraud."[13] Of the 2,216 cases dealt with up to December 31, 1965, compensation has been awarded in 890 cases. Applications were disallowed in 138 cases and an additional 19 applicants withdrew or abandoned their claims. The remainder are still being processed.[14] The vast majority of awards did not exceed $600 in individual cases, though a few reached a figure falling within the range $6,000 to $9,000. In only one case did the compensation exceed $15,000. This was a Scottish case in which the widow of a man stabbed to death in the street received $3,000, and his four children a total of $13,500.

During the period covered by the Board's first report, viz., the 8 months from September 1964 to April 1965, a total of just over $100,000 was paid out in compensation.[15] This modest sum was explained as being attributable to the high proportion of straightforward cases involving comparatively minor injuries, which could be processed quickly. As an informed guess the British Board estimates that its payments of compensation during 1965–1966 may be in the region of $1,500,000.[16]

Around 1,500 completed applications are expected in the current year, a steady rise being noticeable once the existence of the scheme became known to the public. The Board's policy of issuing monthly press releases, including case summaries of some of the successful and unsuccessful applications, has served a variety of useful purposes. It has generated a considerable number of informed editorials and newspaper articles, it has served to convince the sceptics of the justice of the scheme, and, perhaps above all, it has brought home to the general public that long overlooked side of the enforcement of the criminal law, namely, the fate of the victim after sentence has been passed on the offender and the drama of the trial is over. In the latest press release which brings the Board's experience up to December 31, 1965, the expected increase in the number of applications, and the total compensation paid, is strikingly evidenced. The total figure of $100,000 in compensation noted at the end of April 1965 had risen to $913,000 by the end of the year.

5. Characteristics of the Victims of Crimes of Violence

In preparing this article, an analysis was carried out of a sample of 391 cases drawn from the cases reported by the British Criminal Injuries Compensation Board during the first 17 months of its operation.[17] Some of the findings may be

[11]Criminal Injuries Compensation Act, 1963, s. 19.
[12]Cmnd. 2323 of 1964, p. 22
[13]*Loc. cit.*, p. 6.
[14]*Press Release* issued by the Criminal Injuries Compensation Board, dated December 31, 1965.
[15]Cmnd. 2782, p. 4.
[16]*Loc. cit.*
[17]I have to thank Miss Barbara Schloss, research assistant in the Centre of Criminology, for conducting this analysis. The sample is based on all the

of particular interest to those contemplating the introduction of legislation along the lines of the British scheme.

Sex and Age of Victims. Males comprised 78.5 percent of the sample, females representing the balance of 21.5 percent.

The following table shows the percentage of victims falling within specified age groups:

Age	Percent
Under 16	9.2%
17 – 30	35.8%
31 – 40	17.7%
41 – 50	15.1%
51 – 60	12.8%
61 – 87	9.0%

Place Where the Attack or Injury Occurred. In about one-fifth of the cases reported, the place where the offence occurred was not reported. The remaining cases display the following pattern:

Place	Percent
In the street	30%
Other public places, e.g., parks, shops, restaurants, car parks	11.7%
Place of employment	9.0%
Licensed premises or immediately outside	7.4%
Private premises	5.8%
On vehicle or premises of public transportation	5.4%
In victim's own home	5.1%
In social club or adjoining premises	1.8%
In an automobile	1.8%
On the highway	1.3%

Occupation of the Victims. It appears as if the occupation of the victim was noted in the Board's press releases in those instances only where the vulnerability of the offender was increased by reason of the nature of his employment. Thus, the occupations most frequently mentioned are as follow:

Occupation	Percent
Police	7.9%
Public transport worker	3.1%
Service station attendant	2.0%
Post Office employee	1.8%
Caretaker, security guard	1.3%
Barman	1.0%
Lorry driver	.8%
Taxi driver	.8%

Special Categories of Victims. Attention should be drawn to four special categories of victims, in view of the expanded nature of the British scheme to include those who are injured in the course of assisting in the task of law enforcement:

(a) Those who went to the assistance of other victims or potential victims and in the process were themselves injured. There were three cases of this kind in the sample and they received, respectively, compensation amounting to \$850, \$1,050, and \$10,500.

(b) Those who were injured when attempting to arrest single-handed. This group comprised three persons, the levels of compensation ranging from \$220 to \$800.

(c) Those who went to the assistance of the police. So far there appears to have been only one case of this kind, and he was awarded \$3,450.

(d) Where the victim was a member of the police force, a category that could easily be overlooked when examining the theoretical framework of a scheme for victim compensation. At least 31 policemen have been awarded sums ranging from \$100 to \$11,000 with respect to injuries suffered in the execution of their duty.

Juvenile Victims. Juveniles represent an interesting group of their own. Nearly one-half of all the victims who were under 17 years of age received compensation for injuries affecting their vision. Seventeen cases fall into this final group, of whom 10 lost an eye. In the majority of cases the injury was inflicted by another juvenile, the principal instruments being pellets from an air-gun, stones thrown or fired from a sling shot, and bows and arrows. The mean compensation in these cases was \$6,000. Many similar cases involving juveniles were not awarded compensation on the ground that the injury was not directly attributable to the commission of a criminal offense, but arose, for example, as the result of an accident.

6. The Compensation Board and Its Procedure

Here again, a distinct difference in approach is manifest between the British and New Zealand schemes. In New Zealand, the Tribunal ranks as a Commission of Inquiry and is required to sit in public unless there are considerations, e.g., affecting the interests of public morality or the interests of the victim of an

periodic reports issued by the Board, with the exception of the release for February 1965 which was not available.

alleged sexual offence, which justify the hearing being conducted in private.[18] The applicant can appear in person or be represented by his counsel or solicitor. Moreover, in every case the Tribunal is required to state the reasons for its decision.[19]

Informality, on the other hand, may be said to be the key feature of the British scheme. Applications are sifted initially by the staff of the Compensation Board. In addition to describing the incident in which he was injured and the extent of his injuries and loss, the victim is required to sign an authority for the Board to obtain a copy of any statement he made to the police, medical reports from the hospital and the doctor from whom he received treatment, details of payments from his employers and public funds such as sickness or injury benefit. The initial decision whether to allow or dismiss the application and, if necessary, what amount of compensation should be payable, rests in the hands of a single member of the five-member Board. If not satisfied with the decision, the applicant can appeal and he is entitled to a hearing before three members of the Board, excluding the one who made the initial decision. The hearing is informal and in private. There are no set rules of procedure, the rules of evidence do not apply, and the victim is allowed to bring a friend or his legal adviser to assist him in putting his case.

In both Britain and New Zealand the administrative tribunal is entirely responsible for deciding what compensation should be paid in individual cases and their decisions are not subject to appeal or to Ministerial review.[20] All five members of the British Board are legally qualified,[21] but in New Zealand only the chairman is required to be a lawyer.

[18]Criminal Injuries Compensation Act, 1963, s. 12. The Tribunal is also empowered to issue an order restricting press reports of its proceedings.

[19]*Ibid.*, s. 11.

[20]The only qualification exists in the right of appeal on the ground of lack of jurisdiction, which is expressly laid down in the New Zealand Act, s. 16. Presumably, the same principle will apply to the British Compensation Board.

[21]One of the original members of the Board has since become a Justice of the High Court, which may provide some indication of the stature of the Board.

7. Recovery From the Offender

Earlier in this paper attention was drawn to the principle of personal reparation by the offender to the victim which was the foundation of early law. With the passage of time, however, the criminal law has been transformed to the point where the state assumes a pervasive role in every aspect of law enforcement, criminal adjudication, and in the subsequent handling of offenders. The victim occupies a prominent role only during the trial as an essential part of the prosecution's case against the accused. With the handing over of the offender to the state's appointed officials for administering its penal institutions and correctional services the victim's existence and problems are quickly forgotten. The time has come to seriously re-examine modern correctional philosophy in the light of the age-old theory of expiation by the criminal. Effective correctional handling of the offender may well be significantly advanced if the interests of the victim are accorded a more prominent place in the ultimate objective of changing the prisoner's attitude towards his neighbours in society.

The New Zealand statute already recognises this principle by conferring upon its Compensation Tribunal, on the application of the Secretary of Justice, power to make an order directing the offender to refund the whole or part of any compensation paid by the state to the victim. Before making any such order the offender must be given the opportunity to be heard, and proper consideration must be given to his financial position, his employment and future prospects, as well as to his family obligations. The British Compensation Board, it is worth noting, has asked that consideration be given to providing it with the same power of recovery from the offender by action in the courts.

The argument constantly invoked in discussing the feasibility of personal reparation is that the vast majority of those charged with crimes are impecunious and men of straw. Be that as it may, and the data upon which reliable deductions might be made is singularly missing, it is doubtful whether every avenue has yet been adequately explored with a view to ensuring that those who profit by their criminal activities are not permitted to take advantage of their illegally obtained capital and are compelled to make the fullest restitution to their victims, where possible, and if these cannot be identified then to the state itself. Society deserves nothing less and I refuse to believe that criminology is so barren as to be unable to provide a more effective solution to this cardinal problem.[22] Furthermore, I refuse to believe that the acceptance of this fundamental premise runs counter to the rehabilitative approach to corrections. In the words of the notable White Paper "Penal Practice in a Changing Society":[23]

> It may well be that our penal system would not only provide a more effective deterrent to crime, but would also find a greater moral value, if the concept of personal reparation to the victim were added to the concepts of deterrence by punishment and of reform by training. It is also possible to hold that the redemptive value of punishment to the individual offender would be greater if it were made to include a realisation of the injury he had done to his victim as well as to the order of society, and the need to make personal reparation of that injury.

Where the means do not presently exist to fulfill this goal, society must see to it that they are created. If the current Home Office discussions, designed to provide a solution to the administratively complex problem of realistic prisoners' earnings, come to fruition the day may not be too far distant when society in Britain will see offenders placed in a position where they can make substantial reparation to the victims of their misdeeds. Such a landmark in penology would be watched with great interest by other countries, among them Canada and the United States, which are at last awakening to the neglect of past generations to make adequate provision for the blameless victims of crimes of personal violence.

[22]One suggestion, recently put forward to the Royal Commission on the Penal System by a group of senior members of the English Bar, envisages machinery being established which would require a criminal after serving his sentence (1) to prove how he and his family came into possession of money or property, or (2) to satisfy official demands that he account for his postprison affluence.

[23]Cmnd. 645 of 1959, para. 25.

48.

Marvin E. Wolfgang

VICTIM-PRECIPITATED CRIMINAL HOMICIDE

In many crimes, especially in criminal homicide, the victim is often a major contributor to the criminal act. Except in cases in which the victim is an innocent bystander and is killed in lieu of an intended victim, or in cases in which a pure accident is involved, the victim may be one of the major precipitating causes of his own demise. . . .

The law of homicide has long recognized provocation by the victim as a possible reason for mitigation of the offense from murder to manslaughter, or from criminal to excusable homicide. In order that such reduction occur, there are four prerequisites.[1]

(1) There must have been adequate provocation.

(2) The killing must have been in the heat of passion.

(3) The killing must have followed the

Source: Reprinted by special permission of the *Journal of Criminal Law, Criminology and Police Science* (Northwestern University School of Law), Copyright © 1957, Vol. 48, No. 1.

[1]For an excellent discussion of the rule of provocation, from which these four requirements are taken, see: Rollin M. Perkins, "The Law of Homicide," *Journal of Criminal Law and Criminology*, Vol. 36 (March–April, 1946), pp. 412–27; and Herbert Wechsler and Jerome Michael, *A Rationale of the Law of Homicide*, pp. 1280–2. A general review of the rule of provocation, both in this country and abroad, may be found in The Royal Commission on Capital Punishment, *1949–52 Report*, Appendix II, pp. 453-8.

provocation before there had been a reasonable opportunity for the passion to cool.

(4) A causal connection must exist between provocation, the heat of passion, and the homicidal act. Such, for example are: adultery, seduction of the offender's juvenile daughter, rape of the offender's wife or close relative, etc.

Finally (4), Perkins claims that "the adequate provocation must have engendered the heat of passion, and the heat of passion must have been the cause of the act which resulted in death."[2]

DEFINITION AND ILLUSTRATION

The term *victim-precipitated* is applied to those criminal homicides in which the victim is a direct, positive precipitator in the crime. The role of the victim is characterized by his having been the first in the homicide drama to use physical force directed against his subsequent slayer. The victim-precipitated cases are those in which the victim was the first to show and use a deadly weapon, to strike a blow in an altercation—in short, the first to commence the interplay or resort to physical violence.

In seeking to identify the victim-precipitated cases recorded in police files it has not been possible always to determine whether the homicides strictly parallel legal interpretations. In general, there appears to be much similarity. In a few cases included under the present definition, the nature of the provocation is such that it would not legally serve to mitigate the offender's responsibility. In these cases the victim was threatened in a robbery, and either attempted to prevent the robbery, failed to take the robber seriously, or in some other fashion irritated, frightened, or alarmed the felon by physical force so that the robber, either by accident or compulsion, killed the victim. Infidelity of a mate or lover, failure to pay a debt, use of vile names by the victim, obviously means that he played an important role in inciting the offender to overt action in order to seek revenge, to win an argument, or to defend himself. However, mutual quarrels and wordy altercations do not constitute sufficient provocation under law, and they are not included in the meaning of victim-precipitated homicide.

Below are sketched several typical cases to illustrate the pattern of these homicides. Primary demonstration of physical force by the victim, supplemented by scurrilous language, characterizes the most common victim-precipitated homicides. All of these slayings were listed by the Philadelphia Police as criminal homicides, none of the offenders was exonerated by a coroner's inquest, and all the offenders were tried in criminal court.

A husband accused his wife of giving money to another man, and while she was making breakfast, he attacked her with a milk bottle, then a brick, and finally a piece of concrete block. Having had a butcher knife in hand, she stabbed him during the fight.

A husband threatened to kill his wife on several occasions. In this instance, he attacked her with a pair of scissors, dropped them, and grabbed a butcher knife from the kitchen. In the ensuing struggle that ended on their bed, he fell on the knife.

In an argument over a business transaction, the victim first fired several shots at his adversary, who in turn fatally returned the fire.

The victim was the aggressor in a fight, having struck his enemy several times. Friends tried to interfere, but the victim persisted. Finally, the offender retaliated with blows, causing the victim to fall and hit his head on the sidewalk, as a result of which he died.

A husband had beaten his wife on several previous occasions. In the present instance, she insisted that he take her to the hospital. He refused, and a violent quarrel followed, during which he slapped her several times, and she concluded by stabbing him.

During a lover's quarrel, the male (victim) hit his mistress and threw a can of kerosene at her. She retaliated by throwing the liquid on him, and then tossed a lighted match in his direction. He died from the burns.

A drunken husband, beating his wife in their kitchen, gave her a butcher knife and dared her to use it on him. She claimed that if he should strike her once more, she would use the knife, whereupon he slapped her in the face and she fatally stabbed him.

[2] *Ibid.*, p. 425. The term "cause" is here used in a legal and not a psychological sense.

A victim became incensed when his eventual slayer asked for money which the victim owed him. The victim grabbed a hatchet and started in the direction of his creditor, who pulled out a knife and stabbed him.

A victim attempted to commit sodomy with his girlfriend, who refused his overtures. He struck her several times on the side of her head with his fists before she grabbed a butcher knife and cut him fatally.

A drunken victim with knife in hand approached his slayer during a quarrel. The slayer showed a gun, and the victim dared him to shoot. He did.

During an argument in which a male called a female many vile names, she tried to telephone the police. But he grabbed the phone from her hands, knocked her down, kicked her, and hit her with a tire gauge. She ran to the kitchen, grabbed a butcher knife, and stabbed him in the stomach.

THE PHILADELPHIA STUDY

Empirical data for analysis of victim-precipitated homicides were collected from the files of the Homicide Squad of the Philadelphia Police Department, and include 588 consecutive cases of criminal homicide which occurred between January 1, 1948, and December 31, 1952. Because more than one person was sometimes involved in the slaying of a single victim, there was a total of 621 offenders responsible for the killing of 588 victims. . . . The 588 criminal homicides provide sufficient background information to establish much about the nature of the victim-offender relationship. Of these cases, 150, or 26 percent, have been designated, on the basis of the previously stated definition, as VP cases.[3] The remaining 438, therefore, have been designated as non-VP cases.

Thorough study of police files, theoretical discussions of the victim's contribution, and previous analysis of criminal homicide suggest that there may be important differences between VP and non-VP cases. The chi-square test has been used to test the significance in proportions between VP and non-VP homicides and a series of variables. Hence, any spurious association which is just due to chance has been reduced to a minimum by application of this test, and significant differences of distributions are revealed. Where any expected class frequency of less than five existed, the test was not applied; and in each tested association, a correction for continuity was used, although the difference resulting without it was only slight. In this study a value of P less than .05, or the 5 percent level of significance, is used as the minimal level of significant association. Throughout the subsequent discussion, the term *significant* in italics is used to indicate that a chi-square test of significance of association has been made and that the value of P less than .05 has been found. The discussion that follows (with respect to race, sex, age, etc.) reveals some interesting differences and similarities between the two. (Table 13.6.)

RACE

Because Negroes and males have been shown by their high rates of homicide, assaults against the person, etc., to be more criminally aggressive than whites and females, it may be inferred that there are more Negroes and males among VP victims than among non-VP victims. The data confirm this inference. Nearly 80 percent of VP cases compared to 70 percent of non-VP cases involve Negroes, a proportional difference that results in a *significant* association between race and VP homicide.

SEX

As victims, males comprise 94 percent of VP homicides, but only 72 percent of non-VP homicides, showing a *significant* association between sex of the victim and VP homicide.

Since females have been shown by their low rates of homicide, assaults against the person, etc., to be less criminally aggressive than males, and since females are less likely to precipitate their own victimization than males, we should expect more female *offenders* among VP homicides than among non-VP homicides. Such is the case, for the comparative data reveal that females are twice as frequently offenders in VP slayings (29 percent) as they are in non-VP

[3]In order to facilitate reading of the following sections, the *victim-precipitated* cases are referred to simply as VP cases or VP homicides. Those homicides in which the victim was not a direct precipitator are referred to as non-VP cases.

TABLE 13.6

VICTIM-PRECIPITATED AND NON-VICTIM-PRECIPITATED CRIMINAL HOMICIDE BY SELECTED VARIABLES, PHILADELPHIA, 1948–1952

	Total Victims		*Victim-Precipitated*		*Non-Victim-Precipitated*	
	Number	*Percent of Total*	*Number*	*Percent of Total*	*Number*	*Percent of Total*
Race and Sex of Victim						
Both races	*588*	*100.0*	*150*	*100.0*	*438*	*100.0*
Male	449	76.4	141	94.0	308	70.3
Female	139	23.6	9	6.0	130	29.7
Negro	*427*	*72.6*	*119*	*79.3*	*308*	*70.3*
Male	331	56.3	111	74.0	220	50.2
Female	96	16.3	8	5.3	88	20.1
White	*161*	*27.4*	*31*	*20.7*	*130*	*29.7*
Male	118	20.1	30	20.0	88	20.1
Female	43	7.3	1	0.7	42	9.6
Age of Victim						
Under 15	28	4.8	0	—	28	6.4
15–19	25	4.3	7	4.7	18	4.1
20–24	59	10.0	18	12.0	41	9.4
25–29	93	15.8	17	11.3	76	17.3
30–34	88	15.0	20	13.3	68	15.5
35–39	75	12.8	25	16.7	50	11.4
40–44	57	9.7	23	15.3	34	7.8
45–49	43	7.3	13	8.7	30	6.8
50–54	48	8.2	11	7.3	37	8.5
55–59	26	4.4	6	4.0	20	4.6
60–64	18	3.1	7	4.7	11	2.5
65 and over	28	4.7	3	2.0	25	5.7
Total	588	100.0	150	100.0	438	100.0
Method						
Stabbing	228	38.8	81	54.0	147	33.6
Shooting	194	33.0	39	26.0	155	35.4
Beating	128	21.8	26	17.3	102	23.3
Other	38	6.4	4	2.7	34	7.7
Total	588	100.0	150	100.0	438	100.0
Place						
Home	301	51.2	80	53.3	221	50.5
Not Home	287	48.8	70	46.7	217	49.5
Total	588	100.0	150	100.0	438	100.0
Interpersonal Relationship						
Relatively close friend	155	28.2	46	30.7	109	27.3
Family relationship	136	24.7	38	25.3	98	24.5
(Spouse)	(100)	(73.5)	(33)	(86.8)	(67)	(68.4)
(Other)	(36)	(26.5)	(5)	(13.2)	(31)	(31.6)
Acquaintance	74	13.5	20	13.3	54	13.5
Stranger	67	12.2	16	10.7	51	12.8
Paramour, mistress, prostitute	54	9.8	15	10.0	39	9.8
Sex rival	22	4.0	6	4.0	16	4.0
Enemy	16	2.9	6	4.0	10	2.5
Paramour of offender's mate	11	2.0	1	.7	10	2.5
Felon or police officer	6	1.1	1	.7	5	1.3
Innocent bystander	6	1.1	—	—	6	1.5
Homosexual partner	3	.6	1	.7	2	.5
Total	550	100.0	150	100.0	400	100.0
Presence of alcohol during offense						
Present	374	63.6	111	74.0	263	60.0
Not present	214	36.4	39	26.0	175	40.0
Total	588	100.0	150	100.0	438	100.0

TABLE 13.6 (Cont.)

	Total Victims		*Victim Precipitated*		*Non-Victim-Precipitated*	
	Number	*Percent of Total*	*Number*	*Percent of Total*	*Number*	*Percent of Total*
Presence of alcohol in the victim						
Present	310	52.7	104	69.3	206	47.0
Not present	278	47.3	46	30.7	232	53.0
Total	588	100.0	150	100.0	438	100.0
Previous arrest record of victim						
Previous arrest record	*277*	*47.3*	*93*	*62.0*	*184*	*42.0*
Offenses against the person	150	25.5 (54.2)	56	37.3 (60.2)	94	21.4 (50.1)
Other offenses only	127	21.6 (45.8)	37	24.7 (39.8)	90	20.5 (49.9)
No previous arrest record	311	52.7	57	38.0	254	58.0
Total	588	100.0	150	100.0	438	100.0
Previous arrest record of offender						
Previous arrest record	*400*	*64.4*	*81*	*54.0*	*319*	*67.7*
Offenses against the person	264	42.5 (66.0)	49	32.7 (60.5)	215	45.6 (67.4)
Other offenses only	136	21.8 (34.0)	32	21.3 (39.5)	104	22.1 (32.6)
No previous arrest record	221	35.6	69	(46.0)	152	32.3
Total	621	100.0	150	100.0	471	100.0

slayings (14 percent)—a proportional difference which is also highly *significant.*

The number of white female offenders (16) in this study is too small to permit statistical analysis, but the tendency among both Negro and white females as separate groups is toward a much higher proportion among VP than among non-VP offenders. As noted above, analysis of Negro and white females as a combined group does result in the finding of a *significant* association between female offenders and VP homicide.

Age

The age distributions of victims and offenders in VP and non-VP homicides are strikingly similar; study of the data suggests that age has no apparent effect on VP homicide. The median age of VP victims is 33.3 years, while that of non-VP victims is 31.2 years.

Methods

In general, there is a *significant* association between method used to inflict death and VP homicide. Because Negroes and females comprise a larger proportion of offenders in VP cases, and because previous analysis has shown that stabbings occurred more often than any of the other methods of inflicting death,[4] it is implied that the frequency of homicides by stabbing is greater among VP than among non-VP cases. The data support such an implication and reveal that homicides by stabbing account for 54 percent of the VP cases but only 34 percent of non-VP cases, a difference which is *significant.* The distribution of shootings, beatings, and "other" methods of inflicting death among the VP and non-VP cases shows no significant differences. The high frequency of stabbings among VP homicides appears to result from an almost equal reduction in each of the remaining methods; yet the lower proportions in each of these three other categories among VP cases are not separately very different from the proportions among non-VP cases.

[4]Of 588 victims, 228, or 39 percent, were stabbed; 194, or 33 percent, were shot; 128, or 22 percent were beaten; and 38, or 6 percent, were killed by other methods.

Place and Motive

There is no important difference between VP and non-VP homicides with respect to a home/not-home dichotomy, nor with respect to motives listed by the police. Slightly over half of both VP and non-VP slayings occurred in the home. General altercations (43 percent) and domestic quarrels (20 percent) rank highest among VP cases, as they do among non-VP cases (32 and 12 percent), although with lower frequency. Combined, these two motives account for a slightly larger share of the VP cases (3 out of 5) than of the non-VP cases (2 out of 5).

Victim-Offender Relationships[5]

Intra-racial slayings predominate in both groups, but inter-racial homicides comprise a larger share of VP cases (8 per cent) than they do of non-VP cases (5 percent). Although VP cases make up one-fourth of all criminal homicides, they account for over one-third (35 percent) of all inter-racial slayings. Thus it appears that a homicide which crosses race lines is often likely to be one in which the slayer was provoked to assault by the victim. The association between inter-racial slayings and VP homicides, however, is not statistically significant.

Homicides involving victims and offenders of opposite sex (regardless of which sex is the victim or which is the offender) occur with about the same frequency among VP cases (34 percent) as among non-VP cases (37 percent). But a *significant* difference between VP and non-VP cases does emerge when determination of the sex of the victim, relative to the sex of his specific slayer, is taken into account. Of all criminal homicides for which the sex of both victim and offender is known, 88 involve a male victim and a female offender; and of these 88 cases, 43 are VP homicides. Thus, it may be said that 43, or 29 percent, of the 150 VP homicides, compared to 45, or only 11 percent, of the 400 non-VP homicides, are males slain by females. . . .

The proportion that Negro male/Negro male[6] and white male/white male homicides constitute among VP cases (45 and 13 percent) is similar to the proportion these same relationships constitute among non-VP cases (41 and 14 percent). The important contribution of the Negro male as a victim-precipitator is indicated by the fact that Negro male/Negro female homicides are, proportionately, nearly three times as frequent among VP cases (25 percent) as they are among non-VP cases (9 percent). It is apparent, therefore, that Negroes and males not only are the groups most likely to make positive and direct contributions to the genesis of their own victimization, but that, in particular, Negro males more frequently provoke females of their own race to slay them than they do members of their own sex and race.

For both VP and non-VP groups, close friends, relatives, and acquaintances are the major types of specific relationships between victims and offenders. Combined, these three relationships constitute 69 percent of the VP homicides and 65 percent of the non-VP cases. Victims are relatives of their slayers in one-fourth of both types of homicide. But of 38 family slayings among VP cases, 33 are husband-wife killings; while of 98 family slayings among non-VP cases, only 67 are husband-wife killings. This proportional difference results in a *significant* association between mate slayings and VP homicide.

Finally, of VP mate slayings, 28 victims are husbands and only 5 are wives; but of non-VP mate slayings, only 19 victims are husbands while 48 are wives. Thus there is a *significant* association between husbands who are victims in mate slayings and VP homicide. This fact, namely, that *significantly* more husbands than wives are victims in VP mate slayings–means that (1) husbands actually may provoke their wives more often than wives provoke their husbands to assault their respective mates; or, (2) assuming that provocation by wives is as intense and equally as frequent, or even more frequent, than provocation by husbands, then husbands may not receive and define provocation stimuli

[5]Only 550 victim-offender relationships are identified since 38 of the 588 criminal homicides are classified as unsolved, or those in which the perpetrator is unknown.

[6]The diagonal line represents "killed by". Thus, Negro male/Negro male means a Negro male killed a Negro male; the victim precedes the offender.

with as great or as violent a reaction as do wives; or (3) husbands may have a greater felt sense of guilt in a marital conflict for one reason or another, and receive verbal insults and overt physical assaults without retaliation as a form of compensatory punishment; or, (4) husbands may withdraw more often than wives from the scene of marital conflict, and thus eliminate, for the time being, a violent overt reaction to their wives' provocation. Clearly, this is only a suggestive, not an exhaustive, list of probable explanations. In any case, we are left with the undeniable fact that husbands more often than wives are major, precipitating factors in their own homicidal deaths.

Alcohol

The discovery of an association between the presence of alcohol in the homicide situation and Negro male offenders, combined with knowledge of the important contribution Negro males make to their own victimization, suggests an association (by transitivity) between VP homicide and the presence of alcohol. Moreover, whether alcohol is present in the victim or offender, lowered inhibitions due to ingestion of alcohol may cause an individual to give vent more freely to pent up frustrations, tensions, and emotional conflicts that have either built up over a prolonged period of time or that arise within an immediate emotional crisis. The data do in fact confirm the suggested hypothesis above and reveal a *significant* association between VP homicide and alcohol in the homicide situation. Comparison of VP to non-VP cases with respect to the presence of alcohol in the homicide situation (alcohol present in either the victim, offender, or both), reveals that alcohol was present in 74 percent of the VP cases and in 60 percent of the non-VP cases. The proportional difference results in a *significant* association between alcohol and VP homicide. It should be noted that the association is not necessarily a causal one, or that a causal relationship is not proved by the association.

Because the present analysis is concerned primarily with the contribution of the victim to the homicide, it is necessary to determine whether an association exists between VP homicide and presence of alcohol in the victim. No association was found to exist between VP homicide and alcohol in the offender. But victims had been drinking immediately prior to their death in more VP cases (69 percent) than in non-VP cases (47 percent). A positive and *significant* relationship is, therefore, clearly established between victims who had been drinking and who precipitated their own death. In many of these cases the victim was intoxicated, or nearly so, and lost control of his own defensive powers. He frequently was a victim with no intent to harm anyone maliciously, but who, nonetheless, struck his friend, acquaintance, or wife, who later became his assailant. Impulsive, aggressive, and often dangerously violent, the victim was the first to slap, punch, stab, or in some other manner commit an assault. Perhaps the presence of alcohol in this kind of homicide victim played no small part in his taking this first and major physical step toward victimization. Perhaps if he had not been drinking he would have been less violent, less ready to plunge into an assaultive stage of interaction. Or, if the presence of alcohol had no causal relation to his being the first to assault, perhaps it reduced his facility to combat successfully, to defend himself from retaliatory assault and, hence, contributed in this way to his death.

Previous Arrest Record

The victim-precipitator is the first actor in the homicide drama to display and to use a deadly weapon; and the description of him thus far infers that he is in some respects an offender in reverse. Because he is the first to assume an aggressive role, he probably has engaged previously in similar but less serious physical assaults. On the basis of these assumptions several meaningful hypotheses were established and tested. Each hypothesis is supported by empirical data, which in some cases reach the level of statistical significance accepted by this study; and in other cases indicate strong associations in directions suggested by the hypotheses. A summary of each hypothesis with its collated data follows:

(1) In VP cases, the victim is more likely than the offender to have a previous arrest, or police, record. The data show that 62 percent of the victims and 54 percent of the offenders in VP cases have a previous record.

(2) A higher proportion of VP victims than

non-VP victims have a previous police record. Comparison reveals that 62 percent of VP victims but only 42 percent of non-VP victims have a previous record. The association between VP victims and previous arrest record is a *significant* one.

(3) With respect to the percentage having a previous arrest record, VP victims are more similar to non-VP offenders than to non-VP victims. Examination of the data reveals no significant difference between VP victims and non-VP offenders with a previous record. This lack of a significant difference is very meaningful and confirms the validity of the proposition above. While 62 percent of VP victims have a police record, 68 percent of non-VP offenders have such a record, and we have already noted in (2) above that only 42 percent of non-VP victims have a record. Thus, the existence of a statistically *significant* difference between VP victims and non-VP victims and the *lack* of a statistically significant difference between VP victims and non-VP offenders indicate that the victim of VP homicide is quite similar to the offender in non-VP homicide—and that the VP victim more closely resembles the non-VP offender than the non-VP victim.

(4) A higher proportion of VP victims than of non-VP victims have a record of offenses against the person. The data show a *significant* association between VP victims and a previous record of offenses against the person, for 37 percent of VP victims and only 21 percent of non-VP victims have a record of such offenses.

(5) Also with respect to the percentage having a previous arrest record of offenses against the person, VP victims are more similar to non-VP offenders than non-VP victims. Analysis of the data indicates support for this asssmption, for we have observed that the difference between VP victims (37 percent) and non-VP victims (21 percent) is *significant;* this difference is almost twice as great as the difference between VP victims (27 percent) and non-VP offenders (46 percent), and this latter difference is not significant. The general tendency again is for victims in VP homicides to resemble offenders in non-VP homicides.

(6) A lower proportion of VP offenders have a previous arrest record than do non-VP offenders. The data also tend to support this hypothesis, for 54 percent of offenders in VP cases, compared to 68 percent of offenders in non-VP cases have a previous police record.

In general, the rank order of recidivism—defined in terms of having a previous arrest record and of having a previous record of assaults—for victims and offenders involved in the two types of homicide is as follows:

TABLE 13.7

	Percent with Previous Arrest Record	*Percent with Previous Record of Assault*
(1) Offenders in non-VP homicide	68	46
(2) Victims in VP homicide	62	37
(3) Offenders in VP homicide	54	33
(4) Victims in non-VP homicide	42	21

Because he is the initial aggressor and has provoked his subsequent slayer into killing him, this particular type of victim (VP) is likely to have engaged previously in physical assaults which were either less provoking than the present situation, or which afforded him greater opportunity to defer attacks made upon him. It is known officially that over one-third of them assaulted others previously. It is not known how many formerly provoked others to assault them. In any case, the circumstances leading up to the present crime in which he plays the role of victim are probably not foreign to him since he has, in many cases, participated in similar encounters before this, his last episode.

SUMMARY

Criminal homicide usually involves intense personal interaction in which the victim's behavior is often an important factor. As Porterfield has recently pointed out, "the intensity of interaction between the murderer and his victim may vary from complete non-participation on the part of the victim to almost perfect cooperation with the killer in the process of getting killed. . . . It is amazing to note the large number of would-be murderers who become the victim."[7] By defining a VP homicide in terms of the victim's direct, immediate, and positive contribution to his own death, manifested by his being the first to make a physical assault, it has been possible to identify 150 VP cases.

Comparison of this VP group with non-VP cases reveals *significantly* higher proportions of the following characteristics among VP homicide:

(1) Negro victims;
(2) Negro offenders;
(3) male victims;
(4) female offenders;
(5) stabbings;
(6) victim-offender relationship involving male victims of female offenders;
(7) mate slayings;
(8) husbands who are victims in mate slayings;
(9) alcohol in the homicide situation;
(10) alcohol in the victim;
(11) victims with a previous arrest record;
(12) victims with a previous arrest record of assault.

In addition, VP homicides have slightly higher proportions than non-VP homicides of altercations and domestic quarrels; inter-racial slaying, victims who are close friends, relatives, or acquaintances of their slayers. . . .

In many cases the victim has most of the major characteristics of an offender; in some cases two potential offenders come together in a homicide situation and it is probably often only chance which results in one becoming a victim and the other an offender. At any rate, connotations of a victim as a weak and passive individual, seeking to withdraw from an assaultive situation, and of an offender as a brutal, strong, and overly aggressive person seeking out his victim, are not always correct. Societal attitudes are generally positive toward the victim and negative toward the offender, who is often feared as a violent and dangerous threat to others when not exonerated. However, data in the present study—especially that of previous arrest record—mitigate, destroy, or reverse these connotations of victim-offender roles in one out of every four criminal homicides.

[7]Porterfield, Austin L. and Talbert, Robert H., *Mid-Century Crime in Our Culture: Personality and Crime in the Cultural Patterns of American States* (Fort Worth: Leo Potishman Foundation, 1954), pp. 47–8.

49.

MICHAEL FOONER

VICTIM-INDUCED CRIMINALITY

Proposals for compensating victims of violent crime[1] are gaining wide-spread support in the United States, but studies analyzing the behavior of victims suggest that legislators should be alert to the possibilities that some compensation schemes may contribute to the growth of crime and add unwarranted complications to the administration of criminal justice. . . .

The history of crime and punishment in the whole civilized world reveals a steadily increasing concern with the treatment of the criminal, and a virtual blackout of attention to the situation of the victim. For more than 1,000 years prior to the mid-20th century, the victim of crime in our society—and in the administration of justice—has been ignored.

Meanwhile, principles of humane treatment for criminals have been extensively developed and applied. In the United States vast resources are devoted to the care and rehabilitation of the offender. Recently, the 89th Congress passed three crime bills, of which one was aimed at helping police agencies "fight crime" while two were aimed at helping convicted offenders through the easing of parole requirements and the improvement of rehabilitation services. Victims were not provided for.

In the past decade, however, a new line of interest has opened up. The victim has been "discovered," and there are signs of change. Victims, it is being said, are also human; they bleed and suffer, their children and spouses may be deprived of the breadwinner's support.

New Zealand,[2] Britain,[3] California,[4] and New York City[5] have already installed victim-compensation systems and are paying out public money. Many other jurisdictions here and abroad are drafting such legislation.

One observer has suggested that legislators are finding the programs attractive, in the light of mounting public anger over alleged leniency in the treatment of offenders, as a means of placating constituents who demand stern measures against perpetrators of violence. The reasoning may be faulty, but there is public concern, and the sentiment has been gathering momentum.

UNCERTAINTY ABOUT OBJECTIVES

Most people approve the humanitarian motivation of victim-compensation proposals. But there is a serious degree of uncertainty—even a degree of confusion in some quarters—about the specific objectives and proper functioning of the compensation-for-victims concept.

Compassion is but one consideration. Former Associate Justice of the Supreme Court Arthur J. Goldberg, speaking in favor of compensation, declared that the victim of a robbery or assault should be considered to have been "denied protection of the laws" and that "society should assume some responsibility for making him whole."[6] However, there are documented studies

SOURCE: *Science*, September, 1966, pp. 1080–83.

[1]See, for example, C. Reckless and C. L. Newman (eds.), *Interdisciplinary Problems in Criminology: Papers of the American Society of Criminology, 1964* (Columbus, Ohio: College of Commerce and Administration, Ohio State University, 1965), pp. 159–90.

[2]New Zealand Criminal Injuries Compensation Act, No. 134 (1963).

[3]"Compensation for Victims of Crimes of Violence," *Great Britain, Home Office, White Paper* (1964).

[4]"California Statutes of 1965" (SB 1057, McAteer), chap. 1549.

[5]*New York Times,* December 30, 1965.

[6]A. J. Goldberg, James Madison Lecture, New York University School of Law, Feb. 1964, reported in *New York Times,* March 25, 1964.

[those of Von Hentig[7] and Wolfgang,[8] for example] which indicate that the victim himself often contributes to the occurrence of the crime—through his own carelessness, aggressive behavior, or imprudence.

Though some people may consider it paradoxical that criminals should be aided by their victims, this phenomenon is one with which criminologists are familiar. There is a growing literature on the role of the victim in crimes of violence; in addition, similar studies have recently been made in the field of property crimes.[9]

These studies suggest that where, for example, a person has not acted with reasonable self-protective behavior in handling his money, jewelry, or other valuables, and has become the victim of a robbery, he cannot be considered an innocent victim—he has in effect created a "temptation-opportunity" situation, giving the criminal incentive and help.

In popular parlance, "he has himself to blame"; in the explorations of criminology he may begin to look very like an "accomplice" of the criminal. But under current compensation legislation he may be entitled to a cash award for injuries sustained while he was being robbed.

Even where robbery is not involved, the potential for confusion is large if future legislation follows precedents already set. . . . In Britain recently two men got into an argument on a bus; one struck the other, blinding him in one eye and causing him to lose 8 weeks' work; the British Criminal Injuries Compensation Board awarded him $5,660.

Whereas Britain seems to emphasize loss of earnings, California emphasizes need, plus young dependent children. Although hailed as a "pioneer" in concern for unfortunate victims of violent crime, California makes them ineligible for compensation if they are unmarried individuals, childless married couples, elderly people, or individuals unable to pass a public-welfare needs test.

This kind of variation from Britain to California may suggest complexity; equally notable is the potential for confusion. While Goldberg spoke in favor of "society making the victim whole" as a proper rationale for a compensation system, he also is reported to have endorsed the new California law, with its restrictions, and to have called it "beneficial legislation" which deserves to be "widely emulated throughout the country."[10]

UNCERTAINTY ABOUT COSTS

Uncertainty about objectives is matched by uncertainty about costs. Legislators thus far seem not to have concentrated on this aspect of the matter. Notable generosity sometimes is advocated by public officials, but usually with reference to particular cases that receive extensive publicity.

The Wall Street Journal, in an article reporting on compensation proposals,[11] found that "despite voluminous statistics on rising crime rates, there is no way to estimate the total cost of a compensation program." It also quoted a consultant to the California government as saying, "Quite frankly, we don't have the faintest idea what the program will cost. . . ."

SEARCH FOR A THEORY

It seems evident that evaluation of proposals for victim compensation will require consideration of a rather wide spectrum of questions, and that legislators at present have little information on which to base answers. Probably, considerable research is needed on the following points. Is one to be guided solely by considerations of compassion, or does the victim have a "right" to compensation? Should all victims receive compensation, or only those who are in financial straits? How is a victim's financial need to be measured? If a victim is to be compensated, should the offender in some way have, or share, the obligation to pay?

---

[7]H. von Hentig, *The Criminal and His Victim* (New Haven, Conn.: Yale University Press, 1948).

[8]M. E. Wolfgang, *Patterns in Criminal Homicide* (Philadelphia: University of Pennsylvania Press, 1958).

[9]M. Fooner, "The Careless American: A Study in Adventitious Criminality," paper presented at the American Society of Criminology joint annual meeting with the AAAS, Philadelphia, December 29, 1962.

[10]See *New York Times,* July 24, 1965.

[11]G. Mapes, "Pay for Crime Victims: Uncharted Path," *Wall Street Journal,* January 17, 1966.

In the recent literature one may find considerable research on the ways of primitive and ancient peoples but a regrettable paucity of fact related to present-day reality. The Hammurabi code and the wergild of the age of feudalism have a genuine fascination but offer little guidance in a modern street-corner robbery or subway assault. There are a number of basic theories and issues that must be investigated, debated, and resolved after the facts and the consequences have been considered.

For example, from certain points of view compensation might be regarded as a moral and even legal right of the victim. This might be based on the "state duty" theory, which holds that society has a duty to protect its citizens from crime, that occurrence of a crime represents society's failure in the performance of that duty, and that this failure entitles the victim of the crime to a compensatory payment, usually in money.

Moral and legal right might also be established on the "wheel of fortune" theory, based on the assertion that crime is an inherent hazard of our society; that it inevitably falls upon someone, though the particular victim may be "selected" by chance; and that the individual, as victim, should not have to bear his misfortune alone. Under this theory, compensation is a mechanism by which lucky members of society "make it up" to the ones who are unlucky.

Under the "state duty" theory, the local, state, or national government would be obligated to pay, on the basis of an action for damages or an out-of-court settlement; the compensation law would merely systematize and perhaps expedite claims.

Under the "wheel of fortune" theory, there are two basic methods of financing to choose from: a fund appropriated by local, state, or national government or an adaptation of the "social insurance" practice now followed in the United States.

If the social insurance route is chosen, government declares by fiat that crime, like unemployment and old age, is an "insurable hazard" of its citizens; it would collect contributions from them through its taxing powers, and devise a scale of benefits.

If the "insurable hazard" concept is adopted, two other methods are also possible: private insurance, comparable to automobile insurance and a "Blue Cross" type of arrangement.

In contrast to the "right to compensation" concept is the "social welfare" theory, which holds that society ameliorates the distress of its members not as a "right" but as "social policy," if they become widowed, orphaned, or indigent. Victims of crime would be added to the lists of individuals eligible for relief payments under existing state or local welfare systems.

Another approach is more specialized, providing compensation for those harmed when attempting to protect their fellow citizens from criminals, or when cooperating with police. For example, the New York City law which grew out of the strongly publicized case of a man killed when going to the aid of two women being molested in the subway provides a pension for the widow similar to that given one whose husband was a policeman killed in the line of duty.

For the sake of completeness, mention should be made of the theory of individual responsibility—the theory that the criminal should be held financially liable for the injury or death of his victim. Though a few ingenious suggestions have been made for implementing this idea, the concept is largely academic except where the offender is in a high income bracket. Proposals based on this theory seem to evoke the "reparations" concept of our primitive ancestors, or they lean upon avant-garde correctional theory which holds (evidence is yet to be developed) that the offender's payment to the victim will have a psychological effect which will help in his rehabilitation. There are also proposals which extend this concept to parental responsibility for the acts of children; these proposals would be largely academic except in cases where the offender's parents are living and affluent.

Which of these theories or concepts might best serve as a basis for legislation can be determined only after further research. Inevitably such research would include a new exploration of the role of the victim in both criminal phenomena and the administration of justice.

Traditionally, in the administration of justice, the victim of crime has a secondary role. Primary attention usually is focused on the criminal. The victim's function is mainly that of providing information for law enforcement officers, supplying evidence of the criminal act, or being a witness in court proceedings. He is often subjected to inconveniences, indignities, and the harassment of the defense attorney.

One author observes that the victim is "the Cinderella of the criminal procedure." Many have noted the "inequality of treatment" between criminal and victim. Huge sums are spent on shelter, food, medical care, supervision, vocational training, and rehabilitation of offenders, while the victims and their dependents are left to shift for themselves.

PHILOSOPHICAL ISSUES

These are some of the considerations which are lending urgency to what might otherwise be considered a minor problem in the administration of criminal justice. There are, of course, certain philosophical issues, such as that raised by G. O. W. Mueller when he suggests, by way of illustration, that compensation for the family of a murdered man is not socially defensible unless society at the same time provides compensation for a family whose breadwinner is killed by lightning.[12]

Would the administration of criminal justice be seriously affected by proposed systems of victim compensation? If there were no cases other than those in which the victim is clearly an innocent recipient of injury or death at the hands of a criminal, the matter would be simple. But in crimes where there is conflicting testimony, or where there is no credible witness or no apprehended suspect, how should the victim's claim for compensation be adjudicated? How can it be decided whether the injury was caused by an assault, or by an argument, or by a fall due to drunkenness? How can the victim's trial testimony be evaluated if victim compensation is a factor in the case? Standards will have to be developed after careful criminological research.

SUMMARY

In summary, there are certain issues that need to be dealt with if a coherent system of victim compensation is to be created.

1) Is the victim's entitlement to compensation qualified by his behavior in connection with the crime?

If a Texas tycoon visits a clip joint, flashes a fat roll of bills, and gets hit on the head and rolled, is he entitled to compensation? If a man enters into a liaison with another's wife and gets shot by the husband, should his dependents be compensated? If a woman goes walking alone in a disreputable neighborhood and is assaulted, is she entitled to compensation?

Unless the answer to such questions is a flat "yes," the adjudication of victim compensation as a "right" would be embarkation upon a vast sea of confusion.

On the surface it may seem simpler to bypass the issue of "right" and declare for victim compensation as a matter of social policy—a logical extension of the welfare state approach. But the apparent simplicity may quickly prove illusory, in light of the second issue.

2) Is the victim's entitlement to compensation on the basis of indigency to be qualified by the requirement that an offender by apprehended and his guilt determined by a court?

There are two levels to this problem. First, if a severely injured man reports to police that he has been mugged and robbed and if the police cannot apprehend a suspect, how is the administrator of compensation to know that the man is in fact the victim of a crime? The administrator of compensation must determine whether the episode was a criminal act or an argument—and who started it, and who precipitated the violence. What shall be the role of the witnesses, and of investigators? More important is the second level of the problem: How will law-enforcement officials and the courts evaluate the testimony of the victim if compensation of the victim may be at stake?

In the evaluation of proposals for victim compensation, criminologists may need to think very hard about such questions and about the probable effects on the administration of criminal justice.

These are pragmatic problems; there is a third problem which may at this time seem speculative, but is, nevertheless, quite important.

[12]*Journal of Public Law*, Spring 1959.

3) To what extent will a particular proposal for victim compensation contribute to a temptation-opportunity pattern in victim behavior?

In previous studies it has been pointed out that large numbers of our fellow Americans have tended to acquire casual money-handling habits—generically designated "carelessness"—which contribute to the national growth of criminality. How the victim helps the criminal was sketched in reports of those studies.[13]

It was made abundantly clear that human beings in our affluent society cannot be assumed to be prudent or self-protective against the hazards of crime. Even when the "victim" is not overtly acting to commit a crime—as in the case of the property owner who hires an arsonist—he often tempts the offender. Among the victims of burglary—statistically the most prevalent crime in the United States—are a substantial number of Americans who keep cash, jewelry, and other valuables carelessly at home or in hotel rooms to which the burglar has easy access through door or window. Victims of automobile theft—one of the fastest growing classes of crime—include drivers who leave the vehicle or its contents invitingly accessible to thieves. And so on with other classes of crime.

As pointed out in previous studies, when victim behavior follows a temptation-opportunity pattern, it (i) contributes to a "climate of criminal inducements," (ii) adds to the economic resources available to criminal societies, and (iii) detracts from the ability of law-enforcement agencies to suppress the growth of crime.

CONCLUSIONS

It would seem, therefore, that we can draw the following conclusions.

1) If "society should assume some responsibility for making the victim whole," it should also require victim-behavior that will diminish the number of temptation-opportunity situations for offenders. Such behavior could be encouraged through educational programs on citizen defenses against criminality, plus legislative provisions which make victim compensation contingent upon the victim's actions not being contributory to the crime. Similar standards of behavior might be studied for adaptation to casualty insurance practices. The new practices would either be adopted voluntarily or imposed through legislation.

2) The experience of insurance companies probably offers considerable material for study of the victim-compensation problem. Among other things, there is a seeming paradox: if the beneficiary of a life insurance policy causes the death of the insured the claim will not be paid, but with burglary insurance an individual can be careless or imprudent to the point of "inviting" theft and still be compensated for a loss. "Insured" thefts seem to be a law-enforcement problem of growing significance.[14] The relationships between compensation and carelessness and between carelessness and criminal incentives need to be studied for guidance in creating a workable victim-compensation system.

3) Provisions for compensation of the citizen injured while assisting a law officer or while, on his own initiative, restraining an offender can be administered effectively only if standards of citizen behavior are carefully defined. Payment of compensation must be on such a basis as to discourage the vigilante and the busybody. A large-scale educational effort would have to be conducted, so that citizens would know their obligations and rights.[15]

Careful criminological research is needed to help resolve these issues, and to avoid opportunism, contradictions, and serious stresses in public finance.

---

[13]Fooner, *op. cit.*

[14]C. H. Rolph, *Common Sense about Crime and Punishment* (New York: Macmillan, 1961), p. 78.

[15]M. Fooner, *Crime in the Affluent Society: A Summary Statement on Cause of Crime and a Program of Crime Prevention Education,* prepared for the Third United Nations Congress on Crime Prevention and Treatment of Offenders, Stockholm, 1965.

Index of Names

Index of Subjects

THE BOOK MANUFACTURE

Crime in America: Perspectives on Criminal and Delinquent Behavior was typeset by Kopecky Typesetting, Inc., offset printing and binding was by Kingsport Press, Inc. The paper is Perkins & Squier Company's Glatfelter Old Forge. John Goetz designed the text. Charles Kling & Associates designed the cover. The type in this book is Caledonia with Bodoni Bold display.

THE BOOK MANUFACTURE

[illegible] one in American Typewriter [illegible] and [illegible] was typeset by Kopecky Typesetting. Book offset printing and binding was by Kingsport Press, Inc. The paper is [illegible]. John Geer designed the text. [illegible] & Associates designed the cover. The type in this book is Caledonia with Radiant Bold display.